# THE BELLARMINE SERIES

Published by the Jesuit Fathers of
Heythrop College

*General Editor*
## EDMUND F. SUTCLIFFE, S.J.
*Professor Emeritus of Old Testament Exegesis and Hebrew
at Heythrop College*

BY THE SAME AUTHOR

✳

THE BELLARMINE SERIES XVIII

# A
# HISTORY OF PHILOSOPHY

VOLUME VII
FICHTE TO NIETZSCHE

BY
## FREDERICK COPLESTON, S.J.

*Professor at the Pontifical Gregorian University, Rome
and at Heythrop College*

SEARCH PRESS
LONDON

De Licentia Superiorum Ordinis:
JOHN COVENTRY, S.J.
*Praep. Prov. Angliae*

*Nihil obstat:*

T. GORNALL, S.J.
*Censor Deputatus*

*Imprimatur:*

✠ FRANCISCUS
*Archiepiscopus Birmingamiensis*

Birmingamiae
die 26a Junii 1962

*First published 1963*
*Second impression 1965*
*Third impression 1968*
*Fourth impression 1971*

ISBN 0 85532 187 3

PRINTED IN GREAT BRITAIN
BY FLETCHER AND SON LTD, NORWICH
FOR SEARCH PRESS LTD,
85 GLOUCESTER ROAD, LONDON SW7 4SU

# CONTENTS

## PART III

### LATER CURRENTS OF THOUGHT

*Sickness unto Death, Concluding Unscientific Postscript* and *The Concept of Dread.* In the case of quotations from philosophers other than Kierkegaard I have translated the passages myself. But I have frequently given page-references to existing English translations for the benefit of readers who wish to consult a translation rather than the original. In the case of minor figures, however, I have generally omitted references to translations.

# PART I

## POST-KANTIAN IDEALIST SYSTEMS

### CHAPTER I

### INTRODUCTION

*Preliminary remarks—Kant's philosophy and idealist meta-physics—The meaning of idealism, its insistence on system and its confidence in the power and scope of philosophy—The idealists and theology—The romantic movement and German idealism—The difficulty in fulfilling the idealist programme—The anthropomorphic element in German idealism—Idealist philosophies of man.*

1. In the German philosophical world during the early part of the nineteenth century we find one of the most remarkable flowerings of metaphysical speculation which have occurred in the long history of western philosophy. We are presented with a succession of systems, of original interpretations of reality and of human life and history, which possess a grandeur that can hardly be called in question and which are still capable of exercising on some minds at least a peculiar power of fascination. For each of the leading philosophers of the period professes to solve the riddle of the world, to reveal the secret of the universe and the meaning of human existence.

True, before the death of Schelling in 1854 Auguste Comte in France had already published his *Course of Positive Philosophy* in which metaphysics was represented as a passing stage in the history of human thought. And Germany was to have its own positivist and materialist movements which, while not killing metaphysics, would force metaphysicians to reflect on and define more closely the relation between philosophy and the particular sciences. But in the early decades of the nineteenth century the shadow of positivism had not yet fallen across the scene and speculative philosophy enjoyed a period of uninhibited and luxuriant growth. With the great German idealists we find a superb confidence in the power of the human reason and in the scope of philosophy. Looking on reality as the self-manifestation of infinite reason, they thought that the life of self-expression of this reason could be retraced in philosophical reflection. They were not nervous men looking over their shoulders to see if critics were whispering that they were producing poetic effusions under the thin disguise of theoretical philosophy, or that their profundity and obscure language were a mask for lack of clarity of thought. On the contrary, they were convinced that the human spirit had at last come into its own and that the nature of reality was at last clearly revealed to human consciousness. And each set out his vision of the Universe with a splendid confidence in its objective truth.

It can, of course, hardly be denied that German idealism makes on most people today the impression of belonging to another world, to another climate of thought. And we can say that the death of Hegel in 1831 marked the end of an epoch. For it was followed by the collapse of absolute idealism[1] and the emergence of other lines of thought. Even metaphysics took a different turn. And the superb confidence in the power and range of speculative philosophy which was characteristic of Hegel in particular has never been regained. But though German idealism sped through the sky like a rocket and after a comparatively short space of time disintegrated and fell to earth, its flight was extremely impressive. Whatever its shortcomings, it represented one of the most sustained attempts which the history of thought has known to achieve a unified conceptual mastery of reality and experience as a whole. And even if the presuppositions of idealism are rejected, the idealist systems can still retain the power of stimulating the natural impulse of the reflective mind to strive after a unified conceptual synthesis.

Some are indeed convinced that the elaboration of an overall view of reality is not the proper task of scientific philosophy. And even those who do not share this conviction may well think that the achievement of a final systematic synthesis lies beyond the capacity of any one man and is more of an ideal goal than a practical possibility. But we should be prepared to recognize intellectual stature when we meet it. Hegel in particular towers up in impressive grandeur above the vast majority of those who have tried to belittle him. And we can always learn from an outstanding philosopher, even if it is only by reflecting on our reasons for disagreeing with him. The historical collapse of metaphysical idealism does not necessarily entail the conclusion that the great idealists

[1] The fact that there were later idealist movements in Britain, America, Italy and elsewhere does not alter the fact that after Hegel metaphysical idealism in Germany suffered an eclipse.

have nothing of value to offer. German idealism has its fantastic aspects, but the writings of the leading idealists are very far from being all fantasy.

2. The point which we have to consider here is not, however, the collapse of German idealism but its rise. And this indeed stands in need of some explanation. On the one hand the immediate philosophical background of the idealist movement was provided by the critical philosophy of Immanuel Kant, who had attacked the claims of metaphysicians to provide theoretical knowledge of reality. On the other hand the German idealists looked on themselves as the true spiritual successors of Kant and not as simply reacting against his ideas. What we have to explain, therefore, is how metaphysical idealism could develop out of the system of a thinker whose name is for ever associated with scepticism about metaphysics' claim to provide us with theoretical knowledge about reality as a whole or indeed about any reality other than the *a priori* structure of human knowledge and experience.[1]

The most convenient starting-point for an explanation of the development of metaphysical idealism out of the critical philosophy is the Kantian notion of the thing-in-itself.[2] In Fichte's view Kant had placed himself in an impossible position by steadfastly refusing to abandon this notion. On the one hand, if Kant had asserted the existence of the thing-in-itself as cause of the given or material element in sensation, he would have been guilty of an obvious inconsistency. For according to his own philosophy the concept of cause cannot be used to extend our knowledge beyond the phenomenal sphere. On the other hand, if Kant retained the idea of the thing-in-itself simply as a problematical and limiting notion, this was tantamount to retaining a ghostly relic of the very dogmatism which it was the mission of the critical philosophy to overcome. Kant's Copernican revolution was a great step forward, and for Fichte there could be no question of moving backwards to a pre-Kantian position. If one had any understanding of the development of philosophy and of the demands of modern thought, one could only go forward and complete Kant's work. And this meant eliminating the thing-in-itself. For, given Kant's premises, there was no room for an unknowable occult entity supposed to be independent of mind. In other words, the critical philosophy had to

---

[1] I say 'could develop' because reflection on Kant's philosophy can lead to different lines of thought, according to the aspects which one emphasizes. See Vol. VI, pp. 433–4.
[2] See Vol. VI, pp. 268–72, 384–6.

be transformed into a consistent idealism; and this meant that things had to be regarded in their entirety as products of thought.

Now, it is immediately obvious that what we think of as the extramental world cannot be interpreted as the product of conscious creative activity by the human mind. As far as ordinary consciousness is concerned, I find myself in a world of objects which affect me in various ways and which I spontaneously think of as existing independently of my thought and will. Hence the idealist philosopher must go behind consciousness, as it were, and retrace the process of the unconscious activity which grounds it.

But we must go further than this and recognize that the production of the world cannot be attributed to the individual self at all, even to its unconscious activity. For if it were attributed to the individual finite self as such, it would be very difficult, if not impossible, to avoid solipsism, a position which can hardly be seriously maintained. Idealism is thus compelled to go behind the finite subject to a supra-individual intelligence, an absolute subject.

The word 'subject', however, is not really appropriate, except as indicating that the ultimate productive principle lies, so to speak, on the side of thought and not on the side of the sensible thing. For the words 'subject' and 'object' are correlative. And the ultimate principle is, considered in itself, without object. It grounds the subject-object relationship and, in itself, transcends the relationship. It is subject and object in identity, the infinite activity from which both proceed.

Post-Kantian idealism was thus necessarily a metaphysics. Fichte, starting from the position of Kant and developing it into idealism, not unnaturally began by calling his first principle the ego, turning Kant's transcendental ego into a metaphysical or ontological principle. But he explained that he meant by this the absolute ego, not the individual finite ego. But with the other idealists (and with Fichte himself in his later philosophy) the word 'ego' is not used in this context. With Hegel the ultimate principle is infinite reason, infinite spirit. And we can say that for metaphysical idealism in general reality is the process of the self-expression or self-manifestation of infinite thought or reason.

This does not mean, of course, that the world is reduced to a process of thinking in the ordinary sense. Absolute thought or reason is regarded as an activity, as productive reason which posits or expresses itself in the world. And the world retains all the reality which we see it to possess. Metaphysical idealism does not involve the thesis that empirical reality consists of subjective ideas; but it involves the vision of the world and human history as the objective expression of creative reason. This vision was fundamental in the outlook of the German idealist: he could not avoid it. For he accepted the necessity of transforming the critical philosophy into idealism. And this transformation meant that the world in its entirety had to be regarded as the product of creative thought or reason. If, therefore, we look on the need for transforming the philosophy of Kant into idealism as a premiss, we can say that this premiss determined the basic vision of the post-Kantian idealists. But when it comes to explaining what is meant by saying that reality is a process of creative thought, there is room for different interpretations, for the several particular visions of the different idealist philosophers.

The direct influence of Kant's thought was naturally felt more strongly by Fichte than by Schelling or Hegel. For Schelling's philosophizing presupposed the earlier stages of Fichte's thought, and Hegel's absolute idealism presupposed the earlier phases of the philosophies of both Fichte and Schelling. But this does not alter the fact that the movement of German idealism as a whole presupposed the critical philosophy. And in his account of the history of modern philosophy Hegel depicted the Kantian system as representing an advance on preceding stages of thought and as demanding to be itself developed and surpassed in succeeding stages.

In this section reference has been made so far only to the process of eliminating the thing-in-itself and transferring Kant's philosophy into metaphysical idealism. But it was certainly not my intention to suggest that the post-Kantian idealists were influenced only by the idea that the thing-in-itself had to be eliminated. They were also influenced by other aspects of the critical philosophy. For example, Kant's doctrine of the primacy of the practical reason had a powerful appeal for Fichte's strongly-marked ethical outlook. And we find him interpreting the absolute ego as an infinite practical reason or moral will which posits Nature as a field and instrument for moral activity. In his philosophy the concepts of action, of duty and of moral vocation are extremely prominent. And we are perhaps entitled to say that Fichte turned Kant's second *Critique* into a metaphysics, employing his development of the first *Critique* as a means of doing so. With Schelling, however, the prominence given to the philosophy of art, to the role of genius and to the metaphysical significance of aesthetic intuition and artistic creation links him with the third *Critique* rather than with the first or second.

But instead of dwelling at length on the particular ways in which different parts or aspects of Kant's philosophy influenced this or that idealist, it will be more appropriate in our introductory chapter if we take a broader and more general view of the relation between the critical philosophy and metaphysical idealism.

The desire to form a coherent and unified interpretation of reality is natural to the reflective mind. But the actual task to be performed presents itself in different ways at different times. For example, the development of physical science in the post-mediaeval world meant that the philosopher who wished to construct an overall interpretation had to grapple with the problem of reconciling the scientific view of the world as a mechanical system with the demands of the moral and religious consciousness. Descartes was faced with this problem. And so was Kant.[1] But though Kant rejected the ways of dealing with this problem which were characteristic of his philosophical predecessors and offered his own original solution, it is arguable that in the long run he left us with 'a bifurcated reality'.[2] On the one hand we have the phenomenal world, the world of Newtonian science, governed by necessary causal laws.[3] On the other hand there is the supersensuous world of the free moral agent and of God. There is no valid reason for asserting that the phenomenal world is the only reality.[4] But at the same time there is no theoretical proof of the existence of a supersensuous reality. It is a matter of practical faith, resting on the moral consciousness. It is true that in the third *Critique* Kant endeavoured to bridge the gulf between the two worlds to the extent in which he considered this to be possible for the human mind.[5] But it is understandable if other philosophers were not satisfied with his performance. And the German idealists were able to proceed beyond Kant by means of their development and transformation of his philosophy. For if reality is the unified

---

[1] See Vol. IV, pp. 55–6 and Vol. VI, pp. 233–4; 428–9.

[2] Vol. IV, p. 60.

[3] Necessity and causality are for Kant *a priori* categories. But he does not deny, indeed he affirms, that the world of science is 'phenomenally real'.

[4] This is true at least if we refrain from pressing Kant's doctrine of the restricted field of application of the categories to an extent which would exclude any meaningful talk about supersensuous reality, even in the context of moral faith.

[5] See Vol. VI, ch. 15.

process by which absolute thought or reason manifests itself, it is intelligible. And it is intelligible by the human mind, provided that this mind can be regarded as the vehicle, as it were, of absolute thought reflecting on itself.

This condition possesses an obvious importance if there is to be any continuity between Kant's idea of the only possible scientific metaphysics of the future and the idealists' conception of metaphysics. For Kant the metaphysics of the future is a transcendental critique of human experience and knowledge. We can say in fact that it is the human mind's reflective awareness of its own spontaneous formative activity. In metaphysical idealism, however, the activity in question is productive in the fullest sense (the thing-in-itself having been eliminated); and this activity is attributed, not to the finite human mind as such, but to absolute thought or reason. Hence philosophy, which is reflection by the human mind, cannot be regarded as absolute thought's reflective awareness of itself unless the human mind is capable of rising to the absolute point of view and becoming the vehicle, as it were, of absolute thought or reason's reflective awareness of its own activity. If this condition is fulfilled, there is a certain continuity between Kant's idea of the only possible scientific type of metaphysics and the idealist conception of metaphysics. There is also, of course, an obvious inflation, so to speak. That is to say, the Kantian theory of knowledge is inflated into a metaphysics of reality. But the process of inflation retains a certain measure of continuity. While going far beyond anything that Kant himself envisaged, it is not a simple reversion to a pre-Kantian conception of metaphysics.

The transformation of the Kantian theory of knowledge into a metaphysics of reality carries with it, of course, certain important changes. For example, if with the elimination of the thing-in-itself the world becomes the self-manifestation of thought or reason, the Kantian distinction between the *a priori* and the *a posteriori* loses its absolute character. And the categories, instead of being subjective forms or conceptual moulds of the human understanding, become categories of reality; they regain an objective status. Again, the teleological judgment is no longer subjective, as with Kant. For in metaphysical idealism the idea of purposiveness in Nature cannot be simply a heuristic or regulative principle of the human mind, a principle which performs a useful function but the objectivity of which cannot be theoretically proved. If Nature is the expression and manifestation of thought or reason in its movement towards a goal, the process of Nature must be teleological in character.

It cannot indeed be denied that there is a very great difference between Kant's modest idea of the scope and power of metaphysics and the idealists' notion of what metaphysical philosophy is capable of achieving. Kant himself repudiated Fichte's demand for the transformation of the critical philosophy into pure idealism by the elimination of the thing-in-itself. And it is easy to understand the attitude of the neo-Kantians who, later in the century, announced that they had had enough of the airy metaphysical speculations of the idealists and that it was time to return to the spirit of Kant himself. At the same time the development of Kant's system into metaphysical idealism is not unintelligible, and the remarks in this section may have helped to explain how the idealists were able to look on themselves as Kant's legitimate spiritual successors.

3. It will be clear from what has been said about the development of metaphysical idealism that the post-Kantian idealists were not subjective idealists in the sense of holding that the human mind knows only its own ideas as distinct from extramentally existing things. Nor were they subjective idealists in the sense of holding that all objects of knowledge are the products of the finite human subject. True, Fichte's use of the word 'ego' in his earlier writings tended to give the impression that this was precisely what he did hold. But the impression was mistaken. For Fichte insisted that the productive subject was not the finite ego as such but the absolute ego, a transcendental and supra-individual principle. And as for Schelling and Hegel, any reduction of things to products of the individual finite mind was entirely foreign to their thought.

But though it is easily understood that post-Kantian idealism did not involve subjective idealism in either of the senses alluded to in the last paragraph, it is not so easy to give a general description of the movement which will apply to all the leading idealist systems. For they differ in important respects. Moreover, the thought of Schelling in particular moved through successive phases. At the same time there is, of course, a family likeness between the different systems. And this fact justifies one in venturing on some generalizations.

Inasmuch as reality is looked on as the self-expression or self-unfolding of absolute thought or reason, there is a marked tendency in German idealism to assimilate the causal relation to the logical relation of implication. For example, the empirical world is conceived by Fichte and by Schelling (in at any rate the earlier phases of the latter's thought) as standing to the ultimate productive principle in the relation of consequent to antecedent. And this means, of course, that the world follows necessarily from the first productive principle, the priority of which is logical and not temporal. Obviously, there is not and cannot be any question of external compulsion. But the Absolute spontaneously and inevitably manifests itself in the world. And there is really no place for the idea of creation in time, in the sense of there being an ideally assignable first moment of time.[1]

This notion of reality as the self-unfolding of absolute reason helps to explain the idealists' insistence on system. For if philosophy is the reflective reconstruction of the structure of a dynamic rational process, it should be systematic, in the sense that it should begin with the first principle and exhibit the essential rational structure of reality as flowing from it. True, the idea of a purely theoretical deduction does not in practice occupy such an important place in metaphysical idealism as the foreground dialectical process of Fichte and above all Hegel tends to suggest. For idealist philosophy is the conceptual reconstruction of a dynamic activity, a self-unfolding infinite life, rather than a strict analysis of the meaning and implications of one or more initial basic propositions. But the general world-view is embryonically contained in the initial idea of the world as the process of absolute reason's self-manifestation. And it is the business of philosophy to give systematic articulation to this idea, reliving the process, as it were, on the plane of reflective awareness. Hence, though it would be possible to start from the empirical manifestations of absolute reason and work backwards, metaphysical idealism naturally follows a deductive form of exposition, in the sense that it systematically retraces a teleological movement.

Now, if we assume that reality is a rational process and that its essential dynamic structure is penetrable by the philosopher, this assumption is naturally accompanied by a confidence in the power and scope of metaphysics which contrasts sharply with Kant's modest estimate of what it can achieve. And this contrast is

---

[1] Hegel admits the idea of free creation on the level of the language of the religious consciousness. But this language is for him pictorial or figurative.

obvious enough if one compares the critical philosophy with Hegel's system of absolute idealism. Indeed, it is probably true to say that Hegel's confidence in the power and reach of philosophy was unequalled by any previous philosopher of note. At the same time we have seen in the last section that there was a certain continuity between Kant's philosophy and metaphysical idealism. And we can even say, though it is a paradoxical statement, that the closer idealism kept to Kant's idea of the only possible form of scientific metaphysics, the greater was its confidence in the power and scope of philosophy. For if we assume that philosophy is thought's reflective awareness of its own spontaneous activity, and if we substitute a context of idealist metaphysics for the context of Kant's theory of human knowledge and experience, we then have the idea of the rational process, which is reality, becoming aware of itself in and through man's philosophical reflection. In this case the history of philosophy is the history of absolute reason's self-reflection. In other words, the Universe knows itself in and through the mind of man. And philosophy can be interpreted as the self-knowledge of the Absolute.

True, this conception of philosophy is characteristic more of Hegel than of the other leading idealists. Fichte ended by insisting on a divine Absolute which in itself transcends the reach of human thought, and in his later philosophy of religion Schelling emphasized the idea of a personal God who reveals himself to man. It is with Hegel that the idea of the philosopher's conceptual mastery of all reality and the interpretation of this mastery as the self-reflection of the Absolute become most prominent. But to say this is simply to say that it is in Hegelianism, the greatest achievement of metaphysical idealism, that the faith in the power and scope of speculative philosophy which inspired the idealist movement finds its purest and most grandiose expression.

4. Mention has just been made of Fichte's later doctrine of the Absolute and of Schelling's philosophy of religion. And it is appropriate to say something here of the relations between German idealism and theology. For it is important to understand that the idealist movement was not simply the result of a transformation of the critical philosophy into metaphysics. All three of the leading idealists started as students of theology, Fichte at Jena, Schelling and Hegel at Tübingen. And though it is true that they turned very quickly to philosophy, theological themes played a conspicuous role in the development of German idealism. Nietzsche's

statement that the philosophers in question were concealed theologians was misleading in some respects, but it was not altogether without foundation.

The importance of the role played by theological themes in German idealism can be illustrated by the following contrast. Though not a professional scientist Kant was always interested in science. His first writings were mainly concerned with scientific topics,[1] and one of his primary questions was about the conditions which render scientific knowledge possible. Hegel, however, came to philosophy from theology. His first writings were largely theological in character, and he was later to declare that the subject-matter of philosophy is God and nothing but God. Whether the term 'God', as here used, is to be understood in anything approaching a theistic sense is not a question which need detain us at present. The point to be made is that Hegel's point of departure was the theme of the relation between the infinite and the finite, between God and creatures. His mind could not remain satisfied with a sharp distinction between the infinite Being on the one hand and finite beings on the other, and he tried to bring them together, seeing the infinite in the finite and the finite in the infinite. In the theological phase of his development he was inclined to think that the elevation of the finite to the infinite could take place only in the life of love, and he then drew the conclusion that philosophy must in the long run yield to religion. As a philosopher, he tried to exhibit the relation between the infinite and the finite conceptually, in thought, and tended to depict philosophical reflection as a higher form of understanding than the way of thinking which is characteristic of the religious consciousness. But the general theme of the relation between the infinite and the finite which runs through his philosophical system was taken over, as it were, from his early theological reflections.

It is not, however, simply a question of Hegel. In Fichte's earlier philosophy the theme of the relation between the infinite and the finite is not indeed conspicuous, for he was primarily concerned with the completion, as he saw it, of Kant's deduction of consciousness. But in his later thought the idea of one infinite divine Life comes to the fore, and the religious aspects of his philosophy were developed. As for Schelling, he did not hesitate to say that the relation between the divine infinite and the finite is the chief problem of philosophy. And his later thought was profoundly

[1] See Vol. VI, pp. 181-2, 185-7.

religious in character, the ideas of man's alienation from and return to God playing a prominent role.

Being philosophers, the idealists tried, of course, to understand the relation between the infinite and the finite. And they tended to view it according to the analogy of logical implication. Further, if we make the necessary exception for Schelling's later religious philosophy, we can say that the idea of a personal God who is both infinite and fully transcendent seemed to the idealists to be both illogical and unduly anthropomorphic. Hence we find a tendency to transform the idea of God into the idea of the Absolute, in the sense of the all-comprehensive totality. At the same time the idealists had no intention of denying the reality of the finite. Hence the problem which faced them was that of including, as it were, the finite within the life of the infinite without depriving the former of its reality. And the difficulty of solving this problem is responsible for a good deal of the ambiguity in metaphysical idealism when it is a question of defining its relation to theism on the one hand and pantheism on the other. But in any case it is clear that a central theological theme, namely the relation between God and the world, looms large in the speculations of the German idealists.

It has been said above that Nietzsche's description of the German idealists as concealed theologians is misleading in some, respects. For it suggests that the idealists were concerned with reintroducing orthodox Christianity by the backdoor, whereas in point of fact we find a marked tendency to substitute metaphysics for faith and to rationalize the revealed mysteries of Christianity, bringing them within the scope of the speculative reason. To use a modern term, we find a tendency to demythologize Christian dogmas, turning them in the process into a speculative philosophy. Hence we may be inclined to smile at J. H. Stirling's picture of Hegel as the great philosophical champion of Christianity. We may be more inclined to accept McTaggart's view, and also Kierkegaard's, that the Hegelian philosophy undermined Christianity from within as it were, by professing to lay bare the rational content of the Christian doctrines in their traditional form. And we may feel that the connection which Fichte sought to establish between his later philosophy of the Absolute and the first chapter of St. John's Gospel was somewhat tenuous.

At the same time there is no cogent reason for supposing, for instance, that Hegel had his tongue in his cheek when he referred to St. Anselm and to the process of faith seeking understanding.

His early essays showed marked hostility to positive Christianity; but he came to change his attitude and to take the Christian faith under his wing, so to speak. It would be absurd to claim that Hegel was in fact an orthodox Christian. But he was doubtless sincere when he represented the relation of Christianity to Hegelianism as being that of the absolute religion to the absolute philosophy, two different ways of apprehending and expressing the same truth-content. From an orthodox theological standpoint Hegel must be judged to have substituted reason for faith, philosophy for revelation, and to have defended Christianity by rationalizing it and turning it, to borrow a phrase from McTaggart, into exoteric Hegelianism. But this does not alter the fact that Hegel thought of himself as having demonstrated the truth of the Christian religion. Nietzsche's statement, therefore, was not altogether wide of the mark, especially if one takes into account the development in the religious aspects of Fichte's thought and the later phases of Schelling's philosophy. And in any case the German idealists certainly attributed significance and value to the religious consciousness and found a place for it in their systems. They may have turned from theology to philosophy, but they were very far from being irreligious men or rationalists in a modern sense.

5. But there is another aspect of metaphysical idealism which must also be mentioned, namely its relation to the romantic movement in Germany. The description of German idealism as the philosophy of romanticism is indeed open to serious objection. In the first place it suggests the idea of a one-way influence. That is to say, it suggests that the great idealist systems were simply the ideological expression of the romantic spirit, whereas in point of fact the philosophies of Fichte and Schelling exercised a considerable influence on some of the romantics. In the second place, the leading idealist philosophers stood in somewhat different relations to the romantics. We can say indeed that Schelling gave notable expression to the spirit of the romantic movement. But Fichte indulged in some sharp criticism of the romantics, even if the latter had derived inspiration from certain of his ideas. And Hegel had scant sympathy with some aspects of romanticism. In the third place it is arguable that the term 'philosophy of romanticism' would be better applied to the speculative ideas developed by romantics such as Friedrich Schlegel (1772–1829) and Novalis (1772–1801) than to the great idealist systems. At the same time there was undoubtedly some spiritual affinity between

the idealist and romantic movements. The romantic spirit as such was indeed an attitude towards life and the universe rather than a systematic philosophy. One may perhaps borrow Rudolf Carnap's terms and speak of it as a *Lebensgefühl* or *Lebenseinstellung*.[1] And it is perfectly understandable that Hegel saw a considerable difference between systematic philosophical reflection and the utterances of the romantics. But when we look back on the German scene in the first part of the nineteenth century, we are naturally struck by affinities as well as by differences. After all, metaphysical idealism and romanticism were more or less contemporary German cultural phenomena, and an underlying spiritual affinity is only what one might expect to find.

The romantic spirit is notoriously difficult to define. Nor indeed should one expect to be able to define it. But one can, of course, mention some of its characteristic traits. For example, as against the Enlightenment's concentration on the critical, analytic and scientific understanding the romantics exalted the power of the creative imagination and the role of feeling and intuition.[2] The artistic genius took the place of *le philosophe*. But the emphasis which was laid on the creative imagination and on artistic genius formed part of a general emphasis on the free and full development of the human personality, on man's creative powers and on enjoyment of the wealth of possible human experience. In other words, stress was laid on the originality of each human person rather than on what is common to all men. And this insistence on the creative personality was sometimes associated with a tendency to ethical subjectivism. That is to say, there was a tendency to depreciate fixed universal moral laws or rules in favour of the free development of the self in accordance with values rooted in and corresponding to the individual personality. I do not mean to imply by this that the romantics had no concern for morality and moral values. But there was a tendency, with F. Schlegel for example, to emphasize the free pursuit by the individual of his own moral ideal (the fulfilment of his own 'Idea') rather than obedience to universal laws dictated by the impersonal practical reason.

[1] According to Rudolf Carnap, metaphysical systems express a feeling for or attitude towards life. But such terms are much more applicable to the romantic spirit than, say, to Hegel's dialectical system.

[2] Two comments are appropriate here. First, I do not mean to imply that the romantic movement proper followed immediately upon the Enlightenment. But I pass over the intervening phases. Secondly, the generalization in the text should not be interpreted as meaning that the men of the Enlightenment had no understanding at all of the importance of feeling in human life. See, for example, Vol. VI, pp. 24–7.

In developing their ideas of the creative personality some of the romantics derived inspiration and stimulus from Fichte's early thought. This is true of both F. Schlegel and Novalis. But it does not follow, of course, that the use which they made of Fichte's ideas always corresponded with the philosopher's intentions. An example will make this clear. As we have seen, in his transformation of the Kantian philosophy into pure idealism Fichte took as his ultimate creative principle the transcendental ego, considered as unlimited activity. And in his systematic deduction or reconstruction of consciousness he made copious use of the idea of the productive imagination. Novalis seized on these ideas and represented Fichte as opening up to view the wonders of the creative self. But he made an important change. Fichte was concerned with explaining on idealist principles the situation in which the finite subject finds itself in a world of objects which are given to it and which affect it in various ways, as in sensation. He therefore represented the activity of the so-called productive imagination, when it posits the object as affecting the finite self, as taking place below the level of consciousness. By transcendental reflection the philosopher can be aware *that* this activity takes place, but neither he nor anyone else is aware of it *as* taking place. For the positing of the object is logically prior to all awareness or consciousness. And this activity of the productive imagination is certainly not modifiable at the will of the finite self. Novalis, however, depicted the activity of the productive imagination as modifiable by the will. Just as the artist creates works of art, so is man a creative power not only in the moral sphere but also, in principle at least, in the natural sphere. Fichte's transcendental idealism was thus turned into Novalis's 'magical idealism'. In other words, Novalis seized on some of Fichte's philosophical theories and used them in the service of a poetic and romantic extravaganza, to exalt the creative self.

Further, the romantics' emphasis on the creative genius links them with Schelling much more than with Fichte. As will be seen in due course, it was the former and not the latter who laid stress on the metaphysical significance of art and on the role of artistic genius. When Friedrich Schlegel asserted that there is no greater world than the world of art and that the artist exhibits the Idea in finite form, and when Novalis asserted that the poet is the true 'magician', the embodiment of the creative power of the human self, they were speaking in ways which were more in tune with the thought of Schelling than with the strongly ethical outlook of Fichte.

Emphasis on the creative self was, however, only one aspect of romanticism. Another important aspect was the romantics' conception of Nature. Instead of conceiving Nature simply as a mechanical system, so that they would be forced to make a sharp contrast (as in Cartesianism) between man and Nature, the romantics tended to look on Nature as a living organic whole which is in some way akin to spirit and which is clothed in beauty and mystery. And some of them showed a marked sympathy with Spinoza, that is, a romanticized Spinoza.

This view of Nature as an organic totality akin to spirit again links the romantics with Schelling. The philosopher's idea of Nature below man as slumbering spirit and the human spirit as the organ of Nature's consciousness of herself was thoroughly romantic in tone. It is significant that the poet Hölderlin (1770–1843) was a friend of Schelling when they were fellow-students at Tübingen. And the poet's view of Nature as a living comprehensive whole seems to have exercised some influence on the philosopher. In turn Schelling's philosophy of Nature exercised a powerful stimulative influence on some of the romantics. As for the romantics' sympathy with Spinoza, this was shared by the theologian and philosopher Schleiermacher. But it was certainly not shared by Fichte who had a profound dislike for anything approaching a divinization of Nature, which he looked on simply as a field and instrument for free moral activity. In this respect he was anti-romantic in his outlook.

The romantics' attachment to the idea of Nature as an organic living totality does not mean, however, that they emphasized Nature to the detriment, so to speak, of man. We have seen that they also stressed the free creative personality. In the human spirit Nature reaches, as it were, its culmination. Hence the romantic idea of Nature could be and was allied with a marked appreciation of the continuity of historical and cultural development and of the significance of past cultural periods for the unfolding of the potentialities of the human spirit. Hölderlin, for example, had a romantic enthusiasm for the genius of ancient Greece,[1] an enthusiasm which was shared by Hegel in his student days. But special attention can be drawn here to the reawakened interest in

---

[1] It is a mistake to suppose that Hölderlin's attachment to Greece necessarily makes of him a classicist as opposed to a romantic.

the Middle Ages. The man of the Enlightenment had tended to see in the mediaeval period a dark night which preceded the dawn of the Renaissance and the subsequent emergence of *les philosophes.* But for Novalis the Middle Ages represented, even if imperfectly, an ideal of the organic unity of faith and culture, an ideal which should be recovered. Further, the romantics showed a strong attachment to the idea of the spirit of a people (*Volksgeist*) and an interest in the cultural manifestation of this spirit, such as language. In this respect they continued the thought of Herder[1] and other predecessors.

The idealist philosophers not unnaturally shared this appreciation of historical continuity and development. For history was for them the working-out in time of a spiritual Idea, a *telos* or end. Each of the great idealists had his philosophy of history, that of Hegel being particularly notable. As Fichte looked on Nature primarily as an instrument for moral activity, he naturally laid more emphasis on the sphere of the human spirit and on history as a movement towards the realization of an ideal moral world-order. In Schelling's philosophy of religion history appears as the story of the return to God of fallen humanity, of man alienated from the true centre of his being. With Hegel the idea of the dialectic of national spirits plays a prominent role, though this is accompanied by an insistence on the part played by so-called world-historical individuals. And the movement of history as a whole is depicted as a movement towards the realization of spiritual freedom. In general, we can say, the great idealists regarded their epoch as a time in which the human spirit had become conscious of the significance of its activity in history and of the meaning or direction of the whole historical process.

Above all perhaps romanticism was characterized by a feeling for and longing for the infinite. And the ideas of Nature and of human history were brought together in the conception of them as manifestations of one infinite Life, as aspects of a kind of divine poem. Thus the notion of infinite Life served as a unifying factor in the romantic world-outlook. At first sight perhaps the romantics' attachment to the idea of the *Volksgeist* may appear to be at variance with their emphasis on the free development of the individual personality. But there was really no radical incompatibility. For the infinite totality was conceived, generally speaking, as infinite Life which manifested itself in and through finite beings

---

[1] See Vol. VI, pp. 138–46, 172–9.

but not as annihilating them or as reducing them to mere mechanical instruments. And the spirits of peoples were conceived as manifestations of the same infinite Life, as relative totalities which required for their full development the free expression of the individual personalities which were the bearers, so to speak, of these spirits. And the same can be said of the State, considered as the political embodiment of the spirit of a people.

The typical romantic was inclined to conceive the infinite totality aesthetically, as an organic whole with which man felt himself to be one, the means of apprehending this unity being intuition and feeling rather than conceptual thought. For conceptual thought tends to fix and perpetuate defined limits and boundaries, whereas romanticism tends to dissolve limits and boundaries in the infinite flow of Life. In other words, romantic feeling for the infinite was not infrequently a feeling for the indefinite. And this trait can be seen as well in the tendency to obscure the boundary between the infinite and the finite as in the tendency to confuse philosophy with poetry or, within the artistic sphere itself, to intermingle the arts.

Partly, of course, it was a question of seeing affinities and of synthesizing different types of human experience. Thus F. Schlegel regarded philosophy as akin to religion on the ground that both are concerned with the infinite and that every relation of man to the infinite can be said to belong to religion. Indeed art too is religious in character, for the creative artist sees the infinite in the finite, in the form of beauty. At the same time the romantics' repugnance to definite limits and clear-cut form was one of the reasons which led Goethe to make his famous statement that the classical is the healthy and the romantic the diseased. For the matter of that, some of the romantics themselves came to feel the need for giving definite shape to their intuitive and rather hazy visions of life and reality and for combining the nostalgia for the infinite and for the free expression of the individual personality with a recognition of definite limits. And certain representatives of the movement, such as F. Schlegel, found in Catholicism a fulfilment of this need.

The feeling for the infinite obviously constitutes common ground for romanticism and idealism. The idea of the infinite Absolute, conceived as infinite Life, comes to the fore in Fichte's later philosophy, and the Absolute is a central theme in the philosophies of Schelling, Schleiermacher and Hegel. Further, we can say that the German idealists tend to conceive the infinite not as something set over against the finite but as infinite life or activity which expresses itself in and through the finite. With Hegel especially there is a deliberate attempt to mediate between the finite and the infinite, to bring them together without either identifying the infinite with the finite or dismissing the latter as unreal or illusory. The totality lives in and through its particular manifestations, whether it is a question of the infinite totality, the Absolute, or of a relative totality such as the State.

The spiritual affinity between the romantic and idealist movements is thus unquestionable. And it can be illustrated by many examples. For instance, when Hegel depicts art, religion and philosophy as concerned with the Absolute, though in different ways, we can see an affinity between his view and the ideas of F. Schlegel to which reference was made in the last paragraph. At the same time it is necessary to emphasize an important contrast between the great idealist philosophers and the romantics, a contrast which can be illustrated in the following manner.

Friedrich Schlegel assimilated philosophy to poetry and dreamed of their becoming one. In his view philosophizing was primarily a matter of intuitive insights, not of deductive reasoning or of proof. For every proof is a proof of something, and the intuitive grasp of the truth to be proved precedes all argument, which is a purely secondary affair.[1] As Schlegel put it, Leibniz asserted and Wolff proved. Evidently, this remark was not intended as a compliment to Wolff. Further, philosophy is concerned with the Universe, the totality. And we cannot prove the totality: it is apprehended only in intuition. Nor can we describe it in the same way in which we can describe a particular thing and its relations to other particular things. The totality can in a sense be displayed or shown, as in poetry, but to say precisely what it is transcends our power. The philosopher, therefore, is concerned with attempting to say what cannot be said. And for this reason philosophy and the philosopher himself are for the true philosopher a matter for ironic wit.

When, however, we turn from Friedrich Schlegel, the romantic, to Hegel, the absolute idealist, we find a resolute insistence on systematic conceptual thought and a determined rejection of appeals to mystical intention and feeling. Hegel is indeed concerned with the totality, the Absolute, but he is concerned with

[1] Schlegel's view can be compared with the view advanced by some modern writers on metaphysics, that what really matters in a metaphysical system is the 'vision' and that arguments are persuasive devices to commend or put across a vision.

*thinking* it, with expressing the life of the infinite and its relation to the finite in conceptual thought. It is true that he interprets art, including poetry, as having the same subject-matter as philosophy, namely absolute Spirit. But he also insists on a difference of form which it is essential to preserve. Poetry and philosophy are distinct, and they should not be confused.

It may be objected that the contrast between the romantics' idea of philosophy and that of the great idealists is not nearly so great as a comparison between the views of F. Schlegel and Hegel tends to suggest. Fichte postulated a basic intellectual intuition of the pure or absolute ego an idea which was exploited by some of the romantics. Schelling insisted, at least in one stage of his philosophizing, that the Absolute can be apprehended in itself only in mystical intuition. And he also emphasized an aesthetic intuition through which the nature of the Absolute is apprehended not in itself but in symbolic form. For the matter of that, romantic traits can be discerned even within the Hegelian dialectical logic, which is a logic of movement, designed to exhibit the inner life of the Spirit and to overcome the conceptual antitheses which ordinary logic tends to render fixed and permanent. Indeed, the way in which Hegel depicts the human spirit as passing successively through a variety of attitudes and as restlessly moving from position to position can reasonably be regarded as an expression of the romantic outlook. Hegel's logical apparatus itself is alien to the romantic spirit, but this apparatus belongs to the foreground of his system. Underneath we can see a profound spiritual affinity with the romantic movement.

It is not, however, a question of denying the existence of a spiritual affinity between metaphysical idealism and romanticism. We have already argued that there is such an affinity. It is a question of pointing out that, in general, the idealist philosophers were concerned with systematic thought whereas the romantics were inclined to emphasize the role of intuition and feeling and to assimilate philosophy to poetry. Schelling and Schleiermacher stood indeed closer to the romantic spirit than did Fichte or Hegel. It is true that Fichte postulated a basic intellectual intuition of the pure or absolute ego; but he did not think of this as some sort of privileged mystical insight. For him it was an intuitive grasp of an activity which manifests itself to the reflective consciousness. What is required is not some mystical or poetic capacity but transcendental reflection, which is open in principle to all. And in his attack on the romantics Fichte insisted that his philosophy, though demanding this basic intellectual intuition of the ego as activity, was a matter of logical thought which yielded science, in the sense of certain knowledge. Philosophy is the knowledge of knowledge, the basic science; it is not an attempt to say what cannot be said. As for Hegel, it is doubtless true that we, looking back, can discern romantic traits even within his dialectic. But this does not alter the fact that he insisted that philosophy is not a matter of apocalyptic utterances or poetic rhapsodies or mystical intuitions but of systematic logical thought which thinks its subject-matter conceptually and makes it plain to view. The philosopher's business is to understand reality and to make others understand it, not to edify or to suggest meaning by the use of poetic images.

6. As we have seen, the initial transformation of Kant's philosophy into pure idealism meant that reality had to be looked on as a process of productive thought or reason. In other words, being had to be identified with thought. And the natural programme of idealism was to exhibit the truth of this identification by means of a deductive reconstruction of the essential dynamic structure of the life of absolute thought or reason. Further, if the Kantian conception of philosophy as thought's reflective awareness of its own spontaneous activity was to be retained, philosophical reflection had to be represented as the self-awareness or self-consciousness of absolute reason in and through the human mind. Hence it pertained also to the natural programme of idealism to exhibit the truth of this interpretation of philosophical reflection.

When, however, we turn to the actual history of the idealist movement, we see the difficulty encountered by the idealists in completely fulfilling this programme. Or, to put the matter in another way, we see marked divergences from the pattern suggested by the initial transformation of the critical philosophy into transcendental idealism. For example, Fichte starts with the determination not to go beyond consciousness, in the sense of postulating as his first principle a being which transcends consciousness. He thus takes as his first principle the pure ego as manifested in consciousness, not as a thing but as an activity. But the demands of his transcendental idealism force him to push back, as it were, the ultimate reality behind consciousness. And in the later form of his philosophy we find him postulating absolute infinite Being which transcends thought.

With Schelling the process is in a sense reversed. That is to say, while at one stage of his philosophical pilgrimage he asserts the existence of an Absolute which transcends human thought and conceptualization, in his subsequent religious philosophy he attempts to reconstruct reflectively the essence and inner life of the personal Deity. At the same time, however, he abandons the idea of deducing in a *a priori* manner the existence and structure of empirical reality and emphasizes the idea of God's free self-revelation. He does not entirely abandon the idealist tendency to look on the finite as though it were a logical consequence of the infinite; but once he has introduced the idea of a free personal God his thought necessarily departs to a large extent from the original pattern of metaphysical idealism.

Needless to say, the fact that both Fichte and Schelling, especially the latter, developed and changed their initial positions does not by itself constitute any proof that the developments and changes were unjustified. My point is rather that these illustrate the difficulty in carrying through to completion what I have called the idealist programme. One can say that neither with Fichte nor with Schelling is being in the long run reduced to thought.

It is with Hegel that we find by far the most sustained attempt to fulfil the idealist programme. He has no doubt that the rational is the real and the real the rational. And in his view it is quite wrong to speak of the human mind as merely finite and on this ground to question its power to understand the self-unfolding life of the infinite Absolute. The mind has indeed its finite aspects, but it is also infinite, in the sense that it is capable of rising to the level of absolute thought, at which level the Absolute's knowledge of itself and man's knowledge of the Absolute are one. And Hegel makes what is undoubtedly a most impressive attempt to show in a systematic and detailed way how reality is the life of absolute reason in its movement towards the goal of self-knowledge, thus becoming in actual existence what it always is in essence, namely self-thinking thought.

Clearly, the more Hegel identifies the Absolute's knowledge of itself with man's knowledge of the Absolute, the more completely does he fulfil the demand of the idealist programme that philosophy should be represented as the self-reflection of absolute thought or reason. If the Absolute were a personal God, eternally enjoying perfect self-awareness quite independently of the human spirit, man's knowledge of God would be an outside view, so to speak. If, however, the Absolute is all reality, the Universe, interpreted as the self-unfolding of absolute thought which attains self-reflection in and through the human spirit, man's knowledge of the Absolute is the Absolute's knowledge of itself. And philosophy is productive thought thinking itself.

But what is then meant by productive thought? It is arguable at any rate that it can hardly mean anything else but the Universe considered teleologically, that is, as a process moving towards self-knowledge, this self-knowledge being in effect nothing but man's developing knowledge of Nature, of himself and of his history. And in this case there is nothing behind the Universe, as it were, no thought or reason which expresses itself in Nature and human history in the way that an efficient cause expresses itself in its effect. Thought is teleologically prior, in the sense that man's knowledge of the world-process is represented as the goal of the process and as giving it its significance. But that which is actually or historically prior is Being in the form of objective Nature. And in this case the whole pattern of idealism, as suggested by the initial transformation of Kant's philosophy, is changed. For this transformation inevitably suggests the picture of an activity of infinite thought which produces or creates the objective world, whereas the picture described above is simply the picture of the actual world of experience interpreted as a teleological process. The *telos* or goal of the process is indeed depicted as the world's self-reflection in and through the human mind. But this goal or end is an ideal which is never complete at any given moment of time. Hence the identification of being and thought is never actually achieved.

7. Another aspect of the divergences from the natural pattern of post-Kantian idealism can be expressed in this way. F. H. Bradley, the English absolute idealist, maintained that the concept of God inevitably passes into the concept of the Absolute. That is to say, if the mind tries to think the infinite in a consistent manner, it must in the end acknowledge that the infinite cannot be anything else but the universe of being, reality as a whole, the totality. And with this transformation of God into the Absolute religion disappears. 'Short of the Absolute God cannot rest, and, having reached that goal, he is lost and religion with him.'[1] A similar view was expressed by R. G. Collingwood. 'God and the absolute are not identical but irretrievably distinct. And yet they are identical

[1] *Appearance and Reality* (2nd edition), p. 447.

in this sense: God is the imaginative or intuitive form in which the absolute reveals itself to the religious consciousness.'[2] If we preserve speculative metaphysics, we must admit in the long run that theism is a half-way house between the frank anthropomorphism of polytheism on the one hand and the idea of the all-inclusive Absolute on the other.

It is indeed obvious that in the absence of any clear idea of the analogy of being the notion of a finite being which is ontologically distinct from the infinite cannot stand. But let us pass over this point, important as it is, and note instead that post-Kantian idealism in what one might call its natural form is thoroughly anthropomorphic. For the pattern of human consciousness is transferred to reality as a whole. Let us suppose that the human ego comes to self-consciousness only indirectly. That is to say attention is first directed to the not-self. The not-self has to be posited by the ego or subject, not in the sense that the not-self must be ontologically created by the self but in the sense that it must be recognized as an object if consciousness is to arise at all. The ego can then turn back upon itself and become reflectively aware of itself in its activity. In post-Kantian idealism this process of human consciousness is used as a key-idea for the interpretation of reality as a whole. The absolute ego or absolute reason or whatever it may be called is regarded as positing (in an ontological sense) the objective world of Nature as a necessary condition for returning to itself in and through the human spirit.

This general scheme follows naturally enough from the transformation of the Kantian philosophy into metaphysical idealism. But inasmuch as Kant was concerned with human knowledge and consciousness, the inflation of his theory of knowledge into cosmic metaphysics inevitably involves interpreting the process of reality as a whole according to the pattern of human consciousness. And in this sense post-Kantian idealism contains a marked element of anthropomorphism, a fact which it is just as well to notice in view of the not uncommon notion that absolute idealism is much less anthropomorphic than theism. Of course, we cannot conceive God other than analogically; and we cannot conceive the divine consciousness except according to an analogy with human consciousness. But we can endeavour to eliminate in thought the aspects of consciousness which are bound up with finitude. And it is arguable, to put it mildly, that to attribute to the infinite a

[2] *Speculum Mentis*, p. 151.

process of becoming self-conscious is an evident expression of anthropomorphic thinking.

Now, if there is a spiritual reality which is at any rate logically prior to Nature and which becomes self-conscious in and through man, how are we to conceive it? If we conceive it as an unlimited activity which is not itself conscious but grounds consciousness, we have more or less Fichte's theory of the so-called absolute ego.

But the concept of an ultimate reality which is at the same time spiritual and unconscious is not easily understood. Nor, of course, does it bear much resemblance to the Christian concept of God. If, however, we maintain with Schelling in his later religious philosophy that the spiritual reality which lies behind Nature is a personal Being, the pattern of the idealist scheme is inevitably changed. For it cannot then be maintained that the ultimate spiritual reality becomes self-conscious in and through the cosmic process. And inasmuch as Schelling outlived Hegel by more than twenty years we can say that the idealist movement which immediately followed the critical philosophy of Kant ended, chronologically speaking, in a reapproximation to philosophical theism. As we have seen, Bradley maintained that the concept of God is required by the religious consciousness but that, from the philosophical point of view, it must be transformed into the concept of the Absolute. Schelling would have accepted the first contention but rejected the second, at least as understood by Bradley. For in his later years Schelling's philosophy was pretty well a philosophy of the religious consciousness. And he believed that the religious consciousness demanded the transformation of his own former idea of the Absolute into the idea of a personal God. In his theosophical speculations he undoubtedly introduced obvious anthropomorphic elements, as will be seen later. But at the same time the movement of his mind towards theism represented a departure from the peculiar brand of anthropomorphism which was characteristic of post-Kantian idealism.

There is, however, a third possibility. We can eliminate the idea of a spiritual reality, whether unconscious or conscious, which produces Nature, and we can at the same time retain the idea of the Absolute becoming self-conscious. The Absolute then means the world, in the sense of the universe. And we have the picture of man's knowledge of the world and of his own history as the self-knowledge of the Absolute. In this picture, which represents the general line of one of the main interpretations of Hegel's absolute idealism,[1] nothing is added, as it were, to the empirical world except a teleological account of the world-process. That is to say, no existent transcendent Being is postulated; but the universe is interpreted as a process moving towards an ideal goal, namely complete self-reflection in and through the human spirit.

This interpretation can hardly be taken as merely equivalent to the empirical statements that in the course of the world's history man has as a matter of fact appeared and that as a matter of fact he is capable of knowing and of increasing his knowledge of himself, his history and his environment. For presumably none of us, whether materialists or idealists, whether theists, pantheists or atheists, would hesitate to accept these statements. At the very least the interpretation is meant to suggest a teleological pattern, a movement towards human knowledge of the universe, considered as the universe's knowledge of itself. But unless we are prepared to admit that this is only one possible way of regarding the world process and thus to lay ourselves open to the objection that our choice of this particular pattern is determined by an intellectualist prejudice in favour of knowledge for the sake of knowledge (that is, by a particular valuational judgment), we must claim, it appears, that the world moves by some inner necessity towards the goal of self-knowledge in and through man. But what ground have we for making this claim unless we believe either that Nature itself is unconscious mind (or, as Schelling put it, slumbering Spirit which strives towards consciousness or that behind Nature there is unconscious mind or reason which spontaneously posits Nature as a necessary precondition for attaining consciousness in and through the human spirit? And if we accept either of these positions we transfer to the universe as a whole the pattern of the development of human consciousness. This procedure may indeed be demanded by the transformation of the critical philosophy into metaphysical idealism; but it is certainly not less anthropomorphic in character than philosophical theism.

8. In this chapter we have been mainly concerned with German idealism as a theory, or rather set of theories, about reality as a whole, the self-manifesting Absolute. But a philosophy of man is also a prominent feature of the idealist movement. And this is indeed only what one would expect if one considers the metaphysical premisses of the several philosophers. According to

[1] The adequacy of this interpretation of Hegel is highly disputable. But this is a question which need not detain us here.

Fichte, the absolute ego is an unlimited activity which can be represented as striving towards consciousness of its own freedom. But consciousness exists only in the form of individual consciousness. Hence the absolute ego necessarily expresses itself in a community of finite subjects or selves, each of which strives towards the attainment of true freedom. And the theme of moral activity inevitably comes to the fore. Fichte's philosophy is essentially a dynamic ethical idealism. Again, for Hegel the Absolute is definable as Spirit or as self-thinking Thought. Hence it is more adequately revealed in the human spirit and its life than in Nature. And more emphasis must be placed on the reflective understanding of man's spiritual life (the life of man as a rational being) than on the philosophy of Nature. As for Schelling, when he comes to assert the existence of a personal and free God, he occupies himself concurrently with the problem of freedom in man and with man's fall from and return to God.

In the idealist philosophies of man and society insistence on freedom is a conspicuous feature. But it does not follow, of course, that the word 'freedom' is used throughout in the same sense. With Fichte the emphasis is on individual freedom as manifested in action. And we can doubtless see in this emphasis a reflection of the philosopher's own dynamic and energetic temperament. For Fichte man is from one point of view a system of natural drives, instincts and impulses; and if he is looked at simply from this point of view, it is idle to talk about freedom. But as spirit man is not tied, so to speak, to the automatic satisfaction of one desire after another: he can direct his activity to an ideal goal and act in accordance with the idea of duty. As with Kant, freedom tends to mean rising above the life of sensual impulse and acting as a rational, moral being. And Fichte is inclined to speak as though activity were its own end, emphasizing free action for the sake of free action.

But though Fichte's primary emphasis is on the individual's activity and on his rising above the slavery of natural drive and impulse to a life of action in accordance with duty, he sees, of course, that some content has to be given to the idea of free moral action. And he does this by stressing the concept of moral vocation. A man's vocation, the series of actions which he ought to perform in the world, is largely determined by his social situation, by his position, for example, as the father of a family. And in the end we have the vision of a multiplicity of moral vocations converging towards a common ideal end, the establishment of a moral world-order.

As a young man Fichte was an enthusiastic supporter of the French Revolution which he regarded as liberating men from forms of social and political life which hindered their free moral development. But then the question arose, what form of social, economic and political organization is best fitted to favour man's moral development? And Fichte found himself compelled to lay increasing emphasis on the positive role of political society as a morally educative power. But though in his later years reflection on contemporary political events, namely the Napoleonic domination and the war of liberation, was partly responsible for the growth in his mind of a nationalistic outlook and for a strong emphasis on the cultural mission of a unified German State in which alone the Germans could find true freedom, his more characteristic idea was that the State is a necessary instrument to preserve the system of rights as long as man has not attained his full moral development. If man as a moral being were fully developed, the State would wither away.

When we turn to Hegel, however, we find a different attitude. Hegel too was influenced in his youth by the ferment of the French Revolution and the drive to freedom. And the term 'freedom' plays a conspicuous role in his philosophy. As will be seen in due course, he represents human history as a movement towards the fuller realization of freedom. But he distinguishes sharply between negative freedom, as mere absence of restraint, and positive freedom. As Kant saw, moral freedom involves obeying only that law which one gives oneself as a rational being. But the rational is the universal. And positive freedom involves identifying oneself with ends that transcend one's desires as a particular individual. It is attained, above all, by identifying one's particular will with Rousseau's General Will which finds expression in the State. Morality is essentially social morality. The formal moral law receives its content and field of application in social life, especially in the State.

Both Fichte and Hegel, therefore, attempt to overcome the formalism of the Kantian ethic by placing morality in a social setting. But there is a difference of emphasis. Fichte places the emphasis on individual freedom and action in accordance with duty mediated by the personal conscience. We have to add as a corrective that the individual's moral vocation is seen as a member

of a system of moral vocations, and so in a social setting. But in
Fichte's ethics the emphasis is placed on the individual's struggle
to overcome himself, to bring his lower self, as it were, into tune
with the free will which aims at complete freedom. Hegel, however,
places the emphasis on man as a member of political society and on
the social aspects of ethics. Positive freedom is something to be
attained through membership in a greater organic whole. As a
corrective or counterweight to this emphasis we must add that for
Hegel no State can be fully rational unless it recognizes the value
of and finds room for subjective or individual freedom. When at
Berlin Hegel lectured on political theory and described the State in
highfaluting terms, he was concerned with making his hearers
socially and politically conscious and with overcoming what he
regarded as an unfortunate one-sided emphasis on the inwardness
of morality rather than with turning them into totalitarians.
Further, political institutions constitute, according to Hegel, the
necessary basis for man's higher spiritual activities, art, religion
and philosophy, in which the freedom of the spirit reaches its
supreme expression.

What one misses, however, in both Fichte and Hegel is perhaps
a clear theory of absolute moral values. If we talk with Fichte
about action for action's sake, freedom for the sake of freedom,
we may show an awareness of the unique character of each human
being's moral vocation. But at the same time we run the risk of
emphasizing the creative personality and the uniqueness of its
moral vocation at the expense of the universality of the moral law.
If, however, we socialize morality with Hegel, we give it concrete
content and avoid the formalism of the Kantian ethic, but at the
same time we run the risk of implying that moral values and
standards are simply relative to different societies and cultural
periods. Obviously, some would maintain that this is in fact the
case. But if we do not agree, we require a clearer and more adequate
theory of absolute values than Hegel actually provides.

Schelling's outlook was rather different from that either of
Fichte or of Hegel. At one period of his philosophical development
he utilized a good many of the former's ideas and represented the
moral activity of man as tending to create a second Nature, a moral
world-order, a moral world within the physical world. But the
difference between his attitude and Fichte's showed itself in the
fact that he proceeded to add a philosophy of art and of aesthetic
intuition to which he attributed a great metaphysical significance.

With Fichte the emphasis was placed on the moral struggle and on free moral action, with Schelling it was placed on aesthetic intuition as a key to the ultimate nature of reality, and he exalted the artistic genius rather than the moral hero. When, however, theological problems came to absorb his interest, his philosophy of man naturally took on a marked religious colouring. Freedom, he thought, is the power to choose between good and bad. And personality is something to be won by the birth of light out of darkness, that is, by a sublimation of man's lower nature and its subordination to the rational will. But these themes are treated in a metaphysical setting. For example, the views on freedom and personality to which allusion has just been made lead Schelling into theosophical speculation about the nature of God. In turn, his theories about the divine nature react on his view of man.

To return to Hegel, the greatest of the German idealists. His analysis of human society and his philosophy of history are certainly very impressive. Many of those who listened to his lectures on history must have felt that the significance of the past and the meaning of the movement of history were being revealed to them. Moreover, Hegel was not exclusively concerned with understanding the past. As has already been remarked, he wished to make his students socially, politically and ethically conscious. And he doubtless thought that his analysis of the rational State could furnish standards and aims in political life, especially in German political life. But the emphasis is placed on understanding. Hegel is the author of the famous saying that the owl of Minerva spreads her wings only with the falling of the dusk, and that when philosophy spreads her grey on grey, then has a shape of life grown cold. He had a vivid realization of the fact that political philosophy is apt to canonize, as it were, the social and political forms of a society or culture which is about to pass away. When a culture or society has become mature and ripe, or even over-ripe, it becomes conscious of itself in and through philosophical reflection, just at the moment when the movement of life is demanding and bringing forth new societies or new social and political forms.

With Karl Marx we find a different attitude. The business of the philosopher is to understand the movement of history in order to change existing institutions and forms of social organization in accordance with the demands of the teleological movement of history. Marx does not, of course, deny the necessity and value of understanding, but he emphasizes the revolutionary function of understanding. In a sense Hegel looks backward, Marx forward. Whether Marx's idea of the philosopher's function is tenable or not is a question which we need not discuss here. It is sufficient to note the difference between the attitudes of the great idealist and the social revolutionary. If we wish to find among the idealist philosophers something comparable to Marx's missionary zeal, we have to turn to Fichte rather than to Hegel. As will be seen in the relevant chapters, Fichte had a passionate belief in the saving mission of his own philosophy for human society. But Hegel felt, as it were, the weight and burden of all history on his shoulders. And looking back on the history of the world, his primary aim was to understand it. Further, though he certainly did not imagine that history had stopped with the coming of the nineteenth century, he was too historically minded to have much faith in the finality of any philosophical Utopia.

*Life and writings—On looking for the fundamental principle of philosophy; the choice between idealism and dogmatism—The pure ego and intellectual intuition—Comments on the theory of the pure ego; phenomenology of consciousness and idealist metaphysics—The three fundamental principles of philosophy— Explanatory comments on Fichte's dialectical method—The theory of science and formal logic—The general idea of the two deductions of consciousness—The theoretical deduction—The practical deduction—Comments on Fichte's deduction of consciousness.*

1. JOHANN GOTTLIEB FICHTE was born in 1762 at Rammenau in Saxony. He came of a poor family, and in the ordinary course of events he could hardly have enjoyed facilities for pursuing advanced studies. But as a small boy he aroused the interest of a local nobleman, the Baron von Miltitz, who undertook to provide for his education. At the appropriate age Fichte was sent to the famous school at Pforta where Nietzsche was later to study. And in 1780 he enrolled as a student of theology in the University of Jena, moving later to Wittenberg and subsequently to Leipzig.

During his studies Fichte came to accept the theory of determinism. To remedy this sad state of affairs a good clergyman recommended to him an edition of Spinoza's *Ethics* which was furnished with a refutation by Wolff. But as the refutation seemed to Fichte to be extremely weak, the effect of the work was the very opposite of that intended by the pastor. Determinism, however, was not really in tune with Fichte's active and energetic character or with his strong ethical interests, and it was soon replaced by an insistence on moral freedom. He was later to show himself a vigorous opponent of Spinozism, but it always represented for him one of the great alternatives in philosophy.

For financial reasons Fichte found himself compelled to take a post as tutor in a family at Zürich where he read Rousseau and Montesquieu and welcomed the news of the French Revolution with its message of liberty. His interest in Kant was aroused when a student's request for the explanation of the critical philosophy led him to study it for the first time. And in 1791, when returning to Germany from Warsaw, where he had a brief and rather humiliating experience as tutor in a nobleman's family, he visited Kant at Königsberg. But he was not received with any enthusiasm. And he therefore attempted to win the great man's favour by writing an essay to develop Kant's justification of faith in the name of the practical reason. The resulting *Essay towards a Critique of all Revelation* (*Versuch einer Kritik aller Offenbarung*) pleased Kant, and after some difficulties with the theological censorship it was published in 1792. As the name of the author was not given, some reviewers concluded that the essay had been written by Kant. And when Kant proceeded to correct this error and to praise the real author, Fichte's name became at once widely known.

In 1793 Fichte published his *Contributions designed to correct the Judgment of the Public on the French Revolution*. This work won for him the reputation of being a democrat and Jacobin, a politically dangerous figure. In spite of this, however, he was appointed professor of philosophy at Jena in 1794, partly owing to a warm recommendation by Goethe. In addition to his more professional courses of lectures Fichte gave a series of conferences on the dignity of man and the vocation of the scholar, which were published in the year of his appointment to the chair. He was always something of a missionary or preacher. But the chief publication of 1794 was the *Basis of the Entire Theory of Science* (*Grundlage der gesammten Wissenschaftslehre*) in which he presented his idealist development of the critical philosophy of Kant. His predecessor in the chair of philosophy at Jena, K. L. Reinhold (1758–1823), who had accepted an invitation to Kiel, had already demanded that the Kantian criticism should be turned into a system, that is to say, that it should be derived systematically from one fundamental principle. And in his theory of science Fichte undertook to fulfil this task more successfully than Reinhold had done.[1] The theory of science was conceived as exhibiting the systematic development from one ultimate principle of the fundamental propositions which lie at the basis of and make possible all particular sciences or ways of knowing. But to exhibit this development is at the same time to portray the development of creative thought. Hence the theory of science is not only epistemology but also metaphysics.

[1] From about 1797 Reinhold accepted and defended the philosophy of Fichte. But he was a restless spirit, and after a few years he turned to other lines of thought.

But Fichte was very far from concentrating exclusively on the theoretical deduction of consciousness. He laid great stress on the moral end of the development of consciousness or, in more concrete terms, on the moral purpose of human existence. And we find him publishing in 1796 the *Basis of Natural Right* (*Grundlage des Naturrechts*) and in 1798 *The System of Ethics* (*Das System der Sittenlehre*). Both subjects are said to be treated 'according to the principles of the theory of science'. And so no doubt they are. But the works are much more than mere appendages to the *Wissenschaftslehre*. For they display the true character of Fichte's philosophy, that is, as a system of ethical idealism.

Complaints have often been made, and not without reason, of the obscurity of the metaphysical idealists. But a prominent feature of Fichte's literary activity was his unremitting efforts to clarify the ideas and principles of the theory of science.[1] For instance, in 1797 he published two introductions to the *Wissenschaftslehre* and in 1801 his *Sonnenklarer Bericht, A Report, Clear as the Sun, for the General Public on the Real Essence of the Latest Philosophy: An Attempt to compel the Reader to Understand*. The title may have been over-optimistic, but at any rate it bore witness to the author's efforts to make his meaning clear. Moreover, in the period 1801–13 Fichte composed, for his lecture courses, several revised versions of the *Wissenschaftslehre*. In 1810 he published *The Theory of Science in its General Lines* (*Die Wissenschaftslehre in ihrem allgemeinen Umrisse*) and the *Facts of Consciousness* (*Tatsachen des Bewusstseins*, second edition, 1813).

In 1799 Fichte's career at Jena came to an abrupt end. He had already aroused some antagonism in the university by his plans to reform the students' societies and by his Sunday discourses which seemed to the clergy to constitute an act of trespass on their preserves. But his crowning offence was the publication in 1798 of an essay *On the Ground of our Belief in a Divine World-Order* (*Ueber den Grund unseres Glaubens an eine göttliche Weltregierung*). The appearance of this essay led to a charge of atheism, on the ground that Fichte identified God with a moral world-order to be created and sustained by the human will. The philosopher tried to defend himself, but without success. And in 1799 he had to leave Jena and went to Berlin.

In 1800 Fichte published *The Vocation of Man* (*Die Bestimmung*

---

[1] It is perhaps needless to say that the word 'science' must be understood in the sense of 'knowledge' rather than according to the narrower modern use of the term.

*des Menschen*). The work belongs to his so-called popular writings, addressed to the general educated public rather than to professional philosophers; and it is a manifesto in favour of the author's idealist system as contrasted with the romantics' attitude to Nature and to religion. Fichte's exalted language may indeed easily suggest a romantic pantheism, but the significance of the work was understood well enough by the romantics themselves. Schleiermacher, for example, saw that Fichte was concerned with repudiating any attempt to achieve a fusion of Spinozism and idealism, and in a sharply critical review he maintained that Fichte's hostile reaction to the idea of the universal necessity of Nature was really caused by his predominating interest in man as a finite, independent being who had at all costs to be exalted above Nature. In Schleiermacher's opinion Fichte should have sought for a higher synthesis which would include the truth in Spinozism while not denying moral freedom, instead of simply opposing man to Nature.

In the same year, 1800, Fichte published his work on *The Closed Commercial State* (*Der geschlossene Handelsstaat*) in which he proposed a kind of State socialism. It has already been remarked that Fichte was something of a missionary. He regarded his system not only as the philosophical truth in an abstract, academic sense, but also as the saving truth, in the sense that the proper application of its principles would lead to the reform of society. In this respect at least he resembles Plato. Fichte had once hoped that Freemasonry might prove an apt instrument for promoting moral and social reform by taking up and applying the principles of the *Wissenschaftslehre*. But he was disappointed in this hope and turned instead to the Prussian government. And his work was really a programme offered to the government for implementation.

In 1804 Fichte accepted the offer of a chair at Erlangen. But he was not actually nominated professor until April 1805, and he employed the interval by lecturing at Berlin on the *Characteristics of the Present Age* (*Grundzüge des gegenwärtigen Zeitalters*). In these lectures he attacked the view of romantics such as Novalis, Tieck and the two Schlegels. Tieck introduced Novalis to Boehme's writings, and some of the romantics were enthusiastic admirers of the mystical shoemaker of Görlitz. But their enthusiasm was not shared by Fichte. Nor had he any sympathy with Novalis's dream of the restoration of a theocratic Catholic culture. His lectures were also directed against the philosophy of Nature which had been developed by Schelling, his former disciple. But these polemics are in a sense incidental to the general philosophy of history which is sketched in the lectures. Fichte's 'present age' represents one of the epochs in the development of man towards the goal of history described as the ordering of all human relations with freedom according to reason. The lectures were published in 1806.

At Erlangen Fichte lectured in 1805 *On the Nature of the Scholar* (*Ueber das Wesen des Gelehrten*). And in the winter of 1805-6 he gave a course of lectures at Berlin on *The Way to the Blessed Life or The Doctrine of Religion* (*Die Anweisung zum seligen Leben, oder auch die Religionslehre*). At first sight at least this work on religion seems to show a radical change from the philosophy expounded in Fichte's early writings. We hear less about the ego and much more about the Absolute and life in God. Indeed, Schelling accused Fichte of plagiarism, that is, of borrowing ideas from Schelling's theory of the Absolute and trying to graft them on to the *Wissenschaftslehre*, oblivious of the incompatibility between the two elements. Fichte, however, refused to admit that his religious ideas, as set forth in *The Doctrine of Religion*, were in any way inconsistent with his original philosophy.

When Napoleon invaded Prussia in 1806, Fichte offered to accompany the Prussian troops as a lay preacher or orator. But he was informed that the King considered it a time for speaking by acts rather than by words, and that oratory would be better suited for celebrating victory. When events took a menacing turn Fichte left Berlin; but he returned in 1807, and in the winter of 1807-8 he delivered his *Addresses to the German Nation* (*Reden an die deutsche Nation*). These discourses, in which the philosopher speaks in exalted and glowing terms of the cultural mission of the German people,[1] have lent themselves to subsequent exploitation in an extreme nationalist sense. But in justice to him we should remember the circumstances in which they were delivered, namely the period of Napoleonic domination.

The year 1810 saw the foundation of the University of Berlin, and Fichte was appointed dean of the philosophical faculty. From 1811 to 1812 he was rector of the university. At the beginning of 1814 he caught typhus from his wife who had contracted the disease while nursing the sick, and on January 29th of that year he died.

---

[1] A. G. Schlegel had already spoken in a not dissimilar vein of Germany's cultural mission in a course of lectures given in 1803-4.

2. Fichte's initial conception of philosophy has little in common with the romantic idea of the kinship between it and poetry. Philosophy is, or at least ought to be, a science. In the first place, that is to say, it should be a body of propositions which form a systematic whole of such a kind that each proposition occupies its proper place in a logical order. And in the second there must be a fundamental or logically prior proposition. 'Every science must have a fundamental proposition [*Grundsatz*]. . . . And it cannot have more than one fundamental proposition. For otherwise it would be not one but several sciences.'[1] We might indeed wish to question the statement that every science must have one, and only one basic proposition; but this is at any rate part of what Fichte means by a science.

This idea of science is obviously inspired by a mathematical model. Indeed, Fichte takes geometry as an example of a science. But it is, of course, a particular science, whereas philosophy is for Fichte the science of science, that is, the knowledge of knowledge or doctrine of knowledge (*Wissenschaftslehre*). In other words, philosophy is the basic science. Hence the fundamental proposition of philosophy must be indemonstrable and self-evidently true. 'All other propositions will possess only a mediate certainty, derived from it, whereas it must be immediately certain.'[2] For if its fundamental proposition were demonstrable in another science, philosophy would not be the basic science.

As will be seen in the course of the exposition of his thought, Fichte does not actually adhere to the programme suggested by this concept of philosophy. That is to say, his philosophy is not in practice a strict logical deduction such as could in principle be performed by a machine. But this point must be left aside for the moment. The immediate question is, what is the basic proposition of philosophy?

But before we can answer this question we must decide in what direction we are going to look for the proposition which we are seeking. And here, according to Fichte, one is faced with an initial option, one's choice depending on what kind of a man one is. A man of one type will be inclined to look in one direction and a man of another type in another direction. But this idea of an initial option stands in need of some explanation. And the explanation

---

[1] *F*, I, pp. 41–2; *M*, I, p. 170. In this and similar references to Fichte's writings *F* and *M* signify respectively the editions of his *Works* by his son, I. H. Fichte, and F. Medicus.

[2] *F*, I, p. 48; *M*, I, p. 177.

throws light on Fichte's conception of the task of philosophy and of the issue with which contemporary thought is faced.

In his *First Introduction to the Theory of Science* Fichte tells us that philosophy is called upon to make clear the ground of all experience (*Erfahrung*). But the word experience is here used in a somewhat restricted sense. If we consider the contents of consciousness, we see that they are of two kinds. 'We can say in brief: some of our presentations [*Vorstellungen*] are accompanied by the feeling of freedom, while others are accompanied by the feeling of necessity.'[1] If I construct in imagination a griffin or a golden mountain, or if I make up my mind to go to Paris rather than to Brussels, such presentations seem to depend on myself. And, as depending on the subject's choice, they are said to be accompanied by the feeling of freedom. If we ask why they are what they are, the answer is that the subject makes them what they are. But if I take a walk along a London street, it does not depend simply on myself what I see or hear. And such presentations are said to be accompanied by the feeling of necessity. That is to say, they appear to be imposed upon me. The whole system of these presentations is called by Fichte 'experience' even if he does not always use the term in this limited sense. And we can ask, what is the ground of experience? How are we to explain the obvious fact that a very large class of presentations seem to be imposed on the subject? 'To answer this question is the task of philosophy.'[2]

Now, two possibilities lie open to us. Actual experience is always experience of something by an experiencer: consciousness is always consciousness of an object by a subject or, as Fichte sometimes puts it, intelligence. But by a process which Fichte calls abstraction the philosopher can isolate conceptually the two factors which in actual consciousness are always conjoined. He can thus form the concepts of intelligence-in-itself and thing-in-itself. And two paths lie before him. Either he can try to explain experience (in the sense described in the last paragraph) as the product of intelligence-in-itself, that is, of creative thought. Or he can try to explain experience as the effect of the thing-in-itself. The first path is obviously that of idealism. The second is that of 'dogmatism'. And in the long run dogmatism spells materialism and determinism. If the thing, the object, is taken as the fundamental principle of explanation, intelligence will ultimately be reduced to a mere epiphenomenon.

[1] *F*, I, p. 423; *M*, III, p. 7.          [2] *Ibid.*

This uncompromising Either-Or attitude is characteristic of Fichte. There is for him a clear-cut option between two opposed and mutually exclusive positions. True, some philosophers, notably Kant, have endeavoured to effect a compromise, to find, that is to say, a middle path between pure idealism and a dogmatism which ends in deterministic materialism. But Fichte has no use for such compromises. If a philosopher wishes to avoid dogmatism with all its consequences, and if he is prepared to be consistent, he must eliminate the thing-in-itself as a factor in the explanation of experience. The presentations which are accompanied by a feeling of necessity, by the feeling of being imposed upon or affected by an object existing independently of mind or thought, must be accounted for without any recourse to the Kantian idea of the thing-in-itself.

But on what principle is the philosopher to make his choice between the two possibilities which lie open to him? He cannot appeal to any basic theoretical principle. For we are assuming that he has not yet found such a principle but has to decide in what direction he is going to look for it. The issue must, therefore, be decided 'by inclination and interest'.[1] That is to say, the choice which the philosopher makes depends on what kind of a man he is. Needless to say, Fichte is convinced that the superiority of idealism to dogmatism as an explanation of experience becomes evident in the process of working out the two systems. But they have not yet been worked out. And in looking for the first principle of philosophy we cannot appeal to the theoretical superiority of a system which has not yet been constructed.

What Fichte means is that the philosopher who is maturely conscious of his freedom as revealed in moral experience will be inclined to idealism, while the philosopher who lacks this mature moral consciousness will be inclined to dogmatism. The 'interest' in question is thus interest in and for the self, which Fichte regards as the highest interest. The dogmatist, lacking this interest, emphasizes the thing, the not-self. But the thinker who has a genuine interest in and for the free moral subject will turn for his basic philosophical principle to intelligence, the self or ego, rather than to the not-self.

Fichte's preoccupation with the free and morally active self is thus made clear from the start. Underlying and inspiring his theoretical inquiry into the ground of experience there is a profound

[1] *F*, I, p. 433; *M*, III, p. 17.

conviction of the primary significance of man's free moral activity. He continues Kant's insistence on the primacy of the practical reason, the moral will. But he is convinced that to maintain this primacy one has to take the path to pure idealism. For behind Kant's apparently innocent retention of the thing-in-itself Fichte sees the lurking spectre of Spinozism, the exaltation of Nature and the disappearance of freedom. If we are to exorcize this spectre, compromise must be rejected.

We can, of course, detach Fichte's idea of the influence exercised by 'inclination and interest' from his historically-conditioned picture of the initial option with which philosophers are faced. And the idea can then be seen as opening up fascinating vistas in the field of what Karl Jaspers calls 'the psychology of world-views'. But in a book of this kind one must resist the temptation to embark on a discussion of this attractive topic.

3. Assuming that we have chosen the path of idealism, we must turn for the first principle of philosophy to intelligence-in-itself. But it is better to drop this cumbersome term and to speak, as Fichte proceeds to do, of the *I* or ego. We are committed, therefore, to explaining the genesis of experience from the side, so to speak, of the self. In reality Fichte is concerned with deriving consciousness in general from the ego. But in speaking of experience, in the restricted sense explained above, he lays his finger on the crucial difficulty which pure idealism has to face, namely the evident fact that the self finds itself in a world of objects which affect it in various ways. If idealism is incapable of accounting adequately for this fact, it is evidently untenable.

But what is the ego which is the foundation of philosophy? To answer this question we obviously have to go behind the objectifiable self, the ego as object of introspection or of empirical psychology, to the pure ego. Fichte once said to his students: 'Gentlemen, think the wall.' He then proceeded: 'Gentlemen, think him who thought the wall.' Clearly, we could proceed indefinitely in this fashion. 'Gentlemen, think him who thought him who thought the wall', and so on. In other words, however hard we may try to objectify the self, that is, to turn it into an object of consciousness, there always remains an *I* or ego which transcends objectification and is itself the condition of all objectifiability and the condition of the unity of consciousness. And it is this pure or transcendental ego which is the first principle of philosophy.

It is clearly idle to object against Fichte that we cannot find a pure or transcendental ego by peering about. For it is precisely Fichte's contention that the pure ego cannot be found in this way, though it is the necessary condition of our being able to do any peering about. But for this very reason it may appear that Fichte has gone beyond the range of experience (in a wide sense) or consciousness and has failed to observe his own self-imposed limitations. That is to say, having reaffirmed the Kantian view that our theoretical knowledge cannot extend beyond experience, he now seems to have transgressed this limit.

But this, Fichte insists, is not the case. For we can enjoy an intellectual intuition of the pure ego. This is not, however, a mystical experience reserved for the privileged few. Nor is it an intuition of the pure ego as an entity existing behind or beyond consciousness. Rather is it an awareness of the pure ego or *I* principle as an activity within consciousness. And this awareness is a component element in all self-consciousness. 'I cannot take a pace, I cannot move hand or foot, without the intellectual intuition of my self-consciousness in these actions. It is only through intuition that I know that I perform the action. . . . Everyone who ascribes activity to himself appeals to this intuition. In it is the foundation of life, and without it is death.'[1] In other words, anyone who is conscious of an action as his own is aware of himself acting. In this sense he has an intuition of the self as activity. But it does not follow that he is reflectively aware of this intuition as a component element in consciousness. It is only the philosopher who is reflectively aware of it, for the simple reason that transcendental reflection, by which the attention is reflected onto the pure ego, is a philosophical act. But this reflection is directed, so to speak, to ordinary consciousness, not to a privileged mystical experience. Hence, if the philosopher wishes to convince anyone of the reality of this intuition, he can only draw the man's attention to the data of consciousness and invite him to reflect for himself. He cannot show the man the intuition existing in a pure state, unmixed with any component elements; for it does not exist in this state. Nor can he convince the other man by means of some abstract proof. He can only invite the man to reflect on his own self-consciousness and to see that it includes an intuition of the pure ego, not as a thing, but as an activity. 'That there is such a power of intellectual intuition cannot be demonstrated through concepts, nor can its

[1] *F*, 1, p. 463; *M*, 111, p. 47.

nature be developed by means of concepts. Everyone must find i immediately in himself or he will never be able to know it.'[1]

Fichte's thesis can be clarified in this way. The pure ego canno be turned into an object of consciousness in the same way that desire, for example, can be objectified. It would be absurd to sa that through introspection I see a desire, an image and a pure ego For every act of objectification presupposes the pure ego. And fo this reason it can be called the transcendental ego. But it does no follow that the pure ego is an inferred occult entity. For it manifest itself in the activity of objectification. When I say, 'I am walking' I objectify the action, in the sense that I make it object-for-a subject. And the pure *I* reveals itself to reflection in this activity o objectification. An activity is intuited, but no entity behind consciousness is inferred. Hence Fichte concludes that the pur ego is not something which acts but simply an activity or doing 'For idealism the intelligence is a doing [*Thun*] and absolutel nothing else; one should not even call it an active thing [*ei Tätiges*].'[2]

At first sight at least Fichte appears to contradict Kant' denial that the human mind possesses any faculty of intellectua intuition. In particular, he seems to be turning into an object o intuition the transcendental ego which for Kant was simply logical condition of the unity of consciousness and could be neithe intuited nor proved to exist as a spiritual substance. But Ficht insists that his contradiction of Kant is really only verbal. Fo when Kant denied that the human mind possesses any faculty c intellectual intuition, he meant that we do not enjoy any intellectua intuition of supersensible entities transcending experience. An the *Wissenschaftslehre* does not really affirm what Kant denied. Fo it is not claimed that we intuit the pure ego as a spiritual substanc or entity transcending consciousness but simply as an activit within consciousness, which reveals itself to reflection. Furthe apart from the fact that Kant's doctrine of pure apperception gives us at any rate a hint of intellectual intuition, we can easil indicate the place, Fichte claims, at which Kant ought to hav spoken of and admitted this intuition. For he asserted that we ar conscious of a categorical imperative; and if he had considered th matter thoroughly, he should have seen that this consciousnes involves the intellectual intuition of the pure ego as activity

[1] *F*, I, p. 463; *M*, III, p. 47.     [2] *F*, I, p. 440; *M*, III, p. 24.
[3] See Vol. VI, pp. 253–6, 282–6, 391–2.

Indeed, Fichte goes on to suggest a specifically moral approach to the topic. 'In the consciousness of this law . . . is grounded the intuition of self-activity and freedom. . . . It is only through the medium of the moral law that I apprehend *myself*. And if I apprehend myself in this way, I necessarily apprehend myself as self-active. . . .'[1] Once again, therefore, the strongly ethical bent of Fichte's mind finds clear expression.

4. If we look at the matter from the point of view of phenomenology of consciousness, Fichte is, in the opinion of the present writer, perfectly justified in affirming the I-subject or transcendental ego. Hume, looking into his mind, so to speak, and finding only psychical phenomena, tried to reduce the self to the succession of these phenomena.[2] And it is understandable that he acted in this way. For part of his programme was to apply to man the empirical method, as he conceived it, which had proved so successful in 'experimental philosophy' or natural science. But the direction of his attention to the objects or data of introspection led him to slur over the fact, all-important for the philosopher, that psychical phenomena become phenomena (appearing to a subject) only through the objectifying activity of a subject which transcends objectification in the same sense. Obviously, there is no question of reducing the human being to a transcendental or metaphysical ego. And the problem of the relation between the self as pure subject and other aspects of the self is one that cannot be evaded. But this does not alter the fact that a recognition of the transcendental ego is essential to an adequate phenomenology of consciousness. And in regard to this point Fichte shows a degree of insight which Hume lacked.

But Fichte is not, of course, simply concerned with the phenomenology of consciousness, that is, with a descriptive analysis of consciousness. He is concerned also with developing a system of idealist metaphysics. And this point has an important bearing on his theory of the transcendental ego. From a purely phenomenological point of view talk about 'the transcendental ego' no more commits us to saying that there is one and only one such ego than a medical writer's generalizations about 'the stomach' commit him to holding that there is one and only one stomach. But if we propose to derive the whole sphere of the objective, including Nature and all selves in so far as they are objects for a subject, from the transcendental ego, we must either

---

[1] *F*, I, p. 466; *M*, III, p. 50.          [2] See Vol. V, pp. 300–5.

embrace solipsism or interpret the transcendental ego as a supra individual productive activity which manifests itself in all finite consciousnesses. As, therefore, Fichte has no intention of defending solipsism, he is bound to interpret the pure ego as a supra individual absolute ego.

To be sure, Fichte's use of the term *I* or *ego* not unnaturally suggested to many of his readers that he was talking about the individual self or ego. And this interpretation was facilitated by the fact that the more metaphysical aspects of his thought were comparatively inconspicuous in his earlier writings. But the interpretation, Fichte insisted, was erroneous. Lecturing in the winter of 1810–11 and looking back at the criticism that had been levelled against the *Wissenschaftslehre* he protested that he had never intended to say that the creative ego is the individual finite self. 'People have generally understood the theory of science as attributing to the individual effects which could certainly not be ascribed to it, such as the production of the whole material world. . . . They have been completely mistaken: it is not the individual but the one immediate spiritual Life which is the creator of all phenomena, including phenomenal individuals.'[1]

It will be noticed that in this passage the word 'Life' is used instead of 'ego'. Starting, as he did, from the position of Kant and being concerned with transforming it into pure idealism, he not unnaturally began by talking about the pure or absolute ego. But in the course of time he saw that it was inappropriate to describe the infinite activity which grounds consciousness, including the finite self, as itself an ego or subject. However, we need not dwell at present on this point. It is sufficient to note Fichte's protest against what he considered to be a fundamental misinterpretation of his theory. The absolute ego is not the individual finite self but an infinite (better, unlimited) activity.

Fichte's *Wissenschaftslehre* is thus both a phenomenology of consciousness and an idealist metaphysics. And to a certain extent at any rate the two aspects can be separated. Hence it is possible to attach some value to a good deal of what Fichte has to say without committing oneself to his metaphysical idealism. We have already indicated this in regard to the theory of the transcendental ego. But the distinction has a wider field of application.

5. In the second section of this chapter it was remarked that philosophy, according to Fichte, must have a fundamental and

---

[1] *F*, II, p. 607 (not included in *M*).

indemonstrable proposition. And the thought may have occurred to the reader that whatever else the ego may be, it is not a proposition. This is, of course, true. We have still to ascertain what is the basic proposition of philosophy. But we know at any rate that it must be the expression of the original activity of the pure ego.

Now, we can distinguish between the spontaneous activity of the pure ego on the one hand and the philosopher's philosophical reconstruction or thinking of this activity on the other. The spontaneous activity of the pure ego in grounding consciousness is not, of course, itself conscious. As spontaneous activity the pure ego does not exist 'for itself'. It comes to exist for itself, as an ego, only in the intellectual intuition by which the philosopher in transcendental reflection apprehends the ego's spontaneous activity. It is through the act of the philosopher, 'through an activity directed towards an activity ... that the ego first comes to be *originally* [*ursprünglich*] for itself'.[1] In intellectual intuition, therefore, the pure ego is said to posit itself (*sich setzen*). And the fundamental proposition of philosophy is that 'the ego simply posits in an original way its own being'.[2] In transcendental reflection the philosopher goes back, as it were, to the ultimate ground of consciousness. And in his intellectual intuition the pure ego affirms itself. It is not demonstrated as a conclusion from premisses: it is seen as affirming itself and so as existing. 'To *posit itself* and to *be* are, as said of the ego, completely the same.'[3]

But though by means of what Fichte calls an activity directed towards an activity[4] the pure ego is, so to speak, made to affirm itself, the ego's original spontaneous activity is not in itself conscious. Rather is it the ultimate ground of consciousness, that is, of ordinary consciousness, one's natural awareness of oneself in a world. But this consciousness cannot arise unless the non-ego is opposed to the ego. Hence the second basic proposition of philosophy is that 'a non-ego is simply opposited to the ego'.[5] This oppositing must, of course, be done by the ego itself. Otherwise pure idealism would have to be abandoned.

Now, the non-ego of which the second proposition speaks is unlimited, in the sense that it is objectivity in general rather than

---

[1] *F*, I, p. 459; *M*, III, p. 43.     [2] *F*, I, p. 98; *M*, I, p. 292.     [3] *Ibid.*
[4] *Durch ein Handeln auf ein Handeln*. The philosopher's reflection is an activity, a doing. It makes the spontaneous activity of the pure ego relive itself, so to speak, for consciousness.
[5] *F*, I, p. 104; *M*, I, p. 298.

a definite object or set of finite objects. And this unlimited non-ego is opposed to the ego within the ego. For we are engaged in the systematic reconstruction of consciousness; and consciousness is a unity, comprising both ego and non-ego. Hence the unlimited activity which constitutes the pure or absolute ego must posit the non-ego within itself. But if both are unlimited, each will tend, as it were, to fill all reality to the exclusion of the other. They will tend to cancel one another out, to annihilate one another. And consciousness will be rendered impossible. Hence, if consciousness is to arise, there must be reciprocal limitation of ego and non-ego. Each must cancel the other out, but only in part. In this sense both ego and non-ego must be 'divisible' (*theilbar*). And in his *Basis of the Entire Theory of Science* Fichte offers the following formulation of the third basic proposition of philosophy. 'I posit in the ego a divisible non-ego as opposed to a divisible ego.'[1] That is to say, the absolute ego posits within itself a finite ego and a finite non-ego as reciprocally limiting and determining one another. Fichte obviously does not mean that there can be only one of each. Indeed, as will be seen later, he maintains that for self-consciousness the existence of the Other (and so of a plurality of finite selves) is required. His point is that there can be no consciousness unless the absolute ego, considered as unlimited activity, produces within itself the finite ego and the finite non-ego.

6. If we mean by consciousness, as Fichte means by it, human consciousness, the assertion that the non-ego is a necessary condition of consciousness is not difficult to understand. To be sure, the finite ego can reflect on itself, but this reflection is for Fichte a bending back of the attention from the not-self. Hence the non-ego is a necessary condition even of self-consciousness.[2] But we can very well ask why there should be consciousness at all. Or, to put the question in another way, how can the second basic proposition of philosophy be deduced from the first?

Fichte answers that no purely theoretical deduction is possible. We must have recourse to a practical deduction. That is to say, we must see the pure or absolute ego as an unlimited activity striving towards consciousness of its own freedom through moral self-realization. And we must see the positing of the non-ego as a

---

[1] *F*, I, p. 110; *M*, I, p. 305.
[2] We can notice again the distinction between phenomenology and idealist metaphysics. It is one thing to say that the positing (recognition) of the non-ego is a condition of human consciousness. It is another thing to say that the non-ego is posited (produced or created) by the pure or absolute ego.

necessary means to the attainment of this end. True, the absolute ego in its spontaneous activity does not act consciously for any end at all. But the philosopher consciously rethinking this activity sees the total movement as directed towards a certain goal. And he sees that self-consciousness demands the non-ego, from which the otherwise unlimited activity of the ego, comparable to a straight line stretching out indefinitely, can recoil, as it were, onto itself. He sees too that moral activity requires an objective field, a world, in which actions can be performed.

Now, the second basic proposition of philosophy stands to the first as antithesis to thesis. And we have seen that the ego and non-ego tend to cancel one another out, if both are unlimited. It is this fact that drives the philosopher to enunciate the third basic proposition, which stands to the first and second propositions as synthesis to thesis and antithesis. But Fichte does not mean to imply that the non-ego ever exists in such a way that it annihilates the pure ego or threatens to do so. It is because this annihilation would take place if an unlimited non-ego were posited within the ego that we are compelled to proceed to the third proposition. In other words, the synthesis shows what the antithesis must mean if the contradiction between an unlimited ego and an unlimited non-ego is not to arise. If we assume that consciousness is to arise at all, the activity which grounds consciousness must produce the situation in which an ego and a non-ego limit one another.

Looked at under one aspect, therefore, Fichte's dialectic of thesis, antithesis and synthesis[1] takes the form of a progressive determination of the meanings of the initial propositions. And the contradictions which arise are resolved in the sense that they are shown to be only apparent. 'All contradictions are reconciled by determining more closely the contradictory propositions.'[2] Speaking, for example, of the statements that the ego posits itself as infinite and that it posits itself as finite, Fichte remarks that 'were it posited as both infinite and finite in one and the same sense, the contradictions could not be resolved. . . .'[3] The apparent contradiction is resolved by so defining the meanings of the two statements that their mutual compatibility becomes evident. In the case in question we have to see the one infinite activity expressing itself in and through finite selves.

[1] On the hint of a dialectical method in the philosophy of Kant see Vol. VI, pp. 251–2. Kant's antithetical development of the antinomies (pp. 287 f.) is also relevant.
[2] *F*, 1, p. 255; *M*, 1, p. 448.               [3] *Ibid.*

Yet it would not be accurate to say that in actual fact Fichte's dialectic consists simply in the progressive determination or clarification of meanings. For he introduces by the way ideas which cannot be obtained through strict analysis of the initial proposition or propositions. For instance, in order to proceed from the second basic proposition to the third Fichte postulates a limiting activity on the part of the ego, though the idea of limitation cannot be obtained simply through logical analysis of either the first or the second proposition.

This procedure was criticized by Hegel as being insufficiently speculative, that is, philosophical. In Hegel's opinion it was unworthy of a philosopher to offer a deduction which was admittedly no strict theoretical deduction[1] and to introduce, like a *deus ex machina*, undeduced activities of the ego to make possible the transition from one proposition to another.

It can hardly be denied, I think, that Fichte's actual procedure does not square very well with his initial account of the nature of philosophy as a deductive science. At the same time we must remember that for him the philosopher is engaged in consciously reconstructing, as it were, an active process, namely the grounding of consciousness, which in itself takes place unconsciously. In doing so the philosopher has his point of departure, the self-positing of the absolute ego, and his point of arrival, human consciousness as we know it. And if it is impossible to proceed from one step to another in the reconstruction of the productive activity of the ego without attributing to the ego a certain function or mode of activity, then this must be done. Thus even if the concept of limitation is not obtained through strict logical analysis of the first two basic propositions, it is none the less required, from Fichte's point of view, to clarify their meaning.

7. When outlining Fichte's theory of the three basic propositions of philosophy I omitted the logical apparatus which is employed in the *Basis of the Entire Theory of Science* and which figures prominently in some accounts of his philosophy. For this apparatus is not really necessary, as is shown by the fact that Fichte himself omits it in some of the expositions of his system. At the same time something ought to be said about it because it serves to clarify Fichte's idea of the relations between philosophy and formal logic.

In the *Basis of the Entire Theory of Science* Fichte approaches

---

[1] We have noted Fichte's frank admission that no purely theoretical deduction of the second basic proposition is possible.

the first fundamental proposition of philosophy by reflecting on an indemonstrable logical proposition, the truth of which would be admitted by all. This is the principle of identity, stated in the form $A$ *is* $A$ or $A = A$. Nothing is said about the content of $A$; nor is it asserted that $A$ exists. What is asserted is a necessary relation between $A$ and itself. If there is an $A$, it is necessarily self-identical. And this necessary relation between $A$ as subject and $A$ as predicate is referred to by Fichte as $X$.

This judgment is asserted or posited only in and through the $I$ or ego. Thus the existence of the ego is affirmed in its activity of judging, even if no value has been assigned to $A$. 'If the proposition $A = A$ is certain, so also must the proposition $I$ *am* be certain.'[1] In affirming the principle of identity the ego affirms or posits itself as self-identical.

While, therefore, the formal principle of identity is used by Fichte as a means or device for arriving at the first basic proposition of philosophy, the principle of identity is not itself this proposition. Indeed, it is sufficiently obvious that one would not get very far with a deduction or reconstruction of consciousness if one proposed to use the formal principle of identity as a starting-point or foundation.

At the same time the relation between the formal principle of identity and the first basic proposition of philosophy is closer, according to Fichte, than the description of the former as a means or device for arriving at the latter tends to suggest. For the principle of identity is, so to speak, the first basic proposition of philosophy with variables substituted for definite values or content. That is to say, if we took the first basic proposition of philosophy and rendered it purely formal, we would obtain the principle of identity. And in this sense the latter is grounded in the former and derivable from it.

Similarly, what Fichte calls the formal axiom of opposition, $Not-A$ $not = A$, is used to arrive at the second basic proposition. For the positing of $Not$ $-A$ presupposes the positing of $A$ and is thus an oppositing to $A$. And this oppositing takes place only in and through the ego. At the same time the formal axiom of opposition is said to be grounded in the second proposition of philosophy which affirms the ego's oppositing to itself of the non-ego in general. Again, the logical proposition which Fichte calls the axiom of the ground or of sufficient reason, $A$ *in part* $= -A$, *and*

[1] *F*, I, p. 95; *M*, I, p. 289.

*conversely*, is said to be grounded in the third basic proposition of philosophy, in the sense that the former is derived by abstracting definite content from the latter and substituting variables instead.

In brief, therefore, Fichte's view is that formal logic is dependent on and derived from the *Wissenschaftslehre*, and not the other way round. This view of the relation between formal logic and basic philosophy is indeed somewhat obscured by the fact that in the *Basis of the Entire Theory of Science* Fichte starts by reflecting on the principle of identity. But in his subsequent discussion he proceeds to make his view of the derivative character of formal logic quite clear. And this view is in any case entailed by his insistence that the *Wissenschaftslehre* is the fundamental science.

We may add that in his deduction of the fundamental propositions of philosophy Fichte begins to deduce the categories. In his opinion Kant's deduction was insufficiently systematic. If, however, we start with the self-positing of the ego, we can deduce them successively in the course of the reconstruction of consciousness. Thus the first basic proposition gives us the category of reality. For 'that which is posited through the mere positing of a thing . . . is its reality, its essence [*Wesen*]'.[1] The second proposition obviously gives us the category of negation and the third that of limitation or determination.

8. The idea of reciprocal limitation provides the basis for the twofold deduction of consciousness which Fichte considers necessary. Take the statement that the absolute ego posits within itself a finite ego and a finite non-ego as reciprocally limiting or determining one another. This implies two propositions. One is that the absolute ego posits itself as limited by the non-ego. The other is that the absolute ego posits (within itself) the non-ego as limited or determined by the (finite) ego. And these two propositions are respectively the basic propositions of the theoretical and practical deductions of consciousness. If we consider the ego as affected by the non-ego, we can proceed to the theoretical deduction of consciousness which considers what Fichte calls the 'real' series of acts, that is, the acts of the ego as determined by the non-ego. Sensation, for example, belongs to this class of acts. If, however, we consider the ego as affecting the non-ego, we can proceed to the practical deduction of consciousness which considers the 'ideal' series of acts, including, for instance, desire and free action.

[1] *F*, I, p. 99; *M*, I, p. 293.

The two deductions are, of course, complementary, forming together the total philosophical deduction or reconstruction of consciousness. At the same time the theoretical deduction is subordinated to the practical. For the absolute ego is an infinite striving towards self-realization through free moral activity, and the non-ego, the world of Nature, is a means or instrument for the attainment of this end. The practical deduction gives us the reason why the absolute ego posits the non-ego as limiting and affecting the finite ego; and it leads us to the confines of ethics. Indeed, Fichte's theories of rights and of morals are a continuation of the practical deduction as contained in the *Wissenschaftslehre* proper. As already mentioned, Fichte's philosophy is essentially a dynamic ethical idealism.

It is not possible to discuss here all the stages of Fichte's deduction of consciousness. And even if it were possible, it would scarcely be desirable. But in the next two sections some features of the theoretical and practical deductions will be mentioned, to give the reader some idea of Fichte's line of thought.

9. In Fichte's idealist system all activity must be referred ultimately to the ego itself, that is, to the absolute ego, and the non-ego must exist only for consciousness. For to admit the idea of a non-ego which exists quite independently of all consciousness and which affects the ego would be to readmit the idea of the thing-in-itself and to abandon idealism. At the same time it is obvious that from the point of view of ordinary consciousness there is a distinction between presentation (*Vorstellung*) and thing. We have the spontaneous belief that we are acted upon by things which exist independently of the ego. And to all appearances this belief is fully justified. Hence it is incumbent on Fichte to show, in a manner consistent with the idealist position, how the point of view of ordinary consciousness arises, and how from this point of view our spontaneous belief in an objective Nature is in a sense justified. For the aim of idealist philosophy is to explain the facts of consciousness on idealist principles, not to deny them.

Obviously, Fichte must attribute to the ego the power of producing the idea of an independently existing non-ego when in point of fact it is dependent on the ego, so that the non-ego's activity is ultimately the activity of the ego itself. Equally obviously, this power must be attributed to the absolute ego rather than to the individual self, and it must work spontaneously, inevitably and without consciousness. To put the matter crudely,

when consciousness comes on the scene the work must be already
done. It must take place below the level of consciousness. Other
wise it would be impossible to explain our spontaneous belief in a
Nature existing independently of the ego. In other words, for
empirical consciousness Nature must be something given. It is
only the philosopher who in transcendental reflection retraces with
consciousness the productive activity of the absolute ego, which in
itself takes place without consciousness. For the non-philosopher
and for the empirical consciousness of the philosopher himself, the
natural world is something given, a situation in which the finite ego
finds itself.

This power is called by Fichte the power of imagination or, more
appropriately, the productive power of imagination or power of
productive imagination. The power of imagination was prominent
in the philosophy of Kant, where it served as an indispensable link
between sensibility and understanding.[1] But with Fichte it assumes
an all-important role in grounding ordinary or empirical conscious
ness. It is not, of course, a kind of third force in addition to the ego
and non-ego: it is the activity of the ego itself, that is, the absolute
ego. In his earlier writings Fichte may sometimes give the
impression that he is talking about the activity of the individual
self, but when he reviews the development of his thought he protests
that he never meant this.

In what he calls a pragmatic history of consciousness[2] Fichte
pictures the ego as spontaneously limiting its own activity and thus
positing itself as passive, as affected. Its state is then that of
sensation (*Empfindung*). But the ego's activity reasserts itself, as
it were, and objectifies sensation. That is to say, in the outwardly
directed activity of intuition the ego spontaneously refers sensation
to a non-ego. And this act grounds the distinction between
representation or image (*Bild*) and thing. In empirical conscious
ness, the finite self regards the distinction between image and
thing as a distinction between a subjective modification and an
object which exists independently of its own activity. For it is
ignorant of the fact that the projection of the non-ego was the
work of the productive imagination functioning on an infra
conscious level.

Now, consciousness requires not simply an indeterminate non-

---

[1] See Vol. VI, pp. 256–60.
[2] This is given in the *Basis of the Entire Theory of Science*. A more detailed
analysis of some of the stages is given in the *Outline of the Essence of the Theory of
Science*.

ego but definite and distinct objects. And if there are to be distinguishable objects, there must be a common sphere in which and in relation to which objects mutually exclude one another. Hence the power of imagination produces space, extended, continuous and indefinitely divisible, as a form of intuition.

Similarly, there must be an irreversible time series of such a kind that successive acts of intuition are possible and that if a particular act of intuition occurs at any moment, every other possibility is excluded as far as this moment is concerned. Hence the productive imagination conveniently posits time as a second form of intuition. Needless to say, the forms of space and time are produced spontaneously by the activity of the pure or absolute ego: they are not consciously and deliberately posited.

The development of consciousness, however, requires that the product of the creative imagination should be rendered more determinate. And this is effected by means of the powers of understanding and judgment. At the level of understanding the ego 'fixes' (*fixiert*) presentations as concepts, while the power of judgment is said to turn these concepts into *thought* objects, in the sense that they come to exist not only *in* but also *for* the understanding. Both understanding and judgment, therefore, are required for understanding in the full sense. 'Nothing in the understanding, no power of judgment: no power of judgment, nothing in the understanding *for the understanding.* . . .'[1] Sensible intuition is riveted, as it were, to particular objects; but at the level of understanding and judgment we find abstraction from particular objects and the making of universal judgments. Thus in the pragmatic history of consciousness we have seen the ego rising above the unconscious activity of the productive imagination and acquiring, so to speak, a certain freedom of movement.

Self-consciousness, however, requires more than the power to abstract from particular objects in favour of the universal. It presupposes the power to abstract from the object in general, in order to achieve reflection on the subject. And this power of absolute abstraction, as Fichte calls it, is reason (*Vernunft*). When reason abstracts from the sphere of the non-ego, the ego remains, and we have self-consciousness. But one cannot totally eliminate the ego-object and identify oneself in consciousness with the ego-subject. That is to say, pure self-consciousness, in which the I-subject would be completely transparent to itself, is an ideal which

[1] *F*, I, p. 242; *M*, I, p. 435.

can never be actually achieved, but to which one can only approximate. 'The more a determinate individual can think himself (as
object) away, the closer does his empirical self-consciousness
approximate to pure self-consciousness.'[1]

It is, of course, the power of reason which enables the philosopher
to apprehend the pure ego and to retrace, in transcendental
reflection, its productive activity in the movement towards self-
consciousness. But we have seen that the intellectual intuition of
the absolute ego is never unmixed with other elements. Not even
the philosopher can achieve the ideal of what Fichte calls pure self-
consciousness.

10. The practical deduction of consciousness goes behind, as it
were, the work of the productive imagination and reveals its
ground in the nature of the absolute ego as an infinite striving
(*ein unendliches Streben*). True, if we speak of striving, we naturally
tend to think of striving after something. That is to say, we
presuppose the existence of the non-ego. But if we start with the
absolute ego as infinite striving, we obviously cannot presuppose
the existence of the non-ego. For to do this would be to reintroduce
the Kantian thing-in-itself. At the same time striving, Fichte
insists, demands a counter-movement, a counter-striving, a check
or obstacle. For if it met with no resistance, no obstacle or check,
it would be satisfied and would cease to be a striving. But the
absolute ego cannot cease to be a striving. Hence the very nature
of the absolute ego necessitates the positing of the non-ego by the
productive imagination, that is, by the absolute ego in its 'real'
activity.

The matter can be expressed in this way. The absolute ego is to
be conceived as activity. And this activity is fundamentally an
infinite striving. But striving, according to Fichte, implies overcoming, and overcoming requires an obstacle to overcome. Hence
the ego must posit the non-ego, Nature, as an obstacle to be overcome, as a check to be transcended. In other words, Nature is a
necessary means or instrument to the moral self-realization of the
ego. It is a field for action.

Fichte does not, however, proceed directly from the idea of the
ego as striving to the positing of the non-ego. He argues first that
striving takes the determinate form of infra-conscious impulse or
drive (*Trieb*) and that this impulse exists 'for the ego' in the form
of feeling (*Gefühl*). Now, impulse or drive aims, as Fichte puts it, at

---

[1] *F*, I, p. 244; *M*, I, p. 437.

being causality, at effecting something outside itself. Yet it cannot, considered simply as impulse, effect anything. Hence the feeling of impulse or drive is a feeling of constraint, of not-being-able, of being hindered. And the feeling ego is compelled to posit the non-ego as a felt I-know-not-what, a felt obstacle or check. And impulse can then become 'impulse *towards the object*'.[1]

It is worth noting that for Fichte feeling is the basis of all belief in reality. The ego feels impulse or drive as power or force (*Kraft*) which is hindered. The feeling of force and the feeling of hindrance go together. And the total feeling is the foundation of belief in reality. 'Here lies the ground of all reality. Only through the relation of feeling to the ego . . . is reality possible for the ego, whether of the ego or of the non-ego.'[2] Belief in reality is based ultimately on feeling, not on any theoretical argument.

Now, the feeling of impulse as force represents a rudimentary grade of reflection. For the ego is itself the impulse which is felt. Hence the feeling is self-feeling. And in successive sections of the practical deduction of consciousness Fichte traces the development of this reflection. We see, for instance, impulse or drive as such becoming more determinate in the form of distinct impulses and desires, and we see the development in the ego of distinct feelings of satisfaction. But inasmuch as the ego is infinite striving, it is unable to rest in any particular satisfaction or group of satisfactions. And we see it as reaching out towards an ideal goal through its free activity. Yet this goal always recedes. Indeed, it must do so, if the ego is infinite or endless striving. In the end, therefore, we have action for the sake of action, though in his ethical theory Fichte shows how the infinite striving of the absolute ego after complete freedom and self-possession is fulfilled, so far as it can be, through the series of determinate moral actions in the world which it has posited, through, that is to say, the convergence of the determinate moral vocations of finite subjects towards an ideal goal.

In its detailed development Fichte's practical deduction of consciousness is notoriously difficult to follow. But it is clear enough that for him the ego is from the start the morally active ego. That is to say, it is potentially this. And it is the actualization of the ego's potential nature which demands the positing of the non-ego and the whole work of the productive imagination. Behind, as it were, the theoretical activity of the ego lies its nature as striving, as impulse or drive. For example, the production

---

[1] *F*, I, p. 291; *M*, I, p. 483.     [2] *F*, I, p. 301; *M*, I, p. 492.

of the presentation (*Vorstellung*) is the work of the theoretica power, not of the practical power or impulse as such. But the production presupposes the drive to presentation (*der Vorstel lungstrieb*). Conversely, the positing of the sensible world is necessary in order that the fundamental striving or drive can take the determinate form of free moral activity directed towards an ideal goal. Thus the two deductions are complementary, though the theoretical deduction finds its ultimate explanation in the practical. In this sense Fichte endeavours to satisfy in his own way the demands of Kant's doctrine of the primacy of the practical reason

We can also say that in his practical deduction of consciousnes Fichte tries to overcome the dichotomy, present in the Kantian philosophy, between the higher and lower nature of man, between man as a moral agent and man as a complex of instincts and impulses. For it is the self-same fundamental drive which is represented as assuming different forms up to that of free moral activity. In other words, Fichte sees the moral life as a develop ment out of the life of instinct and impulse rather than as a counterblast to it. And he even finds a prefiguring of the categorica imperative on the level of physical longing (*Sehnen*) and desire. In his ethics he has, of course, to allow for the fact that there may be and often is, a conflict between the voice of duty and the claims of sensual desire. But he tries to resolve the problem within the frame work of a unified view of the ego's activity in general.

11. From one point of view Fichte's deduction of consciousnes can be regarded as a systematic exhibition of the conditions of consciousness as we know it. And if it is regarded simply in thi way, questions about the temporal or historical relations between the different conditions are irrelevant. For example, Fichte take it that the subject-object relationship is essential to consciousness And in this case there must be both subject and object, ego and non-ego, if there is to be consciousness. The historical order in which these conditions appear is irrelevant to the validity of thi statement.

But, as we have seen, the deduction of consciousness is also idealist metaphysics, and the pure ego has to be interpreted as supra-individual and transfinite activity, the so-called absolut ego. Hence it is understandable if the student of Fichte ask whether the philosopher regards the absolute ego as positing th sensible world before the finite ego or simultaneously with it o through it.

At first sight at least this may seem to be a silly question. The
emporal, historical point of view, it may be said, presupposes for
'ichte the constitution of empirical consciousness. Hence the
ranscendental deduction of empirical consciousness necessarily
ranscends the temporal and historical order and possesses the
imelessness of a logical deduction. After all, the time-series is
tself deduced. Fichte has no intention of denying the point of view
)f empirical consciousness, for which Nature precedes finite selves.
Ie is concerned with grounding it, not with denying it.

But the matter is not quite so simple. In the Kantian philosophy
t is the human mind which exercises a constitutive activity in
;iving its *a priori* form to phenomenal reality. True, in this
ictivity the mind acts spontaneously and unconsciously, and it
icts as mind as such, as the subject as such, rather than as the
nind of Tom or John. But it is none the less the human mind, not
he divine mind, which is said to exercise this activity. And if we
:liminate the thing-in-itself and hypostatize Kant's transcendental
:go as the metaphysical absolute ego, it is quite natural to ask
vhether the absolute ego posits Nature immediately or through
he infra-conscious levels, as it were, of the human being. After all,
Fichte's deduction of consciousness not infrequently suggests the
;econd of these alternatives. And if this is what the philosopher
:eally means, he is faced with an obvious difficulty.

Happily, Fichte answers the question in explicit terms. At the
beginning of the practical deduction of consciousness he draws
attention to an apparent contradiction. On the one hand the ego
as intelligence is dependent on the non-ego. On the other hand the
:go is said to determine the non-ego and must thus be independent
)f it. The contradiction is resolved (that is, shown to be only
apparent) when we understand that the absolute ego determines
immediately the non-ego which enters into representation (*das
vorzustellende Nicht-Ich*), whereas it determines the ego as
intelligence (the ego as representing, *das vorstellende Ich*) *mediately*,
that is, by means of the non-ego. In other words, the absolute ego
does not posit the world through the finite ego, but immediately.
And the same thing is clearly stated in a passage of the lectures on
*The Facts of Consciousness*, to which allusion has already been
made. 'The material world has been deduced earlier on as an
absolute limitation of the productive power of imagination. But
we have not yet stated clearly and explicitly whether the productive power in this function is the self-manifestation of the one Life

as such or whether it is the manifestation of individual life; whether that is to say, a material world is posited through one self-identical Life or through the individual as such. . . . It is not the individual as such but the one Life which intuits the objects of the material world.'[1]

The development of this point of view obviously requires that Fichte should move away from his Kantian point of departure, and that the pure ego, a concept arrived at through reflection on human consciousness, should become absolute Being which manifests itself in the world. And this is indeed the path which Fichte takes in the later philosophy, to which the lectures on *The Facts of Consciousness* belong. But, as will be seen later, he never really succeeds in kicking away the ladder by which he has climbed up to metaphysical idealism. And though he clearly thinks of Nature as being posited by the Absolute as a field for moral activity, he maintains to the end that the world exists only in and for consciousness. Apart, therefore, from the explicit denial that material things are posited 'through the individual as such', his position remains ambiguous. For though consciousness is said to be the Absolute's consciousness, the Absolute is also said to be conscious through man, and not in itself considered apart from man.

---

[1] *F*, II, p. 614 (not included in *M*).

### CHAPTER III

# FICHTE (2)

*Introductory remarks—The common moral consciousness and the science of ethics—Man's moral nature—The supreme principle of morality and the formal condition of the morality of actions—Conscience as an unerring guide—The philosophical application of the formal moral law—The idea of moral vocation and Fichte's general vision of reality—A community of selves in a world as a condition of self-consciousness—The principle or rule of right—The deduction and nature of the State—The closed commercial State—Fichte and nationalism.*

1. IN the section on Fichte's life and writings we saw that he published the *Basis of Natural Right* in 1796, two years before the publication of *The System of Ethics*. In his opinion the theory of rights and of political society could be, and ought to be, deduced independently of the deduction of the principles of morality. This does not mean that Fichte thought of the two branches of philosophy as having no connection at all with each other. For one thing the two deductions possess a common root in the concept of the self as striving and as free activity. For another thing the system of rights and political society provides a field of application for the moral law. But it was Fichte's opinion that his field is external to morality, in the sense that it is not a deduction from the fundamental ethical principle but a framework within which, and in regard to which, the moral law can be applied. For example, man can have moral duties towards the State and the State should bring about those conditions in which the moral life can develop. But the State itself is deduced as a hypothetically necessary contrivance or means to guard and protect the system of rights. If man's moral nature were fully developed, the State would wither away. Again, though the right of private property receives from ethics what Fichte calls a further sanction, its initial deduction is supposed to be independent of ethics.

One main reason why Fichte makes this distinction between the theory of rights and political theory on the one hand and ethics on the other is that he looks on ethics as concerned with interior morality, with conscience and the formal principle of morality, whereas the theory of rights and of political society is concerned with the external relations between human beings. Further, if the comment is made that the doctrine of rights can be regarded as applied ethics, in the sense that it is deducible as an application of the moral law, Fichte refuses to admit the truth of this contention. The fact that I have a right does not necessarily mean that I am under an obligation to exercise it. And the common good may demand on occasion a curtailment of or limitation on the exercise of rights. But the moral law is categorical: it simply says, 'Do this' or 'Do not do that'. Hence the system of rights is not deducible from the moral law, though we are, of course, morally obliged to respect the system of rights as established in a community. In this sense the moral law adds a further sanction to rights, but it is not their initial source.

In Hegel's opinion Fichte did not really succeed in overcoming the formalism of the Kantian ethics, even if he provided some of the material for doing so. And it was indeed Hegel rather than Fichte who synthesized the concepts of right, interior morality and society in the general concept of man's ethical life. But the chief reason why I have dwelt in the first section of this chapter on Fichte's distinction between the doctrine of rights and ethical theory is that I propose to treat of the philosopher's moral theory before outlining his theory of rights and of the State. And this procedure might otherwise give the erroneous impression that Fichte regarded the theory of rights as a deduction from the moral law.

2. A man can have knowledge, Fichte says, of his moral nature, of his subjection to a moral imperative, in two ways. In the first place he can possess this knowledge on the level of common moral consciousness. That is to say, he can be aware through his conscience of a moral imperative telling him to do this or not to do that. And this immediate awareness is quite sufficient for a knowledge of one's duties and for moral behaviour. In the second place a man can assume the ordinary moral consciousness as something given and inquire into its grounds. And a systematic deduction of the moral consciousness from its roots in the ego is the science of ethics and provides 'learned knowledge'.[1] In one sense, of course, this learned knowledge leaves everything as it was before. It does not create obligation, nor does it substitute a new set of duties for those of which one is already aware through conscience. It will not

[1] *F*, IV, p. 122; *M*, II, p. 516.

give a man a moral nature. But it can enable him to understand his moral nature.

3. What is meant by man's moral nature? Fichte tells us that there is in man an impulsion to perform certain actions simply for the sake of performing them, without regard to external purposes or ends, and to leave undone other actions simply for the sake of leaving them undone, again without regard to external purposes or ends. And the nature of man in so far as this impulsion necessarily manifests itself within him is his 'moral or ethical nature'.[1] To understand the grounds of this moral nature is the task of ethics.

The ego is activity, striving. And as we saw when considering the practical deduction of consciousness, the basic form taken by the striving which constitutes the ego is infra-conscious impulse or drive. Hence from one point of view man is a system of impulses, the impulse which can be ascribed to the system as a whole being that of self-preservation. Considered in this light, man can be described as an organized product of Nature. And as conscious of myself as a system of impulses I can say, 'I find myself as an organized product of Nature.'[2] That is to say, I posit or affirm myself as being this when I consider myself as object.

But man is also intelligence, a subject of consciousness. And as subject of consciousness the ego necessarily tends or is impelled to determine itself through itself alone; that is, it is a striving after complete freedom and independence. Inasmuch, therefore, as the natural impulses and desires which belong to man as a product of Nature aim at satisfaction through some relation to a determinate natural object and consequently appear to depend on the object, we understandably contrast these impulses with the spiritual impulse of the ego as intelligence, the impulse, that is to say, to complete self-determination. We speak of lower and higher desires, of the sphere of necessity and the sphere of freedom, and introduce a dichotomy into human nature.

Fichte does not deny, of course, that such distinctions have, so to speak, a cash value. For one can look at man from two points of view, as object and as subject. As we have seen, I can be conscious of myself as an object in Nature, as an organized product of Nature, and I can be aware of myself as a subject for whose consciousness Nature, including myself as object, exists. To this

---

[1] *F*, iv, p. 13; *M*, ii, p. 407.
[2] *F*, iv, p. 122; *M*, ii, p. 516.

extent Kant's distinction between the phenomenal and noumenal aspects of man is justified.

At the same time Fichte insists that this distinction is not ultimate. For instance, the natural impulse which aims at satisfaction and the spiritual impulse which aims at complete freedom and independence are from the transcendental or phenomenal point of view one impulse. It is a great mistake to suppose that man as an organized product of Nature is the sphere of mere mechanism. As Fichte puts it, 'I do not hunger because food exists for me, but a certain object becomes food for me because I am hungry.'[1] The organism asserts itself: it tends to activity. And it is fundamentally the same impulse to self-activity which reappears in the form of the spiritual impulse to the realization of complete freedom. For this basic impulse cannot be stilled and brought to quiescence by temporary sense satisfaction, but reaches out, as it were, to infinity. It is true, of course, that the basic impulse or striving could not take the form of the higher spiritual impulse without consciousness. Consciousness is indeed a dividing-line between man as an organized product of Nature and man as a rational ego, as spirit. But from the philosophical point of view there is ultimately only one impulse, and man is subject and object in one. 'My impulse as a being of Nature and my tendency as pure spirit: are they two different impulses? No, from the transcendental point of view both are one and the same original impulse which constitutes my being: it is only regarded from two different sides. That is to say, I am subject-object, and in the identity and inseparability of both consists my true being. If I regard myself as an *object*, completely determined through the laws of sense intuition and discursive thinking, then that which is actually my one impulse becomes for me a natural impulse, because from this point of view I myself am Nature. If I regard myself as subject, the impulse becomes for me a purely spiritual impulse or the law of self-determination. All the phenomena of the ego rest simply on the reciprocity of these two impulses, and this is really the reciprocal relation *of one and the same impulse to itself*.'[2]

This theory of the unity of man in terms of one impulse has an important bearing on ethics. Fichte makes a distinction between formal and material freedom. Formal freedom requires only the presence of consciousness. Even if a man always followed his natural impulses as directed to pleasure, he would do so freely,

[1] *F*, IV, p. 124; *M*, II, p. 518.          [2] *F*, IV, p. 130; *M*, II, p. 524.

provided that he did so consciously and deliberately.[1] Material freedom, however, is expressed in a series of acts tending to the realization of the ego's complete independence. And these are moral acts. Now, if we pressed this distinction, we should be faced with the difficulty of giving any content to the moral act. For we should have on the one hand actions performed in accordance with natural impulse, which are rendered determinate by their reference to particular objects, and on the other actions which exclude all determination by particular objects and are performed solely in accordance with the idea of freedom for freedom's sake. And this second class of actions would appear to be completely indeterminate. But Fichte answers that we have to effect a synthesis which is demanded by the fact that the impulse or tendency which constitutes man's nature is ultimately one impulse. The lower impulse or lower form of the one impulse must sacrifice its end, namely pleasure, while the higher impulse or form of the one impulse must sacrifice its purity, that is, its lack of determination by any object.

Expressed in this abstract way Fichte's idea of a synthesis may seem extremely obscure. But the fundamental notion is clear enough. For example, it is clearly not demanded of the moral agent that he should cease to perform all those actions to which natural impulse prompts him, such as eating and drinking. It is not demanded of him that he should try to live as a disembodied spirit. What is demanded is that his actions should not be performed simply for the sake of immediate satisfaction, but that they should be members of a series converging towards the ideal end which man sets before himself as a spiritual subject. In so far as he fulfils this demand man realizes his moral nature.

This suggests, of course, that the moral life involves substituting one end for another, a spiritual ideal for natural satisfaction and pleasure. And this idea may seem to be at variance with Fichte's picture of morality as demanding the performance of certain actions simply for the sake of performing them and the non-performance of other actions simply for the sake of not performing them. But the spiritual ideal in question is for Fichte self-activity, action determined through the ego alone. And his point is that such action must take the form of a series of determinate actions in the

---

[1] There are activities in man, the circulation of the blood for example, of which he is not immediately, but only mediately, conscious. And he cannot be said to control them. But when I am immediately conscious of an impulse or desire, I am free, Fichte takes it, to satisfy or not to satisfy it.

world, though at the same time they must be determined by the ego itself and express its freedom rather than subjection to the natural world. This means in effect that the actions should be performed for the sake of performing them.

One can say, therefore, that Fichte makes a resolute attempt to exhibit the unity of human nature and to show that there is continuity between the life of man as a natural organism and the life of man as spiritual subject of consciousness. At the same time the influence of the Kantian formalism is strongly marked. And it shows itself clearly in Fichte's account of the supreme principle of morality.

4. Speaking of the ego when it is thought only as *object* Fichte asserts that 'the essential character of the ego, by which it is distinguished from everything external to itself, consists in a tendency to self-activity [*Selbstthätigkeit*] for the sake of self-activity; and it is this tendency which is thought when the ego is thought in and for itself without relation to anything outside it'.[1] But it is the ego as subject, as intelligence, which thinks itself as object. And when it thinks itself as a tendency to self-activity for the sake of self-activity, it necessarily thinks itself as free, as able to realize absolute self-activity, as a power of self-determination. Further, the ego cannot conceive itself in this way without conceiving itself as subject to law, the law of determining itself in accordance with the concept of self-determination. That is to say, if I conceive my objective essence as a power of self-determination, the power of realizing absolute self-activity, I must also conceive myself as obliged to actualize this essence.

We have, therefore, the two ideas of freedom and law. But just as the ego as subject and the ego as object, though distinguished in consciousness, are inseparable and ultimately one, so are the ideas of freedom and law inseparable and ultimately one. 'When you think yourself as free, you are compelled to think your freedom as falling under a law; and when you think this law, you are compelled to think yourself as free. Freedom does not follow from the law any more than the law follows from freedom. They are not two ideas, of which the one can be thought as dependent on the other, but they are one and the same idea; it is a complete synthesis.'[2]

[1] *F*, IV, p. 29; *M*, II, p. 423.
[2] *F*, IV, p. 53; *M*, II, p. 447. Kant, Fichte remarks, did not mean that the *thought* of freedom is derived from the thought of law. He meant that faith in the objective validity of the thought of freedom is derived from consciousness of the moral law.

By this somewhat tortuous route Fichte deduces the fundamental principle of morality, 'the necessary idea of the intelligence
that it ought to determine its freedom purely and without exception
in accordance with the concept of independence [*Selbständigkeit*]'.[1]
The free being ought to bring its freedom under a law, namely the
law of complete self-determination or absolute independence
(absence of determination through any external object). And this
law should admit of no exception because it expresses the very
nature of the free being.

Now, a finite rational being cannot ascribe freedom to itself
without conceiving the possibility of a series of determinate free
actions, caused by a will which is capable of exercising real causal
activity. But the realization of this possibility demands an
objective world in which the rational being can tend towards its
goal through a series of particular actions. The natural world, the
sphere of the non-ego, can thus be regarded as the material or
instrument for the fulfilment of our duty, sensible things appearing
as so many occasions for specifying the pure ought. We have already
seen that according to Fichte the absolute ego posits the world as
an obstacle or check which renders possible the recoil of the ego
onto itself in self-consciousness. And we now see the positing of the
world in a more specifically ethical context. It is the necessary condition for the rational being's fulfilment of its moral vocation. Without the world it could not give content, as it were, to the pure ought.

To be a moral action, each of these particular actions must
fulfil a certain formal condition. '*Act always according to your best
conviction of your duty* or *Act according to your conscience*. This is the
formal condition of the morality of our actions. . . .'[2] The will which
so acts is the good will. Fichte is obviously writing under the
influence of Kant.

5. 'Act according to your conscience.' Fichte defines conscience
as 'the immediate consciousness of our determinate duty'.[3] That
is to say, conscience is the immediate awareness of a particular
obligation. And from this definition it obviously follows that
conscience never errs and cannot err. For if conscience is defined
as an immediate awareness of one's duty, it would be contradictory
to say that it can be a non-awareness of one's duty.

It is clear that Fichte wishes to find an absolute criterion of
right and wrong. It is also clear that he wishes, like Kant, to avoid

[1] *F*, iv, p. 59; *M*, ii, p. 453.          [2] *F*, iv, p. 173; *M*, ii, p. 567.
[3] *F*, iv, pp. 173–4; *M*, ii, pp. 567–8.

heteronomy. No external authority can be the required criterion. Further, the criterion must be at the disposal of all, unlearned as well as learned. Fichte fixes, therefore, upon conscience and describes it as an immediate feeling (*Gefühl*). For inasmuch as the practical power has priority over the theoretical power, it is the former which must be the source of conscience. And as the practical power does not judge, conscience must be a feeling.

Fichte's description of conscience as an immediate feeling does indeed fit in with the way in which the ordinary man is accustomed to speak about his moral convictions. A man might say, for example, 'I feel that this is the right thing to do. I feel that any other course of action would be wrong.' And he may very well feel certain about it. At the same time one might wish to comment that feeling is scarcely an unerring criterion of duty. Fichte, however, argues that the immediate feeling in question expresses the agreement or harmony between 'our empirical ego and the pure ego. And the pure ego is our only true being; it is all possible being and all possible truth.'[1] Hence the feeling which constitutes conscience can never be erroneous or deceptive.

To understand Fichte's theory we must understand that he is not excluding from man's moral life all activity by the theoretical power. The ego's fundamental tendency to complete freedom and independence stimulates this power to look for the determinate content of duty. After all, we can and do reflect about what we ought to do in this or that set of circumstances. But any theoretical judgment which we make may be mistaken. The function of argument is to draw attention to the different aspects of the situation under discussion and so to facilitate the attunement, so to speak, of the empirical ego with the pure ego. This attunement expresses itself in a feeling, the immediate consciousness of one's duty. And this immediate awareness puts a stop to theoretical inquiry and argument which might otherwise be prolonged indefinitely.

Fichte will not admit that anyone who has an immediate consciousness of his duty can resolve not to do his duty precisely because it is his duty. 'Such a maxim would be diabolical; but the concept of the devil is self-contradictory.'[2] At the same time 'no man, indeed no finite being so far as we know, is confirmed in good'.[3] Conscience as such cannot err, but it can be obscured or even

---

[1] *F*, IV, p. 169; *M*, II, p. 563.    [2] *F*, IV, p. 191; *M*, II, p. 585.
[3] *F*, IV, p. 193; *M*, II, p. 587.

vanish. Thus the concept of duty may remain, though the consciousness of its connection with some particular action may be obscured. To put the matter crudely, I may not give my empirical ego the chance to click with the pure ego.[1] Further, the consciousness of duty may practically vanish, in which case 'we then act either according to the maxim of self-advantage or according to the blind impulse to assert everywhere our lawless will'.[2] Thus even if the possibility of diabolical evil is excluded, the doctrine of infallibility of conscience does not exclude the possibility of acting wrongly. For I may be accountable for allowing my conscience to become obscured or even to vanish altogether.

According to Fichte, therefore, the ordinary man has at his disposal, if he chooses to make use of it, an infallible criterion for assessing his particular duties, which does not depend on any knowledge of the science of ethics. But the philosopher can inquire into the grounds of this criterion. And we have seen that Fichte offers a metaphysical explanation.

6. Conscience is thus the supreme judge in the practical moral life. But its dictates are not arbitrary and capricious. For the 'feeling' of which Fichte speaks is really the expression of our implicit awareness that a particular action falls inside or outside the series of actions which fulfil the fundamental impulse of the pure ego. Hence even if conscience is a sufficient guide for moral conduct, there is no reason why the philosopher should be unable to show theoretically that actions of a certain type belong or do not belong to the class of actions which lead to the ego's moral goal. He cannot deduce the particular obligations of particular individuals. This is a matter for conscience. But a philosophical application of the fundamental principle of morality is possible, within the limits of general principles or rules.

To take an example. I am under an obligation to act, for only through action can I fulfil the moral law. And the body is a necessary instrument for action. On the one hand, therefore, I ought not to treat my body as if it were itself my final end. On the other hand I ought to preserve and foster the body as a necessary instrument for action. Hence self-mutilation, for example, would be wrong unless it were required for the preservation of the body as a whole. Whether in this or that particular instance self-mutilation is justified is, however, a matter for conscience rather

---

[1] This happens, for example, if I do not really size up the situation but look exclusively at one partial aspect.
[2] *F*, IV, p. 194; *M*, II, p. 588.

than for the philosopher. I can only consider the situation under its different aspects and then act according to my immediate consciousness of my duty, confident, according to Fichte, that this immediate 'feeling' cannot err.

Similarly, one can formulate general rules in regard to the use of the cognitive powers. Fichte's profound respect for the vocation of the scholar is expressed in his insistence on the need for combining complete freedom of thought and research with the conviction that 'knowledge of my duty must be the final end of all my knowledge, all my thought and research'.[1] The synthesizing rule is that the scholar should pursue his researches in a spirit of devotion to duty and not out of mere curiosity or to have something to do.

7. The philosopher, therefore, can lay down certain general rules of conduct as applications of the fundamental principle of morality. But an individual's moral vocation is made up of countless particular obligations, in regard to which conscience is the unerring guide. Thus each single individual has his own real moral vocation, his own personal contribution to make to converging series of actions which tend to realize a moral world-order, the perfect rule of reason in the world. The attainment of this ideal goal requires, as it were, a division of moral labour. And we can reformulate the fundamental principle of morality in this way: 'Always fulfil your moral vocation.'[2]

The general outlines of Fichte's vision of reality should now be clear. The ultimate reality, which can be described, according to our point of view, as the absolute ego or as infinite Will, strives spontaneously towards perfect consciousness of itself as free, towards perfect self-possession. But self-consciousness, in Fichte's view, must take the form of finite self-consciousness, and the infinite Will's self-realization can take place only through the self-realization of finite wills. Hence the infinite activity spontaneously expresses itself in a multiplicity of finite selves or rational and free beings. But self-consciousness is not possible without a non-ego, from which the finite ego can recoil onto itself. And the realization of the finite free will through action requires a world in and through which action is possible. Hence the absolute ego or infinite Will must posit the world, Nature, if it is to become conscious of its own freedom through finite selves. And the moral vocations of finite selves in a common goal can be seen as the way in which the absolute ego or infinite Will moves towards its goal. Nature is

[1] *F*, IV, p. 300; *M*, II, p. 694.     [2] *F*, IV, p. 150; *M*, II, p. 544.

simply the condition, though a necessary condition, for the expression of the moral will. The really significant feature in empirical reality is the moral activity of human beings, which is itself the expression of the infinite Will, the form which the infinite Will, an activity or doing rather than a being which acts, spontaneously and necessarily assumes.

8. We can turn now to the theory of right and the deduction of the State, to a consideration, that is to say, of the framework within which man's moral life is developed. But the theory of right and political theory, treating, as they do, of relations between human beings, presupposes a plurality of selves. Hence it is appropriate to begin by saying a little more about Fichte's deduction of this plurality.

As we have seen, the absolute ego must limit itself in the form of the finite ego if self-consciousness is to arise. But 'no free being becomes conscious of itself without at the same time becoming conscious of other similar beings'.[1] It is only by distinguishing myself from other beings which I recognize as rational and free that I can become conscious of myself as a determinate free individual. Intersubjectivity is a condition of self-consciousness. A community of selves is thus required if self-consciousness is to arise. Intelligence, as existing, is a manifold. In fact it is 'a closed manifold, that is, a *system* of rational beings'.[2] For they are all limitations of the one absolute ego, the one infinite activity.

This recognition of oneself as a member of a community or system of rational beings requires in turn, as a precondition, the sensible world. For I perceive my freedom as manifested in actions which interlock, so to speak, with the actions of others. And for such a system of actions to be possible there must be a common sensible world in which distinct rational beings can express themselves.

9. Now, if I cannot become conscious of myself as free without regarding myself as a member of a community of free rational beings, it follows that I cannot ascribe to myself alone the totality of infinite freedom. 'I limit myself in my appropriation of freedom by the fact that I also recognize the freedom of others.'[3] At the same time I must also conceive each member of the community as limiting the external expression of his freedom in such a way that all other members can express their freedom.

This idea of each member of the community of rational beings limiting the expression of his freedom in such a way that all other

---

[1] *F*, II, p. 143; *M*, IV, p. 143.      [2] *Ibid.*      [3] *F*, III, p. 8; *M*, II, p. 12.

members can also express their freedom is the concept of right. And the principle or rule of right (*Rechtsregel*) is stated by Fichte in this way: 'Limit your freedom through the concept of the freedom of all other persons with whom you come into relation.'[1] The concept of right for Fichte is essentially a social concept. It arises together with the idea of other rational beings who are capable of interfering with one's own activity, and with whose activities one is oneself capable of interfering. If I think away all other rational beings save myself, I have *powers*, and I may have a moral duty to exercise them or some of them. But it is inappropriate in this context to speak of my having a *right* to exercise them. For instance, I have the power of free speech. But if I think away all other rational beings, it is absurd, according to Fichte, to speak of my having a right to free speech. For the concept makes no sense unless I conceive the existence of other beings capable of interfering with my exercise of the power to speak my mind freely. Similarly, it makes no sense to speak of a right to private property except in a social context. True, if I were the only rational being I should have a duty to act and to use material things, expressing my freedom in and through them. I should have possessions. But the concept of the right of private property in the strict sense arises only when I conceive other human beings to whom I have to ascribe similar rights. What can private property mean outside a social context?

Now, though the existence of a community of free selves demands that each member should take the rule of right as the operative principle of his conduct, no individual will is necessarily governed by the rule. Fichte argues, however, that the union of many wills into one can produce a will constantly directed by the rule. 'If a million men are together, it may well be that each one wills for himself as much freedom as possible. But if we unite the will of all in one concept as one will, this will divides the sum of possible freedom into equal parts. It aims at all being free in such a way that the freedom of each individual is limited by the freedom of all the rest.'[2] This union expresses itself in mutual recognition of rights. And it is this mutual recognition which gives rise to the right of private property, considered as the right to exclusive possession of certain things.[3] 'The right of exclusive possession is

---

[1] *F*, III, p. 10; *M*, II, p. 14.    [2] *F*, III, p. 106; *M*, II, p. 110.

[3] It is worth noting that for Fichte rightful ownership of a thing is really the exclusive right to perform certain actions in regard to it. For instance, a farmer's property right in regard to a field is an exclusive right to sow it, plough it, graze cattle on it, and so on.

rought into being *through mutual recognition*: and it does not exist
ithout this condition. All property is grounded on the union of
1any wills into one will.'[1]

10. If the stability of rights rests on sustained common recog-
ition, reciprocal loyalty and trust are required in the persons
oncerned. But these are moral conditions on which one cannot
ount with certainty. Hence there must be some power which can
nforce respect for rights. Further, this power must be the
xpression of the freedom of the human person: it must be
established freely. We thus require a compact or contract whereby
1e contracting parties agree that anyone who infringes the
ghts of another should be treated in accordance with coercive
1w. But such a contract can be effective only when it takes the
orm of the social contract whereby the State is established,[2]
1rnished with the requisite power to secure the attainment of the
nd desired by the general will, namely the stability of the system
f rights and the protection of the freedom of all. The union of all
ills into one thus takes the form of the General Will as embodied
1 the State.

The influence of Rousseau[3] is obvious, both in Fichte's theory of
1e General Will and in his idea of the social contract. But the ideas
re not introduced simply out of reverence for the name of the
rench philosopher. For Fichte's deduction of the State consists in
progressive argument showing that the State is a necessary con-
ition for maintaining relations of right without which a community
f free persons cannot be conceived. And this community is itself
epicted as a necessary condition for the self-realization of the
bsolute ego as infinite freedom. The State must thus be interpreted
s the expression of freedom. And Rousseau's theories of the Social
ontract and General Will lend themselves for this purpose.

Fichte does indeed speak of the State as a totality, and he
ompares it with an organized product of Nature. We cannot say,
1erefore, that the organic theory of the State is absent from
ichte's political thought. At the same time he emphasizes the
1ct that the State not only expresses freedom but also exists to
reate a state of affairs in which each citizen can exercise his
ersonal freedom so far as this is consistent with the freedom of

[1] *F*, III, p. 129; *M*, II, p. 133.
[2] Fichte distinguishes various stages of the social contract, culminating in what
 calls the union-compact, whereby the members of political society become an
ganized totality.
[3] See Vol. VI, chapters 3 and 4.

others. Further, the State, considered as a coercive power, is only
hypothetically necessary. That is to say, it is necessary on the
hypothesis that man's moral development has not reached a point
at which each member of society respects the rights and liberties
of others from moral motives alone. If this condition were fulfilled
the State, as a coercive power, would no longer be necessary.
Indeed, as one of the functions of the State is to facilitate man's
moral development, we can say that for Fichte the State should
endeavour to bring about the conditions for its own demise. To use
Marxist language, Fichte looks forward to the withering away of
the State, at least as an ideal possibility. He cannot, therefore,
regard it as an end in itself.

Given these premises, Fichte naturally rejects despotism. What
may seem surprising in a sympathizer with the French Revolution
is that he also rejects democracy. 'No State may be ruled either
*despotically* or *democratically*.'[1] But by democracy he understands
direct rule by the whole people. And his objection to it is that in a
literal democracy there would be no authority to compel the
multitude to observe its own laws. Even if many citizens were
individually well disposed, there would be no power capable of
preventing the degeneration of the community into an irresponsible
and capricious mob. Provided, however, that the two extremes of
unqualified despotism and democracy are avoided, we cannot say
what form of constitution is the best. It is a matter of politics, not
of philosophy.

At the same time reflection on the possibility of abuse of power
by the civil authority led Fichte to lay great stress on the desirability
of establishing a kind of supreme court or tribunal, the 'Ephorate'.
This would possess no legislative, executive or judicial power in the
ordinary sense. Its function would be to watch over the observance
of the laws and constitution, and in the event of a serious abuse of
power by the civil authority the Ephors would be entitled to
suspend it from the exercise of its functions by means of a State
interdict. Recourse would then be had to a referendum to ascertain
the people's will concerning a change in the constitution, the law
or the government, as the case might be.

That Fichte shows no inclination to deify the State is clear
enough. But his political theory, as so far outlined, may suggest
that he is committed to minimizing the functions of the State by
defending a purely *laissez-faire* policy. But this conclusion does not

[1] *F*, III, p. 160; *M*, II, p. 164.

epresent his mind. He does indeed maintain that the purpose of
he State is to maintain public security and the system of rights.
And from this it follows that interference with the freedom of the
ndividual should be limited to what is required for the fulfilment
f this purpose. But the establishment and maintenance of a
ystem of rights and its adjustment to the common good may
equire a very considerable amount of State activity. It is idle, for
example, to insist that everyone has a right to live by his labour if
conditions are such that many people cannot do so. Further,
hough the State is not the fount of the moral law, it is its business
o promote the conditions which facilitate the moral development
without which there is no true freedom. In particular it should
attend to the matter of education.

11. Hence it is not really so astonishing if in his *Closed Commercial State* we find Fichte envisaging a planned economy. He
presupposes that all human beings have a right not simply to live
out to live a decent human life. And the question then arises how
his right can be most effectively realized. In the first place, as
Plato recognized centuries ago, there must be division of labour,
giving rise to the main economic classes.[1] And in the second place
a state of harmony or balance must be maintained. If one economic
class grows disproportionately large, the whole economy may be
upset. In *The System of Ethics* Fichte emphasized the individual's
duty to choose his profession in accordance with his talents and
circumstances. In *The Closed Commercial State* he is concerned
rather with the common good, and he stresses the State's need to
watch over and regulate the division of labour for the good of the
community. True, changing circumstances will demand changes in
the State's regulations. But supervision and planning are in any
case indispensable.

In Fichte's opinion a balanced economy, once established, cannot
be maintained unless the State has the power to prevent its being
upset by any individual or set of individuals. And he draws the
conclusion that all commercial relations with foreign countries
should be in the hands of the State or subject to strict State control.
'In the rational State immediate trade with a foreign subject
cannot be permitted to the individual citizen.'[2] Fichte's ideal is

---

[1] Fichte assumes that there will be three main economic classes. First, the
producers of the raw materials required for human life. Secondly, those who
transform these raw materials into goods such as clothes, shoes, flour and so on.
Thirdly, the merchants.

[2] *F*, III, p. 421; *M*, III, p. 451.

that of a closed economy in the sense of a self-sufficient economic community.[1] But if there has to be trade with foreign countries, it should not be left to the private initiative and judgment of individuals.

What Fichte envisages, therefore, is a form of national socialism. And he thinks of a planned economy as calculated to provide the material conditions required for the higher intellectual and moral development of the people. In fact, by 'the rational State' (der Vernunftstaat) he really means a State directed according to the principles of his own philosophy. We may not feel particularly optimistic about the results of State patronage of a particular philosophical system. But in Fichte's opinion rulers who were really conversant with the principles of transcendental idealism would never abuse their power by restricting private freedom more than was required for the attainment of an end which is itself the expression of freedom.

12. Regarded from the economic point of view, Fichte can be spoken of as one of Germany's first socialist writers. Politically speaking, however, he moved from an earlier cosmopolitan attitude towards German nationalism. In the Basis of Natural Right he interpreted the idea of the General Will as leading to the idea of the union of all human wills in a universal community, and he looked forward to a confederation of nations. The system of rights, he thought, could be rendered really stable only through the establishment of a world-wide community. And to a certain extent he always retained this wide outlook. For his ideal was always that of the advance of all men to spiritual freedom. But he came to think that the ideals of the French Revolution, which had aroused his youthful enthusiasm, had been betrayed by Napoleon and that the Germans were better qualified than the French for leading mankind towards its goal. After all, were not the Germans best suited for understanding the principles of the Wissenschaftslehre and so for enlightening mankind and teaching it by example what the saving truth could effect? In other words, he thought of Germany as having a cultural mission. And he was convinced that this mission could not be effectively fulfilled without the political unity of the German people. Cultural and linguistic unity go together and no culture can be unified and lasting without the backbone of

---

[1] Fichte's advocacy of a 'closed' commercial State is not based entirely on economic reasons. Like Plato before him, he believes that unrestricted intercourse with foreign countries would hamper the education of the citizens according to the principles of the true philosophy.

political unity. Hence Fichte looked forward to the formation of one German *Reich* which would put an end to the existing division of the Germans into a multiplicity of States. And he hoped for the emergence of a leader who would achieve this political unification of the Germans into one 'rational State'.

If we look back on Fichte's hopes and dreams in the light of Germany's history in the first half of the twentieth century, they obviously tend to appear as sinister and ominous. But, as has already been remarked, we should bear in mind the historical circumstances of his own time. In any case further reflections on this matter can be left to the reader.

# FICHTE (3)

*Fichte's early ideas on religion—God in the first version of the theory of science—The charge of atheism and Fichte's reply— The infinite Will in* The Vocation of Man—*The development of the philosophy of Being, 1801–5*—The Doctrine of Religion— *Later writings—Explanatory and critical comments on Fichte's philosophy of Being.*

1. IN 1790 Fichte wrote some notes or *Aphorisms on Religion and Deism* (*Aphorismen über Religion und Deismus*) which express clearly enough a sense of tension between simple Christian piety and speculative philosophy or, to use a rather hackneyed phrase, between the God of religion and the God of the philosophers. 'The Christian religion seems to be designed more for the heart than for the understanding.'[1] The heart seeks a God who can respond to prayer, who can feel compassion and love; and Christianity fulfils this need. But the understanding, as represented by what Fichte calls deism, presents us with the concept of a changeless necessary Being who is the ultimate cause of all that happens in the world. Christianity offers us the picture of an anthropomorphic Deity, and this picture is well adapted to religious feeling and its exigencies. Speculative philosophy offers us the idea of a change-less first cause and of a system of finite beings which is governed by determinism. And this idea of the understanding does not meet the needs of the heart. True, the two are compatible, in the sense that speculative philosophy leaves untouched the subjective validity of religion. And for the pious Christian who knows little or nothing of philosophy there is no problem. But what of the man whose heart desires a God conceived in human terms but who is at the same time so constituted that the inclination to philosophical reflection is part of his nature? It is all very well to say that he should set limits to philosophical reflection. 'But can he do so, even if he wishes?'

Fichte's own reflection, however, led him in the direction of the Kantian conception of God and of religion rather than in that of deism, which belonged to the pre-Kantian era. And in his *Essay*

[1] *F*, v, p. 5 (not contained in *M*).     [2] *F*, v, p. 8.

*towards a Critique of All Revelation (Versuch einer Kritik aller Offenbarung*, 1792) he attempted to develop Kant's point of view. In particular he made a distinction between 'theology' and religion. The idea of the possibility of a moral law demands belief in God not only as the Power which dominates Nature and is able to synthesize virtue and happiness but also as the complete embodiment of the moral ideal, as the all-holy Being and supreme Good. But assent to propositions about God (such as 'God is holy and just') is not the same thing as religion which 'according to the meaning of the word [*religio*] should be something which *binds* us, and indeed binds us *more strongly* than we would otherwise be bound'.[1] And this binding is derived from the acceptance of the rational moral law as God's law, as the expression of the divine will.

Needless to say, Fichte does not mean that the content of the moral law is arbitrarily determined by the divine will, so that it cannot be known without revelation. Nor does he propose to substitute the concept of heteronomy, of an authoritarian ethics, for the Kantian concept of the autonomy of the practical reason. To justify his position, therefore, he has recourse to the idea of a radical evil in man, that is, to the idea of the ingrained possibility of evil, owing to the strength of natural impulse and passion, and to the idea of the consequent obscuring of man's knowledge of the moral law. The concept of God as the moral legislator and of obedience to the all-holy will of God helps man to fulfil the moral law and grounds the additional element of binding which is peculiar to religion. Further, as the knowledge of God and his law can be obscured, God's revelation of himself as moral legislator is desirable if it is possible.

This may sound as though Fichte is going well beyond Kant. But the difference is much less than may appear at first. Fichte does not decide where revelation is to be found. But he gives general criteria for deciding whether an alleged revelation is really what it claims to be. For example, no alleged revelation can possibly be what it is claimed to be if it contradicts the moral law. And any alleged revelation which goes beyond the idea of the moral law as the expression of the divine will is not revelation. Hence Fichte does not really transcend the limits of Kant's conception of religion. And the sympathy which he was later to show for Christian dogmas is absent at this stage of his thought.

[1] *F*, v, p. 43; *M*, I, p. 12.

Obviously, it can be objected against Fichte's position that t
decide whether revelation really is revelation or not we have firs
to know the moral law. Hence revelation adds nothing except th
idea of fulfilling the moral law as the expression of the all-holy wil
of God. True, this additional element constitutes what is peculia
to religion. But it seems to follow, on Fichte's premises, tha
religion is, as it were, a concession to human weakness. For it i
precisely human weakness which needs strengthening through the
concept of obedience to the divine legislator. Hence if Fichte is no
prepared to abandon the Kantian idea of the autonomy of the
practical reason and if at the same time he wishes to retain and
support the idea of religion, he must revise his concept of God. And
as will be seen presently, his own system of transcendenta
idealism, in its first form at least, left him no option but to de
this.

2. In Fichte's first exposition and explanations of the *Wissen
schaftslehre* there is very little mention of God. Nor indeed is there
much occasion for mentioning God. For Fichte is concerned witl
the deduction or reconstruction of consciousness from a first
principle which is immanent in consciousness. As we have seen, the
pure ego is not a being which lies behind consciousness but ar
activity which is immanent in consciousness and grounds it. And
the intellectual intuition by which the pure ego is apprehended is
not a mystical apprehension of the Deity but an intuitive grasping
of the pure I-principle revealing itself as an activity or doing
(*Thun*). Hence if we emphasize the phenomenological aspect o1
Fichte's theory of science or knowledge, there is no more reason fo1
describing his pure ego as God than there is for so describing Kant's
transcendental ego.

The phenomenological aspect is not indeed the only aspect. In
virtue of his elimination of the thing-in-itself and his transformation
of the critical philosophy into idealism Fichte is bound to attribute
to the pure ego an ontological status and function which was not
attributed by Kant to the transcendental ego as logical condition
of the unity of consciousness. If the thing-in-itself is to be eliminated,
sensible being must be derived, in all the reality which it possesses,
from the ultimate principle on the side of the subject; that is, from
the absolute ego. But the word 'absolute' must be understood as
referring in the first place to that which is fundamental in the
transcendental deduction of consciousness from a principle which
is immanent in consciousness, not as referring to a Being beyond

all consciousness. To postulate such a Being in a system of trans-cendental idealism would be to abandon the attempt to reduce being to thought.

It is true, of course, that the more the metaphysical implications of the theory of the absolute ego are developed, the more does it take on, as it were, the character of the divine. For it then appears as the infinite activity which produces within itself the world of Nature and of finite selves. But while Fichte is primarily engaged in transforming the system of Kant into idealism and in deducing experience from the transcendental ego, it would hardly occur to him to describe this ego as God. For, as the very use of the word 'ego' shows, the notion of the pure, transcendental or absolute ego is so entangled, as it were, with human consciousness that such a description necessarily appears as extremely inappropriate.

Further, the term 'God' signifies for Fichte a personal self-conscious Being. But the absolute ego is not a self-conscious being. The activity which grounds consciousness and is a striving towards self-consciousness cannot itself be conscious. The absolute ego, therefore, cannot be identified with God. What is more, we cannot even think the idea of God. The concept of consciousness involves a distinction between subject and object, ego and non-ego. And self-consciousness presupposes the positing of the non-ego and itself involves a distinction between the I-subject and the me-object. But the idea of God is the idea of a Being in which there is no such distinction and which is perfectly self-luminous quite independently of the existence of a world. And we are unable to think such an idea. We can *talk* about it, of course; but we cannot be said to *conceive* it. For once we try to *think* what is said, we necessarily introduce the distinctions which are verbally denied. The idea of a subject to which nothing is opposed is thus 'the unthinkable idea of the Godhead'.[1]

It should be noted that Fichte does not say that God is impossible. When Jean-Paul Sartre says that self-consciousness necessarily involves a distinction and that the idea of an infinite self-consciousness in which there is perfect coincidence of subject and object without any distinction is a contradictory idea, he intends this as a proof of atheism, if, that is to say, theism is understood as implying the idea which is alleged to be contradictory. But Fichte carefully avoids saying that it is impossible that there should be a God. He appears to leave open the possibility of a

[1] *F*, I, p. 254; *M*, I, p. 448.

Being which transcends the range of human thought and conception. In any case Fichte does not assert atheism.

At the same time it is easily understandable that Fichte was accused of atheism. And we can turn to a brief consideration of the famous atheism controversy which resulted in the philosopher having to abandon his chair at Jena.

3. In his paper *On the Basis of Our Belief in a Divine Providence* (1798) Fichte gave an explicit account of his idea of God. Let us assume first of all that we are looking at the world from the point of view of ordinary consciousness, which is also that of empirical science. From this point of view, that is, for empirical consciousness, we find ourselves as being in the world, the universe, and we cannot transcend it by means of any metaphysical proof of the existence of a supernatural Being. 'The world is, simply because it is; and it is what it is, simply because it is what it is. From this point of view we start with an absolute being, and this absolute being is the world: the two concepts are identical.'[1] To explain the world as the creation of a divine intelligence is, from the scientific point of view, 'simply nonsense' (*totaler Unsinn*). The world is a self-organizing whole which contains in itself the ground of all the phenomena which occur in it.

Now let us look at the world from the point of view of transcendental idealism. The world is then seen as existing only for consciousness and as posited by the pure ego. But in this case the question of finding a cause of the world apart from the ego does not arise. Therefore neither from the scientific nor from the transcendental point of view can we prove the existence of a transcendent divine Creator.

There is, however, a third point of view, the moral. And when looked at from this point of view the world is seen to be 'the sensible material for (the performance of) our duty'.[2] And the ego is seen to belong to a supersensible moral order. It is this moral order which is God. The 'living and operative moral order is itself God. We need no other God, and we cannot conceive any other.'[3] 'This is the true faith; this moral order is the *divine*. . . . It is constructed by right action.'[4] To speak of God as substance or as

[1] F, v, p. 179; M, III, p. 123.
[2] F, v, p. 185; M, III, p. 129.     [3] F, v, p. 186; M, III, p. 130.
[4] F, v, p. 185; M, III, p. 129. It is important to notice the original German text: *Dies ist der wahre Glaube; diese moralische Ordnung ist das Göttliche, das wir annehmen. Er wird construirt durch das Rechtthun.* Grammatically, *Er* (It) should refer to *der wahre Glaube* (the true faith) and cannot refer to *diese moralische Ordnung* (this moral order). Unless, therefore, we are prepared to say that Fichte

personal or as exercising with foresight a benevolent providence
is so much nonsense. Belief in divine providence is the belief that
moral action always has good results and that evil actions can
never have good results.

That such statements led to a charge of atheism is not altogether
surprising. For to most of Fichte's readers God seemed to have
been reduced to a moral ideal. And this is not what is generally
meant by theism. After all, there are atheists with moral ideals.
Fichte, however, was indignant at the accusation and answered it
at considerable length. His replies did not achieve the desired
result of clearing his name in the eyes of his opponents; but this is
irrelevant for our purposes. We are concerned only with what he
said.

In the first place Fichte explained that he could not describe
God as personal or as substance because personality was for him
something essentially finite and substance meant something
extended in space and time, a material thing. In fact, none of the
attributes of things or beings could be predicated of God. 'Speaking
in a purely philosophical manner one would have to say of God:
He is . . . not a being but a *pure activity*, the life and principle of a
supersensible world-order.'[1]

In the second place Fichte maintained that his critics had misunderstood what he meant by a moral world-order. They had
interpreted him as saying that God is a moral order in a sense
analogous to the order created by a housewife when she arranges
the furniture and other objects in a room. But what he had really
meant was that God is an active ordering, an *ordo ordinans*, a living
and active moral order, not an *ordo ordinatus*, something merely
constructed by human effort. God is *ein tätiges Ordnen*, an active
ordering, rather than an *Ordnung*, an order constructed by man.[2]
And the finite ego, considered as acting in accordance with duty, is
'a member of that supersensible world-order'.[3]

In Fichte's idea of God as the moral world-order we can perhaps
see the fusion of two lines of thought. First there is the concept of
the dynamic unity of all rational beings. In the *Basis of the Entire
Theory of Science* Fichte had not much occasion for dwelling on the
plurality of selves. For he was primarily concerned with an abstract

has simply neglected grammatical propriety, we must recognize that he is *not*
saying that God, identified with the moral order, is no more than a creation or
construction of man.
[1] *F*, v, p. 261. (Fichte's *Gerichtliche Verantwortungsschrift* is not printed in *M*.)
[2] *F*, v, p. 382; *M*, III, p. 246.          [3] *F*, v, p. 261.

deduction of 'experience' in the sense already explained. But in the Basis of Natural Right he insisted, as we have seen, on the necessity of a plurality of rational beings. 'Man becomes man only amongst men; and as he can be nothing else but man and would not exist at all if he were not man, *there must be a plurality of men if there is to be man at all*.'[1] Hence Fichte was naturally impelled to reflect on the bond of union between men. In *The Science of Ethics* he was primarily concerned with the moral law as such and with personal morality; but he expressed his conviction that all rational beings have a common moral end, and he spoke of the moral law as using the individual as a tool or instrument for its self-realization in the sensible world. And from this notion there is an easy transition to the idea of a moral world-order which fulfils itself in and through rational beings and unites them in itself.

The second line of thought is Fichte's strongly moralistic conception of religion. At the time when he wrote the essay which occasioned the atheism-controversy he tended, like Kant before him, to equate religion with morality. Not prayer but the performance of one's duty is true religion. True, Fichte allowed that the moral life has a distinguishable religious aspect, namely the belief that whatever appearances may suggest performance of one's duty always produces a good result because it forms part, as it were, of a self-realizing moral order. But, given Fichte's moralistic interpretation of religion, faith in this moral world-order would naturally count for him as faith in God, especially as on his premises he could not think of God as a personal transcendent Being.

This moralistic conception of religion finds clear expression in an essay to which the title *From a Private Paper* (1800) has been given. The place or locus of religion, Fichte asserts, is found in obedience to the moral law. And religious faith is faith in a moral order. In action considered from a purely natural and non-moral point of view man reckons on the natural order, that is, on the stability and uniformity of Nature. In moral action he reckons on a supersensible moral order in which his action has a part to play and which ensures its moral fruitfulness. 'Every belief in a divine being *which contains more* than this concept of the moral order is to that extent imagination and superstition.'[2]

Obviously, those who described Fichte as an atheist were from one point of view quite justified. For he refused to assert what

[1] *F*, III, p. 39; *M*, II, p. 43.      [2] *F*, V, pp. 394–5; *M*, III, p. 258.

heism was generally taken to mean. At the same time his indignant
epudiation of the charge of atheism is understandable. For he did
ot assert that nothing exists except finite selves and the sensible
vorld. There is, at least as an object of practical faith, a super-
ensible moral world-order which fulfils itself in and through man.

4. But if the moral world-order is really an *ordo ordinans*, a
ruly active ordering, it must obviously possess an ontological
tatus. And in *The Vocation of Man* (1800) it appears as the eternal
nd infinite Will. 'This Will binds me in union with itself: it also
inds me in union with all finite beings like myself and is the
ommon mediator between us all.'[1] It is infinite Reason. But
lynamic creative Reason is Will. Fichte also describes it as
reative Life.

If we took some of Fichte's expressions literally, we should
robably be inclined to interpret his doctrine of the infinite Will
n a theistic sense. He even addresses the 'sublime and living Will,
amed by no name and compassed by no concept'.[2] But he still
naintains that personality is something limited and finite and
annot be applied to God. The infinite differs from the finite in
ature and not merely in degree. Further, the philosopher repeats
hat true religion consists in the fulfilment of one's moral vocation.
t the same time this idea of doing one's duty and so fulfilling
ne's moral vocation is undoubtedly infused with a spirit of devout
bandonment to and trust in the divine Will.

To appreciate the role of *The Vocation of Man* in the develop-
nent of Fichte's later philosophy it is important to understand
hat the doctrine of the infinite Will is described as a matter of
aith. This somewhat strange and turgid work, which is introduced
y the remarks that it is not intended for professional philosophers
nd that the *I* of the dialogue portions should not be taken without
nore ado to represent the author himself, is divided into three
arts, entitled respectively *Doubt*, *Knowledge* and *Faith*. In the
econd part idealism is interpreted as meaning that not only
xternal objects but also one's own self, so far as one can have any
lea of it, exist only for consciousness. And the conclusion is drawn
hat everything is reduced to images or pictures (*Bilder*) without
here being any reality which is pictured. 'All reality is transformed
nto a wonderful dream, without a life which is dreamed of and with-
ut a mind which dreams it, into a dream which consists of a dream
f itself. *Intuition* is the dream; *thought*—the source of all the being

[1] *F*, II, p. 299; *M*, III, p. 395.          [2] *F*, II, p. 303; *M*, III, p. 399.

and all the reality which I imagine to myself, of *my* being, my
power, my purpose—is the dream of that dream.'[1] In other words
subjective idealism reduces everything to presentations withou
there being anything which does the presenting or to which the
presentations are made. For when I try to grasp the self for whose
consciousness the presentations exist, this self necessarily become
one of the presentations. Knowledge, therefore, that is, idealis
philosophy, can find nothing abiding, no being. But the mind
cannot rest in such a position. And practical or moral faith, based
on consciousness of myself as a moral will subject to the moral
imperative, asserts the infinite Will which underlies the finite sel
and creates the world in the only way in which it can do so, 'in the
finite reason'.[2]

Fichte thus retains idealism but at the same time goes beyond
the ego-philosophy to postulate the infinite underlying and all
comprehensive Will. And with this postulate the atmosphere, se
to speak, of his original philosophy changes dramatically. I do no
mean to imply that there is no connection. For the theory of the
Will can be regarded as implicit in the practical deduction o
consciousness in the original *Wissenschaftslehre*. At the same tim
the ego retreats from the foreground and an infinite reality, which
is no longer described as the absolute ego, takes its place. 'Only
Reason exists; the infinite in itself, the finite in it and through it
Only in our minds does He create a world, at least that *from whic*
and that *by which* we unfold it: the voice of duty, and harmonious
feelings, intuition and laws of thought.'[3]

As already mentioned, this dynamic panentheistic idealism i
for Fichte a matter of practical faith, not of knowledge. To fulfi
properly our moral vocations, we require faith in a living and activ
moral order which can only be interpreted as infinite dynami
Reason, that is, as infinite Will. This is the one true Being behind
the sphere of presentation, creating and sustaining it through
finite selves which themselves exist only as manifestations of the
infinite Will. The development of Fichte's later philosophy i
largely conditioned by the need to *think* this concept of absolut
Being, to give it philosophical form. In *The Vocation of Man* i
remains within the sphere of moral faith.

5. In the *Exposition of the Theory of Science*[4] which he compose
in 1801 Fichte clearly states that 'all knowledge presupposes . .

---

[1] *F*, II, p. 245; *M*, III, p. 341.        [2] *F*, II, p. 303; *M*, III, p. 399.
[3] *Ibid.*        [4] *Darstellung der Wissenschaftslehre.*

ts own being'.[1] For knowledge is 'a being *for itself* and *in itself*':[2] it
is being's 'self-penetration'[3] and is thus the expression of Freedom.
Absolute knowledge, therefore, presupposes absolute Being: the
former is the latter's self-penetration.

Here we have a clear reversal of the position adopted by Fichte
in the earlier form of his doctrine of knowledge. At first he maintained that all being is being for consciousness. Hence it was not
possible for him to admit the idea of an absolute divine Being
behind or beyond consciousness. For the very fact of conceiving
such a Being made it conditioned and dependent. In other words,
the idea of absolute Being was for him contradictory. Now,
however, he asserts the primacy of Being. Absolute Being comes
to exist 'for itself' in absolute knowledge. Hence the latter must
presuppose the former. And this absolute Being is the divine.

It does not follow, of course, that absolute Being is for Fichte a
personal God. Being 'penetrates itself', comes to knowledge or
consciousness of itself, in and through human knowledge of
reality. In other words, absolute Being expresses itself in and
bears within itself all finite rational beings, and their knowledge
of Being is Being's knowledge of itself. At the same time Fichte
insists that absolute Being can never be wholly understood or
comprehended by the finite mind. In this sense God transcends
the human mind.

Evidently, there is some difficulty here. On the one hand
absolute Being is said to penetrate itself in absolute knowledge.
On the other hand absolute knowledge seems to be ruled out. If,
therefore, we exclude Christian theism, according to which God
enjoys perfect self-knowledge independently of the human spirit,
it appears that Fichte should logically adopt the Hegelian conception of philosophical knowledge as penetrating the inner essence of
the Absolute and as being the Absolute's absolute knowledge of
itself. But in point of fact Fichte does not do this. To the very end
he maintains that absolute Being in itself transcends the reach of
the human mind. We know images, pictures, rather than the
reality in itself.

In the lectures on the *Wissenschaftslehre* which he delivered in
1804 Fichte emphasizes the idea of absolute Being as Light,[4] an
idea which goes back to Plato and the Platonic tradition in metaphysics. This living Light in its radiation is said to divide itself into

---

[1] *F*, II, p. 68; *M*, IV, p. 68.      [2] *F*, II, p. 19; *M*, IV, p. 19.      [3] *Ibid.*
[4] This idea had already been mentioned in the *Wissenschaftslehre* of 1801.

Being and Thought (*Denken*). But conceptual thought, Fichte insists, can never grasp absolute Being in itself, which is incomprehensible. And this incomprehensibility is 'the negation of the concept'.[1] One might expect Fichte to draw the conclusion that the human mind can approach the Absolute only by way of negation. But in point of fact he makes a good many positive statements, telling us, for example, that Being and Life and *ess* are one, and that the Absolute *in itself* can never be subject to division.[2] It is only in its appearance, in the radiation of Light that division is introduced.

In *The Nature of the Scholar* (1806), the published version of lectures delivered at Erlangen in 1805, we are again told that the one divine Being is Life and that this Life is itself changeless and eternal. But it externalizes itself in the life of the human race throughout time, 'an endlessly self-developing life which always advances towards a higher self-realization in a never-ending stream of time'.[3] In other words, this external life of God advances towards the realization of an ideal which can be described, in anthropomorphic language, as 'the Idea and fundamental notion of God in the production of the world, God's purpose and plan for the world'.[4] In this sense the divine Idea is 'the ultimate and absolute foundation of all appearances'.[5]

6. These speculations were worked out more at length in *The Way to the Blessed Life or the Doctrine of Religion* (1806), which comprises a series of lectures delivered at Berlin. God is absolute Being. And to say this is to say that God is infinite Life. For 'Being and Life are one and the same'.[6] In itself this Life is one, indivisible and unchanging. But it expresses or manifests itself externally. And the only way in which it can do this is through consciousness which is the ex-istence (*Dasein*) of God. 'Being ex-ists [*ist da*] and the ex-istence of Being is necessarily consciousness or reflection.'[7] In this external manifestation distinction or division appears. For consciousness involves the subject-object relation.

The subject in question is obviously the limited or finite subject, namely the human spirit. But what is the object? It is indeed Being. For consciousness, the divine *Dasein*, is consciousness of Being. But Being in itself, the immediate infinite Life, transcends the comprehension of the human mind. Hence the object of

[1] F, x, p. 117; M, IV, p. 195.        [2] F, x, p. 206; M, IV, p. 284.
[3] F, VI, p. 362; M, V, p. 17.        [4] F, VI, p. 367; M, V, p. 22.
[5] F, VI, p. 361; M, V, p. 15.        [6] F, V, p. 403; M, V, p. 115.
[7] F, V, p. 539; M, V, p. 251.

onsciousness must be the image or picture or *schema* of the Absolute. And this is the world. 'What does this consciousness contain? I think that each of you will answer: the world and nothing but the world. . . . In consciousness the divine Life is inevitably transformed into an abiding world.'[1] In other words, Being is objectified for consciousness in the form of the world.

Although Fichte insists that the Absolute transcends the grasp of the human mind, he says a good deal about it. And even if the finite spirit cannot know the infinite Life as it is in itself, it can at least know that the world of consciousness is the image or *schema* of the Absolute. Hence there are two main forms of life which lie open to man. It is possible for him to immerse himself in apparent life (*das Scheinleben*), life in the finite and changeable, life directed towards the gratification of natural impulse. But because of its unity with the infinite divine Life the human spirit can never be satisfied with love of the finite and sensible. Indeed, the endless seeking for successive finite sources of satisfaction shows that even apparent life is informed or carried along, as it were, by the longing for the infinite and eternal which is 'the innermost root of all finite existence'.[2] Hence man is capable of rising to true life (*das wahrhaftige Leben*) which is characterized by love of God. For love, as Fichte puts it, is the heart of life.

If it is asked in what this true life precisely consists, Fichte's reply is still given primarily in terms of morality. That is to say, true life consists primarily in a man's fulfilling his moral vocation, by which he is liberated from the servitude of the sensible world and in which he strives after the attainment of ideal ends. At the same time the markedly moralistic atmosphere of Fichte's earlier accounts of religion tends to disappear or at any rate to diminish. The religious point of view is not simply identical with the moral point of view. For it involves the fundamental conviction that God alone is, that God is the one true reality. True, God as he is in himself is hidden from the finite mind. But the religious man knows that the infinite divine Life is immanent in himself, and his moral vocation is for him a divine vocation. In the creative realization of ideals or values through action[3] he sees the image or *schema* of the divine Life.

[1] *F*, v, p. 457; *M*, v, p. 169.    [2] *F*, v, p. 407; *M*, v, p. 119.
[3] In what Fichte calls the higher morality man is creative, seeking actively to realize ideal values. He does not content himself, as in the lower morality, with the mere fulfilment of the successive duties of his state of life. Religion adds belief in God as the one reality and a sense of divine vocation. The life of higher morality is seen as the expression of the one infinite divine Life.

But though *The Doctrine of Religion* is permeated with a religious atmosphere, there is a marked tendency to subordinat the religious point of view to the philosophical. Thus, according to Fichte, while the religious point of view involves belief in th Absolute as the foundation of all plurality and finite existence philosophy turns this belief into knowledge. And it is in accordanc with this attitude that Fichte attempts to show the identit between Christian dogmas and his own system. To be sure, thi attempt can be regarded as the expression of a growth in sympath with Christian theology; but it can also be regarded as an essay i 'demythologization'. For instance, in the sixth lecture Ficht refers to the prologue to St. John's Gospel and argues that th doctrine of the divine Word, when translated into the language o philosophy, is identical with his own theory of the divine ex-istenc or *Dasein*. And the statement of St. John that all things were mad in and through the Word means, from the speculative point o view, that the world and all that is in it exist only in the sphere o consciousness as the ex-istence of the Absolute.

However, with the development of the philosophy of Bein there goes a development in Fichte's understanding of religion From the religious point of view moral activity is love of God an fulfilment of his will, and it is sustained by faith and trust in God We exist only in and through God, infinite Life, and the feeling o this union is essential to the religious or blessed life (*das selig Leben*).

7. *The Way to the Blessed Life* is a series of popular lectures, i the sense that it is not a work for professional philosophers. An Fichte is obviously concerned with edifying and uplifting hi hearers, as well as with reassuring them that his philosophy is no at variance with the Christian religion. But the fundamenta theories are common to Fichte's later writings: they are certainl not put forward simply for the sake of edification. Thus in *Th Facts of Consciousness* (1810) we are told that 'knowledge i certainly not merely knowledge of itself . . . it is knowledge of *Being*, namely of the one Being which truly is, God'.[1] But thi object of knowledge is not grasped in itself; it is splintered, as i were, into forms of knowledge. And 'the demonstration of th necessity of these forms is precisely philosophy or the *Wissen schaftslehre*'.[2] Similarly, in *The Theory of Science in its Genera Outline* (1810) we read that 'only one Being exists purely throug

[1] *F*, ii, p. 685 (not included in *M*).          [2] *Ibid.*

:self, God. . . . And neither within him nor outside him can a new
»eing arise.'[1] The only thing which can be external to God is the
*chema* or picture of Being itself, which is 'God's Being outside his
3eing',[2] the divine self-externalization in consciousness. Thus the
/hole of the productive activity which is reconstructed or deduced
1 the theory of science is the schematizing or picturing of God, the
pontaneous self-externalization of the divine life.

In the *System of Ethics* of 1812 we find Fichte saying that while
rom the scientific point of view the world is primary and the
oncept a secondary reflection or picture, from the ethical point of
'iew the Concept is primary. In fact 'the Concept is ground of the
/orld or of Being'.[3] And this assertion, if taken out of its context,
ppears to contradict the doctrine which we have been considering,
.amely that Being is primary. But Fichte explains that 'the
•roposition in question, namely that the Concept is ground of
3eing, can be expressed in this way: Reason or the Concept is
•ractical'.[4] He further explains that though the Concept or Reason
s in fact itself the picture of a higher Being, the picture of God,
ethics can and should know nothing of this. . . . Ethics must know
1othing of God, but take the Concept itself as the Absolute.'[5] In
•ther words, the doctrine of absolute Being, as expounded in the
*Vissenschaftslehre*, transcends the sphere of ethics which deals
vith the causality of the Concept, the self-realizing Idea or Ideal.

8. Fichte's later philosophy has sometimes been represented as
»eing to all intents and purposes a new system which involved a
»reak with the earlier philosophy of the ego. Fichte himself,
1owever, maintained that it was nothing of the kind. In his view
he philosophy of Being constituted a development of his earlier
hought rather than a break with it. If he had originally meant, as
nost of his critics took him to mean, that the world is the creation
•f the finite self as such, his later theory of absolute Being would
ndeed have involved a radical change of view. But he had never
neant this. The finite subject and its object, the two poles of
onsciousness, had always been for him the expression of an
inlimited or infinite principle. And his later doctrine of the sphere
•f consciousness as the ex-istence of infinite Life or Being was a
levelopment, not a contradiction, of his earlier thought. In other
vords, the philosophy of Being supplemented the *Wissenschaft-
lehre* rather than took its place.

[1] *F*, ii, p. 696; *M*, v, p. 615.       [2] *Ibid.*       [3] *F*, xi, p. 5; *M*, vi, p. 5.
[4] *F*, xi, p. 7; *M*, vi, p. 7.       [5] *F*, xi, p. 4; *M*, vi, p. 4.

It is indeed arguable that unless Fichte was prepared to defenc a subjective idealism which it would have been difficult to dis sociate from a solipsistic implication, he was bound in the long run to transgress his initial self-imposed limits, to go behind conscious ness and to find its ground in absolute Being. Further, he explicitly admitted that the absolute ego, as transcending the subject object relationship which it grounds, must be the identity of subjectivity and objectivity. Hence it is not unnatural that in proportion as he developed the metaphysical aspect of his philo sophy he should tend to discard the word 'ego' as an appropriate descriptive term for his ultimate principle. For this word is too closely associated with the idea of the subject as distinct from the object. In this sense his later philosophy was a development of his earlier thought.

At the same time it is also arguable that the philosophy of Being is superimposed on the *Wissenschaftslehre* in such a way that the two do not really fit together. According to the *Wissenschaftslehr* the world exists only for consciousness. And this thesis really depends on the premiss that being must be reduced to thought or consciousness. Fichte's philosophy of absolute Being, however clearly implies the logical priority of being to thought. True, in his later philosophy Fichte does not deny his former thesis that the world has reality only within the sphere of consciousness. On the contrary, he reaffirms it. What he does is to depict the whole sphere of consciousness as the externalization of absolute Being in itself But it is very difficult to understand this idea of externalization. I we take seriously the statement that absolute Being is and eternally remains one and immutable, we can hardly interpret Fichte as meaning that Being *becomes* conscious. And if the sphere of consciousness is an eternal reflection of God, if it is the divine self consciousness eternally proceeding from God as the Plotinian *Nous* emanates eternally from the One, it seems to follow that there must always have been a human spirit.

Fichte could, of course, depict absolute Being as an infinite activity moving towards self-consciousness in and through the human spirit. But then it would be natural to conceive the infinite Life as expressing itself immediately in objective Nature as a necessary condition for the life of the human spirit. In other words it would be natural to proceed in the direction of Hegel's absolute idealism. But this would involve a greater change in the *Wissen schaftslehre* than Fichte was prepared to make. He does indeed say

hat it is the one Life, and not the individual as such, which
intuits' the material world. But he maintains to the end that the
world, as the image or *schema* of God, has reality only within the
phere of consciousness. And as absolute Being in itself is not
onscious, this can only mean human consciousness. Until this
lement of subjective idealism is abandoned, the transition to the
bsolute idealism of Hegel is not possible.

There is indeed another possibility, namely that of conceiving
bsolute Being as eternally self-conscious. But Fichte can hardly
ake the path of traditional theism. For his idea of what self-
onsciousness essentially involves prevents him from attributing it
o the One. Hence consciousness must be derivative. And this is
uman consciousness. But there can be no being apart from God.
Hence human consciousness must be in some sense the Absolute's
onsciousness of itself. But in what sense? It does not seem to me
hat any clear answer is forthcoming. And the reason is that
Fichte's later philosophy of Being could not be simply super-
mposed on the *Wissenschaftslehre*. A much greater measure of
evision was required.

It may be objected that to interpret Fichte's philosophy as
demanding revision either in the direction of Hegel's absolute
dealism or in that of theism is to fail to do justice to its intrinsic
haracter. And this is true in a sense. For Fichte has his own
thical vision of reality, to which attention has been drawn in these
hapters. We have seen the infinite Will expressing itself in finite
elves for which Nature forms the scene and material for the
ulfilment of their several moral vocations. And we have seen these
vocations converging towards the realization of a universal moral
order, the goal, as it were, of the infinite Will itself. And the
randeur of this vision of reality, of Fichte's dynamic ethical
dealism in its main lines, is not in question. But Fichte did not
ffer his philosophy simply as an impressionistic vision or as
poetry, but as the truth about reality. Hence criticism of his
heories is quite in place. After all, it is not the vision of the
ealization of a universal ideal, a moral world-order, which has
been subjected to adverse criticism. This vision may well possess
n abiding value. And it can serve as a corrective to an interpreta-
ion of reality simply in terms of empirical science. One can
ertainly derive stimulus and inspiration from Fichte. But to draw
profit from him one has to discard a good deal of the theoretical
ramework of the vision.

It has been stated above that Fichte could hardly take the path
of traditional theism. But some writers have maintained that his
later philosophy is in fact a form of theism. And in support of this
contention they can appeal to certain statements which represent
the philosopher's firm convictions and are not simply *obiter dicta* or
remarks calculated to reassure his more orthodox readers or
hearers. For example, Fichte constantly maintains that absolute
Being is unchangeable and that it can suffer no self-diremption. It
is the eternal immutable One; not a static lifeless One but the
fullness of infinite Life. True, creation is free only in the sense that
it is spontaneous; but creation does not effect any change in God.
To be sure, Fichte refuses to predicate personality of God, even if
he frequently employs Christian language and speaks of God as
'He'. But as he regards personality as necessarily finite, he
obviously cannot attribute it to infinite Being. But this does not
mean that he looks on God as infra-personal. God is supra-personal,
not less than personal. In Scholastic language, Fichte has no
analogical concept of personality, and this prevents him from
using theistic terms. At the same time the concept of absolute
Being which transcends the sphere of the distinctions which
necessarily exist between finite beings is clearly a move in the
direction of theism. The ego no longer occupies the central position
in Fichte's picture of reality: its place is taken by infinite Life
which in itself suffers no change or self-diremption.

This is all very well as far as it goes. And it is true that Fichte's
refusal to predicate personality of God is due to the fact that
personality for him involves finitude. God transcends the sphere of
personality rather than falls short of it. But it is also the absence
of any clear idea of analogy which involves Fichte's thought in a
radical ambiguity. God is infinite Being. Therefore there can arise
no being apart from God. If there were such a being, God would not
be infinite. The Absolute is the sole Being. This line of thought
clearly points in the direction of pantheism. At the same time
Fichte is determined to maintain that the sphere of consciousness,
with its distinction, between the finite ego and the world, is in some
sense outside God. But in what sense? It is all very well for Fichte
to say that the distinction between the divine Being and the
divine ex-istence arises only for consciousness. The question
inevitably suggests itself, are finite selves beings or are they not?
If they are not, monism results. And it is then impossible to
explain how consciousness, with the distinctions which it introduces,

rises. If, however, finite selves are beings, how are we to reconcile his with the statement that God is the only Being unless we have recourse to a theory of analogy? Fichte wishes to have things both ways. That is, he wishes to say at the same time that the sphere of consciousness, with its distinction between the finite self and its object, is external to God and that God is the only Being. Hence his position in regard to the issue between theism and pantheism inevitably remains ambiguous. This is not to deny, of course, that the development of Fichte's philosophy of Being conferred on his thought a much greater resemblance to theism than would be suggested by his earlier writings. But it seems to me that if a writer who admires Fichte for his use of the transcendental method of reflection or for his ethical idealism proceeds to interpret his later philosophy as a clear statement of theism, he is going beyond the historical evidence.

If, finally, it is asked whether in his philosophy of Being Fichte abandons idealism, the answer should be clear from what has been already said. Fichte does not repudiate the *Wissenschaftslehre*, and in this sense he retains idealism. When he says that it is the one life, and not the individual subject, which 'intuits' (and so produces) the material world, he is obviously accounting for the fact that the material world appears to the finite subject as something given, as an already constituted object. But he had proclaimed from the beginning that this is the crucial fact which idealism has to explain, and not to deny. At the same time the assertion of the primacy of Being and of the derivative character of consciousness and knowledge is a move away from idealism. Hence we can say that in so far as this assertion proceeded from the exigencies of his own thought, idealism with Fichte tended to overcome itself. But this is not to say that the philosopher ever made a clear and explicit break with idealism. In any case we may well feel that though in recent times there has been a tendency to emphasize Fichte's later thought, his impressive vision of reality is his system of ethical idealism rather than his obscure utterances about absolute Being and the divine *Dasein*.

### CHAPTER V

## SCHELLING (1)

*Life and writings—The successive phases in Schelling's thought —Early writings and the influence of Fichte.*

1. FRIEDRICH WILHELM JOSEPH VON SCHELLING, son of a learned Lutheran pastor, was born in 1775 at Leonberg in Württemberg. A precocious boy, he was admitted at the age of fifteen to the Protestant theological foundation at the University of Tübingen where he became a friend of Hegel and Hölderlin, both of whom were five years older than himself. At the age of seventeen he wrote a dissertation on the third chapter of Genesis, and in 1793 he published an essay *On Myths (Ueber Mythen)*. This was followed in 1794 by a paper *On the Possibility of a Form of Philosophy in General (Ueber die Möglichkeit einer Form der Philosophie überhaupt)*.

At this time Schelling was more or less a disciple of Fichte, a fact which is apparent in the title of a work published in 1795, *On the Ego as Principle of Philosophy (Vom Ich als Prinzip der Philosophie)*. In the same year there appeared his *Philosophical Letters on Dogmatism and Criticism (Philosophische Briefe über Dogmatismus und Kritizismus)*, dogmatism being represented by Spinoza and criticism by Fichte.

But though Fichte's thought formed a point of departure for his reflections, Schelling very soon showed the independence of his mind. In particular, he was dissatisfied with Fichte's view of Nature as being simply an instrument for moral action. And his own view of Nature as an immediate manifestation of the Absolute, as a self-organizing dynamic and teleological system which moves upwards, as it were, to the emergence of consciousness and to Nature's knowledge of herself in and through man, found expression in a series of works on the philosophy of Nature. Thus in 1797 he published *Ideas towards a Philosophy of Nature (Ideen zu einer Philosophie der Natur)*, in 1798 *On the World-Soul (Von der Weltseele)*, and in 1799 a *First Sketch of a System of the Philosophy of Nature (Erster Entwurf eines Systems der Naturphilosophie)* and an *Introduction to the Sketch of a System of the Philosophy of Nature, or On the Concept of Speculative Physics (Einleitung zu dem Entwurf*

94

*ines Systems der Naturphilosophie oder über den Begriff der
*pekulativen Physik*).

It will be noted that the title of the last work refers to speculative
physics. And a similar term occurs in the full title of the work *On
the World-Soul*, the world-soul being said to be an hypothesis of
the higher physics'. One can hardly imagine Fichte giving much
attention to speculative physics. Yet the series of publications on
the philosophy of Nature does not indicate a complete break with
Fichte's thought. For in 1800 Schelling published his *System of
Transcendental Idealism* (*System des transzendentalen Idealismus*)
in which the influence of Fichte's *Wissenschaftslehre* is obvious.
Whereas in his writings on the philosophy of Nature Schelling
moved from the objective to the subjective, from the lowest grades
of Nature up to the organic sphere as a preparation for consciousness, in the *System of Transcendental Idealism* he began with the
ego and proceeded to trace the process of its self-objectification.
He regarded the two points of view as complementary, as is shown
by the fact that in 1800 he also published a *General Deduction of the
Dynamic Process* (*Allgemeine Deduktion des dynamischen Prozesses*),
which was followed in 1801 by a short piece *On the True Concept of
the Philosophy of Nature* (*Ueber den wahren Begriff der Natur-
philosophie*). In the same year he also published *An Exposition of my
System of Philosophy* (*Darstellung meines Systems der Philosophie*).

In 1798 Schelling was appointed to a chair in the University of
Jena. He was only twenty-three, but his writings had won him the
commendation not only of Goethe but also of Fichte. From 1802
to 1803 he collaborated with Hegel in editing the *Critical Journal
of Philosophy*. And during the period of his professorship at Jena
he was in friendly relations with the circle of the romantics, such
as the two Schlegels and Novalis. In 1802 Schelling published,
*Bruno, or On the Divine and Natural Principle of Things* (*Bruno,
oder über das göttliche und natürliche Prinzip der Dinge*) and also a
series of *Lectures on the Method of Academic Study* (*Vorlesungen
über die Methode des akademischen Studiums*) in which he discussed
the unity of the sciences and the place of philosophy in academic
life.

It has been mentioned that in his *System of Transcendental
Idealism* Schelling started with the ego and utilized ideas taken
from Fichte's *Wissenschaftslehre* in his reconstruction of the ego's
self-objectification, for example in morals. But this work culminated
in a philosophy of art, to which Schelling attached great importance.

And in the winter of 1802–3 he lectured at Jena on the philosophy of art. At this time he looked on art as the key to the nature o reality. And this fact alone is sufficient to show the marked difference between Schelling's outlook and that of Fichte.

In 1803 Schelling married Caroline Schlegel after the lega dissolution of her marriage with A. W. Schlegel, and the pair went to Würzburg, where Schelling lectured for a period in the University About this time he began to devote his attention to problems o religion and to the theosophical utterances of the mystical shoe maker of Görlitz, Jakob Boehme.[1] And in 1804 he published *Philosophy and Religion (Philosophie und Religion)*.

Schelling left Würzburg for Munich in 1806. His reflections or freedom and on the relation between human freedom and the Absolute found expression in *Philosophical Inquiries into the Nature of Human Freedom (Philosophische Untersuchungen über das Wesen der menschlichen Freiheit)*, a work which was published in 1809 But by this time his star had begun to grow dim. We have seen that he collaborated with Hegel for a short period in editing a philosophical journal. But in 1807 Hegel, who had previously been little known, published his first great work, *The Phenomenology o Spirit*. And this work not only formed the first stage in its author's rise to fame as Germany's leading philosopher but also represented his intellectual break with Schelling. In particular, Hegel gave a somewhat caustic expression to his opinion of Schelling's doctrine of the Absolute. And Schelling, who was the very opposite o thick-skinned, took this betrayal, as he saw it, very much to heart In the years that followed, as he witnessed the growing reputation of his rival, he became obsessed by the thought that his former friend had foisted on a gullible public an inferior system o philosophy. Indeed, his bitter disappointment at Hegel's rise to a pre-eminent position in the philosophical world of Germany probably helps to explain why, after a remarkable burst of literary activity, he published comparatively little.

Schelling continued, however, to lecture. Thus a course o lectures which he gave at Stuttgart in 1810 is printed in his collected *Works*. In 1811 he wrote *The Ages of the World (Die Zeitalter)*, but the work remained unfinished and was not published during his lifetime.

During the period 1821–6 Schelling lectured at Erlangen. In 1827 he returned to Munich to occupy the chair of philosophy and

[1] For Jakob Boehme (1575–1624) see Vol. III, pp. 270–3.

zestfully set about the congenial task of undermining the influence of Hegel. He had become convinced that a distinction must be made between negative philosophy, which is a purely abstract conceptual construction, and positive philosophy, which treats of concrete existence. The Hegelian system, needless to say, was declared to be an example of the first type.

The death of Schelling's great rival[1] in 1831 should have facilitated his task. And ten years later, in 1841, he was appointed professor of philosophy at Berlin with the mission of combating the influence of Hegelianism by expounding his own religious system. In the Prussian capital Schelling began lecturing as a prophet, as one announcing the advent of a new era. And he had among his audience professors, statesmen and a number of hearers whose names were to become famous, such as Sören Kierkegaard, Jakob Burckhardt, Friedrich Engels and Bakunin. But the lectures were not as successful as Schelling hoped that they would be, and the audience started to diminish. In 1846 he abandoned lecturing, except for occasional discourses at the Berlin Academy. Later he retired to Munich and busied himself with preparing manuscripts for publication. He died in 1854 at Ragaz in Switzerland. His *Philosophy of Revelation* (*Philosophie der Offenbarung*) and *Philosophy of Mythology* (*Philosophie der Mythologie*) were published posthumously.

2. There is no one closely-knit system which we can call Schelling's system of philosophy. For his thought passed through a succession of phases from the early period when he stood very much under the influence of Fichte up to the final period which is represented by the posthumously published lectures on the philosophy of revelation and mythology. There has been no general agreement among historians about the precise number of phases which should be distinguished. One or two have contented themselves with Schelling's own distinction between negative and positive philosophy; but this distinction fails to take account of the variety of phases in his thought before he set about expounding his final philosophy of religion. Hence it has been customary to make further divisions. But though there certainly are distinct phases in Schelling's thought, it would be a mistake to regard these phases as so many independent systems. For there is a visible continuity.

[1] Hegel himself does not seem to have been much concerned with personal rivalries as such; he was absorbed in ideas and in the exposition of what he believed to be the truth. But Schelling took Hegel's criticism of his own ideas as a personal affront.

That is to say, reflection on a position already adopted led Schelling to raise further problems, the solution of which required fresh moves on his part. True, in his later years he emphasized the distinction between negative and positive philosophy. But though he regarded a good deal of his own previous thought as negative philosophy, he stressed the distinction in the course of his polemic against Hegel; and what he desired was not so much a complete rejection of so-called negative philosophy as its incorporation into and subordination to positive philosophy. Further, he claimed that some inkling at least of positive philosophy could be found in his early *Philosophical Letters on Dogmatism and Criticism*, and that even in his first philosophical essays his inclination towards the concrete and historical had manifested itself.

In 1796, when Schelling was twenty-one, he drew up for himself a programme for a system of philosophy. The projected system would proceed from the idea of the ego or self as an absolutely free being by way of the positing of the non-ego to the sphere of speculative physics. It would then proceed to the sphere of the human spirit. The principles of historical development would have to be laid down, and the ideas of a moral world, of God and of the freedom of all spiritual beings would have to be developed. Further, the central importance of the idea of beauty would have to be shown, and the aesthetic character of the highest act of reason. Finally, there would have to be a new mythology, uniting philosophy and religion.

This programme is illuminating. On the one hand it illustrates the element of discontinuity in Schelling's thought. For the fact that he proposes to start from the ego reveals the influence of Fichte, an influence which grew progressively less as time went on. On the other hand the programme illustrates the element of continuity in Schelling's philosophizing. For it envisages the development of a philosophy of Nature, a philosophy of history, a philosophy of art, a philosophy of freedom and a philosophy of religion and mythology, themes which were to occupy his attention in turn. In other words, though Schelling at first gave the impression of being a disciple of Fichte, his interests and bent of mind were already apparent at the beginning of his career.

The upshot of all this is that time spent on discussing exactly how many phases or 'systems' there are in Schelling's philosophizing is time wasted. There certainly are distinct phases, but a genetic account of his thought can do justice to these distinctions without its being implied that Schelling jumped from one self-enclosed system to another. In fine, the philosophy of Schelling is a philosophizing rather than a finished system or succession of finished systems. In a sense the beginning and the end of his pilgrimage coincide. We have seen that in 1793 he published an essay *On Myths*. In his old age he returned to this subject and lectured on it at length. But in between we find a restless process of reflection moving from the ego-philosophy of Fichte through the philosophy of Nature and of art to the philosophy of the religious consciousness and a form of speculative theism, the whole being linked together by the theme of the relation between the finite and the infinite.

3. In his essay *On the Possibility of a Form of Philosophy in General* (1794) Schelling follows Fichte in asserting that philosophy, being a science, must be a logically unified system of propositions, developed from one fundamental proposition which gives expression to the unconditioned. This unconditioned is the self-positing ego. Hence 'the fundamental proposition can only be this: I is I'.[1] In the work *On the Ego as Principle of Philosophy* (1795) this proposition is formulated in the less peculiar form, '*I am I* or *I am*'.[2] And from this proposition Schelling proceeds to the positing of the non-ego and argues that ego and non-ego mutually condition one another. There is no subject without an object and no object without a subject. Hence there must be a mediating factor, a common product which links them together; and this is representation (*Vorstellung*). We thus have the form of the fundamental triad of all science or knowledge, namely subject, object and representation.

The influence of Fichte is obvious enough. But it is worth noting that from the very start Schelling emphasizes the difference between the absolute and the empirical ego. 'The completed system of science starts with the absolute ego.'[3] This is not a thing but infinite freedom. It is indeed one, but the unity which is predicated of it transcends the unity which is predicated of the individual member of a class. The absolute ego is not and cannot be a member of any class: it transcends the concept of class. Further, it transcends the grasp of conceptual thought and can be apprehended only in intellectual intuition.

---

[1] *W*, I, p. 57. References to Schelling's writings are given according to volume and page of the edition of his *Works* by Manfred Schröter (Munich, 1927–8).

Schelling prefers '*I is I*' (*Ich ist Ich*) to 'the ego is the ego' (*das Ich ist das Ich*) on the ground that the ego is given only as *I*.

[2] *W*, I, p. 103.                    [3] *W*, I, p. 100.

None of this contradicts Fichte; but the point is that Schelling's metaphysical interests are revealed from the beginning of his career. Whereas Fichte, starting from the philosophy of Kant, gave so little prominence at first to the metaphysical implications of his idealism that he was widely thought to be taking the individual ego as his point of departure, Schelling emphasizes at once the idea of the Absolute, even if, under Fichte's influence, he describes it as the absolute ego.

It will be noted that in the essay *On the Possibility of a Form of Philosophy in General* Schelling follows Fichte in deducing the presentation or representation. But his real interest is ontological. In the early *Wissenschaftslehre* Fichte declared that the task of philosophy is to explain experience in the sense of the system of presentations which are accompanied by a feeling of necessity. And he did so by showing how the ego gives rise to these presentations through the activity of the productive imagination which works unconsciously, so that for empirical consciousness the world inevitably possesses an appearance of independence. But in his *Philosophical Letters on Dogmatism and Criticism* (1795) Schelling roundly declares that the 'chief business of all philosophy consists in solving the problem of the existence of the world'.[1] In one sense, of course, the two statements come to the same thing. But there is a considerable difference in emphasis between saying that the business of philosophy is to explain the system of presentations which are accompanied by a feeling of necessity and saying that the business of philosophy is to explain the existence of the world. And with the help of a little hindsight at any rate we can discern beneath all the Fichtean trappings of Schelling's early thought the same metaphysical bent of mind which led him to say at a later stage that the task of philosophy is to answer the question, why there is something rather than nothing. True, Fichte himself came to develop the metaphysical implications of his philosophy. But when he did so, Schelling accused him of plagiarism.

Schelling's *Philosophical Letters* is an illuminating work. It is in a sense a defence of Fichte. For Schelling contrasts criticism, represented by Fichte, with dogmatism, represented chiefly by Spinoza. And he comes down on the side of Fichte. At the same time the work reveals the author's profound sympathy with Spinoza and an at any rate latent dissatisfaction with Fichte.

[1] *W*, I, p. 237. This work will be referred to in future simply as *Philosophical Letters*.

Dogmatism, says Schelling, involves in the long run the absolutization of the non-ego. Man is reduced to a mere modification of the infinite Object, Spinoza's substance, and freedom is excluded. It is true that Spinozism, which aims at the attainment of peace and tranquillity of soul through 'quiet self-surrender to the absolute Object',[1] possesses an aesthetic appeal and can exercise a powerful attraction on some minds. But ultimately it means the annihilation of the human being as a free moral agent. Dogmatism has no room for freedom.

But it does not follow that dogmatism can be theoretically refuted. The philosophy of Kant 'has only weak weapons against dogmatism',[2] and can achieve nothing more than a negative refutation. For example, Kant shows that it is impossible to disprove freedom in the noumenal sphere, but he admits himself that he can give no positive theoretical proof of freedom. Yet 'even the completed system of criticism cannot refute dogmatism *theoretically*',[3] even if it can deliver some shrewd blows. And this is not at all surprising. For as long as we remain on the theoretical plane dogmatism and criticism lead, Schelling maintains, to much the same conclusion.

In the first place both systems try to make the transition from the infinite to the finite. But 'philosophy cannot proceed from the infinite to the finite'.[4] We can, of course, invent reasons why the infinite must manifest itself in the finite, but they are simply ways of covering up an inability to bridge the gulf. It appears, therefore, that we must proceed the other way round. But how is this to be done when the traditional *a posteriori* demonstrations have been discredited? Obviously what is required is the suppression of the problem. That is to say, if the finite can be seen in the infinite and the infinite in the finite, the problem of bridging the gulf between them by means of a theoretical argument or demonstration no longer arises.

This need is fulfilled by intellectual intuition, which is an intuition of the identity of the intuiting with the intuited self. But it is interpreted in different ways by dogmatism and criticism. Dogmatism interprets it as an intuition of the self as identical with the Absolute conceived as absolute Object. Criticism interprets it as revealing the identity of the self with the Absolute as absolute Subject, conceived as pure free activity.

[1] *W*, I, p. 208.                    [2] *W*, I, p. 214.
[3] *W*, I, p. 220. The reference is, of course, to Fichte's idealism.
[4] *W*, I, p. 238.

Though, however, dogmatism and criticism interpret intellectua intuition in different ways, the two interpretations lead to muc the same theoretical conclusion. In dogmatism the subject i ultimately reduced to the object, and with this reduction one of th necessary conditions of consciousness is cancelled out. In criticisr the object is ultimately reduced to the subject, and with thi reduction the other necessary condition of consciousness is cancel led out. In other words, both dogmatism and criticism point to th theoretical annihilation of the finite self or subject. Spinoza reduce the finite self to the absolute Object: Fichte reduces it to th absolute Subject or, more precisely (since the absolute ego is no properly a subject), to infinite activity or striving. In both case the self is swamped, so to speak, in the Absolute.

But though from the purely theoretical point of view the tw systems lead by different routes to much the same conclusion their practical or moral demands are different. They expres different ideas of man's moral vocation. Dogmatism demands o the finite self that it should surrender itself to the absolut causality of the divine substance and renounce its own freedom that the divine may be all in all. Thus in the philosophy of Spinoz the self is called on to recognize an already existing ontologica situation, namely its position as a modification of infinite substance and to surrender itself. Criticism, however, demands that mai shall realize the Absolute in himself through constant free activity For Fichte, that is to say, the identity of the finite self with the Absolute is not simply an existing ontological situation which has only to be recognized. It is a goal to be achieved through moral effort. Moreover, it is an always receding goal. Hence even if the philosophy of Fichte points to the identification of the self with the Absolute as a theoretical ideal, on the practical plane it demands unceasing free moral activity, unceasing fidelity to one's personal moral vocation.

In a sense, therefore, the choice between dogmatism and criticism is for the finite self a choice between non-being and being. That is to say, it is a choice between the ideal of self-surrender, of absorption in the impersonal Absolute, of renunciation of personal freedom as illusion, and the ideal of constant free activity in accordance with one's vocation, of becoming more and more the moral agent who rises free and triumphant over the mere object. 'Be! is the highest demand of criticism.'[1] With Spinoza the

---

[1] *W*, I, p. 259.

bsolute Object carries all before it: with Fichte Nature is reduced o a mere instrument for the free moral agent.

Obviously, if a man accepts the demand of criticism, he is hereby committed to rejecting dogmatism. But it is also true that logmatism cannot be refuted, even on the moral or practical plane, n the eyes of the man 'who can tolerate the idea of working at his wn annihilation, of annulling in himself all free causality, and of eing the modification of an object in the infinity of which he sooner of later finds his moral destruction'.[1]

This account of the issue between dogmatism and criticism obviously echoes Fichte's view that the sort of philosophy which a man chooses depends on the sort of man that one is. Further, we can, if we wish, link up Schelling's contention that neither logmatism nor criticism is theoretically refutable and that the choice between them must be made on the practical plane with the view which has sometimes been advanced in much more recent times that we cannot decide between metaphysical systems on the purely theoretical plane but that moral criteria can be used to judge between them when they serve as backgrounds for and tend to promote different patterns of conduct. But for our present purpose it is more relevant to note that though the *Philosophical Letters* was written in support of Fichte and though Schelling comes down ostensibly on his side, the work implies the unspoken, but none the less clear, criticism that both the philosophy of Spinoza and the transcendental idealism of Fichte are one-sided exaggerations. For Spinoza is depicted as absolutizing the object and Fichte as absolutizing the subject. And the implication is that the Absolute must transcend the distinction between subjectivity and objectivity and be subject and object in identity.[2]

In other words, the implication is that some sort of synthesis must be effected which will reconcile the conflicting attitudes of Spinoza and Fichte. Indeed, we can see in the *Philosophical Letters* evidence of a degree of sympathy with Spinoza which was alien to Fichte's mind. And it is in no way surprising if we find Schelling very soon devoting himself to the publication of works on the philosophy of Nature. For the Spinozistic element in the fore-shadowed synthesis will be the attribution to Nature as an organic

---

[1] *W*, I, p. 263.
[2] Fichte himself came to assert that the absolute ego is the identity of subject and object. But he did so partly under the influence of Schelling's criticism. And in any case Fichte's idealism was always characterized, in Schelling's opinion, by an over-emphasis on the subject and on subjectivity.

totality of an ontological status which was denied it by Fichte
Nature will be shown as the immediate objective manifestation o
the Absolute. At the same time the synthesis, if it is to be
synthesis at all, must depict Nature as the expression and mani
festation of Spirit. A synthesis must be idealism, if it is not t
represent a return to pre-Kantian thought. But it must not be
subjective idealism in which Nature is depicted as no more tha
an obstacle posited by the ego in order that it may have somethin
to overcome.

These remarks may perhaps seem to go beyond what the earl
writings of Schelling entitle one to say. But we have already see
that in the programme which Schelling drew up for himself in 1796
very shortly after the writing of *Philosophical Letters*, he explicitl
envisaged the development of a speculative physics or philosoph
of Nature. And it is quite evident that dissatisfaction with Fichte'
one-sided attitude to Nature was already felt by Schelling withi
the period of his so-called Fichtean phase.

### CHAPTER VI

# SCHELLING (2)

*The possibility and metaphysical grounds of a philosophy of Nature—The general outlines of Schelling's philosophy of Nature—The system of transcendental idealism—The philosophy of art—The Absolute as identity.*

1. IT is the growth of reflection, Schelling maintains, that has introduced a rift between the subjective and the objective, the ideal and the real. If we think away the work of reflection, we must conceive man as one with Nature. That is to say, we must conceive him as experiencing this unity with Nature on the level of the immediacy of feeling. But through reflection he has distinguished between the external object and its subjective representation, and he has become an object for himself. In general, reflection has grounded and perpetuated the distinction between the objective external world of Nature and the subjective inner life of representation and self-consciousness, the distinction between Nature and Spirit. Nature thus becomes externality, the opposite of Spirit, and man, as a self-conscious reflective being, is alienated from Nature.

If reflection is made an end in itself, it becomes 'a spiritual malady'.[1] For man is born for action, and the more he is turned in on himself in self-reflection, the less active he is. At the same time it is the capacity for reflection which distinguishes man from the animal. And the rift which has been introduced between the objective and the subjective, the real and the ideal, Nature and Spirit, cannot be overcome by a return to the immediacy of feeling, to the childhood, as it were, of the human race. If the divided factors are to be reunited and the original unity restored, this must be achieved on a higher plane than feeling. That is to say, it must be achieved by reflection itself in the form of philosophy. After all, it is reflection which raises the problem. At the level of ordinary commonsense there is no problem of the relation between the real and the ideal order, between the thing and its mental representation. It is reflection which raises the problem, and it is reflection which must solve it.

[1] *W*, I, p. 663.

One's first impulse is to solve the problem in terms of causal activity. Things exist independently of the mind and cause representations of themselves: the subjective is causally dependent on the objective. But by saying this one simply gives rise to a further problem. For if I assert that external things exist independently and cause representations of themselves in me, I necessarily set myself above thing and representation. And I thus implicitly affirm myself as spirit. And the question at once arises, how can external things exercise a determining causal activity or spirit?

We can indeed attempt to tackle the problem from the other side. Instead of saying that things cause representations of themselves we can say with Kant that the subject imposes its cognitive forms on some given matter of experience and so creates phenomenal reality. But we are then left with the thing-in-itself. And this is inconceivable. For what can a thing possibly be apart from the forms which the subject is said to impose?

There have been, however, two notable attempts to solve the problem of the correspondence between the subjective and the objective, the ideal and the real, without having recourse to the idea of causal activity. Spinoza explained the correspondence by means of the theory of parallel modifications of different attributes of one infinite substance, while Leibniz had recourse to the theory of a pre-established harmony. But neither theory was a genuine explanation. For Spinoza left the modifications of Substance unexplained, while Leibniz, in Schelling's opinion, simply postulated a pre-established harmony.

At the same time both Spinoza and Leibniz had an inkling of the truth that the ideal and the real are ultimately one. And it is this truth which the philosopher is called upon to exhibit. He must show that Nature is 'visible Spirit' and Spirit 'invisible Nature'. That is to say, the philosopher must show how objective Nature is ideal through and through in the sense that it is a unified dynamic and teleological system which develops upwards, so to speak, to the point at which it returns upon itself in and through the human spirit. For, given this picture of Nature, we can see that the life of representation is not something which is simply set over against and alien to the objective world, so that there arises the problem of correspondence between the subjective and the objective, the ideal and the real. The life of representation is Nature's knowledge of

[1] *W*, I, p. 706.

tself; it is the actualization of Nature's potentiality, whereby lumbering Spirit awakens to consciousness.

But can we show that Nature is in fact a teleological system, xhibiting finality? We cannot indeed accept as adequate the purely mechanistic interpretation of the world. For when we consider the organism, we are driven to introduce the idea of finality. Nor can the mind remain content with a dichotomy between two sharply divided spheres, namely those of mechanism and teleology. It is driven on to regard Nature as a self-organizing totality in which we can distinguish various levels. But the question arises whether we are not then simply reading teleology into Nature, first into the organism and then into Nature as a whole. After all, Kant admitted that we cannot help thinking of Nature as if it were a teleological system. For we have a regulative idea of purpose in Nature, an Idea which gives rise to certain heuristic maxims of judgment. But Kant would not allow that this subjective Idea proves anything about Nature in itself.

Schelling is convinced that all scientific inquiry presupposes the intelligibility of Nature. Every experiment, he insists, involves putting a question to Nature which Nature is forced to answer. And this procedure presupposes the belief that Nature conforms to the demands of reason, that it is intelligible and in this sense ideal. This belief is justified if we once assume the general view of the world which has been outlined above. For the idea of Nature as an intelligible teleological system then appears as Nature's self-reflection, as Nature knowing itself in and through man.

But we can obviously ask for a justification of this general view of Nature. And the ultimate justification is for Schelling a meta-physical theory about the Absolute. 'The first step towards philosophy and the indispensable condition for even arriving at it is to understand that the Absolute in the ideal order is also the Absolute in the real order.'[1] The Absolute is the 'pure identity'[2] of subjectivity and objectivity. And this identity is reflected in the mutual interpenetration of Nature and Nature's knowledge of itself in and through man.

In itself the Absolute is one eternal act of knowledge in which there is no temporal succession. At the same time we can distinguish three moments or phases in this one act, provided that we do not look on them as succeeding one another temporally. In the first moment the Absolute objectifies itself in ideal Nature, in the

[1] *W*, I, p. 708.  [2] *W*, I, p. 712.

universal pattern, as it were, of Nature, for which Schelling use
Spinoza's term *Natura naturans*. In the second moment th
Absolute as objectivity is transformed into the Absolute a
subjectivity. And the third moment is the synthesis 'in which thes
two absolutenesses (absolute objectivity and absolute subjectivity
are again one absoluteness'.[1] The Absolute is thus an eternal act o
self-knowledge.

The first moment in the inner life of the Absolute is expressed o
manifested in *Natura naturata*, Nature as a system of particula
things. This is the symbol or appearance of *Natura naturans*, and
as such it is said to be 'outside the Absolute'.[2] The second momen
in the inner life of the Absolute, the transformation of objectivity
into subjectivity, is expressed externally in the world of representa
tion, the ideal world of human knowledge whereby *Natur
naturata* is represented in and through the human mind and th
particular is taken up, as it were, into the universal, that is, o
the conceptual level. We have, therefore, two unities, as Schellin
calls them, objective Nature and the ideal world of representation
The third unity, correlated with the third moment in the inner lif
of the Absolute, is the apprehended interpenetration of the rea
and the ideal.

It can hardly be claimed, I think, that Schelling makes th
relation between the infinite and the finite, between the Absolut
in itself and its self-manifestation, crystal clear. We have seer
indeed that *Natura naturata*, considered as the symbol or appearance
of *Natura naturans*, is said to be outside the Absolute. Bu
Schelling also speaks of the Absolute as expanding itself into the
particular. Clearly, Schelling wishes to make a distinction betweer
the unchanging Absolute in itself and the world of finite particula
things. But at the same time he wishes to maintain that the
Absolute is the all-comprehensive reality. But we shall have to
return later to this topic. For the moment we can content ourselves
with the general picture of the Absolute as eternal essence or Idea
objectifying itself in Nature, returning to itself as subjectivity in
the world of representation and then knowing itself, in and through
philosophical reflection, as the identity of the real and the ideal, of
Nature and Spirit.[3]

---

[1] *W*, I, p. 714. I have used 'absoluteness' to render *Absoluthheit*.
[2] *W*, I, p. 717.
[3] Schelling's picture of the metaphysical basis of a philosophy of Natur
exercised a powerful influence on the thought of Hegel. But it would be in
appropriate to discuss this matter here.

Schelling's justification of the possibility of a philosophy of Nature or of the so-called higher physics is thus admittedly metaphysical in character. Nature (that is, *Natura naturata*) must be ideal through and through. For it is the symbol or appearance of *Natura naturans*, ideal Nature: it is the 'external' objectification of the Absolute. And as the Absolute is always one, the identity of objectivity and subjectivity, *Natura naturata*, must also be subjectivity. This truth is manifested in the process by which Nature passes, as it were, into the world of representation. And the culmination of this process is the insight by which it is seen that human knowledge of Nature is Nature's knowledge of itself. There is really no rift between the objective and the subjective. From the transcendental point of view they are one. Slumbering Spirit becomes awakened Spirit. The distinguishable moments in the supra-temporal life of the Absolute as pure essence are manifested in the temporal order, which stands to the Absolute in itself as consequent to antecedent.

2. To develop a philosophy of Nature is to develop a systematic ideal construction of Nature. In the *Timaeus* Plato sketched a theoretical construction of bodies out of fundamental qualities. And Schelling is concerned with the same sort of thing. A purely experimental physics would not deserve the name of science. It would be 'nothing but a collection of facts, of reports on what has been observed, of what has happened either under natural or under artificially-produced conditions'.[1] Schelling admits indeed that physics as we know it is not purely experimental or empirical in this sense. 'In what is now called physics empiricism [*Empirie*] and science are mixed up.'[2] But there is room, in Schelling's opinion, for a purely theoretical construction or deduction of matter and of the fundamental types of bodies, the inorganic and the organic. Moreover, this speculative physics will not simply assume natural forces, such as gravitation, as something given. It will construct them from first principles.

According to Schelling's intentions at least this construction does not involve producing a fanciful and arbitrary deduction of the fundamental levels of Nature. Rather does it mean letting Nature construct itself before the watchful attention of the mind. Speculative or higher physics cannot indeed explain the basic productive activity which gives rise to Nature. This is a matter for metaphysics rather than for the philosophy of Nature proper. But

[1] *W*, ii, p. 283.                    [2] *Ibid.*

if the development of the natural system is the necessary pro
gressive self-expression of ideal Nature, *Natura naturans*, it mus
be possible to retrace systematically the stages of the process b
which ideal Nature expresses itself in *Natura naturata*. And to d
this is the task of speculative physics. Schelling is obviously wel
aware that it is through experience that we become acquainte
with the existence of natural forces and of inorganic and organi
things. And it is not the philosopher's task to tell us the empirica
facts for the first time, so to speak, or to work out *a priori* a natura
history which can be developed only on the basis of empirica
investigation. He is concerned with exhibiting the fundamenta
and necessary teleological pattern in Nature, in Nature, that is t
say, as known in the first instance by experience and empirica
inquiry. One might say that he is concerned with explaining to u
the why and wherefore of the facts.

To exhibit Nature as a teleological system, as the necessary
self-unfolding of the eternal Idea, involves showing that th
explanation of the lower is always to be found in the higher. Fo
instance, even if from the temporal point of view the inorganic i
prior to the organic, from the philosophical point of view the latte
is logically prior to the former. That is to say, the lower level exist
as a foundation for the higher level. And this is true throughou
Nature. The materialist tends to reduce the higher to the lower
For example, he tries to explain organic life in terms of mechanica
causality, without introducing the concept of finality. But he ha
the wrong point of view. It is not, as he is inclined to imagine, a
question of denying the laws of mechanics or of regarding them a
suspended in the organic sphere, if one introduces the concept o
finality. Rather is it a question of seeing the sphere of mechanic
as the necessary setting for the realization of the ends of Nature i
the production of the organism. There is continuity. For the lowe
is the necessary foundation for the higher, and the latter subsume
the former in itself. But there is also the emergence of something
new, and this new level explains the level which it presupposes.

When we understand this, we see that 'the opposition between
mechanism and the organic sphere disappears'.[1] For we see the
production of the organism as that at which Nature unconsciously
aims through the development of the inorganic sphere, with the
laws of mechanics. And it is thus truer to say that the inorganic is
the organic *minus* than that the organic is the inorganic *plus*. Yet

[1] *W*, I, p. 416.

ven this way of speaking can be misleading. For the opposition
etween mechanism and the organic sphere is overcome not so
uch by the theory that the former exists for the latter as by the
eory that Nature as a whole is an organic unity.

Now, the activity which lies at the basis of Nature and which
xpands' itself in the phenomenal world is infinite or unlimited.
or Nature is, as we have seen, the self-objectification of the infinite
bsolute which, as an eternal *act*, is activity or willing. But if there
s to be any objective system of Nature at all, this unlimited
ctivity must be checked. That is to say, there must be a checking
r limiting force. And it is the interaction between the unlimited
ctivity and the checking force which gives rise to the lowest level
f Nature, the general structure of the world and the series of
odies,[1] which Schelling calls the first potency (*Potenz*) of Nature.
hus if we think of the force of attraction as corresponding to the
hecking force and the force of repulsion as corresponding to the
nlimited activity, the synthesis of the two is matter in so far as
his is simply mass.

But the drive of the unlimited activity reasserts itself, only to
e checked at another point. And the second unity or potency in
he construction of Nature is universal mechanism, under which
eading Schelling deduces light and the dynamic process or the
ynamic laws of bodies. 'The dynamic process is nothing else but
he second construction of matter.'[2] That is to say, the original
onstruction of matter is repeated, as it were, at a higher level. On
he lower level we have the elementary operation of the forces of
ttraction and repulsion and their synthesis in matter as mass. At
he higher level we find the same forces showing themselves in the
henomena of magnetism, electricity and chemical process or the
hemical properties of bodies.

The third unity or potency of Nature is the organism. And on
his level we find the same forces further actualizing their poten-
ialities in the phenomena of sensibility, irritability and repro-
luction. This unity or level of Nature is represented as the synthesis
f the two others. Hence it cannot be said that at any level Nature
s simply lifeless. It is a living organic unity which actualizes its
otentialities at ascending levels until it expresses itself in the
rganism. We must add, however, that there are obviously distin-
uishable levels within the organic sphere itself. On the lower levels

---

[1] *Der allgemeine Weltbau und die Körperreihe; W*, I, p. 718.
[2] *W*, II, p. 320.

reproductivity is particularly conspicuous whereas sensibility is comparatively undeveloped. The individual organisms are lost, as it were, in the species. On the higher levels the life of the senses is more developed, and the individual organism is, so to speak, more of an individual and less a mere particular member of an indefinite class. The culminating point is reached in the human organism which most clearly manifests the ideality of Nature and forms the point of transition to the world of representation or subjectivity, Nature's reflection on itself.

Throughout his construction of Nature Schelling employs the idea of the polarity of forces. But 'these two conflicting forces . . lead to the idea of an *organizing principle* which makes the world a system'.[1] And to this principle we can conveniently give the time-hallowed name of world-soul. It cannot indeed be discovered by empirical investigation. Nor can it be described in terms of the qualities of phenomena. It is a postulate, 'an hypothesis of the higher physics for explaining the universal organism'.[2] This so called world-soul is not in itself a conscious intelligence. It is the organizing principle which manifests itself in Nature and which attains consciousness in and through the human ego. And unless we postulated it, we could not look on Nature as a unified, self developing super-organism.

It may have occurred to the reader to wonder how Schelling's theory of Nature stands to the theory of evolution in the sense of the transformation of forms or the emergence of higher from lower forms. And it is clearly arguable not only that a theory of emergent evolution would fit in very well with Schelling's interpretation but that it is demanded by his view of the world as a self-developing organic unity. Indeed, he explicitly refers to the possibility of evolution. He observes, for instance, that even if man's experience does not reveal any case of the transformation of one species into another, lack of empirical evidence does not prove that such a transformation is impossible. For it may well be that such change can take place only in a much longer period of time than that covered by man's experience. At the same time Schelling goes on to remark, 'however, let us pass over these possibilities'.[3] In other words, while he allows for the possibility of emergent evolution, he is primarily concerned not with a genetic history of Nature but with an ideal or theoretical construction.

This construction is indeed rich in ideas. It echoes much past

peculation about the world. For instance, the pervasive idea of
he polarity of forces recalls Greek speculation about Nature,
while the theory of Nature as slumbering Spirit recalls certain
spects of Leibniz's philosophy. Schelling's interpretation of
Jature also looks forward to later speculation. For example, there
s some family resemblance between Schelling's philosophy of
Jature and Bergson's picture of inorganic things as representing,
s it were, the extinguished sparks thrown off by the *élan vital* in
ts upward flight.

At the same time Schelling's construction of Nature inevitably
ppears so fanciful and arbitrary to the scientific mentality that
here does not seem to be any justification for devoting space here
o further detailed treatment of it.[1] It is not that the philosopher
ails to incorporate into his philosophy of Nature theories and
ypotheses taken from science as he knows it. On the contrary, he
orrows and utilizes ideas taken from contemporary physics,
lectrodynamics, chemistry and biology. But these ideas are fitted
nto a dialectical scheme, and they are often held together by the
pplication of analogies which, however ingenious and perhaps
ometimes suggestive, tend to appear fanciful and far-fetched.
Ience discussion of the details is more a matter for a specialized
reatment of Schelling and of his relations to scientists such as
Jewton and to contemporary writers such as Goethe than for a
eneral history of philosophy.

To say this is not, however, to deny the importance of Schelling's
hilosophy of Nature in its general outlines. For it shows clearly
hat German idealism does not involve subjectivism in the
rdinary sense. Nature is the immediate and objective manifesta-
ion of the Absolute. It is indeed ideal through and through. But
his does not mean that Nature is in any sense the creation of the
uman ego. It is ideal because it expresses the eternal Idea and
ecause it is orientated towards self-reflection in and through the
uman mind. Schelling's view of the Absolute as the identity of
bjectivity and subjectivity demands, of course, that the Absolute's
elf-objectification, namely Nature, should reveal this identity.
3ut the identity is revealed through the teleological pattern of
Jature, not through its reduction to human ideas. Nature's repre-
entation in and through the human mind presupposes the objecti-
ity of the world, though at the same time it presupposes the

[1] The details of Schelling's construction of Nature vary somewhat in his different
vritings on the subject.

intelligibility of the world and its intrinsic orientation to self reflection.

Further, if we prescind from Schelling's rather fanciful speculations about magnetism, electricity and so on, that is, from the details of his theoretical construction of Nature, the general view of Nature as an objective manifestation of the Absolute and as teleological system possesses an abiding value. It is obviously metaphysical interpretation, and as such it can hardly commend itself to those who reject all metaphysics. But the general picture of Nature is not unreasonable. And if we once accept with Schelling and afterwards with Hegel, the idea of a spiritual Absolute, we should expect to find in Nature a teleological pattern, though it does not necessarily follow that we can deduce the forces and phenomena of Nature in the way that Schelling thought that speculative physics is capable of doing.

3. In view of the fact that Schelling's philosophy of Nature represents his divergence from Fichte and his own original contribution to the development of German idealism it is at first sight surprising to find him publishing in 1800 a *System of Transcendental Idealism* in which he starts from the ego and proceeds to elaborate 'the continuous history of self-consciousness'.[1] For it looks as though he is adding to the philosophy of Nature an incompatible system inspired by the influence of Fichte. In Schelling's opinion however, transcendental idealism forms a necessary complement to the philosophy of Nature. In knowledge itself subject and object are united: they are one. But if we wish to explain this identity we have first to think it away. And then we are faced with two possibilities. Either we can start with the objective and proceed towards the subjective, asking how unconscious Nature comes to be represented. Or we can start with the subjective and proceed towards the objective, asking how an object comes to exist for the subject. In the first case we develop the philosophy of Nature showing how Nature develops the conditions for its own self reflection on the subjective level. In the second case we develop the system of transcendental idealism, showing how the ultimate .immanent principle of consciousness produces the objective world as the condition of its attainment of self-consciousness. And the two lines of reflection are and must be complementary. For if the Absolute is the identity of subjectivity and objectivity, it must be possible to start from either pole and to develop a philosophy in

[1] *W*, II, p. 331.

armony with the philosophy developed by starting from the
ther pole. In other words, it is Schelling's conviction that the
nutually complementary characters of the philosophy of Nature
nd the system of transcendental idealism manifest the nature of
he Absolute as identity of subject and object, of the ideal and the
eal.

As transcendental idealism is described as the science of know-
edge, it prescinds from the question whether there is an ontological
eality behind the whole sphere of knowledge. Hence its first
rinciple must be immanent within this sphere. And if we are to
roceed from the subjective to the objective by transcendental
eduction, we must start with the original identity of subject and
bject. This identity within the sphere of knowledge is self-
onsciousness, wherein subject and object are the same. And self-
onsciousness is described by Schelling as the ego. But the term
ego' does not signify the individual self. It signifies 'the act of
*elf-consciousness in general*'.[1] 'The self-consciousness which is our
oint of departure is *one absolute act*.'[2] And this absolute act is a
roduction of itself as object. 'The ego is nothing else but a
roducing which becomes its own object.'[3] It is in fact 'an
ntellectual intuition'.[4] For the ego exists through knowing itself,
nd this self-knowledge is the act of intellectual intuition, which is
the organ of all transcendental thought'[5] and freely produces as
ts object what is otherwise no object. Intellectual intuition and
he production of the object of transcendental thought are one and
he same. Hence a system of transcendental idealism must take the
orm of a production or construction of self-consciousness.

Schelling makes a wider use than Fichte had made of the idea of
ntellectual intuition. But the general pattern of his transcendental
dealism is obviously based on Fichte's thought. The ego is in
self an unlimited act or activity. But to become its own object it
nust limit this activity by setting something over against itself,
amely the non-ego. And it must do so unconsciously. For it is
npossible to explain the givenness of the non-ego within the frame-
ork of idealism unless we assume that the production of the non-
go is an unconscious and necessary production. The non-ego is a
ecessary condition of self-consciousness. And in this sense the
mitation of the infinite or unlimited activity which constitutes the
go must always remain. But in another sense the limitation must

---

[1] *W*, II, p. 374.   [2] *W*, II, p. 388.   [3] *W*, II, p. 370.
[4] *Ibid.*   [5] *W*, II, p. 369.

be transcended. That is to say, the ego must be able to abstra[c]t
from the non-ego and recoil, as it were, on to itself. Self-consciou[s]
ness, in other words, will take the form of human self-consciousne[ss]
which presupposes Nature, the non-ego.

In the first part of the system of transcendental idealism, whic[h]
corresponds to Fichte's theoretical deduction of consciousness i[n]
the *Wissenschaftslehre*, Schelling traces the history of consciou[s]
ness in three main epochs or stages. Many of Fichte's theme[s]
reappear, but Schelling is naturally at pains to correlate h[is]
history of consciousness with the philosophy of Nature. The fir[st]
epoch ranges from primitive sensation up to productive intuitio[n]
And it is correlated with the construction of matter in the phil[o]
sophy of Nature. In other words, we see the production of t[he]
material world as the unconscious activity of Spirit. The secon[d]
epoch ranges from productive intuition up to reflection. The ego [is]
here conscious on the level of sense. That is to say, the sensib[le]
object appears as distinct from the act of productive intuitio[n]
And Schelling deduces the categories of space, time and causalit[y]
A universe begins to exist for the ego. Schelling also occupi[es]
himself with the deduction of the organism as a necessary co[n]
dition for the ego's return on itself. This takes place in the thi[rd]
epoch which culminates in the act of absolute abstraction b[y]
which the ego reflectively differentiates itself from the object [or]
non-ego as such and recognizes itself as intelligence. It has becom[e]
object to itself.

The act of absolute abstraction is explicable only as an act [of]
the self-determining will. And we thus pass to the idea of the eg[o]
or intelligence as an active and free power, and so to the second [or]
practical part of the system of transcendental idealism. Aft[er]
treating of the part played by the consciousness of other selve[s]
other free wills, in the development of self-consciousness Schellin[g]
goes on to discuss the distinction between natural impulse and t[he]
will considered as an idealizing activity (*eine idealisieren[de]
Tätigkeit*), that is, as seeking to modify or change the objecti[ve]
in accordance with an ideal. The ideal belongs to the side of t[he]
subjective: it is in fact the ego itself. Hence in seeking to actuali[ze]
the ideal in the objective world the ego also realizes itself.

This idea sets the stage for a discussion of morality. How, as[ks]
Schelling, can the will, namely the ego as self-determining or sel[f]
realizing activity, become objectified for the ego as intelligenc[e]
That is to say, how can the ego become conscious of itself as wil[l]

The answer is, through a demand, the demand that the ego should will nothing else but self-determination. 'This demand is nothing else but the categorical imperative or the moral law which Kant expresses in this way: you ought to will only that which other intelligences can will. But that which all intelligences can will is only pure self-determination, pure conformity to law. Through the law of morality, therefore, pure self-determination . . . becomes an object for the ego.'[1]

But self-determination or self-realization can be achieved only through concrete action in the world. And Schelling proceeds to deduce the system of rights and the State as conditions for moral action. The State is, of course, an edifice built by human hands, by the activity of the Spirit. But it is a necessary condition for the harmonious realization of freedom by a plurality of individuals. And though it is an edifice built by human hands, it should become a second Nature. In all our actions we count on the uniformity of Nature, on the reign of natural laws. And in our moral activity we ought to be able to count on the rule of rational law in society. That is to say, we ought to be able to count on the rational State, the characteristic of which is the rule of law.

Yet even the best-ordered State is exposed to the capricious and egoistic wills of other States. And the question arises, how can political society be rescued, as far as this is possible, from this condition of instability and insecurity? The answer can be found only in 'an organization which transcends the individual State, namely a federation of all States',[2] which will do away with conflicts between nations. Only in this way can political society become a second Nature, something on which we can count.

For this end to be attained, however, two conditions are required. First, the fundamental principles of a truly rational constitution must be generally acknowledged, so that all individual States will have a common interest in guaranteeing and protecting one another's law and rights. Secondly, individual States must submit themselves to a common fundamental law in the same way that individual citizens submit themselves to the law of their own State. And this means in effect that the federation will have to be a 'State of States',[3] in ideal at least a world-organization with sovereign power. If this ideal could be realized, political society would become a secure setting for the full actualization of a universal moral order.

[1] *W*, II, pp. 573-4.     [2] *W*, II, p. 586.     [3] *W*, II, p. 587.

Now, if this ideal is to be realized at all, it must obviously b
realized within history. And the question arises whether we ca
discern in human history any necessary tendency towards th
attainment of this goal. In Schelling's opinion 'there lies in th
concept of history the concept of endless *progress*'.[1] Obviously, i
this statement meant that the word 'history', as ordinarily usec
necessarily includes as part of its meaning the concept of endles
progress towards a predetermined goal, its truth would be open t
question. But Schelling is looking on history in the light of hi
theory of the Absolute. 'History as a whole is a continual revelatio
of the Absolute, a revelation which gradually discloses itself.'[2] A
the Absolute is the pure identity of the ideal and the real, histor
must be a movement towards the creation of a second Nature,
perfect moral world-order in the framework of a rationally
organized political society. And as the Absolute is infinite, thi
movement of progress must be endless. If the Absolute wer
perfectly revealed in its true nature, the point of view of huma
consciousness, which presupposes a distinction between subjec
and object, would no longer exist. Hence the revelation of th
Absolute in human history must be in principle endless.

But are we not then faced with a dilemma? If on the one han
we assert that the human will is free, must we not admit that ma
can thwart the ends of history and that there is no necessar
progress towards an ideal goal? If on the other hand we assert tha
history necessarily moves in a certain direction, must we not den
human freedom and explain away the psychological feeling o
freedom?

In dealing with this problem Schelling has recourse to the ide
of an absolute synthesis, as he puts it, of free actions. Individual
act freely. And any given individual may act for some purel
private and selfish end. But there is at the same time a hidde
necessity which achieves a synthesis of the apparently unconnectec
and often conflicting actions of human beings. Even if a man act
from purely selfish motives, he will none the less unconsciousl
contribute, even though against his will, to the fulfilment of th
common end of human history.[3]

Up to this point we have been considering briefly the parts o

[1] *W*, II, p. 592.          [2] *W*, II, p. 603.
[3] We can call this a doctrine of divine providence if we like. But at this stage a
any rate of Schelling's thought we should not think of the Absolute as a persona
Deity. The working out of the absolute synthesis is the necessary expression of th
Absolute's nature as pure identity of the ideal and the real.

the system of transcendental idealism which cover more or less the
ground covered by Fichte in his theoretical and practical deductions of consciousness and in his works on the theory of rights and
on ethics, though Schelling makes, of course, some changes and
introduces and develops ideas of his own. But Schelling adds a
third part which is his own peculiar contribution to transcendental
idealism and which serves to underline the difference between his
general outlook and that of Fichte. The philosophy of Nature deals
with slumbering or unconscious Spirit. In the system of transcendental idealism as hitherto outlined we see conscious Spirit
objectifying itself in moral action and in the creation of a moral
world-order, a second Nature. But we have yet to find an intuition
in which the identity of the unconscious and of the conscious, of
the real and of the ideal, is presented in a concrete manner to the
ego itself. And in the third part of the system of transcendental
idealism Schelling locates what he is seeking in aesthetic intuition.
Thus transcendental idealism culminates in a philosophy of art, to
which Schelling attaches great importance. And provided that the
statement is not taken as implying that the philosopher sets out to
minimize the significance of moral activity, we can say that with
Schelling, as contrasted with Fichte, the emphasis shifts from
ethics to aesthetics, from the moral life to artistic creation, from
action for the sake of action to aesthetic contemplation.

From one point of view it would be desirable to treat first of
Schelling's philosophy of art as given in the third part of the
*System of Transcendental Idealism* and later of his aesthetic ideas
as expressed in his lectures on *The Philosophy of Art*. For in the
meantime he had developed his theory of the Absolute, and this
fact is reflected in the lectures. But it is more convenient to outline
his ideas on art in one section, though I shall draw attention to
their historical development.

4. In the *System of Transcendental Idealism* we read that 'the
objective world is only the original, still unconscious poetry of the
Spirit: the universal organon of philosophy—and the keystone of
the whole arch—is *the philosophy of art*'.[1] But the view that the
philosophy of art is 'the true organon of philosophy'[2] stands in
need of some explanation.

In the first place art is grounded on the power of productive
intuition which is the indispensable organ or instrument of transcendental idealism. As we have seen, transcendental idealism

[1] *W*, II, p. 349.          [2] *W*, II, p. 351.

comprises a history of consciousness. But the stages of this histor
are not present from the start to the ego's vision as so many alread
constituted objects at which it only needs to look. The ego c
intelligence has to produce them, in the sense that it has t
re-create or, to use a Platonic term, re-collect them in a systemati
manner. And this task of re-creation or re-collection is performed b
the power of productive intuition. Aesthetic intuition is an activit
of the same power, though there it is directed outwards, as i
were, rather than inwards.

In the second place aesthetic intuition manifests the basic trut
of the unity of the unconscious and the conscious, of the real an
the ideal. If we consider aesthetic intuition from the side of th
creative artist, the genius, we can see that in a real sense he know
what he is doing: he acts consciously and deliberately. Whe
Michelangelo made the statue of Moses, he knew what he was abou
At the same time, however, we can equally well say that the geniu
acts unconsciously. Genius is not reducible to a technical proficienc
which can be imparted by instruction: the creative artist is, as i
were, the vehicle of a power which acts through him. And fc
Schelling this is the same power which operates in Nature. In othe
words, the same power which acts without consciousness in pr
ducing Nature, the unconscious poetry of the Spirit, acts wit
consciousness in producing the work of art. That is to say, it act
through the consciousness of the artist. And this illustrates th
ultimate unity of the unconscious and the conscious, of the real an
the ideal.

The matter can be considered from another point of view. W
can ask why it is that contemplation of a work of art is accompanie
by 'the feeling of infinite satisfaction',[1] why it is that 'ever
impulse to produce is stilled with the completion of the produc
that all contradictions are reconciled and all riddles solved'.[2] I
other words, why is it that in contemplating a work of art th
mind, whether of the artist himself or of someone else, enjoys
feeling of finality, the feeling that nothing should be added c
subtracted, the feeling that a problem is solved, even if the probler
cannot be stated? In Schelling's opinion the answer is that th
completed work of art is the intelligence's supreme objectificatio
of itself to itself, that is, as the identity of the unconscious and th
conscious, the real and the ideal, the objective and the subjectiv
But as the intelligence or ego does not know this reflectively, i

---

[1] *W*, II, p. 615.          [2] *Ibid.*

mply feels a boundless satisfaction, as though some unstated
mystery had been revealed, and ascribes the production of the
work of art to some power which acts through it.

The philosophy of art is thus the culmination of the *System of
Transcendental Idealism*. It will be remembered that transcendental
idealism starts with the idea of the so-called ego or intelligence
considered as an absolute act of self-consciousness in which subject
and object are one. But this absolute act is a producing: it has to
produce its object. And the supreme objectification is the work of
art. True, the organism, as considered in the philosophy of Nature,
is a partial manifestation of the identity of the real and the ideal.
But it is ascribed to an unconscious productive power which does
not work with freedom, whereas the work of art is the expression
of freedom: it is the free ego's manifestation of itself to itself.

Transcendental idealism, as was remarked in the last section,
starts with the first immanent principle within the sphere of
knowledge, namely with the absolute act which becomes an object
for itself, and prescinds from the question whether there is a
reality behind, as it were, this absolute act or ego.[1] But by the
time (1802-3) that Schelling came to deliver the lectures which
were eventually published as the *Philosophy of Art* he had developed
his theory of the Absolute, and we find him emphasizing the
metaphysical significance of the work of art as the finite manifestation of the infinite Absolute. The Absolute is the 'indifference'
(that is to say, the ultimate identity) of the ideal and the real, and
the indifference of the ideal and the real, as indifference, is
expressed in the ideal world through art'.[2] Schelling is not con-
tradicting what he has previously said about art. But in the
lectures he transcends the self-imposed Fichtean limitations of
the *System of Transcendental Idealism* and adopts the frankly
metaphysical point of view which is really characteristic of his
thought.

In *Bruno* (1802) Schelling introduced the notion of divine ideas
and asserted that things are beautiful in virtue of their participation in these ideas. And this theory reappears in the lectures on art.
Thus we are told that 'beauty exists where the particular (the
real) is so in accord with its idea that this idea itself, as infinite,
enters into the finite and is intuited *in concreto*'.[3] Aesthetic
intuition is thus the intuition of the infinite in a finite product of

---

[1] Similarly, the philosophy of Nature starts with the postulated infinite activity
which manifests itself in Nature.
[2] *W*, III, p. 400.                    [3] *W*, III, p. 402.

intelligence. Further, the conformity of a thing with its etern
idea is its truth. Hence beauty and truth[1] are ultimately one.

Now, if the creative genius exhibits in the work of art an etern
idea, he must be akin to the philosopher. But it does not follo
that he is a philosopher. For he does not apprehend the etern
ideas in an abstract form but only through a symbolic mediun
Artistic creation requires the presence of a symbolic world,
world of 'poetic existence'[2] which mediates between the univers;
and the particular. The symbol represents neither the universal ;
such nor the particular as such, but both in unity. We mu;
distinguish, therefore, between the symbol and the image. For th
image is always concrete and particular.

This symbolic world of poetic existence is provided by mytholog
which is 'the necessary condition and primary matter [*Stoff*] of a
art'.[3] Schelling dwells at length on Greek mythology, but he do(
not confine the symbolic world which in his view forms the materi;
for artistic creation to the mythology of the Greeks. He include;
for instance, what he calls Jewish and Christian mythology. Th
Christian mind has constructed its own symbolic world which ha
proved a fruitful source of material for the artist.

This emphasis on mythology in Schelling's account of th
symbolic world of poetic existence may well appear too narrov
But it illustrates Schelling's constant interest in myths as being a
the same time imaginative constructions and intimations c
expressions of the divine. In his later years he makes a distinctio
between myth and revelation. But his interest in the significance c
mythology is a lasting element in his thought. And we shall hav
to return to the subject in connection with his later philosophy o
religion.

In this outline of Schelling's aesthetic philosophy the terms 'arl
and 'artist' have been used in a wider sense than is customary ii
ordinary English. But it would not, I think, be very profitable t
devote space here to Schelling's discussion of the particular fin
arts which he divides into those belonging to the real series, such a
painting and sculpture, and those belonging to the ideal series
such as poetry.[4] For general purposes it is sufficient to understan(
how Schelling makes aesthetic theory an integral part of hi

[1] The reference is obviously to what the Scholastics called ontological truth, a
distinct from logical truth.
[2] *W*, III, p. 419.                    [3] *W*, III, p. 425.
[4] The reader who is interested in this subject can consult the third part o
Schelling's *Philosophy of Art* or, for example, Bernard Bosanquet's *History o*
*Aesthetic*.

hilosophy. In the third *Critique* Kant had indeed discussed the esthetic judgment, and he can be said to have made aesthetics an ntegral part of the critical philosophy. But the nature of Kant's ystem made it impossible for him to develop a metaphysics of art a the way that Schelling does. Kant allowed, it is true, that from he subjective point of view we can see a hint of noumenal reality, f the so-called supersensible substrate. But with Schelling the roduct of artistic genius becomes a clear revelation of the nature f the Absolute. And in his exaltation of the genius, in his partial ssimilation of the artistic genius to the philosopher and his nsistence on the metaphysical significance of aesthetic intuition ve can see clear evidence of his romantic affiliations.

5. In the foregoing sections reference has frequently been made o Schelling's theory of the Absolute as the pure identity of ubjectivity and objectivity, of the ideal and the real. In a sense hese references were premature. For in the preface to his *Exposition f My System of Philosophy* (1801) Schelling speaks of expounding the system of absolute identity'.[1] And this way of speaking shows hat he does not regard himself as simply repeating what he has lready said. At the same time the so-called system of identity can e looked on as an inquiry into and exposition of the metaphysical mplications of the conviction that the philosophy of Nature and he system of transcendental idealism are mutually complementary.

'The standpoint of philosophy,' says Schelling, 'is the standpoint f Reason.'[2] That is to say, philosophical knowledge of things is nowledge of them as they are in Reason. 'I give the name of Reason [*Vernunft*] to the absolute Reason or to Reason in so far as t is conceived as the total indifference of the subjective and bjective.'[3] In other words, philosophy is knowledge of the relation etween things and the Absolute or, as the Absolute is infinite, etween the finite and the infinite. And the Absolute is to be onceived as the pure identity or indifference (lack of all difference) f subjectivity and objectivity.

In attempting to describe the relation between the finite and the nfinite Schelling is in a very difficult position. On the one hand here can be nothing outside the Absolute. For it is infinite reality nd must contain all reality within itself. Hence it cannot be the xternal cause of the universe. 'The absolute identity is not the ause of the universe but the universe itself. For everything which xists is the absolute identity itself. And the universe is everything

[1] *W*, III, p. 9.    [2] *W*, III, p. 11.    [3] *W*, III, p. 10.

which is.'[1] On the other hand, if the Absolute is pure identity, a
distinctions must be outside it. 'Quantitative difference is possibl
only outside the absolute totality.'[2] Hence finite things must b
external to the Absolute.

Schelling cannot say that the Absolute somehow proceeds out
side itself. For he maintains that 'the fundamental error of a
philosophy is the proposition that the absolute identity has reall
gone out of itself. . . .'[3] Hence he is forced to say that it is onl
from the point of view of empirical consciousness that there is
distinction between subject and object and that there are sul
sistent finite things. But this really will not do. For the emergenc
of the point of view of empirical consciousness and its ontologica
status remain unexplained. It is all very well for Schelling to sa
that quantitative difference is posited 'only in appearance'[4] an
that the Absolute is 'in no way affected by the opposition betwee
subjectivity and objectivity'.[5] If appearance is anything at all, i
must, on Schelling's premisses, be within the Absolute. And if it i
not within the Absolute, the Absolute must be transcendent an
unidentifiable with the universe.

In *Bruno* (1802) Schelling makes play with the theory of divin
Ideas, taken over from the Platonic and Neo-Platonic tradition:
Considered from one point of view at least, the Absolute is th
Idea of ideas, and finite things have eternal existence in th
divine Ideas. But even if we are prepared to admit that this theor
of divine Ideas is compatible with the view of the Absolute as pur
identity, a view which is reaffirmed in *Bruno*, there is still th
temporal status of finite things and their quantitative differentia
tion to be explained. In the dialogue Bruno tells Lucian that indivi
dual finite things are separate 'only for you'[6] and that for a ston
nothing proceeds out of the darkness of absolute identity. But w
can very well ask how empirical consciousness, with the distinction
which it involves, can arise either within the Absolute, if it is pur
identity, or outside it, if it is the totality.

Schelling's general point of view is that absolute Reason, as th
identity of subjectivity and objectivity, is self-consciousness, th
absolute act in which subject and object are one. But Reason i
not itself actually self-conscious: it is simply the 'indifference' o
lack of difference between subject and object, the ideal and th
real. It attains actual self-consciousness only in and through huma

---

[1] *W*, III, p. 25.　　　　[2] *W*, III, p. 21.　　　　[3] *W*, III, p. 16.
[4] *W*, III, p. 23.　　　　[5] *Ibid.*　　　　[6] *W*, III, p. 155.

onsciousness, the immediate object of which is the world. In other
words, the Absolute manifests itself or appears in two series of
potencies', the real series, which is considered in the philosophy
of Nature, and the ideal series, which is considered in transcendental
idealism. And from the standpoint of empirical consciousness the
two series are distinct. We have subjectivity on the one hand and
objectivity on the other. And the two together constitute 'the
universe', which, as everything that is, is the Absolute. If, however,
we try to transcend the standpoint of empirical consciousness, for
which distinctions exist, and to grasp the Absolute as it is in itself
rather than in its appearance, we can conceive it only as the
indifference or vanishing-point of all difference and distinctions.
True, the concept has then no positive content. But this simply
shows that by conceptual thought we can apprehend only the
appearance of the Absolute, the absolute identity as it appears in
its 'external' being, and not as it is in itself.

In Schelling's opinion the theory of identity enables him to
transcend all disputes between realism and idealism. For such
controversy assumes that the distinction made by empirical
consciousness between the real and the ideal can be overcome only
by subordinating or even reducing the one to the other. But once
we understand that the real and the ideal are one in the Absolute,
the controversy loses its point. And the system of identity can thus
be called real-idealism (*Realidealismus*).

But though Schelling himself was pleased with the system of
identity, there were others who were not so appreciative. And the
philosopher set himself to explain his position in such a way as to
meet what he regarded as the misunderstandings of his critics.
Further, his own reflections on his position drove him to develop
fresh lines of thought. Maintaining, as he did, that the relation
between the finite and the infinite or the problem of the existence
of the world of things is the fundamental problem of metaphysics,
he could hardly rest content with the system of identity. For it
seemed to imply that the universe is the actualization of the
Absolute, while it also asserted that the distinction between
potentiality and act falls outside the Absolute in itself. Some more
satisfactory account of the relation between the finite and the
infinite was obviously required. But a sketch of Schelling's further
philosophical journeying is best reserved for the next chapter.

### CHAPTER VII

## SCHELLING (3)

*The idea of the cosmic Fall—Personality and freedom in man and God; good and evil—The distinction between negative and positive philosophy—Mythology and revelation—General remarks on Schelling—Notes on Schelling's influence and on some kindred thinkers.*

1. In his work on *Philosophy and Religion* (1804) Schelling explains that the description of the Absolute as pure identity does not mean either that it is a formless stuff, composed of all phenomena fused together, or that it is a vacuous nonentity. The Absolute is pure identity in the sense that it is an absolutely simple infinity. We can approach it in conceptual thought only by thinking away and denying of it the attributes of finite things; but it does not follow that it is in itself empty of all reality. What follows is that it can be apprehended only by intuition. 'The nature of the Absolute *itself*, which as ideal is also immediately real, cannot be known by explanations, but only through intuition. For it is only the composite which can be known by description. The simple must be intuited.'[1] This intuition cannot be imparted by instruction. But the negative approach to the Absolute facilitates the act of intuition of which the soul is capable through its fundamental unity with the divine reality.

The Absolute as ideal manifests or expresses itself immediately in the eternal ideas. Strictly speaking, indeed, there is only one Idea, the immediate eternal reflection of the Absolute which proceeds from it as the light flows from the sun. 'All ideas are one Idea.'[2] But we can speak of a plurality of ideas inasmuch as Nature with all its grades is eternally present in the one Idea. This eternal Idea can be described as the divine self-knowledge. 'But this self-knowledge must not be conceived as a mere accident or attribute of the Absolute-ideal but as itself a subsistent Absolute. For the Absolute cannot be the ideal ground of anything which is not like itself, absolute.'[3]

In developing this theory of the divine Idea, which, as we have

[1] *W*, IV, pp. 15-16.　　　[2] *W*, IV, pp. 23-4.　　　[3] *W*, IV, p. 21.

seen, was first expounded in *Bruno*, Schelling draws attention to its origins in Greek philosophy. No doubt he has also at the back of his mind the Christian doctrine of the divine Word; but the description of the eternal Idea as a second Absolute is more akin to the Plotinian theory of *Nous* than to the Christian doctrine of the second Person of the Trinity. Further, the ideas of the negative approach to the Absolute and of intuitive apprehension of the supreme Godhead also go back to Neo-Platonism, though the first idea at any rate reappears in Scholasticism, as well, of course, as the theory of divine ideas.

However, in spite of its venerable history Schelling's theory of the eternal Idea cannot by itself explain the existence of finite things. For Nature as present in the eternal Idea is *Natura naturans* rather than *Natura naturata*. And from ideas, Schelling sensibly maintains, we can derive by deduction only other ideas. He therefore has recourse to the speculations of Jakob Boehme and introduces the notion of a cosmic Fall. The origin of the world is to be found in a falling-away or breaking-away (*Abbrechen*) from God, which can also be described as a leap (*Sprung*). 'From the Absolute to the real there is no continuous transition; the origin of the sensible world is thinkable only as a complete breaking-away from Absoluteness by means of a leap.'[1]

Schelling does not mean that a part of the Absolute breaks away or splits off. The Fall consists in the emergence of a dim image of an image, resembling the shadow which accompanies the body. All things have their eternal ideal existence in the Idea or divine ideas. Hence the centre and true reality of any finite thing is in the divine Idea, and the essence of the finite thing may thus be said to be infinite rather than finite. Considered, however, precisely as a finite thing, it is the image of an image (that is, an image of the ideal essence which is itself a reflection of the Absolute). And its existence as a distinct finite thing is an alienation from its true centre, a negation of infinity. True, finite things are not simply nothing. They are, as Plato said, a mixture of being and not-being. But particularity and finitude represent the negative element. Hence the emergence of *Natura naturata*, the system of particular finite things, is a Fall from the Absolute.

It must not be thought, however, that the cosmic Fall, the emergence of an image of an image, is an event in time. It is 'as eternal (outside all time) as the Absolute itself and the world of

[1] *W*, IV, p. 28.

Ideas'.[1] The Idea is an eternal image of God. And the sensible world is an indefinite succession of shadows, images of images, without any assignable beginning. This means that no finite thing can be referred to God as its immediate cause. The origin of any given finite thing, a man for instance, is explicable in terms of finite causes. The thing, in other words, is a member in the endless chain of causes and effects which constitutes the sensible world. And this is why it is psychologically possible for a human being to look upon the world as the one reality. For it possesses a relative independence and self-subsistence. But this point of view is precisely the point of view of a fallen creature. From the meta-physical and religious standpoints we must see in the world's relative independence a clear sign of its fallen nature, of its alienation from the Absolute.

Now, if creation is not an event in time, the natural conclusion is that it is a necessary external self-expression of the eternal Idea. And in this case it should be in principle deducible, even if the finite mind is unable actually to perform the deduction. But we have seen that Schelling refuses to allow that the world is deducible even in principle from the Absolute. 'The Fall cannot be, as they say, explained.'[2] Hence the origin of the world must be ascribed to freedom. 'The ground of the possibility of the Fall lies in freedom.'[3] But in what sense? On the one hand this freedom cannot be exercised by the world itself. Schelling may sometimes speak as though the world broke away from the Absolute. But as it is the very existence and origin of the world which are in question, we can hardly conceive it as freely leaping away, as it were, from the Absolute. For *ex hypothesi* it does not yet exist. On the other hand, if we ascribe the timeless origination of the world to a free creative act of God, in a theistic sense, there is no very obvious reason for speaking about a cosmic Fall.

In treating of this problem Schelling appears to connect the Fall with a kind of double-life led by the eternal Idea considered as 'another Absolute'.[4] Regarded precisely as the eternal reflection of the Absolute, as the eternal Idea, its true life is in the Absolute itself. But regarded as 'real', as a second Absolute, as Soul, it strives to produce, and it can produce only phenomena, images of images, 'the nothingness of sensible things'.[5] It is, however, only the *possibility* of finite things which can be 'explained', that is,

[1] *W*, IV, p. 31.  [2] *W*, IV, p. 32.  [3] *W*, IV, p. 30.
[4] *W*, IV, p. 31.  [5] *W*, IV, p. 30.

leduced from the second Absolute. Their actual existence is due to freedom, to a spontaneous movement which is at the same time a lapse.

Creation is thus a Fall in the sense that it is a centrifugal movement. The absolute identity becomes differentiated or splintered on the phenomenal level, though not in itself. But there is also a centripetal movement, the return to God. This does not mean that particular finite material things as such return to the divine Idea. We have seen that no particular sensible thing has God for its immediate cause. Similarly, no particular sensible thing, considered precisely as such, returns immediately to God. Its return is mediate, by means of the transformation of the real into the ideal, of objectivity into subjectivity, in and through the human ego or reason which is capable of seeing the infinite in the finite and referring all images to the divine exemplar. As for the finite ego itself, it represents from one point of view 'the point of furthest alienation from God'.[1] For the apparent independence of the phenomenal image of the Absolute reaches its culminating-point in the ego's conscious self-possession and self-assertion. At the same time the ego is one in essence with infinite Reason, and it can rise above its egoistic point of view, returning to its true centre from which it has been alienated.

This point of view determines Schelling's general conception of history, which is well illustrated by the following oft-quoted passage. 'History is an epic composed in the mind of God. Its two main parts are: first, that which depicts the departure of humanity from its centre up to its furthest point of alienation from this centre, and, secondly, that which depicts the return. The first part is the *Iliad*, the second the *Odyssey* of history. In the first the movement was centrifugal, in the second it is centripetal.'[2]

In grappling with the problem of the One and the Many or of the relation between the infinite and the finite Schelling is obviously concerned with allowing for the possibility of evil. The idea of the Fall and of alienation allows for this possibility. For the human self is a fallen self, entangled, as it were, in particularity; and this entanglement, this alienation from the self's true centre, renders possible selfishness, sensuality and so on. But how can man be really free if the Absolute is the totality? And if there is a real possibility of evil, must it not have a ground in the Absolute itself? If so, what conclusions must we draw about the nature of the

[1] *W*, IV, p. 32.          [2] *W*, IV, p. 47.

Absolute or God? In the next section we can consider Schelling's reflections on these problems.

2. In the Preface to his *Philosophical Inquiries into the Nature of Human Freedom* (1809) Schelling frankly admits that *Philosophy and Religion* was deficient in clarity. He intends, therefore, to give another exposition of his thought in the light of the idea of human freedom.[1] This is especially desirable, he says, in view of the accusation that his system is pantheistic and that there is accordingly no room in it for the concept of human freedom.

As for the charge of pantheism, this is, Schelling remarks, an ambiguous term. On the one hand it might be used to describe the theory that the visible world, *Natura naturata*, is identical with God. On the other hand it might be understood as referring to the theory that finite things do not exist at all but that there is only the simple indifferentiated unity of the Godhead. But in neither sense is Schelling's philosophy pantheistic. For he neither identifies the visible world with God nor teaches acosmism, the theory of the non-existence of the world. Nature is a consequence of the first principle, not the first principle itself. But it is a real consequence. God is the God of the living, not of the dead: the divine Being manifests itself and the manifestation is real. If, however, pantheism is interpreted as meaning that all things are immanent in God, Schelling is quite prepared to be called a pantheist. But he proceeds to point out that St. Paul himself declared that in God we live and move and have our being.

To clarify his position, Schelling reinterprets the principle of identity. 'The profound logic of the ancients distinguished subject and predicate as antecedent and consequent [*antecedens et consequens*] and thereby expressed the real meaning of the principle of identity.'[2] God and the world are identical; but to say this is to say that God is the ground or antecedent and the world the consequent. The unity which is asserted is a creative unity. God is self-revealing or self-manifesting life. And though the manifestation is immanent in God, it is yet distinguishable from him. The consequent is dependent on the antecedent, but it is not identical with it in the sense that there is no distinction between them.

This theory, Schelling insists, in no way involves the denial of human freedom. For by itself it says nothing about the nature of

[1] The revised system is also expounded in the Stuttgart lectures (1810), which are printed together with *Philosophical Inquiries* in the fourth volume of his *Works*.
[2] *W*, IV, p. 234.

the consequent. If God is free, the human spirit, which is his image, is free. If God is not free, the human spirit is not free.

Now, in Schelling's view the human spirit is certainly free. For 'the real and living concept [of freedom] is that it is a power of good and evil'.[1] And it is evident that man possesses this power. But if this power is present in man, the consequent, must it not also be present in God, the antecedent? And the question then arises, whether we are forced to draw the conclusion that God can do evil.

To answer this question, let us first look more closely at the human being. We talk about human beings as persons, but personality, Schelling maintains, is not something given from the start, it is something to be won. 'All birth is birth out of darkness into light',[2] and this general proposition is true of the birth of human personality. There is in man a dark foundation, as it were, the unconscious and the life or urge and natural impulse. And it is on this foundation that personality is built. Man is capable of following sensual desire and dark impulse rather than reason: he is able to affirm himself as a particular finite being to the exclusion of the moral law. But he also has the power of subordinating selfish desire and impulse to the rational will and of developing his true human personality. He can do this, however, only by strife, conflict and sublimation. For the dark foundation of personality always remains, though it can be progressively sublimated and integrated in the movement from darkness to light.

As far as man is concerned, what Schelling has to say on this subject obviously contains a great deal of truth. But stimulated by the writings of Boehme and impelled by the exigencies of his theory of the relation between the human spirit and God, he applies this notion of personality to God himself. There is in God a ground of his personal existence,[3] which is itself impersonal. It can be called will, but it is a 'will in which there is no understanding'.[4] It can be conceived as an unconscious desire or yearning for personal existence. And the personal divine existence must be conceived as rational will. The irrational or unconscious will can be called 'the egoism in God'.[5] And if there were only this will in God, there would be no creation. But the rational will is the will of love, and as such it is 'expansive',[6] self-communicating.

[1] *W*, IV, p. 244.            [2] *W*, IV, p. 252.
[3] It should be noted that the divine Being is now for Schelling a personal Deity and no longer an impersonal Absolute.
[4] *W*, IV, p. 251.            [5] *W*, IV, p. 330.            [6] *W*, IV, p. 331.

The inner life of God is thus conceived by Schelling as a dynami process of self-creation. In the ultimate dark abyss of the divine Being, the primal ground or *Urgrund*, there is no differentiation but only pure identity. But this absolutely undifferentiated identity does not exist as such. 'A division, a difference must be posited, that is, if we wish to pass from essence to existence.'[1] God first posits himself as object, as the unconscious will. But he canno do this without at the same time positing himself as subject, a: the rational will of love.

There is, therefore, a likeness between the divine and the huma conquest of personality. And we can even say that 'God make himself.'[2] But there is also a great difference. And an understanding of this difference shows that the answer to the question whethe God can do evil is that he cannot.

In God the conquest of personality is not a temporal process We can distinguish different 'potencies' in God, different moment in the divine life, but there is no temporal succession. Thus if we say that God first posits himself as unconscious will and then a rational will, there is no question of temporally successive acts 'Both acts are one act, and both are absolutely simultaneous.' For Schelling the unconscious will in God is no more temporally prior to the rational will than the Father is temporally prior to the Son in the Christian theology of the Trinity. Hence, though we can distinguish different moments in the 'becoming' of the divine personality, one moment being logically prior to another, there i no becoming at all in the temporal sense. God is eternally love, and 'in love there can never be the will to evil'.[4] Hence it is meta physically impossible for God to do evil.

But in God's external manifestation the two principles, the lower and the higher wills, are and must be separable. 'If the identity of the two principles were as indissoluble in the human spirit as in God, there would be no distinction (that is, between God and the human spirit); that is to say, God would not manifes himself. Therefore the unity which is indissoluble in God mus be dissoluble in man. And this is the possibility of good and evil.' This possibility has its ground in God, but as a realized possibility it is present only in man. Perhaps one can express the matter by saying that whereas God is necessarily an integrated personality man need not be. For the basic elements are separable in man.

[1] *W*, IV, p. 316.      [2] *W*, IV, p. 324.      [3] *W*, IV, p. 326.
[4] *W*, IV, p. 267.      [5] *W*, IV, p. 256.

It would, however, be erroneous to conclude that Schelling attributes to man a complete liberty of indifference. He is too fond of the idea of antecedent and consequent to admit the concept of freedom as 'a completely indeterminate power of willing one or other of two contradictory things without determining grounds and simply because it is willed'.[1] Schelling rejects this concept and finds the determining ground of a man's successive choices in his intelligible essence or character which stands to his particular acts as antecedent to consequent. At the same time he does not wish to say that it is God who predetermines a man's acts by conceiving him in the eternal Idea. Hence he is forced to depict a man's intelligible character as due to an original self-positing of the ego, as the result of an original choice by the ego itself. He can thus say both that a man's actions are in principle predictable and that they are free. They are necessary; but this necessity is an inner necessity, imposed by the ego's original choice, not a necessity externally imposed by God. 'This inner necessity is itself freedom, the essence of man is essentially *his own act*; necessity and freedom are mutually immanent, as one reality which appears as one or the other only when looked at from different sides. . . .'[2] Thus Judas's betrayal of Christ was necessary and inevitable, given the historical circumstances; but at the same time he betrayed Christ 'willingly and with complete freedom'.[3] Similarly it was inevitable both that Peter would deny Christ and that he would repent of this denial; yet both the denial and the repentance, being Peter's own acts, were free.

If the theory of an intelligible character is given a purely psychological interpretation, it can be made at any rate very plausible. On the one hand we not infrequently say of a given man that he could not act in this or that manner, meaning that such a way of acting would be quite contrary to his character. And if after all he does act in this way, we are inclined to say that his character was not what we supposed. On the other hand we come to know not only other people's characters but also our own through their and our acts. And we might wish to draw the conclusion that in each man there is, as it were, a hidden character which manifests itself progressively in his acts, so that his acts stand to his character in a relation analogous to that between consequent and ground or antecedent. The objection can indeed be made that this presupposes that character is something fixed and settled from the start (by heredity, environment, very early experiences and so on), and that

<hr />

[1] *W*, IV, p. 274.    [2] *W*, IV, p. 277.    [3] *W*, IV, p. 278.

this presupposition is false. But as long as the theory is presented as a psychological theory, it is a matter for empirical investigation. And it is clear that some empirical data count in its favour, even if others tell against it. It is a question of weighing, interpreting and co-ordinating the available evidence.

But Schelling does not present his theory simply as an empirical hypothesis. It is a metaphysical theory. At least it depends in part on metaphysical theories. For example, the theory of identity is influential. The Absolute is the identity of necessity and freedom, and this identity is reflected in man. His acts are both necessary and free. And Schelling draws the conclusion that a man's intelligible essence, which determines his particular acts, must itself have, as it were, an aspect of freedom, in that it is the result of the ego's self-positing. But this original choice of itself by the ego is neither a conscious act nor an act in time. According to Schelling, it is outside time and determines all consciousness, though a man's acts are free inasmuch as they issue from his own essence or self. But it is extremely difficult to see what this primeval act of will can possibly be. Schelling's theory bears some resemblance to M. Sartre's interpretation of freedom in his existentialist philosophy; but the setting is much more meta-physical. Schelling develops Kant's distinction between the intelligible and phenomenal spheres in the light of his theory of identity and of his preoccupation with the idea of ground and consequent, and the resulting theory is extremely obscure. It is indeed clear that Schelling wishes to avoid the Calvinist doctrine of divine predestination on the one hand and the theory of liberty of indifference on the other, while at the same time he wishes to allow for the truths which find expression in these positions. But it can hardly be claimed that the conclusion of his reflections is crystal clear. True, Schelling did not claim that everything in philosophy could be made crystal clear. But the trouble is that it is difficult to assess the truth of what is said unless one understands what is being said.

As for the nature of evil, Schelling experienced considerable difficulty in finding a satisfactory descriptive formula. As he did not look on himself as a pantheist in the sense of one who denies any distinction between the world and God, he felt that he could affirm the positive reality of evil without committing himself to the conclusion that there is evil in the divine Being itself. At the same time his account of the relation between the world and God is being that of consequent or ground to antecedent implies that if evil is a positive reality it must have its ground in God. And the conclusion might be thought to follow that 'in order that evil should not be, God would have not to be himself'.[1] In the Stuttgart lectures Schelling attempts to steer a middle course between asserting and denying the positive reality of evil by saying that it is 'from one point of view nothing, from another point of view an extremely real being'.[2] Perhaps we can say that he was feeling after the Scholastic formula which describes evil as a privation, though a real privation.

In any case evil is certainly present in the world, whatever its precise nature may be. Hence the return to God in human history must take the form of the progressive triumph of good over evil. 'The good must be brought out of darkness into actuality that it may live everlastingly with God; and evil must be separated from the good that it may be cast into not-being. For this is the final end of creation.'[3] In other words, the complete triumph of the rational will over the lower will or urge, which is eternally accomplished in God, is the ideal goal of human history. In God the sublimation of the lower will is eternal and necessary. In man it is a temporal process.

3. We have already had occasion to note Schelling's insistence that from ideas we can deduce only ideas. It is not surprising, therefore, if in his later years we find him emphasizing the distinction, to which allusion was made in the section on his life and writings, between negative philosophy, which is confined to the world of concepts and essences, and positive philosophy, which stresses existence.

All philosophy worthy of the name, Schelling maintains, is concerned with the first or ultimate principle of reality. Negative philosophy, however, discovers this principle only as a supreme essence, as the absolute Idea. And from a supreme essence we can deduce only other essences, from the Idea only other ideas. From a *What* we cannot deduce a *That*. In other words, negative philosophy is quite incapable of explaining the existent world. Its deduction of the world is not a deduction of existents but only of what things must be if they exist. Of being outside God the negative philosopher can only say that 'if it exists, it can exist only in this way and only as such and such'.[4] His thought moves

[1] *W*, IV, p. 295.    [2] *W*, IV, p. 296.
[3] *W*, IV, p. 296.    [4] *W*, V, p. 558.

within the realm of the hypothetical. And this is especially clea
in the case of the Hegelian system which, according to Schelling
by-passes the existential order.

Positive philosophy, however, does not start simply with God a
Idea, as a *What* or essence, but rather with God 'as a pure That',
as pure act or being in an existential sense. And from this suprem
existential act it passes to the concept or nature of God, showin
that he is not an impersonal Idea or essence but a creative person a
Being, the existing 'Lord of being',[2] where 'being' means th
world. Schelling thus connects positive philosophy with the concep
of God as a personal Being.

Schelling does not mean to imply that he is the first to discove
positive philosophy. On the contrary, the whole history c
philosophy manifests the 'combat between negative and positiv
philosophy'.[3] But the use of the word 'combat' must not be mis
understood. It is a question of emphasis and priority rather tha
of a fight to the death between two completely irreconcilable line
of thought. For negative philosophy cannot be simply rejected
No system can be constructed without concepts. And even if th
positive philosopher places the emphasis on existence, he obviousl
does not and cannot disdain all consideration of what exists
Hence we have 'to assert the connection, yes the unity, between th
two',[4] that is, between positive and negative philosophy.[5]

But how, Schelling asks, are we to make the transition fron
negative to positive philosophy? It cannot be made merely b
thinking. For conceptual thought is concerned with essences an
logical deductions. Hence we must have recourse to the will, '
will which demands with inner necessity that God should not be
mere idea'.[6] In other words, the initial affirmation of the divin
existence is based on an act of faith demanded by the will. Th
ego is conscious of its fallen condition, of its state of alienation, an
it is aware that this alienation can be overcome only by God'
activity. It demands, therefore, that God should be not simply
transmundane ideal but an actually existing personal God throug
whom man can be redeemed. Fichte's ideal moral order will no
satisfy man's religious needs. The faith which lies at the basis o

---

[1] *als reines Dass*; W, v, p. 746.    [2] *Ibid.*    [3] *Ibid.*    [4] W, v, p. 746.
[5] Schelling's distinction is similar in certain respects to the distinction mad
by some modern writers, notably Professor Gilson, between essentialist an
existential philosophy, the latter term meaning, not 'existentialism', but philosoph
which lays its fundamental emphasis on being in the sense of existence (*esse*
rather than on being in the sense of essence. But the extent of the similarity i
limited.    [6] W, v, p. 746.

ositive philosophy is faith in a personal creative and redeeming God, not in Fichte's ideal moral order, nor in Hegel's absolute Idea.

At first sight at least Schelling may appear to be repeating Kant's theory of practical or moral faith. But Schelling makes it clear that he regards the critical philosophy as an example of negative philosophizing. Kant does indeed affirm God on faith, but simply as a postulate, that is, as a possibility. Further, Kant affirms God as an instrument, as it were, for synthesizing virtue and happiness. In his religion within the limits of bare reason there is no room for genuine religion. The truly religious man is conscious of his profound need of God, and he is brought by this conscious-ness and by his longing for God to a personal Deity. 'For the person seeks a person.'[1] The truly religious man does not affirm God simply as an instrument for apportioning happiness to virtue: he seeks God for himself. The ego 'demands God himself. *Him, him,* will it have, the God who acts, who exercises providence, who, as being himself real, can meet the reality of the Fall. . . . In this God alone does the ego see the *real* supreme good.'[2]

The distinction between positive and negative philosophy thus turns out to be a distinction between philosophy which is truly religious and philosophy which cannot assimilate the religious consciousness and its demands. Schelling says this quite explicitly with an evident reference to Kant. 'The longing for the real God and for redemption through him is, as you see, nothing else but the expression of the need of *religion*. . . . Without an active God . . . there can be no religion, for religion presupposes an actual, real relationship of man to God. Nor can there be any history in which God is providence. . . . At the end of negative philosophy I have only possible and not actual religion, religion only "within the limits of bare reason". . . . It is with the transition to positive philosophy that we first enter the sphere of religion.'[3]

Now, if positive philosophy affirms the existence of God as a first principle, and if the transition to positive philosophy cannot be made by thinking but only by an act of the will issuing in faith, Schelling obviously cannot turn negative into positive philosophy by supplementing the former by a natural theology in the traditional sense. At the same time there can be what we may call an empirical proof of the rationality of the will's act. For the demand of the religious man is for a God who reveals himself and accomplishes man's redemption. And the proof, if one may so put

[1] *W*, v, p. 748.          [2] *Ibid.*          [3] *W*, v, p. 750.

it, of God's existence will take the form of showing the historica
development of the religious consciousness, the history of man'
demand for God and of God's answer to this demand. 'Positiv
philosophy is historical philosophy.'[1] And this is the reason why i
his later writings Schelling devotes himself to the study of mytho
logy and revelation. He is trying to exhibit God's progressive self
revelation to man and the progressive work of divine redemption

This is not to say that Schelling abandons all his earlie
speculations in favour of an empirical study of the history o
mythology and revelation. As we have seen, his thesis is tha
negative and positive philosophy must be combined. And hi
earlier religious speculations are not jettisoned. For example, i
the essay entitled *Another Deduction of the Principles of Positiv
Philosophy* (1841) he takes as his point of departure 'the un
conditioned existent'[2] and proceeds to deduce the moments o
phases of God's inner life. He does indeed lay emphasis on th
primacy of being in the sense of existence, but the general schem
of his earlier philosophy of religion, with the ideas of the moment
in the divine life, of the cosmic Fall and of the return to God, i
retained. And though in his lectures on mythology and religion h
concerns himself with the empirical confirmation, as it were, of hi
religious philosophy, he never really frees himself from the idealis
tendency to interpret the relation between God and the world as
relation of ground or antecedent to consequent.

The reader may be inclined to share Kierkegaard's disappoint
ment that after making his distinction between negative an
positive philosophy Schelling proceeds to concentrate on the study
of mythology and revelation instead of radically rethinking hi
philosophy in the light of this distinction. At the same time we ca
understand the philosopher's point of view. The philosophy o
religion has come to occupy the central position in his thought
And the self-manifesting impersonal Absolute has become the self
revealing personal God. Schelling is anxious, therefore, to show
that man's faith in God is historically justified and that the history
of the religious consciousness is also the history of the divine self
revelation to man.

4. If, however, we speak of Schelling's philosophy of mythology
and revelation as an empirical study, the word 'empirical' must be
understood in a relative sense. Schelling has not abandoned
deductive metaphysics for pure empiricism. Far from it. For

---

[1] *W*, v, p. 753.      [2] *W*, v, p. 729

xample, the deduction of three 'potencies' in the one God is pre-
upposed. It is also presupposed that if there is a self-manifesting
God, this necessary nature of an absolute Being will be progres-
ively revealed. Hence when Schelling turns to the study of
nythology and revelation, he already possesses the scheme, as it
vere, of what he will find. The study is empirical in the sense that
ts matter is provided by the actual history of religion as known
hrough empirical investigation. But the framework of interpreta-
ion is provided by the supposedly necessary deductions of metaphysics. In other words, Schelling sets out to find in the history of
eligion the self-revelation of one personal God, whose unity does
not exclude three distinguishable potencies or moments. And he
aas, of course, no difficulty in discovering expressions of this
conception of the Deity in the development of religious beliefs from
he ancient mythologies of East and West up to the Christian
logma of the Trinity. Similarly, he has no difficulty in finding
xpressions of the ideas of a Fall and of a return to God.

If Schelling's premises are once assumed, this procedure is, of
course, justified. For, as we have seen, he never intended to
ettison metaphysics, the abstract philosophy of reason, which, to
ase modern jargon, shows us what must be the case if anything is
he case. Hence from Schelling's point of view metaphysical presuppositions are quite in order. For philosophy as a whole is a
combination of negative and positive philosophy. At the same
time Schelling's procedure is doubtless one reason why his philosophy of mythology and revelation exercised comparatively little
nfluence on the development of the study of the history of
religion. This is not to say that metaphysical presuppositions are
llegitimate. Whether one thinks that they are legitimate or
illegitimate obviously depends on one's view of the cognitive value
of metaphysics. But it is easy to understand that Schelling's
*philosophy* of mythology and revelation was looked at askance by
those who wished to free the study of the history of religion from
the presuppositions of idealist metaphysics.

A distinction is drawn by Schelling between mythology on the
one hand and revelation on the other. 'Everything has its time.
Mythological religion had to come first. In mythological religion
we have blind (because produced by a necessary process), *unfree*
and *unspiritual* religion.'[1] Myths are not simply arbitrary and
capricious products of the imagination. But neither are they

[1] *W*, v, p. 437.

revelation, in the sense of a freely-imparted knowledge of God
They can, of course, be consciously elaborated, but fundamentally
they are the product of an unconscious and necessary process
successive forms in which an apprehension of the divine imposes
itself on the religious consciousness. In other words, mythology
corresponds to the dark or lower principle in God, and it has its
roots in the sphere of the unconscious. When, however, we pass
from mythology to revelation, we pass 'into a completely different
sphere'.[1] In mythology the mind 'had to do with a necessary
process, here with something which exists only as the result of an
absolutely free will'.[2] For the concept of revelation presupposes an
act whereby God 'freely gives or has given himself to mankind'.[3]

Inasmuch as mythological religion and revealed religion are both
religion, it must be possible, Schelling insists, to subsume them
under a common idea. And in fact the whole history of the
religious consciousness is a second theogony or birth of God, in the
sense that the eternal and timeless becoming or birth of God in
himself[4] is represented in time in the history of religion. Mythology
as rooted in the unconscious, represents a moment in the divine
life. It logically precedes revelation and is a preparation for it. But
it is not itself revelation. For revelation is essentially God's free
manifestation of himself as infinite, personal and free creator and
lord of being. And, as a free act on God's part, it is not simply a
logical consequence of mythology. At the same time revelation can
be described as the truth of mythology. For mythology is, as it
were, the exoteric element which veils the revealed truth. And in
paganism the philosopher can find mythological representations or
antcipiations of the truth.

In other words, Schelling wishes to represent the whole history
of the religious consciousness as God's revelation of himself, while
at the same time he wishes to leave room for a specifically Christian
concept of revelation. On the one hand revelation, in what we
might perhaps call a weak sense of the term, runs through the
whole history of religion. For it is the inner truth of mythology. On
the other hand revelation in a strong sense of the term is found in
Christianity. For it is in the Christian religion that this inner truth
first comes to the clear light of day. Christianity thus gives the
truth of mythology, and it can be described as the culmination of
historical religion. But it does not follow that Christianity is an

[1] *W*, vi, p. 396.     [2] *Ibid*.     [3] *W*, vi, p. 395.
[4] The reference is to the logically distinguishable 'potencies' in God's inner life.

utomatic consequence of mythology. Mythology as such is, as we
ave seen, a necessary process. But in and through Christ the
ersonal God freely reveals himself. Obviously, if Schelling wishes
o represent the whole history of religion as the temporal represen-
ation of the divine life, it is very difficult for him to avoid asserting
necessary connection between pagan mythology and Christianity.
he former would represent God as unconscious will, while the
atter would represent God as free will, the will of love. At the same
ime Schelling tries to preserve an essential distinction between
mythology and revelation by insisting that the concept of revelation
s the concept of a free act on God's part. Revelation is the truth
f mythology in the sense that it is that at which mythology aims
nd that which underlies the exoteric clothing of myth. But it is in
nd through Christ that the truth is clearly revealed, and it is
evealed freely. Its truth could not be known simply by logical
deduction from the pagan myths.

But though Schelling certainly tries to allow for a distinction
between mythology and revelation, there is a further important
point to make. If we mean by revelation Christianity simply as a
act which stands over against the fact of paganism, there is room
or a higher standpoint, namely that of reason understanding both
mythology and revelation. And this higher standpoint is positive
philosophy. But Schelling is careful to explain that he is not
eferring to a rationalistic interpretation of religion from outside.
He is referring to the activity of the religious consciousness whereby
t understands itself from within. The philosophy of religion is thus
or Schelling not only philosophy but also religion. It presupposes
Christianity and cannot exist without it. It arises within
Christianity, not outside it. 'Philosophical religion is therefore
*historically* mediated through revealed religion.'[1] But it cannot be
simply identified with Christian belief and life as facts. For it takes
these facts as subject-matter for free reflective understanding. In
contrast, therefore, with the simple acceptance of the original
Christian revelation on authority philosophical religion can be
called 'free' religion. 'The free religion is only *mediated* through
Christianity; it is not immediately *posited* by it.'[2] But this does not
mean that philosophical religion rejects revelation. Faith seeks
understanding; but understanding from within does not annul
what is understood.

This process of understanding, of free reflection, has its own

[1] *W*, v, p. 437.        [2] *W*, v, p. 440.

history, ranging through Scholastic theology and metaphysics, up to Schelling's own later religious philosophy. And in this philosophy we can discern Schelling's hankering after a higher wisdom. There was always something of the Gnostic in his mental make-up. Just as he was not content with ordinary physics but expounded a speculative or higher physics, so in later years he expounded an esoteric or higher knowledge of God's nature and of his self-revelation.

It is not surprising, therefore, to find Schelling giving an interpretation of the history of Christianity which in certain respects is reminiscent of the theories of the twelfth-century Abbot Joachim of Flores. According to Schelling there are three main periods in the development of Christianity. The first is the Petrine, characterized by the dominating ideas of law and authority and correlated with the ultimate ground of being in God, which is itself identified with the Father of Trinitarian theology. The second period, the Pauline, starts with the Protestant Reformation. It is characterized by the idea of freedom and correlated with the ideal principle in God, identified with the Son. And Schelling looks forward to a third period, the Johannine, which will be a higher synthesis of the first two periods and unite together law and freedom in the one Christian community. This third period is correlated with the Holy Spirit, the divine love, interpreted as a synthesis of the first two moments in God's inner life.

5. If we look at Schelling's philosophical pilgrimage as a whole, there is obviously a very great difference between its point of departure and its point of arrival. At the same time there is a certain continuity. For we can see how fresh problems arise for him out of positions already adopted, and how his solutions to these problems demand the adoption of new positions which involve modifications in the old or display them in a new light. Further, there are certain pervasive fundamental problems which serve to confer a certain unity on his philosophizing in spite of all changes.

There can be no reasonable objection to this process of development as such, unless we are prepared to defend as reasonable the thesis that a philosopher should expound a rigid closed system and never change it. Indeed, it is arguable that Schelling did not make sufficient changes. For he showed a tendency to retain ideas already employed even when the adoption of a new idea or set of ideas might well have suggested the advisability of discarding them. This characteristic may not be peculiar to Schelling: it is ikely to be found in any philosopher whose thought passed through a variety of distinct phases. But it leads to a certain difficulty in assessing Schelling's precise position at a given moment. For instance, in his later thought he emphasizes the personal nature of God and the freedom of God's creative act. And it is natural to describe the evolution of his thought in its theological aspects as being a movement from pantheism to speculative theism. At the same time his insistence on the divine freedom is accompanied by a retention of the idea of the cosmic Fall and by a persistent inclination to look on the relation between the world and God as analogous to that between consequent and antecedent. Hence, though it seems to me more appropriate to describe his later thought in terms of the ideas which are new rather than in terms of those which are retained for the past, he provides material for those who maintain that even in the last phase of his philosophizing he was a dynamic pantheist rather than a theist. It is, of course, a question partly of emphasis and partly of terminology. But the point is that Schelling himself is largely responsible for the difficulty in finding the precise appropriate descriptive term. However, perhaps one ought not to expect anything else in the case of a philosopher who was so anxious to synthesize apparently conflicting points of view and to show that they were really complementary.

It scarcely needs saying that Schelling was not a systematizer in the sense of one who leaves to posterity a closed and rigid system of the take-it-or-leave-it type. But it does not necessarily follow that he was not a systematic thinker. True, his mind was notably open to stimulus and inspiration from a variety of thinkers whom he found in some respects congenial. For example, Plato, the Neo-Platonists, Giordano Bruno,[1] Jakob Boehme, Spinoza and Leibniz, not to speak of Kant and Fichte, were all used as sources of inspiration. But this openness to the reception of ideas from a variety of sources was not accompanied by any very pronounced ability to weld them all together into one consistent whole. Further, we have seen that in his later years he showed a strong inclination to take flight into the cloudy realm of theosophy and gnosticism. And it is understandable that a man who drew heavily on the speculations of Jakob Boehme can exercise only a very limited appeal among philosophers. At the same time it is

[1] Schelling's theory of the Absolute as pure identity can be regarded as a continuation of Bruno's idea of the infinite as the *coincidentia oppositorum*, an idea which was itself derived from Nicholas of Cusa.

necessary, as Hegel remarks, to make a distinction between Schelling's philosophy and the imitations of it which consist in farrago of words about the Absolute or in the substitution for sustained thought of vague analogies based on alleged intuitiv insights. For though Schelling was not a systematizer in the sense that Hegel was, he none the less thought systematically. That is to say, he made a real and sustained effort to understand his material and to think through the problems which he raised. It was always systematic understanding at which he aimed and which he tried to communicate. Whether he succeeded or not, is another question.

Schelling's later thought has been comparatively neglected by historians. And this is understandable. For one thing, as was remarked in the introductory chapter, Schelling's philosophy of Nature, system of transcendental idealism and theory of the Absolute as pure identity are the important phases of his thought if we choose to regard him primarily as a link between Fichte and Hegel in the development of German idealism. For another thing, his philosophy of mythology and revelation, which in any case belonged to a period when the impetus of metaphysical idealism was already spent, has seemed to many not only to represent a flight beyond anything which can be regarded as rational philo-sophy but also to be hardly worth considering in view of the actual development of the history of religion in subsequent times.

But though this neglect is understandable, it is also perhaps regrettable. At least it is regrettable if one thinks that there is room for a philosophy of religion as well as for a purely historical and sociological study of religions or a purely psychological study of the religious consciousness. It is not so much a question of looking to Schelling for solutions to problems as of finding stimulus and inspiration in his thought, points of departure for independent reflection. And possibly this is a characteristic of Schelling's philosophizing as a whole. Its value may be primarily suggestive and stimulative. But it can, of course, exercise this function only for those who have a certain initial sympathy with his mentality and an appreciation of the problems which he raised. In the absence of this sympathy and appreciation there is a natural tendency to write him off as a poet who chose the wrong medium for the expression of his visions of the world.

6. In the introductory chapter some mention was made of Schelling's relations with the romantic movement as represented by F. Schlegel, Novalis, Hölderlin and so on. And I do not propose

ither to repeat or to develop what was then said. But some
emarks may be appropriate in this last section of the present
hapter on Schelling's influence on some other thinkers both inside
nd outside Germany.

Schelling's philosophy of Nature exercised some influence on
Lorenz Oken (1779–1851). Oken was a professor of medicine at
ena, Munich and Zürich successively; but he was deeply interested
n philosophy and published several philosophical works, such as
*On the Universe (Ueber das Universum)*, 1808. In his view the
philosophy of Nature is the doctrine of the eternal transformation
f God into the world. God is the totality, and the world is the
ternal appearance of God. That is to say, the world cannot have
ad a beginning because it is the expressed divine thought. And
or the same reason it can have no end. But there can be and is
volution in the world.

Schelling's judgment of Oken's philosophy was not particularly
avourable, though he made use of some of Oken's ideas in his
ectures. In his turn Oken refused to follow Schelling into the paths
f his later religious philosophy.

The influence of Schelling's philosophy of Nature was also felt by
ohann Joseph von Görres (1776–1848), a leading Catholic philo-
opher of Munich.[1] But Görres is chiefly known as a religious
hinker. At first somewhat inclined to the pantheism of Schelling's
ystem of identity, he later expounded a theistic philosophy, as in
he four volumes of his *Christian Mysticism (Christliche Mystik*,
836–42), though, like Schelling himself, he was strongly attracted
o theosophical speculation. Görres also wrote on art and on poli-
ical questions. Indeed he took an active part in political life and
nterested himself in the problem of the relations between Church
nd State.

Görres's abandonment of the standpoint represented by
Schelling's system of identity was not shared by Karl Gustav
Carus (1789–1860), a doctor and philosopher who defended
pantheism throughout his career. He is of some importance for his
work on the soul (*Psyche*, 1846) in which he maintains that the key
o the conscious life of the soul is to be found in the sphere of the
unconscious.

Turning to Franz von Baader (1765–1841) who, like Görres, was
n important member of the circle of Catholic thinkers and writers
t Munich, we find a clear case of reciprocal influence. That is to say,

---

[1] Schelling's influence was felt in southern rather than in northern Germany.

though Baader was influenced by Schelling, he in turn influence
the latter. For it was Baader who introduced Schelling to th
writings of Boehme and so helped to determine the direction take
by his thought.

It was Baader's conviction that since the time of Francis Baco
and Descartes philosophy had tended to become more and mor
divorced from religion, whereas true philosophy should have it
foundations in faith. And in working out his own philosoph
Baader drew on the speculations of thinkers such as Eckhart an
Boehme. In God himself we can distinguish higher and low
principles, and though the sensible world is to be regarded as
divine self-manifestation it none the less represents a Fall. Agai
just as in God there is the eternal victory of the higher princip
over the lower, of light over darkness, so in man there should be
process of spiritualization whereby the world would return to Go
It is evident that Baader and Schelling were kindred souls wh
drank from the same spiritual fountain.

Baader's social and political writings are of some interest. I
them he expresses a resolute opposition to the theory of the Sta
as a result of a social compact or contract between individuals. O
the contrary, the State is a natural institution in the sense that
is grounded in and proceeds from the nature of man: it is not th
product of a convention. At the same time Baader strong
attacks the notion that the State is the ultimate sovereign powe
The ultimate sovereign is God alone, and reverence for God an
the universal moral law, together with respect for the huma
person as the image of God, are the only real safeguards again
tyranny. If these safeguards are neglected, tyranny and intoleran
will result, no matter whether sovereignty is regarded as residin
with the monarch or with the people. To the atheistic or secul
power-State Baader opposes the ideal of the Christian State. Th
concentration of power which is characteristic of the secular or th
atheistic national State and which leads to injustice at home an
to war abroad can be overcome only if religion and moralit
penetrate the whole of human society.

One can hardly call Karl Christian Friedrich Krause (1781–183
a disciple of Schelling. For he professed to be the true spiritu
successor of Kant, and his relations with Schelling, when
Munich, were far from friendly. However, he was wont to say th
the approach to his own philosophy must be by way of Schellin
and some of his ideas were akin to those of Schelling. The body

ιe maintained, belongs to the realm of Nature, while the spirit or
go belongs to the spiritual sphere, the realm of 'reason'. This idea
choes indeed Kant's distinction between the phenomenal and
ιoumenal spheres. But Krause argued that as Spirit and Nature,
hough distinct and in one sense opposed, react on one another, we
ιust look for the ground of both in a perfect essence, God or the
ιbsolute. Krause also expounded a 'synthetic' order, proceeding
rom God or the Absolute to the derived essences, Spirit and
ιature, and to finite things. He insisted on the unity of all
ιumanity as the goal of history, and after abandoning his hope of
his end being attained through Freemasonry, issued a manifesto
·roclaiming a League of Humanity (*Menschheitsbund*). In Germany
is philosophy was overshadowed by the systems of the three great
lealists, but it exercised, perhaps somewhat surprisingly, a wide
ιfluence in Spain where 'Krausism' became a fashionable system
f thought.

In Russia Schelling appealed to the pan-Slavist group, whereas
he westernizers were influenced more by Hegel. For instance, in
he early part of the nineteenth century Schelling's philosophy of
ιature was expounded at Moscow by M. G. Pavlov (1773–1840),
·hile the later religious thought of Schelling exercised some
ιfluence on the famous Russian philosopher Vladimir Soloviev
ι853–1900). It would certainly not be accurate to call Soloviev a
isciple of Schelling. Apart from the fact that he was influenced by
ther non-Russian thinkers, he was in any case an original
hilosopher and not the 'disciple' of anyone. But in his tendency
ι theosophical speculation[1] he showed a marked affinity of spirit
ith Schelling, and certain aspects of his profoundly religious
ιought are very similar to positions adopted by the German
hilosopher.

In Great Britain the influence of Schelling has been negligible.
oleridge, the poet, remarks in his *Biographia Literaria* that in
chelling's philosophy of Nature and system of transcendental
lealism he found 'a genial coincidence' with much that he had
orked out for himself, and he praises Schelling at the expense of
ichte, whom he caricatures. But it can hardly be said that
·rofessional philosophers in this country have shown any enthu-
asm for Schelling.

In recent times there has been a certain renewal of interest in

[1] Soloviev made great play with the idea of Wisdom or *Sophia*, as found in the
ιble and also, for instance, in the writings of Boehme.

Schelling's philosophy of religion. For instance, it acted as stimulus in the development of the thought of the Protesta: theologian Paul Tillich. And in spite of Kierkegaard's attitude the has been a tendency to see in Schelling's distinction betwe negative and positive philosophy, in his insistence on freedom ar in his emphasis on existence, an anticipation of some themes existentialism. But though this interpretation has some limit justification, the desire to find anticipations of later ideas illustrious minds of the past should not blind us to the gre differences in atmosphere between the idealist and existentiali movements. In any case Schelling is perhaps most notable for I transformation of the impersonal Absolute of metaphysical idealis into the personal God who reveals himself to the religio consciousness.

### CHAPTER VIII

# SCHLEIERMACHER

*Life and writings—The basic religious experience and its interpretation—The moral and religious life of man—Final remarks.*

. CONCERNED as they were with the Absolute, with the relation etween the infinite and the finite and with the life of the spirit, he three great German idealists naturally devoted attention to eligion as an expression of the finite spirit's relation to the divine eality. And as all three were professors of philosophy and contructors of philosophical systems, it was also natural that they hould interpret religion in the light of the fundamental principles f these systems. Thus in accordance with the spirit of his ethical lealism Fichte tended to reduce religion to ethics,[1] while Hegel ended to depict it as a form of knowledge. Even Schelling, whose hought, as we have seen, became more and more a philosophy of he religious consciousness and who laid emphasis on man's need f a personal God, tended to interpret the development of the eligious consciousness as the development of a higher knowledge. Vith Schleiermacher, however, we find an approach to the hilosophy of religion from the point of view of a theologian and reacher, a man who in spite of his strongly-marked philosophical aterests retained the imprint of his pietistic upbringing and who vas concerned with making a sharp distinction between the eligious consciousness on the one hand and metaphysics and thics on the other.

Friedrich Daniel Ernst Schleiermacher was born at Breslau on Jovember 21st, 1768. His school education was entrusted by his arents to the Moravian Brotherhood. In spite of a loss of faith in ome fundamental Christian doctrines he then proceeded to Halle or the study of theology, though during his first two years at the niversity he interested himself in Spinoza and Kant more than in urely theological subjects. In 1790 he passed his examinations at erlin and then took a post as tutor in a family. From 1794 until he end of 1795 he acted as pastor at Landsberg near Frankfurt on

---

[1] As was mentioned in the account of Fichte's philosophy, the strength of this endency was considerably weaker in his later thought.

the Oder, and from 1796 until 1802 he held an ecclesiastic
position at Berlin.

During this period at Berlin Schleiermacher was in relation wit
the circle of the romantics, particularly with Friedrich Schlege
He shared the general romantic concern with the totality, and l
had a profound sympathy with Spinoza. At the same time he ha
been attracted from an early age by Plato's view of the world a
the visible image of the ideal realm of true being. And Spinoza
Nature was conceived by him as the reality which reveals itself i
the phenomenal world. But as an admirer of Spinoza he was face
with the task of reconciling his philosophical outlook with th
religion which he was commissioned to teach. Nor was this simpl
a matter of satisfying his professional conscience as a Protestar
clergyman. For he was a sincerely religious man who, as alread
remarked, retained the lasting imprint of the piety of his famil
and of his early teachers. He had therefore to think out th
intellectual framework for the religious consciousness as h
conceived it. And in 1799 he published his *Discourses on Religio*
(*Reden über die Religion*), of which there were several subsequer
editions.

This work was followed in 1800 by *Monologues* (*Monologer*
treating of problems connected with the relation between th
individual and society, and in 1801 by Schleiermacher's firs
collection of sermons. Schleiermacher was not, however, wha
would generally be considered an orthodox Protestant theologia
and the years 1802–4 were passed in retirement. In 1803 h
published *Outlines of a Critique of the Doctrine of Morals up t
Present* (*Grundlinien einer Kritik der bisherigen Sittenlehre*). He als
occupied himself with translating into German the dialogues o
Plato, furnished with introductions and notes. The first par
appeared in 1804, the second in 1809 and the third in 1828.

In 1804 Schleiermacher accepted a chair at the University o
Halle. And when Napoleon closed the university, he remained i
the town as a preacher. In 1807, however, he returned to Berli
where he took part in political life and collaborated in the founda
tion of the new university. In 1810 he was appointed professor o
theology in the university and he held this post until his death i
1834. In 1821–2 he published his *Christian Faith according to th
Principles of the Evangelical Church* (*Der christliche Glaube nach de
Grundsätzen der evangelischen Kirche*), a second edition of whicl
appeared in 1830–1. He also published further collections o

ermons. His lecture-courses at the university, which covered not
nly theological but also philosophical and educational themes,
vere published after his death.

2. Thought and being, Schleiermacher maintains, are correla-
ive. But there are two ways in which thought can be related to
eing. In the first place thought can conform itself to being, as in
cientific or theoretical knowledge. And the being which corre-
ponds to the totality of our scientific concepts and judgments is
alled Nature. In the second place thought can seek to conform
eing to itself. And this is verified in the thinking which lies at the
asis of our moral activity. For through moral action we seek to
ealize our ethical ideals and purposes, endeavouring in this way
o conform being to our ideas rather than the other way round.
Thought which aims at knowledge relates itself to a being which
' presupposes; the thought which lies at the root of our actions
elates itself to a being which is to come about through us.'[1] And
he totality of that which expresses itself in thought-directed
ction is called Spirit.

We are thus presented, at first sight at least, with a dualism. On
he one hand we have Nature, on the other Spirit. But though
pirit and Nature, thought and being, subject and object, are
istinct and different notions for conceptual thinking, which is
nable to transcend all distinction and oppositions, the dualism is
ot absolute. The ultimate reality is the identity of Spirit and
Jature in the Universe or God. Conceptual thought cannot
pprehend this identity. But the identity can be felt. And this
eeling is linked by Schleiermacher with self-consciousness. It is
ot indeed reflective self-awareness, which apprehends the identity
f the ego in the diversity of its moments or phases. But at the
asis of reflective self-awareness there lies an 'immediate self-
onsciousness, which equals feeling'.[2] In other words, there is a
undamental immediacy of feeling, at which level the distinctions
nd oppositions of conceptual thought have not yet emerged. We
an speak of it as an intuition. But if we do, we must understand
hat it is never a clear intellectual intuition. Rather is it the
eeling-basis, so to speak, in self-consciousness, and it cannot be
eparated from consciousness of the self. That is to say, the self
oes not enjoy any intellectual intuition of the divine totality as

[1] W, III, p. 59. References to Schleiermacher's writing are given according to
olume and page of the edition of his Works by O. Braun and J. Bauer (4 vols.,
eipzig, 1911–13). This edition consists of selections.
[2] W, III, p. 71.

direct and sole object, but it feels itself as dependent on th
totality which transcends all oppositions.

This feeling of dependence (*Abhängigkeitsgefühl*) is the 'religiou
side'[1] of self-consciousness: it is in fact 'the religious feeling'.[2] Fc
the essence of religion is 'neither thought nor action but intuitio
and feeling. It seeks to intuit the Universe. . . .'[3] And the Universe
as Schleiermacher uses the term, is the infinite divine reality
Hence religion is for him essentially or fundamentally the feelin
of dependence on the infinite.

In this case it is obviously necessary to make a sharp distinctio
between religion on the one hand and metaphysics and ethics o
the other. True, metaphysics and ethics have 'the same subject
matter as religion, namely the Universe and man's relation to it'.
But their approaches are quite different. Metaphysics, say
Schleiermacher with an obvious reference to Fichte's idealism
'spins out of itself the reality of the world and its laws'.[5] Ethic
'develops out of the nature of man and his relation to the Univers
a system of duties; it commands and prohibits actions. . . .'[6] Bu
religion is not concerned with metaphysical deduction, nor is i
concerned with using the Universe to derive a code of duties. It i
neither knowledge nor morality: it is feeling.

We can say, therefore, that Schleiermacher turns his back o
the tendency shown by Kant and Fichte to reduce religion t
morals, just as he rejects any attempt to exhibit the essence c
religion as a form of theoretical knowledge, and that he follow
Jacobi in finding the basis of faith in feeling. But there is a
important difference between Schleiermacher and Jacobi. Fc
while Jacobi grounded all knowledge on faith, Schleiermache
wishes to differentiate between theoretical knowledge an
religious faith and finds in feeling the specific basis of the latter
We can add that though for Schleiermacher the religious conscious
ness stands closer to the aesthetic consciousness than to theoretica
knowledge, the feeling on which the religious consciousness i
based, namely the feeling of dependence on the infinite, is peculia
to it. Hence Schleiermacher avoids the romantic tendency t
confuse the religious with the aesthetic consciousness.

It must not be concluded from what has been said that i
Schleiermacher's view there is no connection at all between religio
on the one hand and metaphysics and ethics on the other. On th

---

[1] *W*, III, p. 72.          [2] *Ibid*.          [3] *W*, IV, p. 240.
[4] *W*, IV, p. 235.          [5] *W*, IV, p. 236.          [6] *Ibid*.

ontrary, there is a sense in which both metaphysics and ethics tand in need of religion. Without the fundamental religious ituition of the infinite totality metaphysics would be left hanging 1 the air, as a purely conceptual construction. And ethics without eligion would give us a very inadequate idea of man. For from the urely ethical point of view man appears as the free and autonomous laster of his fate, whereas religious intuition reveals to him his ependence on the infinite Totality, on God.

Now, when Schleiermacher asserts that religious faith is grounded n the feeling of dependence on the infinite, the word 'feeling' must bviously be understood as signifying the immediacy of this onsciousness of dependence rather than as excluding any intel-ectual act. For, as we have seen, he also talks about 'intuition'. But this intuition is not an apprehension of God as a clearly-onceived object: it is a consciousness of self as essentially dependent n infinite being in an indeterminate and unconceptualized sense. Hence the feeling of dependence stands in need of interpretation on he conceptual level. And this is the task of philosophical theology. t is arguable, of course, that Schleiermacher's account of the basic eligious experience already comprises a conspicuous element of iterpretation. For turning away from the moralism of Kant and he metaphysical speculation of Fichte and inspired by the hought of 'the holy, rejected Spinoza'[1] he identifies that on which he self is felt to depend with the infinite totality, the divine Universe. 'Religion is feeling and taste for the infinite';[2] and of pinoza we can say that 'the infinite was his beginning and end; he Universe was his only and eternal love. . . .'[3] Thus the basic eligious feeling of dependence is initially described in a manner ispired by a romanticized Spinoza. At the same time the influence f Spinoza should not be overestimated. For whereas Spinoza set he 'intellectual love of God' at the summit of the mind's ascent, chleiermacher finds the feeling of dependence on the infinite at the asis of the religious view of the world. And the question arises, ow are we to think or conceive this immediate consciousness of ependence?

A difficulty immediately arises. The basic religious feeling is one f dependence on an infinite in which there are no oppositions, the elf-identical totality. But conceptual thought at once introduces istinctions and oppositions: the infinite unity falls apart into the leas of God and the world. The world is thought of as the totality

---

[1] *W*, IV, p. 243.      [2] *W*, IV, p. 242.      [3] *W*, IV, p. 243.

of all oppositions and differences, while God is conceived a simp
unity, as the existing negation of all opposition and distinction.

As conceptual thought cannot do away altogether with th
distinction to which it necessarily gives rise, it must conceive Go
and the world as correlates. That is to say, it must conceive th
relation between God and the world as one of mutual implicatic
and not as one of mere compresence, nor even as a one-wa
relation of dependence, that is, of the world's dependence on Go
'No God without the world, and no world without God.'[1] At th
same time the two ideas, namely of God and the world, must not l
identified: 'therefore neither complete identification nor comple
separation of the two ideas'.[2] In other words, as conceptual thoug
necessarily conceives the Universe through two ideas, it should no
confuse them. The unity of the Universe of being must be coi
ceived in terms of their correlation rather than of the
identification.

At first sight at least this suggests that for Schleiermacher th
distinction between God and the world exists only for huma
reflection, and that in reality there is no distinction. In point o
fact, however, Schleiermacher wishes to avoid both the reductic
of the world to God and the reduction of God to the world. On th
one hand an acosmistic theory which simply denied any reality t
the finite would be unfaithful to the basic religious consciousnes
For this would inevitably be misinterpreted by a theory which le
nothing at all of which it could be said that it was dependent. O
the other hand a simple identification of God with the spatic
temporal system of finite things would leave no room for an unde:
lying undifferentiated unity. Hence the distinction between Go
and the world must be something more than the expression of
defect in conceptual thought. True, conceptual thought is quit
unable to attain an adequate understanding of the totality, th
divine Universe. But it can and should correct its tendency t
separate completely the ideas of God and the world by conceivin
them as correlates and seeing the world as standing to God i
the relation of consequent to antecedent, as the necessary sel:
manifestation of an undifferentiated unity, or, to use Spinoza
terms, as *Natura naturata* in relation to *Natura naturans*. This i:
as it were, the best that conceptual thought can do, avoiding, tha
is to say, both complete separation and complete identificatior
The divine reality in itself transcends the reach of our concepts.

[1] *W*, III, p. 81.          [2] *W*, III, p. 86.

The really interesting and significant feature in Schleiermacher's philosophy of religion is the fact that it is for him the explicitation of a fundamental religious experience. In interpreting this experience he is obviously influenced by Spinoza. And, like Spinoza, he insists that God transcends all human categories. As God is the unity without differentiation or opposition, none of the categories of human thought, such as personality, can really apply to him. For they are bound up with finitude. At the same time God is not to be conceived as static Substance but as infinite Life which reveals itself necessarily in the world. In this respect Schleiermacher stands closer to Fichte's later philosophy than to the system of Spinoza, while the theory of God or the Absolute as the undifferentiated self-identity to which the world stands as consequent to antecedent resembles the speculations of Schelling. But Schelling's later gnosticism would hardly have met with Schleiermacher's full approval. Religion for Schleiermacher really consists in the appropriation of the basic feeling of dependence on the infinite. It is an affair of the heart rather than of the understanding, of faith rather than knowledge.

3. Though he refuses to ascribe personality to God, except in a symbolic sense, Schleiermacher lays great stress on the value of the individual personality when he is considering human beings as moral agents. The totality, the universal, is indeed immanent in all finite individuals. And for this reason sheer egoism, involving the deification of one finite self, cannot possibly be the moral ideal for man. At the same time every individual is a particular manifestation of God, and he has his own special gifts, his own particularity (*Eigentümlichkeit*). It is thus his duty to develop his individual talents. And education should be directed to the formation of fully developed and harmoniously integrated individual personalities. Man combines in himself Spirit and Nature, and his moral development requires their harmonization. From the metaphysical point of view Spirit and Nature are ultimately one. Hence the human personality cannot be properly developed if we make too sharp a distinction between, say, reason and natural impulse as to imply that morality consists in disregarding or opposing all natural impulses. The moral ideal is not conflict but harmonization and integration. In other words, Schleiermacher has little sympathy with the rigoristic morality of Kant and with his tendency to assert an antithesis between reason and inclination or impulse. If God is the positive negation, so to speak, of all differences and

oppositions, man's moral vocation involves expressing the divine nature in finite form through the harmonization in an integrated personality of reason, will and impulse.

But though Schleiermacher stresses the development of the individual personality, he also insists that individual and society are not contradictory concepts. For particularity 'exists only in relation to others'.[1] On the one hand a man's element of uniqueness, that which distinguishes him from other men, presupposes human society. On the other hand society, being a community of distinct individuals, presupposes individual differences. Hence individual and society imply one another. And self-expression or self-development demands not only the development of one's individual gifts but also respect for other personalities. In other words, every human being has a unique moral vocation, but this vocation can be fulfilled only within society, that is, by man as member of a community.

If we ask what is the relation between morality as depicted by the philosopher and specifically Christian morality, the answer is that they differ in form but not in content. The content of Christian morality cannot contradict the content of 'philosophical' morality, but it has its own form, this form being furnished by the element in the Christian consciousness which mark it off from the religious consciousness in general. And the specific note of the Christian consciousness is that 'all community with God is regarded as conditioned by Christ's redemptive act'.[2]

As regards historical religions, Schleiermacher's attitude is somewhat complex. On the one hand he rejects the idea of a universal natural religion which should be substituted for historical religions. For there are only the latter; the former is a fiction. On the other hand Schleiermacher sees in the series of historical religions the progressive revelation of an ideal which can never be grasped in its entirety. Dogmas are necessary in one sense, namely as concrete symbolic expressions of the religious consciousness. But they can at the same time become fetters preventing the free movement of the spirit. An historical religion such as Christianity owes its origin and impetus to a religious genius, analogous to an artistic genius; and its life is perpetuated by its adherents steeping themselves in the spirit of the genius and in the vital movement which stems from him rather than by subscription to a certain set of dogmas. It is true that as time went on Schleiermacher came to

[1] _W_, II, p. 92.        [2] _W_, III, p. 128.

lay more stress on the idea of the Church and on specifically Christian belief; but he was and remained what is sometimes called a liberal theologian. And as such he has exercised a very considerable influence in German Protestant circles, though this influence has been sharply challenged in recent times by the revival of Protestant orthodoxy.

4. In his attempt to interpret what he regarded as the basic religious consciousness Schleiermacher certainly attempted to develop a systematic philosophy, a coherent whole. But it can hardly be claimed that this philosophy is free from internal strains and stresses. The influence of a romanticized Spinoza, the man possessed by a passion for the infinite, impelled him in the direction of pantheism. At the same time the very nature of the fundamental feeling or intuition which he wished to interpret militated against sheer monism and demanded some distinction between God and the world. For unless we postulate some distinction, how can we sensibly speak of the finite self as conscious of its dependence on the infinite? Again, whereas the pantheistic aspects of Schleiermacher's thought were unfavourable to the admission of personal freedom, in his moral theory and in his account of the relations between human beings he needed and used the idea of freedom. In other words, the pantheistic elements in his metaphysics were offset by his emphasis on the individual in his theories of moral conduct and of society. There was no question of the theory of the divine Universe being reflected in political totalitarianism. On the contrary, quite apart from his admission of the Church as a society distinct from the State, he emphasized the concept of the 'free society', the social organization which gives free play to the expression of the unique character of each individual personality.

The strains in Schleiermacher's philosophy were not, however, peculiar to it. For any philosophy which tried to combine the idea of the divine totality with personal freedom and the idea of an ultimate identity with a full recognition of the value of the distinct finite particular was bound to find itself involved in similar difficulties. But Schleiermacher could hardly evade the problem by saying that the universal exists only in and through the particulars. For he was determined to justify the feeling of dependence on a reality which was not identifiable with the spatio-temporal world. There had to be something 'behind' the world. Yet the world could not be something outside God. Hence he was driven in the same direction taken by Schelling. Perhaps we can

say that Schleiermacher had a profound quasi-mystical consciousness of the One as underlying and expressing itself in the Many
and that this was the foundation of his philosophy. The difficulties
arose when he tried to give theoretical expression to this consciousness. But, to do him justice, he readily admitted that no adequate
theoretical account was possible. God is the object of 'feeling' and
faith rather than of knowledge. Religion is neither metaphysics
nor morals. And theology is symbolical. Schleiermacher had
indeed obvious affinities with the great idealists, but he was
certainly not a rationalist. Religion was for him the basic element
in man's spiritual life; and religion, he insisted, is grounded on the
immediate intuitive feeling of dependence. This feeling of absolute
dependence was for him the food, as it were, of philosophical
reflection. And this is not, of course, a view which can be summarily
dismissed as the amiable prejudice of a man who attributed to the
pious feelings of the heart a cosmic significance which the reflective
reason denies them. For it is at any rate arguable that speculative
metaphysics is, in part at least, a reflective explicitation of a
preliminary apprehension of the dependence of the Many on the
One, an apprehension which for want of a better word can be
described as intuitive.

### CHAPTER IX

# HEGEL (I)

*Life and writings—Early theological writings—Hegel's relations to Fichte and Schelling—The life of the Absolute and the nature of philosophy—The phenomenology of consciousness.*

1. GEORG WILHELM FRIEDRICH HEGEL, greatest of German idealists and one of the most outstanding of western philosophers, was born at Stuttgart on August 27th, 1770.[1] His father was a civil servant. In his school years at Stuttgart the future philosopher did not distinguish himself in any particular way, but it was at this period that he first felt the attraction of the Greek genius, being especially impressed by the plays of Sophocles, above all by the *Antigone*.

In 1788 Hegel enrolled as a student in the Protestant theological foundation of the University of Tübingen where he formed relations of friendship with Schelling and Hölderlin. The friends studied Rousseau together and shared a common enthusiasm for the ideals of the French Revolution. But, as at school, Hegel gave no impression of exceptional ability. And when he left the university in 1793, his certificate mentioned his good character, his fair knowledge of theology and philology and his inadequate grasp of philosophy. Hegel's mind was not precocious like Schelling's: it needed more time to mature. There is, however, another side to the picture. He had already begun to turn his attention to the relation between philosophy and theology, but he did not show his jottings or notes to his professors, who do not appear to have been remarkable in any way and in whom he doubtless did not feel much confidence.

After leaving the university Hegel gained his livelihood as a family tutor, first at Berne in Switzerland (1793-6) and then at Frankfurt (1797-1800). Though outwardly uneventful these years constituted an important period in his philosophical development. The essays which he wrote at the time were published for the first time in 1907 by Hermann Nohl under the title *Hegel's Early Theological Writings* (*Hegels theologische Jugendschriften*), and

[1] This was the year of Kant's inaugural dissertation. It was also the year of birth of Hölderlin in Germany and of Bentham and Wordsworth in England.

something will be said about their content in the next section
True, if we possessed only these essays we should not have any
idea of the philosophical system which he subsequently developed
and there would be no good reason for devoting space to him in
history of philosophy. In this sense the essays are of minor
importance. But when we look back on Hegel's early writings in
the light of our knowledge of his developed system, we can discern
a certain continuity in his problematics and understand better how
he arrived at his system and what was his leading idea. As we have
seen, the early writings have been described as 'theological'. And
though it is true that Hegel became a philosopher rather than a
theologian, his philosophy was always theology in the sense that
its subject-matter was, as he himself insisted, the same as the
subject-matter of theology, namely the Absolute or, in religious
language, God and the relation of the finite to the infinite.

In 1801 Hegel obtained a post in the University of Jena, and his
first published work, on the *Difference between the Philosophical
Systems of Fichte and Schelling* (*Differenz des Fichteschen und
Schellingschen Systems*) appeared in the same year. This work gave
the impression that he was to all intents and purposes a disciple of
Schelling. And the impression was strengthened by his collaboration
with Schelling in editing the *Critical Journal of Philosophy* (1802–3).
But Hegel's lectures at Jena, which were not published before the
present century, show that he was already working out an
independent position of his own. And his divergence from Schelling
was made clear to the public in his first great work, *The Phenomenology of Spirit* (*Die Phänomenologie des Geistes*), which appeared in
1807. Further reference to this remarkable book will be made in
the fifth section of this chapter.

After the Battle of Jena, which brought the life of the university
to a close, Hegel found himself practically destitute; and from
1807 to 1808 he edited a newspaper at Bamberg. He was appointed
rector of the *Gymnasium* at Nuremberg, a post which he held until
1816. (In 1811 he married.) As rector of the *Gymnasium* Hegel
promoted classical studies, though not, we are told, to the detriment
of study of the students' mother tongue. He also gave instruction
to his pupils in the rudiments of philosophy, though more, it
appears, out of deference to the wish of his patron Niethammer
than from any personal enthusiasm for the policy of introducing
philosophy into the school curriculum. And one imagines that most
of the pupils must have experienced great difficulty in under-

tanding Hegel's meaning. At the same time the philosopher ursued his own studies and reflections, and it was during his ojourn at Nuremberg that he produced one of his main works, the *Science of Logic* (*Wissenschaft der Logik*, 1812–16).

In the year in which the second and final volume of this work appeared Hegel received three invitations to accept a chair of philosophy, from Erlangen, Heidelberg and Berlin. He accepted the one from Heidelberg. His influence on the general body of the students does not seem to have been very great, but his reputation as a philosopher was steadily rising. And it was enhanced by the publication in 1817 of the *Encyclopaedia of the Philosophical Sciences in Outline* (*Enzyklopädie der philosophischen Wissenschaften im Grundriss*) in which he gave a conspectus of his system according to its three main divisions, logic, philosophy of Nature and philosophy of Spirit. We may also note that it was at Heidelberg that Hegel first lectured on aesthetics.

In 1818 Hegel accepted a renewed invitation to Berlin, and he occupied the chair of philosophy in the university until his death from cholera on November 14th, 1831. During this period he attained an unrivalled position in the philosophical world not only of Berlin but also of Germany as a whole. To some extent he was looked on as a kind of official philosopher. But his influence as a teacher was certainly not due to his connections with the government. Nor was it due to any outstanding gift of eloquence. As an orator he was inferior to Schelling. His influence was due rather to his evident and uncompromising devotion to pure thought, coupled with his remarkable ability for comprising a vast field within the scope and sweep of his dialectic. And his disciples felt that under his tuition the inner nature and process of reality, including the history of man, his political life and spiritual achievements, were being revealed to their understanding.

During his tenure of the chair of philosophy at Berlin Hegel published comparatively little. His *Outlines of the Philosophy of Right* (*Grundlinien der Philosophie des Rechts*) appeared in 1821, and new editions of the *Encyclopaedia* were published in 1827 and 1830. At the time of his death Hegel was revising *The Phenomenology of Spirit*. But he was, of course, lecturing during the whole of this period. And the texts of his courses, partly based on the collated notes of students, were published posthumously. In their English translations the lectures on the philosophy of art comprise four volumes, those on the philosophy of religion and on the history of philosophy three volumes each, and those on the philosophy of history one volume.

In Hölderlin's opinion Hegel was a man of calm prosaic understanding. In ordinary life at least he never gave the impression of exuberant genius. Painstaking, methodical, conscientious, sociable, he was from one point of view very much the honest *bourgeois* university professor, the worthy son of a good civil servant. At the same time he was inspired by a profound vision of the movement and significance of cosmic and human history, to the expression of which he gave his life. This is not to say that he was what is usually meant by a visionary. Appeals to mystical intuitions and to feelings were abhorrent to him, so far as philosophy at any rate was concerned. He was a firm believer in the unity of form and content. The content, truth, exists for philosophy, he was convinced, only in its systematic conceptual form. The real is the rational and the rational the real; and reality can be apprehended only in its rational reconstruction. But though Hegel had little use for philosophies which took short-cuts, as it were, by appealing to mystical insights or for philosophies which, in his opinion, aimed at edification rather than at systematic understanding, the fact remains that he presented mankind with one of the most grandiose and impressive pictures of the Universe which are to be met with in the history of philosophy. And in this sense he was a great visionary.

2. We have seen that Hegel was attracted by the Greek genius while he was still at school. And at the university this attraction exercised a marked influence on his attitude towards the Christian religion. The theology which he heard from his professors at Tübingen was for the most part Christianity adapted to the ideas of the Enlightenment, that is to say, rationalistic theism with a certain infusion of or tincture of Biblical supernaturalism. But this religion of the understanding, as Hegel described it, seemed to him to be not only arid and barren but also divorced from the spirit and needs of his generation. And he contrasted it unfavourably with Greek religion which was rooted in the spirit of the Greek people and formed an integral part of their culture. Christianity is, he thought, a book-religion, and the book in question, namely the Bible, is the product of an alien race and out of harmony with the Germanic soul. Hegel was not, of course, proposing a literal substitute of Greek religion for Christianity. His point was that Greek religion was a *Volksreligion*, a religion

intimately related to the spirit and genius of the people and forming an element of this people's culture, whereas Christianity, at least as presented to him by his professors, was something imposed from without. Moreover, Christianity was, he thought, hostile to human happiness and liberty and indifferent to beauty.

This expression of Hegel's early enthusiasm for the Greek genius and culture was soon modified by his study of Kant. While not abandoning his admiration for the Greek spirit, he came to regard it as lacking in moral profundity. In his opinion this element of moral profundity and earnestness had been supplied by Kant who had at the same time expounded an ethical religion which was free from the burdens of dogma and Bible-worship. Obviously, Hegel did not mean to imply that mankind had to wait till the time of Kant for the appearance of moral profundity. On the contrary, he attributed a Kantian-like emphasis on morality to the Founder of Christianity. And in his *Life of Jesus* (*Das Leben Jesu*, 1795), which was written while he was a family tutor at Berne, he depicted Christ as being exclusively a moral teacher and almost as an expounder of the Kantian ethics. True, Christ insisted on his personal mission; but according to Hegel he was forced to do so simply because the Jews were accustomed to think of all religions and moral insights as revealed, as coming from a divine source. Hence to persuade the Jews to listen to him at all Christ had to represent himself as the legate or messenger of God. But it was not really his intention either to make himself the unique mediator between God and man or to impose revealed dogmas.

How, then, did Christianity become transformed into an authoritarian, ecclesiastical and dogmatic system? Hegel considered this question in *The Positivity of the Christian Religion* (*Die Positivität der christlichen Religion*), the first two parts of which were composed in 1795–6 and the third somewhat later, in 1798–9. As one would expect, the transformation of Christianity is attributed in large part to the apostles and other disciples of Christ. And the result of the transformation is depicted as the alienation of man from his true self. Through the imposition of dogmas liberty of thought was lost, and through the idea of a moral law imposed from without moral liberty perished. Further, man was regarded as alienated from God. He could be reconciled only by faith and, in Catholicism at least, by the sacraments of the Church.

During his Frankfurt period, however, Hegel's attitude towards

Christianity underwent a certain change, which found expression in *The Spirit of Christianity and Its Fate* (*Der Geist des Christentums und sein Schicksal*, 1800). In this essay Judaism with its legalistic morality becomes the villain of the piece. For the Jew God was the master and man the slave who had to carry out his master's will. For Christ God is love, living in man; and the alienation of man from God, as of man from man, is overcome by the union and life of love. Kant's insistence on law and duty and the emphasis which he lays on the overcoming of passion and impulse seem now to Hegel to express an inadequate notion of morality and to smack in their own way of the master-slave relationship which was characteristic of the Jewish outlook. Christ, however, rises above both Jewish legalism and Kantian moralism. He recognizes, of course, the moral struggle, but his ideal is that morality should cease to be a matter of obedience to law and should become the spontaneous expression of a life which is itself a participation in the infinite divine life. Christ does not abrogate morality in regard to its content, but he strips it of its legal form, substituting the motive of love for that of obedience to law.

It will be noted that Hegel's attention is already directed to the themes of alienation and to the recovery of a lost unity. At the time when he was contrasting Christianity with Greek religion to the detriment of the former he was already dissatisfied with any view of the divine reality as a remote and purely transcendent being. In the poem entitled *Eleusis* which he wrote at the end of his sojourn at Berne and which he dedicated to Hölderlin he expressed his feeling for the infinite Totality. And at Frankfurt he represented Christ as preaching the overcoming of the gulf between man and God, the infinite and the finite, by the life of love. The Absolute is infinite life, and love is the consciousness of the unity of this life, of unity with the infinite life itself and of unity with other men through this life.

In 1800, while still at Frankfurt, Hegel wrote some notes to which Hermann Nohl gave the title *Fragment of a System* (*Systemfragment*). For on the strength of an allusion in a letter from Hegel to Schelling, Nohl and Dilthey thought that the extant notes represented the sketch of a completed system. This conclusion seems to be based on somewhat insufficient evidence, at least if the word 'system' is understood in terms of Hegel's developed philosophy. At the same time the notes are of considerable interest, and deserve some mention.

Hegel is grappling with the problem of overcoming oppositions
r antitheses, above all the opposition between the finite and the
ifinite. If we put ourselves in the position of spectators, the
iovement of life appears to us an infinite organized multiplicity of
nite individuals, that is, as Nature. Indeed, Nature can well be
escribed as life posited for reflection or understanding. But the
idividual things, the organization of which is Nature, are
ransitory and perishing. Thought, therefore, which is itself a form
f life, thinks the unity between things as an infinite, creative life
hich is free from the mortality which affects finite individuals.
nd this creative life, which is conceived as bearing the manifold
ithin itself and not as a mere conceptual abstraction, is called
od. It must also be defined as Spirit (*Geist*). For it is neither an
xternal link between finite things nor the purely abstract concept
f life, an abstract universal. Infinite life unites all finite things
rom within, as it were, but without annihilating them. It is the
iving unity of the manifold.

Hegel thus introduces a term, namely Spirit, which is of great
mportance in his developed philosophy. But the question arises
vhether we are able by conceptual thought so to unify the infinite
nd the finite that neither term is dissolved in the other while at
he same time they are truly united. And in the so-called *Fragment
f a System* Hegel maintains that it is not possible. That is to say,
n denying the gulf between finite and infinite conceptual thought
nevitably tends to merge them without distinction or to reduce
he one to the other, while if it affirms their unity it inevitably
ends to deny their distinction. We can see the necessity for a
ynthesis in which unity does not exclude distinction, but we cannot
eally think it. The unification of the Many within the One without
he former's dissolution can be achieved only by living it, that is,
oy man's self-elevation from finite to infinite life. And this living
process is religion.

It follows from this that philosophy stops short of religion, and
hat in this sense it is subordinate to religion. Philosophy shows us
what is demanded if the opposition between finite and infinite is to
oe overcome, but it cannot itself fulfil this demand. For its fulfil-
nent we have to turn to religion, that is, to the Christian religion.
The Jews objectified God as a being set over above and outside the
inite. And this is the wrong idea of the infinite, a 'bad' infinity.
Christ, however, discovered the infinite life within himself as
source of his thought and action. And this is the right idea of the

infinite, namely as immanent in the finite and as comprising th
finite within itself. But this synthesis can only be lived as Chris
lived it: it is the life of love. The organ of mediation betwee
finite and infinite is love, not reflection. True, there is a passag
where Hegel foreshadows his later dialectical method, but h
asserts at the same time that the complete synthesis transcend
reflection.

Yet if it is presupposed that philosophy demands the over
coming of the oppositions which it posits, it is only to be expecte
that philosophy will itself try to fulfil this demand. And even if w
say that the life of love, the religious life, fulfils the demand
philosophy will attempt to understand what religion does and ho
it does it. It is thus not surprising if Hegel soon tries to accomplis
by reflection what he had previously declared to be impossible
And what he requires for the fulfilment of this task is a new forn
of logic, a logic which is able to follow the movement of life an
does not leave opposed concepts in irremediable opposition. Th
adoption of this new logic signifies the transition from Hegel th
theologian to Hegel the philosopher or, better, from the view tha
religion is supreme and that philosophy stops short of it to the view
that speculative philosophy is the supreme truth. But the problen
remains the same, namely the relation of the finite to the infinite
And so does the idea of the infinite as Spirit.

3. Some six months after his arrival at Jena Hegel published hi
work on the *Difference between the Philosophical Systems of Ficht
and Schelling* (1801). Its immediate aim was twofold; first to sho
that these systems really were different and not, as some peopl
supposed, the same, and secondly to show that the system o
Schelling represented an advance on that of Fichte. But Hegel'
discussion of these topics naturally leads him into general reflection
on the nature and purpose of philosophy.

The fundamental purpose of philosophy, Hegel maintains, i
that of overcoming oppositions and divisions. 'Division [*Entz
weiung*] is the source of *the need of philosophy*.'[1] In the world o
experience the mind finds differences, oppositions, apparen
contradictions, and it seeks to construct a unified whole, to over
come the splintered harmony, as Hegel puts it. True, division and
opposition present themselves to the mind in different forms ir
different cultural epochs. And this helps to explain the peculia

---

[1] *W*, I, p. 44. Unless otherwise stated, references to Hegel's writings will be give
according to volume and page of the jubilee edition of his *Works* by Hermann
Glockner (26 vols., Stuttgart, 1928).

haracteristics of different systems. At one time the mind is
onfronted, for instance, with the problem of the division and
pposition between soul and body, while at another time the same
ort of problem presents itself as that of the relation between
ubject and object, intelligence and Nature. But in whatever
particular way or ways the problem may present itself, the
undamental interest of reason (*Vernunft*) is the same, namely to
ttain a unified synthesis.

This means in effect that 'the Absolute is to be constructed for
onsciousness; such is the task of philosophy'.[1] For the synthesis
must in the long run involve reality as a whole. And it must
overcome the basic opposition between the finite and the infinite,
ot by denying all reality to the finite, not by reducing the
nfinite to the multiplicity of finite particulars as such, but by
ntegrating, as it were, the finite into the infinite.

But a difficulty at once arises. If the life of the Absolute is to be
onstructed by philosophy, the instrument will be reflection. Left
o itself, however, reflection tends to function as understanding
*Verstand*) and thus to posit and perpetuate oppositions. It must
herefore be united with transcendental intuition which discovers
he interpenetration of the ideal and the real, idea and being,
ubject and object. Reflection is then raised to the level of reason
*Vernunft*), and we have a speculative knowledge which 'must be
onceived as identity of reflection and intuition'.[2] Hegel is
evidently writing under the influence of Schelling's ideas.

Now, in the Kantian system, as Hegel sees it, we are repeatedly
onfronted with unreconciled dualisms or oppositions, between
phenomena and noumena, sensibility and understanding, and so
on. Hegel shows therefore a lively sympathy with Fichte's attempt
o remedy this state of affairs. He entirely agrees, for instance,
with Fichte's elimination of the unknowable thing-in-itself, and
egards his system as an important essay in genuine philosophizing.
The absolute principle, the one real foundation and firm standpoint of philosophy is, in the philosophy of Fichte as in that of
Schelling, intellectual intuition or, in the language of reflection,
he identity of subject and object. In science this intuition becomes
he object of reflection, and philosophical reflection is thus itself
ranscendental intuition which makes itself its own object and is
one with it. Hence it is speculation. Fichte's philosophy, therefore,
is a genuine product of speculation.'[3]

[1] *W*, I, p. 50.      [2] *W*, I, p. 69.      [3] *W*, I, pp. 143-4.

But though Fichte sees that the presupposition of speculativ
philosophy is an ultimate unity and starts with the principle o
identity, 'the principle of identity is not the principle of th
system: directly the construction of the system begins, identit
disappears'.[1] In the theoretical deduction of consciousness it i
only the idea of the objective world which is deduced, not the worl
itself. We are left simply with subjectivity. In the practice
deduction we are indeed presented with a real world, but Nature i
posited only as the opposite of the ego. In other words, we are le
with an unresolved dualism.

With Schelling, however, the situation is very different. Fo
'the principle of identity is the absolute principle of the whol
system of Schelling. Philosophy and system coincide: identity i
not lost in the parts, and much less in the result.'[2] That is to say
Schelling starts with the idea of the Absolute as the identity c
subjectivity and objectivity, and it persists as the guiding-idea c
the parts of the system. In the philosophy of Nature Schellin
shows that Nature is not simply the opposite of the ideal but tha
though real, it is also ideal through and through: it is visible Spiri
In the system of transcendental idealism he shows how subjectivit
objectifies itself, how the ideal is also the real. The principle c
identity is thus maintained throughout the whole system.

In his works on the systems of Fichte and Schelling there ar
indeed signs of Hegel's divergence from Schelling. For instance, i
is clear that intellectual intuition does not mean for him a mystica
intuition of a dark and impenetrable abyss, the vanishing-poin
of all differences, but rather reason's insight into antitheses a
moments in the one all-comprehensive life of the Absolute. But a
the work is designed to illustrate the superiority of Schelling'
system to that of Fichte, Hegel naturally does not make explici
his points of divergence from the former's thought. The indepen
dence of his own standpoint is, however, clearly revealed in th
lectures of his Jena period.

In the Jena lectures Hegel argues, for example, that if finite an
infinite are set over against one another as opposed concepts, ther
is no passage from one to the other. A synthesis is impossible. Bu
in point of fact we cannot think the finite without thinking th
infinite: the concept of the finite is not a self-contained an
isolated concept. The finite is limited by what is other than itsel
In Hegel's language, it is affected by negation. But the finite is no

[1] *W*, I, p. 122.          [2] *Ibid.*

imply negation. Hence we must negate the negation. And in
doing so we affirm that the finite is more than finite. That is to say,
it is a moment in the life of the infinite. And from this it follows
that to construct the life of the Absolute, which is the task of
philosophy, is to construct it in and through the finite, showing
how the Absolute necessarily expresses itself as Spirit, as self-
consciousness, in and through the human mind. For the human
mind, though finite, is at the same time more than finite and can
attain the standpoint at which it is the vehicle, as it were, of the
Absolute's knowledge of itself.

To a certain extent, of course, this is in harmony with Schelling's
philosophy. But there is also a major difference. For Schelling the
Absolute in itself transcends conceptual thought, and we must
approach the absolute identity by the *via negativa*, thinking away
the attributes and distinctions of the finite.[1] For Hegel the
Absolute is not an identity about which nothing further can be
said: it is the total process of its self-expression or self-manifestation in and through the finite. It is not surprising, therefore, to
find in the Preface to *The Phenomenology of Spirit* a sharp rejection
of Schelling's view of the Absolute. True, Schelling is not mentioned
by name, but the reference is clear enough. It was clear to Schelling
himself, who felt deeply wounded. Hegel speaks of a monotonous
formalism and abstract universality which are said to constitute
the Absolute. All the emphasis is placed on the universal in the
bare form of identity. 'And we see speculative contemplation
identified with the dissolution of the distinct and determinate, or
rather with hurling it down, without more ado and without
justification, into the abyss of vacuity.'[2] To consider a thing as in
the Absolute is taken to mean considering it as dissolved in an
undifferentiated self-identical unity. But 'to pit this one piece of
knowledge, namely that in the Absolute all is one, against
determinate and complete knowledge or knowledge which at least
seeks and demands completion—to proclaim the *Absolute* as the
night in which, as we say, all cows are black—this is the naïvety of
empty knowledge'.[3] It is not by plunging ourselves into a mystical

---

[1] Needless to say, the reference is to Schelling's philosophical ideas in the first
years of the nineteenth century.
[2] *W*, II, p. 21; *B*, p. 79. In references, as here, to *The Phenomenology of Spirit*
*B* signifies the English translation of this work by J. B. Baillie. But it does not
necessarily follow that the present writer has followed this translation. The like
holds good of other such references to standard English translations, which are
included for the convenience of readers.
[3] *W*, II, p. 22; *B*, p. 79.

night that we can come to know the Absolute. We come to know
only by understanding a determinate content, the self-developing
life of the Absolute in Nature and Spirit. True, in his philosophy of
Nature and in his system of transcendental idealism Schelling
considered determinate contents, and in regard to these content
he attempted a systematic demonstration of the identity of the
ideal and the real. But he conceived the Absolute in itself as being,
for conceptual thought at least, a blank identity, a vanishing-point
of all differences, whereas for Hegel the Absolute is not an
impenetrable reality existing, as it were, above and behind its
determinate manifestations: it *is* its self-manifestation.

4. This point is of great importance for understanding Hegel.
The subject-matter of philosophy is indeed the Absolute. But the
Absolute is the Totality, reality as a whole, the universe. 'Philosophy
is concerned with the true and the true is the whole.'[1] Further,
this totality or whole is infinite life, a process of self-development.
The Absolute is 'the process of its own becoming, the circle which
presupposes its end as its purpose and has its end as its beginning.
It becomes concrete or actual only by its development and through
its end.'[2] In other words, reality is a teleological process; and the
ideal term presupposes the whole process and gives to it its
significance. Indeed we can say that the Absolute is 'essentially a
result'.[3] For if we look on the whole process as the self-unfolding of
an essence, the actualization of an eternal Idea, we can see that it
is the term or end of the process which reveals what the Absolute
really is. True, the whole process is the Absolute; but in a teleological process it is the *telos* or end which shows its nature, its
meaning. And philosophy must take the form of a systematic
understanding of this teleological process. 'The true form in which
truth exists can only be the scientific system of the same.'[4]

Now, if we say that the Absolute is the whole of reality, the
Universe, it may seem that we are committed to Spinozism, to the
statement that the Absolute is infinite Substance. But this is for
Hegel a very inadequate description of the Absolute. 'In my view
—a view which can be justified only through the exposition of the
system itself—everything depends on grasping the true not merely
as *Substance* but as *Subject* as well.'[5] But if the Absolute is subject,
what is its object? The only possible answer is that its object is
itself. In this case it is Thought which thinks itself, self-thinking

[1] *W*, II, p. 24; *B*, p. 81.          [2] *W*, II, p. 23; *B*, p. 81.
[3] *W*, II, p. 24; *B*, p. 81.          [4] *W*, II, p. 14; *B*, p. 70.
[5] *W*, II, p. 22; *B*, p. 80.

hought. And to say this is to say that the Absolute is Spirit, the
nfinite self-luminous or self-conscious subject. The statement that
he Absolute is Spirit is for Hegel its supreme definition.

In saying that the Absolute is self-thinking Thought Hegel is
bviously repeating Aristotle's definition of God, a fact of which he
s, of course, well aware. But it would be a great mistake to assume
hat Hegel is thinking of a transcendent Deity. The Absolute is,
s we have seen, the Totality, the whole of reality; and this totality
s a process. In other words, the Absolute is a process of self-
eflection: reality comes to know itself. And it does so in and
hrough the human spirit. Nature is a necessary precondition of
uman consciousness in general: it provides the sphere of the
bjective without which the sphere of the subjective cannot exist.
3ut both are moments in the life of the Absolute. In Nature the
Absolute goes over into, as it were, or expresses itself in objectivity.
There is no question with Hegel of Nature being unreal or merely
dea in a subjectivist sense. In the sphere of human consciousness
he Absolute returns to itself, that is, as Spirit. And the philo-
ophical reflection of humanity is the Absolute's self-knowledge.
That is to say, the history of philosophy is the process by which the
Absolute, reality as a whole, comes to think itself. Philosophical
eason comes to see the whole history of the cosmos and the whole
istory of man as the self-unfolding of the Absolute. And this
nsight is the Absolute's knowledge of itself.

One can put the matter in this way. Hegel agrees with Aristotle
hat God is self-thinking Thought,[1] and that this self-thinking
Thought is the *telos* or end which draws the world as its final cause.
3ut whereas the self-thinking Thought of Aristotle is, so to speak,
n already constituted self-consciousness which does not depend
n the world, the self-thinking Thought of Hegel is not a trans-
endent reality but rather the universe's knowledge of itself. The
vhole process of reality is a teleological movement towards the
ctualization of self-thinking Thought; and in this sense the
Thought which thinks itself is the *telos* or end of the universe. But
t is an end which is immanent within the process. The Absolute,
he universe or totality, is indeed definable as self-thinking Thought.
3ut it is Thought which comes to think itself. And in this sense we
an say, as Hegel says, that the Absolute is essentially a result.

To say, therefore, that the Absolute is self-thinking Thought is

[1] Hegel frequently speaks of the Absolute as 'God'. But it does not necessarily
ollow from his use of religious language that he looks on the Absolute as a
ersonal Deity in the theistic sense. This question will be discussed later.

to affirm the identity of the ideal and the real, of subjectivity and objectivity. But this is an identity-in-difference, not a blank undifferentiated identity. Spirit sees itself in Nature: it sees Nature as the objective manifestation of the Absolute, a manifestation which is a necessary condition for its own existence. In other words, the Absolute knows itself as the Totality, as the whole process of its becoming; but at the same time it sees the distinction between the phases of its own life. It knows itself as an identity-in-difference, as the unity which comprises distinguishable phases within itself.

As we have seen, the task of philosophy is to construct the life of the Absolute. That is to say, it must exhibit systematically the rational dynamic structure, the teleological process or movement of the cosmic Reason, in Nature and the sphere of the human spirit, which culminates in the Absolute's knowledge of itself. It is not, of course, a question of philosophy trying to do over again or to do better, the work accomplished by empirical science or by history. Such knowledge is presupposed. Rather is it philosophy's task to make clear the basic teleological process which is immanent in the material known in other ways, the process which gives to this material its metaphysical significance. In other words philosophy has to exhibit systematically the self-realization of infinite Reason in and through the finite.

Now if, as Hegel believes, the rational is the real and the real the rational, in the sense that reality is the necessary process by which infinite Reason, the self-thinking Thought, actualizes itself, we can say that Nature and the sphere of the human spirit are the field in which an eternal Idea or an eternal essence manifests itself. That is to say, we can make a distinction between the Idea or essence which is actualized and the field of its actualization. We then have the picture of the eternal Idea or *Logos* manifesting itself in Nature and in Spirit. In Nature the *Logos* goes over, as it were, into objectivity, into the material world, which is its antithesis. In Spirit (the sphere of the human spirit) the *Logos* returns to itself, in the sense that it manifests itself as what it essentially is. The life of the Absolute thus comprises three main phases: the logical Idea or Concept or Notion,[1] Nature and Spirit. And the system of philosophy will fall into three main parts: logic,

[1] The word 'Idea' can have different shades of meaning with Hegel. It may refer to the logical Idea, otherwise called the Concept (*Begriff*) or Notion. It may refer to the whole process of reality, as the actualization of the Idea. Or it may refer primarily to the term of the process.

which for Hegel is metaphysics in the sense that it studies the nature of the Absolute 'in itself', the philosophy of Nature and the philosophy of Spirit. These three parts together form the philosophical construction of the life of the Absolute.

Obviously, if we talk about the eternal Idea 'manifesting itself' in Nature and Spirit, we imply that the *Logos* possesses an ontological status of its own, independently of things. And when Hegel uses, as he so frequently does, the language of religion and speaks of the logical Idea as God-in-himself, he inevitably tends to give the impression that the *Logos* is for him a transcendent reality which manifests itself externally in Nature. But such use of religious language does not necessarily justify this conclusion about his meaning. However, I do not wish to discuss this disputed problem here. For the moment we can leave undecided the question whether or not the self-thinking Thought which forms the culminating category of Hegel's logic can properly be said to exist, that is, independently of the finite. It is sufficient to have noticed the three main parts of philosophy, each of which is concerned with the Absolute. Logic studies the Absolute 'in itself'; the philosophy of Nature studies the Absolute 'for itself'; and the philosophy of Spirit studies the Absolute 'in and for itself'. Together they constitute the complete construction of the life of the Absolute.

Philosophy must, of course, exhibit this life in conceptual form. There is no other form in which it can present it. And if the life of the Absolute is a necessary process of self-actualization, this necessity must be reflected in the philosophical system. That is to say, it must be shown that concept *A* gives rise to concept *B*. And if the Absolute is the Totality, philosophy must be a self-contained system, exhibiting the fact that the Absolute is both Alpha and Omega. A truly adequate philosophy would be the total system of truth, the whole truth, the perfect conceptual reflection of the life of the Absolute. It would in fact be the Absolute's knowledge of itself in and through the human mind; it would be the self-mediation of the Totality. Hence, on Hegelian principles, there would be no question of comparing the absolute philosophy with the Absolute, as though the former were a purely external account of the latter, so that we had to compare them to see whether the philosophy fitted the reality which it described. For the absolute philosophy would *be* the Absolute's knowledge of itself.

But if we say that philosophy must exhibit the life of the Absolute

in conceptual form, a difficulty at once arises. The Absolute is, as
we have seen, identity-in-difference. For instance, it is the
identity-in-difference of the infinite and the finite, of the One and
the Many. But the concepts of infinite and finite, as of the One
and the Many, seem to be mutually exclusive. If, therefore,
philosophy operates with clearly-defined concepts, how can it
possibly construct the life of the Absolute? And if it operates with
vague, ill-defined concepts, how can it be an apt instrument for
understanding anything? Would it not be better to say with
Schelling that the Absolute transcends conceptual thought?

In Hegel's view this difficulty does indeed arise on the level of
understanding (*Verstand*). For understanding posits and perpetu-
ates fixed static concepts of such a kind that it cannot itself
overcome the oppositions which it posits. To take the same example
which has already been given, for understanding the concepts of
the finite and the infinite are irrevocably opposed. If finite, then
not infinite: if infinite, then not finite. But the conclusion to be
drawn is that understanding is an inadequate instrument for the
development of speculative philosophy, not that philosophy is
impossible. Obviously, if the term 'understanding' is taken in a
wide sense, philosophy is understanding. But if the term is taken
in the narrow sense of *Verstand*, the mind, functioning in this way,
is unable to produce the understanding (in the wide sense) which
is, or ought to be, characteristic of philosophy.

Hegel has, of course, no intention of denying that understanding,
in the sense of the mind operating as *Verstand*, has its uses in
human life. For practical purposes it is often important to maintain
clear-cut concepts and oppositions. The opposition between the
real and the apparent might be a case in point. Moreover, a great
deal of scientific work, such as mathematics, is based on *Verstand*.
But it is a different matter when the mind is trying to grasp the
life of the Absolute, the identity-in-difference. It cannot then
remain content with the level of understanding, which for Hegel is
a superficial level. It must penetrate deeper into the concepts
which are categories of reality, and it will then see how a given
concept tends to pass over into or to call forth its opposite. For
example, if the mind really thinks through, so to speak, the concept
of the infinite, it sees it losing its rigid self-containedness and the
concept of the infinite emerging. Similarly, if the mind really
thinks through the concept of reality as opposed to appearance, it
will see the absurd or 'contradictory' character of a reality which

n no way at all appears or manifests itself. Again, for common sense and practical life one thing is distinct from all other things; it is self-identical and negates all other things. And so long as we are not concerned with thinking what this really means, the idea has its practical uses. But once we really try to think it, we see the absurdity of the notion of a completely isolated thing, and we are forced to negate the original negation.

Thus in speculative philosophy the mind must elevate itself from the level of understanding in the narrow sense to the level of dialectical thinking which overcomes the rigidity of the concepts of the understanding and sees one concept as generating or passing into its opposite. Only so can it hope to grasp the life of the Absolute in which one moment or phase passes necessarily into another. But this is obviously not enough. If for the understanding concepts *A* and *B* are irrevocably opposed whereas for the deeper penetration of dialectical thought *A* passes into *B* and *B* into *A*, there must be a higher unity or synthesis which unites them without annulling their difference. And it is the function of reason (*Vernunft*) to grasp this moment of identity-in-difference. Hence philosophy demands the elevation of understanding through dialectical thinking to the level of reason or speculative thought which is capable of apprehending identity-in-difference.[1]

It is perhaps unnecessary to add that from Hegel's point of view it is not a question of producing a new species of logic out of the hat to enable him to establish an arbitrarily preconceived view of reality. For he sincerely believes that dialectical thought gives a deeper penetration of the nature of reality than understanding in the narrow sense can possibly do. For example, it is not for Hegel a question of insisting that the concept of the finite must pass over into or call forth the concept of the infinite simply because of a preconceived belief that the infinite exists in and through the finite. For it is his conviction that we cannot really think the finite without relating it to the infinite. It is not we who do something to the concept, juggling about with it, as it were: it is the concept itself which loses its rigidity and breaks up before the mind's attentive gaze. And this fact reveals to us the nature of the finite: it has a metaphysical significance.

[1] The terms 'understanding' and 'reason' are not used in precisely the same ways by Kant and Hegel. This fact apart, however, the contrast between Kant's mistrust of the flights of reason, coupled with his admission of its practical function, and Hegel's depreciation of understanding, coupled with a recognition of its practical use, well illustrates their respective attitudes to speculative metaphysics.

In his account of dialectical thinking Hegel makes a rather disconcerting use of the word 'contradiction'. Through what he calls the power of the negative a concept of the understanding is said to give rise to a contradiction. That is to say, the contradiction implicit in the concept becomes explicit when the concept loses its rigidity and self-containedness and passes into its opposite. Further, Hegel does not hesitate to speak as though contradictions are present not only in conceptual thought or discourse about the world but in things themselves. And indeed this must be so in some sense if the dialectic mirrors the life of the Absolute. Moreover, this insistence on the role of contradiction is not simply incidental to Hegel's thought. For the emergence of contradiction is the motive force, as it were, of the dialectical movement. The conflict of opposed concepts and the resolution of the conflict in a synthesis which itself gives rise to another contradiction is the feature which drives the mind restlessly onwards towards an ideal term, an all-embracing synthesis, the complete system of truth. And, as we have noted, this does not mean that contradiction and conflict are confined to discourse about reality. When philosophy considers, for example, the history of man, it discovers a dialectical movement at work.

This use of the word 'contradiction' has led some critics of Hegel to accuse him of denying the logical principle of non-contradiction by saying that contradictory notions or propositions can stand together. And in refutation of this charge it has often been pointed out that for Hegel it is precisely the impossibility of being satisfied with a sheer contradiction which forces the mind onwards to a synthesis in which the contradiction is overcome. This answer, however, lays itself open to the retort that Hegel does not share Fichte's tendency to argue that the contradictions or antinomies which arise in the course of dialectical thinking are merely apparent. On the contrary, he insists on their reality. And in the syntheses the so-called contradictory concepts are preserved. In turn, however, it can be replied that though the concepts are preserved, they are not preserved in a relation of mutual exclusiveness. For they are shown to be essential and complementary moments in a higher unity. And in this sense the contradiction is resolved. Hence the simple assertion that Hegel denies the principle of non-contradiction gives a quite inaccurate view of the situation. What Hegel does is to give a dynamic interpretation of the principle in place of the static interpretation which is

haracteristic of the level of understanding. The principle
perates in dialectical thinking, but it operates as a principle of
lovement.

This discussion might be prolonged. But it would be pointless to
o so without first inquiring in what sense Hegel actually under-
tands the term 'contradiction' when he is engaged in working out
is dialectical philosophy rather than in talking abstractly about
ialectical thought. And it is a notorious fact that the result of such
n inquiry is to show that there is no single precise and invariable
ense in which Hegel uses the term. Occasionally indeed we find a
erbal contradiction. Thus the concept of Being is said to give rise
o and pass into the concept of Not-being, while the concept of
Iot-being passes into the concept of Being. And this dialectical
scillation gives rise to the concept of Becoming which synthesizes
Ieing and Not-being. But, as will be seen in the section on Hegel's
ogic in the next chapter, the meaning of this dialectical performance
s easily intelligible, whether we agree or not with what Hegel has
o say. In any case Hegel's so-called contradictions are much more
ften contraries than contradictions. And the idea is that one
ontrary demands the other, an idea which, whether true or false,
oes not amount to a denial of the principle of non-contradiction.
gain, the so-called contradictory or opposed concepts may be
imply complementary concepts. A one-sided abstraction evokes
nother one-sided abstraction. And the one-sidedness of each is
vercome in the synthesis. Further, the statement that every thing
s contradictory sometimes bears the meaning that a thing in a
tate of complete isolation, apart from its essential relations,
rould be impossible and 'contradictory'. Reason cannot remain in
he idea of a completely isolated finite thing. Here again there is no
uestion of denying the principle of non-contradiction.

We have used the word 'synthesis' for the moment of identity-
n-difference in the dialectical advance. But in point of fact the
erms 'thesis', 'antithesis' and 'synthesis' are more characteristic
f Fichte than of Hegel, who seldom uses them. At the same time
he most cursory inspection of the Hegelian system reveals his
reoccupation with triads. Thus there are three main phases in the
onstruction of the life of the Absolute: the logical Idea, Nature
nd Spirit. And each phase is divided and subdivided into triads.
Ioreover, the whole system is, or aims at, a necessary develop-
lent. That is to say, for philosophical reflection one stage reveals
self as demanding the next by an inner necessity. Thus, in theory

at least, if we start with the first category of the *Logic*, the inner
necessity of dialectical development forces the mind to proceed
not simply to the final category of the *Logic* but also to the
ultimate phase of the philosophy of Spirit.

As for Hegel's preoccupation with triadic development, we may
think that it is unnecessary and that it sometimes produces highly
artificial results, but we obviously have to accept it as a fact. But
though it is a fact that he develops his system according to this
pattern, it obviously does not follow that the development always
possesses the character of necessity which Hegel implies that it
ought to have. And if it does not, this is easily understandable. For
when Hegel is concerned, for example, with the life of the Spirit in
art or in religion, he is faced with a multitude of historical data
which he takes over, as it were, from the relevant sources and
which he then interprets according to a dialectical pattern. And it
is clear that there might be various possible ways of grouping and
interpreting the data, no one of which was strictly necessary. The
discovery of the best way will be a matter of reflection and insight
rather than of strict deduction. To say this is not necessarily to
condemn Hegel's practice. For in point of fact his interpretations
of vast masses of data can sometimes be illuminating and are often
stimulating even when we do not agree with them. At the same
time the transitions between the stages of his dialectic are by no
means always of the logical type suggested by his claim that
philosophy is a necessary deductive system, even if the persistent
observance of the same external pattern, namely the triadic
arrangement, tends to obscure the underlying complexity.

Of course, when Hegel claims that philosophy is or ought to be
a necessary deductive system, he does not really mean that it is
the sort of deductive system which could be worked out by a
machine. If it were, then it would belong to the sphere of understanding rather than to that of reason. Philosophy is concerned
with the life of absolute Spirit, and to discern the unfolding of this
life in, say, human history, *a priori* deduction is obviously not
enough. The empirical material cannot be supplied by philosophy,
though philosophy discerns the teleological pattern which works
itself out in this material. At the same time the whole dialectical
movement of the Hegelian system should, in theory at least,
impose itself on the mind by its own inner necessity. Otherwise the
system could hardly be, as Hegel claims that it is, its own justification. Yet it is clear that Hegel comes to philosophy with certain

asic convictions; that the rational is the real and the real the
ational, that reality is the self-manifestation of infinite reason,
nd that infinite reason is self-thinking Thought which actualizes
tself in the historical process. True, it is Hegel's contention that
he truth of these convictions is demonstrated in the system. But it
s arguable that the system really depends upon them, and that
his is one of the main reasons why those who do not share, or at
east are not sympathetically disposed towards, Hegel's initial
onvictions are not much impressed by what we may call his
mpirical confirmation of his general metaphysical scheme. For it
eems to them that his interpretations of the material are governed
y a preconceived scheme, and that even if the system is a
emarkable intellectual *tour de force*, it demonstrates at best only
n what lines we must interpret the various aspects of reality if
ve have already made up our minds that reality as a whole is of a
ertain nature. This criticism would indeed be invalidated if the
ystem really showed that Hegel's interpretation of the process of
eality was the only interpretation which satisfied the demands of
eason. But it may well be doubted whether this can be shown
vithout giving to the word 'reason' a meaning which would beg the
vhole question.

One might perhaps neglect or pass over Hegel's theory of the
ecessity inherent in the dialectical development of the system and
iew his philosophy simply as one of the possible ways of satisfying
he mind's impulse to obtain conceptual mastery over the whole
vealth of empirical data or to interpret the world as a whole and
nan's relation to it. And we could then compare it with other
arge-scale interpretations or visions of the universe and try to find
riteria for judging between them. But though this procedure may
eem eminently reasonable to many people, it does not square with
Iegel's own estimation of his own philosophy. For even if he did
ot think that his presentation of the system of philosophy was the
vhole truth in its final form, he certainly thought that it represented
he highest stage which the Absolute's developing knowledge of
tself had reached up to date.

This may seem to be an extremely bizarre notion. But we have
o bear in mind Hegel's view of the Absolute as identity-in-
ifference. The infinite exists in and through the finite, and infinite
Reason or Spirit knows itself in and through the finite spirit or
nind. But it is not every sort of thinking by the finite mind which
an be said to form a moment in the developing self-knowledge of

the infinite Absolute. It is man's knowledge of the Absolute which is the Absolute's knowledge of itself. Yet we cannot say of any finite mind's knowledge of the Absolute that it is identical with the Absolute's knowledge of itself. For the latter transcends any given finite mind or set of finite minds. Plato and Aristotle, for example, are dead. But according to Hegel's interpretation of the history of philosophy the essential elements in their respective apprehensions of reality were taken up into and persist in the total dialectical movement of philosophy through the centuries. And it is this developing movement which is the Absolute's developing knowledge of itself. It does not exist apart from all finite minds, but it is obviously not confined to any given mind or set of minds.[1]

5. We can speak, therefore, of the human mind rising to a participation in the self-knowledge of the Absolute. Some writers have interpreted Hegel on more or less theistic lines. That is to say, they have understood him to mean that God is perfectly luminous to himself quite independently of man, though man is capable of participating in this self-knowledge. But I have interpreted him here as meaning that man's knowledge of the Absolute and the Absolute's knowledge of itself are two aspects of the same reality. Even, however, on this interpretation we can still speak of the finite mind rising to a participation in the divine self-knowledge. For, as we have seen, it is not every sort of idea and thought in man's mind which can be regarded as a moment in the Absolute's self-knowledge. It is not every level of consciousness which is a participation in the divine self-consciousness. To achieve this participation the finite mind has to rise to the level of what Hegel calls absolute knowledge.

In this case it is possible to trace the successive stages of consciousness from the lowest to the highest levels. And this is what Hegel does in *The Phenomenology of Spirit*, which can be described as a history of consciousness. If we consider the mind and its activity in themselves, without relation to an object, we are concerned with psychology. If, however, we consider mind as essentially related to an object, external or internal, we are concerned with consciousness. And phenomenology is the science of consciousness in this sense. Hegel begins with the natural unscientific consciousness and proceeds to trace the dialectical development of this consciousness, showing how the lower levels

[1] I do not mean to imply that for Hegel philosophy is the only way of apprehending the Absolute. There are also art and religion. But in the present context we are concerned only with philosophy.

e subsumed in the higher according to a more adequate point of
iew, until we reach the level of absolute knowledge.

In a certain sense *The Phenomenology* can be regarded as an
itroduction to philosophy. That is to say, it systematically traces
ie development of consciousness up to the level of what we might
ill the properly philosophical consciousness. But it is certainly
ot an introduction to philosophy in the sense of being an external
reparation for philosophizing. Hegel did not believe that an
itroduction in this sense was possible. And in any case the work is
self an outstanding example of sustained philosophical reflection.
: is, we may say, the philosophical consciousness reflecting on the
henomenology of its own genesis. Moreover, even if the work is
i some sense an introduction to the point of view required by
ie Hegelian system, there is an overlapping. The system itself
nds a place for the phenomenology of consciousness, and *The
'henomenology* contains an outline of a certain amount of material
hich is later treated by Hegel at greater length. The religious
onsciousness is a case in point. Lastly, by no stretch of the
nagination can *The Phenomenology* be described as an introduction
o philosophy in the sense of a work of philosophy-without-tears.
n the contrary, it is a profound work and often extremely
ifficult to understand.

*The Phenomenology* falls into three main parts, corresponding
ith the three main phases of consciousness. The first of these
hases is consciousness of the object as a sensible thing standing
ver against the subject. And it is to this phase that Hegel
ppropriates the name 'consciousness' (*Bewusstsein*). The second
hase is that of self-consciousness (*Selbstbewusstsein*). And here
Iegel has a lot to say about social consciousness. The third phase
: that of Reason (*Vernunft*), which is represented as the synthesis
r unity of the preceding phases on a higher level. In other words,
Reason is the synthesis of objectivity and subjectivity. Needless
o say, each of these main divisions of the work has its subdivisions.
.nd Hegel's general procedure is first to describe the spontaneous
ttitude of consciousness at a given level and then to institute an
nalysis of it. The result of the analysis is that the mind is compelled
o proceed to the next level, considered as a more adequate
ttitude or point of view.

Hegel begins with what he calls sense-certainty, the uncritical
pprehension by the senses of particular objects, which to the
aïve consciousness appears to be not only the most certain and

basic form of knowledge but also the richest. Analysis, he argue
shows that it is in fact a peculiarly empty and abstract form
knowledge. The naïve consciousness feels certain that it is direct
acquainted through sense-apprehension with a particular thin
But when we try to say what it is that we know, that is, to descri
the particular object with which we claim to be immediate
acquainted, we find that we can describe it only in universal ter
which are applicable to other things as well. We can, of cours
attempt to pin the object down, as it were, by using words su
as 'this', 'here', and 'now', accompanying them perhaps with ;
ostensive gesture. But a moment later the same words apply
another object. Indeed, it is impossible, Hegel argues, to give ev
to words like 'this' a genuinely particular significance, howev
much we may wish and try to do so.

We might wish to say that Hegel is simply calling attention to
feature of language. And he is, of course, perfectly well aware th
he is saying something about language. But his main concern
epistemological. He wishes to show that the claim of 'sens
certainty' to be knowledge *par excellence* is a bogus claim. And
draws the conclusion that this level of consciousness, on the pa
towards becoming genuine knowledge, must pass into the level
perception for which the object is a thing conceived as the cent
of distinct properties and qualities. But analysis of this level
consciousness shows that it is not possible, as long as we rema
simply on the level of sense, to reconcile in any satisfactory mann
the elements of unity and multiplicity which are postulated I
this view of the object. And the mind passes, therefore, by vario
stages to the level of scientific understanding which invok
metaphenomenal or unobservable entities to explain sens
phenomena.

For instance, the mind sees sense-phenomena as the manifest
tions of hidden forces. But, Hegel maintains, the mind cannot re
here and proceeds instead to the idea of laws. Yet natural laws a
ways of ordering and describing phenomena; they are n
explicative. Hence they cannot perform the function for whi
they have been invoked, namely to explain sense-phenomen
Hegel obviously does not mean to deny that the concept of natur
laws has a useful function to perform at the appropriate level. B
it does not give the sort of knowledge which, in his opinion, t
mind is seeking.

In the end the mind sees that the whole realm of the met

phenomenal which has been invoked to explain sense-phenomena is the product of the understanding itself. Consciousness is thus turned back on itself as the reality behind the veil of phenomena and becomes self-consciousness.

Hegel begins with self-consciousness in the form of desire (*Begierde*). The self is still concerned with the external object, but it is characteristic of the attitude of desire that the self subordinates the object to itself, seeking to make it minister to its satisfaction, to appropriate it, even to consume it. And this attitude can be shown, of course, in regard to living and non-living things. But when the self is confronted with another self, this attitude breaks down. For the presence of the Other is for Hegel essential to self-consciousness. Developed self-consciousness can arise only when the self recognizes selfhood in itself and others. It must take the form, therefore, of a truly social or we-consciousness, the recognition at the level of self-consciousness of identity-in-difference. But in the dialectical evolution of this phase of consciousness developed self-consciousness is not attained immediately. And Hegel's study of the successive stages forms one of the most interesting and influential parts of *The Phenomenology*.

The existence of another self is, we have mentioned, a condition of self-consciousness. But the first spontaneous reaction of a self confronted with another self is to assert its own existence as a self in face of the other. The one self desires to cancel out or annihilate the other self as a means to the triumphant assertion of its own selfhood. But a literal destruction would defeat its own purpose. For consciousness of one's own selfhood demands as a condition the recognition of this selfhood by another self. There thus arises the master-slave relationship. The master is the one who succeeds in obtaining recognition from the other, in the sense that he imposes himself as the other's value. The slave is the one who sees his own true self in the other.

Paradoxically, however, the original situation changes. And it must do so because of the contradictions concealed in it. On the one hand, by not recognizing the slave as a real person the master deprives himself of that recognition of his own freedom which he originally demanded and which is required for the development of self-consciousness. He thus debases himself to an infra-human condition. On the other hand, by carrying out his master's will the slave objectifies himself through labour which transforms material things. He thus forms himself and rises to the level of true existence.[1]

It is obvious that the concept of the master-slave relationship has two aspects. It can be considered as a stage in the abstract dialectical development of consciousness. And it can also be considered in relation to history. But the two aspects are by no means incompatible. For human history itself reveals the development of Spirit, the travail of the Spirit on the way to its goal. Hence we need not be surprised if from the master-slave relationship in its primary form Hegel passes to an attitude or state of consciousness to which he gives a name with explicit historical associations, namely the Stoic consciousness.

In the Stoic consciousness the contradictions inherent in the slave relationship are not really overcome: they are overcome only to the extent that both master (typified by Marcus Aurelius) and slave (typified by Epictetus) take flight into interiority and exalt the idea of true interior freedom, internal self-sufficiency, leaving concrete relationships unchanged. Hence, according to Hegel, this negative attitude towards the concrete and external passes easily into the Sceptical consciousness for which the self alone abides while all else is subjected to doubt and negation.

But the Sceptical consciousness contains an implicit contradiction. For it is impossible for the sceptic to eliminate the natural consciousness; and affirmation and negation coexist in the same attitude. And when this contradiction becomes explicit, as it must do, we pass to what Hegel calls 'the unhappy consciousness' (*das unglückliche Bewusstsein*), which is a divided consciousness. At this level the master-slave relationship, which has not been successfully overcome by either the Stoic or the Sceptical consciousness, returns in another form. In the master-slave relationship proper the elements of true self-consciousness, recognition of selfhood and freedom both in oneself and in the Other, were divided between two individual consciousnesses. The master recognized selfhood and freedom only in himself, not in the slave while the slave recognized them only in the master, not in himself In the so-called unhappy consciousness, however, the division occurs in the same self. For example, the self is conscious of a gulf between a changing, inconsistent, fickle self and a changeless ideal self. The first appears as in some sense a false self, something

[1] For obvious reasons Hegel's profound analysis of the master-slave relationship contained lines of reflection which found favour with Karl Marx.

⊃ be denied, while the second appears as the true self which is not
et attained. And this ideal self can be projected into an other-
vorldly sphere and identified with absolute perfection, God
ɔnsidered as existing apart from the world and the finite self.[1]
he human consciousness is then divided, self-alienated, 'unhappy'.

The contradictions or divisions implicit in self-consciousness are
vercome in the third phase of *The Phenomenology* when the finite
ubject rises to universal self-consciousness. At this level self-
ɔnsciousness no longer takes the form of the one-sided awareness
f oneself as an individual subject threatened by and in conflict
ith other self-conscious beings. Rather is there a full recognition
f selfhood in oneself and in others; and this recognition is at least
n implicit awareness of the life of the universal, the infinite
pirit, in and through finite selves, binding them together yet not
nnulling them. Present implicitly and imperfectly in the developed
toral consciousness, for which the one rational will expresses
self in a multiplicity of concrete moral vocations in the social
rder, this awareness of the identity-in-difference which is
haracteristic of the life of the Spirit attains a higher and more
xplicit expression in the developed religious consciousness, for
hich the one divine life is immanent in all selves, bearing them in
self while yet maintaining their distinctness. In the idea of a
ving union with God the division within the unhappy or divided
ɔnsciousness is overcome. The true self is no longer conceived as
n ideal from which the actual self is hopelessly alienated, but
ither as the living core, so to speak, of the actual self, which
xpresses itself in and through its finite manifestations.

This third phase of the phenomenological history of conscious-
ess, to which, as we have seen, Hegel gives the general name of
Reason, is represented as the synthesis of consciousness and self-
ɔnsciousness, that is, of the first two phases. In consciousness in
ie narrow sense (*Bewusstsein*) the subject is aware of the sensible
bject as something external and heterogeneous to itself. In self-
ɔnsciousness (*Selbstbewusstsein*) the subject's attention is turned
ack on itself as a finite self. At the level of Reason it sees Nature
s the objective expression of infinite Spirit with which it is itself
nited. But this awareness can take different forms. In the
eveloped religious consciousness the subject sees Nature as the
reation and self-manifestation of God, with whom it is united in

---

[1] Hegel, the Lutheran, tended to associate the unhappy or divided conscious-
ess, in a somewhat polemical way, with mediaeval Catholicism, especially with
s ascetic ideals.

the depth of its being and through whom it is united with oth
selves. And this religious vision of reality is true. But at tl
level of the religious consciousness truth finds expression in tl
form of figurative or pictorial thought (*Vorstellung*), whereas ;
the supreme level of 'absolute knowledge' (*das absolute Wissen*) tl
same truth is reflectively apprehended in philosophical form. Tl
finite subject is explicitly aware of its inmost self as a moment i
the life of the infinite and universal Spirit, as a moment in absolu'
Thought. And, as such, it sees Nature as its own objectificatic
and as the precondition of its own life as actually existing Spiri
This does not mean, of course, that the finite subject considere
precisely as such sees Nature as its own product. Rather does
mean that the finite subject, aware of itself as more than finite, ;
a moment in the innermost life of absolute Spirit, sees Nature as
necessary stage in the onward march of Spirit in its process of sel
actualization. In other words, absolute knowledge is the level ;
which the finite subject participates in the life of self-thinkir
Thought, the Absolute. Or, to put the matter in another way, it
the level at which the Absolute, the Totality, thinks itself ;
identity-in-difference in and through the finite mind of tl
philosopher.

As in the previous main phases of the phenomenology (
consciousness Hegel develops the third phase, that of Reaso;
through a series of dialectical stages. He treats first of observir
Reason which is seen as obtaining some glimpse at any rate of i
own reflection in Nature (through the idea of finality, for example
then as turning inwards in the study of formal logic and (
empirical psychology, and finally as manifesting itself in a seri(
of practical ethical attitudes, ranging from the pursuit of happine:
up to that criticism of the universal moral laws dictated by tl
practical reason which follows from recognition of the fact that
universal law stands in need of so many qualifications that
tends to lose all definite meaning. This sets the stage for tl
transition to concrete moral life in society. Here Hegel moves fro;
the unreflective ethical life in which human beings simply follo'
the customs and traditions of their community to the form (
culture in which individuals are estranged from this unreflectiv
background and pass judgments about it. The two moments a;
synthesized in the developed moral consciousness for which tl
rational general will is not something over and above individua
in society but a common life binding them together as free person

n the first moment, we can say, Spirit is unreflective, as in the
ncient Greek morality before the time of the so-called Sophists.
n the second moment Spirit is reflective but at the same time
stranged from actual society and its traditions, on which it passes
udgment. In the extreme case, as in the Jacobin Terror, it
nnihilates actual persons in the name of abstract freedom. In the
hird moment, however, Spirit is said to be ethically sure of itself.
t takes the form of a community of free persons embodying the
eneral will as a living unity.

This living unity, however, in which each member of the
ommunity is for the others a free self demands an explicit
ecognition of the idea of identity-in-difference, of a life which is
resent in all as their inner bond of unity though it does not
nnihilate them as individuals. It demands, that is to say, an
xplicit recognition of the idea of the concrete universal which
ifferentiates itself into or manifests itself in its particulars while
niting them within itself. In other words, morality passes
ialectically into religion, the moral into the religious conscious-
ess, for which this living unity is explicitly recognized in the form
f God.

In religion, therefore, we see absolute Spirit becoming explicitly
onscious of itself. But religion, of course, has its history; and in
his history we see earlier phases of the dialectic being repeated.
hus Hegel moves from what he calls 'natural religion', in which
he divine is seen under the form of perceptual objects or of
ature, to the religion of art or of beauty, in which, as in Greek
eligion, the divine is seen as the self-conscious associated with the
hysical. The statue, for example, represents the anthropomorphic
eity. Finally, in the absolute religion, Christianity, absolute
pirit is recognized for what it is, namely Spirit; Nature is seen as
divine creation, the expression of the Word; and the Holy Spirit
s seen as immanent in and uniting together finite selves.

But the religious consciousness expresses itself, as we have seen,
n pictorial forms. And it demands to be transmuted into the pure
onceptual form of philosophy which at the same time expresses
he transition from faith to knowledge or science. That is to say,
he pictorial idea of the transcendent personal Deity who saves
an by a unique Incarnation and the power of grace passes into
he concept of absolute Spirit, the infinite self-thinking Thought
hich knows itself in Nature (as its objectification and as the
ondition for its own actualization) and recognizes in the history of

human culture, with its successive forms and levels, its ow
Odyssey. Hegel is not saying that religion is untrue. On th
contrary, the absolute religion, Christianity, is the absolute trutl
But it is expressed in the imaginative or pictorial form which i
correlative to the religious consciousness. In philosophy this trut
becomes absolute knowledge which is 'Spirit knowing itself in th
form of Spirit.'[1] The Absolute, the Totality, comes to know itse
in and through the human spirit, in so far, that is to say, as th
human spirit rises above its finitude and identifies itself with pui
Thought. God cannot be equated with man. For God is Being, th
Totality, and man is not. But the Totality comes actually to kno'
itself in and through the spirit of man; on the level of pictoriz
thought in the evolution of the religious consciousness, on the leve
of science or pure conceptual knowledge in the history of philc
sophy which has as its ideal term the complete truth about realit
in the form of the Absolute's knowledge of itself.

In *The Phenomenology*, therefore, Hegel starts with the lowes
levels of human consciousness and works dialectically upwards t
the level at which the human mind attains the absolute point c
view and becomes the vehicle, as it were, of infinite self-consciou
Spirit. The connections between one level and the next are ofte
very loose, logically speaking. And some of the stages are obviousl
suggested not so much by the demands of a dialectical develop
ment as by Hegel's reflections on the spirits and attitudes c
different cultural phases and epochs. Further, some of the topics c
which Hegel treats strike the modern reader as somewhat odc
There is, for example, a critical treatment of phrenology. At th
same time, as a study of the Odyssey of the human spirit, of th
movement from one attitude or outlook, which proves to be one
sided and inadequate, to another, the work is both impressive an
fascinating. And the correlations between stages of the dialectic c
consciousness and historically-manifested attitudes (the spirit c
the Enlightenment, the romantic spirit, and so on) add to it
interest. One may be suspicious of Hegel's summaries and inte
pretations of the spirits of epochs and cultures, and his exaltatio
of philosophical knowledge may strike one as having a comic;
aspect; but in spite of all reservations and disagreements th
reader who really tries to penetrate into Hegel's thought ca
hardly come to any other conclusion than that *The Phenomenolog*
is one of the great works of speculative philosophy.

[1] *W*, II, p. 610; *B*, p. 798.

### CHAPTER X

# HEGEL (2)

*The logic of Hegel—The ontological status of the Idea or Absolute in itself and the transition to Nature—The philosophy of Nature —The Absolute as Spirit; subjective Spirit—The concept of right —Morality—The family and civil society—The State— Explanatory comments on Hegel's idea of political philosophy— The function of war—Philosophy of history—Some comments on Hegel's philosophy of history.*

. As we have seen, Hegel rejected the view, advanced by Schelling in his so-called system of identity, that the Absolute in tself is for conceptual thought the vanishing-point of all differences, .n absolute self-identity which cannot properly be described except n negative terms and which can be positively apprehended only, f at all, in mystical intuition. Hegel was convinced that the peculative reason can penetrate the inner essence of the Absolute, he essence which manifests itself in Nature and in the history of he human spirit.

The part of philosophy which is concerned with laying bare the nner essence of the Absolute is for Hegel logic. To anyone who is .ccustomed to regard logic as a purely formal science, entirely lissociated from metaphysics, this must seem an extraordinary .nd even absurd point of view. But we have to bear in mind the act that for Hegel the Absolute is pure Thought. This Thought can e considered in itself, apart from its externalization or self-nanifestation. And the science of pure Thought in itself is logic. "urther, inasmuch as pure Thought is the substance, as it were, of eality, logic necessarily coincides with metaphysics, that is, with netaphysics as concerned with the Absolute in itself.

The matter can be made clearer by relating Hegel's conception f logic to Kant's view of transcendental logic. In the philosophy f Kant the categories which give shape and form to phenomena .re *a priori* categories of human thought. The human mind does 
ot create things-in-themselves, but it determines the basic haracter of the phenomenal world, the world of appearance. On Kant's premises, therefore, we have no warrant for assuming that he categories of the human mind apply to reality in itself; their

cognitive function is limited to the phenomenal world. But, as was explained in the introductory chapter, with the elimination of the unknowable thing-in-itself and the transformation of the critical philosophy into pure idealism the categories become the categories of creative thought in the full sense. And if a subjectivist position, threatening to lead to solipsism, is to be avoided, creative thought must be interpreted as absolute Thought. The categories, therefore, become the categories of absolute Thought, the categories of reality. And logic, which studies them, becomes metaphysics. It discloses the essence or nature of the absolute Thought which manifests itself in Nature and history.

Now, Hegel speaks of the Absolute in itself as God in himself. The subject-matter of logic is 'the truth as it is without husk and for itself. One can therefore express the matter by saying that its content is the presentation of God as he is in his eternal essence before the creation of Nature and of a finite spirit.'[1] And this manner of speaking tends to suggest the very odd picture of the logician penetrating the inner essence of a transcendent Deity and describing it in terms of a system of categories. But Hegel's use of religious language can be misleading. We have to remember that, though his Absolute is certainly transcendent in the sense that it cannot be identified with any particular finite entity or set of entities, it is not transcendent in the sense in which the God of Christianity is said to transcend the created universe. Hegel's Absolute is the Totality, and this Totality is depicted as coming to know itself in and through the finite spirit, in so far as the finite spirit attains the level of 'absolute knowledge'. Logic, therefore, is the Absolute's knowledge of itself in itself, in abstraction from its concrete self-manifestation in Nature and history. That is to say, logic is absolute Thought's knowledge of its own essence, the essence which exists concretely in the process of reality.

If we use the word 'category' in a somewhat wider sense than that in which it is used by Hegel himself, we can say, therefore, that his logic is the system of categories. But if we say this, it is essential to understand that the whole system of categories is a progressive definition of the Absolute in itself. Hegel starts with the concept of being because it is for him the most indeterminate and the logically prior concept. And he then proceeds to show how this concept passes necessarily into successive concepts until we

---

[1] W, IV, p. 46; J-S, I, p. 60. The letters J-S signify the English translation of the *Science of Logic* by W. H. Johnston and L. G. Struthers.

reach the absolute Idea, the concept or category of self-knowledge or self-consciousness, self-thinking Thought. But the Absolute is not, of course, a string or chain of categories or concepts. If we ask what the Absolute is, we can answer that it is being. And if we ask what being is, we shall in the end be forced to answer that being is self-thinking Thought or Spirit. The process of showing that this is the case, as worked out by the logician, is obviously a temporal process. But the Absolute in itself does not, to put the matter crudely, start as being at seven in the morning and end as self-thinking Thought at seven in the evening. To say that the Absolute is being is to say that it is self-thinking Thought. But the logician's demonstration of the fact, his systematic dialectical elucidation of the meaning of being, is a temporal process. It is his business to show that the whole system of categories turns in on itself, so to speak. The beginning is the end, and the end is the beginning. That is to say, the first category or concept contains all the others implicitly, and the last is the final explicitation of the first: it gives its true meaning.

The point is easily understood if we employ the religious or theological language which Hegel not infrequently uses. God is being, he is also self-thinking Thought. But the word 'also' is really inappropriate. For to say that God is being is to say that he is self-thinking Thought. The systematic exhibition of this fact by the philosopher is a temporal process. But this temporality obviously does not affect the divine essence in itself. There is, of course, a great difference between Hegel's Absolute and the God of Christian theology. But though Hegel's Absolute is said to be the process of its own becoming, we are not concerned in logic with this actual process, the actualization of the *Logos*: we are concerned with the Absolute 'in itself', with the logical Idea. And this is not a temporal process.

The dialectical movement of Hegel's logic can be illustrated by means of the first three categories. The logically prior concept of the Absolute is the concept of being. But the concept or category of pure being (*reines Sein*) is wholly indeterminate. And the concept of wholly indeterminate being passes into the concept of not-being. That is to say, if we try to think being without any determination at all, we find that we are thinking nothing. The mind passes from being to not-being and from not-being back to being: it can rest in neither, and each disappears, as it were, in its opposite. 'Their truth is thus this *movement* of the immediate disappearing of the one into the other.'[1] And this movement from being to not-being and from not-being to being is becoming. Becoming is thus the synthesis of being and not-being; it is their unity and truth. Being must therefore be conceived as becoming. In other words, the concept of the Absolute as being is the concept of the Absolute as becoming, as a process of self-development.[2]

According to our ordinary way of looking at things a contradiction brings us to a full stop. Being and not-being are mutually exclusive. But we think in this way because we conceive being as determinate being and not-being as the not-being of this determination. Pure being, however, is for Hegel indeterminate, empty or vacuous; and it is for this reason that it is said to pass into its opposite. But contradiction is for Hegel a positive force which reveals both thesis and antithesis as abstract moments in a higher unity or synthesis. And this unity of the concepts of being and not-being is the concept of becoming. But the unity gives rise in turn to a 'contradiction', so that the mind is driven onwards in its search for the meaning of being, for the nature or essence of the Absolute in itself.

Being, not-being or nothing and becoming form the first triad of the first part of Hegel's logic, the so-called logic of being (die Logik des Seins). This part is concerned with the categories of being-in-itself, as distinct from the categories of relation. And the three main classes of categories in this part of logic are those of quality, which include the above-mentioned triad, quantity and measure. Measure is described as the synthesis of quality and quantity. For it is the concept of a specific quantum determined by the nature of the object, that is, by its quality.

In the second main part of the Logic, the logic of essence (die Logik des Wesens), Hegel deduces pairs of related categories, such as essence and existence, force and expression, substance and accident, cause and effect, action and reaction. These categories are called categories of reflection because they correspond with the reflective consciousness which penetrates beneath the surface, as it were, of being in its immediacy. Essence, for example, is conceived as lying behind appearance, and force is conceived as the reality displayed in its expression. In other words, for the reflective

---

[1] W, IV, p. 89; J-S, I, p. 95.
[2] This statement does not contradict what has been said about the non-temporal nature of the logical Absolute. For we are not concerned here with the actual process of the Absolute's self-actualization.

consciousness being-in-itself undergoes self-diremption, breaking up into related categories.

But the logic of essence does not leave us with the division of being into inner essence and outward phenomenal existence. For the last main subdivision is devoted to the category of actuality (*die Wirklichkeit*) which is described as 'the unity of essence and existence'.[1] That is to say, the actual is the inner essence which ex-ists, the force which has found complete expression. If we identify being with appearance, with its external manifestation, this is a one-sided abstraction. But so is the identification of being with a hidden essence underlying appearance. Being as actuality is the unity of the inner and the outer; it is essence manifesting itself. And it must manifest itself.

It is under the general heading of the category of actuality that Hegel deduces the categories of substance and accident, cause and effect, and action and reaction or reciprocal action. And as we have said that his logic is a progressive definition or determination of the nature of the Absolute in itself, the impression may be given that for him there is only one substance and one cause, namely the Absolute. In other words the impression may be given that Hegel embraces Spinozism. But this would be an incorrect interpretation of his meaning. The deduction of the categories of substance and cause is not intended to imply, for example, that there can be no such thing as a finite cause. For the Absolute as actuality is essence manifesting itself; and the manifestation is the universe as we know it. The Absolute is not simply the One. It is the One, but it is also the Many: it is identity-in-difference.

From the logic of essence Hegel passes to the logic of the Concept (*die Logik des Begriffs*) which is the third main part of his work. In the logic of being each category is at first sight independent, standing on its own feet, as it were, even if the dialectical movement of thought breaks down this apparent self-containedness. In the logic of essence we are concerned with obviously related categories, such as cause and effect or substance and accident. We are thus in the sphere of mediation. But each member of a pair of related categories is conceived as mediated 'by another', that is, by something different from itself. The cause, for example, is constituted as a cause by passing into its opposite, namely the effect, which is conceived as something different from the cause. Similarly, the effect is constituted as an

[1] *W*, IV, p. 662; *J-S*, II, p. 160.

effect by its relation to something different from itself, namely the cause. The synthesis of the spheres of immediacy and of mediation by another will be the sphere of self-mediation. A being is said to be self-mediating when it is conceived as passing into its opposite and yet as remaining identical with itself even in this self-opposition. And the self-mediating is what Hegel calls the Concept or the Notion.[1]

Needless to say, the logic of the Notion has three main sub-divisions. In the first Hegel considers the Notion as 'subjectivity', as thought in its formal aspects. And this part corresponds more or less with logic in the ordinary sense. Hegel tries to show how the general idea of being going out from itself and then returning to itself at a higher level is verified in a formal manner in the movement of logical thought. Thus the unity of the universal concept is divided in the judgment and is re-established at a higher level in the syllogism.

Having considered the Notion as subjectivity, Hegel goes on to consider it as objectivity. And as in the first phase or part of the logic of the Notion he finds three moments, the universal concept, the judgment and syllogistic inference, so in this second phase or part he finds three moments, namely mechanism, chemism and teleology. He thus anticipates the main ideas of the philosophy of Nature. But he is concerned here with the thought or concept of the objective rather than with Nature considered as an empirically-given existing reality. The nature of the Absolute is such that it comprises the concept of self-objectification.

Given the character of the Hegelian dialectic, the third phase of the logic of the Notion will obviously be the synthesis or unity on a higher plane of subjectivity and objectivity. As such the Notion is called the Idea. In the Idea the one-sided factors of the formal and the material, the subjective and the objective, are brought together. But the Idea too has its phases or moments. And in the final sub-division of the logic of the Notion Hegel considers in turn life, knowledge and their unity in the absolute Idea which is, as it were, the union of subjectivity and objectivity enriched with rational life. In other words, the absolute Idea is the concept or category of self-consciousness, personality, self-thinking Thought which knows itself in its object and its object as itself. It is thus the category of Spirit. In religious language, it is the concept of God in and for himself, knowing himself as the totality.

[1] As the word 'concept' has too restricted a meaning in English, Hegel's *Begriff* is frequently rendered as 'Notion'.

After a long dialectical wandering, therefore, being has at length revealed itself as the absolute Idea, as self-thinking Thought. The Absolute is being, and the meaning of this statement has now been made explicit. 'The absolute Idea alone is *being*, eternal *life*, *self-knowing truth*, and it is *all truth*. It is the one subject-matter and content of philosophy.'[1] Hegel does not mean, of course, that the logical Idea, considered precisely as such, is the one subject-matter of philosophy. But philosophy is concerned with reality as a whole, with the Absolute. And reality, in the sense of Nature and the sphere of the human spirit, is the process by which the logical Idea or *Logos* actualizes itself. Hence philosophy is always concerned with the Idea.

2. Now, if we speak of the logical Idea or *Logos* as manifesting or expressing itself in Nature and in the sphere of the human spirit, we are obviously faced with the question, what is the ontological status of the logical Idea or the Absolute in itself? Is it a reality which exists independently of the world and which manifests itself in the world, or is it not? If it is, how can there be a subsistent Idea? If it is not, how can we speak of the Idea as manifesting or actualizing itself?

At the end of the *Logic* in the *Encyclopaedia of the Philosophical Sciences*[2] Hegel asserts that the Idea 'in its absolute freedom . . . *resolves* to let its moment of particularity . . . the immediate Idea as its reflected image, go forth freely out of itself as Nature'.[3] In this passage, therefore, Hegel seems to imply not only that Nature is ontologically derived from the Idea but also that the Idea freely posits Nature. And if this implication were taken literally, we should clearly have to interpret the Idea as a name for the personal creative Deity. For it would be preposterous to speak of an Idea in any other sense as 'resolving' to do something.

But consideration of the Hegelian system as a whole suggests that this passage represents an intrusion, as it were, of the way of speaking which is characteristic of the Christian religious consciousness, and that its implications should not be pressed. It seems to be clear enough that according to Hegel the doctrine of

---

[1] *W*, v, p. 328; *J-S*, ii, p. 466.

[2] The *Logic* contained in the *Encyclopaedia* is known as the *Lesser* or *Shorter Logic*, in distinction from the *Greater Logic*, that is, Hegel's *Science of Logic*. Quotations in the last section were from the latter work.

[3] *W*, vi, p. 144; *E*, 191. The letter *E* stands for *Encyclopaedia*. As this work is divided into numbered sections, no reference to particular translations is required. A glance at the number of the relevant volume in the reference to *W* will show whether it is the Heidelberg edition (*W*, vi) or the Berlin edition (*W*, viii–x) which is being referred to.

free creation by God belongs to the figurative or pictorial language of the religious consciousness. It expresses indeed a truth, but it does not do so in the idiom of pure philosophy. From the strictly philosophical point of view the Absolute in itself manifests itself necessarily in Nature. Obviously, it is not constrained to do so by anything external to itself. The necessity is an inner necessity of nature. The only freedom in the *Logos'* self-manifestation is the freedom of spontaneity. And from this it follows that from the philosophical point of view there is no sense in speaking of the Absolute in itself as existing 'before' creation. If Nature is derived ontologically from the Idea, the latter is not temporally prior to the former.[1] Further, though some writers have interpreted Hegel in a theistic sense, as holding, that is to say, that the Absolute in itself is a personal Being, existing independently of Nature and of the sphere of the human spirit, it does not seem to me that this interpretation is correct. True, there are passages which can be cited in support of it. But these passages can equally well be interpreted as expressions of the religious consciousness, as pictorial or figurative statements of the truth. And the nature of the system as a whole clearly suggests that the Absolute attains actual self-consciousness only in and through the human spirit. As has already been explained, this does not mean that human consciousness can be identified without more ado with the divine self-consciousness. For the Absolute is said to know itself in and through the human mind in so far as this mind rises above mere finitude and particularity and reaches the level of absolute knowledge. But the point is that if the Absolute becomes actually existent only in and through the human spirit, the Absolute in itself, the logical Idea, cannot properly be said to 'resolve' to posit Nature, which is the objective precondition for the existence of the sphere of Spirit. If such language is used, it is a concession, as it were, to the mode of thought which is characteristic of the religious consciousness.

If, however, we exclude the theistic interpretation of the Absolute in itself,[2] how are we to conceive the transition from the logical Idea to Nature? If we conceive it as a real ontological transition, that is to say, if we conceive a subsistent Idea as manifesting itself necessarily in Nature, we are obviously attributing

---

[1] Cf., for example, *W*, IX, pp. 51–4; *E*, 247.
[2] The theistic view is certainly admitted by Hegel as far as the religious consciousness and its own characteristic expression are concerned. But we are treating here of the strictly philosophical point of view.

o Hegel a thesis which, to put it mildly, is somewhat odd. We expose him at once to the criticism made by Schelling in his polemic against 'negative philosophy', that from ideas we can deduce only other ideas, and that it is quite impossible to deduce an existing world from an Idea.

It is understandable, therefore, that some writers have endeavoured to exclude altogether the concept of an ontological derivation of Nature from the Idea. The Absolute is the totality, the universe. And this totality is a teleological process, the actualization of self-thinking Thought. The essential nature of this process can be considered in abstraction. It then takes the form of the logical Idea. But it does not exist as a subsistent reality which is logically prior to Nature and which is the efficient cause of Nature. The Idea reflects the goal or result of the process rather than a subsistent reality which stands at its beginning. Hence there is no question of an ontological derivation of Nature from the logical Idea as efficient cause. And the so-called deduction of Nature from the Idea is really an exhibition of the fact, or alleged fact, that Nature is a necessary precondition for the realization of the goal of the total process of reality, the universe's knowledge of itself in and through the human spirit.

It seems to the present writer that the foregoing line of interpretation must be accepted in so far as it denies the separate existence of the logical Idea as a reality quite distinct from the world or as an external efficient cause of the world. For Hegel the infinite exists in and through the finite; the universal lives and has its being, as it were, in and through the particulars. Hence there is no room in his system for an efficient cause which transcends the world in the sense that it exists quite independently of it. At the same time, even though the infinite exists in and through the finite, it is obvious that finite things arise and perish. They are, so to speak, transitory manifestations of an infinite Life. And Hegel certainly tends to speak of the *Logos* as though it were pulsating Life, dynamic Reason or Thought. It exists, it is true, only in and through its manifestations. But inasmuch as it is a continuous Life, Being actualizing itself as what it potentially is, namely Spirit, it is quite natural to look on the passing manifestations as ontologically dependent on the one immanent Life, as an 'outside' in relation to an 'inside'. And Hegel can thus speak of the *Logos* spontaneously expressing itself in or going over into Nature. For Being, the Absolute, the infinite Totality, is not a mere collection of finite

things, but one infinite Life, self-actualizing Spirit. It is th
universal of universals; and even though it exists only in an
through the particulars, it itself persists whereas the particulars d
not. Hence it is perfectly reasonable to speak of the *Logos* a
expressing or manifesting itself in finite things. And inasmuch as '
is absolute Spirit which comes to exist as such through the proces
of its own self-development, material Nature is naturally cor
ceived as its opposite, the opposite which is a precondition for th
attainment of the end or *telos* of the process.

This line of interpretation may seem to be an attempt to hav
things both ways. On the one hand it is admitted that the logica
Idea does not exist as a subsistent reality which creates Natur
from outside, as it were. On the other hand, it is claimed that th
logical Idea, in the sense of the essential structure or meaning c
Being as grasped by the metaphysician, represents a metaphysica
reality which, though it exists only in and through its self
manifestation, is in a certain sense logically prior to its manifesta
tion. But I do not think that we can exclude metaphysics fron
Hegelianism or eliminate altogether a certain element of trans
cendence. The attempt to do this seems to me to make nonsense o
Hegel's doctrine of the infinite Absolute. The Absolute is indeec
the totality, the universe, considered as the process of its own self
development; but in my opinion we cannot escape making a
distinction between inner and outer, between, that is to say, th
one infinite Life, self-actualizing Spirit, and the finite manifesta
tions in and through which it lives and has its being. And in thi:
case we can equally well say that the finite manifestations deriv(
their reality from the one Life which expresses itself in them. I
there is a certain element of ambiguity in Hegel's position, this i:
scarcely surprising. For if there were no such element, his philo
sophy would hardly have given rise to divergent interpretations.

3. 'Nature,' says Hegel, 'is *in itself*, in the Idea, divine. . . . Bui
as it exists, its being does not correspond with its concept.'[1] In the
language of religion, the idea of Nature in the divine mind is
divine, but the objectification of this idea in existing Nature cannot
be called divine. For the fact that the idea is expressed in the
material world, in that which is most unlike God, means that it is
only inadequately expressed. God cannot be adequately mani
fested in the material world. In the language of philosophy, the
Absolute is defined as Spirit. Hence it can manifest itself adequately

---

[1] *W*, VI, p. 147; *E*, 193.

only in the sphere of Spirit. Nature is a precondition of the existence of this sphere, but it is not in itself Spirit, though in its rational structure it bears the imprint of Spirit. One might say with Schelling that it is slumbering Spirit or visible Spirit; but it is not Spirit proper, Spirit as awoken to consciousness of itself.

Spirit is freedom: Nature is the sphere of necessity rather than of freedom. It is also the sphere of contingency (*Zufälligkeit*). For example, it does not exhibit in any uniformly clear-cut way the distinctions postulated by a purely rational pattern. There are, for instance, 'monsters' in Nature which do not conform clearly to any one specific type. And there are even natural species which seem to be due to a kind of Bacchic dance or revel on Nature's part, and not to any rational necessity. Nature appears to run riot as much in the wealth of forms which she produces as in the number of individual members of given species. They elude all logical deduction. Obviously, an empirical explanation of any natural object can be given in terms of physical causality. But to give an empirical explanation in terms of physical causality is not the same thing as to give a logical deduction.

Obviously, Nature cannot exist without particular things. Immanent teleology, for instance, cannot exist without particular organisms. The universal exists only in and through its particulars. But it does not follow that any given individual is logically deducible from the concept of its specific type or from any more general concept. It is not simply a question of its being very difficult or practically impossible for the finite mind to deduce particulars which could in principle be deduced by an infinite mind. For Hegel seems to say that particular objects in Nature are not deducible even in principle, even though they are physically explicable. To put the matter somewhat paradoxically, contingency in Nature is necessary. For without it there could be no Nature. But contingency is none the less real, in the sense that it is a factor in Nature which the philosopher is unable to eliminate. And Hegel ascribes it to 'the *impotence* of Nature'[1] to remain faithful to the determination of the Notion. He is speaking here about the way in which Nature mixes specific types, producing intermediate forms. But the main point is that contingency is ascribed to the impotence of Nature itself and not to the finite mind's incapability of giving a purely rational account of Nature. Whether on his

[1] *W*, IX, pp. 63–4; *E*, 250.

principles Hegel ought to have admitted contingency in Nature is disputable, but the fact that he did so is not open to doubt. And this is why he sometimes speaks of Nature as a Fall (*Abfall*) from the Idea. In other words, contingency represents the externality of Nature in relation to the Idea. And it follows that Nature 'is not to be deified'.[1] Indeed, it is a mistake, Hegel says, to regard natural phenomena such as the heavenly bodies as works of God in a higher sense than the creations of the human spirit, such as works of art or the State. Hegel certainly followed Schelling in attributing to Nature a status which it did not enjoy in the philosophy of Fichte. At the same time he shows no inclination to share the romantic divinization of Nature.

But though Hegel rejects any deification of existing Nature, the fact remains that if Nature is real it must be a moment in the life of the Absolute. For the Absolute is the totality. Hegel is thus placed in a difficult position. On the one hand he has no wish to deny that there is an objective Nature. Indeed, it is essential to his system to maintain that there is. For the Absolute is the identity-in-difference of subjectivity and objectivity. And if there is real subjectivity, there must be real objectivity. On the other hand it is not easy for him to explain how contingency can have any place in a system of absolute idealism. And it is understandable if we can discern a marked tendency to adopt a Platonic position by distinguishing between the inside, as it were, of Nature, its rational structure or reflection of the Idea, and its outside, its contingent aspect, and by relegating the latter to the sphere of the irrational and unreal. There must indeed be an objective Nature. For the Idea must take the form of objectivity. And there cannot be an objective Nature without contingency. But the philosopher cannot cope with this element, beyond registering the fact that it is there and must be there. And what Professor Hegel cannot cope with he tends to dismiss as irrational and so as unreal. For the rational is the real and the real the rational. Obviously, once contingency has been admitted Hegel is driven either to admit some kind of dualism or to slide over the contingent element in Nature as though it were not 'really real'.

However this may be, Nature, in so far as it can be treated by the philosopher, 'is to be considered as a system of stages, of which one proceeds necessarily from the other'.[2] But it must be clearly understood that this system of stages or levels in Nature is a

---

[1] *W*, vi, p. 147; *E*, 193.        [2] *W*, vi, p. 149; *E*, 194.

dialectical development of concepts and not an empirical history
of Nature. It is indeed somewhat amusing to find Hegel dismissing
the evolutionary hypothesis in a cavalier manner.[1] But a physical
hypothesis of this kind is in any case irrelevant to the philosophy
of Nature as expounded by Hegel. For it introduces the idea of
temporal succession which has no place in the dialectical deduction
of the levels of Nature. And if Hegel had lived to a time when the
evolutionary hypothesis had won wide acceptance, it would have
been open to him to say: 'Well, I dare say that I was wrong about
evolution. But in any case it is an empirical hypothesis, and its
acceptance or rejection does not affect the validity of my
dialectic.'

As one would expect, the main divisions of Hegel's philosophy of
Nature are three in number. In the *Encyclopaedia* they are given
as mathematics, physics and organic physics, while in the lectures
on the philosophy of Nature they are given as mechanics, physics
and organics. In both cases, however, Hegel starts with space,
with what is most removed from mind or Spirit, and works
dialectically up to the animal organism which of all levels of
Nature is the closest to Spirit. Space is sheer externality: in the
organism we find internality. Subjectivity can be said to make its
appearance in the animal organism, though not in the form of self-
consciousness. Nature brings us to the threshold of Spirit, but only
to the threshold.

It is hardly worth while following Hegel into the details of his
philosophy of Nature. But attention should be drawn to the fact
that he is not trying to do the work of the scientist all over again
by some peculiar philosophical method of his own. He is concerned rather with finding in Nature as known through observation
and science the exemplification of a dynamic rational pattern. This
may sometimes lead to bizarre attempts to show that natural
phenomena are what they are, or what Hegel believes that they
are, because it is rational and, so to speak, for the best that they
should be what they are. And we may well feel somewhat sceptical
about the value of this kind of speculative or higher physics, as
well as amused at the philosopher's tendency to look down on
empirical science from a superior position. But it is as well to
understand that Hegel takes empirical science for granted, even
if he sometimes takes sides, and not always to the advantage of his
reputation, in controversial issues. It is more a question of fitting

[1] *W*, IX, pp. 59–62; *E*, 249.

the facts into a conceptual scheme than of pretending to deduce the facts in a purely *a priori* manner.

4. 'The Absolute is Spirit: this is the highest definition of the Absolute. To find this definition and to understand its content was, one may say, the final motive of all culture and philosophy. All religion and science have striven to reach this point.'[1] The Absolute in itself is Spirit, but it is potential rather than actual Spirit.[2] The Absolute for itself, Nature, is Spirit, but it is 'self-alienated Spirit',[3] in religious language it is, as Hegel puts it, God in his otherness. Spirit begins to exist as such only when we come to the human spirit, which is studied by Hegel in the third main part of his system, the philosophy of Spirit.

The philosophy of Spirit, needless to say, has three main parts or subdivisions. 'The two first parts of the doctrine of Spirit treat of the finite spirit',[4] while the third part deals with absolute Spirit, the *Logos* in its concrete existence as self-thinking Thought. In this section we shall be concerned only with the first part, to which Hegel gives the title 'subjective Spirit'.

This first part of the philosophy of Spirit is subdivided, according to Hegel's pervasive dialectical scheme, into three subordinate parts. Under the heading of anthropology he treats of the soul (*Seele*) as sensing and feeling subject. The soul is, as it were, a point of transition from Nature to Spirit. On the one hand it reveals the ideality of Nature, while on the other hand it is 'only the *sleep* of the Spirit'.[5] That is to say, it enjoys self-feeling (*Selbstgefühl*) but not reflective self-consciousness. It is sunk in the particularity of its feelings. And it is actual precisely as embodied, the body being the externality of the soul. In the human organism soul and body are its inner and outer aspects.

From the concept of the soul in this restricted sense Hegel passes to the phenomenology of consciousness, resuming some of the themes already treated in *The Phenomenology of Spirit*. The soul of the section on anthropology was subjective spirit considered on its lowest level, as a yet undifferentiated unity. On the level of consciousness, however, subjective spirit is confronted by an object, first by an object regarded as external to and independent of the subject, then, in self-consciousness, by itself. Finally, the subject

---

[1] *W*, VI, p. 228; *E*, 302.
[2] The logical Idea, considered precisely as such, is the category of Spirit, or self-thinking Thought, rather than potential Spirit.
[3] *W*, IX, p. 50; *E*, 247.          [4] *W*, VI, p. 229; *E*, 305.
[5] *W*, VI, p. 232; *E*, 309.

s depicted as rising to universal self-consciousness in which it
recognizes other selves as both distinct from and one with itself.
Here, therefore, consciousness (consciousness, that is, of something external to the subject) and self-consciousness are unified on
a higher level.

The third section of the philosophy of subjective Spirit is
entitled 'mind' or 'spirit' (*Geist*), and it considers the powers or
general modes of activity of the finite spirit as such. We are no
longer concerned simply with slumbering spirit, the 'soul' of the
section on anthropology, nor, as in phenomenology, with the ego
or subject in relation to an object. We have returned from the
finite spirit as term of a relation to spirit in itself but at a higher
level than that of soul. In a sense we are concerned with psychology
rather than with the phenomenology of consciousness. But the
psychology in question is not empirical psychology but a dialectical
deduction of the concepts of the logically successive stages in the
activity of the finite spirit in itself.

Hegel studies the activity of the finite spirit or mind in both its
theoretical and its practical aspects. Under the theoretical aspect
he treats, for instance, of intuition, memory, imagination and
thought, while under the practical aspect he considers feeling,
impulse and will. And his conclusion is that 'the actual free will is
the unity of the theoretical and practical spirit; *free will which
exists for itself as free will*'.[1] He is speaking, of course, of the will as
conscious of its freedom. And this is '*will* as free *intelligence*'.[2] We
can say, therefore, that the concept of Spirit in itself is the concept
of the rational will (*der vernünftige Wille*).

But 'whole regions of the world, Africa and the East, have never
had this idea and do not yet have it. The Greeks and the Romans,
Plato and Aristotle, also the Stoics, did not have it. On the
contrary, they knew only that man is actually free by birth (as a
citizen of Athens or Sparta and so on) or through strength of
character, education or philosophy (the wise man is free even when
he is a slave and in chains). This idea entered the world through
Christianity, according to which the individual *as such* possesses
an *infinite* value, . . . that is, that man *in himself* is destined to the
highest freedom.'[3] This idea of the realization of freedom is a key-
idea in Hegel's philosophy of history.

5. We have seen that the Absolute in itself objectifies or
expresses itself in Nature. So also does Spirit in itself objectify or

---

[1] *W*, x, p. 379; *E*, 481.            [2] *Ibid.*            [3] *W*, x, p. 380; *E*, 482.

express itself, issuing, as it were, out of its state of immediacy. Thus we come to the sphere of 'objective Spirit', the second main part of the philosophy of Spirit as a whole.

The first phase of objective Spirit is the sphere of right (*das Recht*). The person, the individual subject conscious of his freedom, must give external expression to his nature as free spirit; he must 'give himself an external sphere of freedom'.[1] And he does this by expressing his will in the realm of material things. That is to say, he expresses his free will by effectively appropriating and using material things. Personality confers the capacity for having and exercising rights such as that of property. A material thing, precisely because it is material and not spiritual, can have no rights: it is an instrument for the expression of rational will. By its being taken possession of and used a thing's non-personal nature is actually revealed and its destiny fulfilled. Indeed, it is in a sense elevated by being thus set in relation to a rational will.

A person becomes the owner of a thing not by a merely internal act of will but by effective appropriation, by embodying his will in it, as it were.[2] But he can also withdraw his will from the thing, thereby alienating it. And this is possible because the thing is external to him. A man can relinquish his right, for example, to a house. He can also relinquish his right to his labour for a limited time and for a specified purpose. For his labour can then be looked upon as something external. But he cannot alienate his total freedom by handing himself over as a slave. For his total freedom is not and cannot properly be regarded as something external to himself. Nor can his moral conscience or his religion be regarded as an external thing.[3]

In Hegel's somewhat odd dialectical progression the concept of alienation of property leads us to the concept of contract (*Vertrag*). True, alienation of property might take the form of withdrawing one's will, as it were, from a thing and leaving it ownerless. I might alienate an umbrella in this way. But we then remain within the sphere of the abstract concept of property. We advance beyond

[1] *W*, VII, p. 94; *R*, 41. The letter *R* signifies *The Philosophy of Right*. The following number refers to the section. In references to *R* the word 'addition' refers to the additions made by Hegel to the original text. In Professor T. M. Knox's translation these additions are printed after the version of the original text.

[2] Hegel is speaking of the right of property in the abstract. Needless to say, once the concept of society has been introduced the range of legitimate appropriation is restricted.

[3] This refers to religion as something internal. In a state of organized society a man cannot claim inviolability for the external expression of his religious beliefs when such expression is socially harmful.

this sphere by introducing the concept of the unity of two or more individual wills in respect of property, that is, by developing the concept of contract. When a man gives, sells or exchanges by agreement, two wills come together. But he can also agree with one or more persons to possess and use certain property in common for a common end. And here the union of wills, mediated by an external thing, is more evident.

But though contract rests on a union of wills, there is obviously no guarantee that the particular wills of the contracting parties will remain in union. In this sense the union of wills into a common will is contingent. And it comprises within itself the possibility of its own negation. This negation is actualized in wrong. The concept of wrong, however, passes through several phases; and Hegel considers in turn civil wrong (which is the result of incorrect interpretation rather than of evil intent or disrespect of other persons' rights), fraud and crime and violence. The notion of crime brings him to the subject of punishment, which he interprets as a cancellation of wrong, a cancellation which is said to be demanded even by the implicit will of the criminal himself. A criminal, according to Hegel, is not to be treated like an animal which has to be deterred or reformed. As a rational free being, he implicitly consents to and even demands the annulment of his crime through punishment.

Now, it is easy to see how Hegel is led from the concept of contract to that of wrong. For contract, as a free act, involves the possibility of its violation. But it is not so easy to see how the concept of wrong can reasonably be regarded as the unity on a higher plane of the concepts of property and contract. However, it is obvious that Hegel's dialectic is often a process of rational reflection in which one idea leads more or less naturally to another than a process of strictly necessary deduction. And even though he persists in observing his uniform triadic scheme, there is not much point in pressing it.

6. In wrong there is an opposition between the particular will and the universal will, the principle of rightness, which is implicit in the common will expressed in contract. This is true at least of wrong in the form of crime. The particular will negates right, and in doing so it negates the conception or notion of the will, which is universal, the rational free will as such. As we have seen, punishment is the negation of this negation. But punishment is external, in the sense that it is inflicted by an external authority. The

opposition or negation can be adequately overcome only when the particular will is in harmony with the universal will, that is, when it becomes what it ought to be, namely in accord with the concept of the will as raised above mere particularity and selfishness. Such a will is the moral will. We are thus led to make the transition from the concept of right to that of morality (*Moralität*).

It is important to note that the term 'morality' is used by Hegel in a much more restricted sense than it bears in ordinary usage. True, the term can be used in a variety of ways in ordinary language. But when we think of morality, we generally think of the fulfilment of positive duties, especially in a social setting, whereas Hegel abstracts from particular duties, towards the family, for example, or the State, and uses the term for what he calls 'a determination of the will [*Willensbestimmtheit*], so far as it is in the interior of the will in general'.[1] The moral will is free will which has returned on itself, that is, which is conscious of itself as free and which recognizes only itself, and no external authority, as the principle of its actions. As such the will is said to be 'infinite' or universal not only in itself but also for itself. 'The moral stand-point is the standpoint of the will in so far as it is *infinite* not simply *in itself* but *for itself*.'[2] It is the will as conscious of itself as the source of its own principle of action in an unrestricted way. Hegel does indeed introduce in passing the topic of obligation or ought (*Sollen*). For the will considered as a particular finite will may not be in accordance with the will considered as universal; and what is willed by the latter thus appears to the former as a demand or obligation. And, as will be seen presently, he discusses action from the point of view of the responsibility of the subject for its action. But in his treatment of morality he is concerned with the autonomous free will in its subjective aspect, that is, with the purely formal aspect of morality (in the wider sense of the term).

This purely formal treatment of morality is, of course, an unfortunate legacy from the Kantian philosophy. It is all the more important, therefore, to understand that morality, as Hegel uses the term, is a one-sided concept in which the mind cannot rest. It is certainly not his intention to imply that morality consists simply of 'interiority'. On the contrary, it is his intention to show that the purely formal concept of morality is inadequate. And we can say, therefore, that he treats the Kantian ethic as a one-sided

[1] *W*, x, p. 392; *E*, 503.          [2] *W*, vii, p. 164; *R*, 105.

moment in the dialectical development of the full moral consciousness. If, then, we use the term 'morality' to mean the whole ethical
life of man, it would be quite incorrect to say that Hegel makes it
entirely formal and 'interior' or subjective. For he does nothing of
the kind. At the same time it is arguable that in the transition from
morality in the restricted sense (*Moralität*) to the concrete ethical
life (*Sittlichkeit*) some important elements in the moral consciousness are omitted or at least slurred over.

The subjective will externalizes itself in action. But the free will,
as self-determined, has the right to regard as its own action, for
which it can be held accountable, only those acts which stand in
certain relations to it. We can say, therefore, that Hegel raises the
question, for what actions can a person rightly be held accountable?
Or, what are, properly speaking, the actions of a person? But it
must be remembered that Hegel is thinking of the general formal
characteristics of actions, and that he is not concerned at this stage
with indicating where a person's concrete moral duties lie. For
the matter of that, a person can be accountable for bad as well as
for good actions. Hegel is, as it were, going behind the moral
distinction between good and bad to the characteristics of action
which make it possible for us to say that a person has acted
morally or immorally.

In the first place any change or alteration in the world which the
subject brings about can be called his 'deed' (*Handlung*). But he
has the right to recognize as his 'action' (*That*) only that deed
which was the purpose (*Vorsatz*) of his will. The external world is
the sphere of contingency, and I cannot hold myself responsible
for the unforeseeable consequences of my action. It does not follow,
of course, that I can disavow all its consequences. For some
consequences are simply the outward shape which my acting
necessarily assumes, and they must be counted as comprised
within my purpose. But it would be contrary to the idea of the
self-determining free will to hold myself responsible for the
unforeseeable consequences or alterations in the world which are in
some sense my deed but which were certainly not comprised within
my purpose.

Purpose is thus the first phase of morality. The second is
intention (*Absicht*) or, more accurately, intention and welfare or
well-being (*das Wohl*). It seems true to say that we generally use
the words 'purpose' and 'intention' synonymously. But Hegel
distinguishes between them. If I apply a lighted match to

inflammable material in the grate, the natural and foreseen consequence of my action is the ensuing fire. My purpose was to light the fire. But I should not perform this action except in view of an intended end, such as warming myself or drying the room. And my intention is relevant to the moral character of the action. It is not, of course, the only relevant factor. Hegel is far from saying that any sort of action is justified by a good intention. But intention is none the less a moment or relevant factor in morality.

Hegel assumes that intentions are directed to welfare or well-being. And he insists that the moral agent has a right to seek his own welfare, the satisfaction of his needs as a human being. He is not suggesting, of course, that egoism is the norm or morality. But at present we are considering morality apart from its social framework and expression. And when Hegel insists that a man has a right to seek his own welfare, he is saying that the satisfaction of one's needs as a human being belongs to morality and is not opposed to it. In other words, he is defending a point of view comprised in Greek ethics as represented by Aristotle and rejecting the Kantian notion that an act loses its moral value if performed from inclination. In his opinion it is quite wrong to suppose that morality consists in a constant warfare against inclinations and natural impulses.

But though the individual is entitled to seek his own welfare, morality certainly does not consist in the particular will seeking its particular good. At the same time this idea has to be preserved and not simply negated. Hence we must proceed to the idea of the particular will identifying itself with the rational and so universal will and aiming at universal welfare. And the unity of the particular will with the concept of the will in itself (that is, with the rational will as such) is the good (*das Gute*), which can be described as 'the realization of freedom, the absolute final purpose of the world'.[1]

The rational will as such is a man's true will, his will as a rational, free being. And the need for conforming his particular will, his will as this or that particular individual, to the rational will (to his true self, one might say) presents itself as duty or obligation. Inasmuch, therefore, as morality abstracts from all concrete positive duties, we can say that duty should be done for duty's sake. A man ought to conform his particular will to the universal will, which is his true or real will; and he ought to do so

---

[1] *W*, VII, p. 188; *R*, 129.

imply because it is his duty. But this, of course, tells us nothing
bout what a man ought to will in particular. We can only say that
he good will is determined by the subject's inward certainty,
which is conscience (*Gewissen*). 'Conscience expresses the absolute
ight of subjective self-consciousness to know *in itself* and *through
self* what is right and duty, and to recognize nothing as good
ther than what it knows to be good, at the same time assert-
ng that what it knows and wills as good is in truth right and
uty.'[1]

Hegel thus incorporates into his account of morality what we
ay perhaps call the Protestant insistence on inwardness and on
he absolute authority of conscience. But pure subjectivism and
inwardness are really abhorrent to him. And he proceeds immedi-
tely to argue that to rely on a purely subjective conscience is to
e potentially evil. If he had contented himself with saying that a
erson's conscience can err and that some objective norm or
tandard is required, he would have been expounding a familiar
nd easily intelligible position. But he gives the impression of
rying to establish a connection between undiluted moral inward-
ess and wickedness, at least as a possible conjunction. Exaggera-
ion apart, however, his main point is that we cannot give a
efinite content to morality on the level of pure moral inwardness.
o do so, we have to turn to the idea of organized society.

The concepts of abstract right and of morality are thus for
Hegel one-sided notions which have to be unified on a higher level
n the concept of ethical life (*die Sittlichkeit*). That is to say, in the
ialectical development of the sphere of objective Spirit they
eveal themselves as moments or phases in the development of
he concept of concrete ethics, phases which have at the same time
o be negated, preserved and elevated.

Concrete ethics is for Hegel social ethics. It is one's position in
ociety which specifies one's duties. Hence social ethics is the
ynthesis or unity at a higher level of the one-sided concepts of
ight and morality.

7. Hegel's way of dealing with the concrete life is to deduce the
hree moments of what he calls 'the ethical substance' (*die
ittliche Substanz*). These are the family, civil society and the State.
Dne might perhaps expect him to consider man's concrete duties
n this social setting. But what he actually does is to study the
ssential natures of the family, civil society and the State and to

[1] *W*, VII, pp. 196–7; *R*, 137.

show how one concept leads to another. It is not necessary, he remarks, to add that a man has these or those duties towards his family or towards the State. For this will be sufficiently evident from a study of the natures or essences of these societies. In any case it cannot properly be expected of the philosopher that he should draw up a code of particular duties. He is concerned with the universal, with the dialectical development of concepts, rather than with moralizing.

The family, the first moment in 'the ethical substance' or union of moral subjectivity and objectivity, is said to be 'the immediate or natural ethical spirit'.[1] In the social sphere the human spirit, issuing, as it were, out of its inwardness, objectifies itself first of all in the family. This is not to say that in Hegel's opinion the family is a transitory institution which passes away when other types of society have reached their full development. It is to say that the family is the logically prior society inasmuch as it represents the universal in its logically first moment of immediacy. The members of the family are considered as one, united primarily by the bond of feeling, that is, by love.[2] The family is what one might call a feeling-totality. It is, as it were, one person whose will is expressed in property, the common property of the family.

But if we consider the family in this way, we must add that it contains within itself the seeds of its own dissolution. Within the family, considered as a feeling-totality and as representing the moment of universality, the children exist simply as members. They are, of course, individual persons, but they are such *in* themselves rather than *for* themselves. In the course of time, however, they pass out of the unity of family life into the condition of individual persons, each of whom possesses his own plans in life and so on. It is as though the particulars emerge out of the universality of family life and assert themselves as particulars.

The notion of the comparatively undifferentiated unity of the family breaking up through the emergence of particularity is not in itself, of course, the notion of a society. Rather is it the notion of the dissolution or negation of a society. But this negation is itself negated or overcome in what Hegel calls 'civil society' (*die bürgerliche Gesellschaft*) which represents the second moment in the development of social ethics.

[1] *W*, VII, p. 237; *R*, 157.
[2] Obviously, Hegel is not so foolish as to maintain that as a matter of empirical fact every family is united by love. He is talking about the concept or idea essence of the family, what it ought to be.

To understand what Hegel means by civil society we can first picture a plurality of individuals, each of whom seeks his own ends and endeavours to satisfy his own needs. We must then conceive them as united in a form of economic organization for the better furtherance of their ends. This will involve specialization of labour and the development of economic classes and corporations. Further, an economic organization of this kind requires for its stability the institution of law and the machinery of law-enforcements, namely law-courts, a judiciary and police.

Inasmuch as Hegel considers the political constitution and government under the heading of the State and not under that of civil society, we may be inclined to comment that the latter could never exist. For how can there be laws and the administration of justice except in a State? The answer is, of course, that there cannot. But Hegel is not concerned with maintaining that civil society ever existed in the precise form in which he describes it. For the concept of civil society is for him a one-sided and inadequate concept of the State itself. It is the State 'as external State'.[1] That is to say, it is the State with the latter's essential nature omitted.

In other words, Hegel is concerned with the dialectical development of the concept of the State. And he does so by taking two one-sided concepts of society and showing that both represent ideas which are united on a higher plane in the concept of the State. The family, of course, persists in the State. So does civil society. For it represents an aspect of the State, even though it is only a partial aspect. But it does not follow that this aspect, taken in isolation and called 'civil society', ever actually existed precisely as such. The dialectical development of the concept of the State is a conceptual development. It is not equivalent to the statement that, historically speaking, the family existed first, then civil society, then the State, as though these concepts were all mutually exclusive. If we interpret Hegel in this way, we shall probably be inclined to think that he is concerned with expounding a thoroughly totalitarian theory of the State as against, for example, the sort of theory advanced by Herbert Spencer which more or less corresponds, though with certain important qualifications, to the concept of civil society. But though Hegel would doubtless have regarded Spencer's theory of society as very inadequate, he thought of the moment of particularity, represented by the concept of civil

[1] *W*, x, p. 401; *E*, 523.

society, as being preserved, and not simply cancelled out, in the State.

8. The family represents the moment of universality in the sense of undifferentiated unity. Civil society represents the moment of particularity. The State represents the unity of the universal and the particular. Instead of undifferentiated unity we find in the State differentiated universality, that is, unity in difference. And instead of sheer particularity[1] we find the identification of the particular with the universal will. To put the matter in another way, in the State self-consciousness has risen to the level of universal self-consciousness. The individual is conscious of himself as being a member of the totality in such a way that his selfhood is not annulled but fulfilled. The State is not an abstract universal standing over against its members: it exists in and through them. At the same time by participation in the life of the State the members are elevated above their sheer particularity. In other words, the State is an organic unity. It is a concrete universal, existing in and through particulars which are distinct and one at the same time.

The State is said to be 'the self-conscious ethical substance'.[2] It is 'ethical mind as substantial will manifest and clear to itself, which thinks and knows itself and accomplishes what it knows in so far as it knows it'.[3] The State is the actuality of the rational will when this has been raised to the plane of universal self-consciousness. It is thus the highest expression of objective Spirit. And the preceding moments of this sphere are resumed and synthesized in it. For instance, rights are established and maintained as the expression of the universal rational will. And morality obtains its content. That is to say, a man's duties are determined by his position in the social organism. This does not mean, of course, that a man has duties only to the State and none to his family. For the family is not annulled in the State: it is an essential, if subordinate moment in the State's life. Nor does Hegel mean to imply that a man's duties are determined once and for all by an unchangeable social position. For though he insists that the welfare of the whole

[1] To speak of civil society as representing 'sheer particularity' is from one point of view to be guilty of exaggeration. For within civil society itself the antagonism consequent on the emergence and self-assertion of the particulars are partly overcome through the corporations on which Hegel lays stress. But the union of wills among members of a corporation in seeking a common end has also limited universality and prepares the way for the transition to the concept of the State.

[2] *W*, x, p. 409; *E*, 535.          [3] *W*, vii, p. 328; *R*, 257.

ocial organism is paramount, he also insists that the principle of ndividual freedom and personal decision is not annihilated in the State but preserved. The theory of 'my station and its duties', to se Bradley's famous phrase, does not imply acceptance of some ort of caste system.

It is indeed undeniable that Hegel speaks of the State in the most exalted terms. He even describes it, for instance, as 'this ctual God'.[1] But there are several points to be borne in mind. In he first place the State, as objective Spirit, is necessarily 'divine' n some sense. And just as the Absolute itself is identity-in-difference, so is the State, though on a more restricted scale. In the econd place it is essential to remember that Hegel is speaking hroughout of the concept of the State, its ideal essence. He has no ntention of suggesting that historical States are immune from riticism. Indeed, he makes this point quite clear. 'The State is no vork of art; it stands in the world, and so in the sphere of caprice, ontingency and error; it can be disfigured by evil conduct in many espects. But the ugliest human being, the criminal, the diseased nd the cripple, each is still a living man. The positive element, fe, remains in spite of the privation; and it is with this positive lement that we have to do here.'[2]

In the third place we must bear in mind Hegel's insistence on he fact that the mature or well-developed State preserves the rinciple of private liberty in the ordinary sense. He maintains ndeed that the will of the State must prevail over the particular vill when there is a clash between them. And inasmuch as the will f the State, the universal or general will, is for him in some sense he 'real' will of the individual, it follows that the individual's lentification of his interests with those of the State is the ctualization of freedom. For the free will is potentially universal, nd, as universal, it wills the general good. There is a strong dose f Rousseau's doctrines in Hegel's political theory. At the same ime it is unjust to Hegel to draw from the highfaluting way in hich he speaks of the majesty and divinity of the State the onclusion that his ideal is a totalitarian State in which private eedom and initiative are reduced to a minimum. On the contrary, mature State is for Hegel one which ensures the maximum evelopment of personal liberty which is compatible with the overeign rights of the universal will. Thus he insists that while e stability of the State requires that its members should make

[1] *W*, VII, p. 336; *R*, 258, addition.      [2] *Ibid*.

the universal end their end[1] according to their several positions and
capacities, it also requires that the State should be in a real sense
the means to the satisfaction of their subjective aims.[2] As already
remarked, the concept of civil society is not simply cancelled out
in the concept of the State.

In his treatment of the State Hegel discusses first the political
constitution. And he represents constitutional monarchy as being
the most rational form. But he regards a corporative State as more
rational than democracy after the English model. That is to say,
he maintains that the citizens should participate in the affairs of
the State as members of subordinate wholes, corporations or
Estates, rather than as individuals. Or, more accurately, representatives should represent corporations or Estates rather than the
individual citizens precisely as such. And this view seems to be
required by Hegel's dialectical scheme. For the concept of civil
society, which is preserved in that of the State, culminates in the
idea of the corporation.

It has frequently been said that by deducing constitutional
monarchy as the most rational form of political organization
Hegel canonized the Prussian State of his time. But though he
may, like Fichte, have come to regard Prussia as the most
promising instrument for educating the Germans to political self-
consciousness, his historical sense was far too strong to allow him to
suppose that one particular type of constitution could be profitably
adopted by any given nation without regard to its history,
traditions and spirit. He may have talked a good deal about the
rational State, but he was far too reasonable himself to think that
a constitution could be imposed on all nations simply because it
corresponded best with the demands of abstract reason. 'A constitution *develops* out of the spirit of a nation *only* in identity with
this spirit's own development; and it runs through, together with
this spirit, the grades of formation and the alterations required by
its spirit. It is the indwelling spirit and the history of the nation
(and, indeed, the history is simply the history of this spirit) by
which constitutions have been and are made.'[3] Again, 'Napoleon
wished to give the Spaniards, for example, a constitution *a priori*
but the attempt fared badly enough. For a constitution is no mere
artificial product; it is the work of centuries, the idea and the
consciousness of the rational in so far as it has been developed in a

---

[1] It should be remembered that Hegel was partly concerned with educating the
Germans to political self-consciousness.
[2] Cf. *W*, vii, p. 344; *R*, 265, addition.          [3] *W*, x, p. 416; *E*, 540.

people. . . . What Napoleon gave the Spaniards was more rational
than what they had before, and yet they rejected it as something
alien to them.'[1]

Hegel further observes that from one point of view it is idle to
ask whether monarchy or democracy is the best form of government. The fact of the matter is that any constitution is one-sided
and inadequate unless it embodies the principle of subjectivity
(that is, the principle of personal freedom) and answers to the
demands of 'mature reason'.[2] In other words, a more rational
constitution means a more liberal constitution, at least in the
sense that it must explicitly allow for the free development of
individual personality and respect the rights of individuals. Hegel
was by no means so reactionary as has sometimes been supposed.
He did not hanker after the *ancien régime*.

9. It is worth drawing attention to Hegel's general idea of
political theory. His insistence that the philosopher is concerned
with the concept or ideal essence of the State may suggest that in
his opinion it is the philosopher's business to show politicians and
statesmen what they should aim at, by portraying more or less in
detail a supposedly ideal State, subsisting in some Platonic world
of essences. But if we look at the Preface to *The Philosophy of
Right* we find Hegel denying in explicit terms that it is the
philosopher's business to do anything of the kind. The philosopher
is concerned with understanding the actual rather than with
offering political schemes and panaceas. And in a sense the actual
is the past. For political philosophy appears in the period of a
culture's maturity, and when the philosopher attempts to understand the actual, it is already passing into the past and giving
place to new forms. In Hegel's famous words, 'when philosophy
paints its grey on grey, then has a shape of life grown old. And by
this grey on grey it can only be understood, not rejuvenated. The
owl of Minerva spreads its wings only with the falling of the dusk.'[3]

Some thinkers, of course, have supposed that they were
delineating an eternal pattern, a changeless ideal essence. But in
Hegel's opinion they were mistaken. 'Even the Platonic *Republic*,
which passes proverbially as an *empty ideal*, was in essence nothing
but an interpretation of Greek ethical life.'[4] After all, 'every
individual is a son of his time [and] it is just as foolish to suppose

---

[1] *W*, VII, p. 376; *R*, 274, addition.       [2] *W*, VII, p. 376; *R*, 273, addition.
[3] *W*, VII, pp. 36–7; *R*, preface. Marx's equally famous retort was that it is the
philosopher's business to change the world, not simply to understand it.
[4] *W*, VII, p. 33; *R*, preface.

that a philosophy can transcend its contemporary world as it is to suppose that an individual can overleap his own time. . . .'[1]

The clear expression of this view obviously constitutes an answer to those who take too seriously Hegel's apparent canonization of the Prussian State. For it is difficult to suppose that a man who understood very well that Aristotle, for example, canonized the Greek *polis* or City-State at a time when its vigorous life was already on the decline really supposed that the contemporary State of his own period represented the final and culminating form of political development. And even if Hegel did think this, there is nothing in his philosophy as such to warrant his prejudice. On the contrary, one would expect the sphere of objective Spirit to undergo further developments as long as history lasts.

Given this interpretation of political philosophy, the natural conclusion to draw is that the philosopher is concerned with making explicit what we may call the operative ideal of the culture or nation to which he belongs. He is an interpreter of the spirit of his time (*die Zeitgeist*). In and through him the political ideals of a society are raised to the level of reflective consciousness. And a society becomes self-conscious in this way only when it has reached maturity and looks back, as it were, on itself, at a time, that is to say, when a form of life has already actualized itself and is ready to pass into or give way to another.

No doubt, this is partly what Hegel means. His remarks about Plato's *Republic* show that it is. But in this case, it may be asked, how can he at the same time speak of the political philosopher as being concerned with the concept or essence of the State?

The answer to this question must be given, I think, in terms of Hegel's metaphysics. The historical process is the self-actualization of Spirit or Reason. 'What is rational is real and what is real is rational.'[2] And the concept of Spirit is the concept of identity-in-difference at the level of rational life. Objective Spirit, therefore, which culminates in the State tends towards the manifestation of identity-in-difference in political life. And this means that a mature or rational State will unite in itself the moments of universality and difference. It will embody universal self-consciousness or the self-conscious General Will. But this is embodied only in and through distinct finite spirits, each of which as spirit, possesses 'infinite' value. Hence no State can be fully mature or rational (it cannot accord with the concept of the

---

[1] *W*, VII, p. 35; *R*, preface.     [2] *W*, VII, p. 33; *R*, preface.

State) unless it reconciles the conception of the State as an organic totality with the principle of individual freedom. And the philosopher, reflecting on the past and present political organizations, can discern how far they approximate to the requirements of the State as such. But this State as such is not a subsistent essence, existing in a celestial world. It is the *telos* or end of the movement of Spirit or Reason in man's social life. The philosopher can discern this *telos* in its essential outline, because he understands the nature of reality. But it does not follow that he is in a better position, as a philosopher, than is anyone else to prophesy the future or to tell statesmen and politicians what they ought to do. Philosophy always comes too late on the scene to do so.'[1] Plato may indeed have told contemporary Greeks how they ought, in his opinion, to organize the City-State. But he was in any case too late. For the shape of life which he dreamed of reorganizing was growing cold and would before long be ripe for decay. Utopian schemes are defeated by the movement of history.

10. Each State is in relation to other States a sovereign individual and demands recognition as such. The mutual relations between States are indeed partly regulated by treaties and by international law, which presuppose acceptance by the States concerned. But if this acceptance is refused or withdrawn, the ultimate arbiter in any dispute is war. For there is no sovereign power above individual States.

Now, if Hegel was simply registering an obvious empirical fact in the international life of his time, there would be no reason for adverse comment. But he goes on to justify war, as though it were an essential feature of human history. True, he admits that war can bring with it much injustice, cruelty and waste. But he argues that it has an ethical aspect and that it should not be regarded as 'an absolute evil and as a mere external contingent fact'.[2] On the contrary, it is a rational necessity. 'It is *necessary* that the finite, property and life, should be *posited* as contingent. . . .'[3] And this is precisely what war does. It is 'the condition in which we have to take seriously the vanity of temporal goods and things, which otherwise is usually only an edifying phrase'.[4]

It should be noted that Hegel is not simply saying that in war a man's moral qualities can be displayed on an heroic scale, which is obviously true. Nor is he saying merely that war brings home to

---

[1] *W*, vii, p. 36; *R*, preface.                [2] *W*, vii, p. 434; *R*, 324.
[3] *Ibid.*                                        [4] *Ibid.*

us the transitory character of the finite. He is asserting that war is a necessary rational phenomenon. It is in fact for him the means by which the dialectic of history gets, so to speak, a move on. It prevents stagnation and preserves, as he puts it, the ethical health of nations. It is the chief means by which a people's spirit acquires renewed vigour or a decayed political organism is swept aside and gives place to a more vigorous manifestation of the Spirit. Hegel rejects, therefore, Kant's ideal of perpetual peace.[1]

Obviously, Hegel had no experience of what we call total war. And he doubtless had the Napoleonic Wars and Prussia's struggle for independence fresh in his mind. But when one reads the passages in which he speaks of war and dismisses Kant's ideal of perpetual peace it is difficult to avoid the impression, partly comical and partly unpleasant, of a university professor romanticizing a dark feature of human history and decking it out with metaphysical trappings.[2]

11. Mention of international relations and of war as an instrument by which the historical dialectic progresses brings us to the subject of Hegel's concept of world-history.

Hegel distinguishes three main types of history or, rather, historiography. First there is 'original history', that is to say, descriptions of deeds and events and states of society which the historian had before his eyes. Thucydides' history represents this type. Secondly there is 'reflective history'. A general history, extending beyond the limits of the historian's experience, belongs to this type. So, for instance, does didactic history. Thirdly, there is 'philosophical history' or the philosophy of history. This term says Hegel, signifies 'nothing else but the thoughtful consideration of history'.[3] But it can hardly be claimed that this description taken by itself, is very enlightening. And, as Hegel explicitly admits, something more must be said by way of elucidation.

To say that the philosophy of history is the thoughtful consideration of history is to say that a thought is brought to this consideration. But the thought in question, Hegel insists, is not a preconceived plan or scheme into which the facts have somehow to be fitted. 'The only idea which philosophy brings with it [that is, to the contemplation of history] is the simple idea of reason

---

[1] See Vol. VI, pp. 185 and 209.

[2] In justice to Hegel we can recall that he himself had felt the effect of war, its exhibition of the transitoriness of the finite, when he lost his position and belongings at Jena as a result of Napoleon's victorious campaign.

[3] *W*, XI, p. 34; *S*, p. 8. The letter *S* signifies J. Sibree's translation of Hegel lectures on the philosophy of history.

at reason dominates the world and that world-history is thus a
ational process.'[1] As far as philosophy is concerned, this truth is
rovided in metaphysics. But in history as such it is an hypothesis.
ience the truth that world-history is the self-unfolding of Spirit
iust be exhibited as the result of reflection on history. In our
eflection history 'must be taken as it is; we must proceed
istorically, empirically'.[2]

The obvious comment on this is that even if Hegel disclaims
iny desire to force history into a preconceived mould, the thought
r idea which the philosopher brings to the study of history must
bviously exercise a great influence on his interpretation of events.
.ven if the idea is professedly proposed as an empirically verifiable
ypothesis, the philosopher who, like Hegel himself, believes that
s truth has been demonstrated in metaphysics will undoubtedly
e prone to emphasize those aspects of history which seem to offer
upport for the hypothesis. Moreover, for the Hegelian the
ypothesis is really no hypothesis at all but a demonstrated truth.

Hegel remarks, however, that even the would-be 'impartial'
istorians bring their own categories to the study of history.
.bsolute impartiality is a myth. And there cannot be a better
rinciple of interpretation than a proven philosophical truth.
.vidently, Hegel's general idea is more or less this. As the philo-
opher knows that reality is the self-unfolding of infinite reason,
e knows that reason must operate in human history. At the same
ime we cannot tell in advance how it operates. To discover this,
e have to study the course of events as depicted by historians in
he ordinary sense and try to discern the significant rational
rocess in the mass of contingent material. In theological language,
e know in advance that divine providence operates in history.
iut to see how it operates we must study the historical data.

Now, world-history is the process whereby Spirit comes to
ctual consciousness of itself as freedom. Hence 'world-history is
rogress in the consciousness of freedom'.[3] This consciousness is
ttained, of course, only in and through the mind of man. And the
iivine Spirit, as manifested in history through the consciousness
if man, is the World-Spirit (*der Weltgeist*). History, therefore, is
he process whereby the World-Spirit comes to explicit conscious-
iess of itself as free.

But though the *Weltgeist* attains consciousness of itself as free

---

[1] *W*, XI, p. 34; *S*, p. 9.          [2] *W*, XI, p. 36; *S*, p. 10.
[3] *W*, XI, p. 46; *S*, p. 19.

only in and through the human mind, the historian is concerned with nations rather than with individuals. Hence the unit, so to speak, in the concrete development of the World-Spirit is the national spirit or the spirit of a people (*der Volksgeist*). And by this Hegel means in part a people's culture as manifested not only in its political constitution and traditions but also in its morality, art, religion and philosophy. But a national spirit is not, of course, resident simply in legal forms, works of art and so on. It is a living totality, the spirit of a people as living in and through that people. And the individual is a bearer of the *Weltgeist* in so far as he participates in this more limited totality, the *Volksgeist*, which is itself a phase or moment in the life of the World-Spirit.

Hegel does indeed assert that 'in world-history the individuals with whom we have to do are peoples, the totalities which are States'.[1] But he can use the terms 'State' and 'national spirit' more or less interchangeably because the first term signifies for him something much more than the juridical State. He understands by the State in this context a totality which exists in and through its members, though it is not identical with any given set of citizens existing here and now, and which gives concrete form to the spirit and culture of a people or nation.

It should be noted, however, that one important reason why Hegel insists that world-history is concerned with States is that in his view a national spirit exists for itself (that is, as conscious of itself) only in and through the State. Hence those peoples which do not constitute national States are practically excluded from consideration in world-history. For their spirits are only implicit they do not exist 'for themselves'.

Each national spirit, therefore, embodied in a State, is a phase or moment in the life of the *Weltgeist*. Indeed, this World-Spirit is really a *result* of the interplay of national spirits. They are, so to speak, the moments in its actualization. National spirits are limited, finite 'and their fates and deeds in their relations to one another reveal the dialectic of the finitude of these spirits. Out of this dialectic there arises the *Universal Spirit*, the unlimited *World-Spirit* which pronounces its judgment—and its judgment is the highest—upon the finite national spirits. It does so within *world-history* which is the *world's court of* judgment.'[2] The judgment of the nations is for Hegel immanent in history. The actual fate of each nation constitutes its judgment.

---

[1] *W*, XI, p. 40; *S*, p. 14.    [2] *W*, VIII, p. 446; *R*, 340.

Spirit, therefore, in its progress towards full and explicit self-consciousness takes the form of limited and one-sided manifestations of itself, the several national spirits. And Hegel assumes that in any given epoch one particular nation represents in a special way the development of the World-Spirit. 'This people is the dominant people in world-history for this epoch—*and it is only once that it can make its hour strike.*'[1] Its national spirit develops, reaches its zenith and then declines, after which the nation is relegated to the background of the historical stage. Hegel is doubtless thinking of the way in which Spain, for instance, developed into a great empire, with a peculiar stamp and culture of its own, and then declined. But he assumes without more ado that a nation cannot occupy the centre of the stage more than once. And this assumption is perhaps disputable, unless, of course, we choose to make it necessarily true by maintaining that a nation which enjoys a second period of outstanding importance is really a different nation with a different spirit. In any case Hegel's desire to find a particular world-historical nation for each epoch has a narrowing effect on his conception of history.

To say this is not, however, to deny that in his lectures on the philosophy of history Hegel covers a wide field. As he is dealing with world-history, this is obviously bound to be the case. The first part of his work is devoted to the Oriental world, including China, India, Persia, Asia Minor, Palestine and Egypt. In the second part he treats of the Greek world, and in the third of the Roman world, including the rise of Christianity to the position of an historical power (*eine geschichtliche Macht*). The fourth part is devoted to what Hegel calls the Germanic world. The period covered stretches from the Byzantine Empire up to the French Revolution and the Napoleonic Wars inclusively. Mohammedanism receives a brief treatment in this fourth part.

The Orientals, according to Hegel, did not know that man as such is free. And in the absence of this knowledge they were not free. They knew only that *one* man, the despot, was free. 'But for his very reason such freedom is only caprice, ferocity or brutal passion—or a mildness and tameness in the passions which is itself only an accident of Nature or caprice. This *one* is, therefore, only a despot, he is not a free man, a true human being.'[2]

In the Greco-Roman world there arises the consciousness of freedom. But the Greeks and Romans of classical times knew only

[1] *W*, VII, p. 449; *R*, 347.          [2] *W*, XI, p. 45; *S*, p. 18.

that *some* men are free, namely the free men as opposed to the slaves. Even Plato and Aristotle exemplify this inadequate phase in the growth of the consciousness of freedom.

In Hegel's view it was the 'Germanic' peoples who under the influence of Christianity first arrived at the conscious awareness that man as such is free. But though this principle was recognized from the start in Christianity, it does not follow that it immediately found expression in laws, government and political organization and institutions. The awareness of the freedom of the spirit arose first in religion, but a long process of development was required for it to attain explicit practical recognition as the basis of the State. And this process of development is studied in history. The inner consciousness of the freedom of the spirit had to give itself explicit objectification, and here Hegel attributes a leading role to the so-called Germanic peoples.

Now, we have seen that the units to which primary consideration is given in world-history are national States. But it is a notorious fact that Hegel emphasizes the role of what he calls the world-historical individuals (*die weltgeschichtlichen Individuen*), men such as Alexander the Great, Julius Caesar and Napoleon. And this may seem to involve him in some inconsistency. But national spirits and the World-Spirit which arises out of their dialectic exist and live and operate only in and through human beings. And Hegel's point of view is that the World-Spirit has used certain individuals as its instruments in a signal way. In theological language, they were the special instruments of divine providence. They had, of course, their subjective passions and private motives. Napoleon, for example, may have been dominated to a great extent by personal ambition and megalomania. But though the private motives, conscious and unconscious, of a Caesar or a Napoleon are of interest to the biographer and the psychologist, they are not of much importance or relevance for the philosopher of history who is interested in such men for what they accomplished as instruments of the World-Spirit. Nothing great, Hegel remarks, is accomplished in this world without passion. But the passions of the great figures of history are used as instruments by the World-Spirit and exhibit 'the cunning of Reason'. Whatever motives Julius Caesar may have had for crossing the Rubicon his action had an historical importance which probably far transcended anything that he understood. Whatever his private interests may have been, the cosmic Reason or Spirit in its 'cunning' used these nterests to transform the Republic into the Empire and to bring the Roman genius and spirit to the peak of its development.

If we abstract from all questionable metaphysics, Hegel is obviously saying something quite sensible. It is certainly not absurd to claim, for example, that the historian is or ought to be more interested in what Stalin actually accomplished for Russia than in the psychology of that unpleasing tyrant. But Hegel's teleological view of history implies in addition, of course, that what Stalin accomplished *had* to be accomplished, and that the Russian dictator, with all his unpleasant characteristics, was an instrument in the hands of the World-Spirit.[1]

12. In view of the already somewhat inordinate length of this chapter I have no wish either to repeat or to amplify the general remarks about the philosophy of history which I made in the preceding volume.[2] But one or two comments relating to Hegel's concept of world-history may be appropriate.

In the first place, if history is a rational process in the sense of being a teleological process, a movement towards a goal which is determined by the nature of the Absolute rather than by human choice, it may appear that all that occurs is justified by the very fact that it occurs. And if the history of the world is itself the highest court of judgment, the judgment of the nations, it may appear to follow that might is right. For example, if one nation succeeds in conquering another, it seems to follow that its action is justified by its success.

Now, the saying 'might is right' is perhaps generally understood as being an expression of that type of cynical outlook which is manifested by Callicles in Plato's *Gorgias*. For this outlook the notion of a universally obligatory and fundamentally unchanging moral law is the creation of a self-defensive instinct on the part of the weak who try by this means to enslave the strong and free. The really free and strong man sees through this notion of morality and rejects it. He sees that the only right is might. In his judgment the weak, nature's slaves, implicitly admit the truth of this judgment, though they are not consciously aware of the fact. For, individually weak, they try to exercise a collective might by imposing on the strong an ethical code which is of advantage to themselves.

[1] Hegel's answer to any theologically-minded critic is that the theory of the cunning of Reason is in accord with Christianity. For Christianity maintains that God brings good out of evil, using, for instance, Judas's betrayal of Christ in the accomplishment of the Redemption.
[2] See Vol. VI, pp. 422-7.

But Hegel was no cynic. As we have seen, he was convinced of the value of the human person as such, not merely of the value of some human beings. And it can be reasonably claimed that with him it is not so much a question of the cynical view that might is right as of the exaggeratedly optimistic view that in history right, in the form of the rational, is the necessarily dominant factor.

Yet it is arguable, of course, that in the long run it comes more or less to the same thing, even if there is a difference of attitude between Hegel and the cynic. If right always prevails in history, then successful might is justified. It is justified because it is right rather than because it is might; but it is none the less justified. Hegel does indeed allow, for example, that moral judgments can be passed on what he calls world-historical individuals. But he also makes it clear that such judgments possess for him only a purely formal rectitude, as he puts it. From the point of view of a given system of social ethics a great revolutionary, for example, may be a bad man. But from the point of view of world-history his deeds are justified, for he accomplishes what the universal Spirit requires. And if one nation conquers another, its action is justified inasmuch as it is a moment in the dialectic of world-history, whatever moral judgments are passed on the actions of the individuals involved when they are considered, so to speak, in their private capacities. Indeed, world-history is not interested in this second aspect of the situation.

We can say, therefore, that it is Hegel's metaphysical views rather than any cynical outlook which involve him in justifying all the events in which the world-historian or philosopher of history is interested. Hegel argues indeed that he is simply taking seriously and applying to history as a whole the Christian doctrine of divine providence. But there are obvious differences. Once the transcendent God has been transformed into the Hegelian Absolute and judgment has been made purely immanent in history itself, no escape is left from the conclusion that from the world-historical point of view all the events and actions which form moments in the self-manifestation of the Absolute are justified. And moral questions which possess importance from the Christian point of view become practically irrelevant. I do not mean to imply, of course, that this shows of itself that Hegel's point of view is false Nor do I mean to imply that a Christian historian is committed to moralizing. But Hegel's philosophy of history is much more than what historians generally understand by history. It is a metaphysical interpretation of history. And my point is that Hegel's metaphysics drives him to conclusions to which the Christian theologian is not committed. True, Hegel thought that he was giving the philosophical essence, as it were, of the Christian doctrine of providence. But in point of fact this 'demythologization' was a transformation.

Mention of Hegel's metaphysics suggests another comment. If, as Hegel maintains, world-history is the process by which the universal Spirit actualizes itself in time, it is difficult to understand why the goal of the process should not be a universal world-State or world-society in which personal freedom would be perfectly realized within an all-embracing unity. Even if Hegel wishes to insist that the universal is manifested in its particulars and that the particulars in question are national spirits, it would seem that the ideal end of the whole movement should be a world-federation, representing the concrete universal.

Hegel did not, however, adopt this point of view. World-history is for him essentially the dialectic of national spirits, of States, which are the determinate shape which Spirit assumes in history. If we consider Spirit as rising above these particular finite forms, we enter the sphere of absolute Spirit, which will be the theme of the next chapter.

### CHAPTER XI

# HEGEL (3)

*The sphere of absolute Spirit—The philosophy of art—The philosophy of religion—The relation between religion and philosophy—Hegel's philosophy of the history of philosophy— The influence of Hegel and the division between right-wing and left-wing Hegelians.*

1. As we have seen, difficulties arise directly we begin to probe beneath the surface of the outlines of Hegel's system. For example, when we start to inquire into the ontological reference of the logical Idea and the precise relation between the *Logos* and Nature, several possible lines of interpretation present themselves to the mind. But this does not alter the fact that a preliminary statement of the outline of the system can be easily made. The Absolute is Being. Being, considered first (though not in a temporal sense) as the Idea, objectifies itself in Nature, the material world. As the objectification of the Idea, Nature manifests the Idea. At the same time it cannot do so adequately. For Being, the Absolute, is defined as Spirit, as Thought which thinks itself. And it must come to exist as such. It cannot do so in Nature, though Nature is a condition for its doing so. Being comes to exist as Spirit and thus to manifest its essence adequately only in and through the human spirit. But Being as Spirit can be conceived in different ways. It can be conceived 'in itself', in the form of the finite spirit in its inwardness or subjectivity. This is the sphere of subjective Spirit. It can be conceived as issuing out of itself and objectifying itself in the institutions, above all the State, which it posits or creates. This is the sphere of objective Spirit. And it can be conceived as rising above finitude and knowing itself as Being, the totality. And this is the sphere of absolute Spirit. Absolute Spirit exists only in and through the human spirit, but it does so at the level at which the individual human spirit is no longer a finite mind, enclosed in its own private thoughts, emotions, interests and purposes, but has become a moment in the life of the infinite as an identity-in-difference which knows itself as such. In other words, absolute Spirit is Spirit at the level of that absolute knowledge of

which Hegel wrote in *The Phenomenology of Spirit*. And we can thus say that man's knowledge of the Absolute and the Absolute's knowledge of itself are two aspects of the same reality. For Being actualizes itself as concretely existing self-thinking Thought through the human spirit.

For the sake of clarity the following point must be made clear. I am conscious of myself as a finite being: I have, so to speak, my own self-consciousness which is quite different from the self-consciousness of any other human being. But though, like anything else, this subjective self-consciousness must be within the Absolute, it is not at all what Hegel means by absolute knowledge. This arises when I am aware, not simply of myself as a finite individual standing over against other finite persons and things, but rather of the Absolute as the ultimate and all-embracing reality. My knowledge, if I attain it, of Nature as the objective manifestation of the Absolute and of the Absolute as returning to itself as subjectivity in the form of Spirit, existing in and through the spiritual life of man in history, is a moment in absolute self-consciousness, that is, in the self-knowledge of Being or the Absolute.

The matter can be put in this way. We have seen that according to Hegel the World-Spirit arises out of the dialectic of national spirits. And in the comments at the end of the last chapter it was remarked that this view might reasonably be expected to involve the conclusion that the end or goal of history is a universal society, a world-State or at least a world-federation of States. But this was not Hegel's point of view. National spirits are limited and finite. And when the World-Spirit is conceived as rising above this finitude and limitation and existing as infinite Spirit, it must be conceived as knowledge, as self-thinking Thought. We thus pass out of the political sphere. The State is indeed described by Hegel as the self-conscious ethical substance, in the sense that it conceives its own ends and consciously pursues them. But it cannot be described as self-thinking Thought or as personality. Self-thinking Thought is Spirit knowing itself as Spirit and Nature as its objectification and as the condition for its own concrete existence as Spirit. It is the Absolute knowing itself as the Totality, that is, as identity-in-difference: it is infinite Being reflectively conscious of the distinct phases or moments in its own life. It is Spirit set free, as it were, from the limitations of the finitude which characterizes the national spirit.

Absolute Spirit is thus the synthesis or unity of subjective

Spirit and objective Spirit on a higher plane. It is subjectivity and objectivity in one. For it is Spirit knowing itself. But whereas in the spheres of subjective Spirit and objective Spirit we are concerned with the finite Spirit, first in its inwardness, then in its self-manifestation in objective institutions, such as the family and the State, in the sphere of absolute Spirit we are concerned with infinite Spirit knowing itself as infinite. This does not mean that infinite Spirit is something set over against, opposed to and existing entirely apart from the finite spirit. The infinite exists in and through the finite. But in the sphere of absolute Spirit the infinite is reflectively conscious of itself as such. Hence absolute Spirit is not a repetition, so to speak, of subjective Spirit. It is Spirit's return to itself at a higher level, a level at which subjectivity and objectivity are united in one infinite act.

To speak, however, of one infinite act can be misleading. For it suggests the idea of an eternally changeless self-intuition on the part of the Absolute, whereas for Hegel absolute Spirit is the life of the Absolute's developing self-knowledge. It is the process whereby the Absolute actualizes itself precisely as self-thinking Thought. And it does so at three main levels, those of art, religion and philosophy.

What Hegel means by this can most easily be understood if we approach the matter from the point of view of man's knowledge of the Absolute. First, the Absolute can be apprehended under the sensuous form of beauty as manifested in Nature or, more adequately, in the work of art. Hegel thus accepts Schelling's theory of the metaphysical significance of art. Secondly, the Absolute can be apprehended in the form of pictorial or figurative thought which finds expression in the language of religion. Thirdly, the Absolute can be apprehended purely conceptually, that is, in speculative philosophy. Art, religion and philosophy are thus all concerned with the Absolute. The infinite divine Being is, as it were, the content or subject-matter of all three spiritual activities. But though the content is the same, the form is different. That is to say, the Absolute is apprehended in different ways in these activities. As having the same content or subject-matter, art, religion and philosophy all belong to the sphere of absolute Spirit. But the differences in form show that they are distinct phases in the life of absolute Spirit.

The philosophy of absolute Spirit, therefore, consists of three main parts, the philosophy of art, the philosophy of religion and what we may call the philosophy of philosophy. And as Hegel proceeds dialectically, showing how art passes into or demands the transition to religion and how religion in turn demands the transition to philosophy, it is important to understand in what sense the time element enters into this dialectic and in what sense it does not.

In his philosophy of art Hegel does not confine himself to a purely abstract account of the essence of the aesthetic consciousness. He surveys the historical development of art and tries to show a development in the aesthetic consciousness up to the point at which it demands the transition to the religious consciousness. Similarly, in his philosophy of religion he does not confine himself to delineating the essential features or moments of the religious consciousness: he surveys the history of religion from primitive religion up to the absolute religion, Christianity, and endeavours to make clear a dialectical pattern of development in the religious consciousness up to the point at which it demands a transition to the standpoint of speculative philosophy. There is, therefore, a mixture of the temporal and the non-temporal. On the one hand the actual historical developments of art, religion and philosophy are all temporal processes. This is sufficiently obvious. For instance, classical Greek art temporally preceded Christian art, and Greek religion temporally preceded the Christian religion. On the other hand Hegel is not so foolish as to suppose that art ran through all its forms before religion appeared on the scene or that there was no philosophy before the appearance of the absolute religion. He is as well aware as anyone else that Greek temples were associated with Greek religion, and that there were Greek philosophers. The dialectical transition from the concept of art to the concept of religion and from the concept of religion to that of philosophy is in itself timeless. That is to say, it is in essence a conceptual, and not a temporal or historical, progression.

The point can be expressed in this way. Hegel might have confined himself to a purely conceptual movement, in which the only priority involved would be logical, not temporal. But the life of the Spirit is an historical development in which one form of art succeeds another, one stage in the evolution of the religious consciousness succeeds another stage, and one philosophical system succeeds another philosophical system. And Hegel is anxious to show the dialectical patterns exhibited in the history of art, the history of religion and the history of philosophy. Hence the philosophy of absolute Spirit, as he expounds it, cannot abstract from all temporal succession. And it has, therefore, two aspects. It may not indeed be always a simple matter to sort them out. But in any case we only make nonsense of Hegel's doctrine if we take him to mean, for example, that religion started only when art stopped. And whatever some writers may think that Hegel ought to have said, in my opinion he looked on art, religion and philosophy as permanent activities of the human spirit. He may have thought that philosophy is the highest of these activities. But it does not follow that he imagined that man would ever become pure thought.

By way of conclusion to this section it is worth drawing attention to the following point. It is a mistake to think that according to Hegel the State is the highest of all realities and political life the highest activity of man. For, as we have seen, the sphere of objective Spirit leads on to the sphere of absolute Spirit. And while organized society in some form is for Hegel a condition for art, religion and philosophy, these three activities are the highest expression of Spirit. Hegel doubtless exalted the State, but he exalted philosophy still more.

2. Dialectically or logically speaking, the Absolute is manifested first of all in the form of immediacy, under the guise, that is to say, of objects of sense. As such, it is apprehended as beauty, which is 'the sensuous semblance [*Scheinen*] of the Idea'.[1] And this sensuous appearance of the Idea, this shining of the Absolute through the veils of sense, is called the Ideal. Looked at from one point of view the Idea as beauty is, of course, identical with the Idea as truth. For it is the same Absolute which is apprehended as beauty by the aesthetic consciousness and as truth in philosophy. But the forms or modes of apprehension are distinct. Aesthetic intuition and philosophy are not the same thing. Hence the Idea as beauty is termed the Ideal.

While not denying that there can be such a thing as beauty in Nature, Hegel insists that beauty in art is far superior. For artistic beauty is the immediate creation of Spirit; it is Spirit's manifestation of itself to itself. And Spirit and its products are superior to Nature and its phenomena. Hegel confines his attention, therefore, to beauty in art. It may indeed be regrettable that he underestimates natural beauty as a manifestation of the divine. But

---

[1] *W*, XII, p. 160; *O*, I, p. 154. In references to Hegel's lectures on *The Philosophy of Fine Art* the letter *O* signifies the English translation by F. P. B. Osmaston.

iven the construction of his system, he can hardly do anything else
ut concentrate on artistic beauty. For he has left the philosophy of
Jature behind him and is concerned with the philosophy of Spirit.

But, we may ask, if artistic beauty is said to be the sensuous
emblance or appearance of the Idea, what does this proposition
nean? Is it anything more than a high-sounding but vague state-
nent? The answer is fairly simple. The Idea is the unity of
ubjectivity and objectivity. And in the beautiful work of art this
inity is expressed or represented in the union of spiritual content
vith external or material embodiment. Spirit and matter, subjec-
ivity and objectivity, are fused together in a harmonious unity or
ynthesis. 'Art has the task of presenting the Idea to immediate
ntuition in sensuous form, and not in the form of thought or pure
pirituality. And the value and dignity of this presentation lie in
he correspondence and unity of the two aspects of ideal content
ind its embodiment, so that the perfection and excellence of art
ind the conformity of its products with its essential concept
lepend on the degree of inner harmony and unity with which the
deal content and sensuous form are made to interpenetrate.'[1]

Obviously, Hegel does not mean to imply that the artist is
:onsciously aware of the fact that his product is a manifestation
»f the nature of the Absolute. Nor does he mean to imply that a
nan is unable to appreciate the beauty of a work of art unless he
ias this conscious awareness. Both the artist and the beholder may
eel that the product is, so to speak, just right or perfect, in the
ense that to add or subtract anything would be to impair or
lisfigure the work of art. Both may feel that spiritual content and
ensuous embodiment are perfectly fused. And they may both feel
hat the product is in some undefined sense a manifestation of
truth'. But it by no means follows that either of them can state the
netaphysical significance of the work of art, whether to himself or
o anyone else. Nor does this indicate any defect in the aesthetic
:onsciousness. For it is philosophy, and not the aesthetic conscious-
iess, which explicitly or reflectively apprehends the metaphysical
.ignificance of art. In other words, this apprehension arises from
»hilosophical reflection *about* art. And this is something very
lifferent from artistic creation. A great artist may be a very bad
»hilosopher or no philosopher at all. And a great philosopher may
vell be incapable of painting a beautiful picture or composing a
ymphony.

---

[1] *W*, xii, p. 110; *O*, i, p. 98.

In the perfect work of art, therefore, there is complete harmon
between ideal content and its sensuous form or embodiment. Th
two elements interpenetrate and are fused into one. But thi
artistic ideal is not always attained. And the different possibl
types of relation between the two elements give us the fundamenta
types of art.

First we have the type of art in which the sensuous elemen
predominates over the spiritual or ideal content, in the sense tha
the latter has not mastered its medium of expression and does no
shine through the veils of sense. In other words, the artist suggest
rather than expresses his meaning. There is ambiguity and an ai
of mystery. And this type of art is *symbolic* art. It can be found
for example, among the ancient Egyptians. 'It is in *Egypt* that w
have to look for the perfect exemplification of the symbolic mod
of expression, in regard both to its peculiar content and to its form
Egypt is the land of symbol which sets itself the spiritual task o
the self-interpretation of Spirit, without really being able t
fulfil it.'[1] And Hegel finds in the Sphinx 'the symbol of the symboli
itself'.[2] It is 'the objective riddle'.[3]

Hegel subdivides symbolic art into subordinate phases an
discusses the difference between Hindu and Egyptian art and th
religious poetry of the Hebrews. But we cannot follow him int
details. It is sufficient to notice that according to him symbolic ar
is best suited to the early ages of humanity when the world an
man itself, Nature and Spirit, are felt as mysterious and enigmatic

Secondly we have the type of art in which spiritual or idea
content are fused into a harmonious unity. This is *classical* art
Whereas in symbolic art the Absolute is conceived as a mysterious
formless One which is suggested rather than expressed in the worl
of art, in classical art Spirit is conceived in concrete form as th
self-conscious individual spirit, whose sensuous embodiment is th
human body. This type of art, therefore, is predominantly
anthropomorphic. The gods are simply glorified human beings
And the leading classical art is thus *sculpture*, which presents Spiri
as the finite embodied spirit.

Just as Hegel associates symbolic art with the Hindus and
Egyptians, so he associates classical art with the ancient Greeks
In the great works of Greek sculpture we find the perfect marriage
as it were, of Spirit and matter. The spiritual content shines
through the veils of sense: it is expressed, not merely suggested

---

[1] *W*, XII, p. 472; *O*, II, p. 74.    [2] *W*, XII, p. 480; *O*, II, p. 83.    [3] *Ibid.*

in symbolic form. For the human body, as represented by a Praxiteles, is the clear expression of Spirit.

Yet 'classical art and its religion of beauty do not satisfy wholly the depths of the Spirit'.[1] And we have the third main type of art, namely *romantic* art, in which Spirit, felt as infinite, tends to overflow, as it were, its sensuous embodiment and to abandon the veils of sense. In classical art there is a perfect fusion of ideal content and sensuous form. But Spirit is not merely the particular finite spirit, united with a particular body: it is the divine infinite. And in romantic art, which is to all intents and purposes the art of Christendom, no sensuous embodiment is felt to be adequate to the spiritual content. It is not, as in symbolic art, a case of the spiritual content having to be suggested rather than expressed because Spirit has not yet been conceived as such and remains enigmatic, a riddle or problem. Rather is it that Spirit has been conceived as what it is, namely infinite spiritual Life as God, and therefore as overflowing any finite sensuous embodiment.

Romantic art, according to Hegel, is concerned with the life of the Spirit, which is movement, action, conflict. Spirit must, as it were, die to live. That is to say, it must go over into what is not itself that it may rise again to become itself, a truth which is expressed in Christianity, in the doctrine of self-sacrifice and resurrection, exemplified above all in the life, death and resurrection of Christ. The typical romantic arts, therefore, will be those which are best adapted to expressing movement, action and conflict. And these are painting, music and poetry. Architecture is least adapted for expressing the inner life of the Spirit and is the typical form of symbolic art. Sculpture, the typical form of classical art, is better adapted than architecture for this purpose, but it concentrates on the external, on the body, and its expression of movement and life is very limited. In poetry, however, the medium consists of words, that is, of sensuous images expressed in language; and it is best suited for expressing the life of the Spirit.

This asscoiation of particular arts with definite general types of art must not, however, be understood in an exclusive sense. Architecture, for example, is particularly associated with symbolic art because, while capable of expressing mystery, it is of all the fine arts the least fitted for expressing the life of the Spirit. But

---

[1] *W*, XIII, p. 14; *O*, II, p. 180. Note that Hegel here associates a particular type of art with a particular type of religion.

to say this is not to deny that there are forms of architecture which are characteristic of classical and romantic art. Thus the Greek temple, the perfect house for the anthropomorphic deity, is an obvious example of classical architecture, while the Gothic, an example of romantic architecture, expresses the feeling that the divine transcends the sphere of finitude and of matter. In contrast with the Greek temple we can see how 'the romantic character of Christian churches consists in the way in which they arise out of the soil and soar into the heights'.[1]

Similarly, sculpture is not confined to classical art, even if it is the characteristic classical art-form. Nor are painting, music and poetry confined to romantic art. But we cannot follow Hegel any further into his lengthy discussion of the particular fine arts.

Now, if we are considering art simply in itself, we must say that the highest type of art is that in which spiritual content and sensuous embodiment are in perfect harmonious accord. And this is classical art, the leading characteristic form of which is sculpture. But if we are considering the aesthetic consciousness as a stage in the self-manifestation of God or as a level in man's developing knowledge of God, we must say that romantic art is the highest type. For, as we have seen, in romantic art infinite Spirit tends to drop the veils of sense, a fact which becomes most evident in poetry. Of course, as long as we remain in the sphere of art at all, the veils of sense are never completely abandoned. But romantic art provides the point of transition from the aesthetic to the religious consciousness. That is to say, when the mind perceives that no material embodiment is adequate to the expression of Spirit, it passes from the sphere of art to that of religion.[2] Art cannot satisfy the Spirit as a means of apprehending its own nature.

3. If the Absolute is Spirit, Reason, self-thinking Thought, it can be adequately apprehended as such only by thought itself. And we might perhaps expect Hegel to make a direct transition from art to philosophy, whereas in point of fact he makes the transition to philosophy by way of an intermediate mode of apprehending the Absolute, namely religion. 'The sphere of conscious life which is nearest in ascending order to the realm of art is religion.'[3] Obviously, Hegel is not simply concerned with completing a triad, so that the sphere of absolute Spirit may

[1] W, xiii, p. 334; O, iii, p. 91.
[2] To repeat, this transition is dialectical rather than temporal. The Egyptians and the Hindus, for instance, had their own religions as well as their own forms of art.    [3] W, xii, p. 151; O, i, p. 142.

onform to the general pattern of the system. Nor is it simply that
e sees the need for a philosophy of religion in view of the
nportance of religion in the history of mankind, and of the
bvious fact that it is concerned with the divine. The insertion of
eligion between art and philosophy is due above all to Hegel's
onviction that the religious consciousness exemplifies an inter-
nediate way of apprehending the Absolute. Religion in general is
r essentially involves the self-manifestation of the Absolute in the
orm of *Vorstellung*, a word which can be translated in this context
s figurative or pictorial thought. On the one hand the religious
onsciousness differs from the aesthetic in that it *thinks* the
\Absolute. On the other hand the thought which is characteristic of
eligion is not pure conceptual thought as found in philosophy. It
s thought clothed, as it were, in imagery: it is, one may say, the
roduct of a marriage between imagination and thought. A
*Vorstellung* is a concept, but it is not the pure concept of the
hilosopher. Rather is it a pictorial or imaginative concept.

For example, the truth that the logical Idea, the *Logos*, is
bjectified in Nature is apprehended by the religious consciousness
at least in Judaism, Christianity and Mohammedanism) in the
orm of the imaginative or pictorial concept of the free creation of
he world by a transcendent Deity. Again, the truth that the
inite spirit is in essence a moment in the life of infinite Spirit is
pprehended by the Christian consciousness in the form of the
loctrine of the Incarnation and of man's union with God through
Christ. For Hegel the truths are the same in content, but the modes
f apprehension and expression are different in religion and in
hilosophy. For instance, the idea of God in the Christian con-
ciousness and the concept of the Absolute have for Hegel exactly
he same content: they refer to or mean the same reality. But this
eality is apprehended and described in different ways.

As for the existence of God, there is an obvious sense in which
Hegel needs no proof, no proof, that is to say, in addition to his
ystem itself. For God is Being, and the nature of Being is demon-
trated in logic or abstract metaphysics. At the same time Hegel
levotes a good deal of attention to traditional proofs of God's
xistence. Nowadays, he remarks, these proofs have fallen into
liscredit. They are regarded not only as completely antiquated
rom a philosophical point of view but also, from a religious
tandpoint, as irreligious and practically impious. For there is a
trong tendency to substitute unreasoned faith and pious feelings

of the heart for any attempt to give faith a rational foundation
Indeed, so unfashionable has this business of proof become that
'the proofs are here and there hardly even known as historical data
and even by theologians, people, that is to say, who profess to have
a scientific knowledge of religious truths, they are sometime
unknown'.[1] Yet the proofs do not merit this contempt. For the
arose 'out of the need to satisfy thought, reason',[2] and the
represent the elevation of the human mind to God, making explici
the immediate movement of faith.

Speaking of the cosmological proof, Hegel remarks that it
essential defect in its traditional forms is that it posits the finit
as something existing on its own and then tries to make a transitio
to the infinite as something different from the finite. But thi
defect can be remedied if we once understand that 'Being is to b
defined not only as finite but also as infinite.'[3] In other words, w
have to show that 'the being of the finite is not only its being bu
also the being of the infinite'.[4] Conversely, of course, it has to b
shown that infinite Being unfolds itself in and through the finite
The objections against making the transition from the finit
to the infinite or from the infinite to the finite can be met only by
true philosophy of Being which shows that the supposed gul
between the finite and the infinite does not exist. Kant's criticisn
of the proofs then falls to the ground.

This amounts to saying that the true proof of the existence o
God is, as was remarked above, the Hegelian system itself. And t
expound this system is obviously a philosophical task. Hence th
philosophy of religion proper is concerned more with the religiou
consciousness and its mode or modes of apprehending God thai
with proving God's existence.

Considered abstractly, the religious consciousness comprise
three main moments or phases. The first, as the normal scheme o
the Hegelian dialectic would lead one to expect, is the moment o
universality. God is conceived as the undifferentiated universal
as the infinite and only true reality. The second moment is that o
particularity. In conceiving God I distinguish between myself anc
him, between the infinite and the finite. He becomes for me ai
object over against me. And my consciousness of God as 'outside
me or over against me involves the consciousness of myself a

---

[1] W, XVI, p. 361; SS, III, p. 156. In references to Hegel's Lectures on Th
Philosophy of Religion SS signifies the English translation by E. B. Speirs and
J. Burdon Sanderson.    [2] W, XVI, p. 361; SS, III, p. 157.
[3] W, XVI, p. 457; SS, III, p. 259.    [4] W, XVI, p. 456; SS, III, p. 259.

separated or alienated from him, as a sinner. Finally, the third moment is that of individuality, of the return of the particular to the universal, of the finite to the infinite. Separation and alienation are overcome. For the religious consciousness this is accomplished in worship and in the way of salvation, that is, by the variety of means by which man conceives himself as entering into union with God.

The mind thus moves from the bare abstract thought of God to the consciousness of itself and God in separation, and thence to awareness of itself as one with God. And this movement is the essential movement of the religious consciousness. Its three moments or phases, one may note, correspond with the three moments of the Idea.

But religion is not, of course, simply religion in the abstract. It takes the form of definite religions. And in his lectures on the philosophy of religion Hegel traces the development of the religious consciousness through different types of religion. He is primarily concerned with exhibiting a logical or conceptual sequence; but this sequence is developed through reflection on the historical religions of mankind, the existence and nature of which is obviously known by other means than *a priori* deduction. Hegel's concern is to exhibit the dialectical pattern exemplified in the empirical or historical data.

The first main phase of definite or determinate religion is called by Hegel the religion of Nature (*die Naturreligion*), this phrase being used to cover any religion in which God is conceived as less than Spirit. It is subdivided into three phases. First there is immediate religion or magic. Secondly there is the religion of substance, under which heading Hegel considers in turn Chinese religion, Hinduism and Buddhism. Thirdly there are the religions of Persia, Syria and Egypt in which there can be found some glimmering of the idea of spirituality. Thus while in Hinduism Brahman is the purely abstract undifferentiated One, in the Persian religion of Zoroastrianism God is conceived as the Good.

The religion of Nature can be said to correspond with the first moment of the religious consciousness as described above. In the characteristic *Naturreligion*, namely the religion of substance, God is conceived as the undifferentiated universal. This is pantheism in the sense that the finite being is regarded as swallowed up by or as purely accidental to the divine Being. At the same time, though in Hinduism Brahman is conceived in a way corresponding to the

first moment of the religious consciousness, this does not mean
that the other moments are altogether absent.

The second main phase of definite religion is the religion of
spiritual individuality. Here God is conceived as Spirit, but in the
form of an individual person or of individual persons. The inevitable
triad comprises the Jewish, Greek and Roman religions, entitled
respectively the religions of sublimity, beauty and utility. Thus
Jupiter Capitolinus has as his function the preservation of the
safety and sovereignty of Rome.[1]

These three types of religion correspond to the second moment
of the religious consciousness. The divine is conceived as being over
against or apart from the human. In Jewish religion, for example,
God is exalted above the world and man in transcendent sublimity.
At the same time the other moments of the religious consciousness
are also represented. Thus in Judaism there is the idea of man's
reconciliation with God through sacrifice and obedience to the
divine law.

The third main phase of definite religion is absolute religion,
namely Christianity. In Christianity God is conceived as what he
really is, infinite Spirit which is not only transcendent but also
immanent. And man is conceived as united with God by participating in the divine life through the grace received from Christ, the
God-man. Hence the Christian religion corresponds above all with
the third moment of the religious consciousness, which is the
synthesis or unity of the first two moments. God is not looked on
as an undifferentiated unity, but as the Trinity of Persons, a
infinite spiritual Life. And the infinite and finite are not regarded
as set over against one another, but as united without confusion.
As St. Paul says, in him we live and move and have our being.

To say that Christianity is the absolute religion is to say that it
is the absolute truth. And Hegel fulminates against preachers and
theologians who pass lightly over the Christian dogmas or who
whittle them down to suit the outlook of a supposedly enlightened
age. But we must add that Christianity expresses the absolute
truth under the form of *Vorstellung*. There arises, therefore, the
demand for a transition to philosophy which thinks the content of
religion in pure conceptual form. The attempt to do so is, according

---

[1] Evidently, the third member of the triad, the religion of utility, is from one
point of view a degradation of religion. For it practically reduces God to an instrument. At the same time it demands the transition to a higher form of religion.
For example, the admission by Rome of all deities into its pantheon reduces polytheism to an absurdity and demands the transition to monotheism.

o Hegel, the continuation of the pioneer work of men such as St.
Anselm who consciously set out to understand and justify by
necessary reasons the content of faith.

4. As we have seen, the transition from religion to philosophy
is in no way a transition from one subject-matter to another. The
subject-matter is in both cases the same, '*the eternal truth* in its
objectivity, God and nothing but God and the unfolding [*die
Explication*] of God'.[1] In this sense, therefore, 'religion and
philosophy come to the same thing'.[2] 'Philosophy unfolds only
itself when it unfolds religion; and when it unfolds itself, it unfolds
religion.'[3]

The distinction between them lies in the different ways in which
they conceive God, 'in the peculiar ways in which they occupy
themselves with God'.[4] For example, the change from *Vorstellung*
to pure thought involves the replacement of the form of contingency
by that of logical sequence. Thus the theological concept of divine
creation as a contingent event, in the sense that it might or might
not have taken place, becomes in philosophy the doctrine that the
*Logos* is necessarily objectified in Nature, not because the Absolute
is subject to compulsion but because it is what it is. Speculative
philosophy, in other words, strips away the imaginative or
pictorial element which is characteristic of religious thought
and expresses the truth, the same truth, in purely conceptual
form.

It does not follow, however, that philosophy is irreligious. In
Hegel's opinion the notion that philosophy and religion are
incompatible or that the former is hostile or dangerous to the latter
rests on a misconception of their respective natures. Both treat of
God and both are religion. 'What they have in common is that
both are religion; what distinguishes them lies only in the kind and
manner of religion which we find in each.'[5] It is indeed this
difference in their respective ways of apprehending and expressing
the truth which gives rise to the idea that philosophy threatens
religion. But philosophy would be a threat to religion only if it
professed to substitute truth for falsity. And this is not the case.
The truth is the same, though the religious consciousness demands
a mode of expression which must be distinguished from that of
philosophy.

One may be inclined to comment that Hegel uses the term

[1] *W*, xv, p. 37; *SS*, I, p. 19.
[2] *W*, xv, p. 37; *SS*, I, p. 20.
[3] *W*, xv, p. 37; *SS*, I, p. 19.
[4] *W*, xv, p. 38; *SS*, I, p. 20.
[5] *Ibid*.

'religion' ambiguously. For he uses it to cover not only religion experience, faith and cult but also theology. And while a plausib case can be made out for saying that philosophy is not hostile t religious experience as such, or even to pure faith, it mus necessarily be hostile to religion if religion is taken to mean include theology and if philosophy proposes to reveal the un varnished truth, as it were, which is contained in the doctrine which theologians believe to be the best possible expression of th truth in human language.

As regards the first point, Hegel insists that '*knowledge* is a essential part of the Christian religion itself'.[1] Christianity strive to understand its own faith. And speculative philosophy is continuation of this attempt. The difference lies in the fact tha philosophy substitutes the form of pure thought for the form *Vorstellung*, pictorial or figurative thought. But this does not mea that speculative philosophy takes the place of Christianity in th sense that the latter is simply discarded in favour of the forme Christianity is the absolute religion and absolute idealism is th absolute philosophy. Both are true, and their truth is the sam The forms of conception and expression may differ, but it does n follow that Christianity is superseded by absolute idealism. Fc the human being is not simply pure thought: he is by no mean only a philosopher, even if he is a philosopher at all. And for th religious consciousness Christian theology is the perfect expressio of the truth. This is why preachers, who are addressing themselve to the religious consciousness, have no business to tamper wit Christian dogmas. For Christianity is the revealed religion, in th sense that it is the perfect self-manifestation of God to the religiou consciousness.

It is not my intention to imply that Hegel's attitude is consisten with the standpoint of Christian orthodoxy. For I am convince that it is not. I agree with McTaggart, who was not himself Christian believer, when he points out that as an ally of Christianit Hegelianism is 'an enemy in disguise—the least evident but th most dangerous. The doctrines which have been protected from external refutation are found to be transforming themselves til they are on the point of melting away. . . .'[2] Thus Hegel give philosophical proofs of such doctrines as the Trinity, the Fall an the Incarnation. But when he has finished with stating them in th

---

[1] *W*, xv, p. 35; *SS*, I, p. 17.
[2] *Studies in Hegelian Cosmology* (1901 edition), p. 250.

orm of pure thought, they are obviously something very different
rom the doctrines which the Church believes to be the correct
tatement of the truth in human language. In other words, Hegel
nakes speculative philosophy the final arbiter of the inner meaning
f Christian revelation. Absolute idealism is presented as esoteric
hristianity and Christianity as exoteric Hegelianism; and the
mystery insisted on by theology is subordinated to a philosophical
larification which amounts in fact to a transformation.

At the same time there is, in my opinion at least, no cogent
reason for accusing Hegel of personal insincerity. I do not believe
hat when he posed as a champion of orthodoxy he had his tongue
n his cheek. As was noted in the introductory chapter, Benedetto
Croce argued that there could be no valid reason for retaining an
nferior form of thought, namely religion, along with science, art
nd philosophy. If philosophy really gives the inner meaning of
religious beliefs, then religion must give place to philosophy. That
s to say, the two cannot coexist in the same mind. A man may
hink in the categories of religion or he may think in the categories
f philosophy. But he cannot think in both. But while Croce's
omments are by no means without point, it does not necessarily
ollow that they represent Hegel's real, though concealed, opinion.
After all, Croce, though not a believing Catholic, was accustomed
o the idea of ecclesiastical authority as the final arbiter of
religious truth and its statement. And it is perfectly obvious that
Hegel's theory of the relation of speculative philosophy to
Christianity is incompatible with *this* idea. But Hegel was a
Lutheran. And though the superiority of speculative philosophy
o faith is very far from being a Lutheran idea, it was much easier
or him than it would have been for Croce to be sincerely convinced
hat his view of the relation between the absolute philosophy and
he absolute religion was acceptable from the Christian standpoint.
He doubtless thought of himself as continuing the work of the
heologians who in their accounts of the Christian dogmas
ndeavoured to avoid the crudely imaginative forms in which these
ogmas were pictured by the theologically uneducated religious
onsciousness.

5. But the absolute philosophy is no more the only manifestation
f the speculative reason than is the absolute religion the only
nanifestation of the religious consciousness. Just as art and
religion have their history, so has philosophy. And this history is
 dialectical process. From one point of view it is the process by

which infinite Thought comes to think itself explicitly, movin
from one inadequate conception of itself to another and the
uniting them in a higher unity. From another point of view it
the process by which the human mind moves dialectically towarc
an adequate conception of the ultimate reality, the Absolute. Bu
these two points of view represent simply different aspects of or
process. For Spirit, self-thinking Thought, becomes explicit in an
through the reflection of the human mind on the level of absolut
knowledge.

This means, of course, that the different one-sided and ir
adequate concepts of reality which emerge at different stages (
the history of philosophy are taken up and preserved in tr
succeeding higher stages. 'The last philosophy is the result of a
earlier ones: nothing is lost, all principles are preserved.'[1] 'Tr
general result of the history of philosophy is this. First, throughou
all time there has been only one philosophy, the contemporar
differences of which represent the necessary aspects of the or
principle. Secondly, the succession of philosophical systems is n
matter of chance but exhibits the necessary succession of stages i
the development of this science. Thirdly, the final philosophy of
period is the result of this development and is truth in the highes
form which the self-consciousness of Spirit affords. The fina
philosophy, therefore, contains the ones which went before;
embraces in itself all their stages; it is the product and result of a
the philosophies which preceded it.'[2]

Now, if the history of philosophy is the development of th
divine self-knowledge, of absolute self-consciousness, the succe:
sive stages in this history will tend to correspond with the successiv
phases or moments in the Notion or logical Idea. We find, therefor
that Hegel represents Parmenides as the first genuine philosophe:
the man who apprehended the Absolute as Being, while Heraclitu
affirms the Absolute as Becoming. If this is taken as a statemer
of chronological sequence, it is open to criticism. But it illustrate
Hegel's general procedure. Like Aristotle before him, he looks o
his predecessors as bringing to light aspects of truth which ar
preserved, elevated and integrated with complementary aspect
in his own system. Needless to say, the explicit and adequat
recognition of the category of Spirit is reserved for German idealisn

[1] W, xix, p. 685; HS, iii, p. 546. In references to Hegel's Lectures on the Histor
of Philosophy HS signifies the English translation by E. S. Haldane and F. H
Simson.
[2] W, xix, pp. 690–1; HS, iii, pp. 552–3.

nd the philosophies of Fichte and Schelling are treated as
10ments in the development of absolute idealism.

Hegel's history of philosophy is thus an integral part of his
ystem. It is not simply an account of what philosophers have held,
f the factors which influenced their thought and led them to
hink in the ways that they did, and of their influence on their
uccessors and perhaps on society at large. It is a sustained attempt
o exhibit a necessary dialectical advance, a teleological develop-
1ent, in the data of the history of philosophy. And this enterprise
s obviously carried out in the light of a general philosophy. It is
he work of a philosopher looking back on the past from the
antage-point of a system which he believes to be the highest
xpression of the truth up to date and seeing this system as the
ulmination of a process of reflection which, in spite of all contingent
lements, has been in its essential outlines a necessary movement
f Thought coming to think itself. Hegel's history of philosophy is
hus a philosophy of the history of philosophy. If it is objected that
he selection of the essential elements in a given system is governed
y philosophical preconceptions or principles, Hegel can, of course,
nswer that any history of philosophy worthy of the name
ecessarily involves not only interpretation but also a separation
f the essential from the unessential in the light of beliefs about
vhat is philosophically important and what is not. But such an
nswer, though reasonable enough, would not be adequate in the
ontext. For just as Hegel approaches the philosophy of history
vith the belief that the history of mankind is a rational teleological
rocess, so does he approach the history of philosophy with the
onviction that this history is 'the temple of self-conscious reason',[1]
he dialectically continuous and progressive determination of the
dea, 'a logical progress impelled by an inherent necessity',[2] the
ne true philosophy developing itself in time, the dynamic process
f self-thinking Thought.

Does this conception of the history of philosophy imply the
onclusion that for Hegel his philosophy is the final system, the
ystem to end all systems? He has sometimes been represented as
hinking precisely this. But it seems to me that this picture is a
aricature. He does indeed depict German idealism in general, and
is own system in particular, as the highest stage yet reached in
he historical development of philosophy. In view of his interpreta-
ion of the history of philosophy he cannot do anything else. And

[1] *W*, XVII, p. 65; *HS*, I, p. 35.          [2] *W*, XVII, p. 66; *HS*, I, p. 36.

he makes remarks which lend themselves for use by those who wish to ascribe to him the absurd idea that with Hegelianism philosophy comes to an end. 'A new epoch has arisen in the world. It seems that the World-Spirit has now succeeded in freeing itself from all alien objective existence and in apprehending itself at last as absolute Spirit. . . . The strife between the finite self-consciousness and the absolute self-consciousness, which seemed to finite self-consciousness to lie outside it, now ceases. Finite self-consciousness has ceased to be finite, and thereby absolute self-consciousness on the other hand has attained the reality which it formerly lacked.' But though this passage clearly states that absolute idealism is the culmination of all preceding philosophy, Hegel goes on to speak of 'the whole history of the World in general and of the history of philosophy in particular up to the present'.[2] And is it probable that a man who stated roundly that 'philosophy is *its own time expressed in thoughts*'[3] and that it is just as foolish to suppose that a philosophy can transcend its contemporary world as it is to suppose that an individual can overleap his own time seriously thought that philosophy had come to an end with himself? Obviously, on Hegel's principles subsequent philosophy would have to incorporate absolute idealism, even if his system revealed itself as a one-sided moment in a higher synthesis. But to say this is not the same as to deny that there could be or would be any subsequent philosophy.

There is, however, this point. If Christianity is the absolute religion, Hegelianism, as esoteric Christianity, must be the absolute philosophy. And if we take the word 'absolute' in this context as meaning truth in the highest form which it has yet attained rather than as meaning the final or terminal statement of the truth, Christianity is no more the final religion than is Hegelianism the final philosophy. On Hegel's own principles Christianity and absolute idealism stand or fall together. And if we wish to say that Christianity cannot be surpassed whereas Hegelianism can, we cannot at the same time accept Hegel's account of the relation between the two.

6. In view of the comprehensive character of Hegel's system and of the commanding position which he came to occupy in the German philosophical world it is not surprising that his influence was felt in a variety of fields. As one would expect in the case of a man whose thought centred round the Absolute and who appeared

<hr>

[1] *W*, xix, pp. 689–90; *HS*, iii, p. 551.
[2] *W*, xix, p. 690; *HS*, iii, p. 551.      [3] *W*, vii, p. 35; *R*, preface.

ɔ the not too critical or too orthodox observer, to have provided a
ational justification of Christianity in terms of the most up-to-
ate philosophy, his sphere of influence included the theological
eld. For example, Karl Daub (1765–1836), professor of theology
t Heidelberg, abandoned the ideas of Schelling and endeavoured
ɔ use the dialectical method of Hegel in the service of Protestant
ɹeology. Another eminent theologian who was converted or
ɛduced, according as one chooses to regard the matter, by the
ttraction of Hegel was Philipp Konrad Marheineke (1780–1846)
ho became a professor of theology at Berlin and who helped to
dit the first general edition of Hegel's works. In his posthumously
ublished *System of Christian Dogmatics* Marheineke attempted to
ɹanslate Hegelianism into the terms of Christian theology and at
ɹe same time to interpret the content of Christian dogma in the
Iegelian manner. For instance, he represented the Absolute as
ttaining full consciousness of itself in the Church, which was for
im the concrete actualization of Spirit, this Spirit being interpreted
s the Third Person of the Trinity.

The history of ethical systems was studied from an Hegelian
ɔint of view by Leopold von Henning (1791–1866) who followed
Iegel's courses at Berlin and became one of his most fervent
dmirers. In the field of law Hegel's influence was considerable.
'rominent among his disciples was the celebrated jurist Eduard
ɹans (1798–1839) who obtained a chair of law at Berlin and
ublished a well-known work on the right of inheritance.[1] In the
eld of aesthetics Heinrich Theodor Rötscher (1803–71) may be
ɹentioned as one of those who derived inspiration from Hegel. In
ɹe history of philosophy Hegel's influence was felt by such
minent historians as Johann Eduard Erdmann (1805–92), Eduard
eller (1814–1908) and Kuno Fischer (1824–1907). Whatever one
ɹay think of absolute idealism, one cannot deny Hegel's stimulating
ffect on scholars in a variety of fields.

To return to the theological field. We have noted that the
Iegelian system left room for dispute about its precise relation to
hristian theism. And in point of fact controversy arose on this
ɔpic even before Hegel's death, though this event naturally gave
fresh impetus. Some writers, who are generally classified as
elonging to the Hegelian right wing, maintained that absolute
dealism could be legitimately interpreted in a sense compatible
ith Christianity. While Hegel was still alive Karl Friedrich

[1] *Das Erbrecht in weltgeschichtlicher Entwicklung* (1824–35).

Göschel (1784–1861) tried to interpret the philosopher's theory ( the relation between the form of thought peculiar to the religiou consciousness and pure thought or knowledge in such a way as no to imply that religion is inferior to philosophy. And this defence ( Hegel met with a warm response from the philosopher. Afte Hegel's death Göschel published writings designed to show tha Hegelianism was compatible with the doctrines of a personal Go and of personal immortality. Mention can also be made of Ka Ludwig Michelet (1801–93), a Berlin professor, who identified th Hegelian triad with the Persons of the Trinity (as indeed Heg himself had done) and tried to show that there was no incompat bility between Hegelianism and Christian theology.

The left wing was represented, for example, by David Friedric Strauss (1808–74), author of the celebrated *Life of Jesus* (1835 According to Strauss the Gospel stories were myths, and h explicitly connected this view with Hegel's theory of *Vorstellur* and represented his own dissolution of historic Christianity as genuine development of Hegel's thought. He thus provide valuable ammunition for the Christian writers who refused t accept the contention of the right-wing Hegelians that Hegelianis and Christianity were compatible.

The centre of the Hegelian movement can be represented by th name of Johann Karl Friedrich Rosenkranz (1805–79), biographe of Hegel and a professor at Königsberg. As a pupil of bot Schleiermacher and Hegel he tried to mediate between them in h development of the Hegelian system. In his *Encyclopaedia of th Theological Sciences* (1831) he distinguished between speculativ historical and practical theology. Speculative theology exhibi the absolute religion, Christianity, in an *a priori* form. Historic: theology deals with the temporal objectification of this Idea ( concept of the absolute religion. In his evaluation of histor Christianity Rosenkranz was more restrained than Strauss, wh looked on him as belonging to the centre of the Hegelian schoo Later on Rosenkranz attempted to develop Hegel's logic, thoug his efforts in this direction were not much appreciated by oth Hegelians.

We can say, therefore, that the split between right- and lef wing Hegelians concerned first of all the interpretation, evaluatio and development of Hegel's position in regard to religious an theological problems. The right wing interpreted Hegel in a sen: more or less compatible with Christianity, which meant that Go

ad to be represented as a personal, self-conscious Being in his own
ight, so to speak. The left wing maintained a pantheistic inter-
retation and denied personal immortality.

The left wing, however, soon went beyond pantheism to
aturalism and atheism. And at the hands of Marx and Engels the
Iegelian theories of society and history were revolutionized. The
eft wing is thus of much greater historical importance than the
ight wing. But the radical thinkers of the former group must be
ccorded separate treatment and not treated as disciples of Hegel,
who would scarcely have recognized them as such.

Under the heading of the influence of Hegel we might refer, of
ourse, to the British idealism of the second half of the nineteenth
entury and of the first two decades of the present century, to
talian philosophers such as Benedetto Croce (1866–1952) and
Giovanni Gentile (1875–1944) and to recent French works on
Iegel, not to mention other examples of the philosopher's long-
erm influence. But these topics would take us outside the scope of
he present volume. Instead we can turn to consideration of the
eaction against metaphysical idealism and of the emergence of
ther lines of thought in the German philosophical world of the
ineteenth century.

# PART II

## THE REACTION AGAINST METAPHYSICAL IDEALISM

### CHAPTER XII

### EARLIER OPPONENTS AND CRITICS

*Fries and his disciples—The realism of Herbart—Beneke and
psychology as the fundamental science—The logic of Bolzano—
Weisse and I. H. Fichte as critics of Hegel.*

1. THE development of idealism at the hands of Fichte, Schellin
and Hegel was regarded as a great mistake by Jakob Friedric
Fries (1773-1843). In his view the proper and profitable task fc
philosophy was to carry on the work of Kant without turning th
Kantian philosophy into a system of metaphysics. True, Frie
himself made use of the word 'metaphysics', and in 1824 h
published a *System of Metaphysics* (*System der Metaphysik*). Bu
this word meant for him a critique of human knowledge, not
science of the Absolute. To this extent, therefore, he walked in th
footsteps of Kant. Yet at the same time he turned Kant's trans
cendental critique of knowledge into a psychological investigatior
a process of psychological self-observation. Although, therefore
Fries starts with Kant and tries to correct and develop hi
position, the fact that this correction takes the form of psychc
logizing the Kantian critique results in a certain measure c
affinity with the attitude of Locke. For according to Fries w
must investigate the nature and laws and scope of knowledg
before we can tackle problems about the object of knowledge
And the method of pursuing this investigation is empirica
observation.

Fries did not by any means confine his activities to the theor
of knowledge. In 1803 he published a *Philosophical Theory of Righ
(Philosophische Rechtslehre)* and in 1818 an *Ethics (Ethik)*. Hi
political ideas were liberal, and in 1819 he was deprived of his chai
at Jena. Some years later, however, he was nominated to a chair o
mathematics and physics in the same university. He had alread
published some works on natural philosophy and physics, and h

ried to unite the mathematical physics of Newton with the Kantian philosophy as he interpreted it.

In 1832 Fries published a *Handbook of the Philosophy of Religion and of Philosophical Aesthetics* (*Handbuch der Religionsphilosophie und der philosophischen Aesthetik*). As a boy he had been educated in the traditions of pietism, and he maintained to the end an insistence on religious feeling and interior piety. On the one hand we have mathematical and scientific knowledge; on the other and we have the presage of religious and aesthetic feeling, its witness to the Being which lies behind the sphere of phenomena. Practical or moral faith relates us to noumenal reality, but religious and aesthetic feeling gives us a further assurance that the reality behind phenomena is that which moral faith conceives it to be. Fries thus added to Kant's doctrine of practical faith an insistence on the value of religious emotion.

Fries was not without influence. Prominent among his disciples was E. F. Apelt (1812–59), who defended his master's psychological interpretation of Kant and insisted on the need for a close union between philosophy and science.[1] And it is worth mentioning that the celebrated philosopher of religion Rudolf Otto (1869–1937) was influenced by Fries's insistence on the fundamental importance of feeling in religion, though it would be quite incorrect to call Otto a disciple of Fries.

In the early part of the present century the so-called Neo-Friesian School was founded by Leonard Nelson (1882–1927).

2. Among the contemporary opponents of post-Kantian idealism the name of Fries is much less widely known than that of Johann Friedrich Herbart (1776–1841). In 1809 Herbart was nominated to the chair at Königsberg which had once been held by Kant, and he occupied it until 1833 when he went to Göttingen. While in Switzerland (1797–1800) he had known Pestalozzi, and he took a great interest in and wrote on educational subjects. Among his main philosophical works are his *Introduction to Philosophy* (*Einleitung in die Philosophie*, 1813), *Psychology as a Science* (*Psychologie als Wissenschaft*, 1824–5) and *General Metaphysics* (*Allgemeine Metaphysik*, 1828–9).

Herbart once remarked that he was a Kantian of the year 1828. He meant, of course, that though he paid tribute to the work of the great thinker whose chair he then occupied, a good deal of water

[1] Modern logicians rightly look with disfavour on the psychologizing of logic. But the tendency to do this was connected, however mistakenly, with the notion that it was the expression of a scientific attitude.

had flowed under the bridge in the meantime, and that he did n
simply accept the Kantian system as it came from the hands
the master. Indeed, Herbart cannot be called a Kantian in ar
ordinary sense. To be sure, he rejected post-Kantian idealism. B
to regard post-Kantian idealism as a perversion of the thought
Kant is not necessarily the same as to be a Kantian. And in son
respects Herbart's affinities are with the pre-Kantian philosophe
rather than with Kant himself.

When considered under one aspect at least, Herbart's accour
of philosophy has an extremely modern flavour. For he describ
philosophy as the elaboration (*Bearbeitung*) of concepts. A
obvious objection to this description is that no indication is give
of the peculiar subject-matter of philosophy. Any science might
described in this way. But it is Herbart's contention that phil
sophy does not possess a peculiar subject-matter of its ow
alongside the subject-matters of the various particular science
Or, more accurately, we cannot say from the start that philosopl
has a particular field of reality as its peculiar subject-matter. V
must first describe it as the activity of elaborating and clarifyir
concepts.

It is in the course of this activity that the different branches
philosophy arise. For example, if we concern ourselves wit
working out the theory of distinct concepts and their combinatic
and the principles of the clarification of concepts, we are engage
in logic. If, however, we apply logical principles to the clarificatio
of concepts furnished by experience, we are engaged in metaphysic

In Herbart's opinion this work of clarification is essential. F
when the fundamental concepts derived from experience a
submitted to logical analysis, they show themselves to be riddle
with contradictions. Take, for example, the concept of a thing. If
can properly be called a thing, it must be one, a unity. But if v
try to describe it, it is resolved into a plurality of qualities. It
one and many, one and not-one, at the same time. We are thu
faced with a contradiction, and we cannot rest content with it.
is not, however, a question of simply rejecting the concept derive
from experience. For if we sever the link between thought an
experience, we cut ourselves off from reality. What is required is
clarification and elaboration of the concept in such a way that th
contradiction disappears.

Herbart assumes, therefore, that the principle of non-contradi
tion is fundamental. He will have nothing to do with the dialectic

ogic of Hegel which in his opinion blurs this principle. Reality must be without contradiction. That is to say, it must be of such a kind that a true world-view or account of the world would be a harmonious system of mutually consistent and intrinsically non-contradictory concepts. Raw experience, so to speak, does not present us with such a world-view. It belongs to philosophy to construct it by clarifying, modifying and rendering consistent the concepts derived from experience and used in the sciences.

A better way of expressing Herbart's point of view would be to say that reality is of such a kind that a complete account of it would take the form of a comprehensive system of mutually consistent non-contradictory propositions. It is indeed arguable that Hegel himself had a similar ideal of truth, and that he should not be interpreted as having denied the principle of non-contradiction. After all, Herbart too allows contradictions to emerge from our ordinary ways of regarding things and then tries to resolve them. But Hegel speaks as though contradictions were a feature of the process of reality itself, of the life of the Absolute, whereas for Herbart contradictions emerge only from our inadequate ways of conceiving reality: they are not a feature of reality itself. Hence Herbart's view bears more resemblance to that of F. H. Bradley than it does to that of Hegel. And in point of fact Bradley was considerably influenced by Herbart.[1]

Now, let us assume that our ordinary view of things contains or gives rise to contradictions. We regard a rose as one thing and a lump of sugar as another thing. Each seems to be a unity. But when we try to describe them, each dissolves into a plurality of qualities. The rose is red, fragrant and soft; the sugar is white, sweet and hard. In each case we attribute the qualities to a uniting substance or thing. But what is it? If we try to say anything about it, the unity dissolves once more into a plurality. Or, if we say that it underlies the qualities, it seems to be a different thing. We can no longer say that the rose *is* red, fragrant and soft.

According to Herbart, the solution of this problem lies in postulating a plurality of simple and unchangeable entities or substances which he calls 'reals' (*Realen*). They enter into different relations with one another, and phenomenal qualities and changes

---

[1] I am speaking, of course, simply of Bradley's view that our ordinary ways of conceiving and describing things give rise to contradictions, whereas reality itself is a harmonious whole without any contradiction. On the issue between pluralism and monism there is a great difference between Herbart and the British absolute idealist.

correspond to these relations. For instance, the lump of suga
which appears to us as a unit, is composed of a plurality of ur
extended and changeless entities. And the various phenomen;
qualities of the sugar correspond to the relations in which the;
entities stand to one another, while the phenomenal changes in th
sugar correspond to the changing relations between the entitie
We are thus able to harmonize unity and multiplicity, constanc
and change.

After having proposed, therefore, a view of philosophy whic
has been recently fashionable in this country, namely tha
philosophy consists in the clarification of concepts or in conceptu;
analysis, Herbart goes on to raise a problem to which Bradle
subsequently gave a good deal of attention in *Appearance an*
*Reality*. But whereas Bradley, in accordance with the spirit of pos
Kantian idealism, finds the solution in terms of a One whic
'appears' as a multiplicity of things, Herbart has recourse to
pluralistic metaphysics which calls to mind the atoms (
Democritus and the monads of Leibniz. His 'reals' are indee
different from Democritus's atoms in that they are said to posse;
qualities, though these, being metaphenomenal, are unknowabl
Further, though each 'real' is simply and essentially unchangin;
they do not seem to be, like Leibniz's monads, 'windowless'. Fc
each 'real' is said to preserve its self-identity in the face (
disturbances (*Störungen*) from other such entities, so that the;
appears to be some reciprocal influence. At the same time Herbart
theory obviously has affinity with pre-Kantian metaphysics.

The theory of disturbances, each of which calls forth a sel
preservative reaction on the part of the disturbed entity, giv;
rise to some difficulty. For it is not easy to reconcile it with the id;
that space, time and causal interaction are phenomenal. To t
sure, Herbart assumes that phenomenal occurrences are grounde
on and explicable by the behaviour of the 'reals'. And the world (
the 'reals' is not taken to be the static reality of Parmenides. B;
it seems arguable that so far as the postulated relations betwee
'reals' are thought at all, they are inevitably brought into th
phenomenal sphere. For they can hardly be thought except i
terms of relations which are said to be phenomenal.

In any case it is on this metaphysical basis that Herba;
constructs his psychology. The soul is a simple and unextend;
substance or 'real'. It is not, however, to be identified with the pu;
subject or ego of consciousness. The soul, considered simply ;

such, is not conscious at all. Nor is it furnished with any Kantian apparatus of *a priori* forms and categories. All psychical activities are secondary and derived. That is to say, the soul strives to preserve itself in face of disturbances occasioned by other 'reals', and the self-preservative reactions are expressed in sensations and ideas. And mental life is constituted by the relations and inter-actions between sensations and ideas. The idea of distinct faculties can be thrown overboard. For instance, an idea which meets with hindrance can be called a desire, while an idea which is accompanied by a supposition of success can be called a volition. There is no need to postulate appetitive and volitional faculties. The relevant psychical phenomena can be explained in terms of ideas which are themselves explicable in terms of stimuli directly or indirectly caused by the soul's self-preservative reactions to disturbances.

An interesting feature of Herbart's psychology is his theory of the subconscious. Ideas may be associated with one another, but they may also be mutually opposed. In this case a state of tension is set up, and some idea or ideas are forced below the level of consciousness. They then turn into impulses, though they can return to consciousness as ideas. We may also note Herbart's insistence not only that on the conscious level consciousness of objects other than the self precedes self-consciousness but also that self-consciousness is always empirical self-consciousness, conscious-ness of the me-object. There are ego-ideas, but there is no such thing as pure self-consciousness.

Though, however, Herbart's theory of the subconscious is not without historical importance, the salient feature of his psychology is perhaps his attempt to make it a science by mathematicizing it. Thus he assumes that ideas have varying degrees of intensity, and that the relations between them can be expressed in mathematical formulas. When, for example, an idea has been inhibited and forced below the level of consciousness, its return to consciousness will involve the return, according to a mathematically determinable sequence, of associated ideas. And if we possessed sufficient empirical evidence, we could predict the cause of such events. In principle at any rate psychology is capable of being turned into an exact science, the statics and dynamics of the mental life of presentations.

Psychology, therefore, like metaphysics, is concerned with the real. Aesthetics and ethics are concerned with values. The more fundamental of these two is aesthetics. For the ethical judgment is a subdivision of the aesthetic judgment, the judgment of taste which expresses approval or disapproval. But this is not to say that the ethical judgment has no objective reference. For approval and disapproval are grounded in certain relations, and in the case of ethics these are relations of the will, of which Herbart discovers five. In the first place experience shows that we express approval of the relation in which the will is in agreement with a person's inner conviction. That is to say, we express approval in accordance with the ideal of inner freedom.[1] Secondly our approval is given to a relation of harmony between the different tendencies or strivings of the individual will. And our approval is then elicited in accordance with the ideal of perfection. Thirdly we approve the relation in which one will takes as its object the satisfaction of another will. And here it is the ideal of benevolence which informs our judgment. Fourthly approval or disapproval is elicited in accordance with the idea of justice. We disapprove a relation of conflict or disharmony between several wills, while we approve a relation in which each will allows the others to limit it. Fifthly we disapprove a relation in which deliberate good and evil acts are unrecompensed. Here the idea of retribution is operative.

It is in the light of this theory of values that Herbart criticizes the Kantian ethics. We cannot take the categorical imperative as an ultimate moral fact. For we can always ask whence the practical reason or will derives its authority. Behind a command and obedience to it there must be something which warrants respect for the command. And this is found in the recognition of values, the morally beautiful and pleasing.

We cannot enter here into Herbart's educational theory. But it is worth noting that it involves a combination of his ethics with his psychology. Ethics, with its theory of values, provides the end or aim of education, namely character-development. The goal of the moral life is the perfect conformity of the will with moral ideals or values. And this is virtue. But to estimate how this aim is to be pedagogically attained we have to take account of psychology and utilize its laws and principles. The main end of education is moral, but the educator has to build upon the two masses of presentations derived from experience of the world and from social intercourse

[1] Given the psychology outlined above, Herbart does not accept the theory of liberty of indifference. Indeed, he regards the theory as incompatible with the idea of a stable and firm character, the development of which is one of the principal aims of education. But he recognizes, of course, a psychological difference between choosing in accordance with conviction or conscience and being led by impulse or desire to act in a manner contrary to one's conscience.

and environment. The first basis has to be developed into knowledge, the second into benevolence towards and sympathy with others.

Herbart's philosophy clearly lacked the romantic appeal of the great idealist systems. In one sense it was out of date. That is to say, it looked back behind Kant, and its author was out of sympathy with the contemporary prevailing movement in Germany. But in another sense it was very much up to date. For it demanded a closer integration of philosophy and science and looked forward to some of the systems which followed the collapse of idealism and demanded precisely this integration. The most significant features of Herbart's philosophy were probably his psychology and his educational theory. In the second field he helped to provide a theoretical background for the practical ideas of Pestalozzi. In the field of psychology he exercised a stimulative influence. But in view of his idea of psychology as the mechanics of the mental life of sensations and ideas it is as well to remind oneself that he was no materialist. Matter was for him phenomenal. Further, he accepted a form of the argument from design, pointing to a divine supersensible Being.

3. The importance of psychology was even more strongly emphasized by Friedrich Eduard Beneke (1798–1854). Beneke was considerably influenced by the writings of Herbart, but he was certainly not a disciple. He was also influenced by Fries, but above all he derived inspiration from British thought and had a high regard for Locke. He was quite out of sympathy with the dominant idealist philosophy and encountered great difficulties in his academic career. In the end he appears to have committed suicide, an event which elicited some remarks in thoroughly bad taste from Arthur Schopenhauer.

In Beneke's view psychology is the fundamental science and the basis of philosophy. It should not be grounded, as with Herbart, on metaphysics. On the contrary, it is or ought to be grounded on interior experience which reveals to us the fundamental psychical processes. Mathematics is no help and is not required. Beneke was indeed influenced by the associationist psychology, but he did not share Herbart's notion of turning psychology into an exact science by mathematicizing it. He looked rather to the introspective method of the English empiricists.

As for the soul, it is, as Locke rightly claimed, devoid of innate ideas. There are also, as Herbart saw, no distinct faculties in the

traditional sense. But we can discover a number of predisposition
or impulses which can be called faculties if we wish to do so. And
the unity of the self results from the harmonization of these
impulses. Further, pedagogy and ethics, which are both applied
psychology, show how the impulses and predispositions are to be
developed and harmonized in view of a hierarchy of goods or values
determined by a consideration of actions and their effects.

Beneke's philosophy is doubtless very small beer compared with
the grandiose systems of German idealism. At the same time we
can see perhaps in the emphasis which he lays upon impulses as the
fundamental elements in the psychical life and in his tendency to
stress the practical rather than the theoretical some affinity with
the shift towards voluntarism which was given large-scale expression in the metaphysical system of Schopenhauer, the very man
who made caustic remarks about Beneke's suicide. For the matter
of that, Fichte had already emphasized the fundamental role of
impulse and drive.

4. Chronological reasons justify the inclusion in this chapter of
some brief reference to Bernhard Bolzano (1781–1848), even if his
rediscovery as a forerunner in certain respects of modern logical
developments tends to make one think of him as a more recent
writer than he actually was.

Bolzano was born in Prague of an Italian father and German
mother. In 1805 he was ordained priest and soon afterwards he
was appointed to the chair of philosophy of religion in the
University of Prague. But at the end of 1819 he was deprived of
his post, not, as has sometimes been stated, by his ecclesiastical
superiors, but by order of the Emperor in Vienna. The imperial
decree made special mention of Bolzano's objectionable doctrines
on war, social rank and civic disobedience. In point of fact Bolzano
had told the students that war would one day be regarded with
the same abhorrence as duelling, that social differences would in
time be reduced to proper limits, and that obedience to the civil
power was limited by the moral conscience and by the norms of the
legitimate exercise of sovereignty. And though these views may
have been objectionable in the eyes of the Holy Roman Emperor
they were far from being theologically heretical. Indeed, the
ecclesiastical authorities at Prague, when instructed by Vienna to
investigate the case of Bolzano, declared that he was an orthodox
Catholic. However, Bolzano had to abandon teaching and he
devoted himself to a life of study and writing, though he had

some difficulties about publication, at any rate in the Austrian dominions.

In 1827 Bolzano published anonymously a work, commonly called *Athanasia*, on the grounds of belief in the immortality of the soul. His chief work, *Theory of Science: an Essay towards a Detailed and for the most part New Exposition of Logic* (*Wissenschaftslehre: Versuch einer ausführlichen und grösstenteils neuen Darstellung der Logik*) appeared in four volumes in 1837. The *Paradoxes of the Infinite* (*Paradoxen des Unendlichen*) was published posthumously in 1851. In addition he wrote a considerable number of papers on logical, mathematical, physical, aesthetic and political themes, many of them for the Bohemian Society of the Sciences of which he was an active member.

In a short account which he wrote of his intellectual development Bolzano remarked that at no time had he felt inclined to recognize any given philosophical system as the one true philosophy. Referring to Kant, whose first *Critique* he had begun to study in his eighteenth year, he admitted that he found much to approve of in the critical philosophy. At the same time he found much to disagree with and much that was lacking. For example, while he welcomed the distinction between analytic and synthetic propositions, he could not agree with Kant's explanation of the distinction. Nor could he accept the view of mathematical propositions as synthetic propositions based on *a priori* intuitions. For he had himself succeeded in deducing some geometrical truths by analysis of concepts. Mathematics, he thought, is purely conceptual in character, and it should be constructed by a rigorous process of analysis.

This insistence on conceptual analysis and on logical rigour was indeed characteristic of Bolzano. Not only did he find fault with leading philosophers for failing to define their terms,[1] for slovenly conceptual analysis and for lack of consistency in their use of terms, but he also made it clear that in his opinion nobody could be a good philosopher unless he was a good mathematician. Obviously, he was not disposed to regard with a particularly kindly eye the goings-on of the metaphysical idealists.

Further, the tendency of Bolzano's mind was to de-psychologize logic, to formalize it and to set it free from any intrinsic connection with the subject or ego or productive imagination or any other

[1] For instance, he blames Kant for introducing the term 'experience' at the beginning of the first *Critique* without any adequate and unambiguous explanation of the meaning which he attaches to it.

subjective factor. And this tendency shows itself in his theory of the proposition in itself (*der Satz an sich*). A proposition in itself is defined as 'a statement that something is or is not, irrespective of whether this statement is true or false, irrespective of whether anyone has ever formulated it in words, and even irrespective of whether it has ever been present in any mind as a thought'.[1] The idea of propositions in themselves may give rise to some difficulties; but it is clear that for Bolzano the primary element in a proposition is its objective content or meaning. Its being thought or posited by a subject is a secondary factor, irrelevant to the objective meaning.

Bolzano also speaks of the presentation in itself (*die Vorstellung an sich*). This is described as whatever can be a component part in a proposition but which does not by itself constitute a proposition. Hence no presentation or concept can be in itself true or false. For truth and falsity are predicated only of propositions, not of their component parts taken singly. But the meaning or content of a presentation in itself can be analysed; and this can be done without reference to any subject. Logically speaking, the subject is irrelevant. For example, if idea X is conceived by A, B and C, there are three ideas from the psychological point of view but only one from the point of view of the logical analyst who is interested simply in the content of the concept. It seems to me disputable whether the range of meaning of a concept can be analysed in abstraction from the propositions in which it is employed. For meaning is determined by use. But in any case Bolzano's concern with de-psychologizing logic is clear enough.

In the third place Bolzano speaks of the judgment in itself (*das Urteil an sich*). Every judgment expresses and affirms a proposition.

Now, if there are propositions in themselves, there must also be truths in themselves (*Wahrheiten an sich*), namely those propositions which are in fact true. Their truth does not, however, depend in any way on their being expressed and affirmed in judgments by thinking subjects. And this holds good not only of finite subjects but also of God. Truths in themselves are not true because God posits them; God thinks them because they are true. Bolzano does not mean that it is false to say that God makes true factual propositions about the world to be true in the sense that God is creator and thus responsible for there being a world at all. He is looking at the matter from the logician's point of view and

[1] *Theory of Science* (2nd edition, Leipzig, 1929), p. 77.

maintaining that the truth of a proposition does not depend on its being thought by a subject, whether finite or infinite. The truth of a mathematical proposition, for example, depends on the meanings of the terms, not on whether it is thought by a mathematician, human or divine.

As a philosopher, Bolzano rejected Kant's condemnation of metaphysics and maintained that important truths about God and about the spirituality and immortality of the soul could be proved. In his general metaphysical outlook he was influenced by Leibniz. Bolzano did not indeed accept Leibniz's theory of 'windowless' monads; but he shared his conviction that every substance is an active being, its activity being expressed in some form of representation or, as Leibniz puts it, perception. But Bolzano's significance does not lie in his metaphysics but in his work as logician and mathematician. It was his status as a mathematician which first met with recognition, but in modern times tribute has been paid to him as a logician, notably by Edmund Husserl.

5. In the foregoing sections of this chapter we have been concerned with thinkers who stood apart from the movement of post-Kantian metaphysical idealism and followed other lines of thought. We can now consider briefly two philosophers who belonged to the idealist movement but who both developed a critical attitude towards absolute idealism.

(a) Christian Hermann Weisse (1801–66), who was a professor in the University of Leipzig, stood at one time fairly close to Hegel, though he considered that Hegel had exaggerated the role of logic, particularly by trying (according to Weisse's interpretation) to deduce reality from the abstract forms of Being. We require the idea of a personal creative God to make the system tenable.

In his development of a speculative theism Weisse was stimulated by the later religious philosophy of Schelling. And in the *Philosophical Problem of Today* (*Das philosophische Problem der Gegenwart*, 1842) he maintained that Hegel had developed in his logic the negative side of philosophy. The Hegelian dialectic provides us with the idea of the possible Godhead. The logical Absolute is· not the real God, but it is the necessary logical foundation of his reality. Hegel, of course, might have agreed. For the logical Idea as such was not for him the existing divine Being. But what Weisse was concerned to defend was the idea of a personal and free God, whose existence cannot be deduced from the absolute Idea, though it presupposes the validity of the Idea.

That is to say, the divine Being, if there is one, must be self-thinking Thought, a personal and self-conscious Being. But that there is such a Being must be shown in some other way than by *a priori* logical deduction. Further, Weisse tried to show that God cannot be *a* Person, and that we must accept the Christian doctrine of the Trinity.

(*b*) Weisse's criticism of Hegel seemed to be only half-hearted in the eyes of Immanuel Hermann Fichte (1796–1879), son of the famous idealist. The younger Fichte laid emphasis on the individual human personality, and he was strongly opposed to what he regarded as Hegel's tendency to merge the individual in the universal. In Hegelianism as he interpreted it the human person was presented as being no more than a transitory moment in the life of universal Spirit, whereas in his own view the development of personality was the end of creation and man was assured of personal immortality.

The thought of the younger Fichte passed through several stages, from a period when the influence of his father and of Kant was strong to his later concentration on a philosophical anthropology, accompanied by a marked interest in the preconscious aspects of man and in parapsychological phenomena. But the general framework of his philosophy was provided by a speculative theism in which he tried to combine idealist themes with theism and with an emphasis on the human personality. In his *Speculative Theology or General Doctrine of Religion* (*Die spekulative Theologie oder allgemeine Religionslehre*, 1846), which forms the third volume of his trilogy on speculative theism, God is represented as the supreme personal unity of the ideal and the real. The ideal aspect of God is his infinite self-consciousness, while the real aspect is formed by the monads which are the eternal thoughts of God. Creation signifies the act of endowing these monads with free will, with a life of their own. And the development of the human personality is a development of self-consciousness on a basis of preconscious or subconscious levels.

Obviously I. H. Fichte was strongly influenced by the idealist movement. One would hardly expect anything else. But he laid great emphasis on the personal nature of God and on the value and immortality of the human person. And it was in the name of this personalistic idealism that he attacked the Hegelian system in which, he was convinced, finite personality was offered up in sacrifice to the all-devouring Absolute.

### CHAPTER XIII

## SCHOPENHAUER (1)

*Life and writings—Schopenhauer's doctorate dissertation—The world as Idea—The biological function of concepts and the possibility of metaphysics—The world as the manifestation of the Will to live—Metaphysical pessimism—Some critical comments.*

. A PHILOSOPHY'S ability to strike our imaginations by presenting n original and dramatic picture of the universe is obviously not an nfallible criterion of its truth. But it certainly adds greatly to its nterest. It is not, however, a quality which is conspicuously resent in any of the philosophies considered in the last chapter. Ierbart, it is true, produced a general system. But if one had to ingle out the dramatic visions of the world provided by nineteenth-entury philosophers, it would hardly occur to anyone to mention Ierbart. Hegel, yes; Marx, yes; Nietzsche, yes; but not, I think, Ierbart. And still less the sober logician and mathematician 3olzano. In 1819, however, when Herbart was professor at Königsberg and Hegel had recently moved from Heidelberg to 3erlin, there appeared the main work of Arthur Schopenhauer, vhich, though it excited little notice at the time, expressed an nterpretation of the world and of human life that was both triking in itself and opposed in certain important respects to the nterpretations offered by the great idealists. There are indeed ertain family likenesses between the system of Schopenhauer and hose of the idealists. But its author, who never minced words, rofessed an utter contempt for Fichte, Schelling and Hegel, specially the last named, and regarded himself as their great pponent and the purveyor of the real truth to mankind.

Arthur Schopenhauer was born at Danzig on February 22nd, 788. His father, a wealthy merchant, hoped that his son would ollow in his footsteps, and he allowed the boy to spend the years 803-4 in visiting England, France and other countries on the nderstanding that at the conclusion of the tour he would take p work in a business house. The young Schopenhauer fulfilled is promise, but he had no relish for a business career and on his ather's death in 1803 he obtained his mother's consent to his continuing his studies. In 1809 he entered the University o Göttingen to study medicine, but he changed to philosophy in hi second year at the university. As he put it, life is a problem and h had decided to spend his time reflecting on it.

From Göttingen, where he became an admirer of Plato Schopenhauer went in 1811 to Berlin to listen to the lectures o Fichte and Schleiermacher. The former's obscurity was repugnan to him, while the latter's assertion that nobody could be a rea philosopher without being religious elicited the sarcastic commen that nobody who is religious takes to philosophy, as he has no neec of it.

Schopenhauer regarded himself as a cosmopolitan, and at n time was he a German nationalist. Having, as he subsequently said a detestation for all military affairs he prudently left Berlin wher Prussia rose against Napoleon and devoted himself in peacefu retirement to the preparation of a dissertation *On the Fourfold Root of the Principle of Sufficient Reason* (*Ueber die vierfach Wurzel des Satzes vom zureichenden Grunde*) which won for him th doctorate at Jena and was published in 1813. Goethe congratulated the author, and in return Schopenhauer wrote his essay *On Visior and Colours* (*Ueber das Sehen und die Farben*, 1816) in which h more or less supported Goethe against Newton. But apart from th flattering reception accorded it by the great poet the *Fourfold Roo* was practically unnoticed and unsold. The author, however continued to look on it as an indispensable introduction to hi philosophy, and something will be said about it in the next section

From May 1814 until September 1818 Schopenhauer was living at Dresden. And it was there that he composed his main philo sophical work, *The World as Will and Idea* (*Die Welt als Wille unc Vorstellung*). Having consigned the manuscript to the publisher: Schopenhauer left for an art tour of Italy. The work appeared early in 1819, and the author had the consolation of finding tha some philosophers, such as Herbart and Beneke, took notice of it But this consolation was offset by the very small sale of a book which its author believed to contain the secret of the universe.

Encouraged, however, by the fact that his *magnum opus* had not passed entirely unnoticed and eager to expound the truth about the world by word of mouth as well as in writing, Schopenhauer betook himself to Berlin and started lecturing there in 1820 Though he held no university chair, he did not hesitate to choose for his lectures the hour at which Hegel was accustomed to

ecture. The enterprise was a complete failure, and Schopenhauer
left off lecturing after one semester. His doctrine was scarcely
representative of the dominant *Zeitgeist* or spirit of the time.

After some wanderings Schopenhauer settled at Frankfurt on
the Main in 1833. He read widely in European literature, consulted
scientific books and journals, being quick to notice points which
would serve as illustrations or empirical confirmation of his
philosophical theories, visited the theatre and continued writing.
In 1836 he published *On the Will in Nature* (*Ueber den Willen in
der Natur*), and in 1839 he won a prize from the Scientific Society
of Drontheim in Norway for an essay on freedom. He failed,
however, to obtain a similar prize from the Royal Danish Academy
of the Sciences for an essay on the foundations of ethics. One of the
reasons given for the refusal of the prize was the writer's dis-
respectful references to leading philosophers. Schopenhauer had a
great admiration for Kant, but he had the habit of referring to
thinkers such as Fichte, Schelling and Hegel in terms which were,
to put it mildly, unconventional, however amusing his expressions
may be to later generations. The two essays were published together
in 1841 under the title *The Two Fundamental Problems of Ethics*
(*Die beiden Grundprobleme der Ethik*).

In 1844 Schopenhauer published a second edition of *The World
as Will and Idea* with fifty supplementary chapters. In the preface
to this edition he took the opportunity of making quite clear his
views about German university professors of philosophy, just in
case his attitude might not have been sufficiently indicated already.
In 1851 he published a successful collection of essays entitled
*Parerga and Paralipomena*, dealing with a wide variety of topics.
Finally, in 1859 he published a third and augmented edition of his
*magnum opus*.

After the failure of the Revolution of 1848, a revolution for
which Schopenhauer had no sympathy at all, people were more
ready to pay attention to a philosophy which emphasized the evil
in the world and the vanity of life and preached a turning away
from life to aesthetic contemplation and asceticism. And in the
last decade of his life Schopenhauer became a famous man.
Visitors came to see him from all sides and were entertained by his
brilliant conversational powers. And though the German professors
had not forgotten his sarcasm and abuse, lectures were delivered on
his system in several universities, a sure sign that he had at last
arrived. He died in September 1860.

Schopenhauer possessed a great breadth of culture, and he could write extremely well. A man of strong character and will, he was never afraid to express his opinions; and he had a gift of wit. He also possessed a considerable fund of practical sense and business acumen. But he was egoistic, vain, quarrelsome and, on occasion even boorish; and he can hardly be said to have been remarkable for gifts of the heart. His relations with women were not exactly what one expects from a man who discoursed with eloquence on ethical, ascetical and mystical matters; and his literary executors suppressed some of his remarks about the female sex. Further, his theoretical sensitivity to the sufferings of humanity was not accompanied by any very practical efforts to alleviate it. But, as he sagely remarked, it is no more necessary for a philosopher to be a saint than for a saint to be a philosopher. And while as a man he can scarcely be considered as one of the most lovable of philosophers, his outstanding gifts as a writer are, I think, unquestionable.

2. In his doctorate dissertation Schopenhauer writes under the strong influence of Kant. The world of experience is the phenomenal world: it is object for a subject. And as such it is the world of our mental presentations (*Vorstellungen*). But no object is ever presented to us in a state of complete isolation and detachment. That is to say, all our presentations are related to or connected with other presentations in regular ways. And knowledge or science is precisely knowledge of these regular relations. '*Science*, that is to say, signifies a *system* of objects known',[1] not a mere aggregate of presentations. And there must be a sufficient reason for this relatedness or correctedness. Thus the general principle which governs our knowledge of objects or phenomena is the principle of sufficient reason.

As a preliminary enunciation of the principle of sufficient reason Schopenhauer chooses 'the Wolffian formulation as the most general: *Nihil est sine ratione cur potius sit quam non sit*. Nothing is without a reason [*Grund*, ground] why it is.'[2] But he goes on to discover four main types or classes of objects and four main types of relatedness or connection. And he draws the conclusion that there are four fundamental forms of the principle of sufficient reason and that the principle in its general enunciation is an abstraction from them. Hence the title of the dissertation, *On the Fourfold Root of the Principle of Sufficient Reason*.

[1] *W*, I, p. 4. References to Schopenhauer's *Works* are given according to volume and page of the edition by J. Frauenstädt (1877).
[2] *W*, I, p. 5.

The first class of objects or presentations is that of our intuitive, empirical and complete[1] presentations. This may not sound very enlightening; but in the language of ordinary realism the objects in question are the physical objects which are causally related in space and time and which form the subject-matter of natural sciences such as physics and chemistry. According to Schopenhauer, this spatial, temporal and causal relatedness is to be ascribed to an activity of the mind which organizes the matter of phenomena, elementary sensations, according to the *a priori* forms of sensibility, namely space and time, and the pure form of causality which is the only category of the understanding. He thus follows Kant, though the Kantian categories of the understanding are reduced to one. And our knowledge of these presentations, of phenomena or, in realist language, of physical objects, is said to be governed by 'the principle of sufficient reason of becoming, *principium rationis sufficientis fiendi*'.[2]

The second class of objects consists of abstract concepts, and the relevant form of relatedness is the judgment. But a judgment does not express knowledge unless it is true. And 'truth is the relation of a judgment to something different from it, which can be called its ground'.[3] The ground or sufficient reason can be of different types. For instance, a judgment can have as its ground another judgment; and when we consider the rules of implication and inference in a formal way, we are in the province of logic.[4] But in any case the judgment, the synthesis of concepts, is governed by 'the principle of sufficient reason of knowing, *principium rationis sufficientis cognoscendi*'.[5]

The third class of objects comprises 'the *a priori* intuitions of the forms of outer and inner sense, space and time'.[6] Space and time are of such a nature that each part is related in a certain way to another. And 'the law according to which the parts of space and time . . . determine one another I call the principle of sufficient reason of being, *principium rationis sufficientis essendi*'.[7] In time, for example, this is the law of irreversible succession; and 'on this connection of the parts of time rests all counting'.[8] Arithmetic, in other words, rests on the law governing the relations between the

---

[1] Complete in the sense that such presentations comprise both the form and the matter of phenomena. In other words, it is not a question here of abstract concepts.
[2] *W*, I, p. 34.      [3] *W*, I, p. 105.
[4] The implication of this is that Hegel's identification of logic with metaphysics, in the sense of the science of the Absolute, is absurd.
[5] *W*, I, p. 105.      [6] *W*, I, p. 130.
[7] *W*, I, p. 131.      [8] *W*, I, p. 133.

parts of time, while geometry rests on the law governing the respective positions of the parts of space. We can say, therefore that Schopenhauer's third class of objects are mathematical objects, and that the relevant form of the principle of sufficient reason or ground, which governs our knowledge of geometrical and arithmetical relations, is the law, or rather laws, according to which the parts of space and time are respectively related to one another.

The fourth class of objects contains only one member, namely 'the subject of willing considered as object for the knowing subject'.[1] That is to say, the object is the self as source or subject of volition. And the principle governing our knowledge of the relation between this subject and its volitions or acts of will is 'the principle of the ground (or sufficient reason) of acting, *principium rationis sufficientis agendi*; more briefly, the *law of motivation*'.[2] The implication of this is character-determinism. A man acts for motives, and the motives for which he acts have their ground or sufficient reason in his character. We understand the relation between a man's deliberate actions and himself as subject of volition where we see these actions as issuing from the character of the subject. But this subject will be considered later.

Schopenhauer's terminology is based on that of Wolff. But his general position is based on Kant's. The world is phenomenal, object for a subject. And it is the sphere of necessity. True Schopenhauer recognizes different types of necessity. In the sphere of volition, for example, moral necessity rules, which is to be distinguished both from physical and from logical necessity. But within the sphere of presentations as a whole, the relations between them are governed by certain laws, described as distinct roots of the principle of sufficient reason.

It is to be noted, however, that the principle of sufficient reason applies only within the phenomenal sphere, the sphere of objects for a subject. It does not apply to the noumenon, metaphenomenal reality, whatever this may be. Nor can it be legitimately applied to the phenomenal world considered as a totality. For it governs relations *between* phenomena. Hence no cosmological argument for God's existence can be valid, if it is an argument from the world as a whole to God as cause or as sufficient ground of phenomena. And here again Schopenhauer is in substantial agreement with Kant, though he certainly does not follow

[1] *W*, I, p. 140.    [2] *W*, I, p. 145.

Kant in proposing belief in God as a matter of practical or moral faith.

3. The doctorate dissertation which we have just briefly considered appears arid and unexciting in comparison with Schopenhauer's great work *The World as Will and Idea*. Yet Schopenhauer was justified in regarding the former as an introduction to the latter. For his *magnum opus* begins with the statement that 'the world is my idea'.[1] That is to say, the whole visible world or, as Schopenhauer describes it, the sum total of experience is object for a subject: its reality consists in its appearing to or being perceived by a subject. As Berkeley said, the *esse* of sensible things is *percipi*.

The following point should be noticed. The German word translated here by 'idea' is *Vorstellung*. And in the section on Schopenhauer's doctorate dissertation I translated this word by presentation', which is preferable to 'idea'. But the title *The World as Will and Idea* has become so familiar that it seems pedantic to insist on a change. At the same time it is important to understand that Schopenhauer distinguishes between intuitive presentations (*intuitive Vorstellungen*) and abstract presentations (*abstrakte Vorstellungen*) or concepts. And when Schopenhauer says that the world is my idea, he is referring to intuitive presentations. He does not mean, for example, that a tree is identical with my abstract concept of a tree. He means that the tree as perceived by me exists only in relation to me as a percipient subject. Its reality is exhausted, so to speak, in its perceptibility. It is simply what I perceive or can perceive it to be.

Schopenhauer's position can be clarified in this way. Abstract concepts are possessed only by man: intuitive presentations are common to man and animals, at least to the higher animals. There is a phenomenal world not only for man but also for animals. For the conditions of its possibility are present also in the latter, these conditions being the *a priori* forms of sensibility, namely space and time, and the category of the understanding, namely causality. In Schopenhauer's view understanding (*Verstand*) is found also in animals. And the *principium rationis sufficientis fiendi* operates, for instance, in a dog, for which there exists a world of causally related things. But animals do not possess reason (*Vernuft*), the faculty of abstract concepts. A dog perceives things in space and

---

[1] *W*, II, p. 3; *HK*, I, p. 3. In references to *The World as Will and Idea HK* signifies the English translation by R. B. Haldane and J. Kemp.

time, and it can perceive concrete causal relations. But it does not follow that a dog can reflect abstractly about space, time or causality. To put the matter in another way, the statement that the visible world is object for a percipient subject applies as well to a dog as to a man. But it does not follow from this that a dog can know that the statement is true.

It should be added that according to Schopenhauer it was an important discovery of Kant that space and time, as the *a priori* conditions of the visible world, can be intuited in themselves. Hence they can be included in the range of our intuitive presentations which comprise 'the whole visible world, or the whole of experience, together with the conditions of its possibility'.[1] But it does not follow that a dog can intuit space and time in themselves and work out pure mathematics, though there is for it a spatio-temporal world.

Now, if the world is my idea, my body also must be my idea. For it is a visible thing. But we must go further than this. If it is true that the world exists only as object for a subject, it is also true that the percipient subject is correlative with the object. 'For me [Schopenhauer] matter and intelligence are inseparable correlates, existing only for one another, and therefore only relatively . . . the two together constitute *the world as idea*, which is just Kant's *appearance*, and consequently something secondary.'[2] The world as idea or presentation thus comprises both perceiver and perceived. This totality is, as Kant said, empirically real but transcendentally ideal.

For Kant Schopenhauer had a profound respect, and he claimed to be Kant's true successor. But his theory of the phenomenal character of empirical reality was powerfully reinforced by though not derived from, another factor. Shortly after the publication of his doctorate dissertation in 1813 Schopenhauer met at Weimar an Oriental scholar, F. Mayer, who introduced him to Indian philosophical literature. And he retained an interest in Oriental philosophy up to the end of his life. As an old man he meditated on the text of the Upanishads. It is not surprising therefore, if he associated his theory of the world as idea or presentation with the Indian doctrine of Maya. Individual subjects and objects are all appearance, Maya.

Now, if the world is phenomenal, the question arises, what is the noumenon? What is the reality which lies behind the veil of Maya?

[1] *W*, II, p. 7; *HK*, I, p. 7.     [2] *W*, III, pp. 19–20; *HK*, II, p. 181.

And Schopenhauer's discussion of the nature of this reality and
of its self-manifestation forms the really interesting part of his
system. For the theory of the world as idea, though it is in
Schopenhauer's opinion an indispensable part of his philosophy, is
obviously a development of Kant's position, whereas his theory of
the world as will is original[1] and contains the expression of his
characteristic interpretation of human life. Before, however, we
approach this topic, something must be said about his theory of
the practical function of concepts, which possesses an intrinsic
interest of its own.

4. As we have seen, besides intuitive presentations man possesses
also abstract concepts which are formed by reason and presuppose
experience, whether directly or indirectly. But why do we form
them? What is their function? Schopenhauer's answer is that their
primary function is practical. 'The great utility of concepts consists
in the fact that by means of them the original material of knowledge
is easier to handle, survey and order.'[2] In comparison with
intuitive presentations, with immediate perceptive knowledge,
abstract concepts are in a sense poor. For they omit a great deal,
the differences, for example, between individual members of a class.
But they are required if communication is to be possible and if
experimental knowledge is to be retained and handed on. 'The
greatest value of rational or abstract knowledge lies in its com-
municability and in the possibility of retaining it permanently. It
is chiefly on this account that it is so inestimably important for
practice.'[3] Schopenhauer also mentions the ethical importance of
concepts and abstract reasoning. A moral man guides his conduct
by principles. And principles require concepts.

But Schopenhauer is not concerned simply with pointing out
examples of the practical value of concepts. He is also at pains to
show how this practical value is connected with his general theory
of cognition. Knowledge is the servant of the will. Or, to omit
metaphysics for the present, knowledge is in the first instance the
instrument of satisfying physical needs, the servant of the body.
In animals needs are less complicated than in man, and they are
more easily satisfied. Perception is sufficient, especially as Nature
has provided animals with their own means of attack and defence,

[1] Schopenhauer liked to regard his philosophy of the Will as a development of
Kant's doctrine of the primacy of the practical reason or rational will. But the
former's metaphysical voluntarism was really foreign to the latter's mind. It was
Schopenhauer's original creation.
[2] *W*, III, p. 89; *HK*, II, p. 258.          [3] *W*, II, p. 66; *HK*, I, p. 72.

such as the claws of the lion and the sting of the wasp. But with the further development of the organism, in particular of the brain there is a corresponding development of needs and wants. And a higher type of knowledge is required to satisfy them. In man reason appears, which enables him to discover new ways of satisfying his needs, to invent tools, and so on.[1]

Reason, therefore, has a primarily biological function. If one may so speak, Nature intends it as an instrument for satisfying the needs of a more highly complicated and developed organism than that of the animal. But the needs in question are physical needs Reason is primarily concerned with nourishment and propagation with the bodily needs of the individual and species. And it follows from this that reason is unfitted for penetrating through the veil of phenomena to the underlying reality, the noumenon. The concept is a practical instrument: it stands for a number of things belonging to the same class and enables us to deal easily and economically with a vast amount of material. But it is not adapted for going beyond phenomena to any underlying essence or thing-in-itself.

In this case, we may well ask, how can metaphysics be possible. Schopenhauer answers that though the intellect is by nature the servant of the will, it is capable in man of developing to such an extent that it can achieve objectivity. That is to say, though man's mind is in the first instance an instrument for satisfying his bodily needs, it can develop a kind of surplus energy which sets it free, at least temporarily, from the service of desire. Man then becomes a disinterested spectator: he can adopt a contemplative attitude, as in aesthetic contemplation and in philosophy.

Clearly, this claim on behalf of the human mind does not by itself dispose of the difficulty which arises out of Schopenhauer's account of the concept. For systematic and communicable philosophy must be expressed in concepts. And if the concept is fitted for dealing only with phenomena, metaphysics appears to be ruled out. But Schopenhauer replies that metaphysical philosophy is possible provided that there is a fundamental intuition on the level of perceptive knowledge, which gives us direct insight into the nature of the reality underlying phenomena, an insight which philosophy endeavours to express in conceptual form. Philosophy, therefore, involves an interplay between intuition and conceptual

[1] An obvious line of objection is that there is an element of putting the cart before the horse in all this. It might be claimed, that is to say, that it is precisely because man possesses the power of reasoning that he is able to extend the scope and number of his wants and desires.

easoning. 'To enrich the concept from intuition is the constant concern of poetry and philosophy.'[1] Concepts do not provide us with new knowledge: intuition is fundamental. But intuition must be raised to the conceptual level if it is to become philosophy.

Schopenhauer is in a rather difficult position. He does not wish to postulate as the basis of philosophy an exceptional intuition which would be something entirely different from perception on the one hand and abstract reasoning on the other. Hence the intuition of which he is speaking must be on the level of perceptive knowledge. But perception is concerned with individual objects, and so with phenomena. For individuality belongs to the phenomenal sphere. He is forced, therefore, to try to show that even on the level of perception there can be an intuitive awareness of the noumenon, an awareness which forms the basis for philosophical mediation.

Leaving the nature of this intuition for consideration in the next section, we can pause to note how in some respects Schopenhauer anticipates certain Bergsonian positions. For Bergson emphasized the practical function of intelligence and the inability of the concept to grasp the reality of life. And he went on to base philosophy on intuition and to depict the philosopher's task as being partly that of endeavouring to mediate this intuition, so far as this is possible, on the conceptual level. Hence for Bergson as for Schopenhauer philosophy involves the interplay of intuition and discursive or conceptual reasoning. I do not mean to imply that Bergson actually took his ideas from Schopenhauer. For I am not aware of any real evidence to show that he did. The notion that if philosopher $X$ holds views which are similar to his predecessor $Y$, the former must necessarily have borrowed from or been influenced by the latter, is absurd. But the fact remains that though Bergson, when he became aware of the similarity, distinguished between his idea of intuition and that of the German philosopher, there is an obvious analogy between their positions. In other words, the same current or line of thought which found expression in the philosophy of Schopenhauer, when considered under the aspects in question, reappeared in the thought of Bergson. To put the matter in another way, there is some continuity, though there is also difference, between the system of Schopenhauer and the philosophy of Life of which the thought of Bergson is a notable example.

[1] *W*, III, p. 80; *HK*, II, p. 248.

5. Kant maintained that the thing-in-itself, the correlative of the phenomenon, is unknowable. Schopenhauer, however, tells us what it is. It is Will. 'Thing-in-itself signifies that which exists independently of our perception, in short that which properly is. For Democritus this was formed matter. It was the same at bottom for Locke. For Kant it was $=X$. For me it is Will.'[1] And this is one single Will. For multiplicity can exist only in the spatio-temporal world, the sphere of phenomena. There cannot be more than one metaphenomenal reality or thing-in-itself. In other words, the inside of the world, so to speak, is one reality, whereas the outside, the appearance of this reality, is the empirical world which consists of finite things.

How does Schopenhauer arrive at the conviction that the thing-in-itself is Will? To find the key to reality I must look within myself. For in inner consciousness or inwardly directed perception lies 'the single narrow door to the truth'.[2] Through this inner consciousness I am aware that the bodily action which is said to follow or result from volition is not something different from volition but one and the same. That is to say, the bodily action is simply the objectified will: it is the will become idea or presentation. Indeed, the whole body is nothing but objectified will, will as a presentation to consciousness. According to Schopenhauer anyone can understand this if he enters into himself. And once he has this fundamental intuition, he has the key to reality. He has only to extend his discovery to the world at large.

This Schopenhauer proceeds to do. He sees the manifestation of the one individual Will in the impulse by which the magnet turns to the north pole, in the phenomena of attraction and repulsion, in gravitation, in animal instinct, in human desire and so on. Wherever he looks, whether in the inorganic or in the organic sphere, he discovers empirical confirmation of his thesis that phenomena constitute the appearance of the one metaphysical Will.

The natural question to ask is this? If the thing-in-itself is manifested in such diverse phenomena as the universal forces of Nature, such as gravity, and human volition, why call it 'Will'? Would not 'Force' or 'Energy' be a more appropriate term, especially as the so-called Will, when considered in itself, is said to be 'without knowledge and merely a blind incessant impulse', 'an endless striving'?[4] For the term 'Will', which implies rationality

---

[1] *W*, vi, p. 96. From *Parerga und Paralipomena*.
[2] *W*, iii, p. 219; *HK*, ii, p. 406.
[3] *W*, ii, p. 323; *HK*, i, p. 354.                    [4] *W*, ii, p. 195; *HK*, i, p. 213.

eems to be hardly suitable for describing a blind impulse or
triving.

Schopenhauer, however, defends his linguistic usage by main-
aining that we ought to take our descriptive term from what is
est known to us. We are immediately conscious of our own
olition. And it is more appropriate to describe the less well known
a terms of the better known than the other way round.

Besides being described as blind impulse, endless striving,
ternal becoming and so on, the metaphysical Will is characterized
s the Will to live. Indeed, to say 'the Will' and to say 'the Will to
ve' are for Schopenhauer one and the same thing. As, therefore,
mpirical reality is the objectification or appearance of the meta-
hysical Will, it necessarily manifests the Will to live. And
chopenhauer has no difficulty in multiplying examples of this
anifestation. We have only to look at Nature's concern for the
aintenance of the species. Birds, for instance, build nests for
he young which they do not yet know. Insects deposit their eggs
here the larva may find nourishment. The whole series of
henomena of animal instinct manifests the omnipresence of the
Vill to live. If we look at the untiring activity of bees and ants and
sk what it all leads to, what is attained by it, we can only answer
he satisfaction of hunger and the sexual instinct',[1] the means, in
ther words, of maintaining the species in life. And if we look at
aan with his industry and trade, with his inventions and tech-
ology, we must admit that all this striving serves in the first
astance only to sustain and to bring a certain amount of additional
omfort to ephemeral individuals in their brief span of existence,
nd through them to contribute to the maintenance of the species.

All this fits in with what was said in the last section about
chopenhauer's theory of the biological function of reason as
xisting primarily to satisfy physical needs. We noticed indeed
hat the human intellect is capable of developing in such a way
hat it can free itself, at least temporarily, from the slavery of the
Vill. And we shall see later that Schopenhauer by no means
onfines the possible range of human activities to eating, drinking
nd copulation, the means of maintaining the life of the individual
nd of the species. But the primary function of reason manifests
he character of the Will as the Will to live.

6. Now, if the Will is an endless striving, a blind urge or impulse
hich knows no cessation, it cannot find satisfaction or reach a

----

[1] *W*, III, p. 403; *HK*, III, p. 111.

state of tranquillity. It is always striving and never attaining. And this essential feature of the metaphysical Will is reflected in its self-objectification, above all in human life. Man seeks satisfaction happiness, but he cannot attain it. What we call happiness or enjoyment is simply a temporary cessation of desire. And desire, as the expression of a need or want, is a form of pain. Happiness therefore, is 'the deliverance from a pain, from a want';[1] it i 'really and essentially always only *negative* and never positive'.[2] soon turns to boredom, and the striving after satisfaction reasserts itself. It is boredom which makes beings who love one another s little as men do seek one another's company. And great intellectual powers simply increase the capacity for suffering and deepen the individual's isolation.

Each individual thing, as an objectification of the one Will t live, strives to assert its own existence at the expense of other things. Hence the world is the field of conflict, a conflict which manifests the nature of the Will as at variance with itself, as tortured Will. And Schopenhauer finds illustrations of this conflic even in the inorganic sphere. But it is naturally to the organic and human spheres that he chiefly turns for empirical confirmation of his thesis. He dwells, for example, on the ways in which animals of one species prey on those of another. And when he comes to man he really lets himself go. 'The chief source of the most serious evil which afflict man is man himself: *homo homini lupus*. Whoever keeps this last fact clearly in view sees the world as a hell which surpasses that of Dante through the fact that one man must be the devil of another.'[3] War and cruelty are, of course, grist for Schopenhauer's mill. And the man who showed no sympathy with the Revolution of 1848 speaks in the sharpest terms of industrial exploitation, slavery and such like social abuses.

We may note that it is the egoism, rapacity and hardness and cruelty of men which are for Schopenhauer the real justification of the State. So far from being a divine manifestation, the State i simply the creation of enlightened egoism which tries to make the world a little more tolerable than it would otherwise be.

Schopenhauer's pessimism is thus metaphysical in the sense that it is presented as a consequence of the nature of the metaphysical Will. The philosopher is not simply engaged in drawing attention to the empirical fact that there is much evil and suffering in the

---

[1] *W*, II, p. 376; *HK*, I, pp. 411–12.     [2] *Ibid*.
[3] *W*, III, p. 663; *HK*, III, p. 388.

world. He is also indicating what he believes to be the cause of this
empirical fact. The thing-in-itself being what it is, phenomenal
reality must be marked with the black features which we actually
observe. We can, of course, do something to alleviate suffering.
This also is an empirical fact. But it is no good thinking that we can
change the fundamental character of the world or of human life.
If war, for instance, were abolished and if all men's material needs
were met, the result would presumably be, on Schopenhauer's
premises, a condition of intolerable boredom which would be
succeeded by the return of conflict. In any case the prevalence of
suffering and evil in the world is ultimately due to the nature of the
thing-in-itself. And Schopenhauer is not slow to castigate what he
regards as the facile optimism of Leibniz and the way in which the
German idealists, especially Hegel, slur over the dark side of
human existence or, when they admit it, justify it as 'rational'.

7. Needless to say, Schopenhauer thought that his theory of the
phenomenal character of empirical reality fitted in well with his
theory of the Will. That is to say, he thought that having once
accepted Kant's general thesis of the phenomenal character of the
world he could then go on, without inconsistency, to reveal the
nature of the thing-in-itself. But this is questionable.

Take, for example, Schopenhauer's approach to the Will
through inner consciousness. As Herbart remarked, on Schopenhauer's principles the Will, as viewed in inner perception, must be
subject to the form of time: it is known in its successive acts. And
these are phenomenal. We cannot arrive at the Will as a metaphenomenal reality. For in so far as we are conscious of it, it is
phenomenal. True, we can talk about the metaphysical Will. But
in so far as it is thought and spoken about, it must be, it seems,
object for a subject, and so phenomenal.

Schopenhauer does indeed admit that we cannot know the
metaphysical Will in itself, and that it may have attributes which
are unknown by us and indeed incomprehensible to us. But he
insists that it is known, even if only partially, in its manifestation
or objectification, and that our own volition is for us its most
distinct manifestation. In this case, however, the metaphysical
Will seems to disintegrate, as it were, into phenomena, as far as
our knowledge is concerned. And the conclusion seems to follow
that we cannot know the thing-in-itself. To put the matter in
another way, Schopenhauer does not wish to base his philosophy
on a privileged and exceptional intuition of ultimate reality, but

rather on our intuitive perception of our own volition. Yet this intuitive perception seems, on his own premises, to belong to the phenomenal sphere which includes the whole range of the subject-object relationship. In fine, once given the doctrine of *The World as Idea*, the first book of Schopenhauer's *magnum opus*, it is difficult to see how any access to the thing-in-itself is possible. Kant would presumably say that it was impossible.

This line of objection is, I think, justified. But it would, of course, be possible to cut Schopenhauer's philosophy adrift from its Kantian moorings and present it as a kind of hypothesis. The philosopher, let us suppose, was temperamentally inclined to see in a clear light and to emphasize the dark aspects of the world and of human life and history. So far from being secondary features, they seemed to him to constitute the world's most significant and positive aspects. And he considered that analysis of the concepts of happiness and of suffering confirmed this initial vision. On this basis he erected the explanatory hypothesis of the blind and endlessly striving impulse or force which he called the Will. And he could then look round to discover fresh empirical confirmation of his hypothesis in the inorganic, organic and specifically human spheres. Further, the hypothesis enabled him to make some general predictions about human life and history in the future.

It is obviously not my intention to suggest that Schopenhauer would have been willing to surrender his theory of the World as Idea. On the contrary, he laid emphasis on it. Nor is it my intention to suggest that Schopenhauer's picture of the world would be acceptable if it were presented as the lines just indicated above. His analysis of happiness as 'negative', to mention but one point of criticism, seems to me quite untenable. My point is rather that Schopenhauer's philosophy expresses a 'vision' of the world which draws attention to certain aspects of it. And this vision can perhaps be made clearer if his philosophy is expressed in the form of an hypothesis based on an exclusive attention to the aspects in question. To be sure, it is a one-sided vision or picture of the world. But precisely because of its one-sidedness and exaggeration it serves as an effective counter-balance or antithesis to a system such as that of Hegel in which attention is so focused on the triumphant march of Reason through history that the evil and suffering in the world are obscured from view by high-sounding phrases.

### CHAPTER XIV

## SCHOPENHAUER (2)

*Aesthetic contemplation as a temporary escape from the slavery of the Will—The particular fine arts—Virtue and renunciation: the way of salvation—Schopenhauer and metaphysical idealism —The general influence of Schopenhauer—Notes on Eduard von Hartmann's development of Schopenhauer's philosophy.*

. THE root of all evil for Schopenhauer is the slavery of the Will, subservience to the Will to live. But his claim has already been mentioned that the human mind has the capacity for developing beyond the extent required for the satisfaction of physical needs. It can develop, as it were, a surplus of energy over and above the energy required to fulfil its primary biological and practical function. Man is thus able to escape from the futile life of desire and striving, of egoistic self-assertion and conflict.

Schopenhauer describes two ways of escape from the slavery of the Will, the one temporary, an oasis in the desert, the other more lasting. The first is the way of aesthetic contemplation, the way of art; the second is the path of asceticism, the way of salvation. In this section we are concerned with the first, the way of escape through art.

In aesthetic contemplation man becomes the disinterested observer. Needless to say, this does not mean that aesthetic contemplation is uninteresting. If, for example, I regard a beautiful object as an object of desire or as a stimulant to desire, my point of view is not that of aesthetic contemplation: I am an 'interested' spectator. In point of fact I am the servant or instrument of the Will. But it is possible for me to regard the beautiful object neither as itself an object of desire nor as a stimulant to desire but simply and solely for its aesthetic significance. I am then a disinterested, but not an uninterested, spectator. And I am freed, temporarily at least, from the slavery of the Will.

This theory of temporary escape through aesthetic contemplation, whether of natural objects or of works of art, is linked by Schopenhauer with a metaphysical theory of what he calls Platonic Ideas. The Will is said to objectify itself immediately in Ideas

277

which stand to individual natural things as archetypes to copies
They are 'the determinate species or the original unchanging
forms and properties of all natural bodies, both inorganic and
organic, and also the universal forces which reveal themselves
according to natural laws'.[1] There are thus Ideas of natural forces
such as gravity, and there are Ideas of species. But there are no
Ideas of genuses. For while there are natural species, there are
according to Schopenhauer, no natural genuses.

The Ideas of species must not be confused with the immanent
forms of things. The individual members of a species or natural
class are said to be 'the empirical correlative of the Idea'.[2] And the
Idea is an eternal archetype. It is for this reason, of course, that
Schopenhauer identifies his Ideas with the Platonic Forms or
Ideas.

How a blind Will or endless striving can reasonably be said to
objectify itself immediately in Platonic Ideas, is something which
I do not profess to understand. It seems to me that Schopenhauer
sharing the belief of Schelling and Hegel, in spite of his abuse of
them, in the metaphysical significance of art and aesthetic
intuition, and seeing that aesthetic contemplation offers a
temporary escape from the slavery of desire, turns to a philosopher
whom he greatly admires, namely Plato, and borrows from him a
theory of Ideas which has no clear connection with the description
of the Will as a blind, self-tortured impulse or striving. However
it is unnecessary to labour this aspect of the matter. The point is
that the artistic genius is capable of apprehending the Ideas and
of giving expression to them in works of art. And in aesthetic
contemplation the beholder is participating in this apprehension
of the Ideas. He thus rises above the temporal and changing and
contemplates the eternal and unchanging. His attitude is contemplative, not appetitive. Appetite is stilled during aesthetic
experience.

Schopenhauer's exaltation of the role of artistic genius represents
a point of affinity with the romantic spirit. He does not, however
speak very clearly about the nature of artistic genius or about the
relation between the genius and the ordinary man. Sometimes he
seems to imply that genius means not only the ability to apprehend
the Ideas but also the ability to express them in works of art. At
other times he seems to imply that genius is simply the faculty of
intuiting the Ideas, and that the ability to give external expression

[1] *W*, II, p. 199; *HK*, I, p. 219.    [2] *W*, III, p. 417; *HK*, III, p. 123.

) them is a matter of technique which can be acquired by training
nd practice. The first way of speaking fits in best with what is
resumably our normal conviction, namely that artistic genius
ivolves the capacity for creative production. If a man lacked this
apacity, we would not normally speak of him as an artistic genius
r, for the matter of that, as an artist at all. The second way of
)eaking implies that everyone who is capable of aesthetic
ppreciation and contemplation participates in genius to some
xtent. But one might go on to claim with Benedetto Croce that
esthetic intuition involves interior expression, in the sense of
naginative recreation, as distinct from external expression. In
iis case both the creative artist and the man who contemplates
nd appreciates the work of art would 'express', though only the
rst would express externally. However, though it may be possible
) bring together the two ways of speaking in some such manner,
 think that for Schopenhauer artistic genius really involves both
ie faculty of intuiting the Ideas and the faculty of giving
reative expression to this intuition, though this is aided by
echnical training. In this case the man who is not capable of
roducing works of art himself could still share in genius to the
xtent of intuiting the Ideas in and through their external
xpression.

The important point, however, in the present context is that in
esthetic contemplation a man transcends the original subjection
f knowledge to the Will, to desire. He becomes the 'pure will-less
ubject of knowledge, who no longer traces relations in accordance
rith the principle of sufficient reason, but rests and is lost in fixed
ontemplation of the object presented to him, apart from its
onnection with any other object'.[1] If the object of contemplation
s simply significant form, the Idea as concretely presented to
erception, we are concerned with the beautiful. If, however, a
ian perceives the object of contemplation as having a hostile
elation to his body, as menacing, that is to say, the objectification
f the Will in the form of the human body by its power of greatness,
e is contemplating the sublime. That is, he is contemplating the
ublime provided that, while recognizing the menacing character
f the object, he persists in objective contemplation and does not
llow himself to be overwhelmed by the self-regarding emotion of
ear. For instance, a man in a small boat at sea during a terrible
torm is contemplating the sublime if he fixes his attention on the

---

[1] *W*, ii, pp. 209–10; *HK*, i, p. 230.

grandeur of the scene and the power of the elements.[1] But whether a man is contemplating the beautiful or the sublime, he is temporarily freed from the servitude of the Will. His mind enjoys a rest, as it were, from being an instrument for the satisfaction of desire and adopts a purely objective and disinterested point of view.

2. Both Schelling and Hegel arranged the particular fine arts in ascending series. And Schopenhauer too engages in this pastime. His standard of classification and arrangement is the series of grades of the Will's objectification. For example, architecture is said to express some low-grade Ideas such as gravity, cohesion, rigidity and hardness, the universal qualities of stone. Moreover, in expressing the tension between gravity and rigidity architecture expresses indirectly the conflict of the Will. Artistic hydraulics exhibits the Ideas of fluid matter in, for instance, fountains and artificial waterfalls, while artistic horticulture or landscape-gardening exhibits the Ideas of the higher grades of vegetative life. Historical painting and sculpture express the Idea of man, though sculpture is concerned principally with beauty and grace while painting is chiefly concerned with the expression of character and passion. Poetry is capable of representing Ideas of all grades. For its immediate material is concepts, though the poet tries by his use of epithets to bring down the abstract concept to the level of perception and thus to stimulate the imagination and enable the reader or hearer to apprehend the Idea in the perceptible object.[2] But though poetry is capable of representing all grades of Ideas, its chief object is the representation of man as expressing himself through a series of actions and through the accompanying thoughts and emotions.

At the time there was controversy among writers on aesthetics about the range of the concept of fine art. But it would hardly be profitable to enter into a discussion about the propriety or impropriety of describing artistic hydraulics and landscape gardening as fine arts. Nor need we discuss an arrangement of the arts which depends on correlating them with a questionable meta-physical system. Instead we can notice the two following points.

[1] Following Kant, Schopenhauer distinguishes between the dynamical and the mathematically sublime. The man in the boat is contemplating an example of the first type. The mathematically sublime is the statically immense, a great range of mountains, for instance.

[2] For instance, Homer does not simply talk about the sea or the dawn but brings the ideas nearer to the level of perception by the use of epithets such as 'wine-dark' and 'rosy-fingered'.

First, as one would expect, the supreme poetical art is for chopenhauer tragedy. For in tragedy we witness the real iaracter of human life transmuted into art and expressed in ramatic form, 'the unspeakable pain, the wail of humanity, the iumph of evil, the mocking mastery of chance and the irretrievable ill of the just and innocent'.[1]

Secondly, the highest of all arts is not tragedy but music. For iusic does not exhibit an Idea or Ideas, the immediate objectifica-on of the Will: it exhibits the Will itself, the inner nature of the iing-in-itself.[2] In listening to music, therefore, a man receives a irect revelation, though not in conceptual form, of the reality hich underlies phenomena. And he intuits this reality, revealed i the form of art, in an objective and disinterested manner, not as ie caught in the grip of the Will's tyranny. Further, if it were ossible to express accurately in concepts all that music expresses ithout concepts, we should have the true philosophy.

3. Aesthetic contemplation affords no more than a temporary r transient escape from the slavery of the Will. But Schopenhauer ffers a lasting release through renunciation of the Will to live. ndeed, moral progress must take this form if morality is possible t all. For the Will to live, manifesting itself in egoism, self-ssertion, hatred and conflict, is for Schopenhauer the source of vil. 'There really resides in the heart of each of us a wild beast hich only waits the opportunity to rage and rave in order to njure others, and which, if they do not prevent it, would like to estroy them.'[3] This wild beast, this radical evil, is the direct xpression of the Will to live. Hence morality, if it is possible, must ivolve denial of the Will. And as man is an objectification of the Vill, denial will mean self-denial, asceticism and mortification.

Schopenhauer does indeed say that in his philosophy the world ossesses a moral significance. But what he means by this at first ight astonishing statement is this. Existence, life, is itself a crime: t is our original sin. And it is inevitably expiated by suffering and eath. Hence we can say that justice reigns and, adapting Hegel's amous statement, that 'the world itself is the world's court of udgment'.[4] In this sense, therefore, the world possesses a moral ignificance. 'If we could lay all the misery of the world in one

[1] *W*, II, p. 298; *HK*, I, p. 326.
[2] It is for this reason that Schopenhauer condemns imitative music, mentioning Iaydn's *Seasons* as an example.
[3] *W*, VI, p. 230. From *Parerga und Paralipomena*.
[4] *W*, II, p. 415; *HK*, I, p. 454.

scale of the balance and all the guilt of the world in the other, tl
needle would certainly point to the centre.'[1] Schopenhauer speal
as though it were the Will itself which is guilty and the Will itse
which pays the penalty. For it objectifies itself and suffers in i
objectification. And this way of speaking may seem to l
extravagant. For the sufferings of men must be phenomenal c
Schopenhauer's premises: they can hardly affect the thing-i
itself. Passing over this point, however, we can draw from tl
statement that existence or life is itself a crime the conclusion th.
morality, if it is possible, must take the form of denial of the W
to live, of a turning away from life.

Given these premises, it may well appear to follow that tl
highest moral act will be suicide. But Schopenhauer argues tha
suicide expresses a surrender to the Will rather than a denial of i
For the man who commits suicide does so to escape certain evil
And if he could escape from them without killing himself, l
would do so. Hence suicide is, paradoxically, the expression of
concealed will to live. Consequently, denial and renunciation mu
take some form other than suicide.

But is morality possible within the framework of Schopenhauer
philosophy? The individual human being is an objectification
the one individual Will, and his actions are determined. Schope:
hauer draws a distinction between the intelligible and empiric
characters. The metaphysical Will objectifies itself in the individu
will, and this individual will, when considered in itself ar
anteriorly to its acts, is the intelligible or noumenal characte
The individual will as manifested through its successive acts
the empirical character. Now, consciousness has for its object tl
particular acts of the will. And these appear successively. A ma
thus comes to know his character only gradually and imperfectl
in principle he is in the same position as an outsider. He does n
foresee his future acts of will but is conscious only of acts alread
posited. He therefore seems to himself to be free. And this feelir
of freedom is quite natural. Yet the empirical act is really tl
unfolding of the intelligible or noumenal character. The former
the consequence of the latter and determined by it. As Spino;
said, the feeling or persuasion of freedom is really the effect
ignorance of the determining causes of one's actions.

At first sight, therefore, there would seem to be little point i
indicating how people ought to act if they wish to escape from tl

[1] *W*, II, p. 416; *HK*, I, p. 454.

lavery of desire and restless striving. For their actions are
determined by their character. And these characters are objectifications of the Will, which is the Will to live and manifests itself
precisely in desire and restless striving.

Schopenhauer argues, however, that character-determinism
does not exclude changes in conduct. Let us suppose, for example,
that I am accustomed to act in the way most calculated to bring
me financial gain. One day somebody persuades me that treasure
in heaven is more valuable and lasting than treasure on earth. And
my new conviction leads to a change in conduct. Instead of trying
to avail myself of an opportunity to enrich myself at the expense of
Tom Jones I leave the opportunity of financial gain to him. My
friends, if I have any, may say that my character has changed. But
in point of fact I am the same sort of man that I was before. The
actions which I now perform are different from my past actions,
but my character has not changed. For I act for the same sort of
motive, namely personal gain, though I have changed my view
about what constitutes the most gainful line of conduct. In other
words, my intelligible character determines what sort of motives
move me to act; and the motive remains the same whether I am
amassing riches on earth or renouncing them for celestial wealth.

Taken by itself, indeed, this example does not help us to understand how a denial of the Will to live can be possible. For it
illustrates the permanence of egoism rather than the emergence of
radical self-denial. And though it may be useful as indicating a
plausible way of reconciling with the theory of character-
determinism the empirical facts which appear to show the possibility of changes in character, it does not explain how the Will
to live can turn back on itself, in and through its objectification,
and deny itself. But we can pass over this point for the moment.
It is sufficient to note that the idea of changing one's point of view
plays an important role in Schopenhauer's philosophy as it does in
that of Spinoza. For Schopenhauer envisages a progressive seeing
through, as it were, the veil of Maya, the phenomenal world of
individuality and multiplicity. This is possible because of the
intellect's capacity to develop beyond the extent required for the
fulfilment of its primary practical functions. And the degrees of
moral advance correspond with the degrees of penetration of the
veil of Maya.

Individuality is phenomenal. The noumenon is one: a plurality
of individuals exists only for the phenomenal subject. And a man

may, in the first instance, penetrate the illusion of individuality t
the extent that he sets others on the same level as himself and do(
them no injury. We then have the just man, as distinct from th
man who is so enmeshed in the veil of Maya that he asserts himse
to the exclusion of others.

But it is possible to go further. A man may penetrate the veil (
Maya to the extent of seeing that all individuals are really one. Fc
they are all phenomena of the one undivided Will. We then hav
the ethical level of sympathy. We have goodness or virtue which ;
characterized by a disinterested love of others. True goodness ;
not, as Kant thought, a matter of obeying the categoric;
imperative for the sake of duty alone. True goodness is love, *agaf*
or *caritas* in distinction from *eros*, which is self-directed. And lov
is sympathy. 'All true and pure love is sympathy [*Mitleid*], an
all love which is not sympathy is selfishness [*Selbstsucht*]. *Eros* i
selfishness; *agape* is sympathy.'[1] Schopenhauer combined hi
enthusiasm for the Hindu philosophy of Maya with a grea
admiration for the Buddha. And he had perhaps more sympath
with the Buddhist ethic than with more dynamic western concept
of altruism.

We can, however, go further still. For in and through man th
Will can attain such a clear knowledge of itself that it turns fror
itself in horror and denies itself. The human will then ceases t
become attached to anything, and the man pursues the path c
asceticism and holiness. Schopenhauer proceeds, therefore, to extc
voluntary chastity, poverty and self-mortification and holds ou
the prospect of a complete deliverance at death from the servitud
of the Will.

It was remarked above that it is difficult to understand how th
Will's denial of itself is possible. And Schopenhauer recognizes th
difficulty. That the Will, manifested or objectified in the phenc
menon, should deny itself and renounce what the phenomeno;
expresses, namely the Will to live, is, Schopenhauer frankly admit;
a case of self-contradiction. But, contradiction or not, this radica
act of self-denial can take place, even though it happens only i;
exceptional or rare cases. The Will in itself is free. For it is no
subject to the principle of sufficient reason. And in the case of tota
self-denial, total self-renunciation, the essential freedom of th
Will, the thing-in-itself, is made manifest in the phenomenon. I;
other words, Schopenhauer admits an exception to the principle o

[1] *W*, II, p. 444; *HK*, I, p. 485.

determinism. The free metaphysical Will 'by abolishing the nature which lies at the foundation of the phenomenon, while the phenomenon itself continues to exist in time, brings about a contradiction of the phenomenon with itself'.[1] That is to say, the saint does not kill himself; he continues to exist in time. But he totally renounces the reality which lies at the foundation of himself as a phenomenon and can be said to 'abolish it', namely the Will. This is a contradiction, but it is a contradiction which manifests the truth that the Will transcends the principle of sufficient reason.

What, we may ask, is the final end of virtue and holiness? Obviously, the man who denies the Will treats the world as nothing. For it is simply the appearance of the Will, which he denies. And in this sense at least it is true to say that when the Will turns and denies itself, 'our world with all its suns and milky ways is—nothing'.[2] But what happens at death? Does it mean total extinction or not?

'Before us', says Schopenhauer, 'there is indeed only nothingness.'[3] And if, as seems to be the case, there can be no question on his premisses of personal immortality, there is a sense in which this must obviously be true. For if individuality is phenomenal, Maya, then death, the withdrawal, as it were, from the phenomenal world, means the extinction of consciousness. There remains perhaps the possibility of absorption in the one Will. But Schopenhauer seems to imply, though he does not express himself clearly, that for the man who has denied the Will death means total extinction. In life he has reduced existence to a tenuous thread, and at death it is finally destroyed. The man has reached the final goal of the denial of the Will to live.

Schopenhauer does indeed speak of another possibility.[4] As we have already seen, he admits that the thing-in-itself, the ultimate reality, may possibly possess attributes which we do not and cannot know. If so, these may remain when Will has denied itself as Will. Hence there is presumably the possibility of a state being achieved through self-renunciation which does not amount to nothingness. It could hardly be a state of knowledge, for the subject-object relationship is phenomenal. But it might resemble the incommunicable experience to which mystics refer in obscure terms.

[1] *W*, II, p. 339; *HK*, I, p. 371.    [2] *W*, II, p. 487; *HK*, I, p. 532.
[3] *W*, II, p. 486; *HK*, I, p. 531.
[4] Cp. *W*, II, p. 485 and III, pp. 221–2; *HK*, I, p. 530 and II, p. 408.

But though it is open to anyone to press this admission if he wishes, I should not myself care to do so. Partly, I suppose Schopenhauer feels bound to make the admission in view of his own statement that we know the ultimate reality in its self manifestation as Will and not in itself, apart from phenomena. Partly he may feel that the possibility cannot be excluded that the experiences of the mystics are not adequately explicable in terms of his philosophy of the Will. But it would be going too far, were one to represent Schopenhauer as suggesting that either theism or pantheism may be true. Theism he stigmatizes as childish and unable to satisfy the mature mind. Pantheism he judges to be even more absurd and, in addition, to be incompatible with any moral convictions. To identify a world filled with suffering and evil and cruelty with the Godhead or to interpret it as a theophany in a literal sense is utter nonsense, worthy only of a Hegel. Moreover, it leads to a justification of all that happens, a justification which is incompatible with the demands of morality.

In any case, even if the ultimate reality possesses attributes other than those which justify its description as a blind Will, philosophy can know nothing about them. As far as philosophy is concerned, the thing-in-itself is Will. And the denial of the Will thus means for the philosopher the denial of reality, of all that there is, at least of all that he can know that there is. Hence philosophy at any rate must be content with the conclusion: 'no Will; no idea, no world'.[1] If the Will turns on itself and 'abolishes' itself, nothing is left.

4. The reader may perhaps be surprised that the philosophy of Schopenhauer has been considered under the general heading of the reaction to metaphysical idealism. And there is, of course, ground for such surprise. For in spite of Schopenhauer's constant abuse of Fichte, Schelling and Hegel his system undoubtedly belongs in some important respects to the movement of German speculative idealism. Will is indeed substituted for Fichte's Ego and Hegel's *Logos* or Idea, but the distinction between phenomenon and noumenon and the theory of the subjective and phenomenal character of space, time and causality are based on Kant. And it is not unreasonable to describe Schopenhauer's system as transcendental voluntaristic idealism. It is idealism in the sense that the world is said to be our idea or presentation. It is voluntaristic in the sense that the concept of Will rather than that of Reason or

[1] *W*, II, p. 486; *HK*, I, p. 531.

Thought is made the key to reality. And it is transcendental in the sense that the one individual Will is an absolute Will which manifests itself in the multiple phenomena of experience.

But though Schopenhauer's philosophy, when regarded from this point of view, appears as a member of the class of post-Kantian speculative systems which include those of Fichte, Schelling and Hegel, there are also considerable differences between it and the other three philosophies. For example, in the system of Hegel the ultimate reality is Reason, the self-thinking thought which actualizes itself as concrete spirit. The real is the rational and the rational the real. With Schopenhauer, however, reality is not so much rational as irrational: the world is the manifestation of a blind impulse or energy. There are, of course, certain similarities between the cosmic Reason of Hegel and the Schopenhauerian Will. For instance, for Hegel Reason has itself as an end, in the sense that it is thought which comes to think itself, and Schopenhauer's Will also has itself as an end, in the sense that it wills for the sake of willing. But there is a great difference between the idea of the universe as the life of self-unfolding Reason and the idea of the universe as the expression of a blind irrational impulse to existence or life. There are indeed elements of 'irrationalism' in German idealism itself. Schelling's theory of an irrational will in the Deity is a case in point. But with Schopenhauer the irrational character of existence becomes something to be emphasized; it is the cardinal truth rather than a partial truth, to be overcome in a higher synthesis.

This metaphysical irrationalism in Schopenhauer's philosophy may be obscured by his theory of art which sets before us the possibility of transmuting the horrors of existence in the serene world of aesthetic contemplation. But it has important consequences. For one thing there is the substitution of a meta-physically-grounded pessimism for the metaphysically-grounded optimism of absolute idealism. For another thing the deductive character of metaphysical idealism, which is natural enough if reality is regarded as the self-unfolding of Thought or Reason, gives way to a much more empirical approach. To be sure, the comprehensive and metaphysical character of Schopenhauer's philosophy, together with its strongly-marked romantic elements, gives it a family-likeness to the other great post-Kantian systems. At the same time it lends itself very easily to interpretation as a very wide hypothesis based on generalization from empirical data.

And though we naturally and rightly regard it as part of the general movement of post-Kantian speculative metaphysics, it also looks forward to the inductive metaphysics which followed the collapse of absolute idealism.

Further, when we look back on Schopenhauer's system from a much later point in history, we can see in it a transition-stage between the idealist movement and the later philosophies of Life. Obviously, from one point of view the system is simply itself and not a 'transition-stage'. But this does not exclude the point of view which relates the system to the general movement of thought and sees it as a bridge between rationalist idealism and the philosophy of Life in Germany and France. It may be objected, of course, that Schopenhauer emphasizes a no-saying attitude to life. Life is something to be denied rather than affirmed. But Schopenhauer's theory of renunciation and denial is reached only by means of a philosophy which first emphasizes the idea of the Will to live and interprets the world in the light of this idea. Both instinct and reason are described by Schopenhauer as biological instruments or tools, even if he subsequently goes on to speak of the detachment of the human intellect from this practical orientation. Hence he provides the material, as it were, for the substitution of the idea of Life as the central idea in philosophy for that of Thought. Schopenhauer's pessimism no longer appears in the later philosophies of Life; but this does not alter the fact that he brings the idea of Life into the centre of the picture. True, the idea of Life is present in, for example, the philosophies of Fichte and Hegel. But with Schopenhauer the term 'Life' receives a primarily biological significance, and reason (which is also, of course, a form of life) is interpreted as an instrument of Life in a biological sense.

5. After the death of Hegel and after the failure of the Revolution of 1848 the climate of opinion was more prepared for a favourable reconsideration of Schopenhauer's anti-rationalist and pessimistic system, and it became more widely known and won some adherents. Among these was Julius Frauenstädt (1813-79) who was converted from Hegelianism to the philosophy of Schopenhauer in the course of protracted conversations with the philosopher at Frankfurt. He modified somewhat the position of his master, maintaining that space, time and causality are not mere subjective forms and that individuality and multiplicity are not mere appearance. But he defended the theory that the ultimate reality is Will and published an edition of Schopenhauer's writings.

Schopenhauer's writings helped to stimulate in Germany an interest in Oriental thought and religion. Among the philosophers who were influenced by him in this direction we can mention Paul Deussen (1845-1919), founder of the *Schopenhauer-Gesellschaft* (Schopenhauer Society) and a friend of Nietzsche. Deussen occupied a chair in the university of Kiel. In addition to a general history of philosophy he published several works on Indian thought and contributed to bringing about the recognition of Oriental philosophy as an integral part of the history of philosophy in general.

Outside philosophical circles Schopenhauer's influence was considerable. And special mention can be made of his influence on Richard Wagner. The theory that music is the highest of the arts was naturally congenial to Wagner, and he thought of himself as the living embodiment of the Schopenhauerian concept of genius.[1] One cannot, of course, reduce Wagner's outlook on life to Schopenhauer's philosophy. Many of the composer's ideas were formed before he made the acquaintance of this philosophy, and in the course of time he modified and changed his ideas. But when he had been introduced to Schopenhauer's writings in 1854, he sent the philosopher an appreciative letter. And it is said that *Tristan and Isolde* in particular reflects Schopenhauer's influence. One can also mention the writer Thomas Mann as one who owed a debt to Schopenhauer.

Within philosophical circles Schopenhauer's influence was felt more in the form of a stimulus in this or that direction than in the creation of anything which could be called a school. In Germany his writings exercised a powerful influence on Nietzsche in his youth, though he afterwards repudiated Schopenhauer's no-saying attitude to Life. One can also mention the names of Wilhelm Wundt and Hans Vaihinger as philosophers who derived some stimulus from Schopenhauer, though neither man was a disciple of the great pessimist. As for France, it has been already remarked that we must avoid the not uncommon mistake of assuming that similarity of ideas necessarily reveals derivation or borrowing. The development of the philosophy of Life in France explains itself, without the need of involving the name of Schopenhauer. But this does not, of course, exclude a stimulative influence, direct or indirect, by the German philosopher on certain French thinkers.

6. There is at any rate one philosopher of some note whose most

---

[1] Nietzsche, during the halcyon days of their friendship, gave Wagner every encouragement to think this.

obvious affinity is with Schopenhauer and who derived a great deal from him, namely Eduard von Hartmann (1842–1906), a retired artillery officer who gave himself to study and writing. Von Hartmann, who also acknowledged debts to Leibniz and Schelling, endeavoured to develop the philosophy of Schopenhauer in such a way as to lessen the gulf between it and Hegelianism. And he claimed to have worked out his own system on an empirical and scientific basis. His best known work is *The Philosophy of the Unconscious* (*Die Philosophie des Unbewussten*, 1869).

The ultimate reality, according to von Hartmann, is indeed unconscious, but it cannot be, as Schopenhauer thought, simply a blind Will. For the matter of that, even Schopenhauer could not avoid speaking as though the Will had an end in view. Hence we must recognize that the one unconscious principle has two correlative and irreducible attributes, Will and Idea. Or we can express the matter by saying that the one unconscious principle has two co-ordinate functions. As Will it is responsible for the *that*, the existence, of the world: as Idea it is responsible for the *what*, the nature, of the world.

In this way von Hartmann claims to effect a synthesis between Schopenhauer and Hegel. The former's Will could never produce a teleological world-process, and the latter's Idea could never objectify itself in an existent world. The ultimate reality must thus be Will and Idea in one. But it does not follow that the ultimate reality must be conscious. On the contrary, we must turn to Schelling and import the notion of an unconscious Idea behind Nature. The world has more than one aspect. Will manifests itself, as Schopenhauer taught, in pain, suffering and evil. But the unconscious Idea, as Schelling maintained in his philosophy of Nature, manifests itself in finality, teleology, intelligible development and an advance towards consciousness.

Not content with reconciling Schopenhauer, Hegel and Schelling, von Hartmann is also concerned with synthesizing Schopenhauerian pessimism and Leibnizian optimism. The manifestation of the unconscious Absolute as Will gives grounds for pessimism, while its manifestation as Idea gives grounds for optimism. But the unconscious Absolute is one. Hence pessimism and optimism must be reconciled. And this demands a modification of Schopenhauer's analysis of pleasure and enjoyment as 'negative'. The pleasures, for example, of aesthetic contemplation and of intellectual activity are certainly positive.

Now, inasmuch as von Hartmann maintains that the end or *telos* of the cosmic process is the liberation of the Idea from the servitude of the Will through the development of consciousness, we might expect that optimism would have the last word. But though von Hartmann does indeed emphasize the way in which the development of intellect renders possible the higher pleasures, in particular those of aesthetic contemplation, he at the same time insists that the capacity for suffering grows in proportion to intellectual development. For this reason primitive peoples and the uneducated classes are happier than civilized peoples and the more cultured classes.

To think, therefore, that progress in civilization and in intellectual development brings with it an increase in happiness is an illusion. The pagans thought that happiness was attainable in this world. And this was an illusion. The Christians recognized it as such and looked for happiness in heaven. But this too was an illusion. Yet those who recognize it as such tend to fall into a third illusion, namely that of thinking that a terrestrial Paradise can be attained through unending progress. They fail to see two truths. First, increasing refinement and mental development increase the capacity for suffering. Secondly, progress in material civilization and well-being is accompanied by a forgetfulness of spiritual values and by the decadence of genius.

These illusions are ultimately the work of the unconscious principle which shows its cunning by inducing the human race in this way to perpetuate itself. But von Hartmann looks forward to a time when the human race in general will have so developed its consciousness of the real state of affairs that a cosmic suicide will take place. Schopenhauer was wrong in suggesting that an individual can attain annihilation by self-denial and asceticism. What is needed is the greatest possible development of consciousness, so that in the end humanity may understand the folly of volition, commit suicide and, with its own destruction, bring the world-process to an end. For by that time the volition of the unconscious Absolute, which is responsible for the existence of the world, will, von Hartmann hopes, have passed into or been objectified in humanity. Hence suicide on humanity's part will bring the world to an end.

Most people would describe this astonishing theory as pessimism. Not so von Hartmann. The cosmic suicide requires as its condition the greatest possible evolution of consciousness and the triumph of intellect over volition. But this is precisely the end aimed at by the Absolute as Idea, as unconscious Spirit. One can say, therefore, that the world will be redeemed by the cosmic suicide and its own disappearance. And a world which achieves redemption is the best possible world.

There are only two comments which I wish to make on von Hartmann's philosophy. First, if a man writes as much as von Hartmann did, he can hardly avoid making some true and apposite statements, be their setting what it may. Secondly, if the human race destroys itself, which is now a physical possibility, it is much more likely to be due to its folly than to its wisdom or, in von Hartmann's language, to the triumph of Will rather than to that of Idea.

### CHAPTER XV

# THE TRANSFORMATION OF IDEALISM (1)

*Introductory remarks—Feuerbach and the transformation of theology into anthropology—Ruge's criticism of the Hegelian attitude to history—Stirner's philosophy of the ego.*

1. WHEN considering the influence of Hegel we noted that after the philosopher's death there emerged a right and a left wing. And something was said about the differences between them in regard to the interpretation of the idea of God in the philosophy of Hegel and about the system's relation to Christianity. We can now turn to consider some of the more radical representatives of the left wing who were concerned not so much with interpreting Hegel as with using some of his ideas to transform metaphysical idealism into something quite different.

These thinkers are commonly known as the Young Hegelians. This term ought indeed to signify the younger generation of those who stood under the influence of Hegel, whether they belonged to the right or to the left wing or to the centre. But it has come to be reserved in practice for the radical members of the left wing, such as Feuerbach. From one point of view they might well be called anti-Hegelians. For they represent a line of thought which culminated in dialectical materialism, whereas a cardinal tenet of Hegel is that the Absolute must be defined as Spirit. From another point of view, however, the name 'anti-Hegelian' would be a misnomer. For they were concerned to set Hegel on his feet, and even if they transformed his philosophy, they made use, as already mentioned, of some of his own ideas. In other words, they represent a left-wing development of Hegelianism, a development which was also a transformation. We find both continuity and discontinuity.

2. Ludwig Feuerbach (1804–72) studied Protestant theology at Heidelberg and then went to Berlin where he attended Hegel's lectures and gave himself to the study of philosophy. In 1828 he became an unsalaried lecturer (*Privatdozent*) at the university of Erlangen. But finding no prospect of advancement in the academic career he retired into a life of private study and writing. At the time of his death he was living near Nuremberg.

If one were to look only at the titles of Feuerbach's writings, one would naturally conclude that he was first and foremost a theologian, or at any rate that he had strong theological interests. True his earlier works are obviously concerned with philosophy. For example, in 1833 he published a history of modern philosophy from Francis Bacon to Spinoza; in 1837 an exposition and criticism of Leibniz's system; in 1838 a work on Bayle; and in 1839 an essay devoted to criticism of Hegel's philosophy. But then come his important works, such as *The Essence of Christianity* (*Das Wesen des Christentums*, 1841), *The Essence of Religion* (*Das Wesen der Religion*, 1845) and *Lectures on the Essence of Religion* (*Vorlesungen über das Wesen der Religion*, 1851). And these titles, together with such others as *On Philosophy and Christianity* (*Ueber Philosophie und Christentum*, 1839) and *The Essence of Faith in Luther's sense* (*Das Wesen des Glaubens im Sinne Luthers*, 1844), clearly suggest that the author's mind is preoccupied with theological problems.

In a certain sense this impression is quite correct. Feuerbach himself asserted that the main theme of his writings was religion and theology. But he did not mean by this statement that he believed in the objective existence of a God outside human thought. He meant that he was principally concerned with clarifying the real significance and function of religion in the light of human life and thought as a whole. Religion was not for him an unimportant phenomenon, an unfortunate piece of superstition of which we can say that it would have been better if it had never existed and that its effect has been simply that of retarding man's development. On the contrary, the religious consciousness was for Feuerbach an integral stage in the development of human consciousness in general. At the same time he regarded the idea of God as a projection of man's ideal for himself and religion as a temporal, even if essential, stage in the development of human consciousness. He can be said, therefore, to have substituted anthropology for theology.

Feuerbach reaches this position, the substitution of anthropology for theology, through a radical criticism of the Hegelian system. But the criticism is in a sense internal. For it is presupposed that Hegelianism is the highest expression of philosophy up to date. Hegel was 'Fichte mediated through Schelling',[1] and 'the Hegelian philosophy is the culminating point of speculative systematic

[1] *W*, II, p. 180. References to Feuerbach's writings are given according to volume and page of the second edition of his *Works* by Friedrich Jodl (Stuttgart, 1959–60).

philosophy'.[1] But though in the system of Hegel idealism, and indeed metaphysics in general, has attained its most complete expression, the system is not tenable. What is required is to set Hegel on his feet. In particular we have to find our way back from the conceptual abstractions of absolute idealism to concrete reality. Speculative philosophy has tried to make a transition from the abstract to the concrete, from the ideal to the real'.[2] But this was a mistake. The passage or transition from the ideal to the real has a part to play only in practical or moral philosophy, where it is a question of realizing ideals through action. When it is a matter of theoretical knowledge, we must start with the real, with Being.

Hegel, of course, starts with Being. But the point is that for Feuerbach Being in this context is Nature, not Idea or Thought.[3] Being is subject and thought is predicate.'[4] The fundamental reality is spatio-temporal Nature; consciousness and thought are secondary, derived. True, the existence of Nature can be known only by a conscious subject. But the being which distinguishes itself from Nature knows that it is not the ground of Nature. On the contrary, man knows Nature by distinguishing himself from his ground, sensible reality. 'Nature is thus the ground of man.'[5]

We can say indeed with Schleiermacher that the feeling of dependence is the ground of religion. But 'that on which man depends and feels himself to be dependent is originally nothing else but Nature'.[6] Thus the primary object of religion, if we view religion historically and not simply in the form of Christian theism, is Nature. Natural religion ranges from the deification of objects such as trees and fountains up to the idea of the Deity conceived as the physical cause of natural things. But the foundation of natural religion in all its phases is man's feeling of dependence on external sensible reality. 'The divine essence which manifests itself in Nature is nothing else but Nature which reveals and manifests itself to man and imposes itself on him as a divine being.'[7]

Man can objectify Nature only by distinguishing himself from it. And he can return upon himself and contemplate his own essence. What is this essence? 'Reason, will, heart. To a perfect man there belong the power of thought, the power of willing, the

[1] *W*, II, p. 175.    [2] *W*, II, p. 231.
[3] Feuerbach, like Schelling, assumes that Hegel deduces existent Nature from the logical Idea. If this is not assumed, the criticism loses its point.
[4] *W*, II, p. 239.    [5] *W*, II, p. 240.
[6] *W*, VII, p. 434.    [7] *W*, VII, p. 438.

power of the heart.'[1] Reason, will and love in unity constitute the essence of man. Further, if we think any of these three perfections in itself, we think of it as unlimited. We do not conceive, for example the power of thought as being in itself limited to this or that object And if we think the three perfections as infinite, we have the idea of God as infinite knowledge, infinite will and infinite love Monotheism, at least when God is endowed with moral attributes is thus the result of man's projection of his own essence raised to infinity. 'The divine essence is nothing else but the essence of man or, better, it is the essence of man when freed from the limitation of the individual, that is to say, actual corporeal man, objectified and venerated as an independent Being distinct from man himself.'[2]

In *The Essence of Christianity* Feuerbach concentrates on the idea of God as a projection of human self-consciousness, whereas in *The Essence of Religion*, in which religion is considered historic ally, he lays emphasis on the feeling of dependence on Nature a the ground of religion. But he also brings the two points of view together. Man, conscious of his dependence on external reality begins by venerating the forces of Nature and particular natural phenomena. But he does not rise to the concept of personal gods o of God without self-projection. In polytheism the qualities which differentiate man from man are deified in the form of a multiplicity of anthropomorphic deities, each with his or her peculiar charac teristics. In monotheism it is that which unifies men, namely the essence of man as such, which is projected into a transcendent sphere and deified. And a powerful factor in making the transition to some form of monotheism is the consciousness that Nature no only serves man's physical needs but can also be made to serve the purpose which man freely sets before himself. For in this way he comes to think of Nature as existing for him, and so as a unity which embodies a purpose and is the product of an intelligent Creator. But in thinking the Creator man projects his own essence. And if we strip from the idea of God all that is due to this projection, we are left simply with Nature. Hence, though religion is ultimately grounded on man's feeling of dependence on Nature the most important factor in the formation of the concept of an infinite personal Deity is man's projection of his own essence.

Now, this self-projection expresses man's alienation from him self. 'Religion is the separation of man from himself: he sets God

[1] *W*, vi, p. 3.          [2] *W*, vi, p. 17.

over against himself as an opposed being. God is not what man is, and man is not what God is. God is the infinite Being, man the finite; God is perfect, man is imperfect; God is eternal, man is temporal; God is almighty, man is powerless; God is holy, man is sinful. God and man are extremes: God is the absolutely positive, the essence of all realities, while man is the negative, the essence of all nothingness.'[1] Thus by projecting his essence into a transcendent sphere and objectifying it as God man reduces himself to a pitiful, miserable sinful creature.

In this case, of course, religion is something to be overcome. But it does not follow that religion has not played an essential role in human life. On the contrary, man's objectification of his own essence in the idea of God forms an integral stage in the explicit development of his self-awareness. For he has first to objectify his essence before he can become aware of it as *his* essence. And in the highest or most perfect form of religion, namely Christianity, this objectification reaches the point at which it calls for its own overcoming. Man is a social being, and the power of love belongs to his essence. He is an 'I' in relation to a 'Thou'. And in the Christian religion awareness of this fact finds a projected expression in the doctrine of the Trinity. Further, in the doctrine of the Incarnation, the Christian religion has united the word *Man* with the word *God* in the one name *God-Man*, thus making humanity an attribute of the supreme Being'.[2] What remains is to reverse this relation by making Deity an attribute of man. 'The new philosophy has, in accordance with the truth, made this attribute (humanity) the substance; it has made the predicate the subject. The new philosophy is . . . the *truth* of Christianity.'[3]

This last statement recalls to mind Hegel's view of the relation between the absolute religion and the absolute philosophy. But it is certainly not Feuerbach's intention to suggest that 'the new philosophy' can coexist with Christianity in the same mind. On the contrary, the new philosophy abandons the name of Christianity precisely because it gives the rational truth-value of the Christian religion and, in so doing, transforms it from theology into anthropology. Philosophy's elucidation of Christianity is no longer Christianity. Once a man understands that 'God' is a name for his own idealized essence projected into a transcendent sphere, he overcomes the self-alienation involved in religion. And the way then lies open to the objectification of this essence in man's own activity and social life. Man recovers faith in himself and in his own powers and future.

The abandonment of theology involves the abandonment of historic Hegelianism. For 'the Hegelian philosophy is the last place of refuge, the last rational prop of theology'.[1] And 'he who does not give up the Hegelian philosophy does not give up theology'. For the Hegelian doctrine that Nature, reality, is posited by the Idea is simply the *rational* expression of the theological doctrine that Nature has been created by God. . . .'[2] Yet for the overcoming of theology we have to make use of the Hegelian concept of self alienation. Hegel spoke of the return of absolute Spirit to itself from its self-alienation in Nature. For this concept we must substitute that of man's return to himself. And this means 'the transformation of theology into anthropology, and its dissolution therein'. Yet philosophical anthropology is itself religion. For it gives the truth of religion in the highest form that religion has attained. 'What yesterday was still religion is not religion today, and what is accounted atheism today is accounted religion tomorrow.'[4]

With the substitution of anthropology for theology man becomes his own highest object, an end to himself. But this does not mean egoism. For man is by essence a social being: he is not simply *Mensch* but *Mit-Mensch*. And the supreme principle of philosophy is 'the unity between man and man',[5] a unity which should find expression in love. 'Love is the universal law of intelligence and nature—it is nothing else but the realization of the unity of the species on the plane of feeling.'[6]

Feuerbach is obviously alive to the fact that Hegel emphasized man's social nature. But he insists that Hegel had an erroneous idea of the ground of unity in the species. In absolute idealism men are thought to be united in proportion as they become one with the life of universal spirit, interpreted as self-thinking Thought. It is thus on the level of pure thought that human unity is primarily achieved. But here again Hegel needs to be set squarely on his feet. The special nature of man is grounded on the biological level 'on the *reality* of the *difference* between I and Thou',[7] that is, on sexual differentiation. The relation between man and woman manifests unity-in-difference and difference-in-unity. This distinction between male and female is not indeed simply a biological distinction. For it determines distinct ways of feeling and thinking

[1] *W*, II, p. 239.    [2] *Ibid.*    [3] *W*, II, p. 245.    [4] *W*, VI, p. 40.
[5] *W*, II, p. 319.    [6] *W*, II, p. 321.    [7] *W*, II, p. 318.

ınd thus affects the whole personality. Nor is it, of course, the only
vay in which man's social nature is manifested. But Feuerbach
vishes to emphasize the fact that man's nature as *Mit-Mensch* is
grounded on the fundamental reality, which is sensible reality,
ıot pure thought. In other words, sexual differentiation shows that
he individual human being is incomplete. The fact that the 'I'
:alls for the 'Thou' as its complement is shown in its primary and
ıasic form in the fact that the male needs the female and the
emale the male.

One might expect that with this insistence on man's special
ıature, on the unity of the species and on love, Feuerbach would
;o on to develop the theme of a supranational society or to
ıropose some form of international federation. But in point of fact
ıe is sufficiently Hegelian to represent the State as the living unity
ıf men and the objective expression of the consciousness of this
ınity. 'In the State the powers of man divide and develop only to
:onstitute an infinite being through this division and through their
eunion; many human beings, many powers are one power. The
State is the essence of all realities, the State is the providence of
ɲan. . . . The true State is the unlimited, infinite, true, complete,
livine Man . . . the absolute Man.'[1]

From this it follows that 'politics must become our religion',[2]
:hough, paradoxically, atheism is a condition of this religion.
Religion in the traditional sense, says Feuerbach, tends to dissolve
:ather than to unite the State. And the State can be for us an
Absolute only if we substitute man for God, anthropology for
:heology. 'Man is the fundamental essence of the State. And the
State is the actualized, developed and explicit totality of human
ɲature.'[3] Justice cannot be done to this truth if we continue to
project human nature into a transcendent sphere in the form of
the concept of God.

The State which Feuerbach has in mind is the democratic
republic. Protestantism, he remarks, put the monarch in the place
ɔf the Pope. 'The Reformation destroyed *religious* Catholicism,
but in its place the modern era set *political* Catholicism'.[4] The
so-called modern era has been up to now a Protestant Middle Ages.
And it is only through the dissolution of the Protestant religion
that we can develop the true democratic republic as the living
unity of men and the concrete expression of man's essence.

If regarded from a purely theoretical standpoint, Feuerbach's

[1] *W*, II, p. 220.     [2] *W*, II, p. 219.     [3] *W*, II, p. 244.     [4] *W*, II, p. 221.

philosophy is certainly not outstanding. For example, his attempt to dispose of theism by an account of the genesis of the idea of God is superficial. But from the historical point of view his philosophy possesses real significance. In general, it forms part of a movement away from a theological interpretation of the world to an interpretation in which man himself, considered as a social being, occupies the centre of the stage. Feuerbach's substitution of anthropology for theology is an explicit acknowledgement of this. And to a certain extent he is justified in regarding Hegelianism as a half-way house in the process of this transformation. In particular the philosophy of Feuerbach is a stage in the movement which culminated in the dialectical materialism and the economic theory of history of Marx and Engels. True, Feuerbach's thought moves within the framework of the idea of the State as the supreme expression of social unity and of the concept of political rather than of economic man. But his transformation of idealism into materialism and his insistence on overcoming man's self-alienation as manifested in religion prepared the ground for the thought of Marx and Engels. Marx may have criticized Feuerbach severely but he certainly owed him a debt.

3. In view of Feuerbach's preoccupation with the subject of religion the shift of emphasis in the Hegelian left wing from logical, metaphysical and religious problems to problems of a social and political nature is perhaps better illustrated by Arnold Ruge (1802–80). Ruge's first two works, written when he was more or less an orthodox Hegelian, were on aesthetics. But his interest came to centre on political and historical problems. In 1838 he founded the *Hallische Jahrbücher für deutsche Wissenschaft und Kunst*, having among his collaborators David Strauss, Feuerbach and Bruno Bauer (1809–82). In 1841 the review was renamed *Deutsche Jahrbücher für Wissenschaft und Kunst*, and at this time Marx began to collaborate with it. Early in 1843, however, the periodical, which had become more and more radical in tone and had aroused the hostile attention of the Prussian government, was suppressed; and Ruge moved to Paris where he founded the *Deutsch-französische Jahrbücher*. But a break between Ruge and Marx and the dispersal of other contributors brought the life of the new review to a speedy close. Ruge went to Zürich. In 1847 he returned to Germany, but after the failure of the Revolution of 1848 he crossed over into England. In his last years he became a supporter of the new German empire. He died at Brighton.

Ruge shared Hegel's belief that history is a progressive advance towards the realization of freedom, and that freedom is attained in the State, the creation of the rational General Will. He was thus prepared to give full marks to Hegel for having utilized Rousseau's concept of the *volonté generale* and for having grounded the State on the universal will which realizes itself in and through the wills of individuals. At the same time he criticized Hegel for having given an interpretation of history which was closed to the future, in the sense that it left no room for novelty. In the Hegelian system, according to Ruge, historical events and institutions were portrayed as examples or illustrations of a dialectical scheme which worked itself out with logical necessity. Hegel failed to understand the uniqueness and non-repeatable character of historical events, institutions and epochs. And his deduction of the Prussian monarchical constitution was a sign of the closed character of his thought, that is, of its lack of openness to the future, to progress, to novelty.

The basic trouble with Hegel, in Ruge's view, was that he derived the scheme of history from the system. We ought not to presuppose a rational scheme and then derive the pattern of history from it. If we do this, we inevitably end by justifying the actual state of affairs. Our task is rather that of *making* history rational, of bringing, for example, new institutions into being which will be more rational than those already in existence. In other words, in place of Hegel's predominantly speculative and theoretical attitude to history and to social and political life we need to substitute a practical and revolutionary attitude.

This does not mean that we have to abandon the idea of a teleological movement in history. But it does mean that the philosopher should endeavour to discern the movement and demands of the spirit of the time (*der Zeitgeist*) and that he should criticize existing institutions in the light of these demands. Hegel's career fell in the period after the French Revolution, but he had little understanding of the real movement of the *Zeitgeist*. He did not see, for instance, that the realization of freedom of which he talked so much could not be achieved without radical changes in the institutions which he canonized.

We can see in Ruge's attitude an attempt to combine belief in a teleological movement in history with a practical and revolutionary attitude. And his criticism of Hegel was congenial to Marx. The great idealist was primarily concerned with understanding history, with seeing the rational in the real. Ruge and Marx were concerned with making history, with understanding the world in order to change it. But Ruge refused to follow Marx in the path of communism. In his opinion Marx's idea of man was very one-sided, and he opposed to it what he called an integral humanism. It is not only man's material and economic needs which require to be satisfied but also his spiritual needs. However, the break between the two men was by no means due simply to ideological differences.

4. A counterblast to the general movement of thought in left wing Hegelianism came from the somewhat eccentric philosopher Max Stirner (1806–56) whose real name was Johann Kaspar Schmidt. After attending the lectures of Schleiermacher and Hegel at Berlin Stirner taught in a school for a few years and then gave himself to private study. His best known work is *The Individual and His Property* (*Der Einzige und sein Eigentum*, 1845).

At the beginning of this work Stirner quotes Feuerbach's statement that man is man's supreme being and Bruno Bauer's assertion that man has just been discovered. And he invites his readers to take a more careful look at this supreme being and new discovery. What do they find? What he himself finds is the ego, not the absolute ego of Fichte's philosophy but the concrete individual self, the man of flesh and blood. And the individual ego is a unique reality which seeks from the start to preserve itself and so to assert itself. For it has to preserve itself in the face of other beings which threaten, actually or potentially, its existence as an ego. In other words, the ego's concern is with itself.

It is precisely this unique individual ego which most philosophers pass over and forget. In Hegelianism the individual self was belittled in favour of absolute Thought or Spirit. Paradoxically man was supposed to realize his true self or essence in proportion as he became a moment in the life of the universal Spirit. An abstraction was substituted for concrete reality. And Feuerbach's philosophy is tarred with the same brush. To be sure, Feuerbach is right in claiming that man should overcome the self-alienation involved in the religious attitude and rediscover himself. For in Judaism and Christianity freedom, the very essence of man, was projected outside the human being in the concept of God, and man was enslaved. He was told to deny himself and obey. But though Feuerbach is justified in his polemics against religious self-alienation and against the abstractions of Hegelianism, he fails to understand the significance of the unique individual and offers us

nstead the abstraction of Humanity or of absolute Man and the
ulfilment of selfhood in and through the State. Similarly, even if
n humanistic socialism Humanity is substituted for the Christian
God and the Hegelian Absolute, the individual is still sacrificed on
he altar of an abstraction. In fine, the left-wing Hegelians can be
ubjected to the same sort of criticism which they level against
Hegel himself.

In place of such abstractions as Absolute Spirit, Humanity and
he universal essence of man Stirner enthrones the unique and free
ndividual. In his view freedom is realized through owning. And,
as this unique individual, I own all that I can appropriate. This
does not mean, of course, that I have in fact to make everything
my property. But there is no reason why I should not do so, other
than my inability to do it or my own free decision not to do it. I
proceed out of and return into the 'creative nothing', and while I
exist my concern is with myself alone. My endeavour should be
that of expressing my unique individuality without allowing
myself to be enslaved or hampered by any alleged higher power
such as God or the State or by any abstraction such as Humanity
or the universal Moral Law. Subservience to such fictitious
entities weakens my sense of my own uniqueness.

Stirner's philosophy of egoism possesses a certain interest and
significance in so far as it represents the protest of the concrete
human person against the worship of the collectivity or of an
abstraction. Moreover some may wish to see in it some spiritual
affinity with existentialism. And there is at least some ground for
this. It can hardly be said that emphasis on the theme of property
is a characteristic of existentialism, but the theme of the unique
free individual certainly is.[1] Stirner's philosophy has been
mentioned here, however, not for any anticipation of later thought
but rather as a phase in the movement of revolt against metaphysical idealism. One can say perhaps that it represents an
expression of the nominalistic reaction which over-emphasis on the
universal always tends to evoke. It is, of course, an exaggeration.
A healthy insistence on the uniqueness of the individual self is
coupled with a fantastic philosophy of egoism. But the protest
against an exaggeration very often takes the form of an exaggeration in the opposite direction.

Apart, however, from the fact that Stirner was far from being a

[1] Stirner's obscure remarks about 'creative nothing' recall to mind certain
aspects of Heidegger's thought.

great philosopher, his thought was out of harmony with the *Zeitgeist*, and it is not surprising if Marx saw in it the expression of the alienated isolated individual in a doomed bourgeois society. Marx and Engels may have incorporated in their philosophy the very features which Stirner so disliked, substituting the economic class for Hegel's national State, the class war for the dialectic of States, and Humanity for absolute Spirit. But the fact remains that their philosophy was, for good or ill, to possess a great historical importance, whereas Max Stirner is remembered only as an eccentric thinker whose philosophy has little significance except when it is seen as a moment in the perennially recurrent protest of the free individual against the voraciously devouring universal.

### CHAPTER XVI

# THE TRANSFORMATION OF IDEALISM (2)

*Introductory remarks—The lives and writings of Marx and Engels and the development of their thought—Materialism— Dialectical materialism—The materialist conception of history —Comments on the thought of Marx and Engels.*

. CONFRONTED with the thought of Marx and Engels the historian f philosophy finds himself in a rather difficult situation. On the ne hand the contemporary influence and importance of their hilosophy is so obvious that the not uncommon practice of ccording it little more than a passing mention in connection with he development of left-wing Hegelianism scarcely seems to be ustified. Indeed, it might seem more appropriate to treat it as one f the great modern visions of human life and history. On the ther hand it would be a mistake to allow oneself to be so hypno- ized by the indubitable importance of Communism in the modern orld as to tear its basic ideology from its historical setting in ineteenth-century thought. Marxism is indeed a living philosophy 1 the sense that it inspired and gave impetus and coherence to a orce which, for good or ill, exercises a vast influence in the modern vorld. It is accepted, doubtless with varying degrees of conviction, y a great many people today. At the same time it is arguable that :s continued life as a more or less unified system is primarily due o its association with an extra-philosophical factor, a powerful ocial-political movement, the contemporary importance of which obody would deny. It is true, of course, that the connection is not ccidental. That is to say, Communism did not adopt a system of leas which lay outside the process of its own birth and develop- 1ent. But the point is that it is the Communist Party which has aved Marxism from undergoing the fate of other nineteenth- entury philosophies by turning it into a faith. And the historian f nineteenth-century philosophy is justified in dwelling primarily n the thought of Marx and Engels in its historical setting and in rescinding from its contemporary importance as the basic creed f a Party, however powerful this Party may be.

The present writer has therefore decided to confine his attention to some aspects of the thought of Marx and Engels themselves an to neglect, except for some brief references, the subsequen development of their philosophy as well as its impact on th modern world through the medium of the Communist Party. Whe it is a question of an inevitably somewhat overcrowded account o philosophy in Germany during the nineteenth century, thi restriction does not really stand in need of any defence. But as th importance of Communism in our day may lead the reader t think that a more extended treatment would have been desirabl and even that this volume should have culminated in the philo sophy of Marx, it may be as well to point out that to depic Marxism as the apex and point of confluence of nineteenth-centur German philosophical thought would be to give a false historica picture under the determining influence of the political situation i the world today.

2. Karl Marx (1818–83) was of Jewish descent. His father, a liberal Jew, became a Protestant in 1816, and Marx himself wa baptized in 1824. But his father's religious convictions were by n means profound, and he was brought up in the traditions o Kantian rationalism and political liberalism. After his schoc education at Trier he studied at the universities of Bonn anc Berlin. At Berlin he associated with the Young Hegelians, th members of the so-called *Doktorklub*, especially with Bruno Bauer But he soon became dissatisfied with the purely theoretica attitude of left-wing Hegelianism, and this dissatisfaction was in tensified when in 1842 he began to collaborate in editing at Cologn the newly-founded *Rheinische Zeitung*, of which he soon became th chief editor. For his work brought him into closer contact witl concrete political, social and economic problems, and he becam convinced that theory must issue in practical activity, in action if it is to be effective. This may indeed seem to be obvious, even a tautology. But the point is that Marx was already turning away from the Hegelian notion that it is the philosopher's busines simply to understand the world and that we can trust, as it were to the working out of the Idea or of Reason. Criticism of traditiona ideas and existing institutions is not sufficient to change then unless it issues in political and social action. In fact, if religior signifies man's alienation from himself, so also in its own way doe German philosophy. For it divorces man from reality, making hin a mere spectator of the process in which he is involved.

At the same time reflection on the actual situation led Marx to

dopt a critical attitude towards the Hegelian theory of the State.
nd it was apparently in this period, between 1841 and 1843, that
e wrote a criticism of Hegel's concept of the State under the title
*ritik des Hegelschen Staatsrechts*. According to Hegel objective
ɔirit reaches its highest expression in the State, the family and
ivil society being moments or phases in the dialectical develop-
ient of the idea of the State. The State, as the full expression of
ɪe Idea in the form of objective Spirit, is for Hegel the 'subject',
·hile the family and civil society are 'predicates'. But this is to put
ɪings the wrong way round. The family and civil society, not the
tate, are the 'subject': they form the basic realities in human
ɔciety. Hegel's State is an abstract universal, a governmental and
ureaucratic institution which stands apart from and over against
he life of the people. In fact there is a contradiction between
ublic and private concerns. Transposing on to the political plane
·euerbach's idea of religion as an expression of man's self-
lienation, Marx argues that in the State as conceived by Hegel
ɪan alienates his true nature. For man's true life is conceived as
xisting in the State whereas in point of fact the State stands over
gainst individual human beings and their interests. And this
ɔntradiction or gulf between public and private concerns will last
ntil man becomes socialized man and the political State, exalted
y Hegel, gives way to a true democracy in which the social
ɪganism is no longer something external to man and his real
ɪterests.

Marx also attacks Hegel's idea of insistence on private property
s the basis of civil society. But he has not yet arrived at an
xplicit communistic theory. He appeals rather for the abolition of
he monarchy and the development of social democracy. The idea,
owever, of a classless economic society is implicit in his criticism
f Hegel's political State and in his notion of true democracy.
'urther, his concern with man as such and his internationalism
re also implicit in his criticism of Hegel.

Early in 1843 the life of the *Rheinische Zeitung* was brought to a
lose by the political authorities, and Marx went to Paris where he
ollaborated with Ruge in editing the *Deutsch-französische
'ahrbücher*. In the first and only number which appeared he
ublished two articles, one a criticism of Hegel's *Philosophy of
*light*, the other a review of essays by Bruno Bauer on Judaism. In
he first of these articles Marx refers to Feuerbach's analysis of
eligion as a self-alienation on man's part and asks why it occurs.

Why does man create the illusory world of the supernatural an project into it his own true self? The answer is that religio reflects or expresses the distortion in human society. Man political, social and economic life is incapable of fulfilling his tru self, and he creates the illusory world of religion and seeks h happiness therein, so that religion is man's self-administered opiun Inasmuch as religion prevents man from seeking his happines where alone it can be found, it must indeed be attacked. But criticism of religion is of little value if it is divorced from politic and social criticism, for it attacks the effect while neglecting th cause. Further, criticism by itself is in any case inadequate. W cannot change society simply by philosophizing about it. Though must issue in action, that is, in social revolution. For philosophic criticism raises problems which can be solved only in this way. I Marx's language philosophy must be overcome, this overcomin being also the realization (*Verwirklichkung*) of philosophy. It mus leave the plane of theory and penetrate to the masses. And when i does so, it is no longer philosophy but takes the form of a socia revolution which must be the work of the most oppressed class namely the proletariat. By abolishing private property consciousl and explicitly the proletariat will emancipate itself and, togethe with itself, the whole of society. For egoism and social injustice ar bound up with the institution of private property.

In certain obvious respects Marx's way of thinking is influence by Hegel's. For example, the idea of alienation and its overcomin is of Hegelian origin. But it is equally obvious that he rejects th notion of history as the self-manifestation or self-expression of th Absolute defined as Spirit. His concept of theory as realizing itsel through practice or action reminds us indeed of Hegel's concept o the concrete self-unfolding of the Idea. But the fundamenta reality is for him, as for Feuerbach, Nature rather than the Idea o *Logos*. And in his political and economic manuscripts of 184 Marx emphasizes the difference between his own position and tha of Hegel.

True, Marx retains a profound admiration for Hegel. He praise him for having recognized the dialectical character of all proces and for having seen that man develops or realizes himself throug his own activity, through self-alienation and its overcoming. A the same time Marx sharply criticizes Hegel for his idealist concep of man as self-consciousness and for having conceived huma activity as being primarily the spiritual activity of thought. Hege

id indeed look on man as expressing himself outwardly in the
bjective order and then returning to himself on a higher plane.
ut his idealism involved the tendency to do away with the
bjective order by interpreting it simply in relation to conscious-
ess. Hence the process of self-alienation and its overcoming was
or him a process in and for thought rather than in objective
eality.

Whether Marx does justice to Hegel may be open to question.
ut in any case he opposes to the primacy of the Idea the primacy
f sensible reality. And he maintains that the fundamental form of
uman work is not thought but manual labour in which man
lienates himself in the objective product of his labour, a product
hich, in society as at present constituted, does not belong to the
roducer. This alienation cannot be overcome by a process of
hought in which the idea of private property is regarded as a
noment in the dialectical movement to a higher idea. It can be
vercome only through a social revolution which abolishes private
roperty and effects the transition to communism. The dialectical
novement is not a movement of thought about reality: it is the
novement of reality itself, the historical process. And the negation
f the negation (the abolition of private property) involves the
ositive occurrence of a new historical situation in which man's
elf-alienation is overcome in actual fact and not simply for thought.

This insistence on the unity of thought and action and on the
vercoming of man's self-alienation through social revolution and
he transition to communism, an insistence which shows itself in
he articles of 1843 and the manuscripts of 1844, can be regarded,
n part at least, as the result of a marriage between left-wing
Iegelianism and the socialist movement with which Marx came
nto contact at Paris. Dissatisfied with the predominantly critical
nd theoretical attitude of the Young Hegelians, Marx found at
'aris a much more dynamic attitude. For besides studying the
lassical English economists, such as Adam Smith and Ricardo, he
nade the personal acquaintance of German socialists in exile and
f French socialists such as Proudhon and Louis Blanc, as well as
f revolutionaries such as the Russian Bakunin. And even if he
ad already shown an inclination to emphasize the need for action,
his personal contact with the socialist movement had a profound
nfluence upon his mind. At the same time he came to the con-
lusion that though the socialists were more in touch with reality
han were the German philosophers, they failed to make an

adequate appraisal of the situation and its demands. They need an intellectual instrument to give unity of vision, purpose ar method. And though Marx spoke of the overcoming of philosoph and did not regard his own theory of history as a philosophic system, it is clear not only that this is in fact what it became b also that it owed much to a transformation of Hegelianism.

The most important personal contact, however, which Mar made at Paris was his meeting with Engels who arrived in the cit from England in 1844. The two men had indeed met one another couple of years before, but the period of their friendship an collaboration dates from 1844.

Friedrich Engels (1820–95) was the son of a rich industrialis and he took up a position in his father's firm at an early age. Whi doing his military service at Berlin in 1841 he associated with th circle of Bruno Bauer and adopted an Hegelian position. Th writings of Feuerbach, however, turned his mind away fro idealism to materialism. In 1842 he went to Manchester to wor for his father's firm and interested himself in the ideas of the earl English socialists. It was at Manchester that he wrote his study c the working classes in England (*Die Lage der arbeitenden Klasse in England*) which was published in Germany in 1845. He als composed for the *Deutsch-französische Jahrbücher* his *Outlines of Critique of National Economy* (*Umrisse einer Kritik der Nationa. ökonomie*).

An immediate result of the meeting between Marx and Enge in Paris was their collaboration in writing *The Holy Family* (*D heilige Family*, 1845) directed against the idealism of Bruno Baue and his associates who appeared to think that 'criticism' was transcendent being which had found its embodiment in the 'Hol Family', namely the members of Bauer's circle. In opposition t the idealist emphasis on thought and consciousness Marx an Engels maintained that the forms of the State, law, religion an morality were determined by the stages of the class-war.

At the beginning of 1845 Marx was expelled from France an went to Brussels where he composed eleven theses agains Feuerbach, ending with the famous statement that wherea philosophers have only tried to understand the world in differen ways, the real need is to change it. When he had been joined b Engels the two men collaborated in writing *The German Ideolog* (*Die deutsche Ideologie*) which remained unpublished until 1932 The work is a criticism of contemporary German philosophy a:

epresented by Feuerbach, Bauer and Stirner and of the German
ocialists, and it is important for its outline of the materialist
onception of history. The fundamental historical reality is social
nan in his activity in Nature. This material or sensible activity is
nan's basic life, and it is life which determines consciousness, not,
s the idealists imagine, the other way round. In other words, the
undamental factor in history is the process of material or economic
production. And the formation of social classes, the warfare
etween classes and, indirectly, the forms of political life, of law
nd of ethics are all determined by the varying successive modes
f production. Further, the whole historical process is moving
dialectically towards the proletarian revolution and the coming of
ommunism, not the self-knowledge of absolute Spirit or any such
philosophical illusion.

In 1847 Marx published in French his *Poverty of Philosophy*
*Misère de la philosophie*), a reply to Proudhon's *Philosophy of
Poverty* (*Philosophie de la misère*). In it he attacks the notion of
xed categories, eternal truths and natural laws which in his view
s characteristic of bourgeois economics. For example, after
accepting the description of property as theft Proudhon goes on to
nvisage a socialist system which will strip property of this
haracter. And this shows that he regards the institution of private
property as an eternal or natural value and as a fixed economic
ategory. But there are no such values and categories. Nor is there
ny philosophy which can be worked out *a priori* and then applied
o the understanding of history and society. There can be only a
ritical knowledge based on the analysis of concrete historical
ituations. In Marx's view the dialectic is not a law of thought
which is expressed in reality: it is immanent in the actual process
f reality and is reflected in thought when the mind correctly
nalyses concrete situations.

Faithful, however, to his idea of the unity of thought and action,
Marx was by no means content to criticize the shortcomings of
German ideologists such as Bauer and Feuerbach and of socialists
uch as Proudhon. He joined the Communist League and in 1847 was
commissioned, together with Engels, to draw up a summary state-
nent of its principles and aims. This was the famous *Communist
Manifesto* or *Manifesto of the Communist Party* which appeared
n London early in 1848, shortly before the beginning of the series
f revolutions and insurrections which took place in Europe
during that year. When the active phase of the revolutionary

movement started in Germany, Marx and Engels returned t
their native land. But after the failure of the revolution Marx, wh
had been brought to trial and acquitted, retired to Paris, only to b
expelled from France for the second time in 1849. He went t
London where he remained for the rest of his life, receivin
financial aid from his friend Engels.

In 1859 Marx published at Berlin his *Contribution to a Critique c
Political Economy* (*Zur Kritik der politischen Oekonomie*) which i
important, as is also the *Manifesto*, for its statement of th
materialist conception of history. And, again uniting action witl
theory, he founded in 1864 the International Working Men'
Association, commonly known as the First International. Its life
however, was beset with difficulties. For example, Marx and hi
friends considered that it was necessary for authority to b
centralized in the hands of the committee if the proletariat was t
be led successfully to victory, whereas others, such as Bakunin th
anarchist, refused to accept a dictatorship of the central committee
Besides, Marx soon found himself at loggerheads with the Frencl
and German socialist groups. After the congress at The Hague ii
1872 the central committee was transferred to New York at th
instance of Marx. And the First International did not long survive

The first volume of Marx's famous work *Capital* (*Das Kapital*
appeared at Hamburg in 1867. But the author did not continue th
publication. He died in March 1883, and the second and thir
volumes were published posthumously by Engels in 1885 and 189.
respectively. Further manuscripts were published in several part
by K. Kautsky in 1905–10. In the work Marx maintains that th
bourgeois or capitalist system necessarily involves a clas
antagonism. For the value of a community is crystallized labour
as it were. That is to say, its value represents the labour put int
it. Yet the capitalist appropriates to himself part of this value
paying the worker a wage which is less than the value of th
commodity produced. He thus defrauds or exploits the worker
And this exploitation cannot be overcome except by the abolitio
of capitalism. Marx refers, of course, to contemporary abuses i
the economic system, such as the practice of keeping wages as lov
as possible. But exploitation should not be understood only in thi
sense. For if the so-called labour theory of value is once accepted
it necessarily follows that the capitalist system involves exploita
tion or defrauding of the worker. And the payment of high wage.
would not alter this fact.

In 1878 Engels published as a book, commonly known as *Anti-Dühring*, some articles which he had written against the then influential German socialist Eugen Dühring. One chapter was written by Marx. Engels also occupied himself with composing his *Dialectics of Nature* (*Dialektik der Natur*). But he was too taken up with bringing out the second and third volumes of Marx's *Capital* and with efforts to resuscitate the International to be able to finish the work. And it was not published until 1925, when it appeared at Moscow. Engels lacked his friend's philosophical training, but he had wide interests, and it was he rather than Marx who applied dialectical materialism to the philosophy of Nature. The results were not perhaps such as to enhance Engels' reputation as a philosopher among those who do not accept his writings as part of a creed.

Of Engels' other publications mention should be made of his work on *The Origin of the Family, Private Property and the State* (*Der Ursprung der Familie, des Privateigentums und des Staats*, 1884) in which he tries to derive the origin of class divisions and of the State from the institution of private property. In 1888 a series of articles by Engels were published together as a book under the title *Ludwig Feuerbach and the End of the Classical German Philosophy* (*Ludwig Feuerbach und der Ausgang der klassischen deutschen Philosophie*). Engels died of cancer in August 1895.

3. Whether or not Hegel meant that the Concept (*der Begriff*) or logical Idea is a subsistent reality which externalizes or alienates itself in Nature, is a disputable question. But both Marx and Engels understood him in this sense, namely as holding that the Logos is the primary reality which expresses itself in its opposite, namely unconscious Nature, and then returns to itself as Spirit, thus actualizing, as it were, its own essence or definition. Thus in his preface to the second German edition of *Capital* Marx states that 'for Hegel the thought-process, which he goes so far as to transform into an independent Subject under the name "Idea", is the demiurge of the real, the real being simply its external appearance'.[1] And in his book on Feuerbach Engels asserts that with Hegel the dialectic is the self-development of the Concept. The absolute Concept is not only present from eternity—who knows where?—but it is also the real living soul of the whole existent world. . . . It alienates itself in the sense that it transforms itself into Nature where, without consciousness of itself and

[1] *Das Kapital*, I, p. xvii (Hamburg, 1922); *Capital*, II, p. 873 (London, Everyman).

disguised as natural necessity, it goes through a new process of development and finally comes again to self-consciousness in man'.

As against this metaphysical idealism Marx and Engels accepted Feuerbach's thesis that the primary reality is Nature. Thus Engels speaks of the liberating effect of Feuerbach's *Essence of Christianity*, which restored materialism to its throne. 'Nature exists independently of all philosophy; it is the basis on which we human beings, ourselves products of Nature, have grown. Apart from Nature and human beings nothing exists; and the higher beings which our religious fantasy created are only the fantastic reflection of our own essence . . . the enthusiasm was general; we were all for the moment followers of Feuerbach. One can see in the *Holy Family* how enthusiastically Marx welcomed the new conception, and how much he was influenced by it, in spite of all critical reservations'.[2]

In this passage Engels speaks of the re-enthronement of materialism. And both Marx and Engels were, of course, materialists. But this obviously does not mean that they denied the reality of mind or that they identified the processes of thought in a crude manner with material processes. What materialism meant for them was in the first place the denial that there is any Mind or Idea which is prior to Nature and expresses itself in Nature. It was certainly not equivalent to denying that human beings have minds. In his *Dialectics of Nature* Engels speaks of the law of the transformation of quantity into quality, and *vice versa*, as the law by which changes in Nature take place.[3] A transformation of this kind occurs when a series of quantitative changes is succeeded by an abrupt qualitative change. Thus when matter has reached a certain pattern of complicated organization mind emerges as a new qualitative factor.

To be sure, the question of the power of the mind is left somewhat obscure by Marx and Engels. In the preface to his *Critique of Political Economy* Marx makes the famous statement that 'it is not the consciousness of human beings which determines their

[1] *Ludwig Feuerbach*, p. 44 (Stuttgart, 1888); *Ludwig Feuerbach*, edited by C. P. Dutt with an introduction by L. Rudas, p. 53 (London, no date).

[2] *Ludwig Feuerbach*, pp. 12–13 (p. 28). When a translated work is referred to more than once, on all occasions but the first I give the pagination of the translation in brackets, without repeating the title.

[3] It is true that in the *Science of Logic* Hegel passes from the category of quality to that of quantity, but when dealing with measure he speaks of nodal points at which a series of quantitative variations is succeeded by an abrupt qualitative change, a leap. This is succeeded in turn by further quantitative variations until a new nodal point is reached.

eing, but it is, on the contrary, their social being which determines
heir consciousness.'[1] And Engels remarks that 'we conceived the
oncepts in our heads once more from a materialist point of view
s copies of real things, instead of conceiving real things as copies
f this or that stage of the absolute Concept'.[2] And such passages
end to suggest that human thought is no more than a copy or
eflection of material economic conditions or of the processes of
Nature. In other words, they tend to suggest the passive character
f the human mind. But we have already seen that in his theses
gainst Feuerbach Marx asserts that whereas philosophers have
nly tried to understand the world, it is man's business to change
t. Hence it is not really surprising if in the first volume of *Capital*
ve find him comparing the human worker with the spider and the
•ee and remarking that even the worst builder can be distinguished
rom the best bee by the fact that the former conceives the product
f his work before he constructs it whereas the latter does not. In
he human worker there is the will which has an end in view and
vhich externalizes itself.[3] Indeed, if Marx and Engels wish to
naintain, as they do, the need for revolutionary activity, for
orrectly analysing the situation and acting accordingly, they
•bviously cannot maintain at the same time that the mind is no
nore than a kind of pool on the surface of which natural processes
nd economic conditions are passively mirrored. When they are
ngaged in setting Hegel on his feet, that is, in substituting
naterialism for idealism, they tend to stress the copy-idea of
iuman concepts and thought-processes. But when they are
•peaking of the need for social revolution and for its preparation,
hey clearly have to attribute to the human mind and will an
ictive role. Their utterances may not be always perfectly consistent,
out their materialism is basically an assertion of the priority of
natter, not a denial of the reality of mind.

4. Although, however, Marx and Engels regarded their
naterialism as a counterblast to Hegel's idealism, they certainly
lid not look on themselves as being simply opponents of Hegel. For
hey recognized their indebtedness to him for the idea of the
lialectical process of reality, that is, a process by way of negation
ollowed by a negation of the negation, which is also an affirmation
•f a higher stage. Another way of putting the same thing is to say

[1] *Zur Kritik der politischen Oekonomie*, p. xi (Stuttgart, 1897); *Marx-Engels:
Selected Works*, I, p. 363 (London, 1958).
[2] *Ludwig Feuerbach*, p. 45 (p. 54).
[3] *Das Kapital*, I, p. 140 (I, pp. 169–70).

that process or development takes the form of the contradiction of an existing situation or state of affairs, followed by the contradiction of the contradiction, this contradiction being an overcoming of the first. It is not so much a question of thesis, antithesis and synthesis, as of negation and its negation, though the second negation can be regarded as in some sense a 'synthesis', inasmuch as it is a transition to a higher stage in the dialectical process.

This idea of development as a dialectical process is essential to the thought of Marx and Engels. Obviously, a man can accept the thesis of the priority of matter to mind and some form of what is now called emergent evolution without thereby being a Marxist. The materialism of Marx and Engels is dialectical materialism, to use the descriptive term which is now in general use, even if Marx himself did not employ it.

Marx and Engels were indeed at pains to distinguish between their conception of the dialectic and that of Hegel. In their view Hegel, having seen that thought moves dialectically, hypostatized this process as the process of absolute Thought, the self-development of the Idea. Thus the movement of the dialectic in the world and in human history was regarded by Hegel as the reflection or phenomenal expression of the movement of Thought. For Marx and Engels, however, the dialectical movement is found first of all in reality, that is to say, in Nature and history. The dialectical movement of human thought is simply a reflection of the dialectical process of reality. And this reversal of the relation between thought and reality was for them an essential part of the business of setting Hegel on his feet. At the same time Marx and Engels made no secret of the fact that the idea of the dialectic was derived from Hegel. Hence they regarded their materialism as being essentially post-Hegelian materialism, and not as a mere return to an earlier type of materialist theory.

Now, though Marx affirms with Feuerbach the priority of matter to mind, he is not really interested in Nature as such, considered apart from man. Sometimes indeed he seems to imply that Nature does not exist except for man. But this must not be taken as meaning that Nature possesses no ontological reality except as object of consciousness. It would be absurd to interpret Marx as an idealist. What he means is that Nature first exists for man when man differentiates himself from it, though at the same time he recognizes a relation between himself and Nature. An animal is a natural product, and we see it as related to Nature. But the animal is not conscious of these relations as such: they do not exist for it'. Hence Nature cannot be said to exist 'for the animal'. With the emergence of consciousness, however, and the subject-object relation Nature begins to exist for man. And this is essential for what we may call the becoming of man. To be man, man must objectify himself. And he cannot do so, except by distinguishing himself from Nature.

But man is orientated towards Nature in the sense that he has needs which can be satisfied only through objects other than himself. And Nature is orientated towards man in the sense that it is the means of satisfying these needs. Further, man's satisfaction of his needs involves activity or work on his part. And in a sense the spontaneous satisfaction of a basic physical need by appropriating a ready-made object, so to speak, is work. But it is not specifically human work or activity, not at least if it is considered simply as a physical act. A man may, for example, stoop down and drink from a stream to quench his thirst. But so do many animals. Work becomes specifically human when man consciously transforms a natural object to satisfy his needs, and when he employs means or instruments to do so. In other words, the fundamental form of human work and man's fundamental relation to Nature is his productive activity, his conscious production of the means of satisfying his needs. Man is basically economic man, though this is not to say that he cannot be anything but economic man.

Man cannot, however, objectify himself and become man unless he is also object for another. In other words, man is a social being: a relation to his fellows is essential to his being as man. And the basic form of society is the family. We can say, therefore, that the fundamental reality to which Marx directs his attention is productive man as standing in a twofold relation, to Nature and to other human beings. Or, inasmuch as the term 'productive man' already implies a relation to Nature, we can say that the fundamental reality considered by Marx is productive man in society.

For Marx, therefore, man is basically not a contemplative but an active being, this activity being primarily the material one of production. And the relations between man and Nature are not static but changing relations. He uses means of production to satisfy his needs, and therefore fresh needs present themselves, leading to a further development in the means of production. Further, corresponding to each stage in the development of means of production for the satisfaction of man's needs there are social relations between men. And the dynamic interaction between the means or forces of production and the social relations between men constitute the basis of history. Speaking of man's basic physical needs Marx asserts that 'the first historical fact is the production of the means which enable man to satisfy these needs'.[1] But, as we have seen, this leads to the appearance of fresh needs, to a development in the means of production and to new sets of social relations. Hence the so-called first historical fact contains in itself, as it were in germ, the whole history of man. And this history is for Marx the 'locus', so to speak, of the dialectic. But an account of the dialectic of history according to Marx is best reserved for the next section. It is sufficient to note here that his theory of history is materialist in the sense that the basic factor in history is for him man's economic activity, his activity of production to satisfy his physical needs.

Attention has already been drawn to the fact that Engels extended the dialectic to Nature itself, thus developing what may be called a philosophy of Nature. And there has been some dispute about whether this extension was compatible with the attitude of Marx. Of course, if one assumes that for Marx Nature exists for us only as the field for transformation by human work and that the dialectical movement is confined to history, which presupposes a dynamic relation between man and his natural environment, the extension of the dialectic to Nature in itself would constitute not only a novelty but also a change in the Marxist conception of the dialectic. There might perhaps be a dialectical movement in the development of man's scientific knowledge, but this movement could hardly be attributed to Nature in itself, considered apart from man. It would not be merely a case of Marx having concentrated on human history to the practical exclusion of a philosophy of Nature. It would be a case of an exclusion in principle. But it must be remembered that in Marxism the dialectical movement of history is not the expression of the interior movement of absolute Thought: it is the movement of reality itself. It can be reproduced in the human mind, but in the first instance it is the movement of objective reality. Unless, therefore, we choose to press certain of Marx's utterances to the extent of turning him into an idealist, it does not seem to me that his position excludes in

---

[1] *Deutsche Ideologie*, *W*, III, p. 28; *The German Ideology*, p. 16 (Parts I and III translated by W. Lough and C. P. Magill, London, 1942). In references *W* signifies the edition of the *Works* of Marx and Engels published by Dietz Verlag, Berlin 1957 f.

principle the notion of a dialectic of Nature. Moreover, Marx was well aware that his friend was working at a dialectic of Nature, and he appears to have approved or at any rate not to have shown disapproval. So even if it is arguable that Engels was unfaithful to the thought of Marx and that he was laying the foundation of a mechanistic version of dialectical materialism, in which the movement of history would be regarded as simply a continuation of the necessary movement of autodynamic matter, I should not care to commit myself to the assertion that the extension of the dialectic to Nature in itself was excluded by Marx. Given some of his statements, it may be that he ought to have excluded it. But it does not appear that he did so in point of fact.

However this may be, in what he calls his 'recapitulation of mathematics and the natural sciences'[1] Engels was struck by the fact that in Nature nothing is fixed and static but that all is in movement, change, development. And, as he tells us himself, he was particularly impressed by three factors; first, the discovery of the cell, through the multiplication and differentiation of which plant and animal bodies have developed; secondly, the law of the transformation of energy; and, thirdly, Darwin's statement of the theory of evolution. Reflecting on Nature as revealed by contemporary science Engels came to the conclusion that 'in Nature the same dialectical laws of movement assert themselves in the confusion of innumerable changes which govern the apparent contingency of events in history'.[2]

In his *Dialectics of Nature*[3] Engels summarizes these laws as those of the transformation of quantity into quality, of the mutual penetration of opposites and of the negation of the negation. Some often-quoted examples of this last law, the negation of the negation, are to be found in *Anti-Dühring*. Engels speaks, for instance, of the barley-seed which is said to be negated when it sprouts and the plant begins to grow. The plant then produces a multiplicity of seeds and is itself negated. Thus as 'result of this negation of the negation we have again the original barley-seed, though not as such but tenfold, twentyfold or thirtyfold'.[4] Similarly, the larva or caterpillar negates the egg out of which it comes, is transformed in the course of time into a butterfly and is then itself negated in its death.

[1] *Anti-Dühring*, p. xv (Stuttgart, 1919); *Anti-Dühring*, p. 17 (London, 1959, 2nd edition).    [2] *Ibid.*
[3] *Dialektik der Natur*, p. 53 (Berlin, 1952); *Dialectics of Nature*, p. 83 (London, 1954).    [4] *Anti-Dühring*, p. 138 (p. 187).

Whether logical terms such as 'negation' and 'contradiction' are appropriate in this context is, to put it mildly, disputable. But we need not labour this point. Instead we can note that Engels draws an important conclusion in regard to human thought and knowledge from the nature of the twofold field of application of the dialectic, namely Nature and human history.[1] In his view it was Hegel's great discovery that the world is a complex not of finished things but of processes. And it is true both of Nature and of human history that each is a process or complex of processes. From this it follows that human knowledge, as a mirror of this twofold reality, is itself a process which does not and cannot reach a fixed and absolute system of truth. Hegel saw that 'truth lay in the process of knowing itself, in the long historical development of science which rises from lower to ever higher levels of knowledge without ever arriving, through the discovery of a so-called absolute truth, to the point where it can proceed no further, where nothing remains but to lay one's hands on one's lap and wonder at the absolute truth which has been attained'.[2] There is not and cannot be an absolute system of philosophy which only needs to be learned and accepted. Indeed, inasmuch as absolute truth is precisely what philosophers have had in view, we can say that with Hegel philosophy comes to an end. Instead we have a dialectically-advancing progressive scientific knowledge of reality which is always open to further change and development.

Like Marx, therefore, Engels attacks the notion of 'eternal truths'. He finds himself compelled to admit that there are truths which nobody can doubt without being considered mad; for example, that 'two and two make four, that the three angles of a triangle are equal to two right angles, that Paris lies in France, that a man who eats nothing dies of hunger and so on'.[3] But such truths, says Engels, are trivialities or commonplaces. And nobody would dignify them with the solemn title of 'eternal truths' unless he wished to draw from their existence the conclusion that in the field of human history there is an eternal moral law, an eternal essence of justice, and so on. But it is precisely this sort of conclusion which is erroneous. Just as hypotheses in physics and biology are subject to revision and even to revolutionary change, so is morality.

---

[1] Strictly speaking, there are for Engels three fields of application. 'Dialectics is nothing else but the science of the general laws of movement and development in Nature, human society and thought'; *Anti-Dühring*, p. 144 (p. 193).

[2] *Ludwig Feuerbach*, p. 4 (p. 21).          [3] *Anti-Dühring*, p. 81 (p. 122).

Marx and Engels, therefore, did not present their interpretation of reality as being the absolute and final system of philosophy. True, they regarded it as science rather than as speculative philosophy. And this means, of course, that they regarded it as supplanting all previous interpretations, whether idealist or materialist. At the same time science was not for them something which could ever attain a fixed and final form. If reality is a dialectical process, so is human thought, in so far, that is to say, as it reflects reality and does not take refuge in an illusory world of eternal truths and fixed essences.

Taken by itself, this denial of eternal truths, stable positions and final solutions suggests that a detached attitude towards their philosophy would be the appropriate one for Marx and Engels to maintain. But they did not look on it as being simply a theoretical exercise in interpreting the world and history. And it was precisely the detached, theoretical attitude which they decried in Hegel. But the implications of their view of dialectical materialism as a practical instrument or weapon is a topic which must be left aside for the moment.

5. As we have seen, the Marxist theory of history is materialist in the sense that the fundamental situation is depicted as a relation between man, considered as a material being, and Nature: it is man producing by his physical activity the means of satisfying his basic needs. But we must add that historical materialism does not mean only this. It means in addition that man's productive activity determines, directly or indirectly, his political life, his law, his morality, his religion, his art, his philosophy. In the present context materialism does not involve, as has been already remarked, denying the reality of mind or consciousness. Nor does it involve denying all value to the cultural activities which depend on mind. But it maintains that the cultural superstructure in general depends on and is in some sense determined by the economic substructure.

In the economic substructure Marx distinguishes two elements, the material forces of production and the productive relations, the second element depending upon the first. 'In the social production of their life human beings enter into determinate necessary relations which are independent of their will, productive relations [*Produktionsverhältnisse*] which correspond with a determinate stage in the development of their material forces of production [*Produktivkräfte*]. The totality of these productive relations forms the economic structure of society'.[1] In this passage the economic structure of a society is indeed identified with the totality of its productive relations. But inasmuch as these relations are said to correspond with a certain level of development of the productive forces of the society in question, and inasmuch as the emergence of conflicts between the productive forces and the productive relations in a given society is an essential feature in Marx's picture of human history, it is obvious that we must distinguish two main elements in the economic structure of society, a structure which is also described by Marx as a mode of production (*Produktionsweise*).

The term 'material forces of production' (or 'material productive powers') obviously covers all the material things which are used by man as artificial instruments in his productive activity, that is, in the satisfaction of his physical needs, from primitive flint instruments up to the most complicated modern machinery. It also includes natural forces in so far as they are used by man in the process of production. And the term can apparently also cover all such objects as are required for productive activity, even if they do not enter into it directly.[2]

Now, if the term is applied exclusively to things distinct from man himself, man is obviously presupposed. Marx tends to speak of the forces of production as doing this or that, but he is not so stupid as to suppose that these forces develop themselves without any human agency. 'The first condition of all human history is naturally the existence of living human individuals.'[3] And in the *Communist Manifesto* he speaks of the bourgeoisie as revolutionizing the instruments of production and thereby the productive relations. However, in the *German Ideology* he remarks that the production of life, whether of one's own life by work or of that of another through procreation, always involves a social relation, in the sense of the collaboration of several individuals. And after observing that it follows from this that a given mode of production is always linked to a given mode of collaboration, he asserts that this mode of collaboration is itself a 'productive force'.[4] He means, of course, that the social relation between men in the process of production can itself react on men's needs and on the productive forces. But if the mode of collaboration in the labour-process can be reckoned as a productive force, there seems to be no reason why,

[1] *Zur Kritik der politischen Oekonomie*, p. x (I, p. 363).
[2] Cf. *Das Kapital*, I, p. 143 (I, pp. 172–3).
[3] *Deutsche Ideologie*, W, III, p. 20 (p. 7).
[4] *Ibid.*, p. 30 (p. 18).

for example, the proletariat should not be accounted a productive force, even if the term is generally used by Marx for instruments or means of production rather than for man himself.[1] In any case it is notoriously difficult to pin him down to a precise and universal use of such terms.

The term 'productive relations' means above all property-relations. Indeed, in the *Critique of Political Economy* we are told that 'property relations' (*Eigentumsverhältnisse*) is simply a juristic expression for 'productive relations'.[2] However, in general the term 'productive relations' refers to the social relations between men as involved in the labour-process. As we have seen, these relations are said to depend on the stage of development of the productive forces. And the two together constitute the economic substructure.

This economic substructure is said to condition the super-structure. 'The mode of production of material life conditions the social, political and mental (*geistigen*) life-process in general. It is not the consciousness of human beings which determines their being, but it is, on the contrary, their social being which determines their consciousness.'[3] Obviously, the statement that the economic substructure 'conditions' (*bedingt*) the superstructure is ambiguous. The statement is not at all startling if it is taken in a very weak sense. It becomes interesting only in proportion as the meaning of the term 'conditions' approaches 'determines'. And it has indeed frequently been taken in this strong sense. Thus it has been main-tained, for example, that the celestial hierarchy (from God down to the choirs of angels and the company of the saints) of mediaeval theology was simply an ideological reflection of the mediaeval feudal structure which was itself determined by economic factors. Again, the rise of the bourgeoisie and the arrival of the capitalist mode of production were reflected in the transition from Catholi-cism to Protestantism. According to Engels the Calvinist doctrine of predestination reflected the supposed economic fact that in commercial competition success or failure does not depend on personal merits but on incomprehensible and uncontrollable economic powers. Yet it was also Engels who protested that the doctrine of Marx and himself had been misunderstood. They had never meant that man's ideas are simply a pale reflection of

[1] In *The Poverty of Philosophy* Marx says explicitly that the revolutionary proletariat is the greatest of all productive forces. See below, p. 328.
[2] *Zur Kritik der politischen Oekonomie*, p. x (I, p. 363).
[3] *Ibid.*, p. xi (I, p. 363).

economic conditions in the sense that the relation of dependence is exclusively unilateral. Ideas (that is to say, men inspired by ideas) can react on the substructure which has conditioned them.

The fact of the matter is, I think, that in their reversal of the idealist conception of history Marx and Engels not unnaturally emphasized the determining influence of the economic substructure. But, having once stated their vision of the world in terms which suggested that for them the world of consciousness and ideas was simply determined by the mode of economic production, they found themselves compelled to qualify this simple outlook. Political and legal structures are more directly determined by the economic substructure than are ideological superstructures such as religion and philosophy. And human ideas, though conditioned by economic conditions, can react on these conditions. In fact they had to allow for such reaction if they wished to allow for revolutionary activity.

To turn now to a more dynamic aspect of history. According to Marx 'at a certain stage in their development a society's forces of production come into conflict [literally 'contradiction', *Widerspruch*] with the existing productive relations'.[1] That is to say, when in a given social epoch the forces of production have developed to such a point that the existing productive relations, especially property-relations, have become a fetter on the further development of the forces of production, there is a contradiction within the economic structure of society, and a revolution takes place, a qualitative change to a new economic structure, a new social epoch. And this change in the substructure is accompanied by changes in the superstructure. Man's political, juristic, religious, artistic and philosophical consciousness undergoes a revolution which depends on and is subsidiary to the revolution in the economic sphere.

A revolution of this kind, the change to a new social epoch, does not take place, Marx insists, until the forces of production have developed to the fullest extent that is compatible with the existing productive relations and the material conditions for the existence of the new form of society are already present within the old. For this is the state of affairs which comprises a contradiction, namely that between the forces of production and the existing social relations. The qualitative change in the economic structure of society or mode of production does not occur until a contra-

[1] *Zur Kritik der politischen Oekonomie*, p. xi (I, p. 363).

diction has matured, as it were, within the old society through a series of quantitative changes.

Now, if the theory is expressed simply in this way, it gives the impression of being simply a technological and mechanical theory. That is to say, it seems as though social revolution, the transition from one social epoch to another, took place inevitably and mechanically, and as though man's consciousness of the need for a change and his revolutionary activity constituted mere epiphenomena which exercised no real influence on the cause of events. But though this interpretation would fit in with the general doctrine that it is the material conditions of life which determine consciousness and not the other way round, it could scarcely fit in with Marx's insistence on the unity of theory and practice and on the need for the active preparation of the proletariat's revolutionary overthrow of the capitalist economy. Hence, although Marx sometimes tends to speak as though the material forces of production were the real revolutionary agent, we have to introduce the idea of the class war and of human agency.

Marx and Engels envisage at the dawn of history a state of primitive communism in which the land was possessed and tilled by the tribe in common and in which there was no class-division. Once, however, private property had been introduced, a division of society into economic classes soon followed. Marx is aware, of course, that social distinctions in civilized society form a more or less complicated pattern. But his general tendency is to simplify the situation by representing the fundamental distinction as being that between the oppressors and the oppressed, the exploiters and the exploited. In all forms of society, therefore, which presuppose the institution of private property, there is an antagonism between classes, an antagonism now latent, now open. And 'the history of all society hitherto is the history of class struggle'.[1] The State becomes the organ or instrument of the dominant class. So does the law. And the dominant class also tries to impose its own moral conceptions. In the Marxist dialectic of history, therefore, the concept of the class replaces Hegel's concept of the national State, and the class war replaces national wars.[2]

This class war or class struggle becomes particularly significant

[1] *Manifest der kommunistischen Partei*, W, IV, p. 462; *Communist Manifesto*, p. 125 (edit. H. J. Laski, London, 1948). Obviously, this refers to all known history after the passing of primitive communism.
[2] That is to say, the class war is looked on as more fundamental, and national wars are interpreted in economic terms.

at the period when in a given social epoch the forces of production have developed to such a point that the existing social relations especially property-relations, are turned into a drag and a fetter For the hitherto dominant class (individual defections apart endeavours to maintain the existing productive relations, while it is in the interest of a rising class to overthrow these relations. And when the contradiction between the forces of production and the productive relations has been perceived by the rising class whose interest it is to overthrow the existing and antiquated social order revolution takes place. Then the new dominant class in its own turn uses the State and the law as its instruments. This process inevitably continues until private property has been abolished and, with it the division of society into mutually antagonistic classes.

In the preface to his *Contribution to the Critique of Political Economy* Marx observes that we can distinguish in broad outline four progressive social epochs which together form the prehistory (*die Vorgeschichte*) of mankind. The first of these, the asiatic called by Engels the *gens* organization, is that of primitive communism. As we have seen, this was marked by communal ownership of land, associated labour and absence of private property. But with the institution of private property, associated by Engels with the change from matriarchy to patriarchy and with improvements in methods of production, the accumulation of private wealth was rendered possible. It was possible, for example, for a man to produce more than he required for his own needs. Hence there arose a division between rich and poor, and a new form of economic organization was required. If we ask what was the new productive force which was responsible for the transition, special mention is made of iron, though the subject is not developed. In any case the growth of private property and wealth made it necessary for the prospective rich to have labour at their disposal. But as under primitive communism there was no free labour available, slaves had to be obtained through captives in war.

We thus pass to the antique or ancient period, characterized by slavery and by the class antagonism between freemen and slaves. On this economic structure, represented, for instance, by Greece and Rome, there arose corresponding legal and political institutions and the splendid ideological superstructure of the classical world.

Although Marx and Engels mention various historical factors which contributed to the transition from the antique to the feudal epoch, which reached its culminating phase in the Middle Ages, no convincing explanation is offered of the productive force or forces which were responsible for the transition. However, it took place, and the feudal economy was reflected in the political and legal institutions of the time, as well as, though more indirectly, in mediaeval religion and philosophy.

During the mediaeval period a middle class or bourgoisie gradually developed. But its wealth-amassing propensities were hampered by factors such as feudal restrictions and guild regulations, as also by the lack of free labour for hire. With the discovery of America, however, and the opening-up of markets in different parts of the world, a powerful impetus was given to commerce, navigation and industry. New sources of wealth became available, and at the close of the Middle Ages land-enclosure by the nobility and other factors contributed to the formation of a class of dispossessed people ready to be hired and exploited. The time was ripe for a change, and the guild-system was overthrown by the new middle class in favour of the early phase of capitalist society. Finally, steam and machinery revolutionized industry; the world market was opened up; means of communication underwent a remarkable development; and the bourgeoisie pushed into the background the classes which had lingered from the Middle Ages.

In feudal society, as Marx is aware, the pattern of organization was too complicated to permit of its being reduced to one simple class antagonism, as between barons and serfs. But in capitalist society, to which he naturally devotes most of his attention, we can see, Marx argues, a growing simplification. For there has been a tendency for capital to become concentrated in ever fewer hands, in great combines of a more or less international or cosmopolitan character. At the same time many of the small capitalists have sunk into the ranks of the proletariat[1] which has also tended to take on an international character. Hence we are faced by two prominent classes, the exploiters and the exploited. The term 'exploitation' suggests, of course, the imposition of long hours of work for starvation wages. But though Marx does indeed inveigh against the abuses of the earlier phases of the industrial revolution, the primary meaning of the term is for him technical, not emotive. As we have seen, according to the doctrine expounded in *Capital* the whole value of a commodity is, as it were, crystallized labour;

---

[1] This is what Marx says in the *Communist Manifesto* which dates, it should be remembered, from the beginning of 1848.

it is due to the labour expended in its production. Hence the wage-system is necessarily exploitation, irrespective of the amount of the wages paid. For in every case the capitalist filches from the worker. The fact that a given capitalist is a humane man who does his best to improve wages and conditions of work makes no difference to the basic situation which is a necessary antagonism between the two classes.

Now, the bourgeoisie has developed the forces of production to a hitherto unknown and undreamed-of extent. But at the same time it has developed them to the point at which they can no longer co-exist with the existing productive relations. According to Marx, this fact is shown, for example, by the periodic recurrence of economic crises. Hence the time is approaching for the over-throw of the capitalist system. And the task of revolutionary activity, particularly of the Communist Party, is to turn the proletariat from a class in itself, to use Hegelian language, into a class for itself, a class conscious of itself and of its mission. The proletariat will then be able to sweep away the capitalist system, seize the organ of the State and use it to establish the dictatorship of the proletariat which will prepare the way for communist society. In this society the political State will wither away. For the State is an instrument for the maintenance of its own position by a dominant class in face of another class or other classes. And under communism class divisions and the class war will disappear.

In view of the fact that the bourgeoisie itself develops the forces of production we may be inclined to ask, what is the new productive force which emerges and which is fettered by the capitalist mode of production? But Marx is ready with his answer. And in the *Poverty of Philosophy* he tells us that the greatest of all productive forces is 'the revolutionary class itself'.[1] This is the productive force which enters into conflict with the existing economic system and overthrows it by revolution.

Human history is thus a dialectical progress from primitive communism to developed communism. And from one point of view at least the intermediary stages are necessary. For it is through them that the forces of production have been developed and that productive relations have been correspondingly changed in such a manner that developed communism is rendered not only possible but also the inevitable result. But the Marxist theory of history is

---

[1] *W*, IV, p. 181; *The Poverty of Philosophy*, edited by C. P. Dutt and V. Chatto-padhyaya, p. 146 (London, no date); p. 174 (London, 1956).

also an instrument or weapon, not merely a spectator's analysis of historical situations. It is the instrument by which the proletariat, through its vanguard the Communist Party, becomes conscious of itself and of the historical task which it has to perform.

The theory is also, however, a philosophy of man. Marx assumes the Hegelian thesis that to realize himself man must objectify himself. And the primary form of self-objectification is in labour, production. The product is, as it were, man-in-his-otherness. But in all societies based on private property this self-objectification takes the form of self-alienation or self-estrangement. For the worker's product is treated as something alien to himself. In capitalist society it belongs to the capitalist, not to the worker. Further, this economic self-alienation is reflected in a social self-alienation. For membership of a class does not represent the whole man. Whichever class he belongs to, there is, so to speak, something of himself in the other class. Thus class antagonism expresses a profound division, a self-estrangement, in the nature of man. Religion also represents, as Feuerbach said, human self-alienation. But, as we have seen, self-alienation in the religious consciousness is for Marx a reflection of a profounder self-alienation in the social-economic sphere. And this cannot be overcome except through the abolition of private property and the establishment of communism. If self-alienation on the economic and social level is overcome, its religious expression will disappear. And at last the whole man, the non-divided man, will exist. Human ethics will take the place of class ethics, and a genuine humanism will reign.

It follows from this that the overthrow of the capitalist system by the proletariat is not merely a case of the replacement of one dominant class by another. It is indeed this, but it is also much more. The dictatorship of the proletariat is a temporary phase which prepares the way for the classless communist society from which self-alienation will be absent. In other words, by its revolutionary act the international proletariat saves not simply itself but all mankind. It has a messianic mission.

6. There is no great difficulty in giving a certain plausibility to the materialist theory of history. For example, if I wish to illustrate the conditioning by the economic structure of political and legal forms and of the ideological superstructure, there is a large variety of facts to which I can appeal. I can point to the connection between the then existing economic and class structure and the ferocious penalties which were once inflicted in England for theft, or to the

connection between the economic interests of plantation-owners in
the southern States of America and the absence of strong moral
feeling against slavery. I can draw attention to the connection
between the economic life of a hunting tribe and its ideas of life
after death or between class divisions and the lines of the hymn
'The rich man in his castle, the poor man at his gate, God made
them high and lowly and ordered their estate'. I can refer to the
evident influence of Greek political structures on Plato's picture of
the ideal State or, for the matter of that, to the influence of
existing conditions in the world of industry on the thought of Marx
and Engels.

But though the Marxist theory of the relation between the
economic substructure and the superstructure can be rendered
plausible, this plausibility depends in large part on one's selecting
certain data, slurring over others and circumventing awkward
questions. For example, to maintain the theory I have to slur over
the fact that Christianity became the dominant religion in the late
Roman empire and was then accepted by the peoples who built up
the feudal society of the Middle Ages. And I have to avoid awkward
questions about the relation between the development of the
forces of production and the origins of Islam. If such questions
are pressed, I refer to factors which lie outside my original
explanation of the ideological superstructure, while at the same
time I continue to assert the truth of this explanation. And I
blithely admit that the superstructure can itself exercise an
influence on the substructure and that changes can take place in
the former independently of changes in the latter, while at the
same time I refuse to admit that these concessions are inconsistent
with my original position. Why, indeed, should I admit this? For I
have spoken of the relation between the substructure and the
superstructure as a 'conditioning' of the latter by the former. And
I can understand this term in a weak or in a strong sense according
to the demands of the particular situation which I am considering.

We have seen that for Marx and Engels the dialectic is not something imposed on the world from without, the expression of
absolute Thought or Reason. The dialectic as thought is the
reflection of the inner movement of reality, of its immanent laws
of development. And in this case the movement is presumably
necessary and inevitable. This does not mean, of course, that
human thought has no part to play. For there is continuity between
Nature, human society and the world of ideas. We have already

quoted Engels' statement that 'dialectic is nothing else but the science of the general laws of movement and development in Nature, human society and thought'.[1] But the total process would then be the necessary working-out of immanent laws. And in this case there does not seem to be much room for revolutionary activity. Or, rather, revolutionary activity would be a phase of an inevitable process.

From one point of view this mechanical view of the dialectic seems to be required by the conviction of Marx and Engels that the coming of communism is inevitable. But if the dialectic as operating in human history is, as Engels at any rate suggests, continuous with the dialectic as operating in Nature, that is, if it is ultimately a question of the self-development of auto-dynamic matter, it is difficult to see why the process should ever stop or reach a stage where contradictions and antagonisms disappear. Indeed, there is a passage in the *Dialectics of Nature* where Engels remarks that matter goes through an eternal cycle and that with an 'iron necessity' it will exterminate its highest product, namely the thinking mind, and produce it again somewhere else at another time.[2]

But this idea hardly fits in with the apocalyptic aspect of Marxism, which requires the vision of history as moving towards a goal, a terrestrial Paradise. The two ways of looking at the matter are perhaps compatible up to a point. That is to say, it is possible to look on each cycle as leading up to a peak point, as it were. But the more one emphasizes the teleological aspect of history, its movement from primitive communism, the age of innocence, through the Fall, as represented by the introduction of private property and the consequent emergence of selfishness, exploitation and class antagonism, up to the recovery of communism at a higher level and the overcoming of man's self-alienation, so much the more does one tend to reintroduce surreptitiously the notion of the working out of a plan, the realization of an Idea.

In other words, there is a fundamental ambiguity in Marxism. If some aspects are stressed, we have a mechanistic interpretation of the historical process. If other aspects are stressed, the system seems to demand the reintroduction of what Marx and Engels called idealism. Nor is this surprising. For in part Marxism is a transformation of idealism, and elements of this particular source

[1] *Anti-Dühring*, p. 144 (p. 193).    [2] *Dialektik der Natur*, p. 28 (p. 54).

linger on. The alliance between dialectic and materialism is not altogether an easy one. For, as Marx and Engels were well aware, dialectics originally referred to a movement of thought. And though they located the movement of the dialectic primarily in the object of thought and only secondarily and by way of reflection in human thinking, this transposition inevitably tends to suggest that the historical process is the self-development of an Idea. The alternative is to interpret the process as a purely mechanical one.[1]

This is a matter of some importance. Left to itself, so to speak, Marxism tends to divide into divergent lines of thought. It is possible to emphasize the ideas of necessity, inevitability, determinism, and it is possible to emphasize the ideas of deliberate revolutionary activity and of free action. It is possible to emphasize the materialist element, and it is possible to emphasize the dialectical element. It is also possible, of course, to attempt to hold together all these different aspects, in spite of the ambiguities to which this attempt gives rise. But it is significant that even in the Soviet Union different lines of interpretation and development have manifested themselves. If the emergence of these different lines of thought has been held in check, this has been due to the constraining force of the Party Line, to an extra-philosophical factor and not to any intrinsic consistency and lack of ambiguity in the thought of Marx and Engels themselves.

From one point of view criticism of the type suggested in the foregoing paragraphs[2] is beside the point. That is to say, if we choose to regard Marxism as an interesting 'vision' of the world, detailed criticism necessarily seems pedantic and tiresome. Philosophers who provide striking visions of the world are inclined to take one aspect of reality and to use it as a key to unlock all doors. And detailed criticism, it may be said, is out of place. For it is the very exaggeration involved in the vision which enables us to see the world in a new light. When we have done so, we can forget about the exaggeration: the vision has accomplished its purpose. Thus the philosophy of Marx and Engels enables us to see the importance and far-reaching influence of man's economic life, of the so-called substructure. And it is largely because of the exaggerations involved that it can have this effect, breaking the rigidity of other pictures or interpretations of the world. Once we

---

[1] It is probably Engels, with his extension of the dialectic to Nature, who provides most ground for a mechanical interpretation.

[2] The lines of criticism suggested are not, of course, in any way new. They are familiar enough to 'bourgeois' philosophers, that is to say, to objective observers.

have seen what Marx and Engels are drawing attention to, we can forget Marxism as expounded in their writings: the essence of their vision passes into the common outlook. It is pedantic to worry about such detailed questions as the precise relation between freedom and necessity, the precise meaning of 'condition', the exact extent to which morality and values are thought to be relative, and so on.

This attitude is indeed understandable. But the Marxist theory of history is not simply a striking nineteenth-century vision of the world which has made its contribution to human thought and then relapsed into the historical background. It is a living and influential system which professes to be a scientific analysis of historical development, an analysis which permits prediction, and it is at the same time the creed or faith of groups whose importance in the modern world nobody would deny. It is therefore appropriate to point out that the transformation of this philosophy into the dogmatic creed of a powerful Party has arrested the natural development of the different lines of thought to which its diverse aspects might otherwise be expected to have given rise.

The Communist theoretician would perhaps reply that it is not a question of the philosophy of Marx and Engels having been adopted by a Party and transformed into a weapon or instrument. For it was this from the beginning. And it is precisely this fact which distinguishes it from all previous philosophies. Marx always thought of his philosophy as a means of transforming the world and not simply as an interpretation of it. But though this is doubtless true, the question then arises whether Marxism falls under its own concept of ideologies as relative to a passing economic structure or whether it transcends this status and represents absolute truth. If Marxism is relative to the situation in which the proletariat is opposed to the bourgeoisie, it should pass away when this antagonism has been overcome. If, however, it represents absolute truth, how is this claim to be reconciled with what Marx and Engels have to say about eternal truths, natural laws and so on?

And yet all criticism based on the internal ambiguities of the philosophy of Marx and Engels seems in a certain sense to be futile. It may have an effect on those, if any, who are attracted to Marxism simply because they think that it is 'scientific'. But it is not likely to have much effect on those who are primarily attracted by the ideal of human society which Marxism represents. What is needed is the delineation of another ideal, based on a more adequate view of man and his vocation and on a more adequate view of the nature of reality.

The philosophy of Marx and Engels has, of course, undergone some development. Attention has been paid, for example, to the theory of knowledge. And certain modern Thomists seem to think that among contemporary philosophical traditions Marxism, as represented by the philosophers of the Soviet Union, offers them a common basis of discussion because of its insistence on realism in epistemology and ontology. This is a theme which goes beyond the scope of this book. But one may remark that even if realism in the sense intended is common to Thomism and to Marxism, Thomism is for the Marxist an 'idealist' system. For it maintains the priority of Mind or Spirit to matter. And it was precisely this doctrine which Marx and Engels were concerned to deny when they affirmed the truth of materialism.

### CHAPTER XVII

# KIERKEGAARD

*Introductory remarks—Life and writings—The individual and
the crowd—The dialectic of the stages and truth as subjectivity
—The idea of existence—The concept of dread—The influence of
Kierkegaard.*

1. In the chapters on the development of Schelling's thought
mention was made of the distinction which he came to draw
between negative and positive philosophy. The former moves in
the realm of ideas: it is a deduction of concepts or essences. The
latter is concerned with the *that* of things, with existence. Positive
philosophy cannot simply dispense with negative philosophy. At
the same time negative philosophy by itself by-passes actual
existence. And its chief modern representative is Hegel.

Among Schelling's hearers at Berlin, when he expounded this
distinction, was the Dane, Søren Kierkegaard. For the way in
which the German thinker developed his own idea of positive
philosophy Kierkegaard had little sympathy. But he was in full
agreement with Schelling's attack on Hegel. Not that Kierkegaard
was lacking in admiration for Hegel or in appreciation of the
magnitude of his achievement. On the contrary, he regarded Hegel
as the greatest of all speculative philosophers and as a thinker who
had achieved a stupendous intellectual *tour de force*. But this, in
Kierkegaard's opinion, was precisely the trouble with Hegelianism,
namely that it was a gigantic *tour de force* and nothing more. Hegel
sought to capture all reality in the conceptual net of his dialectic,
while existence slipped through the meshes.

Existence, as will be explained presently, was for Kierkegaard
a category relating to the free individual. In his use of the term,
to exist means realizing oneself through free choice between
alternatives, through self-commitment. To exist, therefore, means
becoming more and more an individual and less and less a mere
member of a group. It means, one can say, transcending universality
in favour of individuality. Hence Kierkegaard has scant sympathy
with what he took to be Hegel's view, that a man realizes his true
self or essence in proportion as he transcends his particularity and

becomes a spectator of all time and existence as a moment in the life of universal thought. Hegelianism, in Kierkegaard's opinion, had no place for the existing individual: it could only universalize him in a fantastic manner. And what could not be universalized it dismissed as unimportant, whereas in point of fact it is that which is most important and significant. To merge or sink oneself in the universal, whether this is conceived as the State or as universal Thought, is to reject personal responsibility and authentic existence.

Kierkegaard's emphasis on self-commitment through free choice, a self-commitment whereby the individual resolutely chooses one alternative and rejects another, is an aspect of his general tendency to underline antitheses and distinctions rather than to gloss them over. For example, God is not man, and man is not God. And the gulf between them cannot be bridged by dialectical thinking. It can be bridged only by the leap of faith, by a voluntary act by which man relates himself to God and freely appropriates, as it were, his relation as creature to the Creator, as a finite individual to the transcendent Absolute. Hegel, however, confounds what ought to be distinguished. And his dialectical mediation between the infinite and the finite, between God and man, leaves us in the end with neither God nor man but only with the pale ghost of hypostatized thought, dignified by the name of absolute Spirit.

With this emphasis on the individual, on choice, on self-commitment, Kierkegaard's philosophical thought tends to become a clarification of issues and an appeal to choose, an attempt to get men to see their existential situation and the great alternatives with which they are faced. It is certainly not an attempt to master all reality by thought and to exhibit it as a necessary system of concepts. This idea was quite foreign and repugnant to his mind. In his view speculative systematic philosophy, the greatest example of which was for him absolute idealism, radically misrepresented human existence. The really important problems, that is, the problems which are of real importance for man as the existing individual, are not solved by thought, by adopting the absolute standpoint of the speculative philosopher, but by the act of choice, on the level of existence rather than on that of detached, objective reflection.

As one might expect, Kierkegaard's philosophy is intensely personal. In one sense, of course, every philosopher worthy of the name is a personal thinker. For it is he who does the thinking.

But with Kierkegaard there is a closer connection between his life and his philosophy than in the case of many other philosophers. He does not simply take over traditional problems or the problems most discussed in contemporary philosophical circles and then attempt to solve them in a purely objective and disinterested spirit. His problems arise out of his own life, in the sense that in the first instance they arise for him in the form of alternatives presented for his own personal choice, a choice involving a radical self-commitment. His philosophy is, as it were, a lived philosophy. And one of his objections to Hegelianism is that one cannot live by it. Obviously, Kierkegaard has to universalize. Without universalization there would be only autobiography. At the same time it is abundantly clear that it is the actor who speaks rather than the spectator.

From one point of view this feature of his philosophy constitutes its weakness. That is to say, his thought may appear too subjective, too hostile to objectivity. In fact, some would refuse it the name of philosophy at all. But from another point of view the intensely personal character of Kierkegaard's thought constitutes its strength. For it gives to his writing a degree of seriousness and depth which sets it entirely outside the concept of philosophy as a game or as an academic pastime for those who have the requisite aptitude and inclination.

In view of the fact that Kierkegaard's thought is developed in conscious opposition to Hegelianism or, if preferred, to speculative philosophy as represented by absolute idealism, as well as for chronological reasons, I have included the chapter on his philosophy in this part of the present volume. But if one were to neglect chronology and take effective influence as a standard, one would have to postpone consideration of his thought to a later stage. For though he was one of the most passionate thinkers of his period, he excited very little real interest at the time. A Dane, he was first discovered, so to speak, by the Germans in the first decades of the present century, and he has exercised a profound influence on some phases of the existentialist movement and on modern Protestant theology of the type represented by Karl Barth. Kierkegaard's preoccupation with Hegelianism as the dominant philosophy of his time and cultural milieu constitutes the dating element in his thought. But the ideas which he opposed to Hegelianism have a quite independent significance, and they have exercised a widespread influence in another and later cultural context.

2. Søren Aabye Kierkegaard was born at Copenhagen on May 15th, 1813. He was given an extremely religious upbringing by his father, a man who suffered from melancholia and imagined that the curse of God hung over him and his family.[1] And Kierkegaard was himself affected to some degree by this melancholy, concealed beneath a display of sarcastic wit.

In 1830 Kierkegaard matriculated in the university of Copenhagen and chose the faculty of theology, doubtless in accordance with his father's wishes. But he paid little attention to theological studies and devoted himself instead to philosophy, literature and history. It was at this time that he gained his knowledge of Hegelianism. During this period Kierkegaard was very much the observer of life, cynical and disillusioned, yet devoted to the social life of the university. Estranged from his father and his father's religion, he spoke of the 'stuffy atmosphere' of Christianity and maintained that philosophy and Christianity were incompatible. Religious disbelief was accompanied by laxity in moral standards. And Kierkegaard's general attitude at this time fell under the heading of what he later called the aesthetic stage on life's way.

In the spring of 1836 Kierkegaard appears to have had a temptation to commit suicide, having been overcome by a vision of his inner cynicism. But in June of that year he underwent a kind of moral conversion, in the sense that he adopted moral standards and made an attempt, even if not always successful, to live up to them.[2] This period corresponds to the ethical stage in his later dialectic.

On May 19th, 1838, the year in which his father died, Kierkegaard experienced a religious conversion, accompanied by an 'indescribable joy'. He resumed the practice of his religion and in 1840 he passed his examinations in theology. He became engaged to Regina Olsen, but a year later he broke off the engagement. He evidently thought that he was unsuited for married life, a correct idea one would imagine. But he had also become convinced that he was a man with a mission, and that marriage would interfere with it.

In 1843 Kierkegaard published *Either-Or*, a title which well expresses his attitude to life and his abhorrence of what he took to be Hegel's 'Both-And', *Fear and Trembling* and *Repetition*. These

[1] As a boy, Kierkegaard's father had tended sheep on a Jutland heath. One day afflicted with hunger, cold and loneliness, he had cursed God. And this incident was indelibly printed on his memory.

[2] I do not mean to imply that Kierkegaard had ever led what would be generally understood by a thoroughly immoral life. It was more a question of a change of interior attitude from a rejection to an acceptance of ethical self-commitment.

works were followed in 1844 by *The Concept of Dread* and *Philo-sophical Fragments*, in 1845 by *Stages on Life's Way* and in 1846 by the *Concluding Unscientific Postscript* which, though its name may not suggest it, is a large and weighty tome. He also published some 'edifying discourses' in these years. The works of this period appeared under various pseudonyms, though the identity of the author was well enough known at Copenhagen. As far as the Christian faith was concerned, it was presented from the point of view of an observer, by indirect communication as Kierkegaard put it, rather than from the point of view of an apostle intent on direct communication of the truth.

In the spring of 1848 Kierkegaard enjoyed a religious experience which, as he wrote in his *Journal*, changed his nature and impelled him to direct communication. He did not at once abandon the use of pseudonyms, but with *Anti-Climacus* the change to a direct and positive presentation of the standpoint of Christian faith becomes apparent. The year 1848 saw the publication of *Christian Discourses*, and *The Point of View* was also composed at this time, though it was published only after Kierkegaard's death. *The Sickness unto Death* appeared in 1849.

Kierkegaard was meditating a frontal attack on the Danish State Church which, in his opinion, scarcely deserved any more the name of Christian. For as far as its official representatives at least were concerned, it appeared to him to have watered down Christianity to a polite moral humanism with a modicum of religious beliefs calculated not to offend the susceptibilities of the educated. However, to avoid wounding Bishop Mynster, who had been a friend of his father, Kierkegaard did not open fire until 1854, after the prelate's death. A vigorous controversy ensued in the course of which Kierkegaard maintained that what he represented was simply ordinary honesty. The emasculated Christianity of the established Church should recognize and admit that it was not Christianity.

Kierkegaard died on November 4th, 1855. At his funeral there was an unfortunate scene when his nephew interrupted the Dean to protest against the appropriation by the Danish Church of a man who had so vigorously condemned it.

3. There is an obvious sense in which every human being is and remains an individual, distinct from other persons and things. In this sense of individuality even the members of an enraged mob are individuals. At the same time there is a sense in which the

individuality of the members of such a mob is sunk in a common consciousness. The mob is possessed, as it were, by a common emotion, and it is a notorious fact that a mob is capable of performing actions which its members would not perform precisely as individuals.

This is indeed an extreme example. But I mention it to show in a simple way that we can quite easily give a cash value to the idea of man's being more or less of an individual. One might, of course, take less dramatic examples. Suppose that my opinions are dictated predominantly by what 'one thinks', my emotive reactions by what 'one feels', and my actions by the social conventions of my environment. To the extent that this is the case I can be said to think, feel and act as a member of 'the One', as a member of an impersonal collectivity, rather than as this individual. If, however, I become aware of my anonymous status, so to speak, and begin to form my own principles of conduct and to act resolutely in accordance with them, even if this means acting in a way quite opposed to the customary ways of acting of my social environment, there is a sense in which I can be said to have become more of an individual, in spite of the fact that in another sense I am no more and no less an individual than I was before.

If space permitted, these concepts would obviously require careful analysis. But even in this unanalysed state they may serve to facilitate understanding of the following quotation from Kierkegaard. 'A crowd—not this crowd or that, the crowd now living or the crowd long deceased, a crowd of humble people or of superior people, of rich or of poor, etc.—a crowd in its very concept is the untruth, by reason of the fact that it renders the individual completely impenitent and irresponsible, or at least weakens his sense of responsibility by reducing it to a fraction.' Kierkegaard is not, of course, concerned simply with the dangers of allowing oneself to become a member of a crowd in the sense of mob. His point is that philosophy, with its emphasis on the universal rather than on the particular, has tried to show that man realizes his true essence in proportion as he rises above what is contemptuously regarded as his mere particularity and becomes moment in the life of the universal. This theory, Kierkegaard argues, is false, whether the universal is considered as the State or as the economic or social class or as Humanity or as absolute Thought. 'I have endeavoured to express the thought that the

---

[1] *The Point of View*, p. 114 (translated by W. Lowrie, London, 1939).

mploy the category "race" to indicate what it is to be a man, and
specially as an indication of the highest attainment, is a mis-
nderstanding and mere paganism, because the race, mankind,
iffers from an animal race not merely by its general superiority as
race, but by the *human* characteristic that every single individual
vithin the race (not merely distinguished individuals but every
ndividual) is more than the race. For to relate oneself to God
s a far higher thing than to be related to the race and through the
ace to God.'[1]

The last sentence of this quotation indicates the general
irection of Kierkegaard's thought. The highest self-actualization
f the individual is the relating of oneself to God, not as the
niversal, absolute Thought, but as the absolute Thou. But
urther explanation of what Kierkegaard means by becoming the
ndividual is best reserved for the context of his theory of the three
tages. For the moment it is sufficient to notice that it means the
pposite of self-dispersal in 'the One' or self-submerging in the
niversal, however this may be conceived. The exaltation of the
niversal, the collectivity, the totality, is for Kierkegaard 'mere
aganism'. But he also insists that historic paganism was orientated
owards Christianity, whereas the new paganism is a falling away
r an apostasy from Christianity.[2]

4. In *The Phenomenology of Spirit* Hegel expounded his
nasterly dialectic of the stages by which the mind awakens to self-
onsciousness, to universal consciousness and to the standpoint of
bsolute Thought. Kierkegaard also expounds a dialectic. But it is
adically different from that of Hegel. In the first place it is the
rocess by which spirit is actualized in the form of individuality,
he individual existent, not in the form of the all-comprehensive
niversal. In the second place the transition from one stage to the
ext is accomplished not by thinking but by choice, by an act of
he will, and in this sense by a leap. There is no question of over-
oming antitheses by a process of conceptual synthesis: there is a
hoice between alternatives, and the choice of the higher alternative,
he transition to a higher stage of the dialectic, is a willed self-
ommitment of the whole man.

The first stage or sphere is described as the aesthetic.[3] And it is

---

[1] *Ibid*, pp. 88–9, in Note.
[2] See, for example, *The Sickness unto Death*, pp. 73–4 (translated by W. Lowrie,
rinceton and London, 1941).
[3] This is discussed, for instance, in the first volume of *Either-Or* and in the first
art of *Stages on Life's Way*.

characterized by self-dispersal on the level of sense. The aesthetic man is governed by sense, impulse and emotion. But we must not conceive him as being simply and solely the grossly sensual man. The aesthetic stage can also be exemplified, for instance, in the poet who transmutes the world into an imaginative realm and in the romantic. The essential features of the aesthetic consciousness are the absence of fixed universal moral standards and of determinate religious faith and the presence of a desire to enjoy the whole range of emotive and sense experience. True, there can be discrimination. But the principle of discrimination is aesthetic rather than obedience to a universal moral law considered as the dictate of impersonal reason. The aesthetic man strives after infinity, but in the sense of a bad infinity which is nothing else but the absence of all limitations other than those imposed by his own tastes. Open to all emotional and sense experience, sampling the nectar from every flower, he hates all that would limit his field of choice and he never gives definite form to his life. Or, rather, the form of his life is its very formlessness, self-dispersal on the level of sense.

To the aesthetic man his existence seems to be the expression of freedom. Yet he is more than a psycho-physical organism, endowed with emotive and imaginative power and the capacity for sense enjoyment. 'The soulish-bodily synthesis in every man is planned with a view to being spirit, such is the building; but the man prefers to dwell in the cellar, that is, in the determinants of sensuousness.'[1] And the aesthetic consciousness or attitude to life may be accompanied by a vague awareness of this fact, by a vague dissatisfaction with the dispersal of the self in the pursuit of pleasure and sense enjoyment. Further, the more aware a man becomes that he is living in what Kierkegaard calls the cellar of the building, the more subject he becomes to 'despair'. For he finds that there is no remedy, no salvation, at the level on which he stands. He is faced, therefore, with two alternatives. Either he must remain in despair on the aesthetic level or he must make the transition to the next level by an act of choice, by self-commitment. Mere thinking will not do the trick for him. It is a question of choice; either-or.

The second stage is the ethical. A man accepts determinate moral standards and obligations, the voice of universal reason, and thus gives form and consistency to his life. If the aesthetic stage is

[1] *The Sickness unto Death*, p. 67.

ypified by Don Juan, the ethical stage is typified by Socrates. And
, simple example of the transition from the aesthetic to the moral
onsciousness is for Kierkegaard that of the man who renounces
he satisfaction of his sexual impulse according to passing attraction
.nd enters into the state of marriage, accepting all its obligations.
'or marriage is an ethical institution, an expression of the universal
aw of reason.

Now, the ethical stage has its own heroism. It can produce what
Kierkegaard calls the tragic hero. 'The tragic hero renounces
iimself in order to express the universal.'[1] This is what Socrates
lid, and Antigone was prepared to give her life in defence of the
inwritten natural law. At the same time the ethical consciousness
is such does not understand sin. The ethical man may take account
of human weakness, of course; but he thinks that it can be overcome by strength of will, enlightened by clear ideas. In so far as he
exemplifies the attitude characteristic of the ethical consciousness
is such he believes in man's moral self-sufficiency. Yet in point of
act a man can come to realize his own inability to fulfil the moral
aw as it should be fulfilled and to acquire perfect virtue. He can
come to an awareness of his lack of self-sufficiency and of his sin
ind guilt. He has then arrived at the point at which he is faced
vith the choice or rejection of the standpoint of faith. Just as
despair' forms, as it were, the antithesis to the aesthetic consciousness, an antithesis which is overcome or resolved by ethical self-
commitment, so consciousness of sin forms the antithesis to the
ethical stage, and this antithesis is overcome only by the act of
aith, by relating oneself to God.

To affirm one's relationship to God, the personal and transcendent Absolute, is to affirm oneself as spirit. 'By relating itself
o its own self and by willing to be itself, the self is grounded
ransparently in the Power which constituted it. And this formula
. . is the definition of faith.'[2] Every man is, as it were, a mixture
of the finite and the infinite. Considered precisely as finite, he is
separated from God, alienated from him. Considered as infinite,
nan is not indeed God, but he is a movement towards God, the
novement of the spirit. And the man who appropriates and
affirms his relationship to God in faith becomes what he really is,
the individual before God.

To emphasize the difference between the second and third

[1] *Fear and Trembling*, p. 109 (translated by R. Payne, London, 1939).
[2] *The Sickness unto Death*, p. 216.

stages Kierkegaard uses as a symbol Abraham's willingness to sacrifice his son Isaac at God's command. The tragic hero, such as Socrates, sacrifices himself for the universal moral law; but Abraham, as Kierkegaard puts it, does nothing for the universal 'So we stand in the presence of the paradox. Either the Individual as the Individual can stand in an absolute relation to the Absolute and then ethics is not supreme, or Abraham is lost: he is neither a tragic hero nor an aesthetic hero.'[1] Needless to say, Kierkegaard does not intend to enunciate the general proposition that religion involves the negation of morality. What he means is that the man of faith is directly related to a personal God whose demands are absolute and cannot be measured simply by the standards of the human reason. At the back of Kierkegaard's mind there is doubtless the memory of his behaviour towards Regina Olsen. Marriage is an ethical institution, the expression of the universal. And if ethics, the universal, is supreme, Kierkegaard's conduct was inexcusable. He was justified only if he had a personal mission from God whose absolute demands are addressed to the individual. Obviously, I do not intend to suggest that Kierkegaard is universalizing his own experience in the sense of assuming that everyone has the same specific experience. He universalizes it in the sense that he reflects on its general significance.

As Kierkegaard's dialectic is one of discontinuity, in the sense that the transition from one stage to another is made by choice, by self-commitment, and not through a continuous process of conceptual mediation, he not unnaturally plays down the role of reason and emphasizes that of will when he is treating of religious faith. In his view faith is a leap. That is to say, it is an adventure, a risk, a self-commitment to an objective uncertainty. God is the transcendent Absolute, the absolute Thou; he is not an object the existence of which can be proved. True, God reveals himself to the human conscience in the sense that man can become aware of his sin and alienation and his need of God. But man's response is a venture, an act of faith in a Being who lies beyond the reach of speculative philosophy. And this act of faith is not something which can be performed once and for all. It has to be constantly repeated. It is true that God has revealed himself in Christ, the God-Man. But Christ is the Paradox, to the Jews a stumbling-block and to the Greeks foolishness. Faith is always a venture, a leap.

Looked at from one point of view Kierkegaard's account of the

---

[1] *Fear and Trembling*, p. 171.

standpoint of faith is a vigorous protest against the way in which speculative philosophy, represented principally by Hegelianism, blurs the distinction between God and man and rationalizes the Christian dogmas, turning them into philosophically-demonstrated conclusions. In the Hegelian system 'the qualitative distinction between God and man is pantheistically abolished'.[1] The system does indeed hold out the attractive prospect of 'an illusory land, which to a mortal eye might appear to yield a certainty higher than that of faith'.[2] But the mirage is destructive of faith, and its claim to represent Christianity is bogus. 'The entirely unsocratic tract of modern philosophy is that it wants to make itself and us believe that it is Christianity.'[3] In other words, Kierkegaard refuses to admit that in this life there can be a higher standpoint than that of faith. The vaunted transformation of faith into speculative knowledge is an illusion.

But though in such passages it is Hegelianism which Kierkegaard has principally in mind, there is no adequate ground for saying that he would have had much sympathy with the idea of proving God's existence by metaphysical argument provided that an unequivocally theistic idea of God were maintained. In his view the fact that man is held eternally accountable for belief or disbelief shows that belief is not a matter of accepting the conclusion of a demonstrative argument but rather a matter of will. Catholic theologians would obviously wish to make some distinctions here. But Kierkegaard was not a Catholic theologian. And the point is that he deliberately emphasized the nature of faith as a leap. It was not simply a case of opposition to Hegelian rationalism.

This comes out clearly in his famous interpretation of truth as subjectivity. '*An objective uncertainty held fast in an appropriation-process of the most passionate inwardness is the truth*, the highest truth attainable for an *existing* individual.'[4] Kierkegaard is not denying that there is any such thing as objective, impersonal truth. But mathematical truths, for example, do not concern the 'existing individual' as such. That is to say, they are irrelevant to a man's life of total self-commitment. He accepts them. He cannot do otherwise. But he does not stake his whole being on them. That on which I stake my whole being is not something which I cannot

---

[1] *The Sickness unto Death*, p. 192.
[2] *Concluding Unscientific Postscript*, p. 213 (translated by D. F. Swenson, Princeton and London, 1941).
[3] *The Sickness unto Death*, p. 151.
[4] *Concluding Unscientific Postscript*, p. 182.

deny without logical contradiction or something which is so obviously true that I cannot deny it without palpable absurdity. It is something which I can doubt but which is so important to me that if I accept it, I do so with a passionate self-commitment. It is in a sense *my* truth. 'The truth is precisely the venture which chooses an objective uncertainty with the passion of the infinite. I contemplate the order of nature in the hope of finding God, and I see omnipotence and wisdom; but I also see much else that disturbs my mind and excites anxiety. The sum of all this is an objective uncertainty. But it is for this very reason that the inwardness becomes as intense as it is, for it embraces this objective uncertainty with the entire passion of the infinite.'[1]

Obviously, truth as so described is precisely what Kierkegaard means by faith. The definition of truth as subjectivity and the definition of faith are the same. 'Without risk there is no faith. Faith is precisely the contradiction between the infinite passion of the individual's inwardness and the objective uncertainty.'[2] Kierkegaard does indeed assert more than once that the eternal truth is not in itself a paradox. But it becomes paradoxical in relation to us. One can indeed see some evidence in Nature of God's work, but at the same time one can see much which points in the opposite direction. There is, and remains, 'objective uncertainty', whether we look at Nature or at the Gospels. For the idea of the God-Man is itself paradoxical for the finite reason. Faith grasps the objectively uncertain and affirms it; but it has to maintain itself, as it were, over a fathomless sea. Religious truth exists only in the 'passionate' appropriation of the objectively uncertain.[3]

In point of fact Kierkegaard does not say that there are no rational motives at all for making the act of faith and that it is a purely arbitrary act of capricious choice. But he certainly takes delight in minimizing the rational motives for religious belief and in emphasizing the subjectivity of truth and the nature of faith as a leap. Hence he inevitably gives the impression that faith is for him an arbitrary act of the will. And Catholic theologians at least criticize him on this score. But if we prescind from the theological analysis of faith and concentrate on the psychological aspect of the matter, there is no difficulty in recognizing, whether one is Catholic or Protestant, that there are certainly some who understand very well from their own experience what Kierkegaard is

---

[1] *Concluding Unscientific Postscript*, p. 182.          [2] *Ibid.*
[3] We have to remember that for Kierkegaard faith is a self-commitment to the absolute and transcendent Thou, the personal God, rather than to propositions.

driving at when he describes faith as a venture or risk. And, in general, Kierkegaard's phenomenological analysis of the three distinct attitudes or levels of consciousness which he describes possess a value and a stimulative power which is not destroyed by his characteristic exaggerations.

5. In the passage quoted above which gives Kierkegaard's unconventional definition of truth mention is made of the *existing* individual'. It has already been explained that the term 'existence', as used by Kierkegaard, is a specifically human category which cannot be applied, for example, to a stone. But something more must be said about it here.

To illustrate his use of the concept of existence Kierkegaard employs the following analogy. A man sits in a cart and holds the reins, but the horse goes along its accustomed path without any active control by the driver, who may be asleep. Another man actively guides and directs his horse. In one sense both men can be said to be drivers. But in another sense it is only the second man who can be said to be driving. In an analogous manner the man who drifts with the crowd, who merges himself in the anonymous 'One', can be said to exist in one sense of the term, though in another sense he cannot be said to exist. For he is not the 'existing individual' who strives resolutely towards an end which cannot be realized once and for all at a given moment and is thus in a constant state of becoming, making himself, as it were, by his repeated acts of choice. Again, the man who contents himself with the role of spectator of the world and of life and transmutes everything into a dialectic of abstract concepts exists indeed in one sense but not in another. For he wishes to understand everything and commits himself to nothing. The 'existing individual', however, is the actor rather than the spectator. He commits himself and so gives form and direction to his life. He ex-ists towards an end for which he actively strives by choosing this and rejecting that. In other words, the term 'existence' has with Kierkegaard more or less the same sense as the term 'authentic existence' as used by some modern existentialist philosophers.

If understood simply in this way, the term 'existence' is neutral, in the sense that it can be applied within any of the three stages of the dialectic. Indeed, Kierkegaard says explicitly that 'there are three spheres of existence: the aesthetic, the ethical, the religious'.[1] A man can 'exist' within the aesthetic sphere if he deliberately,

[1] *Concluding Unscientific Postscript*, p. 448.

resolutely and consistently acts as the aesthetic man, excluding alternatives. In this sense Don Juan typifies the existing individual within the aesthetic sphere. Similarly, the man who sacrifices his own inclinations to the universal moral law and constantly strives after the fulfilment of a moral ideal which beckons him ever forward is an existing individual within the ethical sphere. 'An existing individual is himself in process of becoming. . . . In existence the watchword is always *forward*.'[1]

But though the term 'existence' has indeed this wide field of application, it tends to take on a specifically religious connotation. Nor is this in any way surprising. For man's highest form of self-realization as spirit is for Kierkegaard his self-relating to the personal Absolute. 'Existence is a synthesis of the infinite and the finite, and the existing individual is both infinite and finite.'[2] But to say that the existing individual is infinite is not to identify him with God. It is to say that his becoming is a constant striving towards God. 'Existence itself, the act of existing, is a striving . . . (and) the striving is infinite.'[3] 'Existence is the child that is born of the infinite and the finite, the eternal and the temporal, and is therefore a constant striving.'[4] One can say, therefore, that existence comprises two moments: separation or finiteness and constant striving, in this context towards God. The striving must be constant, a constant becoming, because the self-relating to God in faith cannot be accomplished once and for all: it has to take the form of a constantly repeated self-commitment.

It can hardly be claimed that Kierkegaard's definition or descriptions of existence are always crystal clear. At the same time the general notion is intelligible enough. And it is clear that for him the existing individual *par excellence* is the individual before God, the man who sustains the standpoint of faith.

6. In the writings of the existentialists the concept of dread[5] is conspicuous. But the term is used by different writers in different ways. With Kierkegaard it has a religious setting. And in *The Concept of Dread* it has a close association with the idea of sin. However, one can, I think, broaden the range of application and say that dread is a state which precedes a qualitative leap from one stage in life's way to another.

---

[1] *Concluding Unscientific Postscript*, p. 368.
[2] *Ibid.*, p. 350.      [3] *Ibid.*, p. 84.      [4] *Ibid.*, p. 85.
[5] The Germans speak of *Angst*, the French of *angoisse*. Some English writers have employed 'anguish' or even 'anxiety'. I have retained 'dread'. In any case 'fear' should be avoided, for a reason explained in the text.

Dread is defined by Kierkegaard as a '*sympathetic antipathy and an antipathetic sympathy*'.[1] Take the case of the small boy who feels an attraction for adventure, 'a thirst for the prodigious, the mysterious'.[2] The child is attracted by the unknown, yet at the same time is repelled by it, as a menace to his security. Attraction and repulsion, sympathy and antipathy, are interwoven. The child is in a state of dread, but not of fear. For fear is concerned with something quite definite, real or imagined, a snake under the bed, a wasp threatening to sting, whereas dread is concerned with the as yet unknown and indefinite. And it is precisely the unknown, the mysterious, which both attracts and repels the child.

Kierkegaard applies this idea to sin. In the state of innocence, he says, spirit is in a dreaming state, in a state of immediacy. It does not yet know sin. Yet it can have a vague attraction, not for sin as something definite, but for the use of freedom and so for the possibility of sin. 'Dread is the possibility of freedom.'[3] Kierkegaard uses Adam as an illustration. When Adam, in the state of innocence, was told not to eat the fruit of the tree of the knowledge of good and evil under pain of death, he could not know what was meant either by evil or by death. For the knowledge could be obtained only by disobeying the prohibition. But the prohibition awoke in Adam 'the possibility of freedom . . . the alarming possibility of *being able*'.[4] And he was attracted and repelled by it at the same time.

But there is also, Kierkegaard says, a dread in relation to the good. Let us suppose, for example, a man sunk in sin. He may be aware of the possibility of emerging from this state, and he may be attracted by it. But at the same time he may be repelled by the prospect, inasmuch as he loves his state of sin. He is then possessed by dread of the good. And this is really a dread of freedom, if, that is to say, we suppose that the man is in the enslaving grip of sin. Freedom is for him the object of a sympathetic antipathy and an antipathetic sympathy. And this dread is itself the possibility of freedom.

The notion of dread may perhaps become clearer if we can apply it in this way. A man, let us suppose, has become conscious of sin and of his utter lack of self-sufficiency. And he is faced with the possibility of the leap of faith,[5] which, as we have seen, means self-commitment to an objective uncertainty, a leap into the unknown. He is rather like the man on the edge of the precipice

---

[1] *The Concept of Dread*, p. 38 (translated by W. Lowrie, Princeton and London, 1944).     [2] *Ibid.*     [3] *Ibid*, p. 139..     [4] *Ibid.*, p. 40.
[5] 'The opposite of sin is not virtue but faith'; *The Sickness unto Death*, p. 132.

who is aware of the possibility of throwing himself over and who feels attraction and repulsion at the same time. True, the leap of faith means salvation, not destruction. 'The dread of possibility holds him as its prey, until it can deliver him saved into the hands of faith. In no other place does he find repose. . . .'[1] This seems to imply that dread is overcome by the leap. But in so far at least as the maintenance of the standpoint of faith involves a repeated self-commitment to an objective uncertainty, it would appear that dread recurs as the emotive tonality of the repeated leap.

7. Kierkegaard was first and foremost a religious thinker. And though for his actual contemporaries he was pretty well a voice crying in the wilderness, his idea of the Christian religion has exercised a powerful influence on important currents of modern Protestant theology. Mention has already been made of the name of Karl Barth, whose hostility to 'natural theology' is very much in tune with Kierkegaard's attitude towards any invasion by metaphysics into the sphere of faith. It may be said, of course, and with justice, that in the type of theology represented by Karl Barth it is a case not so much of following Kierkegaard as of making a renewed contact with the original well-spring of Protestant thought and spirituality. But inasmuch as some of Kierkegaard's ideas were distinctively Lutheran, this was just one of the effects which his writings could and did exercise.

At the same time his writings are obviously capable of exercising an influence in other directions. On the one hand he had some very hard things to say about Protestantism, and we can discern a movement in his thought not only away from emasculated Protestantism but also from Protestantism as such. It is not my purpose to argue that if he had lived longer, he would have become a Catholic. Whether he would or not is a question which we cannot possibly answer. Hence it is unprofitable to discuss it. But in point of fact his writings have had the effect of turning some people's minds towards Catholicism which, as he remarked, has always maintained the ideal at any rate of what he called No. 1 Christianity. On the other hand one can envisage the possibility of his writings contributing to turn people away from Christianity altogether. One can imagine a man saying, 'Yes, I see the point. Kierkegaard is quite right. I am not really a Christian. And, what is more, I do not wish to be. No leaps for me, no passionate embracing of objective uncertainties.'

[1] *The Concept of Dread*, p. 141.

It is not so surprising, therefore, if in the development of the modern existentialist movement we find certain Kierkegaardian themes divorced from their original religious setting and employed in an atheistic system. This is notably the case in the philosophy of M. Sartre. With Karl Jaspers indeed, who of all the philosophers commonly classified as existentialists[1] stands nearest to Kierkegaard, the religious setting of the concept of existence is to a large extent retained.[2] But the philosophy of M. Sartre reminds us that the concepts of authentic existence, of free self-commitment and of dread are capable of displacement from this setting.

These remarks are certainly not meant to imply that the origins of modern existentialism can be attributed simply to the posthumous influence of Kierkegaard. This would be a gross mis-statement. But Kierkegaardian themes recur in existentialism, though the historical context has changed. And writers on the existentialist movement are perfectly justified in seeing in the Danish thinker its spiritual ancestor, though not, of course, its sufficient cause. At the same time Kierkegaard has exercised a stimulative influence on many people who would not call themselves existentialists or, for the matter of that, professional philosophers or theologians of any kind. As was remarked in the first section of this chapter, his philosophical thought tends to become both an attempt to get men to see their existential situation and the alternatives with which they are faced and an appeal to choose, to commit themselves, to become 'existing individuals'. It is also, of course, a protest in the name of the free individual or person against submergence in the collectivity. Kierkegaard indeed exaggerates. And the exaggeration becomes more evident when the concept of existence is deprived of the religious significance which he gave it. But exaggeration so often serves to draw attention to what is after all worth saying.

[1] Some of these, it is true, have repudiated the label. But we cannot discuss this matter here. In any case, 'existentialism', unless it is confined to the philosophy of M. Sartre, is a portmanteau term.

[2] Jaspers is a professional philosopher and a university professor, whereas it is difficult to imagine the eccentric and passionate Danish thinker as the occupant of any chair. But the life and thought of Kierkegaard (as of Nietzsche) has been for Jaspers a subject of prolonged meditation.

# PART III

## LATER CURRENTS OF THOUGHT

### CHAPTER XVIII

### NON-DIALECTICAL MATERIALISM

*Introductory remarks—The first phase of the materialist movement—Lange's criticism of materialism—Haeckel's monism —Ostwald's energeticism—Empirio-criticism considered as an attempt to overcome the opposition between materialism and idealism.*

1. THE collapse of absolute idealism was soon followed by the ris of a materialistic philosophy which did not stem, as did dialectica materialism, from left-wing Hegelianism but professed to be basec on and to follow from serious reflection on the empirical sciences Science has, of course, no intrinsic connection with philosophica materialism, even if the philosophies of Nature expounded by Schelling and Hegel did little to foster the conviction that th natural complement of science is metaphysical idealism. Further the leading German philosophers, apart from Marx, have certainly not been materialists. Hence I do not propose to devote much space to the nineteenth-century materialist movement in Germany. Bu it is as well to understand that there was such a movement. Anc though it did not represent any profound philosophical thought, i was none the less influential. Indeed, it was precisely because of it lack of profundity and its appeal to the prestige of science that a book such as Büchner's *Force and Matter* enjoyed a wide vogue anc passed through a great number of editions.

2. Among the German materialists prominent in the middle o the nineteenth century were Karl Vogt (1817–95), Heinrich Czolbe (1819–73), Jakob Moleschott (1822–93) and Ludwig Büchner (1824–99). Vogt, a zoologist and professor at Giessen fo a time, is memorable for his statement that the brain secretes thought as the liver secretes bile. His general outlook is indicatec by the title of his polemical work against the physiologist Rudol Wagner, *Blind Faith and Science* (*Kohlerglaube und Wissenschaft*

1854, literally *Faith of a Charcoal-burner and Science*). Rudolf Wagner had openly professed belief in divine creation, and Vogt attacked him in the name of science. Czolbe, author of a *New Exposition of Sensualism* (*Neue Darstellung des Sensualismus*, 1855) and of attacks on Kant, Hegel and Lotze, derived consciousness from sensation, which he interpreted in a manner reminiscent of Democritus. At the same time he admitted the presence in Nature of organic forms which are not susceptible of a purely mechanistic explanation.

Moleschott was a physiologist and doctor who had to abandon his chair at Utrecht in consequence of the opposition aroused by his materialistic theories. Subsequently he became a professor in Italy where he exercised a considerable influence on minds inclined to positivism and materialism. In particular he influenced Cesare Lombroso (1836–1909), the famous professor of criminal anthropology at Turin, who translated into Italian Moleschott's *The Cycle of Life* (*Der Kreislauf des Lebens*, 1852). In Moleschott's view the whole history of the universe can be explained in terms of an original matter, of which force or energy is an intrinsic and essential attribute. There is no matter without force, and no force without matter. Life is simply a state of matter itself. Feuerbach prepared the way for the destruction of all anthropomorphic, teleological interpretations of the world, and it is the task of modern science to continue and complete this work. There is no good reason for making a dichotomy between the natural sciences on the one hand and the study of man and his history on the other. Science can use the same principles of explanation in both cases.

The best known product of the earlier phase of German materialism is probably Büchner's *Force and Matter* (*Kraft und Stoff*, 1855), which became a kind of popular textbook of materialism and was translated into a number of foreign languages. The author condemned out of hand all philosophy which could not be understood by the ordinary educated reader. And for this very reason the book enjoyed considerable popularity. As its title indicates, force and matter are taken as sufficient principles of explanation. The spiritual soul, for example, is thrown overboard.

3. In 1866 Friedrich Albert Lange (1828–75) published his famous *History of Materialism* (*Geschichte des Materialismus*) in which he subjected the materialist philosophy to well-founded criticism from the point of view of a Neo-Kantian. If it is considered simply as a methodological principle in natural science,

materialism is to be affirmed. That is to say, the physicist, for example, should proceed as though there were only material things. Kant himself was of this opinion. The natural scientist is not concerned with spiritual reality. But though materialism is acceptable as a methodological principle in the field of natural science, it is no longer acceptable when it has been transformed into a metaphysics or general philosophy. In this form it becomes uncritical and naïve. For example, in empirical psychology it is quite right and proper to carry as far as possible the physiological explanation of psychical processes. But it is a sure sign of an uncritical and naïve outlook if it is supposed that consciousness itself is susceptible of a purely materialist interpretation. For it is only through consciousness that we know anything at all about bodies, nerves and so on. And the very attempt to develop a materialist reduction of consciousness reveals its irreducible character.

Further, the materialists betray their uncritical mentality when they treat matter, force, atoms and so forth as though they were things-in-themselves. In point of fact they are concepts formed by the mind or spirit in its effort to understand the world. We have indeed to make use of such concepts, but it is naïve to assume that their utility shows that they can properly be made the basis for a dogmatist materialist metaphysics. And this is what philosophical materialism really is.

4. Lange's criticism dealt a telling blow at materialism, all the more so because he did not confine himself to polemics but was at pains to show what was, in his opinion, the valid element in the materialist attitude. But, as one might expect, his criticism did not prevent a recrudescence of materialism, a second wave which appealed for support to the Darwinian theory of evolution as a proved factor which showed that the origin and development of man was simply a phase of cosmic evolution in general, that man's higher activities could be adequately explained in terms of this evolution, and that at no point was it necessary to introduce the notion of creative activity by a supramundane Being. The fact that there is no necessary connection between the scientific hypothesis of biological evolution and philosophical materialism was indeed clear to some minds at the time. But there were many people who either welcomed or attacked the hypothesis, as the case might be, because they thought that materialism was the natural conclusion to draw from it.

The characteristic popular expression of this second phase of the materialist movement in Germany was Haeckel's *The Riddle of the Universe* (*Die Welträtsel*, 1899). Ernst Haeckel (1834–1919) was for many years professor of zoology at Jena, and a number of his works treated simply of the results of his scientific research. Others, however, were devoted to expounding a monistic philosophy based on the hypothesis of evolution. Between 1859, the year which saw the publication of Darwin's *The Origin of Species by Means of Natural Selection*, and 1871, when Darwin's *The Descent of Man* appeared, Haeckel published several works on topics connected with evolution and made it clear that in his opinion Darwin had at last set the evolutionary hypothesis on a really scientific basis. On this basis Haeckel proceeded to develop a general monism and to offer it as a valid substitute for religion in the traditional sense. Thus in 1892 he published a lecture, with additional notes, bearing the title *Monism as Link between Religion and Science* (*Der Monismus als Band zwischen Religion und Wissenschaft*). And similar attempts to find in his monism a fulfilment of man's need for religion can be seen in *The Riddle of the Universe* and in *God-Nature, Studies in Monistic Religion* (*Gott-Natur, Studien über monistische Religion*, 1914).

Reflection on the world has given rise, Haeckel asserts, to a number of riddles or problems. Some of these have been solved, while others are insoluble and are no real problems at all. 'The monistic philosophy is ultimately prepared to recognize only one comprehensive riddle of the universe, the problem of substance.'[1] If this is understood to mean the problem of the nature of some mysterious thing-in-itself behind phenomena, Haeckel is prepared to grant that we are perhaps as unable to solve it as were 'Anaximander and Empedocles 2400 years ago'.[2] But inasmuch as we do not even know that there is such a thing-in-itself, discussion of its nature is fruitless. What has been made clear is 'the comprehensive law of substance',[3] the law of the conservation of force and matter. Matter and force or energy are the two attributes of substance, and the law of their conservation, when interpreted as the universal law of evolution, justifies us in conceiving the universe as a unity in which natural laws are eternally and universally valid. We thus arrive at a monistic interpretation of the universe which is based on the proofs of its unity and of the causal relation between

[1] *Die Welträtsel*, p. 10 (Leipzig, 1908 edition).
[2] *Ibid.*, p. 239.          [3] *Ibid.*

all phenomena. Further, this monism destroys the three principal dogmas of dualistic metaphysics, namely 'God, freedom and immortality'.[1]

Kant's theory of two worlds, the physical, material world and the moral, immaterial world, is thus excluded by the monistic philosophy. But it does not follow that there is no place in monism for an ethics, provided that it is grounded on the social instincts of man and not on some imagined categorical imperative. Monism acknowledges as its highest moral ideal the achievement of a harmony between egoism and altruism, self-love and love of the neighbour. 'Before all others it is the great English philosopher Herbert Spencer whom we have to thank for finding in the theory of evolution a basis for this monistic ethics.'[2]

Haeckel protests that materialism is an entirely inappropriate epithet to apply to his monistic philosophy. For while it does indeed reject the idea of immaterial spirit, it equally rejects the idea of a dead, spiritless matter. 'In every atom both are inseparably combined.'[3] But to say that in every atom spirit and matter (*Geist und Materie*) are combined is really to say that in every atom force and 'stuff' (*Kraft und Stoff*) are combined. And though Haeckel asserts that his philosophy might just as well be labelled spiritualism as materialism, it is evidently what most people would describe as materialism, an evolutionary version of it, it is true, but none the less materialism. His account of the nature of consciousness and reason makes this quite clear, whatever he may say to the contrary.

If the term 'materialism' is objectionable to Haeckel, so also is the term 'atheism'. The monistic philosophy is pantheistic, not atheistic: God is completely immanent and one with the universe. 'Whether we describe this impersonal "Almighty" as "God-Nature" (*Theophysis*) or as "All-God" (*Pantheos*) is ultimately a matter of indifference.'[4] It does not seem to have occurred to Haeckel that if pantheism consists in calling the universe 'God' and if religion consists in cultivating science, ethics and aesthetics as directed respectively towards the ideals of truth, goodness and beauty, pantheism is distinguishable from atheism only by the possible presence of a certain emotive attitude towards the universe in

[1] *Die Welträtsel*, pp. 140, 217 and 240.
[2] *Ibid.*, p. 218. If Haeckel were still alive, he would doubtless express appreciation of the ethical ideas of Professor Julian Huxley.
[3] *Der Monismus*, p. 27 (Stuttgart, 1905 edition).
[4] *Gott-Natur*, p. 38 (Leipzig, 1914).

those who call themselves pantheists which is not present in those who call themselves atheists. Haeckel does indeed make the suggestion that 'as the ultimate cause of all things "God" is the hypothetical "original ground of substance"'.[1] But this concept is presumably the same as that of the ghostly impersonal thing-in-itself which, as we have seen, Haeckel elsewhere dismisses from consideration. Hence his pantheism cannot amount to much more than calling the universe 'God' and entertaining a certain emotive attitude towards it.

5. In 1906 a German Monist Society (Monistenbund) was founded at Munich under the patronage of Haeckel,[2] and in 1912 *The Monist Century* (*Das monistische Jahrhundert*) was published by Ostwald, the then president of the Monist Society.

Wilhelm Ostwald (1853–1932) was a famous chemist, professor of chemistry first at Riga and afterwards at Leipzig, a recipient of the Nobel Prize (1909) and founder of the *Annalen der Natur-philosophie* (1901–21), in the last issue of which there appeared the German text of Ludwig Wittgenstein's *Tractatus logico-philo-sophicus*. In 1906 he resigned from his chair at Leipzig, and in subsequent years he published a considerable number of writings on philosophical topics.

In 1895 Ostwald published a book on *The Overcoming of Scientific Materialism* (*Die Ueberwindung des wissenschaftlichen Materialismus*). But the so-called overcoming of materialism meant for him the substitution of the concept of energy for that of matter. The fundamental element of reality is energy which in a process of transformations takes a variety of distinct forms. The different properties of matter are different forms of energy; and psychic energy, which can be either unconscious or conscious, constitutes another distinct level or form. The different forms or levels are irreducible, in the sense that one distinct form cannot be identified with another. At the same time they arise through transformation of the one ultimate reality, namely energy. Hence 'energeticism' is a monistic theory. It hardly fits in perhaps with Ostwald's own canons of scientific method, which exclude anything approaching metaphysical hypotheses. But when he turned to the philosophy of Nature he was in any case going beyond the limits of empirical science.

6. It is only in its crudest form that materialism involves the

---

[1] *Ibid.*
[2] The Society's guiding idea was that of science as providing a way of life.

assertion that all processes are material. But a philosophy could not be classified as materialist unless it at any rate maintained the priority of matter and that processes which cannot be properly described as material are emergents from matter or epiphenomenal to material processes. Similarly, though idealism does not involve the assertion that all things are ideas in any ordinary sense, a philosophy could not be properly described as a system of meta-physical idealism unless it at any rate held that Thought or Reason or Spirit is prior and that the material world is its expression or externalization. In any case the dispute between materialism and idealism presupposes a *prima facie* distinction between matter and spirit or thought. An attempt is then made to overcome the opposition by subordinating one term of the distinction to the other. One way, therefore, of excluding the dispute between materialism and idealism is to reduce reality to phenomena which cannot properly be described either as material or as spiritual.

We find such an attempt in the phenomenalism of Mach and Avenarius, which is commonly known as empirio-criticism. This is not to say that the two philosophers in question were simply concerned with overcoming the opposition between materialism and idealism. Mach, for instance, was largely concerned with the nature of physical science. At the same time they regarded their phenomenalism as eliminating the dualisms which give rise to metaphysical essays in unification. And it is from this point of view that their theory is considered here.

Richard Avenarius (1843–96), professor of physics at Zürich and author of a *Critique of Pure Experience* (*Kritik der reinen Erfahrung*, 1888–90) and *The Human Concept of the World* (*Der menschliche Weltbegriff*, 1891), sought to reveal the essential nature of pure experience, that is, of experience stripped of all added interpreta-tion. And he found the immediate data or elements of experience in sensations. These depend on changes in the central nervous system which are conditioned by the environment acting either as an external stimulus or by way of the process of nutrition. Further, the more the brain develops, the more is it excited by constant elements in the environment. Thus the impression of a familiar world is produced, a world in which one can feel secure. And increase in these feelings of familiarity and security is accompanied by a decrease in the impression of the world as enigmatic, problematic and mysterious. In fine, the unanswerable problems of metaphysics tend to be eliminated. And the theory of pure experience, with its reduction of both the outer and the inner worlds to sensations, excludes those dichotomies between the physical and the psychical, thing and thought, object and subject, which have formed the basis for such rival metaphysical theories as materialism and idealism.

A similar theory was produced, though by way of a rather different approach, by Ernst Mach (1838–1916) who was for many years a professor in the university of Vienna and published, in addition to works concerned with physical science, *Contributions to the Analysis of Sensations* (*Beiträge zur Analyse der Empfindungen*, 1886), and *Knowledge and Error* (*Erkenntnis und Irrtum*, 1905). Experience is reducible to sensations which are neither purely physical nor purely psychical but rather neutral. Mach thus tries to get behind the distinctions which philosophers have used as a basis for the construction of metaphysical theories. But he is more concerned with purifying physical science from metaphysical elements than with developing a general philosophy.[1] Arising out of our biological needs, science aims at control of Nature by enabling us to predict. For this purpose we have to practise an economy of thought, uniting phenomena by means of the fewest and simplest concepts possible. But though these concepts are indispensable instruments for rendering scientific prediction possible, they do not give us insight into causes or essences or substances in a metaphysical sense.

In *Materialism and Empirio-Criticism* (1909) Lenin maintained that the phenomenalism of Mach and Avenarius leads inevitably to idealism and thence to religious belief. For if things are reduced to sensations or sense-data, they must be mind-dependent. And as they can hardly be dependent simply on the individual human mind, they must be referred to a divine mind.

Historically, the phenomenalism of Mach and Avenarius formed part of the line of thought which issued in the neopositivism of the Vienna Circle in the twenties of the present century. It can hardly be said to have led to a revival of idealism, and much less of theism. It does not follow, however, that Lenin's point of view has nothing to be said for it. For example, as Avenarius had no intention of denying that there were things in some sense before there were human beings, he maintained that sensations could

---

[1] Mach rejects the concept of the ego as a spiritual substance standing over against Nature and interprets the self as a complex of phenomena which are continuous with Nature. But he does not work out this theory in any thorough-going manner, and he admits that the ego is the bond which unites experience.

exist before minds, as possible sensations. But unless the reduction of things to sensations is interpreted as equivalent to the statement, with which not even the most resolute realist would quarrel, that physical objects are in principle capable of being sensed if there is any sentient subject at hand, it becomes difficult to avoid some such conclusion as that drawn by Lenin. One can, of course, try to do so by speaking of *sensibilia* rather than of sensations. But in this case one either reinstates physical objects over against the mind or becomes involved in the same difficulty as before. Besides, it is absurd, in the opinion of the present writer, to reduce the self to a complex or succession of *sensibilia*. For the presence of the self as irreducible to *sensibilia* is a condition of the possibility of attempting such a reduction. Hence one would be left with the self on the one hand and *sensibilia* on the other, in other words with a dualism of the very type which empirio-criticism was concerned to overcome.[1] Mach's attempt to purify physical science from metaphysics is one thing: phenomenalism as a philosophical theory is quite another.

[1] The neopositivist attempted to transform phenomenalism from an ontological into a linguistic theory by saying that the statement that physical objects are sense-data means that a sentence in which a physical object is mentioned can be translated into a sentence or sentences in which only sense-data are mentioned, in such a way that if the original sentence is true (or false) the translation will be true (or false) and *vice versa*. But I do not think that this attempt proved to be successful.

### CHAPTER XIX

# THE NEO-KANTIAN MOVEMENT

*Introductory remarks—The Marburg School—The School of Baden—The pragmatist tendency—E. Cassirer; concluding observations—Some notes on Dilthey.*

1. IN 1865 Otto Liebmann (1840–1912), in his *Kant und die Epigonen*, raised the cry of 'Back to Kant!' This demand for a return to Kant was indeed perfectly understandable in the circumstances. On the one hand idealist metaphysics had produced a crop of systems which, when the first flush of enthusiasm had passed away, seemed to many to be incapable of providing anything which could properly be called knowledge and thus to justify Kant's attitude towards metaphysics. On the other hand materialism, while speaking in the name of science, proceeded to serve up its own highly questionable form of metaphysics and was blind to the limitations placed by Kant to the use which could legitimately be made of scientific concepts. In other words, both the idealists and the materialists justified by their fruits the limitations which Kant had set to man's theoretical knowledge. Was it not desirable, therefore, to turn back to the great thinker of modern times who by a careful critique of human knowledge had succeeded in avoiding the extravagances of metaphysics without falling into the dogmatism of the materialists? It was not a question of following Kant slavishly, but rather of accepting his general position or attitude and working on the lines which he had followed.

The Neo-Kantian movement became a powerful force in German philosophy. It became in fact the academic philosophy or 'School Philosophy' (*Schulphilosophie*), as the Germans say, and by the turn of the century most of the university chairs of philosophy were occupied by people who were in some degree at least representatives of the movement. But Neo-Kantianism assumed pretty well as many shapes as it had representatives. And we cannot possibly mention them all here. Some general indications of the principal lines of thought will have to suffice.

2. A distinction is drawn within the Neo-Kantian movement

between the Schools of Marburg and Baden. The Marburg School can be said to have concentrated principally on logical, epistemological and methodological themes. And it is associated above all with the names of Hermann Cohen (1842–1918) and Paul Natorp (1854–1924).

Cohen, who was nominated professor of philosophy in the university of Marburg in 1876, concerned himself with both the exegesis and the development of Kant's thought. In a wide sense his principal theme is the unity of the cultural consciousness and its evolution, and whether he is writing on logic, ethics, aesthetics or religion[1] it is noticeable that he is constantly referring to the historical development of the ideas which he is treating and to their cultural significance at different stages of their development. This aspect of his thought makes it less formalistic and abstract than Kant's, though the wealth of historical reflections does not facilitate an immediate grasp of Cohen's personal point of view.

In the first volume of his *System of Philosophy* (*System der Philosophie*, 1902–12) Cohen abandons Kant's doctrine of sensibility, the transcendental aesthetic, and devotes himself entirely to the logic of pure thought or pure knowledge (*die reine Erkenntnis*), especially of the pure or *a priori* knowledge which lies at the basis of mathematical physics. True, logic possesses a wider field of application. But 'the fact that logic must have a relation which extends beyond the field of mathematical natural science to the field of the mental sciences (*Geisteswissenschaften*) in no way affects the fundamental relation of logic to knowledge in mathematical natural science'.[2] Indeed, 'the establishment of the relation between metaphysics and mathematical natural science is Kant's decisive act'.[3]

In the second volume, devoted to the ethics of the pure will (*Ethik des reinen Willens*), Cohen remarks that 'ethics, as the doctrine of man, becomes the centre of philosophy'.[4] But the concept of man is complex and comprises the two principal aspects of man, namely as an individual and as a member of society. Thus the deduction of the adequate concept of man moves

[1] In his *System of Philosophy* the idea of God is discussed in the second volume. Cf. also *The Concept of Religion in the System of Philosophy* (*Der Begriff der Religion im System der Philosophie*, Giessen, 1915). The idea of God is depicted as the unifying ideal of truth and perfection.
[2] *System der Philosophie*, I, p. 15 (Berlin, 1922, 3rd edition). The term *Geisteswissenschaften* will be discussed later.
[3] *Ibid.*, p. 9. Cohen is obviously referring to metaphysics in the sense in which Kant accepted metaphysics.
[4] *System der Philosophie*, II, p. 1 (Berlin 1921, 3rd edition).

through several phases or moments until the two aspects are seen as interpenetrating one another. In his discussion of this matter Cohen observes that philosophy has come to look on the State as the embodiment of man's ethical consciousness. But the empirical or actual State is only too evidently the State 'of the ruling classes'.[1] And the power-State (*der Machtstaat*) can become the State which embodies the principles of right and justice (*der Rechtsstaat*) only when it ceases to serve particular class-interests. In other words, Cohen looks forward to a democratic socialist society which will be the true expression of the ethical will of man considered both as a free individual person and as essentially orientated towards social life and the attainment of a common ideal end.

As the whole system of philosophy is conceived 'from the point of view of the unity of the cultural consciousness'[2] and as this consciousness is certainly not completely characterized by science and morals, Cohen devotes the third volume to aesthetics. As Kant saw, a treatment of aesthetics forms an intrinsic part of systematic philosophy.

Natorp, who also occupied a chair at Marburg, was strongly influenced by Cohen. In his *Philosophical Foundations of the Exact Sciences* (*Die philosophischen Grundlagen der exakten Wissenschaften*, 1910) he tries to show that the logical development of mathematics does not require any recourse to intuitions of space and time. His philosophy of mathematics is thus considerably more 'modern' than Kant's. As for ethics, Natorp shared Cohen's general outlook, and on the basis of the idea that the moral law demands of the individual that he should subordinate his activity to the elevation of humanity he developed a theory of social pedagogy. It can also be mentioned that in a well-known work, *Plato's Theory of Ideas* (*Platons Ideenlehre*, 1903), Natorp attempted to establish an affinity between Plato and Kant.

Both Cohen and Natorp endeavoured to overcome the dichotomy between thought and being which seemed to be implied by the Kantian theory of the thing-in-itself. Thus according to Natorp 'both, namely thought and being, exist and have meaning only in their constant mutual relations to one another'.[3] Being is not something static, set over against the activity of thought; it exists only in a process of becoming which is intrinsically related to this activity. And thought is a process which progressively determines

---

[1] *Ibid.*, p. 620.  　　[2] *System der Philosophie*, III, p. 4 (Berlin, 1922).
[3] *Philosophie*, p. 13 (Göttingen, 1921, 3rd edition).

its object, being. But though Cohen and Natorp sought to unite
thought and being as related poles of one process, it would not have
been possible for them to eliminate effectively the thing-in-itself
without deserting the Kantian standpoint and making the
transition to metaphysical idealism.

3. While the Marburg School emphasized inquiry into the
logical foundations of the natural sciences, the School of Baden
emphasized the philosophy of values and reflection on the cultural
sciences. Thus for Wilhelm Windelband[1] (1848–1915) the philosopher is concerned with inquiry into the principles and presuppositions of value-judgments and with the relation between the
judging subject or consciousness and the value or norm or ideal in
the light of which the judgment is made.

Given this account of philosophy, it is obvious that ethical and
aesthetic judgments provide material for philosophical reflection.
The moral judgment, for example, is clearly axiological in character
rather than descriptive. It expresses what ought to be rather than
what is the case in the world. But Windelband includes also logical
judgments. For just as ethics is concerned with moral values, so is
logic concerned with a value, namely truth. It is not everything
which is thought that is true. The true is that which ought to be
thought. Thus all logical thought is guided by a value, a norm. The
ultimate axioms of logic cannot be proved; but we must accept
them if we value truth. And we must accept truth as an objective
norm or value unless we are prepared to reject all logical thinking.

Logic, ethics and aesthetics, therefore, presuppose the values of
truth, goodness and beauty. And this fact compels us to postulate
a transcendental norm-setting or value-positing consciousness
which lies, as it were, behind empirical consciousness. Further,
inasmuch as in their logical, ethical and aesthetic judgments all
individuals appeal implicitly to universal absolute values, this
transcendental consciousness forms the living bond between
individuals.

Absolute values, however, require a metaphysical anchoring
(*eine metaphysische Veränkerung*). That is to say, recognition and
affirmation of objective values leads us to postulate a metaphysical
foundation in a supersensible reality which we call God. And there
thus arises the values of the holy. 'We do not understand by the

[1] Windelband, the well-known historian of philosophy, occupied chairs
successively at Zürich, Freiburg and Strasbourg. In 1903 he was nominated
professor of philosophy at Heidelberg. He was the first major figure of the so-called
Baden School.

holy a particular class of universally valid values, such as the classes constituted by the true, the good and the beautiful, but rather all these values themselves in so far as they stand in relation to a supersensible reality.'[1]

Windelband's philosophy of values was developed by Heinrich Rickert (1863–1936), his successor in the chair of philosophy at Heidelberg. Rickert insists that there is a realm of values which possess reality but cannot properly be said to exist.[2] They possess reality in the sense that the subject recognizes and does not create them. But they are not existing things among other existing things. In value-judgments, however, the subject brings together the realm of values and the sensible world, giving valuational significance to things and events. And though values themselves cannot be properly said to exist, we are not entitled to deny the possibility of their being grounded in an eternal divine reality which transcends our theoretical knowledge.

In accordance with his general outlook Rickert emphasizes the place of the idea of value in history. Windelband had maintained[3] that natural science is concerned with things in their universal aspects, as exemplifying types, and with events as repeatable, that is, as exemplifying universal laws, whereas history is concerned with the singular, the unique. The natural sciences are 'nomothetic' or law-positing, whereas history (that is, the science of history) is 'idiographic'.[4] Rickert agrees that the historian is concerned with the singular and unique, but insists that he is interested in persons and events only with reference to values. In other words, the ideal of historiography is a science of culture which depicts historical development in the light of the values recognized by different societies and cultures.

As far as one particular aspect of his thought is concerned, Hugo Münsterberg (1863–1916), who was a friend of Rickert, can be associated with the Baden School of Neo-Kantianism. In his *Philosophy of Values (Philosophie der Werte*, 1908), he expounded

---

[1] *Einleitung in die Philosophie*, p. 390 (Tübingen, 1914).
[2] In his *System of Philosophy (System der Philosophie*, 1921) Rickert attempts to classify values in six groups or spheres; the values of logic (truth values), aesthetics (values of beauty), mysticism (values of impersonal sanctity or holiness), ethics (moral values), erotics (values of happiness) and religion (values of personal sanctity).
[3] In his *History and Natural Science (Geschichte und Naturwissenschaft*, 1894).
[4] A science is not 'idiographic' by reason simply of the fact that it treats of human beings. Empirical psychology, for instance, treats of human beings, but it is none the less a 'nomothetic' science. In Scholastic language, the distinction is formal rather than material.

the idea of giving meaning to the world in terms of a system of values. But as professor of experimental psychology at Harvard he gave his attention mainly to the field of psychology, where he had been strongly influenced by Wundt.

4. We have seen that Windelband regarded the existence of a supersensible divine reality as a postulate of the recognition of absolute values. At the same time he was concerned to argue that the term 'postulate', as used in this context, means much more than 'useful fiction'. There were, however, some Neo-Kantians who interpreted Kant's postulate-theory in a definitely pragmatist sense.

Thus Friedrich Albert Lange (1828–75), who has already been mentioned as a critic of materialism, interpreted metaphysical theories and religious doctrines as belonging to a sphere between knowledge and poetry. If such theories and doctrines are presented as expressing knowledge of reality, they are open to all the objections raised by Kant and other critics. For we cannot have theoretical knowledge of metaphenomenal reality. But if they are interpreted as symbols of a reality which transcends knowledge and if at the same time their value for life is emphasized, they become immune from objections which have point only if cognitive value is claimed for metaphysics and theology.

The useful-fiction version of the theory of postulates was developed in a more systematic way by Hans Vaihinger (1852–1933), author of the celebrated work *The Philosophy of As-If* (*Die Philosophie des Als-Ob*, 1911). With him metaphysical theories and religious doctrines become only particular instances of the application of a general pragmatist view of truth. Only sensations and feelings are real: otherwise the whole of human knowledge consists of 'fictions'. The principles of logic, for example, are fictions which have proved their real utility in experience. And to say that they are undeniably true is to say that they have been found indispensably useful. Hence the question to ask in regard, say, to a religious doctrine is whether it is useful or valuable to act as though it were true rather than whether it is true. Indeed, the question whether the doctrine is 'really' true or not hardly arises, not simply because we have no means of knowing whether it is true or not but rather because the concept of truth is given a pragmatist interpretation.[1]

[1] To do Vaihinger justice, it must be added that he endeavours to sort out the different ways in which the concepts of 'as-if' and 'fiction' operate. He does not simply throw the principles of logic, scientific hypotheses and religious doctrines indiscriminately into the same basket.

This pragmatist fictionalism evidently goes a long way beyond the position of Kant. Indeed, it really deprives the Kantian theory of postulates of its significance, inasmuch as it does away with the sharp contrast established by Kant between theoretical knowledge on the one hand and the postulates of the moral law on the other. But though I have included Vaihinger among the Neo-Kantians, he was strongly influenced by the vitalism and fiction-theory of Nietzsche on whom he published a well-known work, *Nietzsche as Philosopher* (*Nietzsche als Philosoph*, 1902).

5. As we have seen, Neo-Kantianism was by no means a homogeneous system of thought. On the one hand we have a philosopher such as Alois Riehl (1844–1924), professor at Berlin, who not only rejected decisively all metaphysics but also maintained that value-theory must be excluded from philosophy in the proper sense.[1] On the other hand we have a philosopher such as Windelband who developed the theory of absolute values in such a way as practically to reintroduce metaphysics, even if he still spoke about 'postulates'.

Such differences naturally become all the more marked in proportion as the field of application of the term 'Neo-Kantian' is extended. For instance, the term has sometimes been applied to Johannes Volkelt (1848–1930), professor of philosophy at Leipzig. But as Volkelt maintained that the human spirit can enjoy an intuitive certitude of its unity with the Absolute, that the Absolute is infinite spirit, and that creation can be conceived as analogous to aesthetic production, the propriety of calling him a Neo-Kantian is obviously questionable. And in point of fact Volkelt was strongly influenced by other German philosophers besides Kant.

It will have been noticed that most of the philosophers mentioned lived into the twentieth century. And the Neo-Kantian movement has indeed had one or two eminent representatives in comparatively recent times. Notable among these is Ernst Cassirer (1874–1945) who occupied chairs successively at Berlin, Hamburg, Göteborg and Yale in the United States. The influence of the Marburg School contributed to directing his attention to problems of knowledge. And the fruit of his studies was his three-volume work on *The Problem of Knowledge in the Philosophy and*

---

[1] According to Riehl, a philosophy which deserves to be called scientific must confine itself to the critique of knowledge as realized in the natural sciences. He did not, of course, deny the importance of values in human life; but he insisted that recognition of them is not, properly speaking, a cognitive act and falls outside the scope of scientific philosophy.

*Science of the Modern Era* (*Das Erkenntnisproblem in der Phile sophie und Wissenschaft der neueren Zeit*, 1906–20). This wa followed in 1910 by a work on the concepts of substance an function (*Substanzbegriff und Funktionsbegriff*). Cassirer was strucl by the progressive mathematization of physics, and he conclude that in modern physics sensible reality is transformed into an reconstructed as a world of symbols. Further reflection on th function of symbolism led him to develop a large-scale *Philosoph of Symbolic Forms* (*Philosophie der symbolischen Formen*, 1923–9 in which he maintained that it is the use of symbols which dis tinguishes man from the animals. It is by means of language tha man creates a new world, the world of culture. And Cassirer use the idea of symbolism to unlock many doors. For example, he trie to explain the unity of the human person as a functional unit which unites man's different symbolic activities. He devote special attention to the function of symbolism in the form of myth and he studied such activities as art and historiography in th light of the idea of symbolic transformation.

But though Neo-Kantianism lasted on into the present century it can scarcely be called a twentieth-century philosophy. Th emergence of new movements and lines of thought has pushed i into the background. It is not so much that the subjects witl which it dealt are dead. It is rather that they are treated in differen settings or frameworks of thought. Inquiry into the logic of th sciences and the philosophy of values are cases in point. Furthei epistemology or theory of knowledge no longer enjoys the centra position which Kant and his disciples attributed to it.

This is not to say, of course, that the influence of Kant i exhausted. Far from it. But it is not felt, at any rate on a significan scale, in the continuance of any movement which could appropri ately be called Neo-Kantian. Further, Kant's influence is some times exercised in a direction which is thoroughly un-Kantian. Fo example, while positivists believe that Kant was substantially right in excluding metaphysics from the field of knowledge, ther is a current of thought in modern Thomism which has interpreted and developed Kant's transcendental method for the very un Kantian purpose of establishing a systematic metaphysics.

6. This is a convenient place at which to make a few remark: about Wilhelm Dilthey (1833–1911), who occupied chairs succes sively at Basel, Kiel, Breslau and finally Berlin, where he succeeded Lotze as professor of philosophy. True, though Dilthey entertained

profound admiration for Kant he cannot properly be described
as a Neo-Kantian. He did indeed endeavour to develop a critique
of historical reason (*Kritik der historischen Vernunft*) and a
corresponding theory of categories. And this activity can be
regarded from one point of view as an extension of Kant's critical
work to what the Germans call the *Geisteswissenschaften*. At the
same time he insisted that the categories of the historical reason,
that is, of reason engaged in understanding and interpreting
history, are not *a priori* categories which are then applied to some
raw materials to constitute history. They arise out of the living
penetration by the human spirit of its own objective manifestation
in history. And in general, especially from 1883 onwards, Dilthey
drew a sharp distinction between the abstractness of Kant's
thought and his own concrete approach. However, the fact that
we have already had occasion in this chapter to refer to the
distinction between the natural sciences and the *Geisteswissen-*
*schaften* provides, I think, sufficient reason for mentioning Dilthey
here.

The fact that the term 'mental sciences' is a misleading translation of *Geisteswissenschaften* can easily be seen by considering
the examples given by Dilthey. Alongside the natural sciences,
he says, there has grown up a group of other sciences which
together can be called the *Geisteswissenschaften* or *Kulturwissen-*
*schaften*. Such are 'history, national economy, the sciences of law
and of the State, the science of religion, the study of literature and
poetry, of art and music, of philosophical world-views, and
systems, finally psychology'.[1] The term 'mental sciences' tends to
suggest only psychology. But in a similar list of examples Dilthey
does not even mention psychology.[2] The French are accustomed to
speak of 'the moral sciences'. But in English this term suggests
primarily ethics. Hence I propose to speak of 'the cultural sciences'.
It is true that this term would not normally suggest national
economy. But it is sufficient to say that the term is being used to
cover what Dilthey calls *Kulturwissenschaften* or *Geisteswissen-*
*schaften*.

It is clear that we cannot distinguish between the cultural sciences
on the one hand and the natural sciences on the other by the
simple expedient of saying that the former are concerned with
man whereas the latter are not. For physiology is a natural

---

[1] *Gesammelte Schiften*, VII, p. 79. This collection of Dilthey's *Works* will be
referred to hereafter as *GS*.
[2] *GS*, VII, p. 70.

science; yet it treats of man. And the same can be said o
experimental psychology. Nor can we say simply that the natura
sciences are concerned with the physical and sensible, includin
the physical aspects of man, whereas the cultural sciences ar
concerned with the psychical, the interior, with that which doe
not enter into the sensible world. For it is evident that in the stud
of art, for instance, we are concerned with sensible objects such
as pictures rather than with the psychical states of the artists
True, works of art are studied as objectifications of the huma
spirit. But they are none the less sensible objectifications. Henc
we must find some other way of distinguishing between the tw
groups of sciences.

Man stands in a living felt unity with Nature, and his primar
experience of his physical milieu are personal lived experience
(*Erlebnisse*), not objects of reflection from which man detache
himself. To construct the world of natural science, however, ma
has to prescind from the aspect of his impressions of his physica
milieu under which they are his personal lived experiences; he ha
to put himself out of the picture as far as he can[1] and develop a
abstract conception of Nature in terms of relations of space, time
mass and motion. Nature has to become for him the centra
reality, a law-ordered physical system, which is considered, as i
were, from without.

When, however, we turn to the world of history and culture, th
objectifications of the human spirit, the situation is different. It i
a question of penetration from within. And the individual'
personal lived relations with his own social milieu become o
fundamental importance. For example, I cannot understand th
social and political life of ancient Greece as an objectification o
the human spirit if I exclude my own lived experiences of socia
relations. For these form the basis of my understanding of th
social life of any other epoch. True, a certain unity in the historica
and social life of humanity is a necessary condition of the possibilit
of my own *Erlebnisse* providing a key to the understanding o
history. But the 'original cell of the historical world,'[2] as Dilthe
calls it, is precisely the individual's *Erlebnis*, his lived experienc
of interaction with his own social milieu.

But though what Dilthey calls *Erlebnisse* are a necessar
condition for the development of the cultural sciences, they do no

[1] In the science of physiology man regards himself from an impersonal an
external point of view as a physical object, as part of Nature.
[2] *GS*, VII, p. 161.

by themselves constitute a science of any kind. Understanding (*Verstehen*) is also necessary. And what we have to understand in history and the other cultural sciences is not the human spirit in its interiority, so to speak, but the external objectification of this spirit, its objective expression, as in art, law, the State and so on. We are concerned in other words with the understanding of objective spirit.[1] And to understand a phase of objective spirit means relating its phenomena to an inner structure which finds expression in these phenomena. For example, the understanding of Roman law involves penetrating beneath the external apparatus, so to speak, to the spiritual structure which find expression in the laws. It means penetrating what can be called the spirit of Roman law, just as understanding Baroque architecture would involve penetrating the spirit, the structure of purposes and ideals, which found expression in this style. We can say, therefore, that 'the cultural sciences rest on the relation of lived experience, expression and understanding'.[2] Expression is required because the underlying spiritual structure is grasped only in and through its external expression. Understanding is a movement from the outside to the inside. And in the process of understanding a spiritual object rises before our vision, whereas in the natural sciences a physical object is constructed (though not in the Kantian sense) in the process of scientific knowledge.

We have seen that a man's personal experience of his own social milieu is a necessary condition of his being able to live over again the experience of men in the past. *Erleben* is a condition of the possibility of *Nacherleben*. And the former renders the latter possible because of the continuity and fundamental unity of the developing historical-cultural reality which Dilthey describes as Life (*Leben*). Cultures are, of course, spatially and temporally distinct. But if we conceive the reciprocal relations between persons, under the conditions set by the external world, as a structural and developing unity which persists throughout spatial and temporal differentiations, we have the concept of Life. And in studying this Life the historical reason employs certain categories. As has already been remarked, these categories are not *a priori*

---

[1] Dilthey was influenced by Hegel's concept of 'objective spirit'. But his own use of the term is obviously somewhat different from that of Hegel who classified art and religion under the heading of 'absolute spirit'. Hegel's use of the term is connected, of course, with his idealist metaphysics, for which Dilthey had no use. Further, Dilthey rejected what he regarded as Hegel's *a priori* methods of interpreting history and human culture.

[2] *Auf dem Verhältnis von Erlebnis, Ausdruck und Verstehen; GS*, VII, p. 131.

forms or concepts applied to some raw material: 'they lie in the nature of Life itself'[1] and are conceptualized abstractly in the process of understanding. We cannot determine the exact number of such categories or turn them into a tidy abstract logical scheme for mechanical application. But among them we can name 'meaning, value, purpose, development, ideal'.[2]

These categories should not be understood in a metaphysical sense. It is not a question, for example, of defining the end or meaning of history in the sense of an end which the process of historical development is predestined to attain. It is a question rather of understanding the meaning which Life has for a particular society and the operative ideals which find expression in that society's political and legal institutions, in its art, religion and so on. 'The category of meaning signifies the relations of parts of Life to the whole.'[3] But 'our conception of the meaning of Life is always changing. Each life-plan expresses an idea of the meaning of Life. And the purpose which we set for the future conditions our account of the meaning of the past.'[4] If we say that the task for the future is to achieve this or that, our judgment conditions our understanding of the meaning of the past. And, of course, the other way round as well.

It can hardly be denied that Dilthey's thought contains a prominent element of historical relativism. For example, all world-views or *Weltanschauungen* are partial views of the world, relative to distinct cultural phases. And a study of such world-views or metaphysical systems would exhibit their relativity. At the same time Dilthey does not maintain that there is no universally valid truth at all. And he regards the study of Life, of history as a whole, as a constant approximation to an objective and complete self-knowledge by man. Man is fundamentally an historical being, and he comes to know himself in history. This self-knowledge is never actually complete, but the knowledge which man attains through a study of history is no more purely subjective than is the knowledge attained through the natural sciences. How far Dilthey actually succeeds in overcoming pure historicism is doubtless open to discussion. But he certainly does not intend to assert an extreme relativism which would necessarily invalidate his conception of world-history.

At a time when the natural sciences appear to be threatening to engulf the whole field of knowledge, the question whether and how

[1] *GS*, VII, p. 232.     [2] *Ibid.*     [3] *GS*, VII, p. 233.     [4] *Ibid.*

one could distinguish between the natural and the cultural sciences naturally becomes an issue of importance. And Dilthey's account of the matter was one of the most signal contributions to the discussion. What one thinks of its value seems to depend very largely on one's view of the historian's function. If, for example, one thinks that Dilthey's idea of getting behind the external expression to an inward spiritual structure (the 'spirit' of Roman law, of Baroque art and architecture, and so on) smacks of the transcendental metaphysics which Dilthey himself professed to reject, and if at the same time one disapproves of such transcendental metaphysics, one will hardly be disposed to accept Dilthey's account of the differences between the two groups of sciences. If, however, one thinks that an understanding of man's cultural life does in fact demand this passage from the external phenomena to the operative ideals, purposes and values which are expressed in them, one can hardly deny the relevance of the concepts of *Erleben* and *Nacherleben*. For historical understanding would then necessarily involve a penetration of the past from within, a reliving, so far as this is possible, of past experience, of past attitudes, valuations and ideals. And this would be at any rate one distinguishing characteristic of the historical and cultural sciences. For the physicist can scarcely be said to attempt to relive the experience of an atom or to penetrate behind the relations of infra-atomic particles to a spiritual structure expressed in them. To introduce such notions into mathematical physics would mean its ruin. Conversely, to fail to introduce them into the theory of the cultural sciences is to forget that 'he who explores history is the same who makes history'.[1]

[1] *GS*, VII, p. 278.

### CHAPTER XX

# THE REVIVAL OF METAPHYSICS

*Remarks on inductive metaphysics—Fechner's inductive meta-physics—The teleological idealism of Lotze—Wundt and the relation between science and philosophy—The vitalism of Driesch —Eucken's activism—Appropriation of the past: Trendelenburg and Greek thought; the revival of Thomism.*

1. IN spite of their own excursions into metaphysics both the materialists and the Neo-Kantians were opposed to the idea of metaphysics as a source of positive knowledge about reality, the former appealing to scientific thinking in justification of their attitude, the latter to Kant's theory of the limitations of man's theoretical knowledge. But there was also a group of philosophers who came to philosophy from some branch or other of empirical science and who were convinced that the scientific view of the world demands completion through metaphysical reflection. They did not believe that a valid system of metaphysics could be worked out *a priori* or without regard to our scientific knowledge. And they tended to look on metaphysical theories as hypothetical and as enjoying a higher or lower degree of probability. Hence in their case we can speak of inductive metaphysics.

Inductive metaphysics has, of course, had its notable representatives, above all perhaps Henri Bergson. But there are probably few people who would be prepared to claim that the German inductive metaphysicians of the second half of the nineteenth century were of the same stature as the great idealists. And one of the weak points of inductive metaphysics in general is that it tends to leave unexamined and unestablished the basic principles on which it rests. However, it is as well to realize that we cannot simply divide the German philosophers into two classes, those who constructed metaphysics in an *a priori* manner and those who rejected metaphysics in the name of science or in that of the limitations of the human mind. For there were also those who attempted to achieve a synthesis between science and meta-physics, not by trying to harmonize science with an already-made philosophical system but rather by trying to show that reflection on the world as known through the particular sciences reasonably leads to metaphysical theories.

2. Among the representatives of inductive metaphysics, we can mention Gustav Theodor Fechner (1801–87), for many years professor of physics at Leipzig and celebrated as one of the founders of experimental psychology. Continuing the studies of E. H. Weber (1795–1878) on the relation between sensation and stimulus, Fechner gave expression in his *Elements of Psychophysics* (*Elemente des Psychophysik*, 1860) to the 'law' which states that the intensity of the sensation varies in proportion to the logarithm of the intensity of the stimulus. Fechner also devoted himself to the psychological study of aesthetics, publishing his *Propaedeutics to Aesthetics* (*Vorschule der Aesthetik*) in 1876.

These studies in exact science did not, however, lead Fechner to materialist conclusions.[1] In psychology he was a parallelist. That is to say, he thought that psychical and physical phenomena correspond in a manner analogous to the relation between a text and its translation or between two translations of a text, as he explained in his *Zend-Avesta* (1851) and in his *Elements of Psychophysics*. In fact, the psychical and the physical were for him two aspects of one reality. And in accordance with this view he postulated the presence of a psychical life even in plants, though of a lower type than in animals.[2] Moreover, he extended this parallelism to the planets and stars and indeed to all material things, justifying this panpsychism by a principle of analogy which states that when objects agree in possessing certain qualities or traits, one is entitled to assume hypothetically that they agree also in other qualities, provided that one's hypotheses do not contradict established scientific facts.

This is hardly a very safe rule of procedure, but, to do Fechner justice, it should be added that he demanded some positive ground for metaphysical theories, as distinct from a mere absence of contradiction of scientific facts. At the same time he also made use of a principle which is not calculated to commend his metaphysics in the eyes of anti-metaphysicians or, for the matter of that, of many metaphysicians themselves. I refer to the principle

---

[1] As a youth Fechner went through an atheistic phase, but a book by Oken, one of Schelling's disciples, convinced him that materialism and atheism were by no means entailed by an acceptance of exact science.

[2] In 1848 Fechner published *Nanna, or the Soul-Life of Plants* (*Nanna, oder das Seelenleben der Pflanzen*).

which states that an hypothesis which has some positive ground
and does not contradict any established fact is to be the more
readily embraced the more it renders man happy.[1]

In the spirit of this principle Fechner contrasted what he called
the day-view with the night-view, to the detriment of the latter.
The night-view, attributed not only to the materialists but also to
the Kantians, is the view of Nature as dumb and dead and a
affording no real clue to its teleological significance. The day-view
is the vision of Nature as a living harmonious unity, animated by
a soul. The soul of the universe is God, and the universe considered
as a physical system is the divine externality. Fechner thus uses
his principle of analogy to extend psychophysical parallelism not
only from human beings to other classes of particular things but
also from all particular things to the universe as a whole. He
employs it also as a basis for belief in personal immortality. Our
perceptions persist in memory and enter once again into consciousness. So, we may suppose, our souls persist in the divine memory
but without simple absorption in the Deity.

Panpsychism is indeed a very ancient theory, and it is one
which tends to recur. It is far from being Fechner's private
invention. However, it is difficult to avoid the impression that
when Fechner leaves the purely scientific sphere and embarks on
philosophy he becomes a kind of poet of the universe. But it is
interesting to observe the pragmatist element in his thought. We
have seen that in his view, other things being equal, the theory
which makes for happiness is to be preferred to the theory which
does not. But Fechner does not make it a matter simply of
individual preference. Another of his principles states that the
probability of a belief increases in proportion to the length of its
survival, especially if acceptance of it increases together with the
development of human culture. And it is not surprising that
William James derived inspiration from Fechner.

3. A much more impressive figure as a philosopher is Rudolf
Hermann Lotze (1817–81) who studied medicine and philosophy at
Leipzig, where he also listened to Fechner's lectures on physics. In
1844 he was nominated professor of philosophy at Göttingen and
in 1881, shortly before his death, he accepted a chair of philosophy at Berlin. Besides works on physiology, medicine and

[1] Happiness for Fechner does not mean simply sense-pleasure. It includes joy in
the beautiful, the good and the true and in the religious feeling of union with
God.
[2] Cf. *Die Tagesansicht gegenüber der Nachtansicht*, 1879.

psychology he published a considerable number of philosophical writings.[1] In 1841 there appeared a *Metaphysics*, in 1843 a *Logic*, in 1856-64 a large three-volume work entitled *Microcosm* (*Mikrokosmus*) on philosophical anthropology, in 1868 a history of aesthetics in Germany and in 1874-9 a *System of Philosophy* (*System der Philosophie*). After Lotze's death a series of volumes were published which were based on lecture-notes taken by his students. These covered in outline the fields of psychology, ethics, philosophy of religion, philosophy of Nature, logic, metaphysics, aesthetics and the history of post-Kantian philosophy in Germany. A three-volume collection of his minor writings (*Kleine Schriften*) appeared in 1885-91.

According to Lotze himself it was his inclination to poetry and art which originally turned his mind to philosophy. Hence it can be somewhat misleading to say that he came to philosophy from science. At the same time he had a scientific training at the university of Leipzig, where he enrolled in the faculty of medicine, and it is characteristic of his systematic philosophical thinking that he presupposed and took seriously what he called the mechanical interpretation of Nature.

For example, while recognizing, of course, the evident fact that there are differences in behaviour between living and non-living things, Lotze refused to allow that the biologist must postulate some special vital principle which is responsible for the maintenance and operation of the organism. For science, which seeks everywhere to discover connections which can be formulated in terms of general laws, 'the realm of life is not divided from that of inorganic Nature by a higher force peculiar to itself, setting itself up as something alien above other modes of action . . . but simply by the peculiar kind of connection into which its manifold constituents are woven. . . .'[2] That is to say, the characteristic behaviour of the organism can be explained in terms of the combination of material elements in certain ways. And it is the biologist's business to push this type of explanation as far as he can and not to have recourse to the expedient of invoking special vital principles. 'The connection of vital phenomena demands throughout a mechanical treatment which explains life not by a peculiar principle of operation but by

---

[1] Some of his medico-psychological publications, such as his *Medical Psychology or Physiology of the Soul* (*Medizinische Psychologie oder Physiologie der Seele*, 1852) are of importance for his philosophy.

[2] *Mikrokosmus*, Bk. I, ch. 3, sect. 1 (in 5th German edition, Leipzig, 1896-1909, I, p. 58).

a characteristic application of the general principles of physical process.'[1]

This mechanical interpretation of Nature, which is necessary for the development of science, should be extended as far as possible. And this is as true of psychology as of biology. At the same time we are certainly not entitled to rule out *a priori* the possibility of finding facts of experience which limit the applicability of the mechanical view. And we do find such facts. For example, the unity of consciousness, which manifests itself in the simple act of comparing two presentations and judging them to be like or unlike, at once sets a limit to the possibility of describing man's psychical life in terms of causal relations between distinct psychical events. It is not a question of inferring the existence of a soul as a kind of unalterable psychical atom. It is 'the fact of the unity of consciousness which is *eo ipso* at the same time the fact of the existence of a substance',[2] namely the soul. In other words, to affirm the existence of the soul is neither to postulate a logical condition of the unity of consciousness nor to infer from this unity an occult entity. For recognition of the unity of consciousness is at the same time recognition of the existence of the soul, though the proper way of describing the soul is obviously a matter for further reflection.

Thus there are certain empirical facts which set a limit to the field of application of the mechanical interpretation of Nature. And it is no good suggesting that further scientific advance can abolish these facts or show that they are not facts. This is quite evident in the case of the unity of consciousness. For any further scientific advances in empirical and physiological psychology depend on and presuppose the unity of consciousness. And as for Lotze reflection on the unity of consciousness shows that psychical states must be referred to an immaterial reality as their subject, the point at which the limitation of the mechanical interpretation of man's psychical life becomes decisively evident is also the point at which the need for a metaphysical psychology becomes clear.

It is not, however, Lotze's intention to construct a two-storey system, as it were, in which the mechanical interpretation of material Nature would form the lower storey and a superimposed metaphysics of spiritual reality the higher. For he argues that even as regards Nature itself the mechanical interpretation gives but a

[1] *System der Philosophie*, II, p. 447 (Leipzig, 1912; Bk. 2, ch. 8, sect. 229).
[2] *Ibid.*, p. 481 (sect. 243).

one-sided picture, valid indeed for scientific purposes but inadequate from a metaphysical point of view.

The mechanical interpretation of Nature presupposes the existence of distinct things which are in causal relations of interaction and each of which is relatively permanent, that is, in relation to its own changing states. But interaction between $A$ and $B$ is possible, according to Lotze, only if they are members of an organic unity. And permanence in relation to changing states can best be interpreted on an analogy with the permanent subject of change which is best known to us, namely the human soul as revealed in the unity of consciousness. We are thus led not only to the concept of Nature as an organic unity but also to the idea of things as in some sense psychical or spiritual entities. Further, the ground of this unity must be conceived on an analogy with the highest thing known to us, namely the human spirit. Hence the world of finite spirits is to be conceived as the self-expression of infinite Spirit or God. All things are immanent in God, and what the scientist sees as mechanical causality is simply the expression of the divine activity. God does not create a world and then sit back, as it were, while the world obeys the laws he has given it. The so-called laws are the divine action itself, the mode of God's operation.

From a rather hard-headed starting-point in the mechanical conception of Nature Lotze thus goes on to expound a metaphysical theory which recalls the monadology of Leibniz and which entails the conclusion that space is phenomenal. But though Lotze did indeed derive stimulus from Leibniz and Herbart, he also drew inspiration, as he himself says, from the ethical idealism of Fichte. He was not a disciple of Fichte, and he disapproved of the *a priori* method of the post-Kantian idealists, especially of Hegel. At the same time Fichte's conception of the ultimate principle expressing itself in finite subjects with a view to a moral end exercised a powerful attraction on Lotze's mind. And it is to the philosophy of values that he turns for the key to the meaning of creation. Sense experience tells us nothing about the final cause of the world. But that the world cannot be without end or purpose is a moral conviction. And we must conceive God as expressing himself in the world for the realization of value, of a moral ideal which is being constantly fulfilled in and through the divine activity. As for our knowledge of what this end or aim is, we can come to some knowledge of it only by an analysis of the notion of the Good, of

the highest value. A phenomenological analysis of values is thu
an integral part of philosophy. Indeed, our belief in God's existenc
ultimately rests on our moral experience and appreciation c
value.[1]

God is for Lotze a personal Being. The notion of impersona
spirit he dismisses as contrary to reason. As for the view of Ficht
and other philosophers that personality is necessarily finite an
limited and so cannot be predicated of the infinite, Lotze replie
that it is only infinite spirit which can be personal in the fulles
sense of the word: finitude involves a limitation of personality. A
the same time all things are immanent in God, and, as we have seer
mechanical causality is simply the divine action. In this sense Go
is the Absolute. But he is not the Absolute in the sense that finit
spirits can be considered modifications of the divine substanc
For each exists 'for itself' and is a centre of activity. From
metaphysical point of view, says Lotze, pantheism could b
accepted as a possible view of the world only if it renounced al
inclination to conceive the infinite as anything else but Spirit. Fo
the spatial world is phenomenal and cannot be identified with Go
under the name of Substance. From a religious point of view 'w
do not share the inclination which commonly governs the pan
theistic imagination to suppress all that is finite in favour of th
infinite. . . .'[2]

Lotze's teleological idealism has obvious affinities with the post
Kantian idealist movement. And his vision of the world as a
organic unity which is the expression of infinite Spirit's realizatio
of ideal value may be said to have given fresh life to idealis
thought. But he did not believe that we can deduce a metaphysica
system, descriptive of existent reality, from ultimate principles o
thought or self-evident truths. For the so-called eternal truths o
logic are hypothetical in character, in the sense that they stat
conditions of possibility. Hence they cannot be used as premisse
for an *a priori* deduction of existent reality. Nor can human being
achieve an absolute point of view and describe the whole proces
of reality in the light of a final end which they already know. Man'
metaphysical interpretation of the universe must be based o

---

[1] When discussing the traditional proofs of God's existence, Lotze remarks tha
the immediate moral conviction that that which is greatest, most beautiful an
most worthy has reality lies at the foundation of the ontological argument, just a
it is the factor which carries the teleological argument far beyond any conclusion
which could be logically derived from its assumptions. *Mikrokosmus*, Bk. IX
ch. 4, sect. 2 (5th German edition, III, p. 561).

[2] *Mikrokosmus*, Bk. IX, ch. 4, sect. 3 (5th German edition, III, p. 569).

experience. And, as we have seen, Lotze attributes a profound significance to the experience of value. For it is this experience which lies at the root of the conviction that the world cannot be simply a mechanical system without purpose or ethical value but must be conceived as progressively realizing a spiritual end. This is not to say that the metaphysician, once armed with this conviction, is entitled to indulge in flights of the imagination uncontrolled by logical thinking about the nature of reality. But in the philosopher's systematic interpretation of the universe there will inevitably be much that is hypothetical.

The influence of Lotze was considerable. For instance, in the field of psychology it was felt by Carl Stumpf (1848–1936) and Franz Brentano, of whom something will be said in the last chapter. But it was perhaps in the field of the philosophy of values that his influence was most felt. Among a number of English thinkers who derived stimulus from Lotze we may mention in particular James Ward (1843–1925). In America the idealist Josiah Royce (1855–1916) was influenced by Lotze's personalistic idealism.

4. Among the German philosophers of the second half of the nineteenth century who came from science to philosophy mention must be made of Wilhelm Wundt (1832–1920). After studying medicine Wundt gave himself to physiological and psychological research, and in 1863–4 he published a series of *Lectures on the Human and Animal Soul* (*Vorlesungen über die Menschen- und Tierseele*). After nine years as an 'extraordinary' professor of physiology at Heidelberg he was nominated to the chair of inductive philosophy at Zürich in 1874. In the following year he moved to Leipzig where he occupied the chair of philosophy until 1918. And it was at Leipzig that he founded the first laboratory of experimental psychology. The first edition of his *Outlines of Physiological Psychology* (*Grundzüge der physiologischen Psychologie*) was published in 1874. In the philosophical field he published a two-volume *Logic* in 1880–3,[1] an *Ethics* in 1886, a *System of Philosophy* in 1889,[2] and a *Metaphysics* in 1907. But he did not abandon his psychological studies, and in 1904 he published a two-volume *Psychology of Peoples* (*Völkerpsychologie*) of which a new and greatly enlarged edition appeared in 1911–20.

When Wundt speaks about experimental psychology and the experimental method he is generally referring to introspective

---

[1] An enlarged edition in 3 vols. appeared in 1919–21.
[2] A two-volume edition appeared in 1919.

psychology and the introspective method. Or, more accurately, he regards introspection as the appropriate method of investigation for individual, as distinct from social, psychology. Introspection reveals, as its immediate data, a connection of psychical events or processes, not a substantial soul, nor a set of relatively permanent objects. For no one of the events revealed by introspection remains precisely the same from one moment to another. At the same time there is a unity of connection. And just as the natural scientist tries to establish the causal laws which operate in the physical sphere, so should the introspective psychologist endeavour to ascertain the fundamental laws of relation and development which give content to the idea of psychical causality. In interpreting man', psychical life Wundt lays emphasis on volitional rather than on cognitive elements. The latter are not denied, of course, but the volitional element is taken as fundamental and as providing the key for the interpretation of man's psychical life as a whole.

When we turn from the psychical life as manifested in intro-spection to human societies, we find common and relatively permanent products such as language, myth and custom. And the social psychologist is called on to investigate the psychical energies which are responsible for these common products and which together form the spirit or soul of a people. This spirit exists only in and through individuals, but it is not reducible to them when taken separately. In other words, through the relations of individuals in a society there arises a reality, the spirit of a people, which expresses itself in common spiritual products. And social psychology studies the development of these realities. It also studies the evolution of the concept of humanity and of the general spirit of man which manifests itself, for example, in the rise of universal instead of purely national religions, in the development of science, in the growth of the idea of common human rights, and so on. Wundt thus allots to social psychology a far-reaching programme. For its task is to study from a psychological point of view the development of human society and culture in all its principal manifestations.

Philosophy, according to Wundt, presupposes natural science and psychology. It builds upon them and incorporates them into a synthesis. At the same time philosophy goes beyond the sciences. Yet there can be no reasonable objection to this procedure on the ground that it is contrary to the scientific spirit. For in the particular sciences themselves explanatory hypotheses are constructed which go beyond the empirical data. At the level of knowledge of the understanding (*Verstandeserkenntnis*), the level at which sciences such as physics and psychology arise, presentations are synthesized with the aid of logical method and techniques. At the level of rational knowledge (*Vernunfterkenntnis*) philosophy, especially metaphysics, tries to construct a systematic synthesis of the results of the previous level. At all levels of cognition the mind aims at absence of contradiction in a progressive synthesis of presentations, which form the fundamental point of departure for human knowledge.

In his general metaphysical picture of reality Wundt conceives the world as the totality of individual agents or active centres which are to be regarded as volitional unities of different grades. These volitional unities form a developing series which tends towards the emergence of a total spirit (*Gesamtgeist*). In more concrete terms, there is a movement towards the complete spiritual unification of man or humanity, and individual human beings are called on to act in accordance with the values which contribute to this end. Metaphysics and ethics are thus closely connected, and both receive a natural completion in religious idealism. For the concept of a cosmic process directed towards an ideal leads to a religious view of the world.

5. We have seen that though Lotze went on to develop a metaphysical theory about the spiritual nature of reality, he would not allow that the biologist has any warrant for setting aside the mechanical interpretation of Nature which is proper to the empirical sciences and postulating a special vital principle to explain the behaviour of the organism. When, however, we turn to Hans Driesch (1867–1941) we find this onetime pupil of Haeckel being led by his biological and zoological researches to a theory of dynamic vitalism and to the conviction that finality is an essential category in biology. He became convinced that in the organic body there is an autonomous active principle which directs the vital processes and which cannot be accounted for by a purely mechanistic theory of life.

To this principle Driesch gave the name of *entelechy*, making use of an Aristotelian term. But he was careful to refrain from describing the entelechy or vital principle as psychical. For this term, he considered, is inappropriate in view both of its human associations and of its ambiguity.

Having formed the concept of entelechies Driesch proceeded to

blossom out as a philosopher. In 1907–8 he gave the Gifford
Lectures at Aberdeen, and in 1909 he published his two-volume
*Philosophy of the Organic (Philosophie des Organischen)*. In 1911 he
obtained a chair of philosophy at Heidelberg, and subsequently he
was professor first at Cologne and later at Leipzig. In his general
philosophy[1] the concept of the organism was extrapolated to apply
to the world as a whole, and his metaphysics culminated in the
idea of a supreme entelechy, God. The picture was that of a cosmic
entelechy, the teleological activity of which is directed towards the
realization of the highest possible level of knowledge. But the
question of theism or pantheism was left in suspense.

Through his attack on mechanistic biology Driesch exercised a
considerable influence. But of those who agreed with him that a
mechanistic interpretation was inadequate and that the organism
manifests finality by no means all were prepared to accept the
theory of entelechies. To mention two Englishmen who, like
Driesch, came to philosophy from science and in due course
delivered series of Gifford Lectures, Lloyd Morgan (1852–1936)
rejected Driesch's neo-vitalism, while J. A. Thomson (1861–1933)
tried to steer a middle path between what he regarded as the
metaphysical Scylla of the entelechy theory and the Charybdis of
mechanistic materialism.

6. The philosophers whom we have been considering in this
chapter had a scientific training and either turned from the study
of some particular science or sciences to philosophical speculation
or combined the two activities. We can now consider briefly a
thinker, Rudolf Eucken (1846–1926), who certainly did not come to
philosophy from science but who was already interested as a school-
boy[2] in philosophical and religious problems and who devoted himself to the study of philosophy at the universities of Göttingen and
Berlin. In 1871 he was appointed professor of philosophy at Basel,
and in 1874 he accepted the chair of philosophy at Jena.

Eucken had little sympathy with the view of philosophy as a
purely theoretical interpretation of the world. Philosophy was for
him, as for the Stoics, a wisdom for life. Further, it was for him an
expression of life. In his opinion the interpretation of philosophical
systems as so many life-views (*Lebensanschauungen*) contained a

---

[1] In epistemology Driesch was influenced by Kant, but he departed from
Kantian doctrine by attributing an objective character to the categories, such as
to render possible a metaphysics of reality.
[2] At school Eucken came under the influence of a certain Wilhelm Reuter who
was a disciple of the philosopher Krause.

profound truth, namely that philosophy is rooted in life and continuous with it. At the same time he wished to overcome the fragmentation of philosophy, its falling apart into purely personal reactions to life and ideals for life. And he concluded that if philosophy, as the expression of life, is to possess a more than subjective and purely personal significance, it must be the expression of a universal life which rescues man from his mere particularity.

This universal life is identified by Eucken with what he calls Spiritual Life (*das Geistesleben*). From the purely naturalistic point of view psychical life 'forms a mere means and instrument for the preservation of beings in the hard fight for existence'.[1] Spiritual Life, however, is an active reality which produces a new spiritual world. 'There thus arise whole fields such as science and art, law and morals, and they develop their own contents, their own motive forces, their own laws.'[2] Provided that he breaks with the naturalistic and egoistic point of view man can rise to a participation in this Spiritual Life. He then becomes 'more than a mere point; a universal Life becomes for him his own life'.[3]

Spiritual Life, therefore, is an active reality which operates in and through man. And it can be regarded as the movement of reality towards the full actualization of Spirit. It is, as it were, reality organizing itself from within into a spiritual unity. And as it is through participation in this Life that man achieves real personality, the Life which is the foundation of human personality can be regarded as being itself personal. It is in fact God. 'The concept of God receives here the meaning of an absolute Spiritual Life,'[4] 'the Spiritual Life which attains to complete independence and at the same time to the embracing in itself of all reality.'[5]

Philosophy is or should be the expression of this Life. 'The synthesis of the manifold which philosophy undertakes must not be imposed on reality from without but should proceed out of reality itself and contribute to its development.'[6] That is to say, philosophy should be the conceptual expression of the unifying activity of the Spiritual Life, and it should at the same time contribute to the development of this Life by enabling men to understand their relation to it.

[1] *Einführung in eine Philosophie des Geisteslebens*, p. 9 (Leipzig, 1908).
[2] *Ibid.*, p. 8.
[3] *Grundlinien einer neuen Lebensanschauung*, p. 117 (Leipzig, 1907).
[4] *Der Wahrheitsgehalt der Religion*, p. 138 (Leipzig, 1905, 2nd edition).
[5] *Ibid.*, p. 150.
[6] *Einführung in eine Philosophie des Geisteslebens*, p. 10.

The concept of *das Geistesleben* naturally recalls to mind the philosophy of Hegel. And from this point of view Eucken's thought can be described as neo-idealism. But whereas Hegel emphasized the conceptual solution of problems, Eucken is inclined to say that the important problems of life are solved by action. A man attains to truth in so far as he overcomes the pull of his non-spiritual nature and participates actively in the one Spiritual Life. Hence Eucken described his philosophy as 'activism'.[1] As for the affinities between his own philosophy and pragmatism, Eucken was inclined to interpret pragmatism as involving the reduction of truth to an instrument in the service of 'mere man's' egoistic search for satisfaction and thus as favouring the very fragmentation of philosophy which he wished to overcome. In his view truth is that towards which Spiritual Life actively strives.

In his own day Eucken had a considerable reputation. But what he offers is obviously one more world-view, one more *Lebensanschauung*, rather than an effective overcoming of the conflict of systems. And his philosophy is one in which the element of precise statement and explanation is by no means always conspicuous. It is all very well, for example, to talk about problems being solved by action. But when it is a question of theoretical problems, the concept of solution through action requires much more careful analysis than is given it by Eucken.

7. Hegel, as we have seen, gave a powerful impetus to the study of the history of philosophy. But for him the history of philosophy was absolute idealism in the making or, to express the matter metaphysically, absolute Spirit's progressive understanding of itself. And the historian of philosophy who is thoroughly imbued with Hegelian principles sees in the development of philosophical thought a constant dialectical advance, later systems presupposing and subsuming in themselves earlier phases of thought. It is understandable, however, that there should be other philosophers who look back to past phases of thought as valuable sources of insights which have been later forgotten or overlooked rather than taken up and elevated in succeeding systems.

As an example of the philosophers who have emphasized the objective study of the past with a view to rethinking and re-appropriating its perennially valuable elements we can mention Adolf Trendelenburg (1802–72) who occupied the chair of philosophy at Berlin for many years and exercised a considerable

---

[1] *Einführung in eine Philosophie des Geisteslebens*, p. 155.

influence on the development of historical studies. He applied himself especially to the study of Aristotle, though his historical writings dealt also with Spinoza, Kant, Hegel and Herbart. A vigorous opponent both of Hegel and Herbart, he contributed to the decline of the former's prestige in the middle of the century. And he directed men's attention to the perennially valuable sources of European philosophy in Greek thought, though he was convinced that the insights of Greek philosophy needed to be rethought and appropriated in the light of the modern scientific conception of the world.

Trendelenburg's own philosophy, described by him as the 'organic world-view' (*organische Weltanschauung*) was developed in his two-volume *Logical Inquiries* (*Logische Untersuchungen*, 1840). It owed much to Aristotle, and, as in Aristotelianism, the idea of finality was fundamental. At the same time Trendelenburg endeavoured to reconcile Aristotle and Kant by depicting space, time and the categories as forms both of being and of thought. He also attempted to give a moral foundation to the ideas of right and law in his works on the *Moral Idea of Right* (*Die sittliche Idee des Rechts*, 1849) and *Natural Right on the Foundation of Ethics* (*Naturrecht auf dem Grunde der Ethik*, 1860).

Aristotelian studies were also pursued by Gustav Teichmüller (1832–88) who came under Trendelenburg's influence at Berlin. But Teichmüller subsequently developed a philosophy inspired by Leibniz and Lotze, especially by the former.

Among Trendelenburg's pupils was Otto Willmann (1839–1920) whose mind moved from the thought of Aristotle through criticism of both idealism and materialism to Thomist philosophy. And some allusion can be made here to the reappropriation of mediaeval philosophy, in particular of the thought of St. Thomas Aquinas. It is indeed rather difficult to treat this subject simply within the context of German philosophy in the nineteenth century. For the rise of Thomism was a phenomenon within the intellectual life of the Catholic Church in general, and it can hardly be claimed that the German contribution was the most important. At the same time the subject cannot be simply passed over in silence.

In the seventeenth, eighteenth and early part of the nineteenth centuries philosophy in ecclesiastical seminaries and teaching institutions generally tended to take the form of an uninspired Scholastic Aristotelianism amalgamated with ideas taken from other currents of thought, notably Cartesianism and, later, the philosophy of Wolff. And it lacked the intrinsic vigour which was required to make its presence felt in the intellectual world at large. Further, in the first half of the nineteenth century there were a number of Catholic thinkers in France, Italy and Germany whose ideas, developed either in dialogue with or under the influence of contemporary thought, seemed to the ecclesiastical authorities to compromise, whether directly or indirectly, the integrity of the Catholic faith. Thus in Germany Georg Hermes (1775–1831), professor of theology first at Münster and then at Bonn, was judged by the Church to have adopted far too much from the philosophers whom he tried to oppose, such as Kant and Fichte, and to have thrown Catholic dogma into the melting-pot of philosophical speculation. Again, in his enthusiasm for the revivification of theology Anton Günther (1783–1863) attempted to make use of the Hegelian dialectic to explain and prove the doctrine of the Trinity,[1] while Jakob Froschhammer (1821–93), a priest and a professor of philosophy at Munich, was judged to have subordinated supernatural faith and revelation to idealist philosophy.[2]

In the course of the nineteenth century, however, a number of Catholic thinkers raised the call for a reappropriation of mediaeval thought, and especially of the theological-philosophical synthesis developed in the thirteenth century by St. Thomas Aquinas. As far as Germany was concerned, the revival of interest in Scholasticism in general and Thomism in particular owed much to the writings of men such as Joseph Kleutgen (1811–83), Albert Stöckl (1832–95) and Konstantin Gutberlet (1837–1928). Most of Gutberlet's works appeared after the publication in 1879 of Pope Leo XIII's encyclical letter *Aeterni Patris* in which the Pope asserted the permanent value of Thomism and urged Catholic philosophers to draw their inspiration from it while at the same time developing it to meet modern needs. But Stöckl's *Textbook of Philosophy (Lehrbuch der Philosophie)* had appeared in 1868, and the first editions of Kleutgen's *The Theology of Early Times Defended (Die Theologie der Vorzeit verteidigt)* and *The Philosophy of Early Times Defended (Die Philosophie der Vorzeit verteidigt)* had appeared respectively in 1853–60 and 1860–3. Hence it is not quite accurate to say that Leo XIII inaugurated the revival of

---

[1] Accused by the Church of rationalism, Günther submitted to her judgment.

[2] Froschhammer, who refused to submit to ecclesiastical authority when his views were censured, was later one of the opponents of the dogma of papal infallibility.

Thomism. What he did was to give a powerful impetus to an already existing movement.

The revival of Thomism naturally demanded a real knowledge and understanding not only of the thought of Aquinas in particular but also of mediaeval philosophy in general. And it is natural that the first phase of the revival should have been succeeded by specialist studies in the sphere, such as we associate with the names of Clemens Baeumker (1853–1924) and Martin Grabmann (1875–1949) in Germany, of Maurice De Wulf (1867–1947) in Belgium, and of Pierre Mandonnet (1858–1936) and Étienne Gilson (b. 1884) in France.

At the same time, if Thomism was to be presented as a living system of thought and not as possessing a purely historical interest, it had to be shown, first that it was not entangled with antiquated physics and discarded scientific hypotheses, and secondly that it was capable of development and of throwing light on philosophical problems as they present themselves to the modern mind. In the fulfilment of the first task much was accomplished by the work of Cardinal Mercier (1851–1926) and his collaborators and successors at the university of Louvain.[1] In regard to the fulfilment of the second task we can mention the names of Joseph Geyser (1869–1948) in Germany and of Jacques Maritain (b. 1882) in France.

Having established itself as, so to speak, a respectable system of thought, Thomism had then to show that it was capable of assimilating the valuable elements in other philosophies without self-destruction. But this is a theme which belongs to the history of Thomist thought in the present century.

---

[1] Mercier was not concerned simply with showing that Thomism did not conflict with the sciences. He envisaged the development of Thomism in close connection with the positive and purely objective study of the sciences. An eminent representative of the fulfilment of Mercier's project is the Louvain psychologist Albert Michotte (b. 1881).

### CHAPTER XXI

# NIETZSCHE (1)

*Life and writings—The phases of Nietzsche's thought as 'masks'*
*—Nietzsche's early writings and the critique of contemporary*
*culture—The critique of morals—Atheism and its consequences.*

1. As we have already strayed into the twentieth century, it may seem inappropriate to reserve to this stage of the volume two chapters on a philosopher who died physically in 1900 and, as far as writing was concerned, some ten years previously. But though this procedure is questionable from the chronological point of view, one can also argue in favour of closing a volume on nineteenth-century German philosophy with a thinker who died in 1900 but whose influence was not fully felt until the present century. Whatever one may think about Nietzsche's ideas, one cannot question his vast reputation and the power of his ideas to act like a potent wine in the minds of a good many people. And this is something which can hardly be said about the materialists, Neo-Kantians and the inductive metaphysicians whom we have been considering in the foregoing chapters.

Friedrich Wilhelm Nietzsche was born on October 15th, 1844, at Röcken in Prussian Saxony. His father, a Lutheran pastor, died in 1849, and the boy was brought up at Naumburg in the feminine and pious society of his mother, his sister, a grandmother and two aunts. From 1854 to 1858 he studied at the local *Gymnasium*, and from 1858 to 1864 he was a pupil at the celebrated boarding-school at Pforta. His admiration for the Greek genius was awakened during his schooldays, his favourite classical authors being Plato and Aeschylus. He also tried his hand at poetry and music.

In October 1864 Nietzsche went to the university of Bonn in company with his school friend Paul Deussen, the future orientalist and philosopher. But in the autumn of the following year he moved to Leipzig to continue his philological studies under Ritschl. He formed an intimate friendship with Erwin Rohde, then a fellow student, later a university professor and author of *Psyche*. By this time Nietzsche had abandoned Christianity, and when at Leipzig he made the acquaintance of Schopenhauer's main work one of the features which attracted him was, as he himself said, the author's atheism.

Nietzsche had published some papers in the *Rheinisches Museum*, and when the university of Basel asked Ritschl whether their author was a suitable person to occupy the chair of philosophy at Basel, Ritschl had no hesitation in giving an unqualified testimonial on behalf of his favourite pupil. The result was that Nietzsche found himself appointed a university professor before he had even taken the doctorate.[1] And in May 1869 he delivered his inaugural lecture on *Homer and Classical Philology*. On the outbreak of the Franco-Prussian war Nietzsche joined the ambulance corps of the German army; but illness forced him to abandon this work, and after an insufficient period of convalescence he resumed his professional duties at Basel.

Nietzsche's great consolation at Basel lay in his visits to Richard Wagner's villa on the lake of Lucerne. He had already been seized with admiration for Wagner's music while he was still a student at Leipzig, and his friendship with the composer had a possibly unfortunate effect on his writing. In *The Birth of Tragedy from the Spirit of Music (Die Geburt der Tragödie aus dem Geiste der Musik)* which appeared in 1872, he first drew a contrast between Greek culture before and after Socrates, to the disadvantage of the latter, and then argued that contemporary German culture bore a strong resemblance to Greek culture after Socrates and that it could be saved only if it were permeated with the spirit of Wagner. Not unnaturally, the work met with an enthusiastic reception from Wagner, but the philologists reacted somewhat differently to Nietzsche's views about the origins of Greek tragedy. Wilamowitz-Moellendorff in particular, then a young man, launched a devastating attack against the book. And not even Rohde's loyal defence of his friend could save Nietzsche from losing credit in the world of classical scholarship. Not that this matters much to us today. For it is Nietzsche as philosopher, moralist and psychologist who interests us, not as professor of philology at Basel.

In the period 1873–6 Nietzsche published four essays with the common title *Untimely Meditations* or *Considerations (Unzeitgemässe Betrachtungen)* which is rendered as *Thoughts out of Season* in the English translation of his works. In the first he vehemently attacked the unfortunate David Strauss as a representative of German culture-philistinism, while in the second he attacked the

---

[1] The university of Leipzig thereupon conferred the degree without examination.

idolization of historical learning as a substitute for a living culture. The third essay was devoted to extolling Schopenhauer as an educator, to the disadvantage of the university professors of philosophy, while the fourth depicted Wagner as originating a rebirth of the Greek genius.

By 1876, the date of publication of the fourth essay, entitled *Richard Wagner in Bayreuth*, Nietzsche and Wagner had already begun to drift apart.[1] And his break with the composer represented the end of the first phase or period in Nietzsche's development. If in the first period he decries Socrates, the rationalist, in the second he tends to exalt him. In the first period culture, and indeed human life in general, is depicted as finding its justification in the production of the genius, the creative artist, poet and musician: in the second Nietzsche prefers science to poetry, questions all accepted beliefs and pretty well plays the part of a rationalistic philosopher of the French Enlightenment.

Characteristic of this second period is *Human, All-too-Human* (*Menschliches, Allzumenschliches*) which was originally published in three parts, 1878–9. In a sense the work is positivistic in outlook. Nietzsche attacks metaphysics in an indirect manner, trying to show that the features of human experience and knowledge which had been supposed to necessitate metaphysical explanations or to justify a metaphysical superstructure are capable of explanation on materialistic lines. For instance, the moral distinction between good and bad had its origin in the experience of some actions as beneficial to society and of others as detrimental to it, though in the course of time the utilitarian origin of the distinction was lost sight of. Again, conscience originates in a belief in authority: it is the voice not of God but of parents and educators.

A combination of bad health and dissatisfaction, amounting to disgust, with his professional duties led Nietzsche to resign from his chair at Basel in the spring of 1879. And for the next ten years he led a wandering life, seeking health in various places in Switzerland and Italy, with occasional visits to Germany.

In 1881 Nietzsche published *The Dawn of Day* (*Morgenröte*) in which, as he declared, he opened his campaign against the morality of self-renunciation. And this was followed in 1882[2] by *Joyful*

---

[1] Nietzsche thought, no doubt rightly, that Wagner regarded him as a tool to promote the cause of Wagnerism. But he also came to feel that the real Wagner was not all that he had imagined him to be. The publication of *Parsifal* was for Nietzsche the last straw.

[2] The fifth part of *Joyful Wisdom* was not added until 1887.

*Wisdom (Die fröhliche Wissenschaft)* in which we find the idea of Christianity as hostile to life. The report that God is dead, as Nietzsche puts it, opens up vast horizons to free spirits. Neither book was successful. Nietzsche sent a copy of *The Dawn of Day* to Rohde, but his former friend did not even acknowledge it. And the indifference with which his writings were met in Germany was not calculated to increase Nietzsche's fondness for his fellow countrymen.

In 1881 the idea of the eternal recurrence came to Nietzsche while he was at Sils-Maria in the Engadine. In infinite time there are periodic cycles in which all that has been is repeated over again. This somewhat depressing idea was scarcely new, but it came to Nietzsche with the force of an inspiration. And he conceived the plan of presenting the ideas which were fermenting in his mind through the lips of the Persian sage Zarathustra. The result was his most famous work, *Thus Spake Zarathustra (Also sprach Zarathustra)*. The first two parts were published separately in 1883. The third, in which the doctrine of the eternal recurrence was proclaimed, appeared at the beginning of 1884, and the fourth part was published early in 1885.

*Zarathustra*, with its ideas of Superman and the transvaluation of values, expresses the third phase of Nietzsche's thought. But its poetic and prophetical style gives it the appearance of being the work of a visionary.[1] Calmer expositions of Nietzsche's ideas are to be found in *Beyond Good and Evil (Jenseits von Gut und Böse*, 1886) and *A Genealogy of Morals (Zur Genealogie der Moral*, 1887), which, together with *Zarathustra*, are probably Nietzsche's most important writings. *Beyond Good and Evil* elicited an appreciative letter from Hippolyte Taine, and after the publication of *A Genealogy of Morals*, Nietzsche received a similar letter from Georg Brandes, the Danish critic, who later delivered a course of lectures on Nietzsche's ideas at Copenhagen.

*Beyond Good and Evil* had as its subtitle *Prelude to a Philosophy of the Future*. Nietzsche planned a systematic exposition of his philosophy, for which he made copious notes. His idea of the appropriate title underwent several changes. At first it was to be *The Will to Power, a New Interpretation of Nature* or *The Will to Power, an Essay towards a New Interpretation of the Universe*. In

---

[1] Rudolf Carnap remarks that when Nietzsche wished to take to metaphysics, he very properly had recourse to poetry. Carnap thus looks on *Zarathustra* as empirical confirmation of his own neopositivist interpretation of the nature of metaphysics.

other words, just as Schopenhauer had based a philosophy on the concept of the will to life, so would Nietzsche base a philosophy on the idea of the will to power. Later the emphasis changed, and the proposed title was *The Will to Power, an Essay towards the Trans-valuation of all Values* (*Der Wille zur Macht: Versuch einer Umwerthung aller Werthe*). But in point of fact the projected *magnum opus* was never completed, though *The Antichrist* (*Der Antichrist*) was meant to be the first part of it. Nietzsche's notes for the work which he planned have been published posthumously.

Nietzsche turned aside from his projected work to write a ferocious attack on Wagner, *The Case of Wagner* (*Der Fall Wagner*, 1888), and followed it up with *Nietzsche contra Wagner*. This second essay was published only after Nietzsche's breakdown, as were also other writings of 1888, *The Twilight of the Idols* (*Die Götzen-dämmerung*), *The Antichrist* and *Ecce Homo*, a kind of auto-biography. The works of this year show evident signs of extreme tension and mental instability, and *Ecce Homo* in particular, with its exalted spirit of self-assertion, gives a marked impression of psychical disturbance. At the end of the year definite signs of madness began to show themselves, and in January 1889 Nietzsche was taken from Turin, where he then was, to a clinic at Basel. He never really recovered, but after treatment at Basel and then at Jena he was able to go to his mother's home at Naumburg.[1] After her death he lived with his sister at Weimar. By that time he had become a famous man, though he was hardly in a position to appreciate the fact. He died on August 25th, 1900.

2. In the foregoing section reference has been made to periods or phases in the development of Nietzsche's thought. The philosopher himself, as he looked back, described these phases as so many masks. For example, he asserted that the attitude of a free spirit, that is, of a critical, rationalistic and sceptical observer of life, which he adopted in his second period, was an 'eccentric pose', a second nature, as it were, which was assumed as a means whereby he might win through to his first or true nature. It had to be discarded as the snake sloughs its old skin. Further, Nietzsche was accustomed to speak of particular doctrines or theories as though they were artifices of self-preservation or self-administered tonics. For instance, the theory of the eternal recurrence was a test of

[1] Nietzsche was indeed dogged by bad health and insomnia. And loneliness and neglect preyed on his mind. But it seems probable, in spite of his sister's attempts to deny it, that as a university student he contracted a syphilitic infection and that the disease, after running an atypical course, finally affected the brain.

strength, of Nietzsche's power to say 'yes' to life instead of the Schopenhauerian 'no'. Could he face the thought that his whole life, every moment of it, every suffering, every agony, every humiliation, would be repeated countless times throughout endless time? Could he face this thought and embrace it not only with stoical resignation but also with joy? If so, it was a sign of inner strength, of the triumph in Nietzsche himself of the yea-saying attitude of life.

Obviously, Nietzsche did not say to himself one fine day: 'I shall now pose for a time as a positivist and a coolly critical and scientific observer, because I think that it would be good for my mental health.' It is rather that he seriously attempted to play such a part until, having grown out of it, he recognized it in retrospect as a self-administered tonic and as a mask under which the real direction of his thought could develop unseen. But what was the real direction of his thought? In view of what Nietzsche says about winning through to his true nature, one is inclined, of course, to assume that the doctrine of his later works and of the posthumously-published notes for *The Will to Power* represents his real thought. Yet if we press the theory of masks, we must apply it also, I think, to his third period. As already mentioned, he spoke of the theory of the eternal recurrence as a trial of strength; and this theory belongs to his third period. Further, it was in the third period that Nietzsche explicitly stated his relativistic and pragmatist view of truth. His general theory of truth was indeed social rather than personal, in the sense that those theories were said to be true which are biologically useful for a given species or for a certain kind of man. Thus the theory of Superman would be a myth which possessed truth in so far as it enabled the higher type of man to develop his potentialities. But if we press the idea of masks, we must take such a statement as 'the criterion of truth lies in the intensification of the feeling of power'[1] in a personal sense and apply it to the thought of Nietzsche's third period no less than to that of the first and second periods.

In this case, of course, there remains no 'real thought' of Nietzsche which is statable in terms of definite philosophical theories. For the whole of his expressed thought becomes an

[1] *W*, III, p. 919 (xv, p. 49). Unless otherwise stated, references are given according to volume and page of the three-volume (incomplete) edition of Nietzsche's *Works* by K. Schlechta (Munich, 1954–6). The references in brackets are always to the English translation of Nietzsche's *Works* edited by Dr. Oscar Levy (see Bibliography). The critical German edition of Nietzsche's writings is still unfinished.

instrument whereby Nietzsche as an existing individual, to use Kierkegaard's phrase, seeks to realize his own possibilities. His ideas represent a medium through which we have to try to discern the significance of an existence. We then have the sort of interpretation of Nietzsche's life and work of which Karl Jaspers has given us a fine example.[1]

The present writer has no intention of questioning the value of the existential interpretation of Nietzsche's life and thought. But in a book such as this the reader has a right to expect a summary account of what Nietzsche said, of his public face or appearance, so to speak. After all, when a philosopher commits ideas to paper and publishes them, they take on, as it were, a life of their own and exercise a greater or lesser influence, as the case may be. It is true that his philosophy lacks the impressiveness of systems such as those of Spinoza and Hegel, a fact of which Nietzsche was well aware. And if one wishes to find in it German 'profundity', one has to look beneath the surface. But though Nietzsche himself drew attention to the personal aspects of his thinking and to the need for probing beneath the surface, the fact remains that he held certain convictions very strongly and that he came to think of himself as a prophet, as a reforming force, and of his ideas as 'dynamite'. Even if on his own view of truth his theories necessarily assume the character of myth, these myths were intimately associated with value-judgments which Nietzsche asserted with passion. And it is perhaps these value-judgments more than anything else which have been the source of his great influence.

3. We have already referred to Nietzsche's discovery, when he was a student at Leipzig, of Schopenhauer's *World as Will and Idea*. But though Nietzsche received a powerful stimulus from the great pessimist, he was at no time a disciple of Schopenhauer. In *The Birth of Tragedy*, for example, he does indeed follow Schopenhauer to the extent of postulating what he calls a 'Primordial Unity' which manifests itself in the world and in human life. And, like Schopenhauer, he depicts life as terrible and tragic and speaks of its transmutation through art, the work of the creative genius. At the same time even in his early works, when the inspiration derived from Schopenhauer's philosophy is evident, the general direction of Nietzsche's thought is towards the affirmation of life rather than towards its negation. And when in 1888 he looked back on *The*

---

[1] In his *Nietzsche: Einführung in das Verständnis seines Philosophierens* (Berlin 1936). For Jaspers Nietzsche and Kierkegaard represent two 'exceptions', two embodiments of different possibilities of human existence.

*Birth of Tragedy* and asserted that it expressed an attitude to life which was the antithesis of Schopenhauer's, the assertion was not without foundation.

The Greeks, according to Nietzsche in *The Birth of Tragedy*, knew very well that life is terrible, inexplicable, dangerous. But though they were alive to the real character of the world and of human life, they did not surrender to pessimism by turning their backs on life. What they did was to transmute the world and human life through the medium of art. And they were then able to say 'yes' to the world as an aesthetic phenomenon. There were, however, two ways of doing this, corresponding respectively to the Dionysian and Apollonian attitudes or mentalities.

Dionysus is for Nietzsche the symbol of the stream of life itself, breaking down all barriers and ignoring all restraints. In the Dionysian or Bacchic rites we can see the intoxicated votaries becoming, as it were, one with life. The barriers set up by the principle of individuation tend to break down; the veil of Maya is turned aside; and men and women are plunged into the stream of life, manifesting the Primordial Unity. Apollo, however, is the symbol of light, of measure, of restraint. He represents the principle of individuation. And the Apollonian attitude is expressed in the shining dream-world of the Olympic deities.

But we can, of course, get away from metaphysical theories about the Primordial Unity and Schopenhauer's talk about the principle of individuation, and express the matter in a psychological form. Beneath the moderation so often ascribed to the Greeks, beneath their devotion to art and beauty and form, Nietzsche sees the dark, turgid and formless torrent of instinct and impulse and passion which tends to sweep away everything in its path.

Now, if we assume that life is in itself an object of horror and terror and that pessimism, in the sense of the no-saying attitude to life, can be avoided only by the aesthetic transmutation of reality, there are two ways of doing this. One is to draw an aesthetic veil over reality, creating an ideal world of form and beauty. This is the Apollonian way. And it found expression in the Olympic mythology, in the epic and in the plastic arts. The other possibility is that of triumphantly affirming and embracing existence in all its darkness and horror. This is the Dionysian attitude, and its typical art forms are tragedy and music. Tragedy does indeed transmute existence into an aesthetic phenomenon, but it does not draw a veil over existence as it is. Rather does it exhibit existence in aesthetic form and affirm it.

In *The Birth of Tragedy*, as its title indicates, Nietzsche is concerned immediately with the origins and development of Greek tragedy. But we cannot discuss the matter here. Nor does it matter for our present purposes how far Nietzsche's account of the origins of tragedy is acceptable from the point of view of classical scholarship. The important point is that the supreme achievement of Greek culture, before it was spoiled by the spirit of Socratic nationalism, lay for Nietzsche in a fusion of Dionysian and Apollonian elements.[1] And in this fusion he saw the foundation for a cultural standard. True culture is a unity of the forces of life, the Dionysian element, with the love of form and beauty which is characteristic of the Apollonian attitude.

If existence is justified as an aesthetic phenomenon, the fine flower of humanity will be constituted by those who transmute existence into such a phenomenon and enable men to see existence in this way and affirm it. In other words, the creative genius will be the highest cultural product. Indeed, in the period which we are considering Nietzsche speaks as though the production of genius were the aim and end of culture, its justification. He makes this quite clear in, for instance, his essay on *The Greek State* (*Der griechische Staat*, 1871). Here and elsewhere he insists that the toil and labour of the majority in the struggle of life are justified by forming the substructure on which the genius, whether in art, music or philosophy, can arise. For the genius is the organ whereby existence is, as it were, redeemed.

On the basis of these ideas Nietzsche proceeds to give a highly critical evaluation of contemporary German culture. He contrasts, for example, historical knowledge about past cultures with culture itself, described as 'unity of artistic style in all the expressions of the life of a people'.[2] But his critique of the German culture of his time need not detain us here. Instead we can note two or three general ideas which also look forward to Nietzsche's later thought.

Nietzsche varies the question whether life should dominate knowledge or knowledge life. 'Which of the two is the higher and decisive power? Nobody will doubt that life is the higher and dominating power. . . .'[3] This means that the nineteenth-century culture, characterized by the domination of knowledge and

---

[1] According to Nietzsche, the tragedies of Aeschylus were the supreme artistic expression of this fusion.

[2] *W*, I, p. 140 (I, p. 8).     [3] *W*, I, p. 282 (II, p. 96).

science, is exposed to the revenge, as it were, of the vital forces, the
explosion of which will produce a new barbarism. Beneath the
surface of modern life Nietzsche sees vital forces which are 'wild,
primitive and completely merciless. One looks at them with a
fearful expectancy as though at the cauldron in a witch's kitchen
. . . for a century we have been ready for world-shaking con-
vulsions.'[1] In nineteenth-century society we can see both a
complacency in the condition which man has already reached and
a widespread tendency, fostered by the national State and manifested in the movements towards democracy and socialism, to
promote a uniform mediocrity, hostile to genius. But there is no
reason to suppose that the development of man's potentialities has
reached its term. And the emergence of the latent destructive
forces will pave the way for the rise of higher specimens of
humanity in the form of outstanding individuals.

Obviously, this view involves a supra-historical outlook, as
Nietzsche puts it. It involves, that is to say, a rejection of the
Hegelian canonization of the actual in the name of a necessary self-
manifestation of the *Logos* or Idea, and a vision of values which
transcend the historical situation. The human being is plastic; he
is capable of transcending himself, of realizing fresh possibilities;
and he needs a vision, a goal, a sense of direction. Empirical
science cannot provide this vision. And though Nietzsche does not
say much about Christianity in his early writings, it is clear that
he does not look to the Christian religion as the source of the
requisite vision.[2] There remains philosophy, not indeed as
represented by learned university professors, but in the guise of
the lonely thinker who has a clear vision of the possibilities of man's
self-transcendence and who is not afraid to be 'dangerous'. Once it
has been decided how far things are alterable, philosophy should
set itself 'with ruthless courage to the task of *improving that aspect
of the world which has been recognized as susceptible to being changed*'.[3]
When in later years Nietzsche looks back on these early essays, he

---

[1] *W*, I, p. 313 (II, p. 137).

[2] In *Schopenhauer as Educator* Nietzsche remarks that 'Christianity is certainly
one of the purest manifestations of that impulse towards culture and, precisely,
towards the ever renewed production of the saint'; *W*, I, p. 332 (II, p. 161). But
he goes on to argue that Christianity has been used to turn the mill-wheels of the
State and that it has become hopelessly degenerate. It is clear that he regards the
Christian religion as a spent force. Looking back later on *The Birth of Tragedy*
he sees in its silence about Christianity a hostile silence. For the book in question recognized only aesthetic values, which, Nietzsche maintains, Christianity
denies.

[3] *W*, I, p. 379 (I, p. 120).

sees in this ideal of the philosopher as judge of life and creator of values Zarathustra or himself. It comes to the same thing.

4. A criticism of the ethical attitude in so far as this involves the assertion of a universal moral law and of absolute moral values is implicit in Nietzsche's early writings. We have seen that according to his own statement only aesthetic values were recognized in *The Birth of Tragedy*. And in his essay on David Strauss Nietzsche refers to Strauss's contention that the sum and substance of morality consists in looking on all other human beings as having the same needs, claims and rights as oneself and then asks where this imperative comes from. Strauss seems to take it for granted that the imperative has its basis in the Darwinian theory of evolution. But evolution provides no such basis. The class *Man* comprises a multitude of different types, and it is absurd to claim that we are required to behave as though individual differences and distinctions were non-existent or unimportant. And we have seen that Nietzsche lays stress on outstanding individuals rather than on the race or species.

However, it is in *Human, All-too-Human* that Nietzsche begins to treat of morality in some detail. The work is indeed composed of aphorisms; it is not a systematic treatise. But if we compare the remarks relating to morality, a more or less coherent theory emerges.

It is the first sign that the animal has become man when its notions are no longer directed simply to the satisfaction of the moment but to what is recognized as useful in an enduring manner.[1] But we can hardly talk about morality until utility is understood in the sense of usefulness for the existence, survival and welfare of the community. For 'morality is primarily a means of preserving the community in general and warding off destruction from it'.[2] Compulsion has first to be employed to make the individual conform his conduct to the interests of society. But compulsion is succeeded by the force of custom, and in time the authoritative voice of the community takes the form of what we call conscience. Obedience can become a second nature, as it were, and be associated with pleasure. At the same time moral epithets come to be extended from actions to the intentions of the agents. And the concepts of virtue and of the virtuous man arise. In other words, morality is interiorized through a process of progressive refinement.

[1] *W*, I, p. 502 (VII/I, p. 92).          [2] *W*, I, p. 900 (VII/2, p. 221).

So far Nietzsche speaks like a utilitarian. And his concept of morality bears some resemblance to what Bergson calls closed morality. But once we look at the historical development of morality we see a 'twofold early history of good and evil'.[1] And it is the development of this idea of two moral outlooks which is really characteristic of Nietzsche. But the idea is best discussed in relation to his later writings.

In *Beyond Good and Evil* Nietzsche says that he has discovered two primary types of morality, 'master-morality and slave-morality'.[2] In all higher civilizations they are mixed, and elements of both can be found even in the same man. But it is important to distinguish them. In the master-morality or aristocratic morality 'good' and 'bad' are equivalent to 'noble' and 'despicable', and the epithets are applied to men rather than to actions. In the slave-morality the standard is that which is useful or beneficial to the society of the weak and powerless. Qualities such as sympathy, kindness and humility are extolled as virtues, and the strong and independent individuals are regarded as dangerous, and therefore as 'evil'. By the standards of the slave-morality the 'good' man of the master-morality tends to be accounted as 'evil'. Slave-morality is thus herd-morality. Its moral valuations are expressions of the needs of a herd.

This point of view is expounded more systematically in *The Genealogy of Morals* where Nietzsche makes use of the concept of resentment. The higher type of man creates his own values out of the abundance of his life and strength. The meek and powerless, however, fear the strong and powerful, and they attempt to curb and tame them by asserting as absolute the values of the herd. 'The revolt of the slaves in morals begins with resentment becoming creative and giving birth to values.'[3] This resentment is not, of course, openly acknowledged by the herd, and it can work by devious and indirect paths. But the psychologist of the moral life can detect and bring to light its presence and complex modes of operation.

What we see, therefore, in the history of morals is the conflict of two moral attitudes or outlooks. From the point of view of the higher man there can in a sense be coexistence. That is to say, there could be coexistence if the herd, incapable of anything higher, was content to keep its values to itself. But, of course, it is not content

[1] *W*, I, p. 483 (VII/1, p. 64).          [2] *W*, II, p. 730 (v, p. 227).
[3] *W*, II, p. 782 (XIII, p. 34).

to do this. It endeavours to impose its own values universally. And according to Nietzsche it succeeded in doing this, at least in the West, in Christianity. He does not indeed deny all value to Christian morality. He admits, for instance, that it has contributed to the refinement of man. At the same time he sees in it an expression of the resentment which is characteristic of the herd instinct or slave-morality. And the same resentment is attributed to the democratic and socialist movements which Nietzsche interprets as derivatives of Christianity.

Nietzsche maintains, therefore, that the concept of a uniform universal and absolute moral system is to be rejected. For it is the fruit of resentment and represents inferior life, descending life, degeneracy, whereas the aristocratic morality represents the movement of ascending life.[1] And in place of the concept of one universal and absolute moral system (or indeed of different sets of values, relative to different societies, if each set is regarded as binding all the members of the society) we must put the concept of a gradation of rank among different types of morality. The herd is welcome to its own set of values, provided that it is deprived of the power of imposing them on the higher type of man who is called upon to create his own values which will enable man to transcend his present condition.

When, therefore, Nietzsche speaks of standing beyond good and evil, what he has in mind is rising above the so-called herd-morality which in his opinion reduces everyone to a common level, favours mediocrity and prevents the development of a higher type of man. He does not mean to imply that all respect for values should be abandoned and all self-restraint thrown overboard. The man who rejects the binding force of what is customarily called morality may be himself so weak and degenerate that he destroys himself morally. It is only the higher type of man who can safely go beyond good and evil in the sense which these terms bear in the morality of resentment. And he does so in order to create values which will be at once an expression of ascending life and a means of enabling man to transcend himself in the direction of Superman, a higher level of human existence.

When it comes to describing the content of the new values, Nietzsche does not indeed afford us very much light. Some of the virtues on which he insists look suspiciously like old virtues,

---

[1] The general philosophy of life which these judgments require as a background will be considered later.

though he maintains that they are 'transvalued', that is, made different by reason of the different motives, attitudes and valuations which they express. However, one can say in general that what Nietzsche looks for is the highest possible integration of all aspects of human nature. He accuses Christianity of depreciating the body, impulse, instinct, passion, the free and untrammelled exercise of the mind, aesthetic values, and so on. But he obviously does not call for the disintegration of the human personality into a bundle of warring impulses and unbridled passions. It is a question of integration as an expression of strength, not of extirpation or mortification out of a motive of fear which is based on a consciousness of weakness. Needless to say, Nietzsche gives a very one-sided account of the Christian doctrine of man and of values. But it is essential for him to insist on this one-sided view. Otherwise he would find it difficult to assert that he had anything new to offer, unless it were the type of ideal for man which some of the Nazis liked to attribute to him.

5. In *Joyful Wisdom* Nietzsche remarks that 'the greatest event of recent times—that 'God is dead', that belief in the Christian God has become unworthy of belief—already begins to cast its first shadows over Europe. . . . At last the horizon lies free before us, even granted that it is not bright; at least the sea, *our* sea, lies open before us. Perhaps there has never been so open a sea.'[1] In other words, decay of belief in God opens the way for man's creative energies to develop fully; the Christian God, with his commands and prohibitions, no longer stands in the path; and man's eyes are no longer turned towards an unreal supernatural realm, towards the other world rather than towards this world.

This point of view obviously implies that the concept of God is hostile to life. And this is precisely Nietzsche's contention, which he expresses with increasing vehemence as time goes on. 'The concept *God*', he says in *The Twilight of the Idols*, 'was up to now the greatest *objection* against existence.'[2] And in *The Antichrist* we read that 'with God war is declared on life, Nature and the will to live! God is the formula for every calumny against this world and for every lie concerning a beyond!'[3] But it is unnecessary to multiply quotations. Nietzsche is willing to admit that religion in some of its phases has expressed the will to life, or rather to power; but his general attitude is that belief in God, especially in the God

[1] *W*, ii, pp. 205–6 (x, pp. 275–6).            [2] *W*, ii, p. 978 (xvi, p. 43).
[3] *W*, ii, p. 1178 (xvi, p. 146). Nietzsche is speaking specifically of the Christian concept of God.

of the Christian religion, is hostile to life, and that when it expresses the will to power, the will in question is that of the lower types of man.

Given this attitude, it is understandable that Nietzsche tends to make the choice between theism, especially Christian theism, and atheism a matter of taste or instinct. He recognizes that there have been great men who were believers, but he maintains that nowadays at least, when the existence of God is no longer taken for granted, strength, intellectual freedom, independence and concern for the future of man demand atheism. Belief is a sign of weakness, cowardice, decadence, a no-saying attitude to life. True, Nietzsche attempts a sketch of the origins of the idea of God. And he cheerfully commits the genetic fallacy, maintaining that when it has been shown how the idea of God could have originated, any disproof of God's existence becomes superfluous. He also occasionally alludes to theoretical objections against belief in God. But, generally speaking, the illusory character of this belief is assumed. And the decisive motive for its rejection is that man (or Nietzsche himself) may take the place of God as legislator and creator of values. Considered as a purely theoretical attack, Nietzsche's condemnation of theism in general and of Christianity in particular is worth very little. But it is not an aspect of the matter to which he attaches much importance. As far as theology is concerned, there is no need to bother about such fables. Nietzsche's hatred of Christianity proceeds principally from his view of its supposed effect on man, whom it renders weak, submissive, resigned, humble or tortured in conscience and unable to develop himself freely. It either prevents the growth of superior individuals or ruins them, as in the case of Pascal.[1]

It is indeed noticeable that in his attack on Christianity Nietzsche often speaks of the seductiveness and fascination of Christian beliefs and ideals. And it is clear that he himself felt the attraction and that he rejected it partly in order to prove to himself that 'apart from the fact that I am a *decadent*, I am also the opposite of such a being'.[2] His rejection of God proved to himself his inner strength, his ability to live without God. But from the

---

[1] Nietzsche does occasionally say something in favour of Christian values. But his admissions are by no means always calculated to afford consolation to Christians. For instance, while admitting that Christianity has developed the sense of truth and the ideal of love, he insists that the sense of truth ultimately turns against the Christian interpretation of reality and the ideal of love against the Christian idea of God.

[2] *W*, II, p. 1072 (XVII, p. 12).

purely philosophical point of view the conclusions which he draws from atheism are more important than the psychological factors bearing on his rejection of the Christian God.

Some people have imagined, Nietzsche maintains, that there is no necessary connection between belief in the Christian God and acceptance of Christian moral standards and values. That is to say, they have thought that the latter can be maintained more or less intact when the former has been discarded. We have thus witnessed the growth of secularized forms of Christianity, such as democracy and socialism, which have tried to maintain a considerable part of the Christian moral system without its theological foundations. But such attempts are, in Nietzsche's opinion, vain. The 'death of God' will inevitably be followed, sooner or later, by the rejection of absolute values and of the idea of an objective and universal moral law.

The European man, however, has been brought up to recognize certain moral values which have been associated with Christian belief and, Nietzsche maintains, in a certain sense depend on it. If, therefore, European man loses his faith in these values, he loses his faith in all values. For he knows only 'morality', the morality which was canonized, as it were, by Christianity and given a theological foundation. And disbelief in all values, issuing in the sense of the purposelessness of the world of becoming, is one of the main elements in nihilism. 'Morality was the greatest *antidote* (*Gegenmittel*) against practical and theoretical *nihilism*.'[1] For it ascribed an absolute value to man and 'prevented man from despising himself as man, from turning against life and from despairing of the possibility of knowledge; it was a *means of preservation*'.[2] True, the man who was preserved in this way by the Christian morality was the lower type of man. But the point is that the Christian morality succeeded in imposing itself generally, whether directly or in the form of its derivatives. Hence the breakdown of belief in the Christian moral values exposes man to the danger of nihilism, not because there are no other possible values, but because most men, in the West at least, know no others.

Nihilism can take more than one form. There is, for instance, passive nihilism, a pessimistic acquiescence in the absence of values and in the purposelessness of existence. But there is also active nihilism which seeks to destroy that in which it no longer believes. And Nietzsche prophesies the advent of an active nihilism,

[1] *W*, III, p. 852 (IX, p. 9).          [2] *Ibid.*

showing itself in world-shaking ideological wars. 'There will be wars such as there have never been on earth before. Only from my time on will there be on earth *politics on the grand scale.*'[1]

The advent of nihilism is in Nietzsche's opinion inevitable. And it will mean the final overthrow of the decadent Christian civilization of Europe. At the same time it will clear the way for a new dawn, for the transvaluation of values, for the emergence of a higher type of man. For this reason 'this most gruesome of all guests',[2] who stands at the door, is to be welcomed.

[1] *W*, II, p. 1153 (XVII, p. 132).                [2] *W*, III, p. 881 (IX, p. 5).

### CHAPTER XXII

## NIETZSCHE (2)

*The hypothesis of the Will to Power—The Will to Power as manifested in knowledge; Nietzsche's view of truth—The Will to Power in Nature and man—Superman and the order of rank— The theory of the eternal recurrence—Comments on Nietzsche's philosophy.*

1. '*This world*', Nietzsche asserts, '*is the Will to Power—and nothing else!* And you yourselves too are this Will to Power—and nothing else!'[1] These words are an adaptation of Schopenhauer's statements at the close of his *magnum opus*; and the way in which Nietzsche is accustomed to speak of 'the Will to Power' naturally gives the impression that he has transformed Schopenhauer's Will to Existence or Will to Live into the Will to Power. But though the impression is, of course, correct in a sense, we must not understand Nietzsche as meaning that the world is an appearance of a metaphysical unity which transcends the world. For he is never tired of attacking the distinction between this world, identified with merely phenomenal reality, and a transcendent reality which is 'really real'. The world is not an illusion. Nor does the Will to Power exist in a state of transcendence. The world, the universe, is a unity, a process of becoming; and it is the Will to Power in the sense that this Will is its intelligible character. Everywhere, in everything, we can see the Will to Power expressing itself. And though one can perhaps say that for Nietzsche the Will to Power is the inner reality of the universe, it exists only in its manifestations. Nietzsche's theory of the Will to Power is thus an interpretation of the universe, a way of looking at it and describing it, rather than a metaphysical doctrine about a reality which lies *behind* the visible world and transcends it.

Nietzsche had, of course, Schopenhauer at the back of his mind. But he did not jump straight from his reading of *The World as Will and Idea* to a general theory of the universe. Rather did he discern manifestations of the Will to Power in human psychical processes and then extend this idea to organic life in general. In *Beyond Good and Evil* he remarks that logical method compels us to inquire

[1] *W*, III, p. 917 (xv, p. 432).

whether we can find one principle of explanation, one fundamental form of causal activity, through which we can unify vital phenomena. And he finds this principle in the Will to Power. 'A living thing seeks above all to *discharge* its force—life itself is Will to Power: self-preservation is only one of the indirect and most common *consequences* thereof.'[1] Nietzsche then proceeds to extend this principle of explanation to the world as a whole. 'Granted that we succeed in explaining our whole instinctive life as the development and ramification of *one* fundamental form of will—namely the Will to Power, as *my* thesis says; granted that one could refer all organic functions to this Will to Power, . . . one would have thereby acquired the right to define unequivocally *all* active force as *Will to Power*. The world as seen from within, the world as defined and characterized according to its "intelligible character", would be precisely "Will to Power" and nothing else.'[2]

Thus Nietzsche's theory of the Will to Power is not so much an *a priori* metaphysical thesis as a sweeping empirical hypothesis. If, he says, we believe in the causality of the will, a belief which is really belief in causality itself, 'we *must* make the attempt to posit hypothetically the causality of the will as the only form of causality'.[3] In Nietzsche's intention at least the theory was an explanatory hypothesis, and in his projected *magnum opus* he planned to apply it to different classes of phenomena, showing how they could be unified in terms of this hypothesis. The notes which he made for this work indicate the lines of his thought, and in the next two sections I propose to give some examples of his reflections.

2. 'Knowledge', Nietzsche insists, 'works as an instrument of power. It is therefore obvious that it grows with every increase of power. . . .'[4] The desire of knowledge, the will to know, depends on the will to power, that is, on a given kind of being's impulse to master a certain field of reality and to enlist it in its service. The aim of knowledge is not to know, in the sense of grasping absolute truth for its own sake, but to master. We desire to schematize, to impose order and form on the multiplicity of impressions and sensations to the extent required by our practical needs. Reality is Becoming: it is we who turn it into Being, imposing stable patterns on the flux of Becoming. And this activity is an expression of the Will to Power. Science can thus be defined or described as the

[1] *W*, II, p. 578 (v, p. 20).  [2] *W*, II, p. 601 (v, p. 52).
[3] *Ibid.*  [4] *W*, III, p. 751 (xv, p. 11).

'transformation of Nature into concepts for the purpose of governing Nature'.[1]

Knowledge is, of course, a process of interpretation. But this process is grounded on vital needs and expresses the will to master the otherwise unintelligible flux of Becoming. And it is a question of reading an interpretation into reality rather than of reading it, so to speak, off or in reality. For instance, the concept of the ego or self as a permanent substance is an interpretation imposed upon the flux of Becoming: it is our creation for practical purposes. To be sure, the idea that 'we' interpret psychical states as similar and attribute them to a permanent subject involves Nietzsche in obvious and, in the opinion of the present writer, insoluble difficulties. His general contention is, however, that we cannot legitimately argue from the utility of an interpretation to its objectivity. For a useful fiction, an interpretation which was devoid of objectivity in the sense in which believers in absolute truth would understand objectivity, might be required and thereby justified by our needs.

But there is, according to Nietzsche, no absolute truth. The concept of absolute truth is an invention of philosophers who are dissatisfied with the world of Becoming and seek an abiding world of Being. '*Truth is that sort of error* without which a particular type of living being could not live. The value for *life* is ultimately decisive.'[2]

Some 'fictions', of course, prove to be so useful, and indeed practically necessary, to the human race that they tend to become unquestioned assumptions; for example, 'that there are enduring things, that there are equal things, that there are things, substances, bodies. . . .'[3] It was necessary for life that the concept of a thing or of substance should be imposed on the constant flux of phenomena. 'The beings which did not see correctly had an advantage over those who saw everything "in flux".'[4] Similarly, the law of causality has become so assimilated by human belief that '*not* to believe in it would mean the ruin of our species'.[5] And the same can be said of the laws of logic.

The fictions which have shown themselves to be less useful than other fictions, or even positively harmful, are reputed as 'errors'. But those which have proved their utility to the species and have attained the rank of unquestioned 'truths' become embedded, as

---

[1] *W*, III, p. 440 (xv, p. 105).
[2] *W*, III, p. 844 (xv, p. 20).
[3] *W*, II, p. 116 (x, p. 153).
[4] *W*, II, p. 119 (x, p. 157).
[5] *W*, III, p. 443 (xv, pp. 21–2).

it were, in language. And here lies a danger. For we may be misled by language and imagine that our way of speaking about the world necessarily mirrors reality. 'We are still being constantly led astray by words and concepts into thinking things are simpler than they are, as separate from one another, indivisible and existing each on its own. A philosophical mythology lies hidden in *language* and it breaks out again at every moment, however careful one may be.'[1]

All 'truths' are 'fictions'; all such fictions are interpretations; and all interpretations are perspectives. Even every instinct has its perspective, its point of view, which it endeavours to impose on other instincts. And the categories of reason are also logical fictions and perspectives, not necessary truths, nor *a priori* forms. But the perspectival view of truth admits, of course, of differences. Some perspectives, as we have seen, have proved to be practically necessary for the welfare of the race. But there are others which are by no means necessary. And here the influence of valuations becomes especially evident. For example, the philosopher who interprets the world as the appearance of an Absolute which transcends change and is alone 'really real' expounds a perspective based on a negative evaluation of the world of becoming. And this in turn shows what sort of a man he is.

The obvious comment on Nietzsche's general view of truth is that it presupposes the possibility of occupying an absolute standpoint from which the relativity of all truth or its fictional character can be asserted, and that this presupposition is at variance with the relativist interpretation of truth. Further, this comment by no means loses its point if Nietzsche is willing to say that his own view of the world, and even of truth, is perspectival and 'fictional'.[2] A few moments' reflection is sufficient to show this. Still, it is interesting to find Nietzsche anticipating John Dewey in applying a pragmatist or instrumentalist view of truth to such strongholds of the absolute truth theory as logic. For him, even the fundamental principles of logic are simply expressions of the Will to Power, instruments to enable man to dominate the flux of Becoming.

3. If Nietzsche is prepared to apply his view of truth to alleged eternal truths, he must obviously apply it *a fortiori* to scientific

---

[1] *W*, I, pp. 878–9 (VII/2, p. 192).

[2] No doubt, Nietzsche would admit this in principle, while insisting that his interpretation of the world was the expression of a higher form of the Will to Power. But what is the standard of higher and lower?

hypotheses. The atomic theory, for example, is fictional in character; that is to say, it is a schema imposed on phenomena by the scientist with a view to mastery.[1] We cannot indeed help speaking as though there was a distinction between the seat of force or energy and the force itself. But this should not blind us to the fact that the atom, considered as an entity, a seat of force, is a symbol invented by the scientist, a mental projection.

However, if we presuppose the fictional character of the atomic theory, we can go on to say that every atom is a quantum of energy or, better, of the Will to Power. It seeks to discharge its energy, to radiate its force or power. And so-called physical laws represent relations of power between two or more forces. We need to unify, and we need mathematical formulas for grasping, classifying, mastering. But this is no proof either that things obey laws in the sense of rules or that there are substantial things which exercise force or power. There are simply 'dynamic quanta in a relation of tension to all other dynamic quanta'.[2]

To turn to the organic world. 'A plurality of forces, united by a common nutritive process, we call *Life*.'[3] And life might be defined as 'a lasting form of processes of assertions of force, in which the various combatants on their side grow unequally'.[4] In other words, the organism is an intricate complexity of systems which strive after an increase in the feeling of power. And being itself an expression of the Will to Power, it looks for obstacles, for something to overcome. For example, appropriation and assimilation are interpreted by Nietzsche as manifestations of the Will to Power. And the same can be said of all organic functions.

When treating of biological evolution Nietzsche attacks Darwinism. He points out, for instance, that during most of the time taken up in the formation of a certain organ or quality, the inchoate organ is of no use to its possessor and cannot aid it in its struggle with external circumstances and foes. 'The influence of "external circumstances" is absurdly *overrated* by Darwin. The essential factor in the vital process is precisely the tremendous power to shape and create forms from within, a power which *uses* and *exploits* the environment.'[5] Again, the assumption that natural selection works in favour of the progress of the species and of its better-constituted and individually stronger specimens is

---

[1] Mastery is not to be understood, of course, in a vulgarly utilitarian sense. Knowledge itself is mastery, an expression of the Will to Power.
[2] *W*, III, p. 778 (xv, p. 120).          [3] *W*, III, p. 874 (xv, p. 123).
[4] *W*, III, p. 458 (xv, p. 124).          [5] *W*, III, p. 889 (xv, p. 127).

unwarranted. It is precisely the better specimens which perish and the mediocre which survive. For the exceptions, the best specimens, are weak in comparison with the majority. Taken individually, the members of the majority may be inferior, but when grouped together under the influence of fear and the gregarious instincts they are powerful.

Hence if we based our moral values on the facts of evolution, we should have to conclude that 'the mediocre are more valuable than the exceptional specimens, and that the *decadent* are more valuable than the mediocre'.[1] For higher values we have to look to superior individuals who in their isolation are stimulated to set before themselves lofty aims.

In the field of human psychology Nietzsche finds ample opportunity for diagnosing the manifestations of the Will to Power. For example, he dismisses as quite unfounded the psychological theory presupposed by hedonism, namely the theory that pursuit of pleasure and avoidance of pain are the fundamental motives of human conduct. In Nietzsche's view pleasure and pain are concomitant phenomena in the striving after an increase of power. Pleasure can be described as the feeling of increased power, while pain results from a felt hindrance to the Will to Power. At the same time pain often provides a stimulus to this Will. For every triumph presupposes an obstacle, a hindrance, which is overcome. It is thus absurd to look on pain as an unmixed evil. Man is constantly in need of it as a stimulus to fresh effort and, for the matter of that, as a stimulus to obtaining new forms of pleasure as accompanying results of the triumphs to which pain urges him on.

Though we cannot enter in detail into Nietzsche's psychological analyses, it is worth noting the role played in these analyses by the concept of sublimation. For example, in his view self-mortification and asceticism can be sublimated forms of a primitive cruelty which is itself an expression of the Will to Power. And he raises the question, what instincts are sublimated in, say, the aesthetic view of the world? Everywhere Nietzsche sees the operation, often devious and hidden, of the Will to Power.

4. According to Nietzsche, rank is determined by power. 'It is quanta of power, and nothing else, which determine and distinguish rank.'[2] And one might well draw the conclusion that if the mediocre

---

[1] *W*, III, pp. 748–9 (xv, p. 159).
[2] *W*, x, p. 105 (xv, p. 295). The first reference here is not to the Schlechta edition but to the *Taschen-Ausgabe* published by A. Kroner of Stuttgart, the date of the volume in question being 1921.

majority possesses greater power than individuals who are not mediocre, it also possesses greater value. But this, of course, is by no means Nietzsche's view. He understands power in the sense of an intrinsic quality of the individual. And he tells us, 'I distinguish between a type which represents ascending life and a type which represents decadence, decomposition, weakness'.[1] And even if the mediocre majority, united together, happens to be powerful, it does not, for Nietzsche, represent ascending life.

Yet the mediocre are necessary. For 'a high culture can exist only on a broad basis, on a strongly and soundly consolidated mediocrity'.[2] In fact, from this point of view Nietzsche welcomes the spread of democracy and socialism. For they help to create the requisite basis of mediocrity. In a famous passage in the first part of *Zarathustra* Nietzsche launches an attack against the national State, 'the coldest of all cold monsters'[3] and the new idol which sets itself up as an object of worship and endeavours to reduce all to a common state of mediocrity. But though he condemns the national State from this point of view, namely as preventing the development of outstanding individuals, he none the less insists that the mediocre masses are a necessary means to an end, the emergence of a higher type of man. It is not the mission of the new higher caste or type to lead the masses as a shepherd leads his flock. Rather is it the mission of the masses to form the foundation on which the new so-called lords of the earth can lead their own life and make possible the emergence of still higher types of man. But before this can happen there will come the new barbarians, as Nietzsche calls them, who will break the actual dominion of the masses and thus render possible the free development of outstanding individuals.

As a spur and goal to the potentially higher man Nietzsche offers the myth of Superman (*der Uebermensch*). 'Not "humanity" but *Superman* is the goal.'[4] 'Man is something which must be surpassed; man is a bridge and not a goal.'[5] But this must not be taken to mean that man will evolve into Superman by an inevitable process. Superman is a myth, a goal for the will. 'Superman is the meaning of the earth. Let your will say: Superman *is to be* the meaning of the earth.'[6] Nietzsche does indeed assert that 'man is a rope stretched between animal and Superman—a rope over an abyss'.[7]

---

[1] *W*, III, p. 829 (xv, p. 296).
[2] *W*, III, p. 709 (xv, pp. 302–3).
[3] *W*, II, p. 313 (IV, p. 54).
[4] *W*, III, p. 440 (xv, p. 387).
[5] *W*, II, p. 445 (IV, p. 241).
[6] *W*, II, p. 280 (IV, p. 7).
[7] *W*, II, p. 281 (IV, p. 9).

But it is not a question of man evolving into Superman by a process of natural selection. For the matter of that, the rope might fall into the abyss. Superman cannot come unless superior individuals have the courage to transvalue all values, to break the old table of values, especially the Christian tables, and create new values out of their superabundant life and power. The new values will give direction and a goal to the higher man, and Superman is, as it were, their personification.

If he were taxed with his failure to give a clear description of Superman, Nietzsche might reply that as Superman does not yet exist he can hardly be expected to supply a clear description. At the same time, if the idea of Superman is to act as a spur, stimulus and goal, it must possess some content. And we can say perhaps that it is the concept of the highest possible development and integration of intellectual power, strength of character and will, independence, passion, taste and physique. Nietzsche alludes in one place to 'the Roman Caesar with Christ's soul'.[1] Superman would be Goethe and Napoleon in one, Nietzsche hints, or the Epicurean god appearing on earth. He would be a highly-cultured man, we may say, skilful in all bodily accomplishments, tolerant out of strength, regarding nothing as forbidden unless it is weakness either under the form of 'virtue' or under that of 'vice', the man who has become fully free and independent and affirms life and the universe. In fine, Superman is all that ailing, lonely, tormented, neglected Herr Professor Dr. Friedrich Nietzsche would like to be.

5. The reader of *Zarathustra* may easily and not unnaturally assume that the idea of Superman, if taken in conjunction with that of the transvaluation of values, is the main idea of the book. And he may be inclined to conclude that Nietzsche hopes at least for a constant development of man's potentialities. But Zarathustra is not only the prophet of Superman but also the teacher of the doctrine of the eternal recurrence. Further, in *Ecce Homo* Nietzsche informs us that the fundamental idea of *Zarathustra* is that of the eternal recurrence as 'the highest formula of the yea-saying (attitude to life) which can ever be attained'.[2] He also tells us that this 'fundamental thought'[3] of the work was first presented in the last aphorism but one of *Joyful Wisdom*. If, therefore, the doctrine of the eternal recurrence is the fundamental thought of *Zarathustra*,

[1] *W*, III, p. 422 (xv, p. 380).     [2] *W*, II, p. 1128 (xvII, p. 96).
[3] *Ibid.*

it can hardly be dismissed as a strange excrescence in Nietzsche's philosophy.

To be sure, Nietzsche found the idea of the eternal recurrence somewhat dismaying and oppressive. But, as was remarked earlier, he used the idea as a test of his strength, of his ability to say 'yes' to life as it is. Thus in the relevant aphorism of *Joyful Wisdom* he imagines a spirit appearing to him and telling him that his life, even in all its smallest details, will recur again innumerable times; and he raises the question whether he would be prostrated by this thought and curse the speaker or whether he would welcome the message in a spirit of affirmation of life, inasmuch as the eternal recurrence sets the seal of eternity on the world of Becoming. Similarly, in *Beyond Good and Evil* Nietzsche speaks of the world-approving man who wishes to have the play all over again a countless number of times and who cries *encore* not only to the play but also to the players. And he sets this idea against the 'half-Christian, half-German narrowness and simplicity'[1] with which pessimism was presented in Schopenhauer's philosophy. Again, in the third part of *Zarathustra* Nietzsche speaks of feeling disgust at the thought that even the most inferior man will return and that he himself is to 'come again eternally to this self same life, in its greatest and smallest (events)'.[2] And he proceeds to welcome this return. 'Oh, how should I not be ardent for eternity and for the marriage-ring of rings—the ring of the return?'[3] Similarly, in the notes for his *magnum opus* he speaks several times of the theory of the eternal recurrence as a great disciplinary thought, at once oppressive and liberating.

At the same time the theory is presented as an empirical hypothesis, and not merely as a disciplinary thought or test of inner strength. Thus we read that 'the principle of conservation of energy demands the *eternal* recurrence'.[4] If the world can be looked at as a determinate quantum of force or energy and as a determinate number of centres of force, it follows that the world-process will take the form of successive combinations of these centres, the number of these combinations being in principle determinable, that is, finite. And 'in an infinite time every possible combination would have been realized at some point; further, it would be realized an infinite number of times. And as between each combination and its next recurrence all other possible combinations

[1] *W*, II, p. 617 (v, p. 74).         [2] *W*, II, p. 467 (IV, p. 270).
[3] *W*, II, p. 474 (IV, p. 280).        [4] *W* III, p. 861 (xv, p. 427).

would have to occur, and as each of these combinations conditions the whole sequence of combinations in the same series, a cycle of absolutely identical series would be proved.'[1]

One main reason why Nietzsche lays stress on the theory of the eternal recurrence is that it seems to him to fill a gap in his philosophy. It confers on the flux of Becoming the semblance of Being, and it does so without introducing any Being which transcends the universe. Further, while the theory avoids the introduction of a transcendent Deity, it also avoids pantheism, the surreptitious reintroduction of the concept of God under the name of the universe. According to Nietzsche, if we say that the universe never repeats itself but is constantly creating new forms, this statement betrays a hankering after the idea of God. For the universe itself is assimilated to the concept of a creative Deity. And this assimilation is excluded by the theory of the eternal recurrence. The theory also excludes, of course, the idea of personal immortality in a 'beyond', though at the same time it provides a substitute for this idea, even if the notion of living one's life over again in all its details a countless number of times is unlikely to exercise a more than limited appeal. In other words, the theory of the eternal recurrence expresses Nietzsche's resolute will to this-worldliness, to *Diesseitigkeit*. The universe is shut in, as it were, on itself. Its significance is purely immanent. And the truly strong man, the truly Dionysian man, will affirm this universe with steadfastness, courage and even joy, shunning the escapism which is a manifestation of weakness.

It is sometimes said that the theory of the eternal recurrence and the theory of Superman are incompatible. But it can hardly be claimed, I think, that they are logically incompatible. For the theory of recurrent cycles does not exclude the recurrence of the will to Superman or, for the matter of that, of Superman himself. It is, of course, true that the theory of the eternal recurrence rules out the concept of Superman as the final end of a non-repeatable creative process. But Nietzsche does not admit this concept. On the contrary, he excludes it as being equivalent to a surreptitious reintroduction of a theological manner of interpreting the universe.

6. There have been disciples of Nietzsche who endeavoured to make his thought into a system which they then accepted as a kind of gospel and tried to propagate. But, generally speaking, his

[1] *W*, III, p. 704 (xv, p. 430).

influence has taken the form of stimulating thought in this or that
direction. And this stimulative influence has been widespread. But
it certainly has not been uniform in character. Nietzsche has meant
different things to different people. In the field of morals and values,
for example, his importance for some people has lain primarily in
his development of a naturalistic criticism of morality, while
others would emphasize rather his work in the phenomenology of
values. Others again, of a less academically philosophical turn of
mind, have stressed his idea of the transvaluation of values. In
the field of social and cultural philosophy some have portrayed him
as attacking democracy and democratic socialism in favour of
something like Nazism, while others have represented him as a
great European, or as a great cosmopolitan, a man who was above
any nationalistic outlook. To some he has been primarily the man
who diagnosed the decadence and imminent collapse of western
civilization, while others have seen in him and his philosophy the
embodiment of the very nihilism for which he professed to supply
a remedy. In the field of religion he has appeared to some as a
radical atheist, intent on exposing the baneful influence of religious
belief, while others have seen in the very vehemence of his attack
on Christianity evidence of his fundamental concern with the
problem of God. Some have regarded him first and foremost from
the literary point of view, as a man who developed the potentialities
of the German language; others, such as Thomas Mann, have been
influenced by his distinction between the Dionysian and Apollonian
outlooks or attitudes; others again have emphasized his psychological analyses.

Obviously, Nietzsche's method of writing is partly responsible
for the possibility of diverse interpretations. Many of his books
consist of aphorisms. And we know that in some cases he jotted
down thoughts which came to him on his solitary walks and later
strung them together to form a book. The results are what might
be expected. For instance, reflection on the tameness of bourgeois
life and on the heroism and self-sacrifice occasioned by war might
produce an aphorism or passage in praise of war and warriors,
while on another occasion reflection on the way in which war leads
to the waste and destruction of the best elements of a nation, and
often for no appreciable gain to anyone except a few selfish
individuals, might produce, and indeed did produce, a condemnation of war as stupid and suicidal for both victors and vanquished.
It is then possible for the commentator to depict Nietzsche either

as a lover of war or as almost a pacifist. A judicious selection of texts is all that is required.

The situation is complicated, of course, by the relation between the philosophizing of Nietzsche and his personal life and struggles. Thus while it is possible to confine one's attention to the written word, it is also possible to develop a psychological interpretation of his thought. And, as already noted, there is the possibility of giving an existentialist interpretation of the significance of the whole complex of his life and thought.

That Nietzsche was in some respects an acute and far-seeing thinker is hardly open to question. Take, for example, his excursions into psychology. It is not necessary to regard all his analyses as acceptable before one is prepared to admit that he divined, as it were, a number of important ideas which have become common coin in modern psychology. We have only to recall his notion of concealed operative ideals and motives or his concept of sublimation. As for his use of the concept of the Will to Power as a key to human psychology, an idea which found its classical expression in the psychological theory of Alfred Adler, we can say indeed that it was exaggerated and that the more widely the concept is applied the more indefinite does its content become.[1] At the same time Nietzsche's experimentation with the use of the concept as a key to man's psychical life helped to focus attention on the operation of a powerful drive, even if it is not the only one. Again, as we look back in the light of the events of the twentieth century on Nietzsche's anticipation of the coming of the 'new barbarism' and of world-wars we can hardly fail to recognize that he had a deeper insight into the situation than those of his contemporaries who showed a complacent optimistic belief in the inevitability of progress.

But though Nietzsche was clear-sighted in some respects, he was myopic in others. For instance, he certainly failed to give sufficient attention to the question whether his distinctions between ascending and descending life and between higher and lower types of men did not tacitly presuppose the very objectivity of values which he rejected. It would be open to him, of course, to make it a matter of taste and aesthetic preference, as he sometimes said that it was. But then a similar question can be raised about aesthetic values, unless perhaps the distinction between higher and lower is to become simply a matter of subjective feeling and no claim is

[1] Obviously, similar remarks can be made about Freud's concept of *libido*.

made that one's own feelings should be accepted, as a norm by anyone else. Again, as has already been hinted, Nietzsche failed to give the requisite prolonged consideration to the question how the subject can impose an intelligible structure on the flux of Becoming when the subject is itself resolved into the flux and exists as a subject only as part of the structure which it is said to impose.

As for Nietzsche's attitude to Christianity, his increasingly shrill attack on it is accompanied by an increasing inability to do justice to his foe. And it is arguable that the vehemence of his attack was partly an expression of an inner tension and uncertainty which he endeavoured to stifle.[1] As he himself put it, he had the blood of theologians in his veins. But if we abstract from the shrillness and one-sidedness of his attack on Christianity in particular, we can say that this attack forms part of his general campaign against all beliefs and philosophies, such as metaphysical idealism, which ascribe to the world and to human existence and history a meaning or purpose or goal other than the meaning freely imposed by man himself.[2] The rejection of the idea that the world has been created by God for a purpose or that it is the self-manifestation of the absolute Idea or Spirit sets man free to give to life the meaning which he wills to give it. And it has no other meaning.

The idea of God, whether theistically or pantheistically conceived, thus gives way to the concept of man as the being who confers intelligibility on the world and creates values. But are we to say that in the long run it is the world itself which has, so to speak, the last word, and that man, the moral legislator and conferer of meaning, is absorbed as an insignificant speck in the meaningless cycles of history? If so, man's effort to confer meaning and value on his life appear as a defiant 'No', a rejection

[1] To claim that a professed atheist was 'really' a believer simply because he attacked theism persistently and vehemently would be extravagant and para-doxical. But Nietzsche, who as a boy was profoundly religious, was never indifferent to the problems of Being and of the meaning or purpose of existence. Further, his dialogue, as it were, with Christ, culminating in the final words of *Ecce Homo*, *'Dionysus* versus *the Crucified'*, shows clearly enough that 'the Antichrist' had to do violence to himself, even if he thought of it as a case of transcending his own inclinations to weakness. In spite of his rejection of God he was very far from being what would generally be thought of as an 'irreligious man'.

[2] Nietzsche insists indeed that his main objection against Christianity is against the system of morals and values. At the same time he joins Christianity with German idealism, which he regards as a derivative of Christianity or as a masked form of it, in his attack on the view that the world has a given meaning or goal.

of the meaningless universe, rather than as a yea-saying attitude.[1] Or are we to say that the interpretation of the world as without a given meaning or goal and as a series of endless cycles is a fiction which expresses man's Will to Power? If so, the question whether the world has or has not a given meaning or goal remains open.

A final remark. Professional philosophers who read Nietzsche may be interested principally in his critique of morality or in his phenomenological analyses or in his psychological theories. But it is probably true to say that the attention of the general reader is usually concentrated on the remedies which he offers for the overcoming of what he calls nihilism, the spiritual crisis of modern man. It is the idea of the transvaluation of values, the concept of the order of rank and the myth of Superman which strike their attention. It is arguable, however, that what is really significant in what one may call the non-academic Nietzsche is not his proposed antidotes to nihilism but rather his existence and thought considered precisely as a dramatic expression of a lived spiritual crisis from which there is no issue in terms of his own philosophy.

[1] Unless indeed we understand by a yea-saying attitude an acceptance of the fact of differences between the strong and the weak, as opposed to an attempt to set all on the same level. But in this case a yea-saying attitude should also involve acceptance of the fact that the majority sets limits to the activities of the independent rebels.

### CHAPTER XXIII

# RETROSPECT AND PROSPECT

*Some questions arising out of nineteenth-century German philosophy—The positivist answer—The philosophy of existence —The rise of phenomenology; Brentano, Meinong, Husserl, the widespread use of phenomenological analysis—Return to ontology; N. Hartmann—The metaphysics of Being; Heidegger, the Thomists—Concluding reflections.*

1. KANT endeavoured to overcome what he regarded as the scandal of conflicting metaphysical systems and to set philosophy on a secure basis. And at the beginning of the period covered in this volume we find Fichte insisting that philosophy is the fundamental science which grounds all other sciences. But when Fichte declared that philosophy was the fundamental science, he was referring, of course, to the *Wissenschaftslehre*, that is, to his own philosophy. And his system simply forms one member of the series of highly personal, though interesting and often fascinating, interpretations of reality which span the nineteenth century like a series of mountain peaks. Other examples are the speculative theism of Schelling, the absolute idealism of Hegel, Schopenhauer's philosophy of the world as presentation and will, Kierkegaard's vision of human history and Nietzsche's philosophy of the Will to Power. And it would need a bold man to maintain that the series provides empirical confirmation of the validity of Fichte's claim on behalf of the scientific character of philosophy.

It is indeed arguable that the differences between philosophies, even when these differences are very considerable, do not prove that philosophy has no cognitive value. For it may be that each philosophy expresses a truth, an apprehension of a real aspect of reality or of human life and history, and that these truths are mutually complementary. That is to say, the element of conflict does not arise from any incompatibility between the fundamental ideas which lie at the bases of the different systems, but rather from the fact that each philosopher exaggerates one aspect of the world or of human life and history, thus turning a part into the whole. For example, Marx undoubtedly draws attention to real aspects of man and of human history; and there is no fundamental incompatibility between these aspects and, say, the religious aspects of human existence which are emphasized by Schelling. The incompatibility arises when Marx turns one idea which expresses a partial aspect of man and his history into a key-idea to unlock all doors.

One trouble, however, with this way of looking at things is that it involves whittling down philosophical systems to what amount practically to truisms, and that this process deprives the systems of most of their interest. It can be argued, for example, that Marx's philosophy is of interest precisely because of the element of exaggeration which sets the whole of human history in a certain perspective. If Marxism is whittled down to indubitable truths such as that without man's economic life there could be no philosophy or art or science, it loses a great deal of its interest and all of its provocative character. Similarly, if Nietzsche's philosophy is whittled down to the statement that the will to power or drive to power is one of the influential factors in human life, it becomes compatible with the reduced version of Marxism, but only at the cost of being itself reduced to a fairly obvious proposition.

A possible way of countering this line of argument is to say that the exaggerations in a philosophical system serve a useful purpose. For it is precisely the element of striking and arresting exaggeration which serves to draw attention in a forcible way to the basic truth which is contained in the system. And once we have digested this truth, we can forget about the exaggeration. It is not so much a question of whittling down the system as of using it as a source of insight and then forgetting the instrument by which we attained this insight, unless indeed we need to refer to it again as a means of recovering the insight in question.

But though this is in itself a not unreasonable line of thought, it is of very little use for supporting Fichte's contention that philosophy is the science of sciences. For suppose that we reduce the philosophies of Schopenhauer, Marx and Nietzsche respectively to such statements as that there is a great deal of evil and suffering in the world, that we have to produce food and consume it before we can develop the sciences, and that the will to power can operate in devious and concealed forms. We then have three propositions of which the first two are for most people obviously true while the third, which is rather more interesting, is a psychological proposition. None of them would normally be called a specifically philosophical proposition. The philosophical propositions of

Schopenhauer, Marx and Nietzsche would thus become instruments for drawing attention to propositions of some other type. And this is obviously not at all the sort of thing which Fichte had in mind when he claimed that philosophy was the basic science.

It may be objected that I have been concentrating simply on the outstanding original systems, on the mountain peaks, and neglecting the foothills, the general movements such as Neo-Kantianism. It may be suggested, that is to say, that while it is true that if we are looking for highly personal imaginative interpretations of the universe or of human life we must turn to the famous philosophers, it is also true that in those general movements in which the particular tends to be merged in the universal we can find more plebeian scientific work in philosophy, patient co-operative efforts at tackling separate problems.

But is it true? In Neo-Kantianism, for example, there are, of course, family-likenesses which justify our describing it as a definite movement, distinct from other movements. But once we start to inspect it at close hand we see not only somewhat different general tendencies within the movement as a whole but also a multitude of individual philosophies. Again, in the movement of inductive metaphysics this philosopher uses one idea as a key-idea for interpreting the world while that philosopher uses another. Wundt uses his voluntaristic interpretation of human psychology as a basis for a general philosophy, while Driesch uses his theory of entelechies, derived from reflection on biological processes. True, a sense of proportion and the requirements of mental economy suggest that in many cases individual systems are best forgotten or allowed to sink into the background of a general movement. But this does not alter the fact that the closer we look at the philosophy of the nineteenth century, the more do the massive groupings tend to break up into individual philosophies. Indeed, it is not altogether an exaggeration to say that as the century wears on each professor of philosophy seems to think it necessary to produce his own system.

Obviously, there can be different opinions within the framework of a common conviction about the nature and function of philosophy. Thus the Neo-Kantians were more or less agreed about what philosophy is incompetent to achieve. But though conflicting views about the nature and function of philosophy are not necessarily coextensive with different philosophical views or even systems, there were obviously in nineteenth-century German thought some very different concepts about what philosophy ought to be. For instance, when Fichte said that philosophy ought to be a science, he meant that it should be derived systematically from one fundamental principle. The inductive metaphysicians, however, had a different idea of philosophy. And when we turn to Nietzsche, we find him rejecting the concept of absolute truth and emphasizing the valuational foundations of different kinds of philosophy, the value-judgments themselves depending on the types of men who make them.[1]

Needless to say, the fact that two philosophers differ does not of itself prove that neither is right. And even if they are both wrong, some other philosopher may be right. At the same time the conflicting systems of the nineteenth century, and still more perhaps the conflicting views about the nature and competence of philosophy, show that Kant's attempt to settle once and for all the true nature and function of philosophy was from the historical point of view a failure. And the old questions present themselves to the mind with renewed force. Can philosophy be a science? If so, how? What sort of knowledge can we legitimately expect from it? Has philosophy been superseded by the growth and development of the particular sciences? Or has it still a field of its own? If so, what is it? And what is the appropriate method for investigating this field?

It is not indeed surprising that Kant's judgment about the nature and limits of scientific philosophy should have failed to win universal acceptance. For it was closely related to his own system. In other words, it was a philosophical judgment, just as the pronouncements of Fichte, Hegel, Marx, Nietzsche, Eucken and others were philosophical judgments. In fact, provided that one is not making a statement either about the current conventional use of terms or about the various uses of the word 'philosophy' in history, any pronouncement that one may make about the 'true' nature and function of philosophy is a philosophical statement, one which is made from within philosophy and commits one to or expresses a particular philosophical position.

[1] This view naturally brings to mind Fichte's statement that the kind of philosophy which a man chooses depends on the kind of man that he is. But even if we prescind from the fact that Fichte did not intend this statement to be understood in a sense which would exclude the concept of philosophy as a science and see in it an anticipation of the tendency to subordinate the concept of truth to the concept of human life or existence, in tracing the concrete development of this tendency we find it splitting up into different conceptions of man and of human life and existence. One has only to mention the names of Kierkegaard and Nietzsche, for example.

It is obviously not the intention of the present writer to suggest that no definite philosophical position should be adopted or that it is improper to make philosophical judgments about the nature and function of philosophy. Nor is it his intention to suggest that no good reasons can be adduced in favour of accepting one judgment rather than another. At the same time he does not wish to make an abrupt transition at this moment from the role of historian to the role of one who speaks in the name of a definite philosophical system. He prefers instead to take a brief glance at some of the general lines of answer which have been offered in German thought during the first part of the twentieth century to the type of question mentioned above. This procedure will serve to provide some sort of bridge between past and present.

2. One possible line of answer to questions about the scope of philosophy is to maintain that the particular sciences are the only source of knowledge about the world and that philosophy has no field of its own in the sense that its function is to investigate a special level or type of being. It is indeed perfectly understandable that at one time men sought to acquire knowledge about the world through philosophical speculation. But in the course of their development the various sciences have taken over one part after another of the field of exploration which was once attributed to philosophy. There has thus been a gradual substitution of scientific knowledge for philosophical speculation. And it is no wonder if philosophers who think that they can increase our knowledge of reality by other means than the employment of the scientific method of hypothesis, deduction and verification only succeed in producing conflicting systems which may possess some aesthetic value or emotive significance but which can no longer be seriously considered as possessing cognitive value. If philosophy is to be scientific and not a form of poetry masquerading as science, its function must be purely analytic in character. For example, it may be able to clarify some of the fundamental concepts employed in the sciences and to inquire into scientific methodology, but it cannot go beyond the sciences by adding to or supplementing our scientific knowledge of the world.

This general positivist attitude, the conviction that the empirical sciences are the only reliable source of knowledge about the world, is obviously widespread. In the nineteenth century it attained its classical expression in the philosophy of Auguste Comte, and we have seen that it also found expression, though on a less impressive scale, in the materialist and positivist current of thought in Germany. But we also noted how some of the German philosophers who represented this current of thought went well beyond the particular sciences by developing a general view of reality. Haeckel's monism was a case in point. And it was just this tendency of philosophy to develop into a *Weltanschauung* or world-view which the positivism of the twentieth century was concerned to exclude.

An obvious objection to the reduction of philosophy to the position of a handmaid of science is that there are questions and problems which are not raised by any particular science, which demand answers and which have been traditionally and properly regarded as belonging to the field of philosophical inquiry. The positivist is convinced, of course, that questions about ultimate reality or the Absolute, about the origin of finite existents, and so on have not in fact been answered by the metaphysical philosophers, such as Schelling for instance. But even if one agreed that the questions had not in fact been definitely answered, or even that we were not in a position to answer them, one might still wish to say that the raising and discussion of such questions has a great value. For it helps to show the limits of scientific knowledge and reminds us of the mysteries of finite existence. Hence an effective exclusion of metaphysical philosophy requires the establishment of two complementary theses. It must be shown that metaphysical problems are unanswerable in principle and not merely in the sense that we are not in a position to answer them here and now. And it must further be shown that problems which are unanswerable in principle are pseudo-problems in the sense that they are not real questions at all but verbal expressions which lack any clear meaning.

This is precisely what the neopositivists of the Vienna Circle and their associates set out to show in the twenties of the present century by developing a criterion of meaning, the so-called principle of verifiability, which would effectively exclude metaphysical problems and statements from the class of meaningful problems and statements. Apart from the purely formal propositions of logic and pure mathematics, meaningful propositions were interpreted as empirical hypotheses, the meaning of which was coincident with the thinkable, though not necessarily practically realizable, mode of verification in sense-experience. And as, for instance, we can conceive no empirical verification in sense-experience of the statement of Parmenides that all things are really one changeless being, this statement could not be accepted as meaningful.[1]

As stated in this form, however, the neopositivist criterion of meaning was unable to stand up to criticism, whether from outside or inside the neopositivist movement, and it either came to be interpreted as a purely methodological principle for the purpose of delimiting the range of what could properly be called scientific hypotheses or was so whittled down and explained away that it became quite ineffective for excluding speculative philosophy.

The fact of the matter is, I think, that neopositivism as a philosophy was an attempt to provide a theoretical justification of positivism as a mentality or attitude. And the neopositivist criterion of meaning was heavily loaded with the implicit philosophical presuppositions of this attitude. Further, its effectiveness as a weapon against metaphysical philosophy depended on these presuppositions not being made explicit. For once they have been made explicit, neopositivism stands revealed as one more questionable philosophy. This obviously does not entail the disappearance of positivism as a mentality or attitude. But the whole episode of the rise and criticism (partly autocriticism) of neopositivism had the great advantage of dragging concealed presuppositions into the light of day. It was a question of the positivist mentality, which had become widespread in the nineteenth century, becoming reflectively conscious of itself and seeing its own presuppositions. True, this self-consciousness was attained within the philosophical field and left untouched great areas of the positivist mentality or attitude. But this simply helps to illustrate the need of philosophy, one of the functions of which is precisely to render explicit and subject to critical examination the concealed implicit presuppositions of non-reflective philosophical attitudes.[2]

3. According to the neopositivists, philosophy can become scientific, but only at the cost of becoming purely analytic and relinquishing any claim to increase our factual knowledge of

---

[1] That is to say, the statement might be expressive and evocative of emotive attitudes, thus possessing 'emotive' significance; but according to strict neopositivist principles it would be meaningless in the sense that it would be incapable of being either true or false.

[2] A bibliography of neopositivism is provided in *Logical Positivism* (an anthology), edited by A. J. Ayer, Glencoe, Ill., and London, 1959. Some writings illustrating the discussion of the principle of verifiability, together with a selected bibliography, can be found in *A Modern Introduction to Philosophy* edited by P. Edwards and A. Pap, pp. 543–621, Glencoe, Ill. 1957. Cf. also *Contemporary Philosophy*, by F. C. Copleston, pp. 26–60, London, 1956, for a critical discussion of neopositivism.

reality. Another possible way of describing the function and nature of philosophy is to say that it has a field of its own, inasmuch as it is concerned with Being, and at the same time to deny that it is or can be a science, whether a universal science or a special science alongside the particular empirical sciences. In one sense philosophy is what it always has been, namely concerned with Being (*das Sein*) as distinct from *die Seienden*. But it was a mistake to suppose that there can be a science of Being. For Being is unobjectifiable; it cannot be turned into an object of scientific investigation. The primary function of philosophy is to awaken man to an awareness of Being as transcending beings and grounding them. But as there can be no science of Being, no metaphysical system can possess universal validity. The different systems are so many personal decipherings of unobjectifiable Being. This does not mean, however, that they are valueless. For any great metaphysical system can serve to push open, as it were, the door which positivism would keep shut. Thus to speak of the scandal of conflicting systems betrays a misconception of the true nature of philosophy. For the objection is valid only if philosophy, to be justified at all, should be a science. And this is not the case. True, by claiming that philosophy is a science, the metaphysicians of the past have themselves provided the ground for talk about the scandal of different and incompatible systems. But once this claim is relinquished and we understand the true function of metaphysics as being that of awakening man to an awareness of the enveloping Being in which he and all other finite existents are grounded, the ground for scandal disappears. For that there should be different personal decipherings of transcendent Being is only what one ought to expect. The important thing is to see them for what they are and not to take the extravagant claims of their authors at their face value.

This point of view represents one aspect of the philosophy of Professor Karl Jaspers (b. 1883). But he combines acceptance of the Kantian contention that speculative metaphysics cannot provide us with theoretical knowledge with a theory of 'existence' which shows the influence of Kierkegaard. The human being can be objectified and studied scientifically by, say, the physiologist and the psychologist. The individual is then exhibited as classifiable in this or that way. But when looked at from the point of view of the free agent himself, from within the life of free choice, the individual is seen as this unique existent, the being who freely transcends what he already is and creates himself, as it were, through the exercise of his freedom. Indeed, from this point of view man is always in the making, his own making: *Existenz* is always possible existence, *mögliche Existenz*. Of man regarded under this aspect there can be no scientific study. But philosophy can draw attention to or illuminate 'existence' in such a way as to enable the existing individual to understand what is meant in terms of his own experience. It can also draw attention to the movement by which, especially in certain situations, the individual becomes aware both of his finitude and of the enveloping presence of Being as the Transcendent in which he and all other beings are grounded. But as transcendent Being can be neither objectified nor reduced to the conclusion of a demonstration or proof, the man who becomes aware of it as the unobjectifiable complement and ground of finite beings is free either to affirm it with Kierkegaard, through what Jaspers calls 'philosophical faith', or to reject it with Nietzsche.

We cannot enter into further descriptions of the philosophy of Karl Jaspers,[1] as it has been mentioned less for its own sake than as one of the ways of depicting the nature and functions of philosophy which have been exemplified in German thought during the first half of the twentieth century. It should be noted, however, that Jaspers, like Kant before him, endeavours to place belief in human freedom and in God beyond the reach of scientific criticism. Indeed, we can see an evident recurrence of Kantian themes. For example, Jaspers' distinction between man as seen from the external scientific point of view and man as seen from the internal point of view of 'existence' corresponds in some way to the Kantian distinction between the phenomenal and noumenal levels. At the same time there are also evident differences between Kant and Jaspers. For instance, Kant's emphasis on the moral law, on which practical faith in God is grounded, disappears, and the Kierkegaardian concept of the existing individual comes to the fore. Besides, Jaspers' 'philosophical faith', which is a more academic version of Kierkegaard's leap of faith, is directed towards God as Being, not, as with Kant, to the idea of God as an instrument for synthesizing virtue and happiness.

An obvious objection to Jaspers' way of setting metaphysics beyond the reach of scientific criticism is that in speaking at all

---

[1] As a sympathetic study one can recommend *Karl Jaspers et la philosophie de l'existence*, by M. Dufrenne and P. Ricoeur, Paris, 1947.

about freedom and, still more, about Being he is inevitably objectifying what according to him cannot be objectified. If Being is really unobjectifiable, it cannot be mentioned. We can only remain silent. But one might, of course, employ Wittgenstein's distinction and say that for Jaspers philosophy tries to 'show' what cannot be 'said'. Indeed, Jaspers' emphasis on the 'illuminating' function of philosophy points in precisely this direction.

4. For the neopositivists, philosophy can be scientific, but by the very fact of becoming scientific it is not a science in the sense of having a field peculiar to itself. For Jaspers philosophy has in a sense a field of its own,[1] but it is not a science and moves on a different plane from those of the sciences. The phenomenologists, however, have tried both to assign to philosophy a field or fields and to vindicate its scientific character.

(i) In a few notes on the rise of phenomenology there is no need to go back beyond Franz Brentano (1838–1917). After studying with Trendelenburg Brentano became a Catholic priest. In 1872 he was appointed to a chair at Würzburg, and in 1874 at Vienna. But in 1873 he had abandoned the Church, and his status as a married ex-priest did not make his life as a university professor in the Austrian capital an easy one. In 1895 he retired from teaching and took up residence at Florence, moving to Switzerland on the outbreak of the First World War.

In 1874 Brentano published a book bearing the title *Psychology from the Empirical Standpoint* (*Psychologie vom empirischen Standpunkt*).[2] Empirical psychology, he insists, is not a science of the soul, a term which has metaphysical implications, but of psychical phenomena. Further, when Brentano talks about empirical psychology, it is descriptive rather than genetic psychology which he has in mind. And descriptive psychology is for him an inquiry into psychical acts or acts of consciousness as concerned with 'inexistent' objects, that is, with objects as contained within the acts themselves. All consciousness is consciousness *of*. To think is to think of something, and to desire is to desire something. Thus every act of consciousness is 'intentional': it 'intends' an object. And

---

[1] The term 'philosophy of existence' suggests that *Existenz* constitutes this field. But Jaspers insists more on Being, the illumination of 'existence' being the path to the awareness of Being. Being, however, is not a field for scientific investigation by philosophy, though the philosopher may be able to reawaken or keep alive the awareness of Being.

[2] Among other writings we can mention *On the Origin of Moral Knowledge* (*Vom Ursprung der sittlichen Erkenntnis*, 1889), *On the Future of Philosophy* (*Ueber die Zukunft der Philosophie*, 1893) and *The Four Phases of Philosophy* (*Die vier Phasen der Philosophie*, 1895).

we can consider the object precisely as intended and as inexistent, without raising questions about its extramental nature and status.

This theory of the intentionality of consciousness, which goes back to Aristotelian-Scholastic thought, is not in itself a subjectivist theory. The descriptive psychologist, as Brentano interprets his function, does not say that the objects of consciousness have no existence apart from consciousness. But he considers them only as inexistent, for the good reason that he is concerned with psychical acts or acts of consciousness and not with ontological questions about extramental reality.

Now, it is clear that in considering consciousness one can concentrate either on the inexistent objects of consciousness or on the intentional reference as such. And Brentano tends to concentrate on the second aspect of consciousness, distinguishing three main types of intentional reference. First there is simple presentation, in which there is no question of truth or falsity. Secondly there is judgment which involves recognition (*Anerkennen*) or rejection (*Verwerfen*), in other words affirmation or denial. Thirdly there are the movements of the will and of feelings (*Gemütsbewegungen*), where the fundamental attitudes or structures of consciousness are love and hate or, as Brentano also says, of pleasure and displeasure.

We may add that just as Brentano believed that there are logical judgments which are evidently true, so did he believe that there are moral sentiments which are evidently correct or right. That is to say, there are goods, objects of moral approval or pleasure, which are evidently and always preferable. But from the point of view of the rise of phenomenology the important feature of Brentano's thought is the doctrine of the intentionality of consciousness.

(ii) Brentano's reflections exercised an influence on a number of philosophers who are sometimes grouped together as the Austrian School, such as Anton Marty (1847–1914), a professor at Prague, Oskar Kraus (1872–1942), a pupil of Marty and himself a professor at Prague, and Carl Stumpf (1848–1936), who was a noted psychologist and had Edmund Husserl among his pupils.

Special mention, however, must be made of Alexius Meinong (1853–1920) who studied under Brentano at Vienna and subsequently became professor of philosophy at Graz. In his theory of objects (*Gegenstandstheorie*) Meinong distinguished different types of objects. In ordinary life we generally understand by the term 'objects' particular existing things such as trees, stones, tables, and so on. But if we consider 'objects' as objects of consciousness, we can easily see that there are other types as well. For example, there are ideal objects, such as values and numbers, which can be said to possess reality though they do not exist in the sense in which trees and cows exist. Again, there are imaginary objects such as a golden mountain or the king of France. There is no existing golden mountain and there has been no king of France for many years. But if we can talk about golden mountains, we must be talking about something. For to talk about nothing is not to talk. There is an object present to consciousness, even if there is no corresponding extramentally existent thing.

Bertrand Russell's theory of descriptions was designed to circumvent Meinong's line of argument and to depopulate, as it were, the world of objects which are in some sense real but do not exist. However, this is irrelevant to our present purpose. The main point is that Meinong's theory helped to concentrate attention on objects considered precisely as objects of consciousness, as, to use Brentano's term, inexistent.

(iii) The effective founder of the phenomenological movement was, however, neither Brentano nor Meinong but Edmund Husserl (1859–1938). After having taken his doctorate in mathematics Husserl attended Brentano's lectures at Vienna (1884–6) and it was Brentano's influence which led him to devote himself to philosophy. He became professor of philosophy at Göttingen and subsequently at Freiburg-im-Breisgau where Martin Heidegger was one of his pupils.

In 1891 Husserl published a *Philosophy of Arithmetic* (*Philosophie der Arithmetik*) in which he showed a certain tendency to psychologism, that is, to grounding logic on psychology. For example, the concept of multiplicity, which is essential for the concept of number, is grounded on the psychical act of binding together diverse contents of consciousness in one representation. This view was subjected to criticism by the celebrated mathematician and logician Gottlob Frege (1848–1925) and in his *Logical Investigations* (*Logische Untersuchungen*, 1900–1) Husserl maintained clearly that logic is not reducible to psychology.[1] Logic is concerned with the sphere of meaning, that is, with what is meant (*gemeint*) or intended, not with the succession of real psychical acts. In other words, we must distinguish between consciousness

[1] In his rejection of psychologism Husserl was probably influenced not only by Frege but also by Bolzano (see pp. 256–9).

as a complex of psychical facts, events or experiences (*Erlebnisse*) and the objects of consciousness which are meant or intended. The latter 'appear' to or for consciousness: in this sense they are phenomena. The former, however, do not appear: they are lived through (*erlebt*) or experienced. Obviously, this does not mean that psychical acts cannot themselves be reduced to phenomena by reflection; but then, considered precisely as appearing to consciousness, they are no longer real psychical acts.

This involves a distinction between meanings and things, a distinction which is of considerable importance. For failure to make this distinction was one of the main reasons why the empiricists found it necessary to deny the existence of universal concepts or ideas. Things, including real psychical acts, are all individual or particular, whereas meanings can be universal. And as such they are 'essences'.

In the work which in its English translation bears the title *Ideas: General Introduction to Pure Phenomenology* (*Ideen zu einer reinen Phänomenologie und phänomenologischen Philosophie*, 1913) Husserl calls the act of consciousness *noesis* and its correlative object, which is meant or intended, *noema*. Further, he speaks of the intuition of essences (*Wesensschau*). In pure mathematics, for example, there is an intuition of essences which gives rise to propositions which are not empirical generalizations but belong to a different type, that of *a priori* propositions. And phenomenology in general is the descriptive analysis of essences or ideal structures. There could thus be, for example, a phenomenology of values. But there could also be a phenomenological analysis of the fundamental structures of consciousness, provided, of course, that these structures are 'reduced' to essences or *eidē*.

A point insisted on by Husserl is the suspension of judgment (the so-called *epoche*) in regard to the ontological or existential status or reference of the objects of consciousness. By means of this suspension existence is said to be 'bracketed'. Suppose, for example, that I wished to develop a phenomenological analysis of the aesthetic experience of beauty. I suspend all judgment about the subjectivity or objectivity of beauty in an ontological sense and direct my attention simply to the essential structure of aesthetic experience as 'appearing' to consciousness.

The reason why Husserl insists on this suspension of judgment can be seen by considering the implications of the title of one of his writings, *Philosophy as Strict Science* (*Philosophie als strenge*

*Wissenschaft*, 1910–11). Like Descartes before him, Husserl wished
to put philosophy on a firm basis. And in his opinion this meant
going behind all presuppositions to that which one cannot doubt
or question. Now, in ordinary life we make all sorts of existential
assumptions, about, for instance, the existence of physical objects
independently of consciousness. We must therefore prescind from
or bracket this 'natural attitude' (*natürliche Einstellung*). It is not
a question of saying that the natural attitude is wrong and its
assumptions unjustified. It is a question of methodologically
prescinding from such assumptions and going behind them to
consciousness itself which it is impossible either to doubt or to
prescind from. Further, we cannot, for example, profitably discuss
the ontological status of values until we are quite clear what we
are talking about, what value 'means'. And this is revealed by
phenomenological analysis. Hence phenomenology is fundamental
philosophy: it must precede and ground any ontological philosophy,
any metaphysics.

As already hinted, Husserl's employment of the *epoche* bears a
resemblance to Descartes' use of methodological doubt. And in
point of fact Husserl saw in Descartes' philosophy a certain measure
of anticipation of phenomenology. At the same time he insisted
that the existence of a self in the sense of a spiritual substance or
as Descartes put it, a 'thinking thing' (*res cogitans*) must itself be
bracketed. True, the ego cannot be simply eliminated. But the
subject which is required as correlative to the object of consciousness is simply the pure or transcendental ego, the pure subject as
such, not a spiritual substance or soul. The existence of such a
substance is something about which we must suspend judgment,
so far as pure phenomenology is concerned.

The methodological use of the *epoche* does not by itself commit
Husserl to idealism. To say that the existence of consciousness is
the only undeniable or indubitable existence is not necessarily to
say that consciousness is the only existent. But in point of fact
Husserl proceeds to make the transition to idealism by trying to
deduce consciousness from the transcendental ego and by making
the reality of the world relative to consciousness. Nothing can
be conceived except as an object of consciousness. Hence the object
must be constituted by consciousness.[1]

Already discernible in *Ideas*, this idealistic orientation of

---

[1] Constituting an object can mean making it an object *for* consciousness. And
this does not necessarily mean idealism. Or it can be taken to refer to a creative

Husserl's thought became more marked in *Formal and Transcendental Logic* (*Formale und transzendentale Logik*, 1929) where logic and ontology tend to coincide, and in *Cartesian Meditations* (*Méditations cartésiennes*, 1931). It is understandable that this transition to idealism did not favour the acceptance by other phenomenologists of Husserl's original insistence on the *epoche*. Martin Heidegger, for example, decisively rejected the demand for the *epoche* and attempted to use the phenomenological method in the development of a non-idealistic philosophy of Being.

(iv) Phenomenological analysis is capable of fruitful application in a variety of fields. Alexander Pfänder (1870–1941) applied it in the field of psychology, Oskar Becker (b. 1889), a disciple of Husserl, in the philosophy of mathematics, Adolf Reinach (1883–1917) in the philosophy of law, Max Scheler (1874–1928) in the field of values, while others have applied it in the fields of aesthetics and the religious consciousness. But the use of the method does not necessarily mean that the user can be called a 'disciple' of Husserl. Scheler, for example, was an eminent philosopher in his own right. And phenomenological analysis has been practised by thinkers whose general philosophical position is markedly different from Husserl's. One has only to mention the French existentialists Jean-Paul Sartre (b. 1905) and Maurice Merleau-Ponty (b. 1908) or indeed the contemporary Thomists.

It is not unreasonable to argue that this widespread use of phenomenological analysis not only constitutes an eloquent testimony to its value but also shows that it is a unifying factor. At the same time it is also arguable that the fact that Husserl's demand for the *epoche* has generally been disregarded or rejected and that phenomenology has been used within the frameworks of different philosophies rather than as a foundation for a philosophy to put an end to conflicting systems shows that it has not fulfilled Husserl's original hopes. Besides, the nature of what is called phenomenological analysis can itself be called in question. For example, though the relations between continental phenomenology and the conceptual or 'linguistic' analysis practised in England is one of the main themes which permit a fruitful dialogue between groups of philosophers who in other respects may find it difficult to understand one another, one of the principal issues in such a dialogue is precisely the nature of what is called phenomenological activity by which things are given the only reality they possess, namely as related to consciousness, as consciousness-dependent. It is the transition to this second meaning which involves idealism.

analysis. Is it legitimate to speak of a phenomenological analysis of 'essences'? If so, in what precise sense? Is phenomenological analysis a specifically philosophical activity? Or does it fall apart into psychology on the one hand and so-called linguistic analysis on the other? We cannot discuss such questions here. But the fact that they can be raised suggests that Husserl was as over-optimistic as Descartes, Kant and Fichte before him in thinking that he had at last overcome the fragmentation of philosophy.

5. We have seen that at the turn of the century Neo-Kantianism was the dominant academic philosophy or *Schulphilosophie* in the German universities. And one obviously associates with this tradition a concern with the forms of thought and of the judgment rather than with objective categories of things. Yet it was a pupil of Cohen and Natorp at Marburg, namely Nicolai Hartmann (1882–1950), who expressed in his philosophy what we may call a return to things and developed an impressive realist ontology. And though it would be out of place to dwell here at any length on the ideas of a philosopher who belonged so definitely to the twentieth century, some general indication of his line of thought will serve to illustrate an important view of the nature and function of philosophy.

In his *Principles of a Metaphysics of Knowledge (Grundzüge einer Metaphysik der Erkenntnis*, 1921) Nicolai Hartmann passed from Neo-Kantianism to a realist theory of knowledge, and in subsequent publications he developed an ontology which took the form of an analysis of the categories of different modes or levels of being. Thus in his *Ethics (Ethik*, 1926) he devoted himself to a phenomenological study of values, which possess ideal being, while in *The Problem of Spiritual Being (Das Problem des geistigen Seins*, 1933) he considered the life of the human spirit both in its personal form and in its objectification. *A Contribution to the Foundation of Ontology (Zur Grundlegung der Ontologie*, 1935), *Possibility and Actuality (Möglichkeit und Wirklichkeit*, 1938), *The Construction of the Real World. Outline of the General Doctrine of Categories (Der Aufbau der realen Welt. Grundriss der allgemeinen Kategorienlehre*, 1940) and *New Ways in Ontology (Neue Wege der Ontologie*, 1941) represent general ontology, while in *Philosophy of Nature (Philosophie der Natur*, 1950) special attention is paid to the categories of the inorganic and organic levels.[1]

[1] We can also mention the posthumously-published works, *Teleological Thought (Teleologisches Denken*, 1951) and *Aesthetics (Aesthetik*, 1953), a study of beauty and aesthetic values.

In general, therefore, Hartmann's thought moves from a study of the universal structural principles or categories of being, such as unity and multiplicity, persistence and becoming or change, to regional ontologies, that is, to the analysis of the specific categories of inorganic being, organic being and so on. And to this extent he distinguishes between being-there (*Dasein*) and being-thus-or-thus (*Sosein*). But his ontology takes throughout the form of a phenomenological analysis of the categories exemplified in the beings given in experience. The idea of subsistent being, in the sense of the infinite act of existence, *ipsum esse subsistens*, is entirely foreign to his thought. And any metaphysics of transcendent being, in the sense in which God is transcendent, is excluded. Indeed, metaphysics for Hartmann deals with insoluble problems, whereas ontology in his sense is perfectly capable of attaining definite results.

Hartmann's ontology, therefore, is an overcoming of Neo-Kantianism inasmuch as it involves a study of the objective categories of real being. It is an overcoming of positivism inasmuch as it assigns to philosophy a definite field of its own, namely the different levels or types of being considered precisely as such. And though Hartmann employs the method of phenomenological analysis, he is not involved in that restriction to a subjective sphere to which an observance of Husserl's *epoche* would have condemned him. At the same time his ontology is a doctrine of categories, not a metaphysics of Being (*das Sein*) as grounding beings (*die Seienden*). In his view scientific philosophy has no place for an inquiry into Being which goes beyond a study of beings as beings. There is indeed the ideal being of values which are recognized in varying degrees by the human mind. But though these values possess ideal reality, they do not, as such, exist. And existent beings are those which form the world.

6. (i) The recall of philosophy to the thought of Being (*das Sein*) is principally represented in contemporary German thought by that enigmatic thinker, Martin Heidegger (b. 1889). According to Heidegger the whole of western philosophy has forgotten Being and immersed itself in the study of beings.[1] And the idea of Being has meant either an empty and indeterminate concept, obtained by thinking away all the determinate characteristics of beings, or the supreme being in the hierarchy of beings, namely God. Being as the Being of beings, as that which is veiled by beings and as that

[1] Obviously, Nicolai Hartmann is included in this judgment.

which grounds the duality of subject and object that is presupposed by the study of beings, is passed over and forgotten: it remains hidden, veiled. Heidegger asks, therefore, what is the meaning of Being? For him this is not a grammatical question. It is to ask for an unveiling of the Being of beings.

The very fact that man can ask this question shows, for Heidegger, that he has a pre-reflective sense of Being. And in the first part of *Being and Time* (*Sein und Zeit*, 1927) Heidegger sets out to give a phenomenological-ontological analysis of man as the being who is able to raise the question and who is thus open to Being. What he calls fundamental ontology thus becomes an existential analysis of man as 'existence' (*Dasein*). But though Heidegger's aim is in this way to bring Being to show itself, as it were, he never really gets further than man. And inasmuch as man's finitude and temporality are brought clearly to light, the work not unnaturally tends to give the impression, even if incorrect, that Being is for the author essentially finite and temporal. The second part of *Being and Time* has never been published.

In Heidegger's later writings we hear a great deal about man's openness to Being and of the need for keeping it alive, but it can hardly be said that he has succeeded in unveiling Being. Nor indeed would he claim to have done so. In fact, though Heidegger proclaims that the world in general and philosophers in particular have forgotten Being, he seems unable to explain clearly what they have forgotten or why this forgetfulness should be as disastrous as he says it is.

(ii) Heidegger's pronouncements about Being, as distinct from his existential analysis of man, are so oracular that they cannot be said to amount to a science of Being. The idea of metaphysics as a science of Being is most clearly maintained by the modern Thomists, especially by those who employ what they call the transcendental method. Inspired by Kant and, more particularly (inasmuch as Kant is concerned only with the transcendental deduction of the forms of thought) by German idealists such as Fichte, the transcendental method contains two main phases. To establish metaphysics as a science it is necessary to work backwards, as it were, to a foundation which cannot itself be called in question; and this is the reductive phase or moment.[1] The other

[1] Some see the proper starting-point in an analysis of the judgment as an act of absolute affirmation. So, for example, J. B. Lotz in *Das Urteil und das Sein. Eine Grundlegung der Metaphysik* (Pullach bei München, 1957) and *Metaphysica operationis humanae methodo transcendentali explicata* (Rome, 1958). Others go

phase consists in the systematic deduction of metaphysics from the ultimate starting-point.

In effect the transcendental method is used by the philosophers in question to establish Thomist metaphysics on a secure foundation and deduce it systematically, not to produce a new system of metaphysics as far as content is concerned, still less to discover startling new truths about the world. Hence to the outsider at least it seems to be a question of putting the same old wine into a new bottle. At the same time it is obvious that the question of scientific method inevitably tends to loom large and to grow in importance in proportion as emphasis is placed, as with the Thomists under discussion, on the task of converting man's unreflective and implicit apprehension of Being into systematically-grounded explicit knowledge.

7. This admittedly sketchy outline of some currents in thought in German philosophy during the first half of the twentieth century does not afford much ground for saying that the divergencies of systems and tendencies has been at last overcome. At the same time it suggests that in order to justify its claim to be more than a mere handmaid of the sciences philosophy must be metaphysical. If we assume that the aspects of the world under which it is considered by the particular sciences are the only aspects under which it can properly be considered, philosophy, if it is to continue to exist at all, must concern itself either with the logic and methodology of the sciences or with the analysis of ordinary language. For it obviously cannot compete with the sciences on their own ground. To have a field of its own other than analysis of the language of the sciences or of ordinary language, it must consider beings simply as beings. But if it confines itself, as with Nicolai Hartmann, to an inquiry into the categories of the different levels of finite being as revealed in experience, the crucial question of the being or existence of beings is simply passed over. And unless this question is ruled out as meaningless, there can be no justification for this neglect. If, however, the question is once admitted as a genuine philosophical question, the problem of the Absolute comes once more into the foreground. And in the long run Schelling will be shown to be justified in claiming that no more important philosophical problem can be conceived than that of the relation of finite existence to the unconditioned Absolute.

behind the judgment to the *question*, what is the ultimate foundation of all knowledge and judgment? So E. Coreth in *Metaphysik. Eine methodisch-systematische Grundlegung* (Innsbruck, Vienna and Munich, 1961).

This reference to Schelling is not equivalent to a demand for a return to German idealism. What I have in mind is this. Man is spirit-in-the-world. He is in the world not only as locally present in it but also as, by nature, involved in it. He finds himself in the world as dependent on other things for his life, for the satisfaction of his needs, for the material of his knowledge, for his activity. At the same time, by the very fact that he conceives himself as a being in the world he stands out from the world: he is not, as it were, totally immersed in the world-process. He is an historical being, but in the sense that he can objectify history he is a supra-historical being. It is not, of course, possible to make a complete separation between these two aspects of man. He is a being in the world, a 'worldly' being, as standing out from the world; and he stands out from the world as a being in the world. Considered as spirit, as standing out from the world, he is able, and indeed impelled, to raise metaphysical problems, to seek a unity behind or underlying the subject-object situation. Considered as a being involved in the world, he is naturally inclined to regard these problems as empty and profitless. In the development of philosophical thought these divergent attitudes or tendencies recur, assuming different historical, and historically explicable, forms. Thus German idealism was one historically-conditioned form assumed by the metaphysical tendency or drive. Inductive metaphysics was another. And we can see the same fundamental tendency reasserting itself in different ways in the philosophies of Jaspers and Heidegger.

On the plane of philosophy each tendency or attitude seeks to justify itself theoretically. But the dialectic continues. I do not mean to imply that there is no means of discriminating between the proffered justifications. For example, inasmuch as man can objectify himself and treat himself as an object of scientific investigation, he is inclined to regard talk about his standing out from the world or as having a spiritual aspect as so much nonsense. Yet the mere fact that it is he who objectifies himself shows, as Fichte well saw, that he cannot be completely objectified, and that a phenomenalistic reduction of the self is uncritical and naïve. And once reflective thought understands this, metaphysics begins to reassert itself. Yet the pull of the 'worldly' aspect of man also reasserts itself, and insights once gained are lost sight of, only to be regained once more.

Obviously, reference to two tendencies or attitudes based on the dual nature of man would be a gross over-simplification if it were taken to be a sufficient key to the history of philosophy. For in explaining the actual development of philosophy very many factors have to be taken into account. Yet even if there is no simple repetition in history, it is only to be expected that persistent tendencies should constantly tend to recur in varying historical shapes. For, as Dilthey remarked, he who understands history also made history. The dialectic of philosophy reflects the complex nature of man.

The conclusion may appear to be pessimistic, namely that there is no very good reason to suppose that we shall ever reach universal and lasting agreement even about the scope of philosophy. But if fundamental disagreements spring from the very nature of man himself, we can hardly expect anything else but a dialectical movement, a recurrence of certain fundamental tendencies and attitudes in different historical shapes. This is what we have had hitherto, in spite of well-intentioned efforts to bring the process to a close. And it can hardly be called undue pessimism if one expects the continuation of the process in the future.

# APPENDIX

## A SHORT BIBLIOGRAPHY

### General Works

Abbagnano, N. *Storia della filosofia:* II, *parte seconda.* Turin, 1950.

Adamson, R. *The Development of Modern Philosophy, with other Lectures and Essays.* Edinburgh, 1908 (2nd edition).

Alexander, A. B. D. *A Short History of Philosophy.* Glasgow, 1922 (3rd edition).

Bosanquet, B. *A History of Aesthetic.* London, 1892.

Bréhier, E. *Histoire de la philosophie:* II, *deuxième partie.* Paris, 1944. (Bréhier's work is one of the best histories of philosophy, and it contains brief, but useful, bibliographies.)

    *Histoire de la philosophie allemande.* Paris, 1933 (2nd edition).

Castell, A. *An Introduction to Modern Philosophy in Six Problems.* New York, 1943.

Catlin, G. *A History of the Political Philosophers.* London, 1950.

Collins, J. *A History of Modern European Philosophy.* Milwaukee, 1954. (This work by a Thomist can be highly recommended. It contains useful bibliographies.)

    *God in Modern Philosophy.* London, 1960. (In the relevant period this work contains treatments of Hegel, Feuerbach, Marx and Kierkegaard.)

De Ruggiero, G. *Storia della filosofia:* IV, *la filosofia moderna. L'età del romanticismo.* Bari, 1943.

    *Hegel.* Bari, 1948.

Deussen, P. *Allgemeine Geschichte der Philosophie:* II, 3, *Neuere Philosophie von Descartes bis Schopenhauer.* Leipzig, 1922 (3rd edition).

Devaux, P. *De Thalès à Bergson. Introduction historique à la philosophie.* Liège, 1948.

Erdmann, J. E. *A History of Philosophy:* II, *Modern Philosophy*, translated by W. S. Hough. London, 1889, and subsequent editions.

Falckenberg, R. *Geschichte der neuern Philosophie.* Berlin, 1921 (8th edition).

Fischer, K. *Geschichte der neuern Philosophie.* 10 vols. Heidelberg, 1897–1904. (This work includes separate volumes on Fichte, Schelling, Hegel and Schopenhauer, as listed under these names.)

Fischl, J. *Geschichte der Philosophie*, 5 vols. III, *Aufklärung und deutscher Idealismus.* IV, *Positivismus und Materialismus.* Vienna, 1950.

Fuller, B. A. G. *A History of Philosophy.* New York, 1945 (revised edition).

Hegel, G. W. F. *Lectures on the History of Philosophy*, translated by E. S. Haldane and F. H. Simson. Vol. III. London, 1895. (Hegel's history of philosophy forms part of his system.)

Heimsoeth, H. *Metaphysik der Neuzeit*. Munich, 1929.

Hirschberger, J. *The History of Philosophy*, translated by A. Fuerst, 2 vols. Milwaukee, 1959. (The second volume treats of modern philosophy.)

Höffding, H. *A History of Philosophy* (modern), translated by B. E. Meyer, 2 vols. London, 1900 (American reprint, 1924).
　　　*A Brief History of Modern Philosophy*, translated by C. F. Sanders, London, 1912.

Jones, W. T. *A History of Western Philosophy: II, The Modern Mind*. New York, 1952.

Klimke, F., S.J. and Colomer, E., S.J. *Historia de la filosofía*. Barcelona, 1961 (3rd edition).

Marías, J. *Historia de la filosofía*. Madrid, 1941.

Meyer, H. *Geschichte der abendländischen Weltanschauung: IV, Von der Renaissance zum deutschen Idealismus: V, Die Weltanschauung der Gegenwart*. Würzburg, 1950.

Oesterreich, T. K. *Die deutsche Philosophie des XIX Jahrhunderts*. Berlin, 1923 (reproduction, 1953). (This is the fourth volume of the new revised edition of Ueberweg's *Grundriss der Geschichte der Philosophie*. It contains extensive bibliographies and is useful as a work of reference.)

Randall, H., Jr. *The Making of the Modern Mind*. Boston, 1940 (revised edition).

Rogers, A. K. *A Student's History of Philosophy*. New York, 1954 (3rd edition reprinted). (A straightforward textbook.)

Russell, Bertrand. *History of Western Philosophy and its connection with Political and Social Circumstances from the Earliest Times to the Present Day*. London, 1946, and reprints.
　　　*Wisdom of the West. An Historical Survey of Western Philosophy in its Social and Political Setting*. London, 1959. (For German philosophy in the nineteenth century the last-named work is to be preferred to the first.)

Sabine, G. H. *A History of Political Theory*. London, 1941. (A valuable study of the subject.)

Schilling, K. *Geschichte der Philosophie: II, Die Neuzeit*. Munich, 1953. (Contains useful bibliographies.)

Souilhé, J. *La philosophie chrétienne de Descartes à nos jours*. 2 vols. Paris, 1934.

Thilly, F. *A History of Philosophy*, revised by L. Wood. New York, 1951.

Thonnard, F. J. *Précis d'histoire de la philosophie.* Paris, 1941 (revised edition).

Turner, W. *History of Philosophy.* Boston and London, 1903.

Vorländer, K. *Geschichte der Philosophie: II, Philosophie der Neuzeit.* Leipzig, 1919 (5th edition).

Webb, C. C. J. *A History of Philosophy.* (Home University Library.) London, 1915 and reprints.

Windelband, W. *A History of Philosophy, with especial reference to the Formation and Development of its Problems and Conceptions,* translated by J. A. Tufts. New York and London, 1952 (reprint of 1901 edition). (This notable work treats the history of philosophy according to the development of problems.)

> *Lehrbuch der Geschichte der Philosophie,* edited by H. Heimsoeth with a concluding chapter, *Die Philosophie im 20 Jahrhundert mit einer Uebersicht über den Stand der philosophie-geschichtlichen Forschung.* Tübingen, 1935.

Wright, W. K. *A History of Modern Philosophy.* New York, 1941.

*Chapter I: General Works Relating to the German Idealist Movement*

Benz, R. *Die deutsche Romantik,* Leipzig, 1937.

Cassirer, E. *Das Erkenntnisproblem in der Philosophie und Wissenschaft der neueren Zeit: III, Die nachkantischen Systeme.* Berlin, 1920.

Delbos, V. *De Kant aux Postkantiens.* Paris, 1940.

Flügel, O. *Die Religionsphilosophie des absoluten Idealismus: Fichte, Schelling, Hegel, Schopenhauer.* Langensalza, 1905.

Gardeil, H.-D. *Les étages de la philosophie idéaliste.* Paris, 1935.

Groos, H. *Der deutsche Idealismus und das Christentum.* Munich, 1927.

Hartmann, N. *Die Philosophie des deutschen Idealismus.* Berlin, 1960. 2nd edition (originally 2 vols., 1923–9).

Haym, R. *Die romantische Schule.* Berlin, 1928 (5th edition).

Hirsch, E. *Die idealistische Philosophie und das Christentum.* Gütersloh, 1926.

Kircher, E. *Philosophie der Romantik.* Jena, 1906.

Kroner, R. *Von Kant bis Hegel.* 2 vols. Tübingen, 1921–4. (This work and that of N. Hartmann are classical treatments of the subject, from different points of view.)

Lutgert, W. *Die Religion des deutschen Idealismus und ihr Ende.* Gütersloh, 1923.

Maréchal, J., S.J. *Le point de départ de la métaphysique.* Cahier IV: *Le système idéaliste chez Kant et les postkantiens.* Paris, 1947.

Michelet, C. L. *Geschichte der letzten Systeme der Philosophie in Deutschland von Kant bis Hegel.* 2 vols. Berlin, 1837-8.
    *Entwicklungsgeschichte der neuesten deutschen Philosophie.* Berlin, 1843.

### Chapters II–IV: Fichte

*Texts*

*Sämmtliche Werke*, edited by I. H. Fichte. 8 vols. Berlin, 1845-6.
*Nachgelassene Werke*, edited by I. H. Fichte. 3 vols. Bonn, 1834-5.
*Werke*, edited by F. Medicus. 6 vols. Leipzig, 1908-12. (This edition does not contain all Fichte's works.)
*Fichtes Briefwechsel*, edited by H. Schulz. 2 vols. Leipzig, 1925.
*Die Schriften zu J. G. Fichte's Atheismus-streit*, edited by H. Lindau. Munich, 1912.
*Fichte und Forberg. Die philosophischen Scriften zum Atheismus-streit*, edited by F. Medicus. Leipzig, 1910.
*The Science of Knowledge*, translated by A. E. Kroeger. Philadelphia, 1868; London, 1889.
*New Exposition of the Science of Knowledge*, translated by A. E. Kroeger. St. Louis, 1869.
*The Science of Rights*, translated by A. E. Kroeger. Philadelphia, 1869; London, 1889.
*The Science of Ethics*, translated by A. E. Kroeger. London, 1907.
*Fichte's Popular Works*, translated, with a memoir of Fichte, by W. Smith. 2 vols. London, 1889 (4th edition).
*Addresses to the German Nation*, translated by R. F. Jones and G. H. Turnbull. Chicago, 1922.
*J. G. Fichtes Leben und literarischer Briefwechsel*, by I. H. Fichte. Leipzig, 1862 (2nd edition).

*Studies*

Adamson, R. *Fichte.* Edinburgh and London, 1881.
Bergmann, E. *Fichte der Erzieher.* Leipzig, 1928 (2nd edition).
Engelbrecht, H. C. *J. G. Fichte: A Study of His Political Writings with special Reference to His Nationalism.* New York, 1933.
Fischer, K. *Fichtes Leben, Werke und Lehre.* Heidelberg, 1914 (4th edition).
Gogarten, F. *Fichte als religiöser Denker.* Jena, 1914.
Gueroult, M. *L'évolution et la structure de la doctrine de la science chez Fichte.* 2 vols. Paris, 1930.
Heimsoeth, H. *Fichte.* Munich, 1923.
Hirsch, E. *Fichtes Religionsphilosophie.* Göttingen, 1914.
    *Christentum und Geschichte in Fichtes Philosophie.* Göttingen, 1920.

Léon, X. *La philosophie de Fichte*. Paris, 1902.
    *Fichte et son temps*. 2 vols. (in 3). Paris, 1922–7.
Pareyson, L. *Fichte*. Turin, 1950.
Rickert, H. *Fichtes Atheismusstreit und die kantische Philosophie*. Berlin, 1899.
Ritzel, W. *Fichtes Religionsphilosophie*. Stuttgart, 1956.
Stine, R. W. *The Doctrine of God in the Philosophy of Fichte*. Philadelphia, 1945 (dissertation).
Thompson, A. B. *The Unity of Fichte's Doctrine of Knowledge*. Boston, 1896.
Turnbull, G. H. *The Educational Theory of Fichte*. London, 1926.
Wallner, F. *Fichte als politischer Denker*. Halle, 1926.
Wundt, M. *Fichte*. Stuttgart, 1937 (2nd edition).

## *Chapters V–VII: Schelling*

*Texts*

*Sämmtliche Werke*, edited by K. F. A. Schelling. *Erste Abteilung*, 10 vols., 1856–61; *Zweite Abteilung*, 4 vols. 1856–8. Stuttgart and Augsburg.
*Werke*, edited by M. Schröter. 6 vols. Munich, 1927–8; 2 supplementary vols. Munich, 1943–56.
*Of Human Freedom*, translated by J. Gutman. Chicago, 1936.
*The Ages of the World*, translated by F. Bolman, Jr. New York, 1942.
*The Philosophy of Art: An Oration on the Relation between the Plastic Arts and Nature*, translated by A. Johnson. London, 1845.
*Essais*, translated by S. Jankélévitch. Paris, 1946.
*Introduction à la philosophie de la mythologie*, translated by S. Jankélévitch. Paris, 1945.

*Studies*

Bausola, A. *Saggi sulla filosofia di Schelling*. Milan, 1960.
Benz, E. *Schelling, Werden und Wirkung seines Denkens*. Zürich and Stuttgart, 1955.
Bréhier, E. *Schelling*. Paris, 1912.
Dekker, G. *Die Rückwendung zum Mythos. Schellings letzte Wandlung*. Munich and Berlin, 1930.
Drago del Boca, S. *La filosofia di Schelling*. Florence, 1943.
Fischer, K. *Schellings Leben, Werke und Lehre*. Heidelberg, 1902 (3rd edition).
Fuhrmans, H. *Schellings letzte Philosophie. Die negative und positive Philosophie im Einsatz des Spätidealismus*. Berlin, 1940.
    *Schellings Philosophie der Weltalter*. Düsseldorf, 1954.

Gibelin, J. *L'ésthetique de Schelling d'après la philosophie de l'art.* Paris, 1934.

Gray-Smith, R. *God in the Philosophy of Schelling.* Philadelphia, 1933 (dissertation).

Hirsch, E. D., Jr. *Wordsworth and Schelling.* London, 1960.

Jankélévitch, V. *L'odysée de la conscience dans la dernière philosophie de Schelling.* Paris, 1933.

Jaspers, K. *Schelling: Grösse und Verhängnis.* Munich, 1955.

Knittermeyer, H. *Schelling und die romantische Schule.* Munich, 1929.

Koehler, E. *Schellings Wendung zum Theismus.* Leipzig, 1932 (dissertation).

Massolo, A. *Il primo Schelling.* Florence, 1953.

Mazzei, V. *Il pensiero etico-politico di Friedrich Schelling.* Rome, 1938.

Noack, L. *Schelling und die Philosophie der Romantik.* Berlin, 1859.

Schulz, W. *Die Vollendung des deutschen Idealismus in der Spätphilosophie Schellings.* Stuttgart and Cologne, 1955.

Watson, J. *Schelling's Transcendental Idealism.* Chicago, 1892 (2nd edition).

For a further bibliography see: *Friedrich Wilhelm Joseph von Schelling. Eine Bibliographie,* by G. Schneeberger. Bern, 1954.

## Chapter VIII: Schleiermacher

*Texts*

*Werke,* Berlin, 1835–64. (Section I, theology, 13 vols.; Section II, sermons, 10 vols.; Section III, philosophy, 9 vols.)

*Werke* (selections), edited by O. Braun. 4 vols. Leipzig, 1910–13.

*Addresses on Religion,* translated by J. Oman. London, 1894.

*The Theology of Schleiermacher, a Condensed Presentation of His Chief Work 'The Christian Faith',* by G. Cross. Chicago, 1911.

*Studies*

Baxmann, R. *Schleiermacher, sein Leben und Wirken.* Elberfeld, 1868.

Brandt, R. B. *The Philosophy of Schleiermacher.* New York, 1941.

Dilthey, W. *Leben Schleiermachers.* Berlin, 1920 (2nd edition).

Fluckinger, F. *Philosophie und Theologie bei Schleiermacher.* Zürich, 1947.

Keppstein, T. *Schleiermachers Weltbild und Lebensanschauung.* Munich, 1921.

Neglia, F. *La filosofia della religione di Schleiermacher.* Turin, 1952.

Neumann, J. *Schleiermacher.* Berlin, 1936.

Reble, A. *Schleiermachers Kulturphilosophie.* Erfurt, 1935.

Schultz, L. W. *Das Verhältnis von Ich und Wirklichkeit in der religiösen Antropologie Schleiermachers.* Göttingen, 1935.

Schutz, W. *Schleiermacher und der Protestantismus.* Hamburg, 1957.

Visconti, L. *La dottrina educativa di F. D. Schleiermacher.* Florence, 1920.

Wendland, I. *Die religiöse Entwicklung Schleiermachers.* Tübingen, 1915.

*Texts*      *Chapters IX–XI: Hegel*

*Werke,* Jubiläumsausgabe, edited by H. G. Glockner. 26 vols. Stuttgart, 1927–39. The first 20 vols., containing Hegel's writings, are a reprint of the 1832–87 edition (19 vols.). Vols. 21–2 contain Glockner's *Hegel* and Vols. 23–6 his *Hegel-Lexikon.*

*Sämmtliche Werke, kritische Ausgabe,* edited by G. Lasson and J. Hoffmeister. This critical edition, originally published at Leipzig (F. Meiner), was begun by G. Lasson (1862–1932) in 1905. On Lasson's death it was continued by J. Hoffmeister, and from 1949 it was published at Hamburg (F. Meiner). It was planned to contain 24 (later 26 and then 27) vols. Some of the vols. went through several editions. For example, a third edition of Vol. 2 (*Die Phänomenologie des Geistes*) appeared in 1929 and a third edition of Vol. 6 (*Grundlinien der Philosophie des Rechts*) in 1930. The total work remains unfinished.

*Sämmtliche Werke, neue kritische Ausgabe,* edited by J. Hoffmeister. This edition, planned to contain 32 vols., is published at Hamburg (F. Meiner) and is designed both to complete and to supersede the Lasson-Hoffmeister edition, now known as the *Erste kritische Ausgabe.* The situation is somewhat complicated as some of the volumes of the Lasson-Hoffmeister edition are being taken over by the new critical edition. For instance, the first part of Hoffmeister's edition of Hegel's *Vorlesungen über die Geschichte der Philosophie,* which was published in 1940 as Vol. 15*a* in the *Kritische Ausgabe,* becomes Vol. 20 in the *Neue kritische Ausgabe.* Again, the first volume of Hoffmeister's edition of letters written by and to Hegel (1952) bore the title *Kritische Ausgabe* and mention was made of Lasson as the original editor, whereas the second volume (1953) bore the title *Neue kritische Ausgabe* and no mention was made of Lasson. (The *Briefe von und an Hegel* form Vols. 27–30 in the new critical edition.)

*Hegels theologische Jugendschriften,* edited by H. Nohl. Tübingen, 1907.

*Dokumente zu Hegels Entwicklung,* edited by J. Hoffmeister. Stuttgart, 1936.

*G. W. F. Hegel: Early Theological Writings,* translated by T. M. Knox with an introduction by R. Kroner. Chicago, 1948.

*The Phenomenology of Mind,* translated by J. Baillie. London, 1931 (2nd edition).

*Encyclopaedia of Philosophy*, translated and annotated by G. E. Mueller New York, 1959.

*Science of Logic*, translated by W. H. Johnston and L. G. Struthers. 2 vols. London, 1929. (This is the so-called 'Greater Logic' of Hegel.)

*The Logic of Hegel, translated from the Encyclopaedia of the Philosophical Sciences*, translated by W. Wallace. Oxford, 1892 (2nd edition). (This is the so-called 'Lesser Logic'.)

*Hegel's Philosophy of Mind, translated from the Encyclopaedia of the Philosophical Sciences*, translated by W. Wallace. Oxford, 1894.

*The Philosophy of Right*, translated and annotated by T. M. Knox. Oxford, 1942.

*Philosophy of History*, translated by J. Sibree. London, 1861.

*The Philosophy of Fine Art*, translated by F. P. B. Osmaston. 4 vols. London, 1920.

*Lectures on the Philosophy of Religion, together with a Work on the Proofs of the Existence of God*, translated by E. B. Speirs and J. B. Sanderson. 3 vols. London, 1895 (reprint 1962).

*Lectures on the History of Philosophy*, translated by E. S. Haldane and F. H. Simpson. 3 vols. London, 1892–6.

## Studies

Adams, G. P. *The Mystical Element in Hegel's Early Theological Writings*. Berkeley, 1910.

Aspelin, G. *Hegels Tübinger Fragment*. Lund, 1933.

Asveld, P. *La pensée religieuse du jeune Hegel. Liberté et aliénation.* Louvain, 1953.

Baillie, J. *The Origin and Significance of Hegel's Logic*. London, 1901.

Balbino, G. *Der Grundirrtum Hegels*. Graz, 1914.

Brie, S. *Der Volksgeist bei Hegel und die historische Rechtsschule.* Berlin, 1909.

Bullinger, A. *Hegelsche Logik und gegenwärtig herrschender antihegelische Unverstand*. Munich, 1901.

Bülow, F. *Die Entwicklung der Hegelschen Sozialphilosophie*. Leipzig, 1920.

Caird, E. *Hegel*. London and Edinburgh, 1883. (This is still an excellent introduction to Hegel.)

Cairns, H. *Legal Philosophy from Plato to Hegel*. Baltimore, 1949.

Coreth, E., S.J. *Das dialektische Sein in Hegels Logik*. Vienna, 1952.

Cresson, A. *Hegel, sa vie, son œuvre*. Paris, 1949.

Croce, B. *What is Living and What is Dead in the Philosophy of Hegel*, translated by D. Ainslie. London, 1915.

Cunningham, G. W. *Thought and Reality in Hegel's System*. New York, 1910.

De Ruggiero, G. *Hegel*. Bari, 1948.

Dilthey, W. *Die Jugendgeschichte Hegels*. Berlin, 1905. (Contained in Dilthey's *Gesammelte Schriften*, IV; Berlin, 1921.)

Dulckeit, G. *Die Idee Gottes im Geiste der Philosophie Hegels*. Munich, 1947.

Emge, C. A. *Hegels Logik und die Gegenwart*. Karlsruhe, 1927.

Findlay, J. N. *Hegel. A Re-Examination*. London, 1958. (A sympathetic and systematic account of Hegel's philosophy, in which the metaphysical aspect is minimized.)

Fischer, K. *Hegels Leben, Werke und Lehre*. 2 vols. Heidelberg, 1911 (2nd edition).

Foster, M. B. *The Political Philosophies of Plato and Hegel*. Oxford, 1935.

Glockner, H. *Hegel*. 2 vols. Stuttgart. (Vols. 21 and 22 in Glockner's edition of Hegel's *Works* mentioned above.)

Grégoire, F. *Aux sources de la pensée de Marx: Hegel, Feuerbach*. Louvain, 1947.
 *Études hégéliennes*. Louvain, 1958.

Häring, T. *Hegel, sein Wollen und sein Werk*. 2 vols. Leipzig, 1929–38.

Haym, R. *Hegel und seine Zeit*. Leipzig, 1927 (2nd edition).

Heimann, B. *System und Methode in Hegels Philosophie*. Leipzig, 1927.

Hoffmeister, J. *Hölderlin und Hegel*. Tübingen, 1931.
 *Goethe und der deutsche Idealismus. Eine Einführung zu Hegels Realphilosophie*. Leipzig, 1932.
 *Die Problematik des Völkerbundes bei Kant und Hegel*. Tübingen, 1934.

Hyppolite, J. *Genèse et structure de la Phénomenologie de l'Esprit de Hegel*. Paris, 1946. (A very valuable commentary.)
 *Introduction à la philosophie de l'histoire de Hegel*. Paris, 1948.
 *Logique et existence: Essai sur la logique de Hegel*. Paris, 1953.

Iljin, I. *Die Philosophie Hegels als kontemplative Gotteslehre*. Bern, 1946.

Kojève, A. *Introduction à la lecture de Hegel*. Paris, 1947 (2nd edition). (The author gives an atheistic interpretation of Hegel.)

Lakebrink, B. *Hegels dialektische Ontologie und die thomistiche Analektik*. Cologne, 1955.

Lasson, G. *Was heisst Hegelianismus?* Berlin, 1916.
 *Einführung in Hegels Religionsphilosophie*. Leipzig, 1930. (This book constitutes an introduction to Vol. 12 of Lasson's critical edition of Hegel's *Works*, mentioned above. There are similar introductions by Lasson; for example, *Hegel als Geschichtsphilosoph*, Leipzig, 1920.)

Litt, T. *Hegel. Versuch einer kritischen Erneuerung.* Heidelberg, 1953.

Lukács, G. *Der junge Hegel. Ueber die Beziehungen von Dialektik und Oekonomie.* Berlin, 1954 (2nd edition). (The author writes from the Marxist point of view.)

Maggiore, G. *Hegel.* Milan, 1924.

Maier, J. *On Hegel's Critique of Kant.* New York, 1939.

Marcuse, M. *Reason and Revolution: Hegel and the Rise of Social Theory.* New York, 1954 (2nd edition).

McTaggart, J. McT. E. *Commentary on Hegel's Logic.* Cambridge, 1910.

    *Studies in the Hegelian Dialectic.* Cambridge, 1922 (2nd edition).

    *Studies in Hegelian Cosmology.* Cambridge, 1918 (2nd edition).

Moog, W. *Hegel und die Hegelsche Schule.* Munich, 1930.

Mure, G. R. G. *An Introduction to Hegel.* Oxford, 1940. (Stresses Hegel's relation to Aristotle.)

    *A Study of Hegel's Logic.* Oxford, 1950.

Negri, A. *La presenza di Hegel.* Florence, 1961.

Niel, H., S.J. *De la médiation dans la philosophie de Hegel.* Paris, 1945. (A study of Hegel's philosophy in the light of the pervading concept of mediation.)

Nink, C., S.J. *Kommentar zu den grundlegenden Abschnitten von Hegels Phänomenologie des Geistes.* Regensburg, 1931.

Ogiermann, H. A., S.J. *Hegels Gottesbeweise.* Rome, 1948.

Olgiati, F. *Il panlogismo hegeliano.* Milan, 1946.

Pelloux, L. *La logica di Hegel.* Milan, 1938.

Peperzak, A. T. B. *Le jeune Hegel et la vision morale du monde.* The Hague, 1960.

Pringle-Pattison, A. S. (=A. Seth). *Hegelianism and Personality.* London, 1893 (2nd edition).

Reyburn, H. A. *The Ethical Theory of Hegel: A Study of the Philosophy of Right.* Oxford, 1921.

Roques, P. *Hegel, sa vie et ses œuvres.* Paris, 1912.

Rosenkranz, K. *G. W. F. Hegels Leben.* Berlin, 1844.

    *Erläuterungen zu Hegels Enzyklopädie der Philosophie.* Berlin, 1870.

Rosenzweig, F. *Hegel und der Staat.* 2 vols. Oldenburg, 1920.

Schmidt, E. *Hegels Lehre von Gott.* Gütersloh, 1952.

Schneider, R. *Schellings und Hegels schwäbische Geistesahnen.* Würzburg, 1938.

Schwarz, J. *Die anthropologische Metaphysik des jungen Hegel.* Hildesheim, 1931.

    *Hegels philosophische Entwicklung.* Frankfurt a. M., 1938.

Specht, E. K. *Der Analogiebegriff bei Kant and Hegel.* Cologne, 1952.

Stace, W. T. *The Philosophy of Hegel*. London, 1924 (new edition, New York, 1955). (A systematic and clear account.)

Steinbüchel, T. *Das Grundproblem der Hegelschen Philosophie*. Vol. 1. Bonn, 1933. (The author, a Catholic priest, died before the completion of the work.)

Stirling, J. H. *The Secret of Hegel*. London, 1865.

Teyssedre, B. *L'ésthetique de Hegel*. Paris, 1958.

Vanni Rovighi, S. *La concezione hegeliana della Storia*. Milan, 1942.

Wacher, H. *Das Verhältnis des jungen Hegel zu Kant*. Berlin, 1932.

Wahl, J. *Le malheur de la conscience dans la philosophie de Hegel*. Paris, 1951 (2nd edition). (A valuable study.)

Wallace, W. *Prolegomena to the Study of Hegel's Philosophy and especially of his Logic*. Oxford, 1894 (2nd edition).

Weil, E. *Hegel et l'état*. Paris, 1950.


*Chapters XIII–XIV: Schopenhauer*

Texts

*Werke*, edited by J. Frauenstädt. 6 vols. Leipzig, 1873–4 (and subsequent editions). New edition by A. Hübscher, Leipzig, 1937–41.

*Sämmtliche Werke*, edited by P. Deussen and A. Hübscher. 16 vols. Munich, 1911–42.

*On the Fourfold Root of the Principle of Sufficient Reason, and On the Will in Nature*, translated by K. Hillebrand. London, 1907 (revised edition).

*The World as Will and Idea*, translated by R. B. Haldane and J. Kemp. 3 vols. London, 1906 (5th edition).

*The Basis of Morality*, translated by A. B. Bullock. London, 1903.

*Selected Essays*, translated by E. B. Bax. London, 1891.


Studies

Beer, M. *Schopenhauer*. London, 1914.

Caldwell, W. *Schopenhauer's System in Its Philosophical Significance*. Edinburgh, 1896.

Copleston, F. C., S.J. *Arthur Schopenhauer, Philosopher of Pessimism*. London, 1946.

Costa, A. *Il pensiero religioso di Arturo Schopenhauer*. Rome, 1935.

Covotti, A. *La vita a il pensiero di A. Schopenhauer*. Turin, 1909.

Cresson, A. *Schopenhauer*. Paris, 1946.

Faggin, A. *Schopenhauer, il mistico senza Dio*. Florence, 1951.

Fauconnet, A. *L'ésthetique de Schopenhauer*. Paris, 1913.

Frauenstädt, J. *Schopenhauer-Lexikon*. 2 vols. Leipzig, 1871.

Grisebach, E. *Schopenhauer*. Berlin, 1897.

Hasse, H. *Schopenhauers Erkenntnislehre*. Leipzig, 1913.

Hübscher, A. *Arthur Schopenhauer. Ein Lebensbild.* Wiesbaden, 1949 (2nd edition).

Knox, I. *Aesthetic Theories of Kant, Hegel and Schopenhauer.* New York, 1936.

McGill, V. J. *Schopenhauer, Pessimist and Pagan.* New York, 1931.

Méry, M. *Essai sur la causalité phénoménale selon Schopenhauer.* Paris, 1948.

Neugebauer, P. *Schopenhauer in England, mit besonderer Berüktsichtigung seines Einflusses auf die englische Literatur.* Berlin, 1931.

Padovani, U. A. *Arturo Schopenhauer: L'ambiente, la vita, le opere.* Milan, 1934.

Robot, T. *La philosophie de Schopenhauer.* Paris, 1874.

Ruyssen, T. *Schopenhauer.* Paris, 1911.

Sartorelli, F. *Il pessimismo di Arturo Schopenhauer, con particolare riferimento alla dottrina del diritto e dello Stato.* Milan, 1951.

Schneider, W. *Schopenhauer.* Vienna, 1937.

Seillière, E. *Schopenhauer,* Paris. 1912.

Simmel, G. *Schopenhauer und Nietzsche.* Leipzig, 1907.

Siwek, P., S.J. *The Philosophy of Evil* (Ch. X). New York, 1951.

Volkelt, J. *Arthur Schopenhauer, seine Persönlichkeit, seine Lehre, seine Glaube.* Stuttgart, 1907 (3rd edition).

Wallace, W. *Schopenhauer.* London, 1891.

Whittaker, T. *Schopenhauer.* London, 1909.

Zimmern, H. *Schopenhauer: His Life and Philosophy.* London, 1932 (revised edition). (A short introduction.)

Zint, H. *Schopenhauer als Erlebnis.* Munich and Basel, 1954.

## Chapter XV: Feuerbach

### Texts

*Sämmtliche Werke,* edited by L. Feuerbach (the philosopher himself). 10 vols. Leipzig, 1846–66.

*Sämmtliche Werke,* edited by W. Bolin and F. Jodl. 10 vols. Stuttgart, 1903–11.

*The Essence of Christianity,* translated by G. Eliot. New York, 1957. (London, 1881, 2nd edition, with translator's name given as M. Evans.)

### Studies

Arvon, H. *Ludwig Feuerbach ou la transformation du sacré.* Paris, 1957.

Bolin, W. *Ludwig Feuerbach, sein Wirken und seine Zeitgenossen.* Stuttgart, 1891.

Chamberlin, W. B. *Heaven Wasn't His Destination: The Philosophy of Ludwig Feuerbach.* London, 1941.

Engels, F. *Ludwig Feuerbach and the Outcome of Classical German Philosophy.* (Contained in *Karl Marx, Selected Works,* edited by C. P. Dutt. See under Marx and Engels.)

Grégoire, F. *Aux Sources de la pensée de Marx, Hegel, Feuerbach.* Louvain, 1947.

Grün, K. *Ludwig Feuerbach in seinem Briefwechsel und Nachlass.* 2 vols. Leipzig, 1874.

Jodl, F. *Ludwig Feuerbach.* Stuttgart, 1904.

Lévy, A. *La philosophie de Feuerbach et son influence sur la littérature allemande.* Paris, 1904.

Lombardi, F. *Ludwig Feuerbach.* Florence, 1935.

Löwith, K. *Von Hegel bis Nietzsche.* Zurich, 1941.

Nüdling, G. *Ludwig Feuerbachs Religionsphilosophie.* Paderborn, 1936.

Rawidowicz, S. *Ludwig Feuerbachs Philosophie.* Berlin, 1931.

Schilling, W. *Feuerbach und die Religion.* Munich, 1957.

Secco, L. *L'etica nella filosofia di Feuerbach.* Padua, 1936.

## Chapter XVI: Marx and Engels

*Texts*

*Marx-Engels, Historisch-kritische Gesamtausgabe: Werke, Schriften, Briefe,* edited by D. Ryazanov (from 1931 by V. Adoratsky). Moscow and Berlin. This critical edition, planned to contain some 42 vols., was undertaken by the Marx-Engels Institute in Moscow. It remains, however, sadly incomplete. Between 1926 and 1935 there appeared 7 vols. of the writings of Marx and Engels, with a special volume to commemorate the fortieth anniversary of Engels' death. And between 1929 and 1931 there appeared 4 vols. of correspondence between Marx and Engels.

*Karl Marx–Friedrich Engels, Werke.* 5 vols. Berlin, 1957–9. This edition, based on the one mentioned above, covers the writings of Marx and Engels up to November 1848. It is published by the Dietz Verlag. And a large number of the works of Marx and Engels have been reissued in this publisher's Library of Marxism-Leninism (*Bücherei des Marximus-Leninismus*).

*Gesammelte Schriften von Karl Marx und Friedrich Engels,* 1852–1862, edited by D. Ryazanov. 2 vols. Stuttgart, 1920 (2nd edition). (Four volumes were contemplated.)

*Aus dem literarischen Nachlass von Karl Marx, Friedrich Engels und Friedrich Lassalle,* 1841–1850, edited by F. Mehring. 4 vols. Berlin and Stuttgart, 1923 (4th edition).

*Karl Marx. Die Frühschriften,* edited by S. Landshut. Stuttgart, 1953.

*Der Briefwechsel zwischen F. Engels und K. Marx,* edited by A. Bebel and E. Bernstein. 4 vols. Stuttgart, 1913.

A number of the writings of Marx and Engels have been translated into English for the Foreign Languages Publishing House in Moscow and have been published in London (Lawrence and Wishart). For example: Marx's *The Poverty of Philosophy* (1956), Engels' *Anti-Dühring* (1959, 2nd edition) and *Dialectics of Nature* (1954), and *The Holy Family* (1957) by Marx and Engels.

Of older translations one can mention the following. Marx: *A Contribution to the Critique of Political Economy* (New York, 1904); *Selected Essays*, translated by H. J. Stenning (London and New York, 1926); *The Poverty of Philosophy* (New York, 1936). Engels: *The Origin of the Family, Private Property and the State* (Chicago, 1902); *Ludwig Feuerbach* (New York, 1934); *Herr Dühring's Revolution in Science*, i.e. *Anti-Dühring* (London, 1935). Marx and Engels: *The German Ideology* (London, 1938).

There are several English translations of *Capital*. For example: *Capital*, revised and amplified according to the 4th German edition by E. Untermann (New York, 1906), and the two-volume edition of *Capital* in the Everyman Library (London), introduced by G. D. H. Cole and translated from the 4th German edition by E. and C. Paul.

Of the English editions of *The Communist Manifesto* we can mention that by H. J. Laski: *Communist Manifesto: Socialist Landmark*, with an introduction (London, 1948).

## Other Writings

*Marx-Engels. Selected Correspondence.* London, 1934.

*Karl Marx. Selected Works*, edited by C. P. Dutt. 2 vols. London and New York, 1936, and subsequent editions.

*Karl Marx. Selected Writings in Sociology and Social Philosophy*, edited by T. Bottomore and M. Rubel. London, 1956.

*Three Essays by Karl Marx*, translated by R. Stone. New York, 1947.

*Karl Marx and Friedrich Engels. Basic Writings on Politics and Philosophy*, edited by L. S. Feuer. New York, 1959.

## Studies

Acton, H. B. *The Illusion of the Epoch, Marxism-Leninism as a Philosophical Creed.* London, 1955. (An excellent criticism.)

Adams, H. P. *Karl Marx in His Earlier Writings.* London, 1940.

Adler, M. *Marx als Denker.* Berlin, 1908.

*Engels als Denker.* Berlin, 1921.

Aron, R., and Others. *De Marx au Marxisme.* Paris, 1948.

Aron, H. *Le marxisme.* Paris, 1955.

Baas, E. *L'humanisme marxiste.* Paris, 1947.

Barbu, Z. *Le développement de la pensée dialectique.* (By a Marxist.) Paris, 1947.

Bartoli, H. *La doctrine économique et sociale de Karl Marx*. Paris, 1950.

Beer, M. *Life and Teaching of Karl Marx*, translated by T. C. Partington and H. J. Stenning. London, 1934 (reprint).

Bekker, K. *Marx's philosophische Entwicklung, sein Verhältnis zu Hegel*. Zürich, 1940.

Berdiaeff, N. *Christianity and Class War*. London, 1934.
        *The Origin of Russian Communism*. London, 1937.

Berlin, I. *Karl Marx*. London, 1939 and subsequent editions. (A useful small biographical study.)

Bober, M. *Karl Marx's Interpretation of History*. Cambridge (U.S.A.), 1927.

Bohm-Bawerk, E. von. *Karl Marx and The Close of His System*. London, 1898.

Boudin, L. B. *Theoretical System of Karl Marx in the Light of Recent Criticism*. Chicago, 1907.

Bouquet, A. C. *Karl Marx and His Doctrine*. London and New York, 1950. (A small work published by the S.P.C.K.)

Calvez, J.-V. *La pensée de Karl Marx*. Paris, 1956. (An outstanding study of Marx's thought.)

Carr, H. *Karl Marx. A Study in Fanaticism*. London, 1934.

Cornu, A. *Karl Marx, sa vie et son œuvre*. Paris, 1934.
        *The Origins of Marxian Thought*. Springfield (Illinois), 1957.

Cottier, G. M.-M. *L'athéisme du jeune Marx: ses origines hégéliennes*. Paris, 1959.

Croce, B. *Historical Materialism and the Economics of Karl Marx*, translated by C. M. Meredith. Chicago, 1914.

Desroches, H. C. *Signification du marxisme*. Paris, 1949.

Drahn, E. *Friedrich Engels*. Vienna and Berlin, 1920.

Gentile, G. *La filosofia di Marx*. Milan, 1955 (new edition).

Gignoux, C. J. *Karl Marx*. Paris, 1950.

Grégoire, F. *Aux sources de la pensée de Marx: Hegel, Feuerbach*. Louvain, 1947.

Haubtmann, P. *Marx et Proudhon: leurs rapports personels, 1844–47*. Paris, 1947.

Hook, S. *Towards the Understanding of Karl Marx*. New York, 1933.
        *From Hegel to Marx*. New York, 1936.
        *Marx and the Marxists*. Princeton, 1955.

Hyppolite, J. *Études sur Marx et Hegel*. Paris, 1955.

Joseph, H. W. B. *Marx's Theory of Value*. London, 1923.

Kamenka. E. *The Ethical Foundations of Marxism*. London, 1962.

Kautsky, K. *Die historische Leistung von Karl Marx*. Berlin, 1908.

Laski, H. J. *Karl Marx*. London, 1922.

Lefebvre, H. *Le matérialisme dialectique*. Paris, 1949 (3rd edition).
        *Le marxisme*. Paris, 1958. (By a Marxist author.)

Leff, G. *The Tyranny of Concepts: A Critique of Marxism.* London, 1961.

Lenin, V. I. *The Teachings of Karl Marx.* New York, 1930.
*Marx, Engels, Marxism.* London, 1936.

Liebknecht, W. *Karl Marx, Biographical Memoirs.* Chicago, 1901.

Loria, A. *Karl Marx.* New York, 1920.

Löwith, K. *Von Hegel bis Nietzsche.* Zürich, 1947.

Lunau, H. *Karl Marx und die Wirklichkeit.* Brussels, 1937.

Marcuse, H. *Reason and Revolution.* London, 1941.

Mandolfo, R. *Il materialismo storico in Friedrich Engels.* Genoa, 1912.

Mascolo, D. *Le communisme.* Paris, 1953. (By a Marxist.)

Mayer, G. *Friedrich Engels.* 2 vols. The Hague, 1934 (2nd edition).

Mehring, F. *Karl Marx: the Story of His Life,* translated by E. Fitzgerald. London, 1936. (The standard biography.)

Meyer, A. G. *Marxism. The Unity of Theory and Practice. A Critical Essay.* Cambridge (U.S.A.) and Oxford, 1954.

Nicolaievsky, N. *Karl Marx.* Philadelphia, 1936.

Olgiati, F. *Carlo Marx.* Milan, 1953 (6th edition).

Pischel, G. *Marx giovane.* Milan, 1948.

Plenge, J. *Marx und Hegel.* Tübingen, 1911.

Robinson, J. *An Essay in Marxian Economics.* London, 1942.

Rubel, M. *Karl Marx. Essai de biographie intellectuelle.* Paris, 1957.

Ryazanov, D. *Karl Marx and Friedrich Engels.* New York, 1927.
*Karl Marx, Man, Thinker and Revolutionist.* London, 1927.

Schlesinger, R. *Marx: His Time and Ours.* London, 1950.

Schwarzschild, L. *Karl Marx.* Paris, 1950.

Seeger, R. *Friedrich Engels.* Halle, 1935.

Somerhausen, L. *L'humanisme agissant de Karl Marx.* Paris, 1946.

Spargo, J. *Karl Marx. His Life and Work.* New York, 1910.

Tönnies, F. *Marx. Leben und Lehre.* Jena, 1921.

Touilleux, P. *Introduction aux systèmes de Marx et Hegel.* Tournai, 1960.

Tucker, R. C. *Philosophy and Myth in Karl Marx.* Cambridge, 1961.

Turner, J. K. *Karl Marx.* New York, 1941.

Vancourt, R. *Marxisme et pensée chrétienne.* Paris, 1948.

Van Overbergh, C. *Karl Marx, sa vie et son œuvre. Bilan du marxisme.* Brussels, 1948 (2nd edition).

Vorländer, K. *Kant und Marx.* Tübingen, 1911.
*Marx Engels und Lassalle als Philosophen.* Stuttgart, 1920.

Wetter, G. A. *Dialectical Materialism* (based on 4th German edition). London, 1959. (This outstanding work is devoted mainly to the development of Marxism-Leninism in the Soviet Union. But the author treats first of Marx and Engels.)

## Chapter XVII: Kierkegaard

### Texts

*Samlede Vaerker*, edited by A. B. Drachmann, J. L. Herberg and H. O. Lange. 14 vols. Copenhagen, 1901-6. A critical Danish edition of Kierkegaard's *Complete Works* is being edited by N. Thulstrup. Copenhagen, 1951 ff. A German translation of this edition is being published concurrently at Cologne and Olten. (There are, of course, previous German editions of Kierkegaard's writings.)

*Papirer (Journals)*, edited by P. A. Heiberg, V. Kuhr and E. Torsting. 20 vols. (11 vols. in 20 parts). Copenhagen, 1909-48.

*Breve (Letters)*, edited by N. Thulstrup. 2 vols. Copenhagen, 1954.

There is a Danish *Anthology* of Kierkegaard's writings, *S. Kierkegaard's Vaerker i Udvalg*, edited by F. J. Billeskov-Jansen. 4 vols. Copenhagen, 1950 (2nd edition).

English translations, mainly by D. F. Swenson and W. Lowrie, of Kierkegaard's more important writings are published by the Oxford University Press and the Princeton University Press. Exclusive of the Journals (mentioned separately below) there are 12 vols. up to date, 1936-53. Further references to individual volumes are made in the footnotes to the chapter on Kierkegaard in this book.

*Johannes Climacus*, translated by T. H. Croxall. London, 1958.

*Works of Love*, translated by H. and E. Hong. London, 1962.

*Journals* (selections), translated by A. Dru. London and New York, 1938 (also obtainable in Fontana Paperbacks).

*A Kierkegaard Anthology*, edited by R. Bretall. London and Princeton, 1946.

*Diario*, with introduction and notes by C. Fabro (3 vols., Brescia, 1949-52), is a useful Italian edition of selections from Kierkegaard's *Journals* by an author who has also published an *Antologia Kierkegaardiana*, Turin, 1952.

### Studies

Bense, M. *Hegel und Kierkegaard*. Cologne and Krefeld, 1948.

Bohlin, T. *Sören Kierkegaard, l'homme et l'œuvre*, translated by P. H. Tisseau. Bazoges-en-Pareds, 1941.

Brandes, G. *Sören Kierkegaard*. Copenhagen, 1879.

Cantoni, R. *La coscienza inquieta: S. Kierkegaard*. Milan, 1949.

Castelli, E. (editor). Various Authors. *Kierkegaard e Nietzsche*. Rome, 1953.

Chestov, L. *Kierkegaard et la philosophie existentielle*, translated from the Russian by T. Rageot and B. de Schoezer. Paris, 1948.

Collins, J. *The Mind of Kierkegaard*. Chicago, 1953.

Croxall, T. H. *Kierkegaard Commentary*. London, 1956.

Diem, H. *Die Existenzdialektik von S. Kierkegaard*. Zürich, 1950.

Fabro, C. *Tra Kierkegaard e Marx*. Florence, 1952.

Fabro, C., and Others. *Studi Kierkegaardiani*. Brescia, 1957.

Friedmann, K. *Kierkegaard, the Analysis of His Psychological Personality*. London, 1947.

Geismar, E. *Sören Kierkegaard. Seine Lebensentwicklung und seine Wirksamkeit als Schriftsteller*. Göttingen, 1927.

    *Lectures on the Religious Thought of Sören Kierkegaard*. Minneapolis, 1937.

Haecker, T. *Sören Kierkegaard*, translated by A. Dru. London and New York, 1937.

Hirsch, E. *Kierkegaardstudien*. 2 vols. Gütersloh, 1930–3.

Höffding, H. *Sören Kierkegaard als Philosoph*. Stuttgart, 1896.

Hohlenberg, J. *Kierkegaard*. Basel, 1949.

Jolivet, R. *Introduction to Kierkegaard*, translated by W. H. Barber. New York, 1951.

Lombardi, F. *Sören Kierkegaard*. Florence, 1936.

Lowrie, W. *Kierkegaard*. London, 1938. (A very full bibliographical treatment.)

    *Short Life of Kierkegaard*. London and Princeton, 1942.

Martin, H. V. *Kierkegaard the Melancholy Dane*. New York, 1950.

Masi, G. *La determinazione de la possibilità dell' esistenza in Kierkegaard*. Bologna, 1949.

Mesnard, P. *Le vrai visage de Kierkegaard*. Paris, 1948.

    *Kierkegaard, sa vie, son œuvre, avec un exposé de sa philosophie*. Paris, 1954.

Patrick, D. *Pascal and Kierkegaard*. 2 vols. London, 1947.

Roos, H., S.J. *Kierkegaard et le catholicisme*, translated from the Danish by A. Renard, O.S.B. Louvain, 1955.

Schremf, C. *Kierkegaard*. 2 vols. Stockholm, 1935.

Sieber, F. *Der Begriff der Mitteilung bei Sören Kierkegaard*. Würzburg, 1939.

Thomte, R. *Kierkegaard's Philosophy of Religion*. London and Princeton, 1948.

Wahl, J. *Études kierkegaardiennes*. Paris, 1948 (2nd edition).

## Chapters XXI–XXII: Nietzsche

*Texts*

A complete critical edition of Nietzsche's writings and correspondence, *Nietzsches Werke und Briefe, historisch-kritische Ausgabe*, was begun at Munich in 1933 under the auspices of the Nietzsche-Archiv. Five volumes of the *Werke* (comprising the *juvenilia*) appeared between 1933 and 1940, and four volumes of the *Briefe* between 1938 and 1942. But the enterprise does not seem to be making much progress.

*Gesammelte Werke, Grossoktav Ausgabe.* 19 vols. Leipzig, 1901–13. In 1926 R. Oehler's *Nietzsche-Register* was added as a 20th vol.

*Gesammelte Werke, Musarionausgabe.* 23 vols. Munich, 1920–9.

*Werke*, edited by K. Schlechta. 3 vols. Munich, 1954–6. (Obviously incomplete, but a handy edition of Nietzsche's main writings, with lengthy selections from the *Nachlass*.)

There are other German editions of Nietzsche's *Works*, such as the *Taschenausgabe* published at Leipzig.

*Gesammelte Briefe.* 5 vols. Berlin and Leipzig, 1901–9. A volume of correspondence with Overbeck was added in 1916. And some volumes, such as the correspondence with Rohde, have been published separately.

*The Complete Works of Friedrich Nietzsche*, translated under the general editorship of O. Levy. 18 vols. London, 1909–13. (This edition is not complete in the sense of containing the *juvenilia* and the whole *Nachlass*. Nor are the translations above criticism. But it is the only edition of comparable scope in the English language.)

Some of Nietzsche's writings are published in *The Modern Library Giant*, New York. And there is the *Portable Nietzsche*, translated by W. A. Kaufmann. New York, 1954.

*Selected Letters of Friedrich Nietzsche*, edited by O. Levy. London. 1921.

*The Nietzsche-Wagner Correspondence*, edited by E. Förster-Nietzsche. London, 1922.

*Friedrich Nietzsche. Unpublished Letters.* Translated and edited by K. F. Leidecker. New York, 1959.

*Studies*

Andler, C. *Nietzsche: sa vie et sa pensée.* 6 vols. Paris, 1920–31.

Banfi, A. *Nietzsche.* Milan, 1934.

Bataille, G. *Sur Nietzsche. Volonté de puissance.* Paris, 1945.

Bäumler, A. *Nietzsche der Philosoph und Politiker.* Berlin, 1931.

Benz, E. *Nietzsches Ideen zur Geschichte des Christentums.* Stuttgart, 1938.

Bertram, E. *Nietzsche. Versuch einer Mythologie.* Berlin, 1920 (3rd edition).

Bianquis, G. *Nietzsche en France.* Paris, 1929.

Bindschedler, M. *Nietzsche und die poetische Lüge.* Basel, 1954.

Brandes, G. *Friedrich Nietzsche.* London, 1914.

Brinton, C. *Nietzsche.* Cambridge (U.S.A.) and London, 1941.

Brock, W. *Nietzsches Idee der Kultur*. Bonn, 1930.

Chatterton Hill, G. *The Philosophy of Nietzsche*. London, 1912.

Copleston, F. C., S.J. *Friedrich Nietzsche, Philosopher of Culture*. London, 1942.

Cresson, A. *Nietzsche, sa vie, son œuvre, sa philosophie*. Paris, 1943.

Deussen, P. *Erinnerungen an Friedrich Nietzsche*. Leipzig, 1901.

Dolson, G. N. *The Philosophy of Friedrich Nietzsche*. New York, 1901.

Drews, A. *Nietzsches Philosophie*. Heidelberg, 1904.

Förster-Nietzsche, E. *Das Leben Friedrich Nietzsches*. 2 vols. in 3. Leipzig, 1895–1904.
    *Der junge Nietzsche*. Leipzig, 1912.
    *Der einsame Nietzsche*. Leipzig, 1913. (These books by Nietzsche's sister have to be used with care, as she had several axes to grind.)

Gawronsky, D. *Friedrich Nietzsche und das Dritte Reich*. Bern, 1935.

Goetz, K. A. *Nietzsche als Ausnahme. Zur Zerstörung des Willens zur Macht*. Freiburg, 1949.

Giusso, L. *Nietzsche*. Milan, 1943.

Halévy, D. *Life of Nietzsche*. London, 1911.

Heidegger, M. *Nietzsche*. 2 vols. Pfulligen, 1961.

Jaspers, K. *Nietzsche: Einführung in das Verständnis seines Philosophierens*. Berlin, 1936. (The two last-mentioned books are profound studies in which, as one might expect, the respective philosophical positions of the writers govern the interpretations of Nietzsche.)

Joël, K. *Nietzsche und die Romantik*. Jena, 1905.

Kaufmann, W. A. *Nietzsche: Philosopher, Psychologist, Antichrist*. Princeton, 1950.

Klages, L. *Die psychologischen Errungenschaften Nietzsches*. Leipzig, 1930 (2nd edition).

Knight, A. H. J. *Some Aspects of the Life and Work of Nietzsche, and particularly of His Connection with Greek Literature and Thought*. Cambridge, 1933.

Lannoy, J. C. *Nietzsche ou l'histoire d'un égocentricisme athée*. Paris, 1952. (Contains a useful bibliography, pp. 365–92.)

Lavrin, J. *Nietzsche. An Approach*. London, 1948.

Lea, F. A. *The Tragic Philosopher. A Study of Friedrich Nietzsche*. London, 1957. (A sympathetic study by a believing Christian.)

Lefebvre, H. *Nietzsche*. Paris, 1939.

Lombardi, R. *Federico Nietzsche*. Rome, 1945.

Lotz, J. B., S.J. *Zwischen Seligkeit und Verdamnis. Ein Beitrag zu dem Thema: Nietzsche und das Christentum*. Frankfurt a. M., 1953.

Löwith, K. *Von Hegel bis Nietzsche*. Zürich, 1941.
    *Nietzsches Philosophie der ewigen Wiederkehr des Gleichen*. Stuttgart, 1956.

Ludovici, A. M. *Nietzsche, His Life and Works*. London, 1910.
 *Nietzsche and Art*. London, 1912.
Mencken, H. L. *The Philosophy of Friedrich Nietzsche*. London, 1909.
Mess, F. *Nietzsche als Gesetzgeber*. Leipzig, 1931.
Miéville, H. L. *Nietzsche et la volonté de puissance*. Lausanne, 1934.
Mittasch, A. *Friedrich Nietzsche als Naturphilosoph*. Stuttgart, 1952.
Molina, E. *Nietzsche, dionisiaco y asceta*. Santiago (Chile), 1944.
Morgan, G. A., Jr. *What Nietzsche Means*. Cambridge (U.S.A), 1941.
 (An excellent study.)
Mügge, M. A. *Friedrich Nietzsche: His Life and Work*. London, 1909.
Oehler, R. *Nietzsches philosophisches Werden*. Munich, 1926.
Orestano, F. *Le idee fondamentali di Friedrich Nietzsche nel loro progressivo svolgimento*. Palermo, 1903.
Paci, E. *Federico Nietzsche*. Milan, 1940.
Podach, E. H. *The Madness of Nietzsche*. London, 1936.
Reininger, F. *Friedrich Nietzsches Kampf um den Sinn des Lebens*. Vienna, 1922.
Reyburn, H. A., with the collaboration of H. B. Hinderks and J. G. Taylor. *Nietzsche: The Story of a Human philosopher*. London, 1948. (A good psychological study of Nietzsche.)
Richter, R. *Friedrich Nietzsche*. Leipzig, 1903.
Riehl, A. *Friedrich Nietzsche, der Künstler und der Denker*. Stuttgart, 1920 (6th edition).
Römer, H. *Nietzsche*. 2 vols. Leipzig, 1921.
Siegmund, G. *Nietzsche, der 'Atheist' und 'Antichrist'*. Paderborn, 1946 (4th edition).
Simmel, G. *Schopenhauer und Nietzsche*. Leipzig, 1907.
Steinbüchel, T. *Friedrich Nietzsche*. Stuttgart, 1946.
Thibon, G. *Nietzsche ou le déclin de l'esprit*. Lyons, 1948.
Vaihinger, H. *Nietzsche als Philosoph*. Berlin, 1905 (3rd edition).
Wolff, P. *Nietzsche und das christliche Ethos*. Regensburg, 1940.
Wright, W. H. *What Nietzsche Taught*. New York, 1915. (Mainly excerpts.)

# INDEX

(The principal references are in heavy type. Asterisked numbers refer to bibliographical information. References in ordinary type to a continuous series of pages, e.g. 195–8, do not necessarily indicate continuous treatment. References to two persons together are usually under the person criticized or influenced. Footnote abbreviations given in italics, e.g. *B*, are referred to the pages explaining them.)

316; Marxism 307, 316, 320,
324ff, 331; *also* 250f, 284f, 346
*and below*
contradiction, principle of *see* non-
contradiction
contradictions, reconciliation of:
Fichte 47, 57; Hegel 166, 176,
184f, 192; Herbart 251
contraries: Hegel 177
Copenhagen 338f, 393
Copernican revolution 3
Coreth, E. 439*
corporations: Hegel 212n, 214
corporativism: Hegel 214
correspondence theory of knowledge
106
creation: Fichte 9, 80, 92; Hegel 9,
196, 235, 239; Schelling 9, 128f,
132, 135f, 143; *also* 258ff, 298,
353f, 367, 419
purpose of 135, 260, 379
creative nothing: Stirner 302
creative human powers: Nietzsche
392, 396, 398, 403; *also* 15f,
279
creaturehood acknowledged: Kierkegaard 336, 341
crime and the criminal: Hegel 205,
213
critical philosophy of Kant: Fichte
3–6, 7f, 15, 32f, 39–42, 44, 52,
56ff, 60, 64, 78f; Hegel 5, 10,
167, 189f; Schelling 101, 123,
137; *also* 248ff, 257
German idealism and 10, 21, 23–6
*See also* Kant
criticism: Schelling 94, 100–3
Croce, Benedetto (1866–1952) 241,
247, 279
cruelty: Nietzsche 412; Schopenhauer 274, 286
cult, worship: Hegel 237, 240
cultural sciences *see Geisteswissenschaften*
culture, cultures: Fichte 74; Hegel
30, 202, 216, 220; Nietzsche
391f, 398, 399n, 413f; *also* 16,
321, 362f, 368, 370f, 382
German culture 74, 391, 398
history and 365, 370f, 398
'cunning of reason': Hegel 222,
223n; *also* 291
curiosity: Fichte 68
custom 382, 400

cycles of history *see* eternal recurrence
Czolbe, Heinrich (1819–73) 352f

Danzig 261
darkness and light: Baader 146;
Schelling 131
Darwin, Charles (1809–82), Darwinism: Nietzsche 400, 411f; *also*
319, 354f
*Dasein*: Fichte 86, 88, 93; N. Hartmann 437; Heidegger 438
*See also* existence
Daub, Karl (1765–1836) 245
dawn, new: Nietzsche 406
day-view and night-view: Fechner
376
death: Kierkegaard 349; Schopenhauer 281, 284f
decadence: Nietzsche 404, 406,
412f, 417
deduction: Fichte 48, 50f, 119, *see
also* transcendental D. *below*,
*and* consciousness, D. of; Hegel
48, 168, 178, 199, 201, 203, 259,
301; Kant 11, 438; Schelling
22, 116, 127f, 135f, 139, 335;
*also* 259f, 287, 362, 439
consciousness, D. of *see* consciousness, D. of
Nature, D. of: Hegel 168f, 197;
Schelling 109–14
transcendental D: Fichte 57, 78,
438; *also* 115, 438f
definition: Bolzano 257
deification: Feuerbach 295
deism: Fichte 76
demiurge 313
democracy: Cohen 363; Feuerbach
299; Fichte 72; Hegel 214f;
Marx 307; Nietzsche 399, 402,
405, 413, 417
Democritus (B.C. 460–370) 252, 272,
353
demythologization: Fichte 88;
Hegel 225, 241; *also* 12
dependence, feeling of: Feuerbach
295f; Schleiermacher **152f**, 155,
157f, 295
Descartes, René (1596–1650) 6, 434
descriptions, theory of 432
desire: Fichte 50, 55f, 61; Hegel
183; Schopenhauer 270, 274,